THE ECONOMY OF HAPPINESS

THE ECONOMY
OF
HAPPINESS

BY

JAMES MACKAYE

BOSTON
LITTLE, BROWN, AND COMPANY
1906

Copyright, 1906,
By JAMES MACKAYE.

All Rights Reserved

Published September, 1906

To S. S. P.

PREFACE

The philosophy of common sense had its origin in ancient Greece, its most conspicuous expositor during antiquity being Aristotle. In modern times its development has been due almost entirely to the English philosophers of the 17th and 18th centuries, of whom Hobbes, Locke, Berkeley, Hume and Bentham are the chief representatives, the so-called "common sense" metaphysic of Reid and Hamilton embodying a doctrine less worthy of such a designation than that of their profounder predecessors, Berkeley and Hume. The present work aims to be a contribution to the English school of philosophy.

The industrial renaissance which began with the 19th century initiated a critical period in the political philosophy of the western world. Two divergent avenues of development had been proposed in the latter part of the 18th century — one by Adam Smith in "The Wealth of Nations," which appeared in 1776 — the other by Jeremy Bentham in "The Principles of Morals and Legislation," which appeared in 1789. The first led to commercialism — the second to utilitarianism. At this critical period arose the dominant political thinker of the 19th century — John Stuart Mill. It was for him to determine the trend of political thought of the century. He determined it. Failing to appreciate Bentham's discovery of the nature of intuitionism, Mill evolved an inconsistent theory of utility entirely incapable of application. Thus deflected from the path of common sense, and influenced, no doubt, by the ideals of his age, Mill followed Adam Smith into commercialism and perpetuated the separation of politics and morality.

In this manner it has come about that the prevailing school of political philosophy has but one God — Production, and Mill is its prophet. He who seeks the overthrow of our present political paganism therefore must deal with the arch-offender himself, and hence in the following work Mill appears as the spokesman of his school. It is easy to destroy the dogmas of commercialism, but not easy to construct a practical substitute therefor; yet nothing less is required of him who would guide the practices of society by the theory of utility. In submitting to criticism the system herein expounded, therefore, I deem myself entitled to a judgment which will weigh the difficulties of the attempt in the same scale with its defects.

JAMES MACKAYE.

Cambridge, Mass., March 10, 1906.

TABLE OF CONTENTS

INTRODUCTION

PAGE

Problem of Happiness. Solvable by common sense. Scope of common sense. Suggested order of reading book 1

BOOK I

THE PRINCIPLES OF COMMON SENSE

CHAPTER I

INTELLIGIBILITY

Utility of undertaking. Right and wrong — unintelligibility of. Meaning of meaning. Requirements of intelligibility. Origin of language. Meaning — how ascertained. Terms — concrete and abstract. Table of elementary experiences. Definable and indefinable terms. Co-ordinates of experience. Nature of definition. Real and verbal definition. First requirement of intelligibility. Second requirement of intelligibility. Sufficient intelligibility. Third requirement of intelligibility. Summary 7

CHAPTER II

TRUTH

Nature of relation. Expectation. Extension of its meaning. Conjunctions — only expectables. Expression of expectation. Kinds of propositions. Valid and invalid expectations. The scientific method. Sources of knowledge. Nature of inference. Deduction. The principle of contradiction. Nature of certainty. Inference by conversion. Inference by opposition. Inference by syllogism. Rules of the syllogism. Induction. Observation. Assumption of existence. Similarity of relation. Principle of the uniformity of nature. The law of causation. Canons of induction. Degree of expectation. Probability. Expression of probability. Direct probability. Inverse probability. Assumption of a fair sample. Formula of Laplace. Extension of Laplace's formula. Empirical and derivative laws. The inductive syllogism. Probable deduction. Combination of evidence. The peithosyllogism or belief-judgment. Nature of a reason for a belief, etc. Difficulties in application of the theory of probabilities. First cause. Nature of hypothesis. Verification. Utility of understanding logic. Nature of reality or existence. Misunderstanding thereof due to unintelligibility of terms. Similar misunderstanding of nature of right and wrong . . 33

CONTENTS

CHAPTER III
UTILITY

PAGE

Voluntary acts — classification of. Diversity of meaning of right and wrong. Intuitional and utilitarian meanings. Nature of pleasure and pain. Modes of variation of pleasure and pain. Determinants of preference. Pain as a determinant. Unit of intensity of pain. Quantity of pain. Pleasure as a determinant. Unit of intensity of pleasure. Quantity of pleasure. Relation of pleasure and pain as determinants. Correct and incorrect preference. Principle of preference. Curve of happiness. Composition of happiness curves. Absolute right and wrong. The chresyllogism or use-judgment. Nature of a reason for an act, etc. Definition of right and wrong. Utility of understanding the theory of utility. Nature of utility. Distribution of happiness. Dilemma of distribution. Relation of means to ends. Confusion of means and ends. Free will. Fatalism. Nature of common sense 101

CHAPTER IV
ERROR

Nature of error. Abnormal and normal error. Logomania. Verbal emasculation. Proteromania. Pathomania. Variation of moral standards — inconsistency of. Disguises for custom. Standard of inalienable rights of individuals — disguise for custom. Inconsistency with common sense. Standard of natural law. Inconsistency with common sense. Disguise for custom. Economic standard. Inconsistency with common sense. Practomania or production-madness. Disguise for custom. Standard of conservatism. Nature of caution. Inconsistency of standard with common sense. Accelerative policies. No substitute for common sense. End or object of utility 160

BOOK II

THE TECHNOLOGY OF HAPPINESS
PART ONE — THEORETICAL

CHAPTER V
THE FACTORS OF HAPPINESS

Application of common sense. End of utility to be sought by employment of means available. Justice. Analogy of politics with steam engineering technology. Three factors of economy in steam generation. Three factors of economy in happiness generation. End of utility attained by successive approximations. Technology of happiness expressible only in general rules 187

CONTENTS xi

CHAPTER VI

THE FIRST FACTOR OF HAPPINESS

PAGE

Man as a happiness producing mechanism. In primary and secondary capacity. Health. Adjustability. Intelligence. Will. Altruism. Determinants of foregoing characteristics. Inheritance. Racial improvement by selection — effectiveness of. Transmissibility of mental and moral characteristics. Racial improvement by education. Acquired characters. Question of their inheritability. Injuries and functional variations. Effects of germinal experience. Acquired characters not inheritable. Confusion of effects of education with those of inheritance. Racial deterioration — not through education, but through selection. Deteriorating effect of civilization. Education. Means of individual improvement. Objects of. Academic education. Dogmatic influences affecting it. Technical education. Freedom from dogmatism. Education of will. Education in altruism. Function of the church. Theological foundation of morality. Dogmatism — theological and political. Comparison of common sense and other judgments. Origin of dogmatism. Universal distinction between common sense and dogmatism. Origin of conscience. Function of conscience. Dilemma of Intuitionism. Influence of intuitionism on morals. Cause of survival of mediævalism. Educational importance of comprehension of significance of dilemma of intuitionism. Danger of dogmatism. Antidote therefor. Advantages of dogmatism — not to be overestimated 196

CHAPTER VII

THE SECOND FACTOR OF HAPPINESS

Possibility of the adjustment of external conditions. Nomenclature of subject. Productive and consumptive acts. Their varieties. Desiderata. Their varieties. Producing and consuming ratio. Law of self-support. Modes of increasing the margin of self-support. Production. Unpleasantness of average labor. Labor cost. Measurement of production. Efficiency of production. Law of fatigue of production. Law of diminishing returns of labor. Law of increasing returns of labor. Machinery. Origin of. Definition of a machine. Preparatory and final development. Individualistic and socialistic production. Efficiency of socialistic production. Effect on skill and interest of laborers. Labor-saving machinery. Sentient and non-sentient factors of production. Possible modes of utilizing machinery. Consumption. Effect of production-madness. Law of fatigue of consumption. Fallacies connected therewith. Capacity of man for pain greater than for pleasure. Effects of retrospection and anticipation. Efficiency of consumption. Average individual. Self-supporting life. Law of diminishing returns of happiness. Ideal and actual in technology. Curve A — utility of. Curve B. Distribution of production and consumption. Nature of self-sufficiency. Curve C. Mode of calculating daily or yearly

xii   CONTENTS

                                                                    PAGE
happiness output of an average individual. The indicative ratio.
Bearing of law of diminishing returns of happiness on question of
its distribution 266

CHAPTER VIII
THE THIRD FACTOR OF HAPPINESS

Defective economy of consumption of industrial states. Remedy therefor. Essential increase in efficiency of production. Effect of increase and decrease of population on labor cost. Effect on happiness output of a community. Beneficent equilibrium. Determination of just number of population. Effect of change in efficiencies of production and consumption on point of beneficent equilibrium. Efficiency of conversion. Luxurious tastes — low economy of. Simple tastes — high economy of. Variety of taste. Effect of increase in efficiency of conversion on population. Analysis of the factors of happiness. Primary and secondary adjustments. The elements of happiness. Tests of the social system 318

CHAPTER IX
LIBERTY

Confusion of terms. Nominal liberty. Opportunity. Real liberty. The co-essentials of liberty. Objections. Universal human motives. Law — mode of operation of. The adaptive principle. Legal liberty. Paternalism. Relation of legal to real liberty. Theory of *laissez faire* — fallacy of. Rule of utility. Relation of liberty to production and consumption. No necessary relation between utility and inaction. Custom. Property — useful and not useful. Common sense in law. Legal and moral right. Function of government. Nature of society. 333

BOOK III
THE TECHNOLOGY OF HAPPINESS
PART TWO — APPLIED

CHAPTER X
THE SOCIAL MECHANISM

Object of utility attainable only through appropriate social mechanism. Anarchy. Oligarchy. Democracy. Difficulties of democracy. Direct and indirect democracy. Rights of posterity. Characteristics of modern nations. Four forms of democratic mechanism 355

CONTENTS xiii

CHAPTER XI
COMPETITION

Nature of competition. Individualism and anti-individualism. The capitalistic system — characteristics of. Four classes of opposed interests under the capitalistic system. The labor problem. Proposed remedies. Effect of competition on the first element of happiness. Natural selection in nature. In society. Confusion of the goal of man with that of nature. Law of the survival of the incompetent. Competition and education. Effect of competition on the second element of happiness. Resignation not desirable. Dissatisfaction of laborers. Dissatisfaction of capitalists. Competition and health. The third element of happiness. Effect of competition on the fourth element of happiness. Stimulus to development of machinery. To development of inferior products and impositions. The morals of trade. Effect of competition on the fifth element of happiness. Difference between effect upon directive and executive laborers. Labor organizations. Limitation of output. Labor disturbances. Effect of competition on the sixth element of happiness. Distribution of wealth in the United States. Unequal distribution a universal symptom of competition. Cause of. Effect of competition on the seventh element of happiness. Nominal and real wages. Tendency of wages to a minimum and labor time to a maximum. Loss of leisure. Objections — not valid. Army of unemployed. Tendency of indicative ratio to a minimum. Crises. Need of foreign markets. Effect of competition on the eighth element of happiness. The Law of Malthus. Offset to the Law of Malthus. Laws of migration. Popular fallacy concerning population. Happiness of average man. New York as an example. Methods of testing its happiness output. Negative output generally conceded. Conclusion therefrom. Attractions of city. Ideal of a large population. Natural equilibrium. Proposed method of averting. Effects of unrestricted competition. Operation of law of increasing returns alone cannot avert natural equilibrium. India as an example. Possibilities of increase of population in the United States. Increase of population in the United States and the principal countries of Europe 1800–1900. Population and natural resources. Consistent practomania vs. consistent common sense. Comparison of competition with a just social system. Complete failure of competition to meet the tests furnished by the elements of happiness 361

CHAPTER XII
PRIVATE AND PUBLIC MONOPOLY

Evolution of competition into monopoly. Pools. Trusts. Holding companies. Artificial competition. Pseudo-socialism — difficulties of. Socialism. Nature and object of. Socialism and corruption. Socialism and political power. Socialism and efficiency of production. Efficiency of government management. Public utilities. Popular misunderstanding of socialism. Confusion with anarchism. Confusion with communism. Confusion of socialism in production with socialism in consumption. Misunderstanding of morals of socialism. Insufficiency of remedies for competition . . 409

CHAPTER XIII

PANTOCRACY

First essential of an economic social system. Profit — functions of. Substitute for profit. Constructibility of happiness engine — guarantee of. Divisions of pantocracy. Public ownership. Regulation of output. Regulation of distribution. Labor exchange. Adaptation of supply of and demand for labor. Means of. Bureau of inspection. Organization of commodity producing industries. Disposition of funds. Disposition of personnel. Function of wage earners and wage system. Conditional compensation. Function of directors. Sample industry. Six possible conditions of an industry. Supplied and overstimulated industries. Change in producing time. Industrial coefficient. Calculation of standard number of commodities and standard time. Calculation of required increase in personnel. Calculation of prices. Rise in prices — causes of. Simultaneous benefit to producer and consumer in operation of overstimulated industries. Magnitude of effects. Supplied and unstimulated industries. Supplied and understimulated industries. Calculation of prices in. Fall of wages in. Automatic adjustment of. Fluctuating industries. Unsupplied and overstimulated industries. Existence of, implies abolition of poverty. Automatic adjustment of. Improvement of conditions in backward industries. Unsupplied and unstimulated and understimulated industries. Division of working time. Means of insuring invariable adjustment of supply to demand. Provision for expansion of industry. Mode of selecting directors of industry. Mode of determining industrial coefficient. Application to insurance. Foundation of improvement in the arts. Stupidity of present system. Department of industrial improvement. Organization of research. Medical and psychical research. Organization of invention. Board of improvement. Functions of. Universal insurance. National education — importance of. Amount of education determined by efficiency of production. Stimulus to study. Academic education. Instruction in common sense. Objections to. Technical education. Reaction upon the advance of science. Effect of pantocracy on the first element of happiness. Suspension of the law of the survival of the incompetent. Influence on education. Effect of pantocracy on the second element of happiness. Hopefulness in labor. Discouragement to pursuit of wealth. Influence on health. The third element of happiness. Effect of pantocracy on the fourth element of happiness. Stimulus to improvement in the arts. Comparison with competition. Adequacy of conditional compensation. Superiority of pantocracy. Effect of pantocracy on the fifth element of happiness. Identity of interests of those engaged in industry. Disappearance of the labor problem. Stimulus to zeal in work. Comparison with capitalism. Effect of pantocracy on the sixth element of happiness. Large fortunes impossible under pantocracy. Perfect equality in distribution of wealth not sought. Effect of pantocracy on the seventh element of happiness. Emancipation of society from toil. Growth of the humanities and the refinements of life universal. Comparison with effect of competition. Effect of pantocracy on the eighth element of happiness. Suspension of the Law of Malthus. Cure of poverty. Husbandry and economic development of natural resources. Contrast of pantocracy and competition. Possible modes of escaping pain produced by society. Necessity of changing the social system. Delusions of practomania. Commercialism vs. utilitarianism 429

CHAPTER XIV

THE NEXT STEP

Danger of conservatism. Contrast with common sense. Provisional test of pantocracy. Conditions requisite for its success in the United States. Immigration problem. Delusion respecting effects of blending races. Application of common sense to the immigration problem. Effect on posterity. Opportunity of America. Immigration and the Law of Malthus. Protection. Influence on standard of living in America. Improvement in arts no protection. Effect of restriction on dissipation of natural resources. Initiation of pantocracy. Qualifications required in initial stages. Care in extension of the system. Means of transforming private into public monopoly. Confiscation. Destructive competition. Purchase. Acquisition by issue of non-inheritable bonds. Necessity of restriction on the right of bequest. Acquisition by payment of diminishing interest. Centralization safe with direct legislation. Extension of the Golden Rule. Inconsistency of asceticism. Patriotism vs. humanitarianism. *Laissez faire* theory of free trade. Utilitarian theory of free trade. Comparison of their effects upon output of happiness. Foreign trade unnecessary for the United States. Effect of utilitarian theory of free trade on immigration. Injustice of fatalism and sentimentalism. Abolition of war. Humanitarianism. Primitiveness of present treatise. Principles of criticism. Test of practicability. Shallowness of current criticism. Science to solve the problem of happiness 492

THE ECONOMY OF HAPPINESS

INTRODUCTION

Human intelligence from the time of its origin has been engaged in the attempt to solve one great problem — the problem of happiness — and it has failed to solve it. Throughout history the activities of nature and of man have combined to develop the world's potentiality for pain and to leave undeveloped the world's potentiality for pleasure. However hopeful for a happier end, men's acts have not been adapted to its attainment. Hence the great problems of every age, though manifold in form, are one in substance. To-day as always, the omnipresent problem is how to avoid unhappiness and achieve happiness. The being for whom this problem has no interest is not sentient.

If men have failed to solve the problem of happiness it is because they do not know how to solve it. It is not because they lack the will, but because they lack the knowledge. The numerous abortive attempts to cure the ills common to mortality have disposed many persons to the belief that they are incurable — that what has so long been sought in vain must be in its nature so elusive as to be unattainable, and he who presumes to make a frontal attack on the great problem and offer a general solution of it is viewed with suspicion. He is regarded as a dreamer, crank, or nostrum-monger, whose cure-all may safely be spurned as the product of shallowness and presumption. I have no disposition to question the justice of this common judgment, nor to ignore the experience on which it is founded — yet whatever odium attaches to him who attempts a general solution of the problem of happiness I cannot consistently avoid, for in the work to follow I attempt to formulate precisely such a cure-all, precisely such a universal panacea, as critics delight to deride, and in submitting it to the public, do so with complete consciousness of the risk such a course involves. The panacea I propose is *common sense,* and I claim that it will cure all the ills which *can* be cured by any means whatever, and that it offers a complete solution of the problem of happiness. Moreover I claim that there is no other solution, and that the many substitutes which have been proposed and practised will prove in the future, as they have in the past, to be delusions.

But perhaps it may be suspected that in offering common sense as a universal panacea, I am seeking to avoid the responsibility of an ambitious claim by perpetrating a platitude. Anything may be labeled common sense — the name is free to whomsoever cares to employ it, and it is as easy for a sophist to prate of common sense as for a corruptionist to prate of patriotism. Before the solution proposed can be taken seriously then, it must be ascertained what we are really talking about — whether about a word or something more than a word. It is only reasonable to challenge such a claim as I have made by the direct question: Just what do you mean by *common sense?* To judge from the mode in which the term is most often applied, it appears to mean that kind of sense the absence of which men frequently notice in others, but never notice in themselves. Is this the variety of sense to which I have reference? No — it is not; for though this variety of sense is common, it is not common sense.

By the term *common sense* I refer to a kind of sense susceptible of tests which are independent of the convictions of any man or assemblage of men. Its rigorous application removes any problem from the realm of opinion, though not from that of probability. It is my purpose in Book I to offer an analysis of common sense which will, in the measure required by the design of this work, disclose the tests specified.

When we ask a question beginning with the word *why,* that for which we inquire is a *reason,* and reasons are of two classes, and only two. (1) Reasons for beliefs or expectations. (2) Reasons for acts or policies. To ask a question beginning with the word *why,* is to ask either " Why do you *believe* or *expect*"? or " Why do you *do?* " *Common sense postulates that reasons are the tests of beliefs or acts, and that beliefs or acts are not the tests of reasons. Hence the primary concern of common sense is with the nature of a reason.* The common quality of reasonable beliefs is *truth.* The common quality of reasonable acts is *utility.* Hence it is with the nature of truth and utility that common sense is primarily concerned. Could the nature of utility be independently comprehended, a comprehension of the nature of truth would be superfluous, for the ultimate object of common sense is identical with that of utility. But utility, as will subsequently be shown, is indeterminate in the absence of truth. Truth, however, may be communicated or expressed only by means of symbols, verbal or otherwise; and these symbols may or may not be adapted to their purpose. The common quality of symbols adapted to the expression of truth is *intelligibility,* and it is a quality as often replaced by unintelligibility in speech, as truth and utility are replaced by untruth and inutility in beliefs and acts respectively. A comprehension of its nature is essential to a comprehension of the nature of a reason. Common sense then is concerned first with the *nature of intelligibility,* second with the *nature of truth,* and third with the *nature of utility,* and to the discussion of each of these subjects I shall devote a separate chapter. Having ascertained what common sense is in Book I, I shall in Books II and III seek to apply it; not indeed to the problem of happiness in its totality — that would be to discuss every subject of human interest — but to that phase of the problem which concerns the fundamental policies of society.

Before making this attempt, however, it is only fair to warn the reader that I shall not discuss the subjects of greatest popular interest — the concrete applications of common sense — until Book III is reached. It has been my effort to make the earlier parts of the work as interesting and intelligible as the nature of the subject would permit, but despite the best intentions, I fear Book I will prove dry — some portions of it very dry — to the general reader. Book II is better, though the exposition of the Law of Diminishing Returns of Happiness is perhaps rather irksome. As this work seeks to reach, and if possible interest, the class of general readers, or rather such portions thereof as may concern themselves with the great social problems of the present age, I deem it no impropriety to offer some advice to those who are more interested in the applications than the abstractions of philosophy. If apprehensive of being bored by a discussion of logical or ethical theory, I suggest that they first read, or at least peruse, Book III. If what is there expressed appears to lack common sense, I recommend that they read Book II in which are developed the principles applied in Book III. If common sense seems still to be conspicuously absent, Book I, which seeks to develop the philosophy of common sense from the constitution of the mind itself, should be read. If it appears that the principles therein expounded, or any of them, are departed from in Books II and III, I recommend that the reader specifically locate the point of departure, for if common sense has been departed from at all, it must be at some particular point. If such a point is discoverable, then our solution of the problem of happiness is to that extent invalidated. If not, then either common sense has not been departed from, or its nature has been misapprehended. Should the reader come to the latter conclusion, it might be well for him to satisfy himself just where the misapprehension has occurred. This can be done by comparing the principles of common sense as I have expounded them with the principles as they are, and noticing the point or points of divergence. This in turn requires a knowledge of the principles *as they are* — a knowledge not to be acquired " by intuition."

Should criticism show that the following analysis does not embody the true principles of common sense, I shall be compelled to acknowledge the defeat of my primary purpose in offering it; but even should it do no more than stimulate the search for those principles, it will, in that degreee, have contributed to the solution of the problem of happiness.

BOOK I
THE PRINCIPLES OF COMMON SENSE

CHAPTER I

INTELLIGIBILITY

It is customary for those whose purpose it is to expound, to commence their task with a demonstration that the exposition they have in mind is one which it is useful to undertake. Such a demonstration on the part of the present expounder would be one of peculiar difficulty, since as his purpose is an examination into the nature of usefulness and the formulation of precepts sanctioned by that examination, an attempt by him to conform to custom would necessitate the demonstration that a knowledge of the nature of usefulness is useful. But fortunately that which makes the task difficult makes it superfluous, since those who admit the proposition will require no demonstration, and those who deny it, admit by their denial that they speak without meaning.

For a thing to be useful it must be a means to some end and the end must be a good or desirable one. Hence the quality of usefulness in a means implies a quality of goodness or desirability in the end. But means are employed for the attainment of ends only by intelligent beings and the employment of a means to an end by an intelligent being is called a voluntry act. Usefulness then is a quality present or absent in voluntary acts, and as usefulness in a means requires goodness in an end we are led to inquire what kinds of acts will lead to good ends. This is clearly the old question as to what constitutes the difference between right and wrong — a question as old as philosophy.

Kant tells us that the object of philosophy is to supply the answer to three questions: What can I know? What ought I to do? and For what may I hope? Three questions which every philosopher attempts to answer, but so far without success in securing the acquiescence of the world. Were we able to supply an answer to the second query there would be no further question as to the difference between right and wrong, for it is universally conceded that we ought to do right and ought not to do wrong. To many persons it may seem strange that at this late date in the world's history we are still inquiring as to the difference between right and wrong. Surely that must have been settled long ago. At any rate, we hear men of intelligence, clergymen, statesmen, publicists, predicating rightness, usefulness, or desirability of this act or policy, and wrongness, uselessness, or undesirability of that one, with an assurance which, it would seem, must be born of an intimate knowledge of just what the qualities are which are so confidently predicated. And yet a little examination forces upon us the suspicion that, after all, their knowledge cannot be so complete as the confidence they express in their convictions might lead us to believe; for we find that from a consideration of the same data different men come to different conclusions as to what is right and what is wrong. Can any given act or policy be both right and wrong? From what we see and hear around us it would seem so. If we ask the next educated man we meet to explain this apparent anomaly, he will probably inform us that these differences in opinion depend upon different "points of view"; and by the delivery of this judgment will doubtless feel assured that the mystery is at once cleared up. Judging by my own experience, men believe that any paradox may be explained by saying that it all depends upon the point of view. But with all deference to the potence of the phrase, we are constrained to inquire: Does ten times one make ten, or does it depend upon the point of view? If it does, then we see at once what is meant by the phrase. It merely refers to the fact that whether ten times one is ten or not, depends upon the meaning of the words — something that a child might have told us. If it does not, then clearly a knowledge of right and wrong does not rest on a foundation so universally conceded to be sound as does a knowledge of the multiplication table. If it did, there would be no more controversy about the one than there is about the other. The fact is that just what men predicate of acts or policies when they predicate rightness or wrongness of them, is practically always unknown even to those making the predication. This may appear an astonishing assertion, yet the fact must be, and generally has been, admitted by everyone who examines the subject.

In the introduction to his essay on "Utilitarianism," published in 1861, John Stuart Mill uses the following language:

"There are few circumstances among those which make up the present condition of human knowledge, more unlike what might have been expected, or more significant of the backward state in which speculation on the most important subjects still lingers, than the little progress which has been made in the decision of the controversy respecting the criterion of right and wrong. From the dawn of philosophy, the question concerning the *summum bonum*, or what is the same thing, concerning the foundation of morality, has been accounted the main problem in speculative thought, has occupied the most gifted intellects, and divided them into sects and schools, carrying on a vigorous warfare against one another. And after more than two thousand years the same discussions continue, philosophers are still ranged under the same contending banners, and neither thinkers nor mankind at large seem nearer to being unanimous on the subject, than when the youth Socrates listened to the old Protagoras, and asserted (if Plato's dialogue be grounded on a real conversation) the theory of utilitarianism against the popular morality of the so-called sophist."

The condition thus described is the same to-day as it was when the words were uttered. The subject, though the most important to which the attention of the human mind may be directed, is in such a degree obscure that, save for the accident of common traditions, men have no common ground upon which judgments concerning right and wrong may be founded — no criterion by which a good act may be distinguished from a bad one. Now is there anything in the nature of the question which makes it inaccessible to human investigation — is it essentially unknowable — or has there been some constant source of error or confusion operating in the past, which has thwarted the efforts of those who have sought to penetrate the obscurity surrounding it? In this essay I shall attempt to establish a presumption that the first hypothesis is incorrect, and the second one correct.

To settle the question of right and wrong requires that we separate human acts into two, or into three classes: either, into (1) Right, (2) Wrong; or into (1) Right, (2) Wrong, (3) Neither Right nor Wrong; and further requires that we establish some specific criterion by which we may be able to determine to which of these classes any particular act belongs. Now in general how do we go to work to ascertain whether or not any particular thing belongs to any particular class? Obviously by first ascertaining the characteristics of the thing and of the class. How, for example, should we ascertain whether a stone picked up on the roadside belonged to the class *rock* or not? We must first know what we mean by a *rock*, must we not? We certainly could not ascertain if we did not know.

Suppose we define a rock to be a firmly coherent mixture of minerals. If upon examining our stone we find it to be a firmly coherent mixture of minerals, then we know it belongs to the class rock — if we find it to consist of a single mineral, we know it does not belong to that class. This is simple enough. Now suppose we desire to ascertain whether any particular act belongs to the class *right act,* how shall we proceed? Evidently by first ascertaining what is meant by the word *right.* In examining the acts which men call right, however, it appears that there must be considerable confusion in the minds of those who use the term, for while by their language implying the existence of a common test for right and wrong, they never mention what it is or quote anyone who does. Of course, unless we know the meaning of right it is absurd to attempt to ascertain whether any particular act is right or not, nor is it of any service to suggest that the meaning of the word cannot be specified because men disagree as to just what is signified by it. This is only to assert that rightness is something or other about which men disagree. Such an assertion does not distinguish the quality of rightness from the taste of tripe, and leaves us just as wise as we were before anything was said. There can then be no doubt that the first thing to be done in attempting to settle the question of right and wrong is to ascertain the meanings of the terms. This appears reasonable, but how shall we know when we have ascertained them? How shall we distinguish between a real and a spurious meaning? Of course many attempts have been made to give the words *right* and *wrong* a meaning. Every dictionary claims to do it, but examination shows that the definitions or synonyms they supply are not necessarily, or even generally, meanings. Hence, following the process outlined above, it looks as if we should first have to proceed to discover what we mean by a *meaning;* and this is in fact what we must do.

Now it is obvious that we know something about what we mean by a meaning, but it is not so obvious that we might not with profit know more; and *there is reason to believe that the failure to sufficiently examine the nature of meaning, and to apply the knowledge so gained, has in the past been a constantly operating source of confusion, obscuring not only the question of right and wrong, but the whole domain of philosophy,* and has been the cause of the justly merited discredit in which such subjects are held by many thinkers. Metaphysics is notoriously barren. Its cultivation has been compared to the occupation of milking a he goat into a sieve. Well might Newton say, "Physics, beware of metaphysics," for should the methods of metaphysics be introduced into physics there would be an end to its usefulness. In metaphysics we too commonly find the chaos which we should expect to find in geometry if we began the study of that science without defining any of the terms used; endeavoring, for example, to prove that an equilateral triangle is equiangular without knowing what is meant by the words *angle* or *triangle*. The terms used in philosophy are, to be sure, much more difficult to adequately define, but their definition, when possible, is for that reason not the less imperative.

Words are either equally intelligible or they are not. He who denies that words, or their equivalent symbols, vary in intelligibility denies the possibility of a communicable philosophy — he denies the possibility of any communication between sentient beings, and by his very denial convicts himself of inconsistency. He who admits it, admits that there is something which makes, or may make, one word more intelligible than another — he admits that intelligibility is a specific, testable quality of words. Philosophers have a definite test for the consistency of propositions, but none for the intelligibility of terms. The principle of contradiction supplies a criterion of the forms of propositions; a principle of intelligibility is required as a criterion of their substance, and to a communicable philosophy the second principle is as essential as the first.

There are three requirements which every useful symbol of communication, whether verbal or otherwise, must possess. (1) It must have meaning. (2) When used as a means of intercommunication, i. e., of communication between individuals, it must not mislead. (3) When used as a means of intra-communication, i. e., of communication within the mind of a single individual, it must not mislead. It is obvious that these requirements call for more or less conformity to usage, but strict conformity they do not call for. If they did, equivocality and avocality (p. 31) would be requirements of intelligibility. In attributing particular meanings to terms, as much conformity to usage as the infirmities of usage will permit should be sought, but where the issue is between usage and intelligibility it should always be decided in favor of the latter.

Intelligibility is evidently a useful quality of words, but it is not the only useful quality. Usefulness in words may be either of sound, or of sense. Of the first quality we shall have no occasion to treat — it is of importance to poets and rhetoricians, but not to logicians. Usefulness of sense, on the other hand, is of such importance that communicable knowledge would be impossible in its absence. Language has arisen among men because it could serve them, just as any other tool or device has arisen. Words are the signs of ideas or other experiences and are used primarily to communicate the ideas or other experiences in one mind to another. The idea or other experience of which a word (or clause) is the sign is called the *meaning* of that word (or clause). Had it been of no service to men to communicate their experiences language would not have arisen. Therefore it is those experiences which it is of use to communicate which will find expression in words. The experiences which men have occasion to communicate most frequently they will attempt to communicate easily. We should therefore expect to find the most common and conspicuous objects of, or distinctions in, experience expressed by single words rather than by clauses, and this is what we do find. The words, *I, you, earth, sun, hand, north, south, up, down,* illustrate such common words. Common or conspicuous classes of objects, such as *men, animals, trees, houses, clouds,* etc., among general terms and common qualities of objects, such as *wetness, dryness, blueness, hardness, coldness,* etc., among abstract terms are also represented by single words. For most of the less common objects, classes of objects, qualities, or combinations of qualities, no distinctive term is used. Were it so, the number of words in a language would become immeasurably great. Appropriate combinations of the words expressive of the more common objects of experience or their qualities — i. e., clauses, are used to designate these subordinate experiences. There is a word for *building,* applicable to any building, but there is no single word for *building with green blinds,* or *four-story building,* or *building with thirty windows,* though had these objects been sufficiently common among the experiences of men, there is no reason why a separate name should not have been devised for any or all of them. Wherever it has been sufficiently serviceable to have them, distinct names *have* been devised. A building used as a dwelling is called a *house,* one used for worship a *church,* one used for purposes of trade a *store, shop* or *warehouse,* one used for incarceration a *prison,* etc. The reason why buildings are thus classed or given distinctive names according to the purpose to which they are put, rather than according to their color or the number of rooms they contain, is because the first method is found by experience to be useful and the second is not. There is sufficient occasion to call attention to the distinctions expressed by the first method of classification, while the occasions for calling attention to the second are so infrequent that a descriptive phrase suffices to express them. No people will ever have a name for any object or class of objects of which they have no experience. The Esquimaux have no name for *banana, elephant, jungle, coral* or *pineapple.* The aborigines of Central Africa probably have no name for *ocean, locomotive* or *newspaper,* and before the advent of Europeans they probably had no name for *clothes.* But all peoples have names for *sun* and *moon,* for *day* and *night,* for *food, water* and *fire,* for these are familiar to all. In fact we may be quite certain that all conspicuous objects of, or distinctions in, experience which are from their nature universally familiar, will generally be represented in language by single words, and *vice versa* words common to all languages may be expected to represent experiences which are everywhere considered worthy of emphasis. But whatever a word may signify, it is essential that it shall not signify one thing to him who utters it and a totally different thing to him who hears it uttered. There must be some understanding between men as to what particular symbols, verbal or written, shall represent particular experiences, and any confusion in this understanding will be likely to defeat the very purpose which symbols are devised to serve.

There are two methods by which a mutual understanding as to the meaning of words may be attained — *definition* and *exemplification.* The first method makes the meaning plain by associating in an appropriate manner the word to be defined with other words whose meaning is already known; the second, by associating the word directly with the experience of which it is the sign, or with some sensible representation of it; as when children are taught the meanings of the words *cat, dog, man, tree, house,* by associating the words with pictures of the appropriate objects, or with the objects themselves. We may also exemplify by means of words — as when we convey the meaning of the word *horse* to a foreigner by telling him that it is the animal to be observed drawing vehicles in the street. The meaning of words is best conveyed where both methods are employed, one supplementing the other, for each has its advantages. A definition is not an enumeration of all the qualities of a thing or class of things, but only of so many of them and no more, as are necessary to distinguish the thing or class of things from other things or classes of things, and the number and degree of the qualities which it is essential to specify will depend upon the degree of resemblance between the object defined, and other objects of experience from which, for the purpose in hand, it is convenient to distinguish it. The care required in exemplification is dependent upon similar considerations.

In discussing the subject of intelligibility there is one class of words which we shall have no occasion to consider; such words, for example, as *the, quite, and, of, slowly,* and conjunctions, prepositions, and adverbs in general. They are what the schoolmen called *syncategorematic* words, or words which have no meaning by themselves, but only when combined with other words. They represent nothing of which anything may be predicated.

The principal class of words which we shall have occasion to discuss are what is known as *terms* or *names*. They may consist of one or more words. Hobbes has defined a name as follows: "A name is a word taken at pleasure to serve for a mark, which may raise in our mind a thought like to some other thought which we had before, and which, being pronounced to others, may be to them a sign of what thought the speaker had before in his mind." This definition evidently conforms to our notion of the nature of meaning, and is sufficiently explicit for our purposes.

Terms are generally divided for purposes of definition into two classes, *concrete* and *abstract* terms. Concrete terms are the names of things; abstract terms the names of qualities of things. *Apple* is a concrete term; the form, the flavor, the color and all the other qualities of the apple are represented by abstract terms. The form has no single term to represent it, as in any actual apple the form is very complex; to the flavor is given the name *tartness* or *sweetness* according as it is a tart or a sweet apple; to the color is assigned the term *redness, greenness,* etc., according to circumstances, and so with the other qualities, and when all the qualities of the apple have been enumerated, the apple is completely described, for the apple and the sum of the qualities of the apple are the same thing, and even two apples, or two other material objects whose qualities are identical, except for a difference in their location in space, or time, or both, will be distinguishable by the difference in quality implied by such a difference in location. Were they identical in their location in space and time they would not be two objects, but one. This is all we mean when we say two objects cannot occupy the same space at the same time, for under such conditions they would, by definition, be one.

As any object or thing is merely a combination of qualities, so any concrete term is merely a short symbol for expressing the combination of several — perhaps a great many — abstract terms; it is a sort of compound abstract term. In fact all, or almost all, our experiences consist of compound impressions or ideas, often of great complexity, and this is particularly true of visual experiences. Objects seen are generally recognized as consisting of a very complex association of sensations of form and color. To enter into any detailed discussion of the psychology of sensation would take us too far away from our present subject. Suffice it to say that compound qualities, of which objects are limiting cases, are recognized as consisting of simple qualities related to one another by what is termed the relation of co-existence. In the idea of an apple, for example, we recognize the qualities of *redness, hardness, sourness,* and others associated together as elements constituting the experience of an apple, but in such a term as *redness* we can recognize no constituents. The first is an example of a *compound,* the second of an *elementary experience*. In the degree in which compound experiences contain the same elements they are similar; in the degree in which they contain different elements they are dissimilar. Two experiences consisting of the same elements, including location in space and time, would, as already explained, be indistinguishable, that is, they would be one experience.

Although elementary experiences, also called *simple perceptions,* are indefinitely numerous, they all belong to a few classes. According to Huxley the following table of the mind's contents includes them all. (I have slightly modified his classification.)

TABLE OF THE CONTENTS OF THE MIND.

(1) Impressions.
    A. Sensations.
        a Smell
        b Taste
        c Hearing
        d Sight
        e Touch
        f Resistance (the muscular sense)
        g Pleasure
        h Pain

B. Relations.
   a Co-existence
   b Succession
   c Similarity
   d Dissimilarity

(2) Ideas.
Copies, or reproductions in memory of the foregoing.[1]

Impressions characterized by the sensations designated a, b, c, d, e and f are called *phenomena*. All other experiences are *non-phenomena*.

If the above list represents the complete contents of the mind, it is evident that all men can think of, or speak of, must be included in it; and he who seeks a foundation for philosophy, whether speculative or practical, must find it here. But without debating the question as to whether or not the list *is* complete, it is clear that it includes the principal classes of elementary experiences, and I shall base no conclusion upon assumptions which depend for their validity upon its completeness. If then a term is, as Hobbes has told us, a word "to serve for a mark, which may raise in our mind a thought . . . which, being pronounced to others, may be to them a sign of what thought the speaker had before in his mind," or if, as the authors of the Port Royal Logic assert, "Words are sounds, distinct and articulate which men have taken as signs to express what passes in their mind," then *terms must represent some elementary experience or combination of such*, since they are all that can be in the mind, and hence, if our list is complete, it must include, not only all of which men can think, but all to which names can be applied, and if it is not complete, it does not mean that terms do not represent experiences, but merely that one or more elements of experience are absent from the list.

Mill gives the following list of "Nameable Things," with such remarks as he deems appropriate:

"1st. Feelings, or States of Consciousness.
"2nd. The Minds which experience those feelings.
"3rd. The Bodies, or external objects which excite certain of those feelings, together with the powers or properties whereby they excite them; these latter (at least) being included rather in

[1] Essay on Hume, p. 85.

compliance with common opinion, and because their existence is taken for granted in the common language from which I cannot prudently deviate, than because the recognition of such powers or properties as real existences appears to be warranted by a sound philosophy.

"4th and last. The Successions and Co-existences, the Likenesses and Unlikenesses, between feelings or states of consciousness. Those relations, when considered as subsisting between other things, exist in reality only between the states of consciousness which those things, if bodies, excite, if minds, either excite or experience." [1]

A short inspection of this "Classification of Existences" must convince anyone that it is as hopelessly confused as the Categories of Aristotle which it is designed to replace. If indeed, contrary to our claim, names do refer to something not to be found among the contents of the mind, it is obvious that such as do so cannot be defined or exemplified, since these are processes for directing the attention of one mind to a portion of its contents similar to that which is engaging, or has engaged, the attention of another. It would, I apprehend, be difficult to say what can be meant by the meaning of a name, if Mill's category of nameable things be accepted, unless indeed, it is intended to represent his manner of classifying the contents of the mind, and such a supposition would seem to be precluded by his inclusion of "States of Consciousness" in the first category. Words are, or should be, the signs of ideas or impressions, and a term which does not represent something in experience has no meaning at all; its only use is in its sound. A term useless in sense is merely a meaningless term. A term useful in sense is one which has a meaning — i. e., one that symbolizes something in experience. Now the definition of a term is an enumeration of the qualities essential to distinguish the class of experiences represented by the term from other classes of experiences; hence it is obvious that terms which represent the elements of experience cannot be defined, since, as they do not consist of a combination, no enumeration is possible. They cannot be expressed in terms of simpler experiences. Elementary experiences then, are expressed in *indefinable* terms — all others are expressed in *definable* terms — and, as all compound experiences are but combinations of elementary ones, it follows that all definable terms, in their last analysis, must be expressible in indefinable terms;

[1] System of Logic, Longmans, Green and Co., 1889, p. 49.

and if we find the definition of a term not expressed in terms thus indefinable, we may know that the definition has not been reduced to what we may denominate its lowest terms.

It is well to call attention here to the fact that although elementary experiences may not be expressible in simpler terms, they are not necessarily simple, if we mean by simple having no quality common to other experiences. Red and green, for example, are called different kinds of colors — that is, they are both colors or possess the common quality of color; but we are quite unable to think of a color which is not some particular color. The sound of a flute is not a compound of the quality *sound* with some other quality x. Red is not a combination of some simple quality which we may term y with the quality *color* — as an apple is a combination of the color *red* with the quality of *oblate-sphericalness* and numerous others. In the case of the apple we are able to separate these qualities from one another, and to recognize the object called an apple as their sum; but when we speak of kinds of sounds or kinds of smells or kinds of tastes, the word *kind* does not imply a relation of combination. Yet it must be admitted that red, yellow, green, etc., have some quality in common, otherwise we should not apply to them the common term — *color*. Red, for instance, resembles green more than it resembles the shape of a sphere or of a cube. By what do we recognize this difference in resemblance? It is convenient to answer this question by saying that it is by means of the presence or absence of the quality *color* that we do so. On the other hand, the experience of red and the shape of a sphere resemble one another more than either of them resembles the taste of a pickle or the sound of a horn. They therefore have a common quality, absent in the taste or sound — a quality to which we give the name *visuality*. That is, red is a kind of color, color is a kind of visuality, or visual experience, visuality is a kind of sense (one of the senses), and classed with the others by reason of the common quality of sensuality, and sensuality is a kind of experience — the common quality of experiences is known as *consciousness,* and it is the only absolutely simple quality of experience.

In order to have words adapted to express the relation between such qualities as red and color, or taste and different kinds of tastes, and to enable us to distinguish between the undissociable relation by them exemplified, and the dissociable relation exemplified by the various qualities, *redness, tartness, hardness,* etc., whose combination we call an apple, we shall denominate qualities related in the latter manner *abstractable* qualities, whereas those related in the former manner we shall call *unabstractable*. Hence an elementary quality of experience is not an absolutely simple one, but a compound of unabstractable qualities, none of which are definable.

Now while terms which stand for elementary experiences cannot be defined, they may easily be exemplified. The term *red*, for instance, may be exemplified by pointing out that it stands for the quality present in a brick and a brilliant sunset, but absent in an evergreen tree and a sheet of white paper. Although the qualities of visuality and of color would be present in the first two examples, they would not be absent in the second two. The quality *red* is the only one which would fulfil the conditions. Similarly the odor of ammonia cannot be defined, but it may easily be exemplified. Of course, the table on page 15 is that for a person of normal faculties. It would not hold good for a blind or a deaf person, for example. To a person blind from birth, it would be impossible to convey the meaning of any term representing a visual experience, since the elementary experiences could not be exemplified, and the same is true of a person deaf from birth with regard to terms expressive of sensations of sound. In fact the communication of meaning, in its last analysis, is dependent upon the power to exemplify, and a definition not founded upon exemplifiable elements of experience can never get beyond the verbal stage. From these considerations it appears that *a term incapable of definition can have a meaning, but that one incapable both of definition and of exemplification cannot.*

Experiences are characterized, and may be designated, by the absence of qualities as well as by their presence. Thus such terms as *colorless* or *odorless* are employed to express the absence of color and of odor respectively. The word *nothing* is employed to express the absence of all quality; that is, *nothing* is that which is inexpressible in terms of experience.

It would be a useless, if not a hopeless, task to express all terms in indefinable terms; it is seldom if ever necessary to do so, because although all elementary terms are capable of being made familiar to a person of normal faculties, they are not the only terms that are, for there are many familiar terms that are not elementary. It is well, however, to keep in mind the fact that a term not defined in terms of elementary experience, is only proximately defined, and if, in its use, we find ourselves or others led to perplexing or unexpected conclusions, we should at once suspect our definition, for in the inadequate definition of terms is to be found the most elusive of all sources of confusion.

It seems to some persons inexpedient to examine into the meanings of the words used in an argument. If such a one in the course of a discussion is asked to explain the meaning of some term he has used, and gives it perhaps in words no less unfamiliar than those already employed, and is requested to define his definition, he is likely to claim that such a mode of criticising an argument is illegitimate, and that we should not attempt to define all words. A smilar impression is shared by some logicians. The author of the Port Royal Logic remarks:

"I say, further, that it would be impossible to define all words; for, in order to define a word, we must of necessity have others which may designate the idea to which we may attach that word; and if we still wish to define the words which we have employed for the explication of it, we should still have need of others and so on to infinity. It, therefore, is necessary that we stop at some primitive terms which cannot be defined; and it would be as great a fault to wish to define too much as not to define enough, because by one or the other we should fall into that confusion which we pretend to avoid."[1]

Now if we have made no mistake in our apprehension of the nature of definition, the "primitive terms which cannot be defined" are those representing elementary experiences; hence if A is defined in terms of B, B in terms of C, C in terms of D, etc., the process cannot be carried on to infinity, but must stop when it has arrived at the indefinable but exemplifiable terms representing elementary experiences; and if necessary we are entitled to inquire into the meaning of terms used in discussion to any degree requisite to convert a verbal into a real definition (p. 24). It is obvious that such a succession of inquiries, if carried on in bad faith, can make discussion impossible — it is always easy for bad faith to find means of escaping an argument which it cannot meet — but this is no reason why discussion in good faith should not be permitted any degree of latitude in inquiring into the meaning of terms: indeed it would be preposterous to deny the propriety of such inquiry, since, should we do so, the sophist could, without fear of in-

[1] The Port Royal Logic, 5th edition; Edinburg, p. 85.

terruption, make inferences of any degree of absurdity by a succession of fallacies of equivocation. But while it may be perfectly proper, it is not often expedient to attempt to reduce definitions to their lowest terms; our effort should be to reduce them to terms *sufficiently* (p. 28) low. Pascal in the Port Royal Logic has well expressed the proper course as follows:

" The most perfect method available to men consists not in defining everything and demonstrating everything, nor in defining nothing and demonstrating nothing, but in pursuing the middle course of not defining things which are clear and understood by all persons, but of defining all others; and of not proving truths known to all persons, but of proving all others."

Whatever else may be meant by the word *personality,* it certainly refers to a succession of states of consciousness, not, to be sure, isolated and distinct from one another, but melting the one into the other in what Professor James has called a " stream of consciousness " normally discontinuous only during periods of sleep. It is convenient to be able to refer to particular portions of this stream, and to any particular portion is given the name of a *state of consciousness,* or we may call it, an *experience.* It is better, however, in general, to apply the name *experience* to some specified portion of a state of consciousness, co-existent with other portions, though we may include the whole as a special case. Thus the same state of consciousness generally contains many experiences. For example, we may be eating, while at the same time listening to conversation, looking about us, and walking up and down. Under these circumstances, we have simultaneous experiences of taste, hearing, sight, touch (of our feet on the ground) and of the muscular sense, and each of these by centering our condition thereupon may be found to consist of several, perhaps a great number, of experiences which we may — unless unabstractable — consider as distinct, and in subsequent contemplation separate from the experiences with which they were co-existent.

When a state of consciousness is thus divisible into two or more co-existent portions, each may be called the *associate* of the others, so that if we have occasion to fix our attention on any particular experience — call it A — which is recognized as bearing, or having borne, the relation of co-existence to other experiences — B, C, D, etc., then B, C, D, etc., may be called the *associates* of A. The relation of the state of consciousness of which A is a component to those which precede and succeed it, we shall call its *location in time,* or simply its *location* — the location of A being the same as the location of its associates. Thus if d is the state of consciousness of which A is a component and it is one of a series of consecutive states, b, c, d, e, f, etc., then b, c, will be its immediate *antecedents,* e, f, its immediate *consequents* and the position which d occupies in the total sequence of which b, c, d, e, f, etc., are a portion is its *location.* The associates and the location of A will collectively be called its *primary co-ordinates,* as they completely fix its place as a component of personality. By its *secondary co-ordinates* we shall refer to the relations of simultaneity and succession which it bears to the experiences of other beings.

In actual experience elementary sensations do not occur in haphazard association, one combination on the whole being as frequently experienced as another, but certain combinations are much more common and frequently occurring than others, and indeed of the immeasurable number of possible combinations, relatively few are encountered in experience. Certain constant combinations continually recur, and the great variety of experience consists of these constant combinations with which, from moment to moment, variable qualities associate themselves. In the world of experience, expressible in terms of sight and touch for example, we find continually present the combination of qualities which is expressed by the term *space.* However our sensations of sight may vary, these qualities persist, and on analysis may be recognized as elements of all our varying visual experiences of the world of external things. Certain other constant qualities added to those of space give us the association of experiences which we call *matter,* for matter possesses all the qualities of space — in fact is a peculiar kind of space — just as a liquid is a peculiar kind of matter. Matter in turn by the addition of qualities is classified into solid, liquid and gaseous, and these into their manifold varieties until we get all possible forms of visible and tangible nature. To those combinations which occur associated most commonly, and to their principal modes of change, distinct names are given, and thus language arises. The first objects of experience to receive names were probably those most familiar and to which it was most serviceable to refer. Later, names for classes of objects, or general names, arose, and in the course of time the more restricted classes of objects were merged in more comprehensive,

CHAP. I]　　　　　INTELLIGIBILITY　　　　　23

until in developed languages such names as *object* or *thing* are to be found, which in ordinary usage are comprehensive enough to include any concrete combination of visible and tangible experiences whatever. The recognition of an object as belonging to, or included in, a class of similarly constituted objects resembling one another in certain specific attributes, and of this class in turn as belonging to a greater class, and so on, is of considerable service in the consideration of the nature of definition. Let us consider the following series of definitions:

(1) An oak is a tree which bears acorns.

(2) A tree is a plant with a trunk, and perennial in duration.

(3) A plant is an organism, devoid of consciousness under all circumstances.

(4) An organism is a material body possessed of life.

(5) A material body is an existence which occupies, but is not space.

(6) An existence is anything real.

Without inquiring into the intrinsic merit of these definitions, let us call attention to several points illustrated by them.

First, they are (with the exception of No. 6) expressed in a form which definitions in general may be made to assume, viz.: A is a kind of B — An oak is a kind of tree, A tree is a kind of plant, A plant is a kind of organism, etc. In the language of logic a definition has three parts: (1) The *species* which is the thing or class of things defined. (2) The *genus*, a class of things having greater extension (see below) than the species, and serving to exclude the species from all classes of things not included in the genus. (3) The *difference*, consisting of one or more qualities distinguishing the species from other members of the genus. Thus in definition No. 2, *tree* is the species, *plant* the genus, and the *quality of perennialness and those implied in the possession of a trunk,* the difference. The genus distinguishes a tree from all things not plants; the difference from all plants not trees. No. 6 would probably never serve the purpose of a real definition. It is not in logical form and is no more than a statement of the equivalency of synonyms.

Second, they illustrate what is called the *extension* and the *intension* of terms. Concrete terms have two kinds of meaning: (1) The meaning in *extension* or the sum of the things of which the term is the name, e. g., the word *tree* is the name of any and all trees wherever found, and (2) The meaning in *intension* or the sum of the qualities which distinguish the thing or class of things of which the term is the name from all other things or classes of things, e. g., the qualities implied in the term *tree* added to, or combined with, the quality of bearing acorns, distinguish oaks from all other things whatever. The fact that whatever bears acorns is always an oak does not make the attributes of a tree any the less an essential part of the definition of an oak, since in the absence of these attributes, or any of them, any acorn-bearing object would not be called an oak. The definitions also illustrate what is universally true, viz., that, as the extension increases, the intension decreases, and *vice versa*. The term *plant*, for example, is the name of many more objects than the term *tree;* but the term *tree* possesses or implies a greater number of qualities than the term *plant*. The first has the greater extension, the second the greater intension. Terms are said to *denote* their extension and *connote* their intension.

Third, they may be made to illustrate the difference between *real* and *verbal* definitions, than which no distinction in the theory of definition is more crucial. As we have pointed out on page 17, to know the meaning of a term is to know its intension, i. e., the qualities which distinguish the object for which it is a name from other objects, but these qualities are either one or more of the elementary perceptions recorded on page 15, or some combination or class of combinations of them. Therefore, to know the meaning of a term is to know the sum of the elementary experiences by which the objects of experience for which it is a name are distinguished from other objects of experience. This does not necessarily, though it does frequently, mean that these are the experiences which we will have if we encounter the object; neither does it mean that these experiences are reproduced in consciousness when we hear the term and apprehend its meaning. What it does mean is, that should we encounter the combination of elementary experiences implied by the term, we should recognize them as the object of which the term is the name. We might encounter an oak, for example, and yet from the definition alone might not recognize it, strictly speaking, from one encounter, we could not — yet we certainly would, if of normal faculties, perceive a combination of sensations in its presence, and sensibly the same combination as that received by a person whose observation of the tree had been sufficient for him to have determined it to be an oak. On the other hand, on hearing an oak spoken of, the recognition of the meaning of the term would not necessarily involve any definite image of an oak arising in our mind. We might think only of some symbol, such as the word *oak*, and if the term recognized had been one of slight intension like the term *matter*, we almost certainly would have thought of some symbol. It is scarcely possible that the image of matter should have arisen in our minds, since it can hardly be said to have an image. If, however, by sufficiently long continued observation of an object we satisfied ourselves that it was a tree, namely, possessed a trunk and lived for a series of years, and furthermore observed that it bore acorns, we should recognize it as the object to which the name *oak* was applied. Moreover, we should not have been able to make these necessary observations had we been devoid of the faculties (of sight) through which the elementary sensations of which the observations were the sum, were felt, nor should we have been able to recognize the sensations so felt as those implied in the term *oak*, had we been ignorant of what sensations were implied by that term. Such terms as *peculiarity, demonstrativeness, awkwardness*, etc., are subject to the same rule. On encountering a combination of elementary experiences implied by one or another of these terms we should either recognize it as one to which the term was applicable, or we should not. If we did, the term would have a meaning for us; otherwise it would not. The uncertainty which we feel about such terms is but the evidence that they are vague, that is, have no very definite and delimitable meaning.

A definable term is simply a short symbol or abbreviation for its definition, and its definition may be substituted for it in any proposition without altering the import of the proposition, just as in algebra the values of x and y may be substituted for them in any equation without altering the truth of the equation. Thus the word *plant* is a short method of saying " an organism devoid of consciousness under all circumstances," just as 4×4 is a short method of saying $4+4+4+4$ and 4^4 is a short method of saying $4 \times 4 \times 4 \times 4$. We thus express in a single term 4^4 what in the notation $4 \times 4 \times$ . . . it takes four terms to express, and had we substituted the first mode of notation $4+4+$ . . . we should require sixty-four terms to express what is expressed by 4^4 in one. Now a similar convenience attaches to the terms used in language. Few definable terms, except those of very slight intension, would bear expression in elementary terms without becoming unuseable and unintelligible from their very length. We may illustrate this in a partial manner, sufficient to suggest the inconvenience involved, by expressing the term *oak* in terms obtained by substituting for the several genera in the series of definitions we are considering, the definitions as given. Thus — An oak is an existence, which occupies but is not space, possessed of life, devoid of consciousness under all circumstances, with a trunk, and perennial in duration, which bears acorns. This merely suggests what the definition would become were we first to define every term in it, including those employed, in stating the several differences, in indefinable terms. Should we have the patience and ingenuity to do so, the definition would extend over several pages, and be completely unintelligible, nor could we construct a useful definition in terms of elementary experience of any term with such great intension as the term *oak*. These considerations afford us insight into the mechanism of thought itself. They show us that not only is our capacity for expressing thought to others limited by the symbols available, but our capacity for thinking as well. If anyone will observe himself while thinking out a subject of any complexity, he will find he is in reality talking to himself, and those familiar with several languages will in this process, by preference, employ the language most familiar. Although we cannot express with any precision in terms of elementary experience what we mean by the term *oak*, yet we are confident that when we encounter the appropriate experiences in combination we shall recognize that they are those implied in that term, and this, of course, we could not do, were we ignorant of what they were. When a person is thus able to recognize the experiences implied in a term and connect them with the term as constituting its meaning, we shall say that the term is one *familiar* to him, and it is this which we shall imply by the adjective *familiar* when qualifying the sense of a term. It too often happens that a word familiar in sound is assumed to be familiar in sense, when it is not — hence the necessity of strict definition.

Now suppose there are two persons, A and B, to whom we submit the definition: "An oak is a tree which bears acorns." And suppose A to be familiar with the terms *tree* and *acorns*, and B to be unfamiliar with them and with the word *oak*, but both A and B to be familiar with the other words of the definition. Then A may be said to have a *real* knowledge, B to have a *verbal* knowledge of the meaning of the term *oak*. B, if he understood the language, would know that the word *oak* was a short method of expressing the succession of articulate sounds " A tree which bears acorns " but this knowledge would not help him in communicating his experiences to others, or of apprehending the experiences which they might seek to communicate to him. To him, the definition would be of precisely the same value as the expression: " An x is a y which bears zs." A, on the other hand, would have not only the verbal knowledge possessed by B, but his familiarity with the terms in which the definition was expressed would enable him to use the term *oak* to achieve the ends which words are intended to achieve — those namely, of thinking and of communicating thought. To convert B's verbal knowledge into a real one, we should have to continue defining the words *tree, acorn,* etc., until we reached words with which he was familiar, or we should have to teach him their meaning by exemplification, and thus by directly associating the term with the combination of elementary experiences which it represented, make him familiar with it.

The foregoing discussion having revealed the real nature of meaning, we are prepared to reduce the information now in our possession to definite criteria.

To satisfy the first requirement of intelligibility it is necessary and sufficient that a term symbolize something in experience. Thus if the term x symbolize one or more combinations of elementary experiences to one person A and symbolize the same or different combinations to a second person B the first requirement of intelligibility is satisfied. The term has meaning.

To satisfy the second requirement it is necessary that whatever combination of elementary experiences the term x signifies to A, it shall signify to B a combination such that when used in communication between A and B neither shall be misled. The processes which insure the fulfilment of the second requirement are definition and exemplification. Hence the necessity we have been under of discussing them. The extent to which these processes must be employed to achieve sufficient similarity between A's meaning of the term x and B's meaning thereof will depend upon the use to which the term is to be put. A term is useful in sense only when it is employed in the expression of probability. Therefore, in this part of our discussion, we shall be forced to anticipate the chapter following in a slight degree. It is there shown that probability is the name of a quality common to expectations having a specific origin, and that the expression of these expectations is embodied in propositions which include two or more terms. What concerns us here is that the necessary degree of similarity between A's meaning of the term x and B's meaning of that term will depend upon what expectation it is to be used to express in communication between A and B. Now all that is necessary in order to meet the second requirement of intelligibility is that the similarity in meanings signified by a term shall be such, that the expectations which it is employed to express shall be the same in the mind of the person to whom said expectations are communicated, as in that of the person who communicates them. This does not mean that the expectations in both minds must be identical, but simply that the expectations designed to be expressed must be identical. When this condition is fulfilled the term will not be misleading — when it is not, the term will be misleading — and thus the implication of the adjective *misleading* is made plain. It is apparent then, that for some purposes very little similarity in the meanings of a term is required to prevent the expression of misleading expectations, and that for other purposes great similarity is required. For example, if A understood by the term *potato* that which is generally understood, viz., a certain edible tuber; and B understood by the same term a very different thing, viz., that which is generally called a pumpkin, the meaning of the term would be sufficiently similar in the minds of A and B if the expectation to be communicated was expressed by the proposition " Potatoes are good to eat," for this is true both of potatoes and pumpkins; but if the expectation to be communicated was that embodied in the proposition " Potatoes grow beneath the ground," the meanings would not be sufficiently similar, for this is not true of pumpkins.

Now a term which can meet the second requirement of intelligibility I shall denominate a *sufficiently* defined or exemplified term, one which cannot meet it I shall call *insufficiently* defined or exemplified; or I may refer to the distinction as that between terms sufficiently and insufficiently *intelligible* or *familiar*. Thus by clearing up the meaning of the word *misleading* as applied to the connotation of terms, the second requirement of intelligibility is made definite and it is now apparent that there may be any degree of confusion in the meaning of a term so long as the propositions in which it is employed are such as to be valid whichever of the various meanings are attributed to it. Intelligibility does not require that terms always be understood in exactly the same meaning. If it did, few terms outside of mathematics would be intelligible and the bulk of the words in all languages would be useless. I have not, for example, attempted to define or exemplify every term used, or to be used, in this work. It would obviously be impossible. The common knowledge of a language among men implies greater or less similarity among the meanings which they attach to the terms occurring in that language. If any term used in communication is insufficiently defined or exemplified for the purpose to which it is put, it will inevitably lead to misapprehension, but everyone who seeks to communicate thought by language is compelled to trust the definition or exemplification of the great majority of the terms he uses to the common processes which constitute the acquisition of a common language. These processes do not insure the fulfilment of the second requirement of intelligibility, and hence arises confusion which can only be remedied by carefully fixing the meaning of those terms which cause the trouble. Such terms I shall attempt to sufficiently define or exemplify, but others I shall leave alone, thus following the counsel of Pascal of "not defining things which are clear and understood by all persons, but of defining all others." Care in the definition of terms, however, involves one difficulty. By restricting the use of words to certain definite meanings they are no longer available as means of expressing the distinct, though related, meanings to which usage extends them. Hence these meanings are left with no means of verbal expression. In mathematics this dilemma would cause no difficulty, since additional symbols would be brought into requisition wherewith to express them; but such a policy is scarcely practical outside of mathematics since it would introduce into language too many strange and unfamiliar terms. Therefore I have, in a number of instances in this work, used terms in meanings not identical with those I have attributed to them, but in all cases have been careful to employ them in such a context as not to mislead. In a bare outline of the principles of intelligibility, such as this chapter pretends to be, it would be impractical to formulate a nomenclature sufficiently extensive to eliminate all equivocal terms. To discover equivocality in the terms used in this exposition then does not constitute a criticism thereof, since the vital question is not, are the terms used in any degree equivocal? but, are they *sufficiently* equivocal to mislead?

Another mode of criticism which cannot be deemed valid as applied to an exposition of the character of this one is that which makes usage the test of terminology. As the object of language is to communicate thought, the all too common method of criticizing definitions according as they do or do not conform to usage, results in deflecting the most important of issues into the barren realm of purely verbal controversy. The meanings of terms should be judged according as they are or are not adapted to bring clearly before the mind the important objects of, and distinctions in, experience; not as to whether they are or are not in conformity with this or that usage. Failure to apprehend this matter leads to verbal emasculation, a subject discussed in Chapter 4.

The second requirement of intelligibility, so far as I am aware, admits of no more specific expression than that which I have employed. In general this requirement can only be met when we have knowledge of the substance of propositions. Relationships to the form of propositions are indeed discoverable, but I deem them scarcely worth discussion in this essay.

Having thus prescribed the conditions required to meet the second requirement of intelligibility, we may proceed to inquire what conditions are required to meet the third. We have observed that the operation of thinking is essentially an operation of talking to one's self. The formulation of propositions is the function of a different mental faculty from that which tests their validity. In the operation of thinking we have a condition equivalent to that of communicating thought — the situation is practically the same as when one person submits propositions to another. Hence the conditions necessary to meet the third requirement of intelligibility are the same as those required to meet the second, and the absence of these conditions will cause a person to mislead himself in the same way that they will cause one person to mislead another. If the reader doubts that this be so, I recommend that he attempt to express to himself what he means by such words as *cause, existence, matter* — and if he can at the first attempt specify the qualities, and the only qualities, which he implies by those terms, so successfully as to stand every subsequent test which he may apply, it will prove him a person of extraordinary analytical acumen. If he fails to recognize what qualities he himself implies by those terms, can he avoid admitting that his knowledge of his own meaning may be insufficient for communicating certain thoughts, even to himself? No one can long have observed the operations of the human mind, his own or others, without noticing with what facility men mislead themselves with words, and this would not occur if the requirements of intelligibility were fulfilled. But a yet more significant phenomenon is to be observed than the confusion of one meaning with another. Men frequently perform mental operations resulting in the formulation of purely verbal propositions which are neither true nor untrue but simply unmeaning. By inducing similar barren manipulations of terms in other minds they may construct a whole series of verbal propositions which have the form of doctrines, but being devoid of any element of expectation are incapable of symbolizing truths. Approval of a formula is thus mistaken for belief in a proposition.

The word *sufficient* as applied to terms which meet the second requirement of intelligibility I shall apply in the same sense to terms which meet the third requirement. That is, a term used in thought is *sufficiently* defined or exemplified, *sufficiently* intelligible or familiar, if it conveys the expectations in the expression of which it occurs without misleading the thinker. The word *insufficient* will be employed with a correlative meaning.

It may be said of any term in common use that it either has one and only one meaning, or it has not. If it has, it is called a *univocal* term. If it has not, it is either *equivocal* or *avocal* (Lat. *a* or *ab* = not: *vox* = a voice, a word) that is, it has more than one meaning or less than one. If it is avocal, its only usefulness consists in its sound. If it is equivocal, it will be useful for some purposes but not for others, and whether it is safe to use it or not will depend upon whether it fulfils, or fails to fulfil, the appropriate requirement of intelligibility.

To summarize: terms are used either for inter-communication or intra-communication. To satisfy the necessary and sufficient conditions of intelligibility, they must, if of the first class, fulfil the first, and second: if of the second class, the first and third requirements of intelligibility. Terms may on this basis be classified into (a) Inter-intelligible (b) Inter-unintelligible; and into (c) Intra-intelligible (d) Intra-unintelligible.

Inter-univocal terms all belong to class (a). Inter-equivocal terms may belong to class (a) or to class (b). Inter-avocal terms belong to class (b). Similarly intra-univocal terms all belong to class (c). Intra-equivocal terms may belong to class (c) or class (d). Intra-avocal terms belong to class (d).

While it would be very convenient if all men employed the same terms with one meaning and only one, this is not absolutely necessary for inter- or intra-communication. If the conditions of sufficient intelligibility are met confusion will be avoided — but *let no one cherish the delusion that because terms are sufficiently intelligible for some purposes that they will be sufficiently intelligible for all purposes*. The examples which we shall hereafter encounter will, I believe, leave no excuse for such an error.

Of all insufficiently intelligible words, *right* and *wrong* are the most important. In attempting to discuss their meaning, we found it necessary first to discover the meaning of the word *meaning* itself. This we have done, but before our goal is attained a still more difficult subject must be discussed which will constitute the theme of the next chapter.

CHAPTER II

TRUTH

As all with which the philosophy of common sense concerns itself is mind, and as the object of the present chapter is to disclose the nature of truth, the attainment of that object will require a further examination of the Table of the Contents of the Mind (p. 15). It will there be observed that the several classes of experience are divided into (A) Sensations and (B) Relations. The basis for the classification is sufficiently obvious. Any particular sensation of sight, taste, touch, pleasure, pain, etc., may be experienced independently of any other, but perceptions of relation are derivative, and arise from the comparison or association of at least two impressions or ideas. The perception of similarity cannot be experienced until at least two impressions or ideas which, on comparison, exhibit that quality, have arisen in the mind, and the same is true of the perceptions of dissimilarity, and of co-existence and succession. To experiences which thus arise from the comparison of experiences we give the name of *relations* and those enumerated in the table are the four classes of elementary, or indefinable, relations. By the name *impression* we shall designate only those vivid experiences characteristic of perceptions of the external world, and following Hume we shall give to other kinds of perceptions, consisting largely of the less vivid copies or derivative combinations of impressions supplied by the imagination, the name *ideas*. If we examine ideas, we shall find that they consist of a great many classes. To two of these I desire to call attention. (1) Those consisting of copies of simple perceptions recognized as being combined in a manner similar to some combination which has in the past been experienced — these we call *memories*. (2) Those consisting of copies of simple perceptions cognized as being combined in a manner similar to some combination which is in the future to be experienced — these we call *expectations*. Both of these classes of ideas may vary much in definiteness, from vivid copies to obscure adumbrations, from distinct images to mere suggestive symbols.

As illustrating the symbolic character of expectations it may be noted that the anticipation of such severe physical pain as that of having a tooth pulled, in itself involves no pain — or at any rate none resembling that expected.

Expectations may be copies of memories, or they may not be. The perception of succession is common to both expectations and memories, but it is clearly not the only perception implied by the terms, for if it were we should be unable to distinguish between them. It is, however, an unabstractable quality of both classes of experiences, and they may be considered as two kinds of perceptions of succession, just as we may consider green and red as two kinds of sensations of color.

To express the particular class of experiences which will form the principal subject of this chapter no single word in our language has as yet been devised. The term *expectation,* however, is the nearest approach to it: hence for the purpose of this exposition I propose to give to that term an extension of meaning, independent of usage, by means of which the theory of the nature of truth herein maintained may be expounded. In thus extending the meaning of a term already well known and slightly, if at all, ambiguous, I am but adopting the method commonly employed in expounding mathematics, of enlarging the implication of such terms as *product, power, root,* etc., as higher and higher branches of the subject are reached, and the gain in usefulness which justifies the extension in the latter case, justifies it in the former.

The term *expectation* as already defined then, I shall regard as referring to but one subdivision of the class of experiences to the expression of which I shall extend it. In its implication as already given, it is subject to the three following restrictions. (1) It refers only to personal experiences — the anticipated experience and the expectation thereof must be felt by the same individual, they are part of the same sequence. (2) It refers only to actual experiences — to those actually expected. (3) It refers only to future experiences. The extension I propose giving the term may be said to consist of the removal of these three restrictions. Hence I shall exemplify the extension in three divisions.

(1). Under the term *expectation* I shall include not only anticipations of personal experiences, but anticipations of the experiences of other beings. The distinction is between "what I may expect" and "what others may expect." Such expectations I shall call *impersonal* as distinguished from *personal.* An impersonal expectation is *definite* if the person or being whose experience is expected is specifiable; *indefinite* if unspecifiable. When we say we expect our brother John will have dyspepsia tomorrow, we express a definite impersonal expectation. When we say we expect an eclipse of the sun will be observed in Africa on the fifteenth of the month, we express an indefinite impersonal expectation.

(2). Under the term *expectation* I shall include, not only anticipations of actual experiences or such as are anticipated under the actual conditions expected, but also of such as would be experienced were those conditions different. The distinction is between "what is expected" and "what might be expected." Such expectations I shall call *conditional* as distinguished from *unconditional*. When we say we expect to see the sun rise tomorrow, we express an unconditional expectation. When we say we might expect to see it rise if we were awake early enough, we express a conditional expectation. One peculiarity, and that an important one, of conditional expectations is that they may be entertained of experiences possible in the imagination only — a point discussed on page 93.

(3). Under the term *expectation* I shall include not only anticipations of experiences which may or might be felt in the future, but also of such as were or might have been felt in the past — and in the case of impersonal expectations of such as may or might be felt at present. The first distinction is between "what is expected" and "what it is expected was or would have been." Such we may call *past* as distinguished from *future* expectations. The second distinction is between "what is expected" and "what it is expected is or would be." Such we may call *present* as distinguished from *future* expectations. When we say we expect Socrates drank poison, we express a past expectation. When we say we expect our brother John is eating lobster salad in the next room, we express a present expectation.

Two kinds of restrictions upon expectables are from what has preceded readily discoverable. (1) That due to the absence of some faculty, such as sight, hearing, or touch. (2) That due to the relation of contradiction, the presence of one quality implying the absence of its contradictory. The one restricts the *kinds* of perceptions which may enter into an expectation: the other restricts the *combinations* in which they may enter. In other words, we are unable to expect a conjunction between elementary experiences or combinations thereof which we have not experienced, as a man blind from birth is unable to expect a conjunction including the color yellow; and we are equally unable to expect a conjunction between contradictory qualities, as between *hard* and *not hard, white* and *not white,* when these terms refer to the same object or portion thereof.

In order to avoid troublesome explanations, iterations, and circumlocutions, I shall generally in the exposition to follow speak of expectations as if they were always personal, actual, and future, but the theorems which I shall establish concerning them will not be restricted to that class of expectations, but will be true of expectations in general, and may be applied thereto by noting the manner in which I have extended the meaning of the term. As future expectations are by far the most important class, particularly for the purpose which this work has in view, little will be lost in failing to adapt our mode of expression to expectations of the past and present.

The words *horse, wall, star, hardness, dryness,* etc., obviously express no expectation. It cannot be said that alone they express anything capable of being expected or not expected, and it is indeed clear that a single term cannot express an expectation. If, however, we say " The wall is hard " we have evidently expressed something capable of being expected. That which is expected is a *conjunction* between the qualities implied by the term *wall* with the quality of hardness; and it is true in general that *the only expectable things are conjunctions, or the absence of conjunctions, between elementary experiences or combinations thereof.* Even in the expectation expressed by such a proposition as " I am to see my friend " the impressions implied by the phrase " my friend " are expected to be conjoined with definite, though perhaps unspecifiable, primary coordinates. Indeed if they were not, the expectation would not be recognized as a personal one. The elementary experiences or combinations thereof between which conjunction is expected (or observed) are called the *members* of the conjunction.

The verbal symbol or expression of an expectation is called a *proposition.* Categorical propositions, which are those most commonly employed in logic, always consist of three parts; two terms and an expression of relation. The first term is called the *subject* and connotes one member of the conjunction, the second is called the *predicate* and connotes the other, and the word which expresses conjunction between them (always some form of the verb " to be ") is called the *copula.* That expectations are adapted to expression in this particular form results from the manner in which experiences are distributed. We have already suggested that although all combinations of elementary experiences are imaginable except contradictory ones, yet in fact all combinations do not occur with equal frequency in experience; but that certain combinations are much more frequent than others. To the most common or conspicuous combinations distinct names are awarded, and thereby the world of experience is divided into a great number of classes. The names of these classes are called *general terms*. The words, *planet, house, man, material thing, volition, emotion,* are examples of general terms. A general term, however, may be expressed by a phrase, and often is. Thus such a phrase as "Persons employed for the purpose of keeping the peace" would be a general term. Now the classes of objects of experience of which general terms are the names may or may not be mutually exclusive. When we say a class of objects is distinguished by the qualities A, B, C, D, we do not mean that no member of the class has any other qualities, but merely that all members have these. Similarily a class characterized by the qualities a, b, c, d, may have many other qualities besides. If we designate the first class by X and the second by Y, it is evident that X and Y may have members in common or they may not. That is, X and Y may overlap each other in extension in any degree limited by mutual exclusion on the one hand, and by complete inclusion or identity on the other. The amount of this overlap determines the degree of completeness of conjunction in intension, and by the use of quantitative propositions may be expressed to various degrees of precision; but in order to make matters simple, it is usual in formal logic to treat only four forms of proposition.

To express complete inclusion logicians employ the form — All Xs are Ys, affirming inclusion and denying exclusion. To express mutual exclusion they employ the form — No Xs are Ys, affirming exclusion and denying inclusion. It might be expected that the most convenient way of expressing a partial overlap would be by the proposition — Some Xs are Ys and some are not, and this in some cases might be a convenient form. For the purposes of logic, however, it is found best to express a partial inclusion or exclusion by two different forms of proposition, viz.: (1) Some Xs are Ys, and (2) Some Xs are not Ys. A very little consideration will make evident the reason why these forms are generally more convenient than the preceding. When we have discovered that there is an overlap between classes X and Y and desire to express that discovery it is most convenient to say — Some Xs are Ys. While it might be true that some Xs are Ys and some are not, it is obvious that it would require more observation to justify such an assertion than it would the first form, since the simple discovery that some Xs are Ys does not necessarily imply that some are not. Hence the proposition — Some Xs are Ys, affirms inclusion without denying exclusion. The same considerations of convenience have dictated the form — Some Xs are not Ys, which affirms exclusion without denying inclusion. These four forms of propositions have been named as follows:

(1) All Xs are Ys is called a Universal Affirmative Proposition.

(2) No Xs are Ys is called a Universal Negative Proposition.

(3) Some Xs are Ys is called a Particular Affirmative Proposition.

(4) Some Xs are not Ys is called a Particular Negative Proposition.

And in one or more of these forms it is possible to express any or all expectations, personal or impersonal. Particular propositions frequently occur with such words as *most, many, a few, a very few* in place of the word *some,* thus designating more or less closely how large a proportion of the class denominated by the subject is referred to, and De Morgan has considered propositions of this character in his discussion of the numerically definite syllogism.

To exemplify the four different classes of propositions perhaps we cannot do better than to employ the diagrams first used by Euler in illustrating the method by which the different forms of propositions express inclusion and exclusion. (See Fig. 1.) The diagrams will explain themselves. The letters in brackets are those which it is customary to use in place of the names of the various propositions. Thus A is merely a short way of saying Universal Affirmative proposition, E a short way of saying Universal Negative proposition, etc. The examples are as follows:

(1) Universal Affirmative. (A) All men are mammals.
(2) Particular Affirmative. (I) Some trees are evergreens.
(3) Universal Negative.   (E) No men are immortal beings.
(4) Particular Negative.   (O) Some coins are not silver objects.

CHAP. II]   TRUTH   39

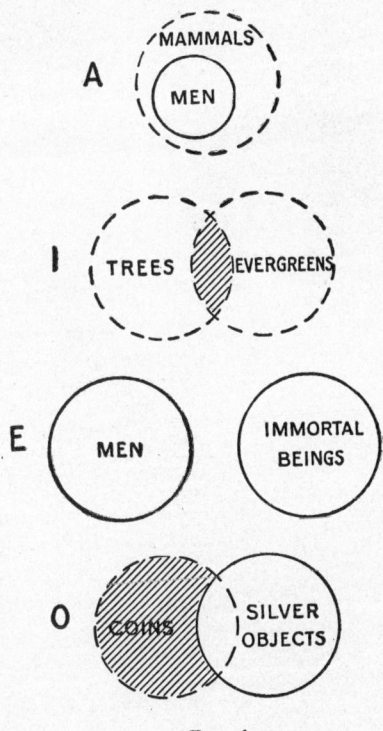

Fig. I.

In order to remove all doubt, I have in the case of propositions I and O shaded those portions of the diagram which represent the conjunctions predicated by the corresponding propositions. Thus I affirms that a portion at least of the class *trees* is identical with a portion at least of the class *evergreens;* and O affirms that a portion at least of the class *coins* is identical with a portion at least of the class *not silver objects*.

A term is said to be *distributed* when it refers to all the members of a class; *undistributed* when it refers to some of the members only. In the diagrams I have enclosed the undistributed terms in dotted lines and by reference to them the following table, showing in which forms of proposition the subject or predicate is distributed and in which undistributed, may be verified.

			Subject	Predicate
Universal	Affirmative	A	Distributed	Undistributed
	Negative	E	Distributed	Distributed
Particular	Affirmative	I	Undistributed	Undistributed
	Negative	O	Undistributed	Distributed

It may appear obscure why O distributes its predicate, but if we remember that the proposition — Some As are not Bs, may equally well be expressed by the proposition — Some As are not any or all Bs, we see that the predicate refers to the whole class of Bs.

Perhaps a few words ought to be said about three kinds of categorical propositions which might, when encountered, be considered different from any I have mentioned.

(1) Identical propositions, such as — A is A, or — A is B, when B is a synonym of A, would be represented by a diagram consisting of one circle, since as the subject and predicate are identical the circles representing them would coincide. Such propositions express complete conjunction.

(2) Singular propositions, such as — Agamemnon was a Greek, in which a singular term is the subject are special cases of universal affirmative propositions. A singular term is only the limiting case of a general term, and in a singular proposition the subject may be said to be distributed, since it refers to the whole class, consisting to be sure of but one object.

(3) Definitions are expressed in the form of categorical propositions. They are in fact identical propositions, but give us information about words only. They are not therefore the less important, for without the knowledge expressed by them, we could neither think clearly on any but the simplest subjects, nor could we communicate thought.

Precisely the same expectations as are expressed in propositions of strict categoric form may be expressed in other forms. For instance, the proposition — Some metals are not combustible substances, would usually be expressed in the form — Some metals are not combustible — the word *substances* being understood, but although expectations may be expressed in various forms, all of them may be reduced to some one of the four mentioned.

Euler's diagrams enable us to see how well adapted the form of expression embodied in a proposition is to stand as a symbol for an expectation. If X represents the assemblage of qualities implied in the definition of the subject, Y the assemblage of qualities implied in the definition of the predicate, then a proposition of form A conveys the knowledge that whenever X is encountered, Y is to be expected; form I, that sometimes when X is encountered Y is to be expected; form E that whenever X is encountered Y is not to be expected; form O that sometimes when X is encountered, Y is not to be expected. Hence to have the knowledge implied in any of these propositions means that we are able to prophesy one quality or set of qualities from another, to tell from qualities observed what other qualities may be observed; in other words to foresee, and foresight is the immediate object of knowledge. Thus by the proposition — All ice is cold, we should be led to expect the experience of cold should we touch an object having qualities of colorlessness, transparency, polish, etc., characteristic of ice, and similarly with the qualities implied by the terms *men* and *mammals,* or *trees* and *evergreens,* occurring in the examples recently given.

Now it is an observation familiar to all that expectations are sometimes fulfilled or realized, and sometimes are not. How should we designate a being whose expectations were always fulfilled: whose every expectation as to what is to be, or what might have been, experienced at any time or place, is, or would be, verified? Should we not call such a being *omniscient,* or *all-knowing?* If so, then a being whose expectations are such as always to be verified is one possessed of all knowledge — at least, concerning the things of which he entertains expectations. But suppose we expect a series of events A, B, C, D, and also expect a series of events E, F, G, H, and suppose the events A, B, C, D, occur, but E, F, G, H, do not. Would it not be said, in general, that of the events A, B, C, D, we had knowledge, but of the events E, F, G, H, we thought we had knowledge, but did not have it? If so, then knowledge would seem to consist of a certain kind of expectation, viz. of any expectation which will be, or would have been, fulfilled.

It is obviously of the utmost importance to our inquiry — as indeed it is to all inquiries — that we should understand the nature of knowledge and be able, if possible, to distinguish knowledge from that which is not knowledge but appears to be; for it is unnecessary to suggest that our conduct is at least largely, and as we hope to show, ought to be wholly, guided by our knowledge of its consequences. Is there then any means of testing expectations whereby those which will be fulfilled may be distinguished from those which will not? Are there any means of avoiding the latter class of expectations? If so, what are they? In other words, how are we to distinguish knowledge, from that which is not knowledge but appears to be? If such a test is to be discovered it obviously must be found by an examination of past experience, since this is all that is open to our examination. That is, expectations may be tested only by memories; we can have knowledge of the future only from an examination of the past, and we shall in the course of this chapter show how such an examination may reveal the test which we seek.

Let us call expectations which will be fulfilled *valid* expectations: Those which will not, let us call *invalid* expectations — the words *valid* and *invalid* applying also to the propositions expressive of each kind respectively. The question asked in the last paragraph may now be expressed thus: Is there any way in which a valid expectation or proposition may be distinguished from an invalid one?

This query may be answered by saying that no infallible, or invariably successful, method has thus far been found; but a method which in the past has given excellent results, and is likely to give them in the future has been discovered, and is capable of formulation. This is known as the *inductive* or *scientific* method, and before we can sufficiently comprehend the nature of truth, of which we are in search, it will be necessary to understand its principles.

In order to do this, we must begin at the beginning and again consider certain classes into which expectations may be divided. They may first be classified as (1) Those established by the inductive method. (2) Those not so established. Consideration of the first class will be postponed until the nature of the method designated is revealed. Members of the second class are known as *intuitions* and may, for the purpose we have in view, be further classified in two ways. First as (1) *Universal intuitions,* or those common to all minds, and not functions of the location in space or time of the individuals who experience them. (2) *Local intuitions,* or those not common to all minds, but functions of the location in space or time of the individuals who experience them. Second, they may be classified as (1) *Ineradicable intuitions,* or those the contradictory of which are unexpectable or incapable of being conceived. (2) *Eradicable in-*

tuitions, or those the contradictory of which *are* expectable or capable of being conceived.

Now the scientific method postulates that all knowledge is derived from two sources (1) *Observation* and (2) *Universal Intuition.* The mental processes by which expectations are derived from these sources are known as *inferences.* Inferences which conform to the rules of the inductive method are called *correct* inferences and claim to lead to valid expectations or knowledge. Correct inferences are distinguished from incorrect by a class of experiences called *reasons,* citable in support of the former, but not citable in support of the latter kind of inference. To reveal the nature of a reason for an inference, or the expectation resulting therefrom, is the object of *logic.*

Correct inferences may be divided into two kinds: (1) Processes for deriving valid expectations from observations. (2) Processes for deriving one valid expectation from one or more others. The first kind of inference is called *induction,* the second *deduction,* and on the basis of this classification logic is divided into *inductive* and *deductive logic.*

All knowledge is founded upon experience — observation precedes expectation. Hence should we treat the subject of logic in what might be called its natural order, we should consider first how expectations may be correctly derived from observations. This, however, would not be the most readily comprehensible method of treatment, so I shall first treat of the modes whereby one expectation may correctly be derived from others, that is, of deduction.

Deduction: Deduction is a mental process depending upon the so-called LAWS OF THOUGHT, expressible as follows:
    (1) *The Law of Identity: Whatever is, is.*
    (2) *The Law of Contradiction: Nothing can both be and not be.*
    (3) *The Law of Excluded Middle: Everything must either be or not be.*

Should the words in which are expressed the axioms, or self-evident truths, of mathematics be sufficiently defined, it would appear that they are special cases of the laws of thought, and these laws have one common characteristic, viz., whoever denies any of them contradicts himself. Hence we shall refer to these laws as if they constituted one law, to which we shall give the name — the LAW OR PRINCIPLE OF CONTRADICTION. It is a universal ineradicable intuition. It is said to be *certain.* When I experience the sensation of a red color, a sweet taste, or any other sensation or perception, there can be no doubt that I experience it. It is certain that any combination of qualities is always conjoined with itself; in other words, that what is, is. Hence to say that a universal ineradicable intuition is a certainty gives us no information about a universal ineradicable intuition, but it does about the meaning of the word *certainty*. As a contradiction is, so far as I know, the only relation between perceptions which is universally unthinkable, I shall confine the meaning of the word *certainty* to the laws of thought: in short, by a *certainty* I shall mean the contradiction of a contradiction, and any proposition involving such a relation I shall call *certain*. By an *inconceivability* or *impossibility*, on the other hand, I shall simply mean a contradiction, and any proposition involving a contradiction is the expression of an impossibility.

A certainty may be considered as a special case of an expectation, distinguished from all others by the fact that its contradictory is not only unexpected, but unexpectable. Certainty is also called *absolute truth*. It is a special case of truth, and as purely deductive inference deals with absolute truth alone, I shall provisionally identify truth with absolute truth.

Although certainties are tenacious convictions of all men, tenacity of conviction is no test of certainty. This is proved by the existence of local ineradicable intuitions, involving a corresponding local certainty. They consist of various doctrines, usually of a theological character, which are confined to certain localities or periods of history. There is no reason known to me for believing that intuitions of this class have any particular relation to knowledge, except that they are mistaken for it. No one knows how many there are of them, and their status is very doubtful. It is claimed by many Christian theologians that the proposition — God exists, or — God is an existing Being, is the expression of an ineradicable intuition; that is, it is not possible for them to think or imagine otherwise; and Mohammedan theologians would doubtless affirm that the proposition — There is but one God and Mahomet is His prophet, embodied an ineradicable intuition, or fixed conviction of theirs. Now an intuition of this class cannot be profitably discussed; hence when someone tells us in good faith that he has such an intuition, we can say no more than that it is one not shared by many others — that it is a purely local affair. It cannot be usefully disputed however. All we can say is — " If you have that kind of an intuition, then that is the kind of an intuition you have." The origin of local intuitions will be disclosed in Chapter 6.

Deductive inference may be divided into (1) *Immediate inference,* (2) *Mediate inference.* Immediate inference may be divided into (a) *Inference by conversion,* (b) *Inference by opposition.* Mediate inference is accomplished by an operation whose expression is called a *syllogism,* and hence may be called *syllogistic inference.*

Inference by conversion: If we glance at the diagrams on page 39 we shall see that besides expressing the proposition with which each is associated they express equally well the following propositions: No. 1 is equivalent to the proposition — Some mammals are men. No. 2 is equivalent to the proposition — Some evergreens are trees. No. 3 is equivalent to the proposition — No immortal beings are men. No. 4 is equivalent to the proposition — Some not silver objects are coins.

These are called the *converse* of the corresponding propositions, the subjects and predicates being interchanged. The process is called *conversion,* and by its use we are able to infer from the proposition — All men are mammals to the proposition — Some mammals are men; from the proposition — Some trees are evergreens to the proposition — Some evergreens are trees, etc.; or stating the matter in general terms, we may from a proposition of the form A infer a converse proposition of the form I; from I we may infer the converse in the form I; from E the converse in the form E; and from O the converse in the form I. Now it may appear to the reader that the change from Some trees are evergreens to Some evergreens are trees, is too simple and obvious to be called an inference. The two propositions appear to say the same thing. Even the change from All men are mammals to Some mammals are men, though not quite so simple, is hardly much of an inference, and there has arisen some controversy as to whether these are really inferences. Indeed there has been considerable discussion among logicians as to whether any of the processes of deductive inference really pass from one truth to another; for, say the critics, the conclusion merely expresses what was already involved or implicitly contained in the premises. The discussion apparently arises from the failure of logicians to sufficiently define the words *inference* and *truth.* When it is once understood that a truth is merely a kind of expectation, and that deductive inference is merely a process whereby one expectation arouses or excites another, the controversy is seen to be an idle one. Each person must decide for himself, and it would be impossible for another to decide for him, whether the proposition — Some mammals are men does, or does not, arouse expectations different from those aroused by the proposition — All men are mammals. Now some men might say it did, and some might say it did not. Hence to be on the safe side, all correct changes of propositions which are, or might be, adapted to arouse the appropriate expectations are called inferences. Were it to be admitted that no new truth could be arrived at by deductive inference because the conclusion is always involved in the premises, then it would have to be admitted that the *pons asinorum*, for example, is not a different truth from that expressed by the axioms and definitions of plane geometry, for this proposition is implied or involved in those axioms and definitions; nevertheless it undoubtedly arouses expectations not aroused by them, and hence is a new and different truth. This matter will become clearer as we proceed.

Referring to the converted propositions on page 45, let us attempt to deny them while affirming the propositions from which they were derived by conversion.

To deny No. 1 we should have to affirm: No mammals are men.

To deny No. 2 we should have to affirm: No evergreens are trees.

To deny No. 3 we should have to affirm: Some immortal beings are men.

To deny No. 4 we should have to affirm: No not silver objects are coins.

Let us now compare the diagrams of these denials with the diagrams of the originals on page 39. (See Fig. 2.)

A glance at these contrasted diagrams shows that the propositions which they respectively express are inconsistent with one another: that in affirming them both we contradict ourselves. To affirm that no mammals are men is to affirm that no men are mammals, and to affirm this, and at the same time affirm that all men are mammals, is to affirm that men are mammals and not mammals, that what is, is not. This is a contradiction in terms, and of course expresses nothing which it is possible to expect. Of two contradictory propositions we cannot expect both, though if they are not contradictions in terms we may think we can, because of the confusion in meaning of the propositions, and it is a common thing for persons to assert belief in contradictions. Those, for instance, who assert the omniscience

CHAP. II] TRUTH 47

and omnipotence of God while denying the doctrine of pre-
destination do this. Every inconsistency is, in fact, an implicit
or explicit contradiction.

These considerations show that we are able from a given

Diagrams of the original prop-   Diagrams of the denials of the cor-
          ositions.   responding converted propositions.

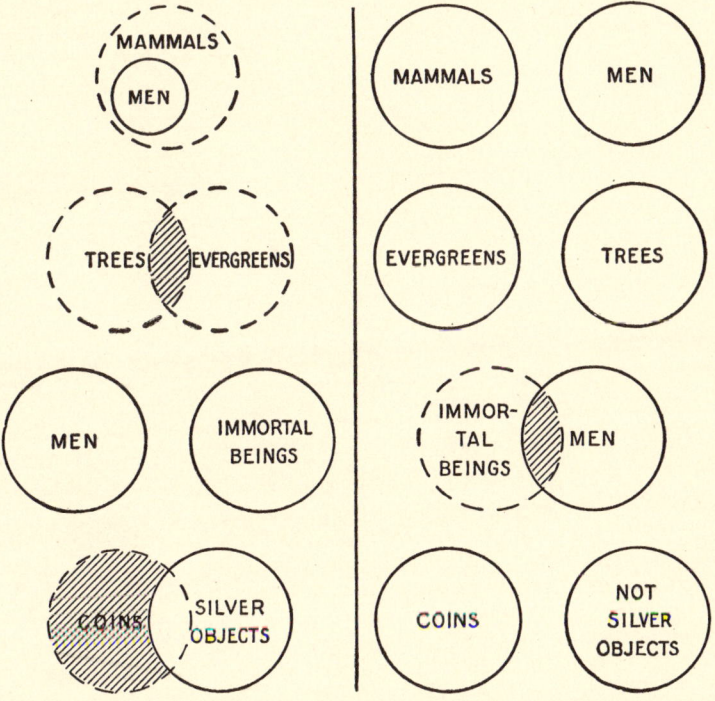

Fig. 2.

proposition to derive other propositions, the denial of which involves the denial of the given proposition. This leads us to
the principle in accordance with which one expectation may be
derived or deduced from another, viz.: *Any proposition A which
bears a relation to a proposition B, such that the denial of A*

involves the denial of B, is a deduction or proposition deducible from B.

A simple extension of this rule can be made to cover cases in which one expectation is derived from two or more other expectations, viz: *Any proposition A which bears a relation to two or more propositions B, C, D, &c., such that the denial of A involves the denial of one, though not a specifiable one, of the propositions B, C, D, &c., is a deduction or proposition deducible from said propositions.*

Inference by Opposition: By the opposition of propositions the relation of opposition which the four forms of categorical propositions A, I, E, O, bear to one another is referred to. For example, if I know the proposition — All men are mammals — to be true, I can immediately infer that the proposition — Some men are mammals — is true, and the propositions — No men are mammals — and — Some men are not mammals — are false, i. e., not true. Similarly if I know the proposition — Some metals are not combustible — to be true, I can infer that the proposition — All metals are combustible — is false, though I cannot infer anything concerning the truth or falsity of the propositions — Some metals are combustible — and — No metals are combustible; that is, they remain doubtful. Similar inferences may be made from propositions of the forms I and E. The relations of opposition and the inferences possible from these relations are shown in the following table, taken from Jevons. It applies, of course, only to propositions having the same subject and predicate:

	A is	E is	I is	O is
If A be true	true	false	true	false
If E be true	false	true	false	true
If I be true	doubtful	false	true	doubtful
If O be true	false	doubtful	doubtful	true

Inference by Syllogism: Proceeding now to mediate deduction, suppose we consider two propositions: Say — All mammals are vertebrates — and — All men are bipeds. Can we infer anything more from these in conjunction than we can infer from them separately? Apparently not. They have nothing in common by which to compare them. They are quite unrelated propositions. But suppose we should change the predicate of the last proposition, so that the propositions became — All mammals are vertebrates — and — All men are mammals. From these two propositions it is obvious that we may infer that — All men are vertebrates. We have been enabled to make this inference because the two propositions have a common term, *mammals,* and by comparing the other two terms with this common term an expressible relation may be found between men and vertebrates. By comparing the diagrams of the three propositions, the justification of the inference is made plain to the eye:

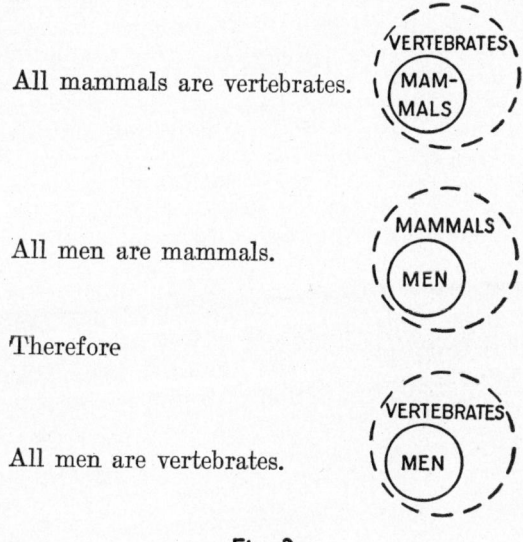

All mammals are vertebrates.

All men are mammals.

Therefore

All men are vertebrates.

Fig. 3.

The relation between the three, and the reason why the inference is possible explains itself. If vertebrates include all mammals, and mammals all men, obviously vertebrates include all men. In all cases in which the appropriate relation of inclusion or exclusion between two classes by means of a third class can be established, inferences of this kind may be drawn. Fig. 4 furnishes an example in which one of the premises is particular.

All metals are elements.

Some metals are incombustible substances.

Therefore

Some incombustible substances are elements.

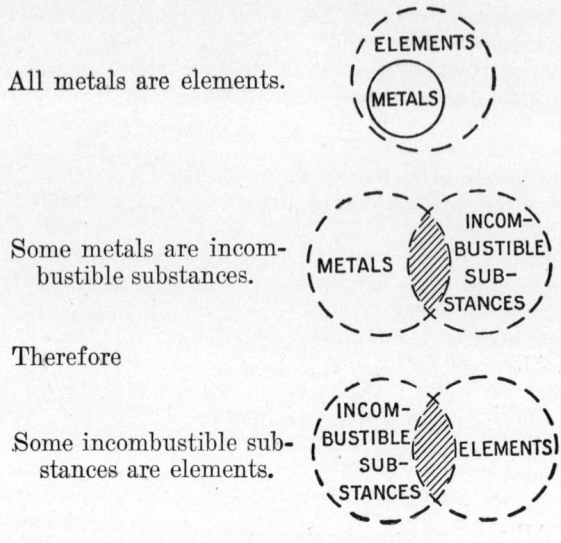

Fig. 4.

An inference of the character here illustrated, wherein two propositions containing but three terms between them enable us to draw an inference which could not be drawn from the propositions separately is called a *syllogism*. The two propositions from which the inference is made are known as the *premises;* the proposition inferred from them is the *conclusion*. The term common to the premises is called the *middle term,* and through its *mediation* the inference is made possible. The predicate of the conclusion is called the *major term,* and its subject the *minor term*. The middle or mediating term, of course, never occurs in the conclusion. The premise containing the major term is called the *major premise* — that containing the minor term the *minor premise*.

A syllogism is evidently a deduction. To deny the conclusion is equivalent to denying one of the premises. Hence to affirm the premises and deny the conclusion involves a contradiction. By combining the four forms of categorical propositions, A, I, E, O, two by two, in all possible variations, logicians have discovered that there are just nineteen different ways in which a conclusion may be correctly inferred from two premises. To each of these ways a Latin name has been given and these names may be found in any logic. They do not concern us here. It has been discovered, however, that in all nineteen forms of syllogism the premises and conclusion are so related to one another as to conform to the following rules, as formulated by Jevons:

1. Every syllogism has three and only three terms.

These terms are called the major term, the minor term, and the middle term.

2. Every syllogism contains three, and only three propositions.

These propositions are called the major premise, the minor premise, and the conclusion.

3. The middle term must be distributed once at least, and must not be ambiguous.

4. No term must be distributed in the conclusion which was not distributed in one of the premises.

5. From negative premises nothing can be inferred.

6. If one premise be negative, the conclusion must be negative; and *vice versa,* to prove a negative conclusion, one of the premises must be negative.

From the above rules may be deduced two subordinate rules, which it will nevertheless be convenient to state at once.

7. From two particular premises no conclusion can be drawn.

8. If one premise be particular, the conclusion must be particular.

These are called the *Rules of the Syllogism*. All correct syllogisms obey them. Hence, if we find a conclusion related to its premises in a manner which does not conform to these rules we may know it is not a correct syllogism; that it is not a correct deduction, although it may appear to be one. In saying that a syllogism which does not conform to the rules of the syllogism is incorrect, no more information is conveyed about the characteristics of a syllogism than was conveyed about the laws of thought by the assertion that they were certain. In other words, we *mean* by a correct syllogism one which conforms to the rules just given, and by a correct deduction one which conforms to these rules or those given for making immediate deductions. Incorrect deductions are called *fallacies,* and as their many varieties are discussed in every book on logic I need not discuss them here.

Letting this brief discussion of deduction suffice, let us consider the more complicated kind of inference known as induction.

Induction: In examining the nature of deduction we have had occasion to point out how from one or more valid expectations others might be derived, but the methods there discussed did not suggest how an expectation was to be derived from something not an expectation. The premises of any given deduction may be the conclusions of former deductions, but if we trace back such a series of deductions we must finally arrive at propositions not established by deduction. How then can such propositions be established? Experience alone can establish them, and it is of the mode by which experience establishes the fundamental propositions which are the ultimate premises of all deduction that inductive logic treats.

In the consideration of inductive logic, two methods of classifying experience will be useful:

First, experiences may be divided into (1) Personally observable experiences, which of necessity are confined to one person, such as pleasure, pain, volition, etc. (2) Impersonally observable experiences or those which more than one person may observe, such as result from the observation of the animate and inanimate objects which surround us, and their movements.

Second, experiences may be divided into (a) Those involving a perception of relation. (b) Those not involving a perception of relation.

Of these two latter classes, the first only is capable of expression in a proposition and experiences of this class are the foundations of all knowledge. Logicians in treating of inductions generally confine their inquiries to experiences of phenomena, and in the discussion which follows I shall do likewise. The application to non-phenomenal experiences will, however, be sufficiently clear. The principles are the same for both.

Now all knowledge of phenomena is derived from experience of phenomenal impressions. An impersonally observable relation among phenomenal impressions I shall call a *phenomenal conjunction* or, for brevity, simply a *conjunction*. In an assemblage of conjunctions having one member in common, said member is called the *common member*. The others are called *conjoined members*. A conjunction having a beginning is called an *event*. A conjunction not necessarily observed but expected to be observable, is called an *observability*. To predicate the *occurrence* of a conjunction is to predicate its observability. A conjunction actually observed is called an *observation,* and observations are the foundation of all knowledge of phenomena. It is from this particular kind of experience that such knowledge arises. But here we meet a difficulty. It has been asserted that observations of phenomena possess the quality of impersonal observability. Can we be certain that such a quality is always possessed by them? To this question we must answer No. It is impossible to assure ourselves beyond all doubt that the things we observe about us are observable by others, or even that experiences other than our own exist. No method has ever been suggested, for example, whereby we may, with certainty, distinguish between the impressions of a dream and those of waking life. Purely imaginary impressions of phenomena such as those observed in delirium are of no value in induction, because they do not possess the quality of impersonal observability. This quality is, in fact, assumed. It will appear later that such an assumption is equivalent to *assuming that the phenomena whose observation constitutes the basis of knowledge, exist;* and this ASSUMPTION OF EXISTENCE may be called the First Inductive Postulate. It is a universal intuition. Phenomenal experiences which do not involve this assumption are called *pure observations.*

Now a conjunction being an observable relation, must involve one or more of the perceptions of relation enumerated on page 16, viz., *similarity, dissimilarity, co-existence* or *succession.* In the theory of knowledge the most important of these relations is the first, for it is from the detection and classification of the similarities among the chaos of dissimilarities which constitute experience that knowledge emerges. To perceive the relation of similarity is to perceive one or more identical qualities in two objects of experience, and Jevons, identifying science with knowledge, remarks: " Science arises from the discovery of identity amidst diversity." Similarities of relation are observable as well as similarities of other impressions. Thus we may observe: (a) Similar similarities, (b) Similar dissimilarities, (c) Similar co-existences, (d) Similar successions.

From the first two of these (a) and (b) our concepts of magnitude (including number) are derived. No detailed discussion of this matter will be undertaken here, because it is already sufficiently clear in the minds of most persons. From the second two (c) and (d) all other knowledge is derived. Of course similarities of similarity and dissimilarity must co-exist with, or succeed one another in the mind, and thus all conjunctions may be classed either as of co-existence, or as of succession. Let us see how similarities of co-existence or succession give rise to valid expectations, that is to knowledge, and as an example let us examine a simple similarity of co-existence.

Suppose we observe a block of transparent material having a vitreous lustre, and on touching it observe a sensation of cold such as is imparted by ice. Were it our first experience with a piece of ice the sensation of cold would be entirely unexpected. Never before having observed a similar co-existence of qualities we should have no expectation of observing it. Had we, on the other hand, had experience with ice, the co-existence of coldness, with the vitreous lustre and other sensible properties of ice, would be expected, and upon observing the latter set of qualities, we should expect the sensation of coldness which in previous observations had co-existed with them. When we see the sun shining we expect all objects to cast shadows; when we hear the wind roar in the trees we expect to see their branches moving; when we perceive the odor of a rose we expect that that flower is, or might be, observable in the vicinity; when we drop a coin on a hard object we expect to hear it ring; and we might enumerate any number of similar relations between observation and expectation, all alike having arisen from previous experience of the appropriate similarities of co-existence or succession, some of narrow and some of wide application.

The reader may notice that should we observe the conjunction between the other sensible properties of ice and its coldness even once, we should thereafter expect (in some degree) a similar conjunction; and he may deem that such a fact contravenes our assertion; for one observation of a co-existence can give rise to no perception of similarity of co-existence. Instead of contravening our assertion this objection confirms it since, on examination, the expectation generated by one observed conjunction is seen to depend upon a principle of very wide applicability which is itself founded upon observations of similarity. It has been observed in a vast number of cases that where a particular conjunction between certain qualities is observed once, that a similar conjunction will be observed many times or perhaps always: hence where a new conjunction of a more or less similar kind is observed once, we expect it to be observed again, since this is a generic character of such conjunctions. Had this principle not itself been established by observation, a single conjunction of the character specified would establish no expectation.

Now what assumption, if any, is involved in the expectations we have cited? Why is it that when a conjunction has been one or more times observed, the observation of one member of the conjunction will generate an expectation that the other member is observable? The fact is, no reason can be given why expectations thus generated should be fulfilled. We simply discover that they are, or are likely to be. The assumption common to all expectations of this character is a universal one, and I shall call it the Second Inductive Postulate. It is denominated the PRINCIPLE OF THE UNIFORMITY OF NATURE — *an assumption that the unobserved will resemble the observed;* that unobserved observabilities will be similar to observed observabilities. By the aid of this universal intuition observations made at one place and time may give rise to valid expectations about other places and times, and it is, in fact, postulated, consciously or unconsciously, in practically every deliberate act of men and animals. We do not reach out our hand to take up our hat, we do not turn our head in order to look at something, we do not draw a chair to the table, we do not perform a single act of dressing, eating, walking, or indeed any act which is not automatic, without assuming the uniformity of nature. The act is controlled by our expectation of its consequences, and a consequence implies a previously observed similarity or uniformity of succession; though to be sure in some very familiar acts like those of walking, or reading, the appropriate movements of the legs or the eyes have been performed so often as to have become in part automatic. Now why is the uniformity of nature so universally postulated? Apparently because it is so uniformly observed. In the case of the observation of ice already cited, the uniform association of transparency, etc., with the feeling of cold led to an expectation of uniformity of coexistence, and uniformities of succession similarly generate expectations of succession. Both are acquired from experience and from experience only. Beings who have had no experience perform few, if any, deliberate acts, and the acts performed are so similar as to lead many persons to class them as automatic or instinctive, rather than deliberate. Thus young mammals perform complicated movements in the act of suckling, and newly hatched chickens will eat meal without any previous experience, but these inexperienced beings never can perform any other acts than those which any of their fellows can perform, and moreover the acts performable are always related to their necessities in such a manner as to lead to the belief that nature has built into their nervous structure substitutes for expectation which cause them to perform these acts as automatically in response to the appropriate stimulus, as the acts of the heart are performed in response to an increase of muscular exertion.

With the possible exception of the act of suckling then, newly born infants perform no deliberate acts. Their crying even is automatic, and the spasmodic movements of their arms and legs are utterly aimless. Indeed, even after they have had enough experience to know the use of their hands their judgment is so defective that they will attempt to grasp the moon with the same apparent expectation of success as that with which they attempt to grasp a rattle within reach. It is only by continued experience that they gradually learn to distinguish valid from invalid expectations, and to the end of their lives they never learn to perfectly distinguish between them. Similarly were a person who from birth had been without the sense of smell suddenly endowed with it he would not from the odor of a rose be led to any expectation of its visible presence. Should a person deaf from birth have his hearing restored he would not on hearing laughter infer mirth. Should a person blind from birth gain his sight, he would as deliberately walk against a tree or a wall as a blind man. He would observe the tree, but the visible impression would generate no expectation and hence would not influence his acts; in the absence of experience the visible impression would not be associated with the tangible impressions which he would receive on colliding with the tree. After a few such encounters, however, the expectation would be generated, and when his experience had enabled him to distinguish solid objects he would avoid such encounters as experience indicated were harmful.

It is sometimes assumed that the principle of the uniformity of nature is deducible from another one called the *law of causation*. Let us examine this important law and incidentally test the validity of the assumption.

At any particular time or place the external universe is in some particular condition; the objects of nature have a particular distribution; the material world a definite configuration; the possible sensible observabilities are determinate; all phenomena are particular phenomena. A *phenomenal condition* is simply an observable phenomenon. The internal world is similarly definite: non-phenomenal experience may be of one kind or another, but it is of some definite, particular, kind at every moment in the life of every being. A *mental condition* is simply an observed non-phenomenon. The term *condition* refers to either a phenomenal or non-phenomenal condition.

By the *total cause* of an event I mean a combination of conditions in the concurrence of which the event will occur, but in the absence of any of which the event will not occur. Mill's definition of a cause is very similar to that here given of a total cause. It is as follows:

"The cause, then, philosophically speaking, is the sum total of the conditions positive and negative taken together; the whole of the contingencies of every description, which being realized, the consequent invariably follows." [1]

By *a* cause of an event I shall mean any condition among those constituting a total cause. By *the* cause I shall mean some conspicuous cause, or one which it is useful to locate or consider. The *effect* is simply the event which invariably follows the concurrence of the conditions constituting a total cause.

The *law of causation* asserts (1) That the same total cause is always followed by the same effect or event. (2) That every event is preceded by a total cause. Hence the relation between the two, and consequently between a cause and its effect is independent of time.

Metaphysicians divide causes into two classes, *efficient* and *sensible* causes. That to which we here refer is the sensible cause — what Minto calls "The perceptible antecedent of a perceptible consequent." Efficient causes will be discussed later.

The first half of the law of causation may be expressed thus: Let T represent the location in time of an event X, and let A, B, C, D, E, &c., be the conditions under which X has occurred, but in the absence of any of which, and of any other total cause, it would not have occurred; then the concurrence of A, B, C, D, E, &c., is a total cause of X, and the law of causation asserts that if at some other time T, the conditions A, B, C, D, E, &c., again concur, that X will occur also, that is, that the relation between a total cause A, B, C, D, E, &c., and its effect is independent of their location in time; provided, of course, that which is referred to as the event does not include some particular location in time in its meaning.

Although the law of causation asserts that the concurrence of conditions constituting a total cause is invariably followed by the same effect or effects, it does not assert that the same effect may not be preceded by more than one total cause. Most, if not

[1] System of Logic, p. 217.

all, events may be caused in more than one way. Thus we may cause a billiard ball to move either by striking it with some solid object, by directing a blast of air against it, by tipping the table upon which it rests, and other ways might be suggested. Of course, many of the conditions constituting these various causes are the same, and in assuming that an event may be caused, there is always a certain class of conditions or combination of conditions which are assumed absent, those namely, which are causes of the absence of the event; that is, we assume the absence of counter-acting causes. Thus in our assumption that a billiard ball could be moved in the modes suggested we assumed, among other things, that the ball was not attached to the table by some means or other.

The sum of the conditions with which an event is actually associated, and in the absence of any of which, and of all other total causes, it would not have occurred, I shall call the *actual total cause*. The sum of those with which it might have been associated, and in the absence of any of which, and of all other total causes, it would not have occurred, I shall call a *possible total cause*. An actual total cause is thus, of course, always a possible total cause. Corresponding to actual and possible total causes there are *actual* and *possible* causes. This distinction is so familiar as to require no exemplification.

The second part of the law of causation may then be stated thus: Let X be any event, and let A, B, C, D, E, &c., F, G, H, I, J, &c., K, L, M, N, O, &c., . . . represent all of its possible total causes. Then, whenever X occurs, some one of said possible total causes has preceded it. This is merely to assert that any, and therefore every, event has some total cause.

We shall generally speak of the relation between a possible cause and its effect as the relation between cause and effect. Thus not only is it true that the same effect may have many causes but it is equally true that the same cause may have many effects. In fact, any and every event to be observed or experienced is an effect. Hence every cause which has a beginning is itself an effect, and every effect may be a cause. Every event occurring in the present is an effect of a long series of causes — the occurrences of to-day are but effects of causes set in operation centuries ago, and those in turn of previous causes — the endless chain of causation emerging from an impenetrable past, is lost in an impenetrable future.

From this explanation of the law of causation it is evident that those who contend that the principle of the uniformity of nature is deducible from it, claim in effect that all conjunctions are events, for an event must be something which has a beginning. Without stopping to examine the argument of Mill that there are many uniformities of co-existence independent of causation, one example of such a uniformity may be mentioned which would seem to nullify this claim. According to the law of the conservation of matter, matter can neither be created nor destroyed. Now in material bodies the properties of inertia and gravity are invariably conjoined. Hence if we accept the law mentioned we have here a uniformity which, having had no beginning, could have had no cause. But without dwelling upon this example it would appear from an examination of our own minds that the idea of nature's uniformity does not spring from that of causation, but that, on the contrary, the idea of causation arises from the observed uniformity of nature. In fact, the notion has doubtless been suggested by the observation of similarities of succession, the antecedent member being called a cause, the consequent member an effect. Such is the view of Hume, who says:

" 'Tis therefore by EXPERIENCE only, that we can infer the existence of one object from that of another. The nature of experience is this. We remember to have had frequent instances of the existence of one species of objects; and also remember, that the individuals of another species of objects have always attended them, and have existed in a regular order of contiguity and succession with regard to them. Thus we remember to have seen that species of object we call flame, and to have felt that species of sensation we call heat. We likewise call to mind their constant conjunction in all past instances. Without any farther ceremony, we call the one cause and the other effect, and infer the existence of the one from the other. In all those instances, from which we learn the conjunction of particular causes and effects, both the causes and effects have been perceived by the senses, and are remembered: But in all cases, wherein we reason concerning them, there is only one perceived or remembered, and the other is supplied in conformity to our past experience.

" Thus in advancing we have insensibly discovered a new relation betwixt cause and effect. . . . This relation is their CONSTANT CONJUNCTION. Contiguity and succession are not sufficient to make us pronounce any two objects to be cause and effect, unless we perceive, that these two relations are preserved in several instances." [1]

[1] A Treatise of Human Nature; David Hume, Book I, p. 87. Clarendon Press, Oxford, 1896.

We shall presently seek to demonstrate that the contention of Hume here quoted has not, as some persons apparently believe, been invalidated through the invention of *efficient* causes by confused metaphysicians.

The law that unsupported bodies fall toward the earth does not receive universal acceptance by authority of the law of causation. Ignorant savages and even animals accept it. It is a uniformity observed and therefore expected, and should a cause for such occurrences be discovered to-morrow it would not materially increase our conviction that unsupported bodies will fall toward the earth. Many other instances might be cited which prove that laws involving causation stand on precisely the same ground as other empirical laws.

Uniformities of causation are special cases of the uniformity of nature. The law of universal causation is, in fact, the most comprehensive and important of empirical laws, and like other products of induction it does not attain to certainty: it is by no means universally accepted; indeed those who hold to the doctrine of free will reject it, and they include some of the best minds of the age. Nevertheless, examination of our own minds and of the acts of others makes it obvious that though sometimes rejected in theory, it is universally postulated in practice, and that in all the familiar affairs of life it constitutes a guide to expectation and conduct.

Accepting the law of causation, we may expect to find experiences varying together in such a manner that we may distinguish such as are causally related from such as are not. Hence in general, it may be said that when things are observed to vary together and persist in so doing that the relation is either that between cause and effect, or that between effects of the same cause, for many uniformities of co-existence are inferrible from uniformities of succession, though all are not. The methods commonly used in distinguishing between events which are related causally and those which are not have been condensed by Mill into five rules or guides to observation, known as *Canons of Induction.* On page 57 I have given Mill's definition of a cause. It will therefore be best to give the canons in the words of Mill. They are as follows:

(1) The Method of Agreement.

"If two or more instances of the phenomenon under investigation have only one circumstance in common, the circumstance in which alone all the instances agree is the cause (or effect) of the given phenomenon."

(2) The Method of Difference.

"If an instance in which the phenomenon under investigation occurs, and an instance in which it does not occur, have every circumstance in common save one, that one occurring only in the former; the circumstance in which alone the two instances differ is the effect, or the cause, or an indispensable part of the cause, of the phenomenon."

(3) The Joint Method of Agreement and Difference.

"If two or more instances in which the phenomenon occurs have only one circumstance in common, while two or more instances in which it does not occur, have nothing in common save the absence of the circumstance, the circumstance in which alone the two sets of instances differ is the effect, or the cause, or an indispensable part of the cause, of the phenomenon."

(4) The Method of Residues.

"Subduct from any phenomenon such part as is known by previous inductions to be the effect of certain antecedents, and the residue of the phenomenon is the effect of the remaining antecedents."

(5) The Method of Concomitant Variations.

"Whatever phenomenon varies in any manner whenever another phenomenon varies in some particular manner, is either a cause or an effect of that phenomenon, or is connected with it through some fact of causation."

Such phenomena as appear to vary quite independently of one another are, on the other hand, probably not causally related, or at any rate only remotely so. Mill gives numerous illustrations of the use of his canons, but it would occupy too much space to enumerate them here, and many examples will occur to the reader. The first two canons are those in most use. They are the ones by which the thousand and one uniformities whereby our daily acts are guided have, in the main, been discovered. Mill only mentions causal relations between phenomena, but they may as easily be traced among non-phenomena. In trains of thought wherein one idea suggests another, uniformities may be observed which, tested by the rules embodied in Mill's canons, will be found to be those of cause and effect. Indeed the most conspicuous and important of causes, viz. volition, and the most conspicuous and important of effects, viz. pleasure and pain, are non-phenomenal.

So far our expression of the postulate of the uniformity of nature has been indefinite. It assumes that the unobserved will resemble the observed, but does not make clear how close the resemblance will be. Let us examine this question.

It has been remarked that should we on some given occasion observe a transparent object that looked like ice and remember that on former occasions such an object had always felt cold to the touch, we should expect it to be cold to the touch on the given occasion. That is, by the reiterated experience of the conjunction of two qualities A and B such that when A is experienced, B always is, an expectation of B arises whenever A is observed. Suppose, however, that on some occasion, we should touch a transparent object inferred to be ice, and fail to find it cold, but on touching a piece of it to our tongue should perceive a saline taste, such as rock salt imparts. What effect would such an experience have on our expectation next time we perceived a transparent object that looked like ice? Should we expect the absence of cold and the presence of a saline taste, or the absence of a saline taste and the presence of cold? If asked whether our expectation of cold was the same as before, we doubtless would reply that it was not, but was less than before. If asked whether our expectation of a saline taste was the same as before, we would reply that it was greater, since before experiencing the taste conjoined with the transparent object resembling ice, we had no expectation of it at all. Such replies clearly imply that expectation may vary in degree — may be greater or less. In other words, if we call the degree of expectation of cold a and the degree of expectation of a saline taste b, then a and b are two magnitudes capable of varying, and as we have seen they will vary with a variation in remembered experience.

Sometimes when we say we expect a certain experience we mean that we expect it in a greater degree than we expect its absence. This is obviously not the meaning in which we have just employed the term, since, on observing a transparent object we expect both a sensation of cold and a saline taste. Now we do not expect both in conjunction, and clearly we cannot expect the former more than the latter, and at the same time the latter more than the former. Hence our degrees of expectation either must be equal or one must be greater than the other. The experience of such co-existent expectations — sometimes of a great number of them — is familiar to everyone. They are often called probabilities, and admit of an indefinite number of degrees, but as we shall presently point out, degree of expectation and degree of probability may or may not refer to the same quantity. On page 41 it has been noted that knowledge is but a name for valid expectation. De Morgan says: " It may seem strange to treat knowledge as a magnitude in the same manner as length, or weight, or surface. This is what all writers do who treat of probability, and what all their readers have done long before they ever saw a book on the subject." Had De Morgan but asked himself what he meant by knowledge he would not have found it strange that it was a variable magnitude like length, or weight, or surface, for expectation is thus obviously variable. Again he says " By degree of probability we really mean, or ought to mean, degree of belief." And Huxley says " To have an expectation of a given event and to believe that it will happen are only two modes of stating the same fact."

Now unless De Morgan and Huxley are far astray in these assertions there is some important relation between probabilities, beliefs and expectations; hence unless we desire confusion in thought, we must distinguish clearly the meanings of these and other common terms, and if usage supplies none, we are at liberty to supply them ourselves, on the principle that verbal derelicts on the ocean of obscurity are at the service of him who first brings them into the port of intelligibility.

The term *expectation* has already been exemplified. By *probability,* or *presumption,* is meant the measure of an expectation's validity, its chance or frequency of fulfilment in the long run, and as this varies in degree, it is capable of numerical expression. Usage, however, has with such persistence extended the meaning of the term *probability* to designate propositions of higher degrees of validity that it would be impractical to attempt the suppression of the term's equivocality. It need not, however, mislead us if we are careful that the context shall reveal which meaning is intended. Probability being the measure of an expectation's validity is clearly something of importance, and the formulation of a convenient method of expressing it is next required.

A certainty, as we have already explained, is something we cannot do otherwise than expect; an impossibility we cannot do otherwise than not expect. Hence the probability of the former may be deemed a maximum; of the latter a minimum. To represent degree of probability therefore, suppose we call the maximum probability 1 and the minimum 0. Then all other probabilities must lie between these two; i. e., they must be represented by common fractions. It is obvious that expectations themselves may be represented in a similar manner by means of fractions, and the deviation of the degree of an expectation from the degree of its probability, is a measure of its invalidity.

By a *belief* I shall mean an expectation greater than one-half; by a *rational* or *valid belief* I shall mean an expectation having a probability greater than one-half. To probabilities greater than one-half and to the propositions expressive thereof, I shall apply the term *truth*.

Now we are all interested in ascertaining what propositions are true and what are not — we desire a guide to expectation, such that we may acquire expectations which will, at least generally, be fulfilled, and may avoid acquiring those which will not, for obviously we should then have a convenient guide to conduct. In order to see how such a guide is obtainable and in what degree it is a safe one, let us consider some simple cases, which will incidentally bring out more clearly the nature of a probability.

Direct, or Deductive Probability: Any given conjunction must either occur or it must not; i. e., the probability of its occurring added to that of its not occurring is a certainty. Hence if the probability of a given conjunction occurring is two-thirds, the probability of its not occurring must be one-third, so that $\frac{2}{3}+\frac{1}{3}=1$, or in general, if the probability of a conjunction occurring is a, the probability of its not occurring is $1-a$. This theorem which is deducible directly from the law of contradiction may receive more general expression thus: *The probability of the occurrence of at least one among several mutually exclusive conjunctions is the sum of the probabilities of the conjunctions.*

Two or more conjunctions are said to be *independent* when the occurrence or non-occurrence of any one does not affect the probability of the occurrence of any of the others. Otherwise they are *dependent*. Dependent conjunctions are always causally related, though the relation may be a remote one. Thus the fact that a coin, known to be of normal construction, has fallen heads, once, twice, thrice, or any number of times in succession, does not affect the probability that it will fall heads the next time, since the first events cannot causally affect the last one; the events are indeed independent; but if we are told by one who has means of knowledge that the coin is a loaded one, the event of being thus told will increase the probability that the next fall will be heads, because we infer that a causal relation between the structure of the coin and the information of our informant exists. Such events are dependent.

If we toss up an ordinary coin, our expectation that it will fall heads is no greater and no less than that it will fall tails, and this equality of expectation has been generated by a process hereafter to be discussed from previous observation of the behavior of symmetrical objects under the influence of gravity. The probability of throwing heads and of throwing tails is, in fact, one-half, since the coin must fall either one or the other, i.e., the sum of the probabilities must be 1, and no reason why it should fall heads rather than tails or *vice versa* can be adduced. Let us next inquire what the probability is that a coin will fall heads (or tails) twice in succession. To discover this we first ascertain in how many different ways it would be possible for it to fall. These ways are: (1) first toss, heads, second toss, heads, (2) first toss, tails, second toss, tails, (3) first toss, heads, second toss, tails, (4) first toss, tails, second toss, heads; and no reason is known why any one of these combinations is not as likely as any other. Of these four different ways, only one would give heads twice in succession, while three would not. The probability of any one being equal to the probability of any other, and the sum of the probabilities being equal to 1, we are required to find that fraction which multiplied by four will give one. This fraction is $\frac{1}{4}$: hence $\frac{1}{4}$ is the probability that any one of the four possible combinations will occur; hence it is the probability that heads will fall twice in succession. It is obvious that this reasoning can be applied to any number of equally probable independent conjunctions; that is, if it is admitted that out of a given number q of equally probable independent conjunctions, there are p ways in which a specified conjunction x may occur, the probability of the occurrence of x is $\frac{p}{q}$; or the theorem may be stated thus: *If a conjunction may occur in m ways and fail in n ways, and all these ways are equally probable, the probability of the conjunction is* $\frac{m}{m+n}$

In order to obtain a useful corollary from this theorem let us assume two independent conjunctions, A and B to have the probabilities $\frac{a}{b}$ and $\frac{c}{d}$ respectively. What is the probability that both will occur? Now if b is the possible number of independent conjunctions (all equally probable) among which A can occur, and d the possible number among which B can occur, then it is clear that in combination with any single conjunction among those represented by b, every single conjunction among those represented by d can occur; and hence with each of the b conjunctions, all of the d conjunctions can occur, so that the possible number of the combinations of conjunctions is $b \times d$. The same reasoning shows that the possible number of the conjunctions of A and B is $a \times c$. Hence the probability of the compound conjunction A B is $\frac{a \times c}{b \times d}$. For example, if we consider three independent and equally probable events, m, n, o, and also three other independent and equally probable events, p, q, r, it is clear that the possible conjunctions of events (by twos) is nine, as follows: mp, mq, mr, np, nq, nr, op, oq, or, or $3 \times 3 = 9$. Now if but one event among the first group m, n, o, can occur, the probability that it be m is $\frac{1}{3}$ (similarly for n or o) and under the same conditions the probability of p (or q or r) is $\frac{1}{3}$. Examining the nine possible conjunctions we see that there is only one between m and p. Hence the probability that the conjunction mp will occur is $\frac{1}{9}$ or $\frac{1}{3} \times \frac{1}{3}$. The same reasoning would permit us to establish the same results concerning the probability of any number of given events or conjunctions. Hence the corollary may be expressed thus: *The probability of the conjunction of any number of independent conjunctions is the product of their separate probabilities.* Thus the probability that in tossing up a coin, heads will fall three times in succession is, by this rule, $\frac{1}{8}$, or ten times in succession is $\frac{1}{1024}$.

The above theorem may readily be extended to include dependent conjunctions, for if a, b, c, d, e, &c., are a series of conjunctions, b depending upon the occurrence of a, c upon the occurrence of b, etc., then the probability that b will occur is the probability that a having occurred b will occur; the probability that c will occur is the probability that a and b having both occurred c will occur, &c.; hence: If p_1 *be the probability that a conjunction a will occur, and when it has occurred,* p_2

is the probability that b will occur, and when a and b have occurred, p_3 is the probability that c will occur, &c., the probability that all will occur is $p_1 \times p_2 \times p_3$, &c. An example of the application of this theorem is given on page 71.

One of the methods commonly used to exemplify the theory of probabilities is that of a mixture of different colored balls in a ballot box. If such a box contains A white balls, B black balls, C red balls, &c., it is obvious from what has been said, that the probability of drawing a white ball is, in general, $\frac{A}{A+B+C+\&c.}$; of drawing a black ball is $\frac{B}{A+B+C+\&c.}$; and so on. Of this convenient analogy we shall presently make use.

The preceding discussion of direct probabilities, showing modes whereby we may proceed from one probability to another, has purposely been made brief, because it is to be found more fully expanded in any elementary work on probabilities and a multiplication of derivative propositions here would be superfluous. The theorems established will be sufficient for the purpose we have in view — the discovery of how degree of probability depends upon observation, a subject we are now prepared to discuss.

Inverse, or Inductive Probability: It has already been remarked that when a conjunction between phenomena is observed, an expectation is generated that the conjunction will be observable again. When a transparent block is observed to be cold, even once, it generates an expectation that the properties so conjoined will be conjoined again. When the conjunction is observed twice, three times, ten times, one thousand times, etc., without ever failing, the expectation is correspondingly strengthened. When the conjunction is observed to fail once, twice, three times, ten times, or a thousand times, it diminishes the expectation correspondingly. If out of one hundred times in which a transparent block had been observed, we had found that in eighty cases it had turned out to be ice, and in twenty rock salt, what would be the probability that the next time we saw a transparent block it would be ice or rock salt? How would the relative frequency of observation affect expectation?

Let us first state the problem generally and then supply a general answer. The problem is: From a knowledge of the relative frequency with which a series of conjunctions of phenomena having a common member have been observed, to determine the probability that the next conjunction will or will not be a particular one. If the conjunctions have been as follows:

A B — m_1 times; A C — m_2 times; A D — m_3 times; A E — m_4 times; &c., what is the chance that A will be conjoined (simultaneously or successively) with B, C, D, E, &c., respectively, next time it is observed? If we compare the conjoined members B, C, D, E, &c., to different colored balls (say B a white ball, C a black one, D a red one, and E a green one) and the common member A, to the operation of drawing a ball from a ballot box, we are then in the position of a person who, standing before a ballot box of infinite capacity and unknown contents draws m_1 white balls, m_2 black ones, m_3 red ones, and m_4 green ones from it, and is required from these drawings to judge of the character of the next one. Nature offers to man just such a ballot box of infinite capacity and (antecedent to experience) unknown contents, and his knowledge of its contents and of the character of future drawings is based on the character and relative frequency of past drawings. By the analysis of how our common sense proceeds, we may see how the postulate of the uniformity of nature permits us to form judgments.

When the contents of the ballot box is known, it is easy from theorems already established to calculate the probability of drawing any particular ball or combination of balls. We have now the inverse problem. From the character of the balls drawn, we have to infer the probable character of the contents of the ballot box, and from this to deduce the probable character of the next draw. Let us make a provisional assumption, viz. that the sample drawn is a fair sample of the contents of the box, that is, that the ratio of the white, black, red or green balls in the box to the total number of balls therein is the same as that among the balls drawn. If this assumption is a correct one, the character of the contents of the box is at once revealed by the drawings, since it is this ratio, together with the color of the various balls, which we mean by "the character of the contents." If m_1, m_2, m_3, and m_4 are the number of white, black, red and green balls respectively drawn, then from page 65, the probability of drawing a white ball next time is $\frac{m_1}{m_1+m_2+m_3+m_4}$; of a black ball, $\frac{m_2}{m_1+m_2+m_3+m_4}$; and so with the rest. With the assumption we have made it is easy to infer the character of the contents of the box and the probability of the next draw; but what authority, if any, have we for the assumption? Suppose for a moment that we are drawing from a finite ballot box, containing, let us say, fifty white, ninety black, one hundred and thirty red, and two hundred and twenty green balls. Then the smallest number of drawings which can yield a fair sample will be forty-nine; five white, nine black, thirteen red, and twenty-two green. It is obvious then, that in a box in which the balls are varied and numerous, a small number of drawings cannot give us a fair sample. If the balls are well mixed, however, it is equally obvious that a large number of drawings will give a sample which differs only in a slight degree from a fair sample, and indeed, when we assert the probability under given conditions of a given conjunction to be P, we simply assert that if the conditions recur some large number of times R, that the given conjunction will, on the average, occur about $P \times R$ times.

From the illustration last cited we see that the assumption that a given finite sample drawn from a ballot box is a fair sample is not necessarily the most probable assumption. Laplace by mathematical methods which I shall make no attempt to explain here, has shown what the most probable assumption is.[1] The results of his investigations may be given as follows:

If the common member (A) of a conjunction has been observed conjoined with the member B m_1 times, the member C m_2 times, &c., the total number of different members with which it has been observed thus conjoined being r, and the total number of observations m_1, m_2, &c., being n; then the probabilities, p_1, p_2, &c., that when next observed A will be conjoined with B, C, &c., respectively, are:

$$p_1 = \frac{m_1 + 1}{n + r + 1}; \quad p_2 = \frac{m_2 + 1}{n + r + 1} \quad \&c.$$

If compared with the formula arising from the assumption that the sample drawn is a fair one, viz. $p_1 = \frac{m_1}{n}$ it will be found to depart from it in any considerable degree only when the number of observed conjunctions is small absolutely, or when it is small compared with the number of different conjoined members. Again comparing the empirical observation of the conjunction of events to drawing balls from a huge ballot box, we may return to the old problem on page 67. The qualities of transparency, vitreous lustre, etc., have been observed conjoined with the sensation of cold eighty times, and with a

---

[1] Those who are interested in this matter may find it discussed in Laplace's Theorie des Probabilities. Also a condensation in Todhunter, History of Probability, p. 554 — and considerably simplified in De Morgan's Essay on Probability, Chap. 3. Jevons gives a non-mathematical treatment of the subject in The Principles of Science.

saline taste twenty times. From these observations to determine the probability that the next observation will reveal a conjunction with a cold feeling or a saline taste respectively. Calling the probability of the first conjunction p_1, and of the second p_2, we have by Laplace's Formula $p_1 = \frac{81}{103} = .7864$; $p_2 = \frac{21}{103} = .2039$. By the assumption that the samples are fair ones, we have $p_1 = \frac{80}{100} = .80$; $p_2 = \frac{20}{100} = .20$. The percentage error of p_1 by the latter formula is only about 1.7% too large, and that of p_2 is only about 1.9% too small. Had the number of observations been increased to 800 and 200 respectively, we should have had the same result by the second formula, and by Laplace's formula should have had: $p_1 = \frac{801}{1003} = .7986$; $p_2 = \frac{201}{1003} = .2004$. And obviously, it is universally the case that, as the number of observations increases, the results of the two formulæ continually approach coincidence. An infinite number of observations would result in complete coincidence. This reveals the most conspicuous source of error in the second formula. It is evident that no finite number of observations could ever make it certain that some conjunction different from any previously observed might not be observed in the future. Now it is certain that all conjunctions to be observed will be either some one of those already observed or they will not — the assertion that the conjunction will be some particular conjunction is a certainty. Hence the sum of the several probabilities must be 1, representing certainty. If we add p_1 and p_2, as obtained from the second formula, viz. .80 and .20, we find that they already equal 1, which is equivalent to asserting that no other conjunction than those observed *can* be observed. This is obviously asserting more than the observations can justify, since (to return to the ballot box analogy) had the box contained white, black, and red balls in the ratio of eighty to twenty to one, one hundred drawings would have been insufficient to afford a fair sample, and we should, in assuming that it could, have assumed, perhaps, that because we had drawn no red ball, that it was impossible to draw one. Laplace's Formula, on the other hand, is subject to no such error. If we add together p_1 and p_2 as obtained from his formula, viz. .7864 and .2039, we obtain .9903. Subtracting this from 1, we find that the probability that the next observation will be of some conjunction different from either observed before is .0097 when the total observations have been 100, whereas by the time that the observations have been increased to 1000, this probability has diminished to .001, which is the mathematical method of asserting, what the simplest common sense confirms, that there is a better chance of observing all the conjunctions that are to be observed when the observations have been many than when they have been few.

Applying the theorem given on page 66 to the Formula of Laplace we obtain as an extension of that formula an expression for the probability of any number of repetitions of the occurrence of a given conjunction. Thus in the formula $p_1 = \dfrac{m_1+1}{n+r+1}$, if the probability that the conjunction whose occurrence has been observed m_1 times will in the future occur y times in succession, is represented by P, we have:

$$P = \frac{m_1+1}{n+r+1} \times \frac{m_1+2}{n+r+2} \times \; \cdot \; \cdot \; \frac{m_1+y}{n+r+1}$$

and it is obvious that, by application of the same theorem, it would be equally easy to establish a formula for the probability of the occurrence of any of the $r-1$ other conjunctions in succession, or for any successive combination of them. Remembering that probabilities are always common fractions, and that the formula for a succession of conjunctions is in the form of a product, it is evidently a rule universally valid that the probability of a succession of conjunctions decreases as the number of members of the succession increases.

As an example of the application of the formulæ we have been discussing, we may cite the illustrations given by Jevons, as follows:

"When an event has happened a very great number of times, its happening once again approaches nearly to certainty. Thus if we suppose the sun to have arisen demonstratively one thousand million times, the probability that it will rise again, on the ground of this knowledge merely, is $\dfrac{1,000,000,000+1}{1,000,000,000+1+1}$ But then the probability that it will continue to rise for as long a period as we know it to have risen is only $\dfrac{1,000,000,000+1}{2,000,000,000+1}$ or almost exactly $\tfrac{1}{2}$. The probability that it will continue so rising a thousand times as long is only about $\dfrac{1}{1,001}$. The lesson which we may draw from these figures is quite that which we should adopt on other grounds, namely that experience never affords certain knowledge, and that it is exceedingly improbable that events will always happen as we observe them. Inferences pushed far beyond their data soon lose any considerable probability. De Morgan has said 'No finite experience whatsoever can justify us in saying that the future shall coincide with the past in all time to come, or that there is any probability for such a conclusion.'"[1]

It will be noticed that the only conjunctions the probabilities of which we have attempted to evaluate are such as have a common member. The reason why we have not discussed those having no common member is because comparison of such conjunctions neither increases nor decreases the probability of their future occurrence. Thus should we observe the conjunction between the coldness and the other sensible qualities of ice, and also that between the hardness and the other sensible properties of diamond, the comparison of these two conjunctions would add nothing to, and subtract nothing from, our knowledge of the probability of their future conjunction. It is true of two conjunctions having no common member, as of two propositions having no common term, that no more can be inferred from them conjointly than can be inferred from them separately.

The ordinary uniformities of conjunction familiar to everyone, expressed in such propositions as: Grass is green: Water is not dry: Clouds often indicate rain: etc., are generally referred to as *facts,* a term having several other meanings besides. When such facts are of considerable importance, or are used much in scientific discussion, they are called *laws* or *principles*. I shall make no attempt to distinguish laws into classes on such a basis, but shall consider them all as expectations whose probability it is of interest to ascertain.

A uniformity of conjunction or law which is not deducible from any other law or laws can only be established by observation, and its probability is measurable only by the Formula of Laplace, or some extension thereof. Such a uniformity is called an *empirical law*. A uniformity which is deducible from one or more others is called a *derivative law*. That from which either kind of law is inferred is called *evidence*. The evidence which establishes empirical laws is called *aposteriori* evidence and consists of observations of the conjunctions whose uniformity is predicated by the law. Any portion of this evidence is called a *reason aposteriori,* and is adjudged a good or a bad reason, according as it tends or does not tend to establish a high degree of probability for the law or the expectation expressed by it. The evidence which establishes derivative laws is called *apriori* evidence, and consists of the propositions constituting the premises, immediate or remote, from which the law

[1] Principles of Science; p. 299.

is deducible, and any assemblage of such propositions, so related as to conform to the rules of deduction and having the law as a conclusion, is called a *reason apriori,* and is adjudged a good or a bad reason by the same rule as that applicable to a reason *aposteriori.* How it comes about that propositions conforming to the rules of deduction are capable of establishing anything but a certainty will be explained on page 76.

All the fundamental laws of nature, such as those of gravitation, thermodynamics, the conservation of matter, and even the law of causation itself, are empirical laws. They are simply statements of the results of observation. They cannot be inferred from other uniformities and no cause can be assigned for them. No one has ever been able to give a reason why every particle of matter should attract every other particle with a force varying directly as the mass, and inversely as the square of the distance. No one has ever been able to give a reason why the quantity of energy in an isolated system is constant as asserted by the first law of thermodynamics, nor why an isolated system is not reversible, as asserted by the second; nor has any reason ever been proposed why matter can neither be created nor destroyed. Many other uniformities are to be observed in nature which are purely empirical. No reason *apriori,* for example, can be cited why water is colorless, why graphite is black, why diamond is hard, why gold has a high specific gravity — these are simply observed uniformities. In these and similar empirical laws (referring to Laplace's Formula) m_1 would be a very high number — millions, or billions, or even more, in some of the laws cited, n would be the same number, and r would be 1. That is, they are laws with no observed exceptions, or universal laws. Besides these there are general laws, which have exceptions, sometimes very few, sometimes a good many. An example of the first kind would be: Most crows are black. A few white crows have been observed, say one in a hundred thousand. Suppose, for the sake of illustration, that the number of different crows which have been observed were 10,000,000,000; then according to Laplace's Formula, the probability that the next crow observed by any person would be black, would be:

$$\frac{9{,}999{,}900{,}001}{10{,}000{,}000{,}003} = .99998999980$$

From these examples it is apparent that the numerical data required for the application of Laplace's formula are seldom available. It is misleading to express the uniformities established by observation in terms more accurate than the data which establishes them can justify. Hence the expression of observed uniformities assumes, in general, such forms as: All As are Bs: Most As are Bs: Some As are Bs: A few As are not Bs: etc. Thus it is clear that unless we are to extend inferences far beyond their data the assumption that the conjunctions observed are fair samples of the unobserved will, in general, be as accurate as the assumption involved in the Formula of Laplace. But this is only a more exact way of saying that the conjunctions observed will be similar to the conjunctions unobserved. In other words, the assumption which underlies all empirical laws is that of the uniformity of nature. Thus this universal assumption permits us to infer from the observed to the unobserved, or as logicians usually express it, from the known to the unknown; but it must never be forgotten that the probability of the inference is determinable only by means of the Formula of Laplace. In truth *Laplace's Formula is the quantitative expression of the postulate of the Uniformity of Nature.* The qualitative expression simply tells us that the unobserved will be similar to the observed. Laplace's Formula tells us, within the limits of human foresight, *how* similar it will be.

We are now in a position to completely comprehend the nature of the *inductive syllogism,* the formal expression of inductive inference. Let us take the historic example furnished by Whately.

 This, that, and the other magnet attract iron.
 This, that, and the other magnet are all magnets.
 Therefore all magnets attract iron.

Thus expressed, it is clear that the minor premise is absurd. Let us throw it into the form justified by human experience.

 This, that, and the other magnet attract iron.
 This, that, and the other magnet are fair samples of all magnets.
 Therefore all magnets attract iron.

The conclusion of this, as of all inductive syllogisms, is an empirical law, whose major premise is an expression of observed conjunctions, and whose minor premise is an expression of the uniformity of nature. If the major premise records phenomenal observations it involves the assumption of existence. As we know the reservation with which we assert the observed conjunctions to be fair samples of the unobserved, the nature of the inductive syllogism is completely comprehended.

There is another possible kind of inductive inference, known as *perfect induction*. It is of the form — A is an X, B is an X, C is an X; therefore A, B, and C are Xs. An example would be: Peter was an apostle, John was an apostle, James was an apostle; therefore, Peter, John, and James were apostles. Mill denominates these inferences, if inferences they are, as " Inductions improperly so-called." They are merely a mode of recording observations and their validity does not require the postulate of the uniformity of nature.

Now it is apparent that having established a series of empirical laws, we may, by the method of deduction derive other laws or uniformities from them. Suppose, for example, that by the inductive method we establish the following uniformities:

(1) Iron is the most magnetic metal.
(2) Iron has an atomic weight of fifty-six.

From these propositions, empirically established, we may deduce the conclusion that the most magnetic metal has an atomic weight of fifty-six. Similarly we may establish by experiment that:

(1) Lithium is the lightest metal known.
(2) Lithium has an atomic weight of seven.

and from these premises may deduce the conclusion that the lightest metal known has an atomic weight of seven. Combining the first conclusion with the second and with the known relation between seven and fifty-six, we infer by deduction that the most magnetic metal has an atomic weight eight times that of the lightest metal. Thus from four uniformities established by observation, we have deduced three others, the truth of which was involved in that of their premises.

As empirical laws are never anything more than probable, the conclusions derived by deduction from them, i. e., derivative laws, can never be anything but probable; in fact, except in immediate inferences, they are, in general, less probable than the premises from which they are derived. Thus in the last syllogism, suppose the probability of the minor premise: Lithium is the lightest metal known, to be .9995 — and that of the major premise: Lithium has an atomic weight of seven, to be .9200. Then it is clear from the theorem on page 66 that the conclusion: The lightest metal known has an atomic weight of seven, will have a probability equal to the product of the probabilities of its premises: namely, $.9200 \times .9995 = .91954$, and similar reasoning applies to syllogisms in general, or to combinations thereof. Hence the probability of any conclusion is the product of the probabilities of its premises (assuming them independent), which involves the assertion that the probability of a derivative law is the product of the probabilities of the (independent) empirical laws from which it is thus deduced.

Propositions, though sometimes useful in expressing invalid expectations — as in works of fiction — are, so far as they concern the logician, useful only in the expression of truth. In dealing with departments of thought whose premises are confined to definitions and axioms, propositions express absolute truth or certainty — their probability always equals unity. Such departments of thought include pure mathematics and deductive logic, which are known as *exact sciences*. The objects of experience with which these sciences deal are called *ideal* and are not to be discovered in the world of real phenomena. A perfect circle, for example, is the only kind of a circle with which geometry is concerned, and of which the propositions of geometry hold true; but a perfect circle has never been observed in nature. When propositions established by observation enter into inference, certainty vanishes, since such propositions never have a probability equal to unity. Nevertheless they are still useful in the expression of truth, though not of absolute truth. In all departments of thought except the exact sciences then, a proposition is called true if it expresses a probability greater than one-half. If this be so however, it is clear that from two true premises an untrue conclusion may be deduced, since it is easily possible that two probabilities, each greater than one-half may have a product less than one-half. Hence, when we are dealing with any department of thought except that consisting of the exact sciences, a ninth rule of the syllogism must be added to the eight given on page 51, viz.

9. The product of the probabilities of the premises must be greater than one-half.

Of course when one premise of a syllogism is a definition or axiom, the conclusion has a probability equal to that of the other premise. In such cases, although we do not deal with certain premises, we deal with certain inference. A similar certainty of inference obviously obtains in the case of immediate inferences.

Now all that can affect probability, i. e., all evidence, is either *aposteriori* or *apriori*; either inductive or deductive; it is derived directly or indirectly from experience. But it is clear that the probability of a given proposition is not always — or even often — derived from one set of observations, or from one line of deduction. The evidence is usually derived from several separate sources, and the total probability of the proposition will be that which results from combining the evidence thus separately accumulated. To learn how this may be done we need but apply principles already established. Let us see first how to combine *aposteriori* evidence.

It is apparent that the series of observations of an assemblage of conjunctions having a common member will establish the same probability for the empirical law which predicates the uniformity of those conjunctions, whether made at one place and time, or at several places and times, unless there is reason *apriori* for expecting that the uniformity is a function of space and time. Thus, ignoring the *apriori* probabilities concerned, the proposition — All iron is magnetic — would be as probable, had the observations which established it been made at one place and time, as it is now when established by observations made at many places and times. Hence, using our symbols with the meaning already given them in the discussion of the Formula of Laplace, if the *aposteriori* probability of a given law is from source A equal to $\dfrac{m_1 + 1}{n_1 + r_1 + 1}$ from source B equal to $\dfrac{m_2 + 1}{n_2 + r_2 + 1}$, &c., the maximum number of different conjoined members of the conjunctions observed being r, then the total *aposteriori* probability from the several sources will be equal to

$$\frac{m_1 + m_2 + m_3 + \ldots \&c. + 1}{n_1 + n_2 + n_3 + \ldots \&c. + r + 1}$$

In seeking to ascertain the correct mode of combining the evidence from several sources of *apriori* evidence, we must distinguish between *dependent* and *independent* sources. The sources are independent if the occurrence or non-occurrence of the conjunctions predicated in the case of any one does not affect the probability of the occurrence of the conjunctions predicated in the case of any other. Thus suppose a given person X to be the heir of three, and only three persons, B, C, and D, and that we desire to ascertain the probability that X will receive a bequest. Suppose the several persons concerned to be of such ages that the probability that B will die before X is $\frac{3}{4}$, that C will die before him is $\frac{2}{3}$, and that D will die before him is $\frac{1}{2}$. The only way in which X can fail to receive the bequest is for B, C, and D all to die after he does. By the theorem on page 64 the probability that B will die after him is $\frac{1}{4}$, that C will die after him is $\frac{1}{3}$, and that D will die after him is $\frac{2}{3}$. The probability that all three events will occur is, according to the theorem on page 66 $\frac{1}{4} \times \frac{1}{3} \times \frac{2}{3} = \frac{1}{18}$. But if $\frac{1}{18}$ is the probability that X will fail to receive a bequest, then by the theorem first cited, the probability that he will receive one is $1 - \frac{1}{18} = \frac{17}{18}$, which is the probability sought.

Similarly to ascertain the total probability of the occurrence of a conjunction as determined by several independent, *apriori* sources of evidence, first ascertain the probability of its non-occurrence as determined by each source; the product of these will be the total probability of its non-occurrence, and if this be subtracted from unity the remainder will be the probability of its occurrence. That is, if the probability of the occurrence of a certain conjunction is from source (1) equal to $\frac{a}{b}$, from source (2) equal to $\frac{c}{d}$, from source (3) equal to $\frac{e}{f}$, &c. then the total probability of its occurrence is equal to

$$1 - \left[(1 - \frac{a}{b}) \times (1 - \frac{c}{d}) \times (1 - \frac{e}{f}) \text{ \&c.} \right]$$

or more briefly

$$1 - \frac{(b-a)(d-c)(f-e)}{bdf} \text{ \&c.}$$

If the different sources of evidence are not independent, then the probability resulting from combining them will be a function of the particular mode of dependence and will involve the application of the theorem on page 66. As this will vary in each particular case, no general expression for it can be formulated.

To combine *aposteriori* and *apriori* evidence precisely the same operations are employed as in combining the evidence from different *apriori* sources. That is, if the total probability of a conjunction from all *aposteriori* sources is $\frac{A}{B}$, and the total probability from all *apriori* sources is $\frac{C}{D}$, and the probabilities are independently established, then the total probability *aposteriori* and *apriori* is:

$$1 - \left[(\frac{B-A}{B})(\frac{D-C}{D}) \right]$$

As in the former case, if the probabilities are dependent, no general expression can be formulated, but each case must be treated by itself according to the principles of probability herein set forth.

The method described in this chapter of applying universal intuitions to observations as a means to the establishment of probabilities, and the method of combining or assembling these probabilities, is the so-called *scientific* or *inductive* method. No other method has ever been suggested for distinguishing expectations which will from those which will not be fulfilled, and to the mental operations involved in applying it to experience, I shall give the name *Belief-judgment,* or *Peithosyllogism* (Gr. πείθω = believe : συλλογισμός = judgment) because by such an operation, and by no other, the validity of beliefs may be tested.

The nature of truth, probability, reasonableness, correctness, knowledge, etc., and their relation to untruth, improbability, unreasonableness, incorrectness, ignorance, etc., is now, I believe, plainer than heretofore, and a brief reiteration, rendering clearer these relationships may be tolerated.

If the numerical value of a belief-judgment is one-half, it is indicative of *doubt:* if it is more than one-half, it is indicative of *truth:* if it is less than one-half it is indicative of *improbability.* As a *belief* is an expectation greater than one-half, a *correct belief* is a valid expectation greater than one-half, and as a *disbelief* is an expectation less than one-half, a *correct disbelief* is a valid expectation less than one-half, An *untruth* is an improbability expressed as a truth. The *knowledge* of an individual is great or small as the number and extension of the valid expectations held by him are great or small, and *ignorance* is the absence of knowledge. A *reason* is simply a piece of evidence *apriori* or *aposteriori;* and when we say a proposition is *true* or expresses a *truth,* we mean there is reason to believe it rather than its contradictory — there is more evidence for it than against it. Similarly when we say it expresses either an *improbability* or an *untruth,* we mean we have reason to disbelieve it rather than its contradictory, for the reasonableness of a belief is measured by its probability as determined by a belief-judgment. Furthermore, when sufficient reason for a proposition can be adduced, and not otherwise, the proposition may properly be said to be one which *should* or *ought* to be believed, and thus the signification of these words in their application to belief and expectation is established.

Truth does not mean certainty nor *untruth* impossibility. Were these terms mere synonyms for *certainty* and *impossibility* respectively, they would be of little service in symbolizing the expectations of beings not omniscient. Assuming they were such synonyms, the only truth would be the law of contradiction and the only untruth would be its denial. Truth is merely the name of the higher degrees of probability, and to distinguish between greater or less degrees of truth, it is convenient to speak of propositions that are *certainly true, almost certainly true, probably true,* etc., and the same words are employed to distinguish degrees of untruth.

By a proposition, as by a word, men can express only what is in their mind; the meaning of a proposition is limited by the meaning of the words which compose it. It is customary to draw a distinction between *thinking* and *knowing* a thing. The distinction is merely one of degree. In the ordinary acceptation of the terms to *know,* or to be *certain* of a thing, is merely to have a strong expectation of it: to *think* or *believe* without being certain is to have a less strong expectation. It is obvious that no more than this can be meant, for this is all it is possible for a person to have in his mind. He cannot mean more by his words than it is possible for words to mean. For anyone to claim he is certain (as I define that term) of anything except the laws of thought, which are by definition certain, is to claim that he is omniscient, though he may say that if A is B and if C is B, then he is certain that A is C, but this is conditional certainty. It is certainty with an *if.* It is certainty of inference only. The distinction between certainty and probability is not alone one of degree, but of origin.

It must not be overlooked that the presumptions established by a belief-judgment are those established by the inductive and deductive evidence at the time and place available. No one can form judgments more probable than his means of information permit. It is absurd to assert that presumptions can be established upon data which are not available. Thus truths established by common sense at one period of history may, by data subsequently discovered, be converted into untruths, but if all men employ the method of common sense in inferring from such evidence as is available to them, they will have done the best that a fallible being can do, and no man can do better than the best he can. If the expectations aroused by adhering to common sense are found to be mistaken and fail to be fulfilled, it is not the fault of the method employed, but is an unavoidable consequence of man's fallibility; and hence cannot be avoided by the employment of any method short of one which will render him infallible. Similarly if in computing the area of a piece of land, an engineer employs the data given him by his transit and other means of information, and applies to these data the rules of multiplication, division, and the other required rules of mathematics, he has used the method of common sense, and if he makes a mistake because of defective data, or through an error of computation, it is not the fault of the rules he has used, but a consequence of human fallibility. No one proposes to reject the multiplication table because school boys sometimes make mistakes in multiplication.

The mathematical theory of probabilities is not, except in particular cases, at all easy of application. Such mathematical geniuses as Pascal, Leibnitz, and Bernouilli, fell into the most elementary errors in their attempts to apply it; and even some of the methods of Laplace have been questioned. Though without doubt a powerful instrument of investigation strict precautions are required in its use, because of the ease with which it leads the unwary astray. The difficulties of the theory arise chiefly from two sources.

First: in determining whether the members of a conjunction are really *the same* or not. The conditions actually observed in the case of any observation are always but a small proportion of those observable, and in specifying what constitutes any member of a conjunction there is always danger of including too little. For example, should we make a series of observations on the eastern coast of America by which we established the uniform conjunction of rainy weather with easterly winds, our expectations would fail to be fulfilled should we therefrom be led to expect a like uniformity of conjunction on the western coast. The common member of the assemblage of observations concerned would include too little if expressed by the term *easterly winds*. The expression should be *easterly winds on the eastern coast of the continent*. With this member of the conjunction, the conjoined member *rainy weather* is very uniformly associated, but not with the too restricted member first named. Unwarrantable restriction of the conditions specified as constituting one or both members of a conjunction leads to inferences not justified by the data actually observed, and such unwarrantable restriction often causes mistakes in applying the theory of probabilities. In fact, two conjunctions can never be absolutely and identically the same, since to be so they would have to be the same in space and time, which would constitute them one conjunction instead of two.

Second: in determining whether conjunctions are really independent or not. It is this difficulty which has most often led mathematicians astray, and which renders imperative the great care so generally required in applying the formulæ of the theory of probabilities. D'Alembert, for instance, failed to perceive that the probability of any given combination was the same when coins are thrown successively as when thrown simultaneously. He perceived an independence in the one case which he failed to perceive in the other. Difficulties of this nature are often met in problems involving probabilities, and for examples thereof I refer the reader to any advanced algebra.

Although there can be no doubt that conjunctions occur which appear to be completely independent of one another, and the probabilities of which can be calculated on the assumption of independence, yet there is reason to believe that such results are due to the complication, and not to the absence, of causal relations. As with the progress of science the sphere of human knowledge is enlarged and the universe of human ignorance invaded, the probability continually increases that truly independent conjunctions do not exist. Not only is the law of universal causation everywhere verified, but as the investigation of phenomena proceeds, a marvelously significant and interesting unity is discovered throughout nature. Uniformities formerly isolated and apparently independent, turn out to be but special cases of more comprehensive uniformities. Laws tend to pass from the empirical to the derivative class. The discovery of the law of universal gravitation by Newton and his successors, combined with the experiments of Cavendish and others on the attraction of terrestrial bodies, has shown that the fall of a stone and the movements of the heavenly bodies are but two examples of the same uniformity. The labors of Clausius, Maxwell, and others indicate that the atmosphere in which we live, and move, and breathe, is a microcosm of bodies obeying essentially the same laws of gravitation and inertia as those which control the galaxy of stars which constitutes the visible universe. The researches of scores of investigators have established a strong presumption that every phenomenal change, whether in this world or in others, occurs in strict conformity with the two laws of thermodynamics, or rather of energetics, which have already been mentioned, and the spectroscope shows that the same kinds of matter familiar to us on earth, hydrogen, sodium, calcium, iron, &c., exist in the sun and stars and possess properties there similar to those that they possess here.

The progressive discovery of these, and many other evidences of the unity of nature, inevitably suggests that could knowledge be sufficiently extended, it might lead to the discovery of some all comprehensive law or necessity of nature, of which all observed or observable conjunctions are special cases. The nature of this obscurely conceived necessity is, of course, unknown — perhaps to beings of our restricted faculties it is unknowable — but the probability of its existence is forced upon the attention of him who contemplates the steady replacement of empirical by derivative laws. However vaguely we may cognize this all inclusive uniformity, in the comprehension of whose nature the secrets of creation would be revealed, its existence must have been coeval with the existence of the universe and its operation or authority coextensive therewith. Thus thought of it appears as a sort of primeval necessity, a First Cause, from which all things have proceeded, of which all occurrences are the effects, and from a knowledge of which all conjunctions would be deducible.

To symbolize the First Cause thus inferred, the name *God* is perhaps as appropriate as any other, since it is with some such concept that thinkers, whether scientific or otherwise, are more and more tending to associate that extremely equivocal, yet awe-connoting term. Thus employed, however, it must not be confused with the meaning attached to it by dogmatic theologians, inheriting their concepts from the crude anthropomorphism prevalent in the childhood of the world, which represents God as a manlike personality, subject to jealousy, anger, and other infirmities of human nature. It is perhaps natural that in the ignorance and intellectual isolation of a primitive world, man should thus create God in his own image, and conceive of the universe as anthropocentric, just as a dog would conceive of it as canocentric, or a cat as felocentric. Science in its investigation of that "mighty sum of things forever speaking" constituting the observable universe is led to no such concept. It can discover no evidence that the First Cause of all things is a magnified man. The language which nature, the product of God, speaks, is not a human language, nor in its interpretation is there any suggestion of an anthropomorphic origin of creation. It is supremely shallow to test the limitations of nature by the limitations of man. In the present incomplete state of our knowledge we must content ourselves with patiently and persistently groping for a clearer comprehension of the presumed First Cause, which is perhaps after all beyond our capacity ever to know: which may, in the words of Herbert

Spencer, be "no more representable in terms of human consciousness than human consciousness is representable in terms of a plant's functions."

It is apparent to anyone that the expectations constituting an individual's knowledge are not present to his consciousness at all times. They are stored up, as it were, in his mind, and it is only because experiences in general tend to suggest former experiences in some degree similar, that they can be made available when required. As particular problems are suggested by the events of life, the mind is constrained to seek their solution by the application of knowledge already acquired, and this application is accomplished by means of what are known as *hypotheses*. The degree of probability of a conjunction is determined by a belief-judgment, but the operation of the mind involved therein is not the only mental operation included in inductive processes. The assembling of observations to establish an empirical law we may denominate *simple induction*. The equally common inductive process involved in the application of knowledge to particular problems, we may call *compound induction*. It requires simple induction as an essential antecedent, and its nature may readily be revealed.

An *hypothesis* is a guess or assumption suggested or generated by an observation, and so related thereto that the presence of said hypothesis in the mind leads, or should lead, to the expectation of the observation. An hypothesis is either a previously established, or an assumed, uniformity or law of nature, or some deduction therefrom, and, if reasonable, is said to *explain* the observation which generates it; for when an observation is such that we might reasonably have expected it, it is said to be *explained* or to have received an *explanation*. We are perpetually making hypotheses at almost every moment of our waking life. This may easily be shown. Ordinarily as we go about our daily affairs, we feel no surprise at what we perceive about us. If we feel none it is because ordinary occurrences are not unexpected, and if they are not it must be because we have reason, or at least believe we have reason, to expect them. I do not mean that we anticipate all our observations, but that ordinary commonplace observations instinctively generate hypotheses which anticipate astonishment. Were this not the case, we should find ourselves deliberately seeking explanations of sights and sounds as much among familiar, as among unfamiliar, surroundings.

A simple example will make plain the universality of hypotheses: Suppose we go to see an exhibition of strength. Among other things, we observe lying upon the floor of the stage a large dumb-bell. We are asked what it is made of, and reply without hesitation, "of iron." This is obviously only an hypothesis, and is founded upon the previous uniformity attested by memory, with which objects whose appearance is that of a dumb-bell have possessed the properties of iron. The performer now appears, and with great evidence of effort raises the dumb-bell above his head and receives the applause of the audience. On the hypothesis that the dumb-bell is of iron the feat is an extraordinary one. Presently a small woman comes upon the stage, and taking up the dumb-bell tosses it about with no effort whatever. For a moment we are astonished. Why? Because on the hypothesis that the dumb-bell is of iron, the ease with which a woman handles it is inexplicable; but the next moment we have formulated another hypothesis — we have guessed again — and our astonishment disappears. This time we guess that the dumb-bell is a mere imitation, made of papier-mache, intended as a joke to deceive the audience, and we select this new hypothesis because it will explain the new observation. Such a deception as described is successful, only because the generation of hypotheses by observation is universal. Now an hypothesis is an expectation, and as it is generated by observation, it is an induction. Whether it is a correct one or not depends upon its probability as determined by a belief-judgment.

To illustrate how such a probability is determined, we may quote Jevons' example. Be it observed, however, that he does not employ the Formula of Laplace, but the closely related formula which we adopted as a provisional assumption on page 68. By converting $\dfrac{p_1}{p_1 + p_2 + p_3}$ into $\dfrac{p_1 + 1}{p_1 + p_2 + p_3 + 4}$, &c., the required correction may be made. Jevons' statement is correct for his assumption, viz., that it is "certain that one or other of the supposed causes exists," but this can never be certain.

"If an event can be produced by any one of a certain number of different causes, the probabilities of the existence of these causes as inferred from the event, are proportional to the probabilities of the event as derived from these causes. In other words, the most probable cause of an event which has happened is that which would most probably lead to the event, supposing the cause to exist; but all other possible causes are also to be taken into account with probabilities proportional to the probability that the event would have happened if the cause existed. Suppose, to fix our ideas clearly, that E is the event, and C_1 C_2 C_3 are the three only conceivable causes. If C_1 exist, the probability is p_1 that E will follow; if C_2 and C_3 exist, the like probabilities are respectively p_2 and p_3. Then as p_1 is to p_2, so is the probability of C_1 being the actual cause to the probability of C_2 being it; and, similarly, as p_2 is to p_3, so is the probability of C_2 being the actual cause to the probability of C_3 being it. By a very simple mathematical process we arrive at the conclusion that the actual probability of C_1 being the cause is

$$\frac{p_1}{p_1 + p_2 + p_3}$$

and the similar probabilities of the existence of C_2 and C_3 are

$$\frac{p_2}{p_1 + p_2 + p_3} \quad \text{and} \quad \frac{p_3}{p_1 + p_2 + p_3}$$

The sum of these three fractions amounts to unity, which correctly expresses the certainty that one cause or other must be in operation.

"We may thus state the result in general language. If it is certain that one or other of the supposed causes exists, the probability that any one does exist is the probability that if it exists the event happens, divided by the sum of all the similar probabilities." [1]

The method thus described is that by which we determine the antecedent probability of an hypothesis as tested by one, or one class, of its presumed effects. It may as readily be applied to the process of verification. This process depends on the principle that a given cause has many effects. Hence if the cause assumed is the true one, we may expect other effects than the one first observed. The effects thus made probable *apriori* may be searched for, and if found, the hypothesis is said to be *verified,* i. e., *verification* consists of the observation of effects deduced from a hypothesis, and may be of many degrees. In fact, all possible hypotheses as to the causes of an event are in some degree verified if the event occurs, since they would not be possible causes if the event was not deducible from them with some degree of probability. Thus suppose that an event E is observed, and that several hypotheses as to its cause are proposed. Call the hypothetical causes C_1, C_2, C_3, &c. The hypothesis which assumes C_1 to be the cause of E may then be provisionally accepted and other effects E_1, E_2, E_3, &c. deduced from it. That is, if C_1 is the cause actually in operation E_1, E_2, E_3, &c. should be observable since they are effects of C_1. If they are

[1] Principles of Science; p. 279.

observed, the provisional hypothesis is verified. If not, it is unverified, and a provisional hypothesis assuming C_2 to be the cause is adopted and the same means is employed to verify it as in the case of the first hypothesis. After testing all proposed hypotheses in this manner, that one is adopted as the correct one which is best verified by experience. The mental process involved in making an hypothesis and seeking its verification is that referred to as *compound induction.* Its expression is called a *hypothetical syllogism,* examples of which will be found in Chapter 6. Of course the more completely the results predicted and those observed agree, the more perfectly is an hypothesis verified. On the other hand, the more completely they disagree, the more perfectly is it refuted; but no finite amount of experience can completely verify or refute an hypothesis — all hypotheses are provisional, and must be, so long as man is not omniscient. Many, however, are put so far beyond a reasonable doubt as to be for all practical purposes, certain.

We here terminate our necessarily brief exposition of the inductive method of arriving at truth. It is the method which science persistently pursues and is identical with that which men pursue in the familiar affairs of life. Under such conditions it is known as *common sense.* In fact, *science is but consistent common sense.* It is common sense applied as rigorously to unfamiliar as to familiar things, and the fact that men so generally fail to recognize it as such, indicates with what unfortunate uniformity the application of common sense is restricted to the commonest concerns of life. Nothing is more frequently asserted than the uselessness of logic, largely perhaps because its forms are unfamiliar. We do not see men in their daily affairs constructing syllogisms and applying canons of induction. Logic, therefore, may be well enough to divert impractical philosophers, but it is of no real service in an active world. Nine men out of ten reason thus, and the less they know of logic, the more positive they are that it is useless. No less brilliant a mind than that of Lord Macaulay shared this view, and incidentally proved the value of logic by attempting to disprove it. His method was the common one of demonstrating that a knowledge of the logical method is superfluous by citing a number of cases in which it is superfluous; just as it is easy to show that a knowledge of reading and writing is superfluous, because people can cook, and eat, and plant potatoes, and draw water, without such knowledge.

It is probable that should a farmer be offered a compass to guide him about his farm he would laugh at the offer, and say that such an instrument was useless to him, as he could find his way over such familiar ground without it, and it need not be denied that for such a purpose a compass would be superfluous. But suppose the farmer should claim that it was equally superfluous to serve as a guide in a neighboring trackless forest. It is obvious that should he act on this expectation he would, in endeavoring to penetrate the forest, be in danger of losing his way, and perhaps dying of starvation. Now men apply common sense well enough to common things, but to uncommon things they appear to think that some sort of uncommon sense is better adapted. Thus they are led into innumerable errors and absurdities, some conspicuous examples of which will be examined in the succeeding pages.

Before leaving the theme of this chapter it will be well to examine with some care a subject of extraordinary philosophic interest which our analysis of the nature of inference, if sound, should enable us to comprehend. It has been suggested to the minds of men by the assumption involved in the first inductive postulate. We have shown that a reason or assemblage of reasons is that by which truth is to be distinguished from untruth and we have already considered how reasons are related to explanation. Experience, if explained at all, must be explained by other experience. When we use the term *why* in relation to the validity or invalidity of an expectation — to the truth or falsity of a proposition — that for which we inquire is a reason or explanation, and when we ask: "Why is this or that experience to be expected," our only answer can be: "Because this or that experience has been observed."

Now the question to which the metaphysical mind constantly recurs is: Why do we have experience? and particularly: Why do we have experience of phenomena? What is the reason for, or explanation of, the occurrence of experience itself? If the answer which the metaphysician desires to this question is the answer which we generally desire when we use the word *why,* then that which he desires is an explanation. But this could scarcely satisfy him, since it would merely amount to saying that we have experience because we have it.

Some metaphysicians appear to claim, however, that an explanation may be given of phenomenal experience — that is, of phenomena. At any rate, they seem to think that they can tell us about something which has some sort of relation, not precisely specified, to an explanation. They claim that phenomena are related in a manner expressible by the term *causal* to something or other to which they give the name of a *noumenon* or *thing-in-itself,* sometimes called a *substance* or an *efficient cause.* Of this thing-in-itself they postulate existence, and thus *explain* phenomena by reference to it; for say they, as the noumenon exists and is an efficient cause of phenomena, it is clear that phenomena are explained, for when we can show that a cause exists, it is obvious that we have shown a reason for the effect. If asked why they postulate a cause at all, they reply that everything must have a cause and therefore phenomena must have one. Moreover they point out that different beings perceive the same phenomena under the same conditions, and this can only be explained on the assumption that their perceptions are due to the same cause. De Morgan expresses this view in the following words:

" Our most convincing communicable proof of the existence of other things (things-in-themselves) is, not the appearance of objects, but the necessity of admitting that there are other minds besides our own. The external inanimate objects might be creations of our own thought, of thinking and perceptive function; they are so sometimes, as in the case of insanity, in which the mind has frequently the appearance of making the whole or part of its own external world. But when we see other beings performing similar functions to those which we ourselves perform, we come so irresistibly to the conclusion that there must be other sentients like ourselves, that we should rather compare a person who doubted it to one who denied his own existence than to one who simply denied the real external existence of the material world.

" When once we have admitted different and independent minds, the reality of external objects (external to all those minds) follows as of course. For different minds receive impressions at the same time which their power of communication enables them to know are similar, so far as any impressions, one in each of two different minds, can be known to be similar. There must be a *somewhat* independent of those minds, which thus acts upon them all at once and without any choice of their own. This *somewhat* is what we call an external object." [1]

That we have reason to believe that other minds than our own exist is obvious, nor is it worth while to discuss what the reasons are. No one considers that a stone gives evidence of sentience, and everyone considers that a horse or a man does,

[1] Formal Logic, p. 28.

To admit the existence of other minds is not difficult. It is merely to admit the existence of states of consciousness made up of elements similar to (or even different from) our own, differently distributed in co-existence and succession from any to which our memories testify. We believe, that is, we have a strong expectation, that such minds exist, but like our other expectations, this one does not attain to certainty — to deny it does not involve a contradiction — as the denial of the existence of our own minds does. De Morgan, however, says that "when once we have admitted different and independent minds the reality of external objects (external to all those minds) follows as of course." We can neither concede nor deny this conclusion until we know what it means. What is it that "follows as of course"? Nothing less than the "reality of external objects." Now we know fairly well what "external objects" are — they are those objects of experience expressible in terms of visible and tangible sensation — at least it would be to such an object that any person would point, were he asked for an example of an external object.

An examination of De Morgan's words would lead us to the belief that he disagreed with this commonly accepted view of the meaning of the term *external object*. Apparently he believes that an external object is some kind of a *"somewhat,"* whatever that may be, and is itself imperceptible. On this supposition it is a mystery how external objects ever came to be named at all. Let us ignore for the moment De Morgan's mode of expression — for it is but a mode of expression — and assume that he admits the ordinary meaning of the term. Thus assuming, we are told that "it follows as of course" that external objects possess a certain quality the name of which is "reality." The only interest which the term *reality* has to a logician is confined to its sense. Its sound has no interest to him. He therefore feels himself entitled to ask — "What does it mean?" It would be generally conceded that the terms *existence* and *reality* imply the same quality — the quality common to *existences* and *realities,* as distinguished from *non-existences* and *unrealities*. An unreal existence is simply a non-existence. The question then is, what is meant by the term *existence?* (We might have selected the term *reality* but *existence* is the commoner of the two.) It is a term continually used, and its equivalent is to be found in practically all well developed languages. The distinction between existence and non-existence is evidently a conspicuous one in the minds of

men, and in the ordinary affairs of life it is not misunderstood.
And yet how many persons can give a definition of the term
existence? Not many, I apprehend. Yet the first person we
meet on the street will prove by his acts that he knows what the
term implies, just as he knows, in general, what the term *truth*
implies, though he cannot define it. How then is it that men
may be misled by terms so well understood? It is for the old
reason: that a meaning sufficient for one purpose is insufficient
for another. For ordinary purposes no definition at all of the
term *truth* is sufficient — the examples of truths which men
carry in their memories are sufficient for such purposes; but
just as soon as we depart from familiar things, and attempt to
reason about things remote and unfamiliar, truth must have
some sort of definition or we shall soon be confusing it with
untruth. Similarly with the term *existence*. Its definition is
even less essential than that of truth. Its exemplification in
the experience of men has been complete. It would seem that
anything specifically observable is an example of an existence —
yet such assertions as that just quoted from De Morgan (and
it is but one example of many such) make it evident that there
may be purposes for which a definition of the term is required.
Let us examine the matter.

There is one meaning of the word *existence* which is obvious
at once. It is universally conceded that anything actually experienced is an example of an existence — an existing experience
is merely an experience — that is, in the broadest meaning of
the term, an existence is merely an experience or set of experiences. But it is a second meaning of the term which gives rise
to most of the confusion. Does the external world exist? Does
matter exist? It is this question which has perplexed philosophers since the time of Plato. The answer to it, as has been
said, depends upon what we mean by *existence*. If it does not
so depend then it would be as sensible to ask: Does the external
world x? Does matter x? Now I apprehend little difficulty
in discovering what is generally meant by existence. It may
be discovered by observing under what conditions men employ
the term, and under what conditions they withhold it, and then
observing what distinction in experience corresponds to the distinction between the terms *existence* and *non-existence,* as thus
actually applied. If there are many such distinctions, the terms
are equivocal — if there are not, they are not. This is, in fact,
the method by which we should ascertain the accepted meaning

of any term such as *coat, house, egg, tree,* etc. Let us apply the test.

Suppose we should inform a friend that a large mahogany dining table *existed* in the adjoining room. Suppose he should thereupon go thither and observe a table answering that description. He would then agree with us that the table existed there, would he not? Suppose, on the other hand, that after carefully examining the room, he could observe nothing of the kind there. He would then disagree with our assertion that a table existed there, would he not? Suppose that upon failing to observe the table, he returned to us and said that we must have been mistaken about the existence of the table since he had failed to observe it; and suppose we replied to him thus: "I did not say you would observe the table in the next room — I merely said that it *existed* there." Would not such a speech cause our friend surprise? Would he not be constrained to inquire —" If in saying that the table *existed* there you did not imply that it was *observable* there, what did you imply?" And if he should so inquire, what answer could we make? The reader may think of an intelligible and sufficient answer, but I can think of none. On the other hand, suppose we informed our friend that the table did not exist in the next room; would he not have deemed our assertion mistaken if he had observed it there? In this case then, *existence* evidently implied *observability,* and if we examine the matter, I think we shall agree that it implied nothing more, since the observance of the table would have been sufficient to have justified the predication of its existence — its non-observance sufficient to have justified the predication of its non-existence. It will be noticed that the observability thus implied by the term *existence* is an impersonal observability — it is no part of the meaning of the term that any specified individual shall observe the thing of which existence is predicated. Of course, the example cited is but one; hence I recommend the reader to test it as thoroughly as he feels inclined. Let him note anything which he experiences through the senses, sight, hearing, touch, etc., by which we are made cognizant of that portion of our experiences known as *external,* and satisfy himself whether or not he ever observes a non-existence. If so, what does it look like, or sound like, or feel like? In thus testing his experiences he may come to the conclusion that he can, and often has, observed non-existences; and will therefore perhaps conclude that *existence* and *observability* cannot mean the same thing; and this perhaps will perplex him,

The confusion thus produced is an instructive example of what a simple equivocality in terms may do to throw the mind off the track. The term *existence* is, indeed, much more equivocal than at first sight appears, and it is this defect in the term which causes the trouble — not any inconsistency in the nature of things. The reader might notice, for example, that a shadow may be observed; and yet it is not an existence as a stone or block of wood is. In this latter use of the term, *existence* certainly does not mean *observability* but means tangible as well as visible observability — the identity of sound leading to a confusion in sense. The original meaning, however, remains, for an observed shadow certainly would not be called a non-existent one; thus, in one meaning of the term, shadows exist, and in another they do not. It simply depends on how we find it convenient to apply the term. In dreams also, observability does not seem to imply existence, a source of difficulty which we shall presently consider. I shall confine the meaning of the term *existence* to its broader, though not its broadest, sense, that is, an (external) *existence* is merely that which is to be observed, and the common quality of existences is (*impersonal*) *observability*. An existence is merely a phenomenon, and we have simply to notice under what conditions people apply the term to become satisfied that this is what is generally meant by it, though it sometimes is restricted in its application to visible and tangible phenomena only. Nor is the term confined to phenomena actually observed, but is extended to include things which it would be physically impossible for men to observe. Thus an astronomer would agree that mountains *exist* on the other side of the moon, but hotels do not; though he is aware that no one known to him is in a position to make observations of the other side of the moon. Nevertheless he believes that should anyone be in a position to observe, he would observe the presence of mountains and the absence of hotels; hence he predicates the *existence* of the first and the *non-existence* of the second. An (external) existence then is merely a phenomenon.

Now if we revert to De Morgan's assumed assertion that external objects have the quality of reality or existence, we see that it amounts to nothing more than the assertion that objects observable have the quality of observability, which is no more than saying that what is, is. Can this be all he meant? Apparently not, and I apprehend that the reader will, at this point, be inclined to object that I have all along been confusing two things — the *phenomenon* with the *cause* of the phenomenon;

that the qualities of existence and of observability are not the same quality, but that the first is a cause of the second; that an external object as De Morgan says is not a phenomenon but the cause of a phenomenon. This objection might serve the purpose which a similar line of thought has served so often — of confusing the whole matter — were it not for two things: first the perfectly palpable fact that what everyone, except a metaphysician, agrees in calling an external object is a phenomenon, as the simplest test with the next man we meet will show; and second, that we have taken the precaution to learn the nature of a cause. Now a cause is either a non-phenomenal experience like volition, or it is a phenomenon. To which of these classes does the cause of phenomena — the so-called *efficient cause* belong? Obviously not to the second, that would be asserting that phenomena are caused by other phenomena (which is, in general, true enough), whereas the metaphysician appears to be seeking that which is the cause of *all* phenomena as distinguished from that which causes particular phenomena. Neither does it belong to the first class — at any rate there is nothing in the term "*somewhat*" to suggest such a thing, or to lead us to the belief that efficient causes are of this class, and still more difficult would it be to discover evidence of such a cause. But if it belongs to neither of these classes, it is not a cause at all. In fact, if we inquire whether the meaning of such a term as *efficient cause* or *thing-in-itself* may be expressed in terms of experience, the metaphysicians tell us that it cannot; but if it cannot, then the term cannot satisfy the first requirement of intelligibility; in other words, it must either be a meaningless term, or a synonym of the word *nothing*. (See p. 19.) The latter is the more plausible supposition, for if we ask a metaphysician by what perceptible quality or qualities a *thing-in-itself* is to be distinguished from nothing, he is quite unable to say. Indeed, we are forced to the conclusion that what metaphysicians try to refer to by the words *substance, efficient cause, noumenon, thing-in-itself,* is some peculiar kind of nothing. If it can neither be defined nor exemplified, what else can it be? It does not clear up the obscurity to say an efficient cause is one kind of cause. By so doing we may attain a similarity of sound, but not of sense. It would be quite as illuminating to say that circles are of two kinds, *round* circles and *square* circles, as to say that causes are of two kinds, *sensible* causes and *efficient* causes. When we have discovered the cause of a thing, we are said to have explained it, but to discover that phenomena are due to an efficient cause is to discover that the cause of something is nothing; for as metaphysicians postulate existence of an efficient cause, and this latter term being the equivalent of the term *nothing* in meaning, they are led to the conclusion that nothing exists, and as the cause exists, the effect must follow, or from the existence of nothing the existence of something " follows as of course." And by thus expressing the unknown, not only by the still more unknown, but by the utterly unknowable and unintelligible, they appear to think some sort of *explanation* is afforded. To such implied inanity have the greatest intellects been led, simply from their failure to sufficiently define such words as *existence, cause, explanation,* and indeed the moment a sufficient definition of the one word *existence* is established, the whole metaphysical structure falls like a house of cards, for it is a verbal structure only.

When we once have clearly in mind the meaning of the words *existence* or *reality,* the reality of external objects " follows as of course " as De Morgan says, but reality is not a quality of the so-called efficient causes of phenomena, but of phenomena themselves. This was, in fact, the contention of Bishop Berkeley. His main contribution to philosophy was, in substance, to provide a definition of the word *matter.* The popular notion that he denied its existence is based upon his objection to the metaphysical use of the term *exist.* Thus he says:

" I do not argue against the existence of any one thing that we can apprehend either by sense or reflection. That the things I see with my eyes and touch with my hands do exist, really exist, I make not the least question. The only thing whose existence we deny is that which *Philosophers* call Matter or corporeal substance. And in doing of this there is no damage done to the rest of mankind, who, I dare say, will never miss it. The Atheist indeed will want the colour of an empty name to support his impiety; and the Philosophers may possibly find they have lost a great handle for trifling and disputation.

" If any man thinks this detracts from the existence or reality of things, he is very far from understanding what hath been premised in the plainest terms I could think of." [1]

In discussing the application of such a term as *exist* we are dealing with two distinct questions — one of philosophy and

[1] A Treatise Concerning the Principles of Human Knowledge, Vol. I., p. 276. The Works of Geo. Berkeley, Clarendon Press, Oxford, 1901.

one of etymology. The "coxcombs" who "vanquish Berkeley with a grin," by their acts prove that they agree with his philosophy, though they express disagreement with his etymology. This is of small consequences, however, except as again illustrating how easily men make inferences from the sound instead of the sense of words.

A brief consideration of the phenomena of dreams will clinch our claims and convince any clear minded man of the invulnerability of Berkeley's position. In dreams we observe persons and things and yet deny that they are *existing* persons and things. Now just what do we admit and what do we deny? That the experiences, the pure observations exist (using the word *exist* in its broadest meaning) we do not deny. The sensations experienced are experienced: thus much is certain and is admitted. But while dreaming, we draw from these experiences certain inferences — the same in fact which we should draw from the same experiences if we had them when awake. The pure observations generate expectations that the objects perceived are, or might be, observable by other beings than ourselves — concerning them we have impersonal expectations, and impute to them the quality of impersonal observability and therefore (while dreaming) of *existence*. It is this inference which, on awakening, we declare to be incorrect — it is this expectation which we admit to be, or to have been, invalid. In other words, we admit the pure observation to be a real one, but deny the truth of the inferences from it. We deny the first inductive postulate. Thus in the phenomena of dreams we have the strongest confirmation of our previous assertion that certainty is not a quality of expectation, or truth in general. The quality of external existence is an inferred quality, and hence however strong our expectation that the external world exists, we cannot in fact ever be certain of it. The common admission that after all life may turn out to be a dream is conclusive evidence of this; for were we really certain of the existence of the external world we could not admit such an hypothesis, any more than we could admit that what is is not. While the quality common to external existences is merely impersonal observability, the question as to whether that quality is, or is not, associated with any given phenomenon must always remain in the realm of probability. In no proposition can a man express more than what he thinks or expects, and this is as true of the proposition *Phenomena are existing phenomena* as it is of any other proposition. Certainties are confined to the laws of thought.

We have digressed into the discussion of this subject principally to show the vital necessity of intelligibility. Words which should be the servants of the mind, when applied to abstract subjects, frequently reverse their position, and the intellect becomes the slave of its symbols — language becomes an instrument for concealing truth, not only from him who hears it, but from him who employs it in thought. In such subjects indeed, words are too often not the signs of ideas or impressions, but the substitutes for them. There is a well known aphorism to the effect that metaphysics is a disease of language. Our diagnosis confirms this view, and indicates that the disease consists of atrophy of intelligibility.

Having proceeded thus far in the discussion, perhaps it will be as well to briefly clear up my own position. It may be asked — "If you abandon the notion of an efficient cause as the explanation of phenomena, what do you substitute for it?" In other words, how are we to answer the question which persists in spite of repeated failures to answer it: Why do we have experiences of phenomena at all? Now clearly to answer this question we must first understand just what it is that we are inquiring for. Is it an explanation? If so, the answer must be in terms of experience, but this will not do, since that by which we explain experience would be the very thing for which we seek an explanation, and if not in terms of experience, the answer would certainly be incomprehensible, since it would be meaningless. It is clearly not an explanation that we desire; yet metaphysicians appear to assume that it is, and increase the confusion by attempting to answer the question as they would other questions beginning with the word *why*. Of course, they fall into the absurdities we have mentioned, and their readers are tempted to express a wish similar to that of the puzzled Byron when he spoke of Coleridge

> . . . "explaining metaphysics to the nation —
> I wish he would explain his explanation."

Once conceded, however, that this question does not call for an explanation and things become clearer. Its resemblance to a question which does call for an explanation becomes apparent. When we ask a question like — Why does paraffine float? or Why did the Campanile at Venice fall? we are conscious of what may be called a sensation of interrogation — a species of uncertainty or doubt. When we receive the replies: Because its specific gravity is less than water; or Because its foundations were decayed; this sensation disappears, and it is characteristic of an explanation that, among other things, it is capable of dispelling a sensation of interrogation. Now when we ask the question: Why do we have experience of phenomena — of the external world? we are conscious of a sensation of interrogation — a feeling of doubt or wonder. Hence we conclude that an explanation is what we desire as an answer, and to those who have not closely inquired into the nature of explanation, a reply having the form of an explanation may suffice to dispel that sensation. Therefore when men are told that phenomena are to be observed or experienced because *things-in-themselves* exist which are *efficient* causes of phenomena, the sensation of interrogation may thereby be dispelled, but it has not been dispelled by an explanation, any more than in the familiar story of the lady who inquired of the doctor why morphine put people to sleep, and received the reply that it was because it had a soporific effect — yet both replies may suffice to dispel the sensation of interrogation. The sensation is dispelled by the sound of the reply, and not by its sense. Indeed the whole discussion has arisen over a mere mode of expression. To say that phenomena are observable because they are efficiently caused is only another way of saying that they are observable; just as to say that morphine induces sleep because it has a soporific effect is only another way of saying that it induces sleep. The alleged explanation is thus but a synonym disguised as an explanation.

It not only appears impossible for us to give an answer to the question — Why do we have experience of phenomena? but we cannot even imagine what the nature of a reasonable answer to such a question would be. It is probable that no combination of words could, by their sense alone, dispel the sensation of interrogation which we undoubtedly feel on making this inquiry. Like the question — Why are we unable to imagine a contradiction? it is unanswerable. In attempting to answer such questions the mind encounters limits beyond which it cannot penetrate. An explanation is an expression of the unfamiliar in terms of the familiar — hence things, than which none are more familiar, admit of no explanation.

It is the effort of science to perfect our knowledge of all that the universe contains; but deeply as knowledge may penetrate, it cannot take us beyond experience. The efforts of metaphysicians, as of theologians, to transcend experience has but resulted in absurdity. The restrictions imposed by our faculties cannot be removed. Although we cannot explain the unexplainable, our examination has sufficed to show the untenable position both of the materialistic and the theistic metaphysic.

The materialist who claims that the sum of phenomena is efficiently caused by a substance called *matter* simply speaks without meaning. Matter, the *phenomenon,* exists, but matter, the *noumenon,* does not. The theist who claims that the sum of phenomena is caused by mind also speaks without meaning, if he means, or attempts to mean, that mind is an efficient cause; whereas if he means that it is a sensible cause, he speaks without evidence No; creation is not the *product* of mind — it *is* mind. *The external universe is but the common mind of sentient beings.*

The significance of the first inductive postulate is now more apparent. To make the assumption involved therein is to assume that the objects of experience which we observe are a portion of that section of our minds which we share, or can share, directly with other beings, and if we are mistaken in this assumption, it is obvious that any expectations generated by said objects of experience are devoid of validity and of no value to ourselves or our fellow sentients.

The confusion in the meaning of the word *existence* which apparently has misled metaphysicians, even some of the acutest among them, such as Kant, to predicate existence of so-called *noumena* or *things-in-themselves,* has in reality led to little, if any, practical difficulty. To be sure, it has put philosophers to much trouble, and led to the writing of thousands of pages of meaningless propositions, but in practical affairs the meaning of the word is so well known that the confusion of metaphysicians has had little effect upon the conduct of men. As much cannot be said of the confusion which has always been prevalent about the meaning of the word *truth.* But among all words by the misunderstanding of which abominations have been nurtured and disasters multiplied, the words *right* and *wrong* must be assigned the first place. These words are so immediately related to the mental processes which control the conduct of man that their definition is more vital to his interests than any others to be found in language. Says Sidney Smith:

"Definition of words has been commonly called a mere exercise of grammarians: but when we come to consider the innumerable murders, proscriptions, massacres, and tortures, which men have inflicted on each other from mistaking the meaning of words, the exercise of definition certainly begins to assume rather a more dignified aspect."

Let it be admitted that the words *right* and *wrong* must be defined before they can be useful and at once it becomes possible to formulate a guide to conduct based on common sense alone, adequate to serve as the foundation of a moral system, as applicable to public as to private acts, and at the same time completely consistent with itself. Let men continue in the future, as they have in the past, to be guided by the sound instead of by the sense of their words, and two thousand years hence they will be floundering as helplessly as they were two thousand years ago when "the youth Socrates listened to the old Protagoras" with so little profit. We have come a long way to reach our original inquiry once more, but it will be worth the journey if it has convinced us of the necessity of critically examining the symbols by which thought, and through thought, conduct is directed.

If there is a difference between right and wrong it must be some particular difference. It will not do to define the words in terms as vague as themselves. To adequately examine the subject requires that we divest our minds of dogmatism and determine the meanings of the words *right* and *wrong* by judgment, and not by feeling, just as we would determine the meaning of such words as *tree,* or *rock,* or *apple pie.* This attitude of mind is essential to the inquiry at hand, but unfortunately it seems almost unattainable by the untrained, or even by the trained, faculties of men, so powerful are the obsessions which possess the mind in the domain of morals. However, we can do no more than utter the warning — the inquiry must be undertaken without prejudice or it might as well be abandoned at the outset. We invite the reader to carefully watch for, and unreservedly discount, any and all effects of moral prepossession as they may make themselves apparent in the analysis which follows, and we recommend that he analyze with equal care the origin of the sentiments of approval or disapproval which the views here expounded may arouse in himself.

CHAPTER III

UTILITY

Human acts may be divided for the convenience of our inquiry into two classes: (1) Voluntary. (2) Involuntary. When a person in acting can select one from two or more possible alternative acts, his act is voluntary; otherwise involuntary.

The term *volition* expresses the well recognized combination of desire and expectation invariably present as an antecedent to such acts as stepping over an obstruction in our path, bowing to an acquaintance, or driving a nail — but invariably absent as an antecedent to such acts as fainting, winking at a sudden sound, or such as are performed by a victim of St. Vitus's dance. Tested by Mill's second canon then, volition is recognized as causally related to the first class of acts, but not to the second class. Hence the first are called *voluntary* — the second *involuntary* acts. The latter class of acts have no part in this inquiry.

Voluntary acts are either of the body or of the mind. In deliberately entering upon a train of thought, we perform a voluntary mental act. The attention is directed to a certain subject, and the association of ideas carries the mind onward. The voluntary acts most commonly discussed by psychologists are those of the body. That which it is most important to note about voluntary acts is that they are controlled by expectations. In the absence of expectation it is clear that no act with a purpose is possible.

When a sentient being voluntarily moves his arms or legs or lips or any other part of his body, it is because he desires to produce some other change, either in the external world about him or in his own or other minds; hence he must already have had in mind an expectation of how his act would effect the change desired, and if the expectation is a valid one it must have been derived from a previous knowledge of cause and effect — a knowledge only to be obtained by experience. Thus we see why knowledge affects conduct. It is because voluntary acts are controlled by expectations; and we see also how vital it is that the expectations which thus control conduct shall be valid ones, and as valid expectations are to be obtained by the scientific method only, we are able to perceive how helpless an individual or nation must be which attempts to distinguish between valid and invalid expectations — between truth and untruth — by an appeal to anything except common sense. Their means will have no prospect whatever of being adapted to their ends. It is because, and only because, of this intimate relation between knowledge and conduct that we have been compelled to make an analysis of the nature of knowledge. Right and wrong are qualities present or absent in voluntary acts; truth and untruth are qualities present or absent in expectations; expectations control voluntary acts, and no one can understand the distinction between right and wrong until he understands the distinction between truth and untruth. This will become clearer when we have considered just how conduct is dependent upon probability or presumption.

To avoid any misunderstanding at the start as to what we are seeking, the distinction between character and conduct should be noticed. *Conduct* consists of the voluntary acts of an individual. *Character* is a cause of conduct. We shall first direct our attention to the meanings of the words *right* and *wrong* as they apply to conduct. We shall not neglect their application to character, but shall postpone consideration of the question in order to avoid a confusion of issues. The two inquiries are closely related but separable.

Voluntary acts may be divided into two classes: (1) Right. (2) Not right. It is a common practice among men to divide the second class — the class of not right acts itself, into two classes, viz.: (a) Wrong. (b) Neither right nor wrong. This provides three classes, in one of which every possible voluntary act must fall, viz.: (1) Right. (2) Wrong. (3) Neither right nor wrong. The existence of class 3 may be debated; that of classes 1 and 2 is removed from the realm of debate by the admission that there is a difference in the meaning of the words *right* and *wrong*. Our inquiry now narrows itself to the question: What determines to which of these three classes an act shall be assigned?

Should we ask a casual acquaintance whether it is wrong to steal, he would doubtless reply that it is, and he would make a similar reply should we ask him whether it is wrong to lie or to commit murder. There are many other classes of acts which he would classify as wrong. Should we then ask him *why* they are wrong, his reply would depend upon his intelligence and training, but we should probably receive one of four replies:

(1) That they are wrong because they are wrong.
(2) That they are wrong because they offend God.
(3) That they are wrong because they offend the conscience of him who commits them.
(4) That they are wrong because they cause pain or prevent pleasure, or both.

If our acquaintance be mystically inclined he might say they are wrong because they tend toward imperfection, or defeat the ends of evolution, or violate natural or spiritual law, or are out of harmony with the universe, or are inconsistent with the higher life. Indeed it would be impossible to enumerate the responses which might be received to such an inquiry, and were we, in order to arrive at a solution of our problem, compelled to consider them all, our task would be a hopeless one. No such necessity, however, exists. Of such replies as those last suggested no notice need be taken. They belong to a class of expressions which for all purposes of accurate inquiry are practically meaningless, or if they have any ascertainable meaning, it would, on examination, doubtless be found to be the same as that involved in some one of the four replies first named. We may say with Aristotle — "To sift all opinions would be perhaps rather a fruitless task; so it shall suffice to sift those which are most generally current, or thought to have some reason in them."

Now of the four replies I have enumerated it is obvious that the first is a mere reiteration of the original assertion and does not answer the question. Yet it is probable that many, and perhaps most, persons would be unable to give any better reply. Children and persons of untrained mind would be almost sure to return such an answer. When we ask the question — Why are these acts wrong? we are asking for some characteristic, common to the several acts which leads men to apply to them a common term, viz., *wrong* or *wrongness*. To fail to mention such a common characteristic then, is to fail to answer the question; and indeed we may say that when we find the meaning of the term *wrongness,* if it turns out to be the name of more than one characteristic or combination of characteristics of an act, it will prove it to be an equivocal term which should, before it is used in discussion, or as a guide to conduct, be separated into two or more terms. At any rate, it is obvious that we shall not find the meaning of the word *wrong* in answer No. 1.

When we turn to No. 2 we shall find that it affords as little information useful for our purpose as No. 1, for if we inquire how men are to know what acts offend God, and what do not, we shall be informed that this knowledge is gained through revelation. A revelation is, however, a local intuition, and as local intuitions are not derived from a peithosyllogism, they cannot be accepted as grounds of expectation or belief. In the case of revelation it is particularly obvious that local intuitions cannot lead to truth, since if the various revelations upon which the many theological systems of the present and past ages are, or have been, founded are examined it will be found that the acceptance of some necessitates the rejection of others. As revelations claim to be above, and exempt from, deductive or inductive test, it may be admitted for the sake of argument that no means are available whereby the validity of any may be tested. Hence, if our judgment is unprejudiced, we shall estimate all revelations as equally valid; but as some are inconsistent with others, some at least must be invalid; therefore, an impartial judgment must pronounce them all invalid. This narrows the discussion to Nos. 3 and 4.

In ethics there are two main schools, each with its own view of the nature of right and wrong — what may be called the *intuitional* school, and the *utilitarian* school. Those who adhere to the first contend that men are able to tell the difference between right and wrong by a so-called *moral sense,* just as they would tell the difference between red and blue by the sense of sight. The distinction is recognized by something like an intuition, in that it is a law unto itself, recognizing no extrinsic authority. I shall therefore call them *intuitionists.* They maintain that the distinction between *right* and *wrong* is identical with that between *conscientious* and *unconscientious;* the approval of conscience being a test of right — its disapproval a test of wrong. No. 3 therefore would represent the answer of an intuitionist. As intuitionism will be fully considered in Chapter 6, and its inadequacy as a standard of conduct made evident, we need not discuss it here.

Those who adhere to the second school are called *utilitarians.* No. 4 would represent the answer of a utilitarian, and by investigation of the grounds upon which it is founded the real difference between right and wrong may be discovered. I propose therefore to make a critical examination of the sensations of pleasure and pain in order, if possible, to express the utilitarian definitions of right and wrong with a precision heretofore wanting.

The words *happiness, pleasure, gratification,* etc., have reference to a characteristic of experience which, though perfectly familiar, is indefinable. To one who had never experienced pleasure the word could not be defined, because it is incapable of expression in terms of other kinds of experience, just as we could never explain what is implied by the words *red* or *green* to a man unfamiliar with the sense of sight, or express the taste of sugar in terms of sound. In short, it is an elementary experience. The words *unhappiness, pain, disagreeableness,* etc., are likewise expressive of an elementary experience, familiar to all, but indefinable. Both of these classes of sensation will be found among elementary impressions in the table on page 15. In spite of their familiarity, however, the words *pleasure* and *pain* are somewhat indefinite. Many persons would make a distinction between pleasure and comfort, for example; they would distinguish a condition which was painful from one which was merely uncomfortable. But it would be conceded that an experience sufficiently uncomfortable is painful; that is, a resemblance is recognizable between an uncomfortable and a painful experience, and as no resemblance will be perceived between experiences which have nothing in common, it follows that painful and uncomfortable experiences have some common quality.

What is implied by the word *pain* will be sufficiently exemplified if we say that it is the sensation common to a toothache, the taste of soap, the feeling of nausea, and the sensation experienced on hearing of the death of a friend. In other words, that in which all painful or disagreeable experiences of whatever degree or kind from acute agony to mild discomfort, from a bad taste to a sad thought, resemble one another, I shall in this work denominate *pain;* it is the quality common to all so-called painful or disagreeable experiences, and is the means by which we recognize them as a distinct class of experiences, to be distinguished from all others by this common quality.

Similarly the word *pleasure* will be sufficiently exemplified if we say that it is the sensation common to melodious sounds, the odor of roses, the taste of a good dinner, and the feeling experienced when one hears of a large legacy being left him — the last not indeed universally familiar, but easily imaginable. That is, I shall denominate by the word *pleasure,* the quality common to all pleasurable experiences from the highest degree of happiness to the faintest element of satisfaction, from the pleasure derived from the odor of a flower to that derived from performing a virtuous act — the quality by which we recognize pleasurable experiences as constituting a class distinguished from all experiences in which the quality is absent. I shall employ the words *pleasure* and *happiness* and *pain* and *unhappiness* respectively, as synonyms in the implications thus illustrated. As is obvious, mental and physical experiences of pain and pleasure respectively are classed together, for mental unhappiness and physical unhappiness, however divergent, must have a common quality or we should perceive no resemblance whatever between them, and the same is true of mental and physical happiness

Keeping these meanings in mind, it may be said that most of the experiences of men are either painful or pleasurable, but there are also many which belong to a third category which we may call *neutral*. With such experiences neither pain nor pleasure is associated. As we descend in the animal scale neutral conditions of consciousness doubtless more and more preponderate, until in such animals as oysters and worms they constitute almost the whole life of the animal.

Painful and pleasurable experiences, like other experiences, have, in the first place, definite associates and a definite location (p. 21). A point of particular interest to determine is in what degree pleasure or pain may be abstracted from their associates, for connected with this is the question of whether these qualities vary in kind or not. There is a good deal of confusion on this subject in ethics, and, as I apprehend, it arises from uncertainty in the meaning of the word *kind*. Let us, for brevity of expression, consider painful experiences only, in attempting to clear up this question.

That pain may be separated from some of its associates is so plain as to require no particular consideration. If we are suffering say from rheumatism, and at the same time are reading a book, we are in no danger of assuming that the experiences involved in reading are inseparably associated with rheumatism. When we compare what are commonly called *kinds* of pain, however, things are not so plain. In bad tastes and smells, in discordant sounds and disagreeable sights, for example, can we abstract the pain from the sensations of taste, smell, sound and sight respectively? Are we experiencing kinds of pain, as well as kinds of taste, sound, etc., or are we experiencing pain abstractably associated with taste, smell, touch and sight respectively? I think it may be said that, in some cases at least, we may certainly abstract the pain from the associated sensations. To anyone with eyes made sensitive by disease, even a moderate light causes sharp pain; yet in time of health exactly the same light causes no pain, and on comparison of the two experiences, it is quite impossible to detect any difference in them (beside the difference in co-ordinates) except that one is painful, the other is not. In such a case, pain is clearly abstractable from elements of experience with which it is closely associated, and many other cases might be cited. When we come to pains of touch, however, it is doubtful if pain much exceeding what we should call discomfort can be abstracted, and pains of a high degree of intensity, whatever their associates, appear to be unabstractable, at least generally. Pleasures are probably more frequently abstractable than pains, but of both pain and pleasure it is safe to say that they are sometimes abstractable and sometimes not, and therefore, that they may vary in kind. The type of unabstractability discussed in this connection is not identical with that discussed in Chapter 1. Nevertheless the two qualities are sufficiently similar to be classed together.

For convenience of expression I shall mean by *a pain* or *a pleasure* a painful or pleasurable experience, and the words *pains* and *pleasures* will be used as the plurals of *a pain* and *a pleasure* and not of *pain* or *pleasure*. Pain is a quality, and a single quality of experiences, and hence properly has no plural, and the same is true of pleasure.

Besides their variation in association and location, pleasures and pains may vary in two other ways — in *intensity* and in *duration*. The expressions *intensity of pain* and *intensity of pleasure* are evidently indefinable though easily exemplifiable. So familiar are they, however, that no examples are required. By the *duration* of a pain or pleasure I shall mean simply the number of seconds, minutes, or other time units, which it endures. Pleasures and pains then, may vary (1) In *association,* (2) In *location,* (3) In *intensity,* (4) In *duration,* and moreover they may vary in any one, any two, any three, or all four ways at once.

It is a doctrine which has often been suggested that expectations of pleasure and pain determine all the voluntary acts of an individual, and by some this doctrine has been supposed to be an essential part of utilitarian systems. Jeremy Bentham held this view. He opens his essay on the Principles of Morals and Legislation as follows:

"Nature has placed mankind under the governance of two sovereign masters, *pain* and *pleasure*. It is for them alone to point out what we ought to do, as well as to determine what we shall do. On the one hand the standard of right and wrong, on the other the chain of causes and effects are fastened to their throne. They govern us in all we do, in all we say, in all we think; every effort we can make to throw off our subjection will serve but to demonstrate and confirm it. In words a man may pretend to adjure their empire: but in reality he will remain subject to it all the while. The *principle* of *utility* recognizes this subjection, and assumes it for the foundation of that system, the object of which is to rear the fabric of felicity by the hands of reason and of law."

I believe such a supposition to be erroneous. Certainly quantities of pain or pleasure (p. 114) are not invariable determinants of acts, though immediate intensities may be. It would, however, take an extended induction to establish such a principle. Acts are often determined by habit, or by impulses, the quantity of pleasure or pain involved in which have no particular value in determining the act. Later philosophers, observing that Bentham had fallen into error in his primary assumption as to the universality of pleasure and pain as motives, have concluded that his whole system in consequence must fall. This conclusion is too hasty. The nature of right and wrong and the nature of what motives do, as a matter of fact, actuate men, are two distinct subjects of inquiry. Separating them is all the difference between what is and what ought to be. But although many acts are not determined by considerations of pleasure or pain, it is an obvious fact that many are, and it is of interest to inquire in those cases in which pleasure and pain do decide voluntary acts, just what relation the kind, intensity, duration, and location of the pains and pleasures involved, bear to the decision.

In order to determine this let us imagine a being invariably guided by motives of pleasure and pain to whose attention are presented two and only two experiences, both painful, to one of which he is by physical necessity constrained to submit, and between which he is called upon to choose. Call the experiences A and B. Let us assume (1) that A and B are precisely alike as to kind, duration, and location, but differ in intensity, A having greater intensity than B. Which will our imaginary being prefer; that is, which will he voluntarily select? Obviously B. Assume (2) A and B to be exactly alike as to kind, intensity and location, but different in duration, A having greater duration than B. Again he will select B. To these conclusions I deem everyone will agree. Assume (3) A and B to be alike as to intensity, duration and location, but different in kind. Which then will he select? To this question we should at first be inclined to reply "That depends upon his taste; some kinds of pain would be selected by some people, other kinds by others." This is doubtless so, but suppose we should ask a person who, under these conditions, said he preferred A to B, *why* he preferred it. Would he not reply that it was because the kind of pain involved in A was *less* painful or disagreeable to him than that involved in B? He certainly would not prefer it because it was *more* painful. Now to say that B is more painful than A is to say that B differs from A in intensity, or duration of pain, or in both; but on our assumption A and B do not differ in intensity or duration, but only in kind. Hence A and B must be equally painful. Under these circumstances it is safe to assert that between A and B there would be no preference — our supposed being would have no choice between them. A selection between such alternatives could be made only on grounds which have nothing to do with the pleasure or pain involved therein and this sort of choice is precluded by our hypothesis. The idea that *kinds* of pain or pleasure commonly determine acts is a wide-spread but erroneous one. The error involved will, I believe, be more clearly apprehended by reading what is said on page 296, Chapter 7. Assume (4) that A and B are alike in intensity, duration, and kind, but differ in location, and let us suppose that B is further in the future than A, i. e., more remote, in time, from the moment of decision. Would these data be sufficient to enable us to predict the decision of our supposed being? Let us examine the three possible cases: (A) He might have no choice, a fact so obvious that we need not discuss it: (B) He might prefer A to B: or (C) He might prefer B to A. Suppose he preferred A to B. Should he be asked the reason for his preference, his reply probably would be that he would in this way get the pain over the sooner. Suppose he preferred B to A. Should he again be asked the reason for his preference, he would doubtless reply that he dreaded the experience, and hence desired to postpone it as long as possible. It is a matter of familiar experience that decisions on both these grounds are of frequent occurrence in daily life. No others occur to me which appear to depend upon the location of painful experiences, and upon their location alone. It is plain, however, that it is not location isolated from its effects which induces them. Examination of our own minds convinces us that when intensity or duration of pain influences our decisions, it is not because they are *causes* of something we would avoid; it is because they *are* something we would avoid; but this is not the case with decisions determined by location. Hence while location itself may never determine acts, yet considerations inseparable from it sometimes do. Such decisions I shall regard as determined by location, since for the purposes of this analysis the distinction is of no consequence. Nevertheless, the fact that decisions, and deliberate decisions, on both the grounds mentioned are a matter of common occurrence, confirms what we have already asserted — that degrees of pleasure and pain do not always decide acts, for although the first at foundation is a decision based upon considerations of the magnitude of pain, the second certainly is not.

From this examination then, it appears that when pains alone determine acts it is always either the intensity, the duration, or the location in time of the pain, and never the kind which controls the decision.

Let us next assume two painful experiences A and B, which do not vary in location, and which therefore determine preference according to their intensity or duration or both, to vary both in intensity and duration. Two cases are possible: (1) One is greater in both duration and intensity than the other, say A than B, (2) One is greater in intensity than the other, but less in duration. In the first case it is obvious that B would be preferred. In the second case it is equally obvious that we shall have no grounds for decision until we know the relative degrees of intensity and duration. Both elements of experience have very various degrees. How shall we express them? It is a simple matter to express degrees of duration. They may be expressed in seconds, minutes, hours, days, or any other convenient unit, and greater or less duration may be indicated very exactly by the greater or less number of units employed in its expression. But has anyone ever heard of a unit of intensity of pain? I think not. To suggest such a thing would to many persons appear grotesque. Yet in daily life we frequently compare one degree of intensity with another; we speak of *slight, moderate, considerable, great,* and *agonizing* pain, and by various qualifying adjectives may express intermediate degrees of intensity. Such modes of expression suggest that a scale of intensity might be constructed which would express degrees of intensity, as seconds, minutes, etc., express degrees of duration, and as inches, feet, etc., express those of length. A unit is simply a convenience for comparing different magnitudes of the same kind. To be sure, some units cannot be very accurately determined and among them one of pain intensity would have to be included; but the question of the accuracy of a unit and of its utility need not be confounded, though doubtless the more accurately determined a unit, the better. Nevertheless, as I think I can make some matters plainer by the use of such a unit, I shall adopt one. A unit and a mode of using it may, I believe, be suggested which will permit us to compare and express pain intensities with more accuracy at least, than such terms as *slight, great, acute,* etc., express them. Suppose our unit to be the intensity of pain, (in its generic sense of course) produced by placing upon the tip of the tongue one centigram of sulphate of quinine. The taste is one of intense bitterness. Should we take, say a whole gram and communicate the taste to the whole of the tongue and roof of the mouth, the intensity of pain caused thereby would be very considerable. Should the reader care to test the unit of intensity given, he may readily do so. To render it more definite we may call the unit of intensity the average intensity felt between the fifth and fifteenth second after placing the drug on the tongue; and the unit thus defined let us call a *pathon,* (Gr. $\pi\acute{\alpha}\theta$os = pain).

I am aware that the intensity of pain produced by the means suggested would be different in different people, but except in rare cases, I do not think it would be very different, and with the same person, it would be different at different times. As psychological investigations have shown, the sensibility of persons to agencies producing either pain or pleasure varies with various vital conditions — the state of health, the rapidity of circulation, the activity of the senses, and the stimulus at the moment applied to them, etc., and even depends upon what the person had for dinner and how many hours he slept the night before. We may, however, by keeping these causes of variation sensibly constant very nearly eliminate the error and render the unit sufficiently accurate for practical purposes. As I shall draw no conclusions the validity of which will depend upon the accurate determination of pain or pleasure intensities any attempt to fix an accurate unit would be superfluous. At any rate, the unit suggested is only one of many which might be suggested.

Let us suppose now we desire to estimate the intensity of a certain pain at a certain moment in terms of this unit. As most pains vary in intensity from moment to moment we must, of course, confine our attention to their intensity at some particular moment, or if we desire the average intensity over a certain definite interval, we may, if we please, direct our attention to the estimation of such an average intensity. Assume that we desire to estimate the intensity of a headache at its height. Assume further that the headache is over and that we estimate its intensity from memory. To determine it we should ask ourselves this question: "What is the greatest number of minutes for which you would endure the pain of unit intensity — one pathon — rather than endure that of the headache for one minute?" After weighing the question, suppose we should answer — *one*. What would this tell us about the intensity of the pain? Clearly, it would show that it was of intensity one pathon, or unit intensity, i. e., of the same intensity as the unit, since we estimate that between suffering the headache for one minute and suffering the unit intensity of pain for the same time there is no choice. Suppose our answer to have been *five*. This would indicate a headache of greater intensity than the first answer indicated, since it would mean that between suffering the headache for one minute, and suffering the unit intensity of pain for a period five times as long there would be no choice. Could we correctly say that the pain of the headache was five times as intense? This would depend upon what the phrase *five times* or *n times as intense* means. I am not aware that, in this connection, such a phrase has ever been given a definite meaning. Therefore, I consider myself entitled to give it one, and I shall mean by the *intensity* of a given pain the greatest number of time units (minutes for instance) for which we would endure the unit intensity of pain in preference to enduring the given pain for one time unit. The unit of time we use is obviously a matter of indifference, provided it be not so short that our experience would give us no means of making use of it in comparison. For example, were we asked to represent in memory the difference between an experience of any kind, painful or otherwise, lasting one one-hundredth of a second and one lasting two one-hundredths, we probably could not do it without special training. By this definition then, a painful experience, physical or mental, may be said to have intensity n at the moment M if n is the greatest number of minutes (or other units of time) for which we would endure unit intensity of pain (one pathon) in preference to enduring that of the given painful experience (assuming its intensity to remain the same as at the moment M) for one minute, (or other time unit). If n = 5 then the pain is of intensity 5 or five times as intense as unit intensity. If n = $\frac{1}{2}$, then the intensity is $\frac{1}{2}$, etc. Of course, intensities represented by fractions are those of pains whose intensity is less than, and therefore preferable to, unit intensity. From this example the mode of measuring the average intensity of pain over a given interval will be obvious.

Using the above method of estimating intensities, we might under different circumstances arrive at very different estimates. Suppose, for example, that in the first case cited we had given our estimate as to the intensity of our headache at the very time we were experiencing it, instead of estimating from memory, and suppose then and there we applied to our tongue the centigram of quinine in the manner specified, and thus compared the experiences direct; we should obviously be in a better position to estimate their relative intensities than if we made our estimate from memory. We might, under these conditions, by careful attention, estimate the intensity of the headache to be only four instead of five. Similarly if we were asked to estimate how much higher one building was than another we should be able to come nearer the truth if we saw them side by side than if we had to compare their heights from the memory of how each had appeared to us separately. What then do we mean by the numerical value of a pain intensity? What conditions shall we specify as those under which our estimate of intensity shall be considered the correct one? We can only answer this by saying — under those in which the opportunity of comparing the given intensity with the unit intensity is most perfect. Just what these conditions are we do not know, and never shall know completely, but we do know some of them, and psychological investigation will doubtless, in the future, permit us to approximate them more and more nearly. This may to some persons appear like an admission that the evaluation of pain intensities is impossible. It is, if we mean their perfect evaluation, but this is not what we mean. Pain intensities can never be more than estimated or approximated; but then, this is true of the evaluation of all quantities whatever, though some may be approximated more closely than others. The period of rotation of the earth, equal to one sidereal day, may, with the help of a chronograph, be measured to within a hundredth of a second, or with an error of little less than 00.00001 per cent. On the other hand, the distance of the star Sirius can, with the best instruments, be measured only to within some hundreds of billions of miles, involving an error which may be as much as thirty or forty per cent, and our estimate of the distance of stars with a less parallax may not be nearer the truth than several hundred per cent. The indefiniteness of the unit then need not concern us, since we have discussed it more with the intention of attaining clear apprehension than for any other object. The fact that it is theoretically measurable is sufficient for our purposes, and having established the concept of intensity as a measurable magnitude, we are now in a position to define quantity of pain.

Quantity of pain and *quantity* of pleasure are the most important magnitudes known to sentient beings. By them the importance of all other magnitudes, and of all other experiences, actual or possible, always should be judged. *Quantity of pain* varies directly as the intensity and the duration, and *is measured by the product of the intensity into the duration.* Hence if, in any painful experience, P represents the average intensity expressed in pathons and M the duration expressed in minutes, the quantity will be represented by P × M pathon-minutes. In just the same way, if we desire to measure the quantity of energy yielded in a given time by a steam engine we must know the power, or intensity of work, and the duration, or the time during which the power is exerted. Thus if the power is P horse-power, and the duration T minutes, the quantity of energy will be represented by P × T horse-power-minutes. What in the theory of units are known as the *dimensions* of energy are thus strictly comparable to what with propriety may be called the *dimensions* of pain (and pleasure). The intensity of painful experiences may be called the *intensity* dimension, the duration may be called the *capacity* dimension, and a similar distinction obtains in the case of pleasurable experiences.

As we have noted, preference varies inversely as duration in painful experiences whose intensity is the same. Therefore, it is obvious that preference as between two or more painful experiences of the same location is determined by quantity alone. Reverting now to the question on page 110 we see that the answer depends upon whether A or B yields the greater quantity of pain. If A gives the greater quantity, then B is preferred and *vice versa;* or in general, if A and B are two painful experiences, and P_1 P_2 are their respective intensities, and M_1 M_2 their respective durations, A will be preferred to B when $P_1 M_1 < P_2 M_2$ and B preferred to A when $P_1 M_1 > P_2 M_2$. This is merely asserting in mathematical language that a person when choosing between two painful experiences of the same location, and considering the pain involved in them alone, will always choose that which is less painful. It may seem as if we had come rather a long road merely to reach this simple and readily admitted result, but the utility of taking the long road will appear later. In order to comprehend the utilitarian doctrine, the relation of intensity to quantity of pain or pleasure must be recognized as well as the fact that, in common with probabilities, they are definite measurable magnitudes like time, length, area, or weight.

We have now, I believe, examined every possible case in which preference is determined by the consideration of painful experiences only, and find, in general, that it is independent of the kind of experience, and — with the exceptions noted — of its location in time, but is dependent upon, and generally determined by, the quantity of pain involved, the smaller quantity always being preferred to the greater.

If now we examine pleasurable experiences or pleasures, we shall find that they also may vary in four different ways — in intensity, in duration, in kind, in location — in this respect being similar to painful ones; and again preference is determined, in general, by quantity of pleasure; but while we prefer the less quantity of pain, we prefer the greater quantity of pleasure. Corresponding to this antithesis, a correlated exception is found depending upon location, for it is a frequent experience that quantity of pleasure is sometimes sacrificed, in order to obtain immediate rather than remote realization, and such sacrifice, whatever we may think about its wisdom, is evidently deliberate.

We might, if we pleased, devise a unit of pleasure, as we have one of pain, and thus measure intensities and quantities of pleasure as we did similar magnitudes in the case of pain. We shall, however, adopt a more convenient method of measurement. Admitting that, in general, of two pains we prefer that least in quantity, and of two pleasures that greatest in quantity, let us next inquire how preference is determined when we choose between experiences of pain and pleasure.

Two cases are recognizable: (1) When the alternatives are such that location in time may enter into the decision, (2) When they are not. The first class of cases are indeterminate, because no universal rule is discoverable which will inform us when, in the decisions of a fallible being, location will prevail and when it will not. Therefore Class (1) need not be discussed. Class (2) is divisible into four cases: (a) When one alternative involves pain and no pleasure: the other pleasure and no pain. (b) When both alternatives involve both pleasure and pain. (c) When one alternative involves pleasure only: the other both pleasure and pain. (d) When one alternative involves pain only: the other both pleasure and pain.

In case (a) it will be readily admitted that the second alternative involving pleasure but no pain will be preferable.

Case (b) requires more careful discussion. Suppose two alternatives A and B to be alike in the kind, location, and duration of their pleasure and pain, but different in the relative intensity of each. For example, alternative A might be that of listening to a concert one hour long while suffering from a headache whose average intensity, let us say, is $\frac{1}{2}$ pathon. Alternative B, an experience exactly similar except that the headache has an intensity 1 pathon. It is obvious that in this case, alternative A in which the pleasure is the same while the pain is only one-half that of B will be preferred. Let us now suppose the headache of the same average intensity, but one concert to be one hour and one-half in length — the other, one hour; that is, the kinds, locations and relative intensities[1] are the same, but the durations are different. We have seen that when pleasure alone is concerned the greater duration is preferred to the less, whereas when pain alone is concerned the contrary is the case. How is it when pleasure and pain both are involved? The answer can be obtained only by consulting our own minds. Any one so doing will, I believe, answer the question by saying that if the average intensity of pleasure during the interval is more than equivalent to the average intensity of pain, the longer interval will be preferred: if it is less than equivalent, the shorter interval. But what do we mean by *equivalent?* The expression appears to imply that pain intensities and pleasure intensities may be compared with respect to their magnitude, and it is probable that if we examine into the process of comparison as it actually occurs in

---

[1] The relative intensities could, in practice, hardly remain the same under the conditions named, owing to the operation of a cause discussed in Chapter 7, but we will suppose in the longer concert the music to be somewhat better, so that the average intensity of pleasure afforded by it remains the same as in the shorter concert.

our experience we shall agree that the nature of equivalence may be expressed thus: When a given pleasurable experience bears a relation to a given painful experience of equal duration, such that, in order to attain the first, we would be willing to undergo an amount of pain equal to, but not exceeding, the second, then the intensity of pleasure involved in the first experience is equivalent to the intensity of pain involved in the second. If this be so, we may dispense with the necessity of formulating a separate unit of pleasure intensity and use for our unit that intensity which is equivalent to a pathon. This we may call an *anti-pathon* or *hedon* (Gr. ἡδονή = pleasure) and if we refer to page 112 and there recall how pain intensities are compared with each other, we shall see that two pathons are equivalent to two hedons, and in general, that n pathons are equivalent to n hedons, where n represents any positive number, integral or fractional; and just as a pathon is equivalent to a hedon in intensity, so a pathon-minute or hour is equivalent to a hedon-minute or hour in quantity. In fact, pain stands in the same relation to pleasure that a negative quantity stands to a positive. Both may be measured by units of the same kind, but opposite in sign. Thus we may condense the separate units of pleasure and pain into one and call it a *pathedon;* if positive it expresses pleasure, if negative, pain. Pain intensities and quantities may be compared with pleasure intensities and quantities by means of preference, just as we compare the relative intensities of pleasure or of pain with one another, and any uncertainty found in the one unit will be found in the other.

Suppose now in the question under discussion, the average intensity of pain to be x pathons and of pleasure y hedons, then we may answer the question by saying that if x is greater than y in numerical magnitude, we shall prefer the shorter concert, if y is greater than x, the longer. It is obvious that in the first case, we should experience a less surplus of pain by selecting the shorter duration, and in the second a greater surplus of pleasure by selecting the longer, and the surplus is one of quantity in each case. In fact, it follows generally that of two or more alternatives, involving both pleasure and pain, similar in location, that one is preferred which involves the greatest surplus of pleasure, or if none involve a surplus of pleasure, that one is preferred which involves the least surplus of pain. These considerations enable us to perceive that case (a) is merely a particular example of case (b); for a purely pleasurable experience is one in which the pleasure is expressed by some positive number of hedon-minutes, while the pain is expressed by 0 pathon-minutes, while an experience purely painful would be one the pain of which would be expressible by some positive number of pathon-minutes, and the pleasure of which would be expressible by 0 hedon-minutes. With these considerations clearly in mind, we may under case (b) (p. 116) class the possible subordinate cases as follows:

(1) Quantities of pain and pleasure equivalent: no surplus of pain or pleasure — no preference.
(2) Equal surplus of pain — no preference.
(3) Equal surplus of pleasure — no preference.
(4) Unequal surplus of pain:
    (a) A greater surplus than B — B preferred.
    (b) B greater surplus than A — A preferred.
(5) Unequal surplus of pleasure:
    (a) A greater surplus than B — A preferred.
    (b) B greater surplus than A — B preferred.
(6) A surplus of pleasure: B surplus of pain — A preferred.
(7) B surplus of pleasure: A surplus of pain — B preferred.

Like case (a), cases (c) and (d) may be considered special examples of case (b) in which the pleasure or pain of one alternative is reduced to zero, and are governed by the same principles. That is, under the conditions specified, preference is always determined by quantity — pleasure prevailing over pain, the greater pleasure over the less, and the less pain over the greater.

It seems from our examination beginning on page 108 that in the very numerous cases in which preference is determined by considerations of pleasure and pain alone, (cases so numerous that some writers have suggested that they include all cases of the determination of preference), that preference is never determined by the kind of pleasure and pain, but always by quantity or location in time, and when determined by location, immediate pleasures and remote pains are, at least among the less deliberative beings, generally preferred to remote pleasures and immediate pains. The most frequently occurring and conspicuous cases of this sacrifice of quantity to location are those in which a small but immediate benefit is preferred to a great but remote one, and those in which an alternative involving an immediate temporary pain, and a remote but permanent pleasure, is rejected for one involving less or no pain, but also less or no pleasure. Many examples of such decisions will occur to everyone. They are generally regarded as due to lack of foresight on the part of those making them, and indeed are far more common among animals, children, and ignorant persons than among beings more mature and farseeing. Among adults, sometimes considerations of quantity, sometimes those of location prevail, depending much upon the degree of remoteness of the benefits or injuries involved, as well as upon the magnitude of the surplus of the pleasure or pain. As the experience of men increases and their decisions become more deliberate, preference tends more and more to be decided by the sign or quantity of the surplus alone, pleasure always prevailing over pain, the less pain over the greater, and the greater pleasure over the less, independent of location. On the other hand, to beings governed more by impulse than by judgment, location is more often the controlling factor. Such a relation between maturity of judgment and the character of the motives controlling acts suggests a significant distinction.

In the foregoing analysis it has been our endeavor to learn by what characteristics of painful or pleasurable experiences preference *is* determined. Would it be proper to inquire if these characteristics are those by which it *should* or *ought* to be determined? In this class of decisions does what *is* coincide with what *ought to be?* In order that the question may be answered without prejudice, at this point, I suggest that the reader, if so inclined, reinspect the various cases we have cited, and himself decide which he thinks, on grounds of pure self-interest, are correct, and which incorrect decisions — which should, and which should not be made — remembering that these are the decisions of a being acting in his own interest alone, since by our hypothesis acts affecting the interests of other beings are not among those physically possible. There can be little doubt of the result of such an inspection. Those in which quantity determines preference will be pronounced *right* or *correct* decisions; those in which location determines it, *wrong* or *incorrect.* In other words, a man should, when acting in his own interest, select that alternative which yields the greatest quantity of pleasure, if any can yield pleasure, and if none can, then he should select that yielding the least quantity of pain. Those whose decisions are otherwise determined are said to act against their own interest — their decisions are said to be different from what they should, or ought to be. This is the simplest common sense, and will, I believe, be universally admitted. In short, the use of the terms *right, wrong, should* and *ought, correct* and *incorrect,* in the above connection will be conceded to be in general conformity with usage. If so, we have a generally conceded meaning of these words as applied to a very numerous and important class of voluntary acts, viz. a right act, or the one among the possible alternatives which should be selected, is that act resulting in the greatest surplus of pleasure, if pleasure be attainable, or if it be unattainable, then it is that resulting in the least surplus of pain. A wrong act is a not-right act, or one selected from considerations different from those which determine the selection of a right act. As numerous illustrations of right and wrong decisions of this character will occur to the reader, none need be cited here. If, however, he will consider a number of such illustrations an important characteristic of them all will be obvious. None of them appear to involve the fulfilment or violation of any moral obligation, or to be a matter with which conscience has any concern. In other words, although they involve a distinction between what should be and what should not be — between right and wrong acts or decisions — they involve no distinction between conscientious acts and unconscientious acts. Hence we should feel inclined to express this distinction as one between *correct* and *incorrect* acts rather than between right and wrong ones. The significance of this peculiarity of terms expressive of acts affecting the interests of one person only, will become apparent in Chapter 6.

In the foregoing discussion we have considered experiences involving pain, pleasure, or both, as the determinants of preference when the alternatives were between two specific experiences which differed from each other in kind alone, intensity alone, duration alone, location alone, or quantity alone, and such a mode of investigation was necessary in order to discover just what characteristics of pleasurable or painful experiences govern preference, for if we had considered particular experiences which varied in kind, intensity, duration, and location, at the same time, we obviously could not have learned by which of these characteristics preference was determined. Life, however, does not consist of a series of isolated and independent experiences. Discontinuity of consciousness occurs, of course, notably in sleep, but, in general, one state of consciousness melts into the next without any break in continuity. By an experience we mean any portion of this continuous flow of experience contemplated by itself, and in the foregoing examination we have not placed any restriction upon the duration of this portion; for anything we have said, any of the experiences cited may have lasted as well a year as a second. It is true that we have not specifically discussed the effect of a series of discontinuous painful or pleasurable experiences, but I anticipate no traverse of the assertion that whether the experiences are continuous or discontinuous, dependent or independent, the testimony of consciousness informs us that preference under the conditions postulated, is determined by the principles which have been pointed out, and moreover, these are as applicable when three, four, ten, or an indefinite number of alternatives are open to us, as they are when the alternatives are confined to two. That is, in deciding between two or more experiences involving pleasure or pain, or both, to ourselves alone, that one should be selected which involves the greatest algebraic surplus of pleasure. This may be considered in the nature of a universal moral intuition, because it is independent of all local, fortuitious, or transient determinants of preference. I shall call it the LAW OR PRINCIPLE OF PREFERENCE.

In addition to the principles established, but one postulate is required to enable us to represent diagrammatically the variation of happiness throughout the life of an individual, viz. that at every moment of his life the intensity of the pleasure or pain felt is of some particular value (which may be zero), and I apprehend no dissent from such a proposition; for the only alternative would be to assert that it was of no particular value; in other words, was of two or more values at the same time — an assertion of doubtful intelligibility.

Keeping in mind then the definition of our unit of intensity given on page 111, let us attempt to construct in Fig. 5 a diagram representing the course of the life of an individual, so far as it involves pleasure or pain, for one day of twenty-four hours. Distances measured horizontally, or along the X axis, (X − X) represent periods of time, and the twenty-four divisions into which the diagram is divided by vertical lines, each represent an hour in that day; the line marked Y − Y (the Y axis) representing noon, the morning hours being represented to the left, the afternoon hours to the right of the noon line. Intensities are measured vertically, pleasure being represented by distances above the X axis, pain by distances below it. The heavy horizontal lines divide the diagram into pathedons, those measured above the line being positive, those below negative. Points on the X axis represent zero intensity, or a condition where neither pain nor pleasure is experienced. At times when

122 THE PRINCIPLES OF COMMON SENSE [Book I

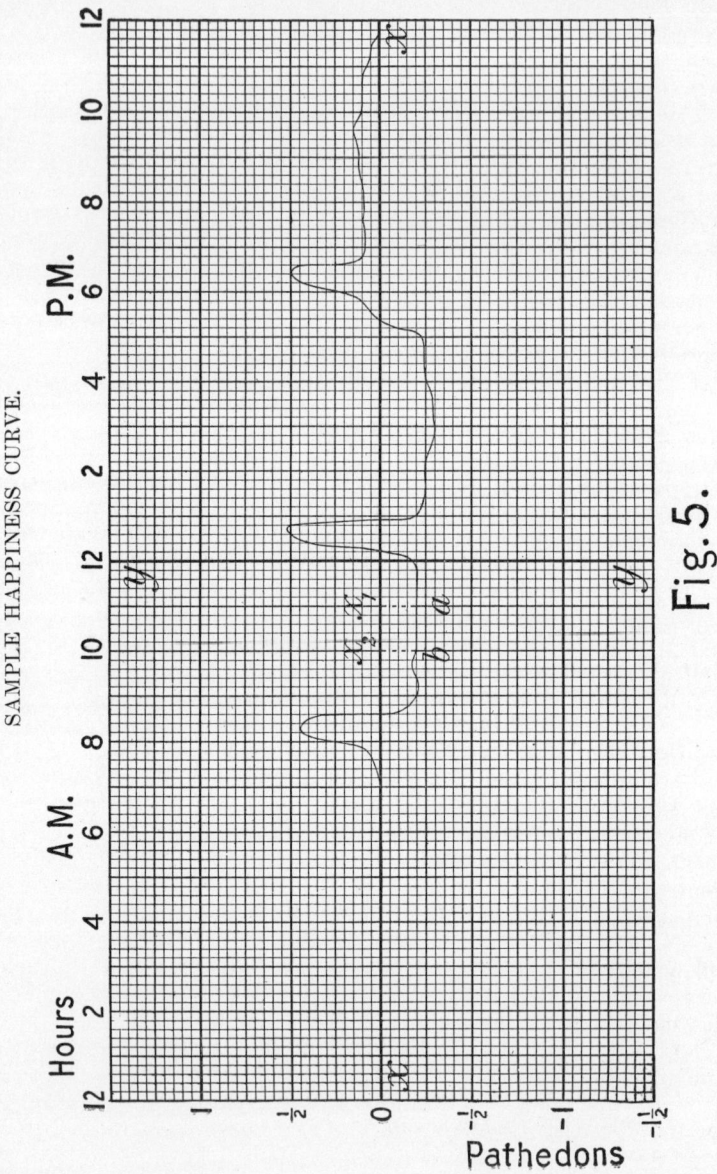

Fig. 5.

pain and pleasure are felt simultaneously the value recorded represents the difference of intensity, or resultant. It is clear then, from the postulate formulated on the preceding page, that for every moment of time in the life of the given individual during the day represented there is a pain or pleasure intensity of some particular value which may be represented on the diagram by a perpendicular erected at the point on the X axis representing that moment. If the intensity is one of pleasure, the perpendicular will be in a positive direction or upward from the X axis; if it is one of pain, it will be downward or negative: the length of the perpendicular will represent the degree of intensity of pleasure or pain.

Suppose now such a perpendicular to be erected at points representing, say every second during the twenty-four hours, and that a line be drawn connecting the ends of these perpendiculars. A curve more or less like that in the diagram would thus be traced, and would represent completely the variation of pleasure and pain of that individual during that day. The interpretation of the curve is very simple. If we suppose it to represent the life of a clerk, say on some normal business day, we see that for the first seven hours the curve is coincident with the X axis, representing a condition painless and pleasureless — in fact, we may easily infer that during those hours he was asleep, and that his sleep was dreamless. He awakes at seven, and the anticipation of a good breakfast, together with the bodily well being that is felt in health, causes the curve to rise slightly while he is dressing. The considerable rise from eight to eight-thirty indicates the breakfast hour, which is evidently a satisfactory one. Going to his daily work, which if it is that of the average clerk is uninteresting enough, pleasure gives place to indifference, and then to a condition to which unconsciousness is preferable — the curve crosses the X axis and for about three hours he drudges at his task with slight fluctuations of ennui until the approach of the noon hour, when anticipation of freedom and lunch causes the curve to recross the X axis and assume positive values again. These increase during the meal, for in healthy persons eating is an enjoyable occupation. The afternoon is a repetition of the morning, and the curve gradually rising, recrosses the X axis about five o'clock. At five-thirty he leaves his place of business and has dinner between six and six-forty-five. We will suppose that he reads and talks to his family in the evening, which accounts for the distinctly positive values of the curve from dinner time to eleven o'clock. Supposing him to get to sleep at eleven-forty-five, the day closes as it began with the curve coincident with the X axis.

It is obvious that curves of this character, sufficiently magnified could be made to show every fluctuation in the intensity of happiness of every sentient being during every day of its life. The curve given is purposely made very simple, and is intended merely as an example. Owing to our assumption of good health and freedom from all care the curve expresses (algebraically) greater happiness than on normal days would be experienced. It incidentally expresses also, what I believe to be probably true, that in the life of the average working individual more pleasure is obtained from eating than from any other one source, and perhaps than from all other sources combined.

The happiness curve thus exemplified expresses not only diurnal variations of pleasure and pain intensity, but also the quantities of pleasure and pain experienced during the day recorded, and expresses them as accurately as it does their intensities. To discover how this is, let us examine the curve shown in Fig. 5 between ten and eleven A. M. and suppose, for the sake of clearness, that between these hours the degree of pain (or boredom) remains constant. This would, of course, be represented by the curve remaining parallel with the X axis and below it. Now as quantity of pain (or pleasure) is proportional to intensity and duration, it is proportional to their product, and using the units defined on page 117 it is equal to their product. It is therefore equal to the area represented on the curve by x_1 x_2 a b, since this, on our assumption, must be a rectangle whose area is equal to the intensity measured by x_1 a, multiplied by the duration, measured by x_1 x_2. Not only does this represent the quantity of pain experienced between ten and eleven A. M., but by an inspection of the diagram, we see that the intensity is $-\frac{1}{5}$ pathedon and is constant. An intensity of $-\frac{1}{5}$ pathedon experienced for one hour will give a quantity of $-\frac{1}{5}$ pathedon-hours or -12 pathedon-minutes, and hence the diagram not only represents to the eye the quantity of pain thus experienced, but gives us the means of expressing it in definite units. If now we suppose the rectangle x_1 x_2 a b divided by vertical lines into sixty equal rectangles, the area of each of these will represent $-\frac{1}{5}$ pathedon-minute, and in each of these, as in the larger rectangle, the quantity of pain experienced during a particular time interval is seen to be represented by an area on the diagram bounded by the curve, the X axis, and the two vertical lines (ordinates) representing the pain intensities at the beginning and end of the interval respectively. We have shown that this must be true of an interval during which the intensity remains constant. By using the methods of the integral calculus it may be shown that the rule is equally valid when the intensity is continuously varying; that is, the area between the curve, the X axis and the ordinates which mark off the given interval, will always be the measure of the quantity of pain (or pleasure) whether constant or continuously varying. This is proved in every work on calculus — its demonstration would be out of place here — nor need the reader fear that the demonstration would not apply to such intangible things as pleasure and pain. The proof, as given, applies to any unvarying or continuously varying succession of magnitudes whatever their nature. All that we have done in the above examination is to theoretically ascertain, in a concrete case, the *definite integral of happiness* — in this case negative, namely, the sum of all the successive quantities of pain experienced by a sentient being between two definite moments in time, and we have found it to be -12 pathedon-minutes. The accuracy with which we may thus determine the quantity of pain (or pleasure) by integration depends upon how accurately the curve represents the actual variation of pain or pleasure during the interval considered — and it depends upon nothing else. It is obvious that the method explained of obtaining the quantity of pain experienced between any two moments in time is equally available in obtaining quantities of pleasure, so that by measuring on Fig. 5 the several areas between the curve and the X axis above that axis — the positive areas — we may obtain the quantity of pleasure experienced during the day by the individual whose life it represents. By measuring the similar areas below the X axis — the negative areas — we may obtain the quantity of pain experienced during the same time. By subtracting the sum of the negative areas from the sum of the positive areas, or *vice versa,* we shall get the surplus of pleasure or pain, whichever it may be. In the curve shown, the quantity of pleasure is 83 hedon-minutes, the quantity of pain 108 pathon-minutes, giving a surplus of pain of 25 pathon-minutes for the day.

At this point, I apprehend the reader may be inclined to ask — What is the use of all this? Of what service can the plotting of such imaginary data be? It can but seek to represent the unknown, if not the unreal. In reply to such criticism, it may be said that the object for which the explanation is introduced does not depend for its fulfilment upon an accurate knowledge of any particular curve, and is therefore unaffected by the uncertainty incident to any attempt to plot one. It is introduced primarily to give our ideas precision and to enable us to comprehend the exact meaning which we intend giving the words *right* and *wrong*. The fact then that no one has in his or her possession the data for accurately constructing such a curve is of small consequence. All we require to know is that throughout the life of every sentient being the succession of values which the pain or pleasure intensities assume are definite values, and would, therefore, if plotted, result in a curve having the characteristics pointed out. We do not need to know what the values are, but only that they are definite or particular values, and this it would be very difficult to deny. It certainly does not follow from the fact that the values of these intensities are unknown that they therefore have no values. If so, we should be justified in asserting that because we do not know the number of horses, or cows, or sheep, in the United States that therefore there is no particular number; or that because the distance of the polar star from the earth is unknown, that it is therefore at no particular distance. What Professor Donkin says about the practical difficulty of accurately expressing degrees of belief or expectation applies equally well to the difficulty of expressing degrees of intensity of pain and pleasure. He says:

"I do not see on what ground it can be doubted that every definite state of belief concerning a proposed hypothesis, is in itself capable of being represented by a numerical expression, however difficult or impracticable it may be to ascertain its actual value. It would be very difficult to estimate in numbers the vis viva of all the particles of a human body at any instant; but no one doubts that it is capable of numerical expression." [1]

It is apparent then that such a curve as we have represented would be constructible, had we the requisite knowledge, for every sentient being in creation during every hour of its life.

Suppose a sentient and intelligent being to be able to forecast the course of the curve for the day next ensuing in his own

[1] "Philosophical Magazine," 4th Series, Vol. 1, p. 354.

life. Suppose him to discover that the sum of the negative areas representing quantity of pain exceeds in magnitude the sum of the positive areas representing quantity of pleasure. Would he or would he not wish to live through such a day? that is, would he or would he not prefer such a day to oblivion for an equal period? Or suppose he had already lived through the day, would he or would he not desire to live the day over again, or rather, live over again a day in which the quantities of pain and pleasure were exactly the same? To answer this question four points must first be settled. (1) Is his choice decided by considerations of pleasure and pain alone? (2) Is he an egotist, one, namely, who considers the effect of acts on himself alone? (3) Is what he *would* decide coincident with what he *should* decide — that is, will he recognize and act upon what he would, if the question were entirely impersonal, decide to be the right or correct course of action? (4) Will any event presumed to occur during the day affect the surplus of pleasure or pain on any or all subsequent days? If we suppose the first three questions to be answered in the affirmative, and the last in the negative, it follows from our definition of equivalent quantities of pleasure and pain that he would prefer to omit the day from his life — he would consider it to be not worth living. Suppose now that instead of forecasting a single day, our hypothetical being was able to forecast his whole subsequent life and discovered that when completely summed up, it showed an excess of negative area — a surplus of pain. This would eliminate the necessity of having the knowledge mentioned in the fourth condition, since there would then be no subsequent days. Again, let us assume the remaining questions are answered in the affirmative, and again we are forced to the conclusion that he would prefer oblivion — in this case prefer death to life. Now it is evident that few persons, even when they are practically certain that their subsequent life will result in a surplus of pain, prefer death to life. This is equivalent to saying that with a majority of persons the third condition above mentioned is not fulfilled, that men do not, in such cases, act in their own interest. Indeed, their decisions are not based on reason, but on instinct — an instinct common to both men and animals. Hence their acts are not controlled by considerations of pleasure and pain, but by the fear of death. In assuming therefore that in the case of our supposed being condition 3 is fulfilled, we are assuming that he is without the fear of death.

128   THE PRINCIPLES OF COMMON SENSE   [Book I

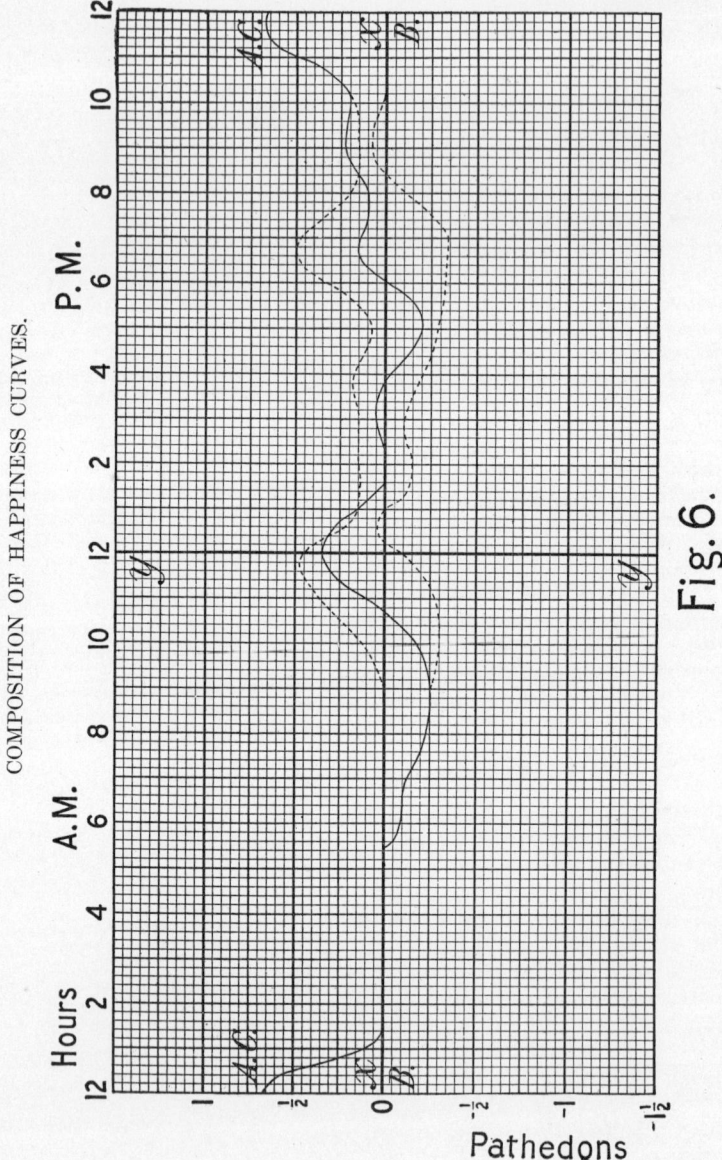

Fig. 6.

Let us now turn our attention to Fig. 6. It represents the curve of happiness of two individuals for a particular day. The dotted lines A—A and B—B are the two individual curves. The solid line C—C is a derivative curve whose characteristic is that the position of every point upon it is determined by the algebraic sum of the happiness values of the two individual curves at points corresponding to it in time. For example, let us take the point on the curve C—C corresponding to the time 4 P. M. It is fixed as follows: The happiness value of the curve A—A for that moment in time is .18 pathedon; that of the curve B—B is −.205 pathedon. Their algebraic sum will therefore be $.18 - .205 = -.025$ pathedon, which determines the position of the point of the curve C—C for 4 P. M. All other points on the curve are determined in a similar manner. At times when only one individual is conscious the resultant curve is coincident with the curve of the other individual. When neither is conscious it is coincident with the X axis. It thus happens in the example given, that the termini of the curves A—A and C—C are coincident. The curve C—C then represents the happiness curve of an individual who experiences, in his own person, the pain and pleasure experienced by the individuals whose curves are A—A and B—B separately, that is, his sensations of pleasure and pain are the resultants of theirs, and the happiness value of his day, measured in units of quantity, is the algebraic sum of the happiness value of theirs. If now, the happiness curve D—D of a third individual (not shown) were represented on the diagram, it obviously could be combined with C—C as A—A and B—B were combined with one another to give C—C, and the resulting curve would represent the algebraic sum of the diurnal happiness values of all three individuals. Similarly four, five, or any number of curves could be combined until curves representing the happiness of a community, a nation, of all mankind, or of all sentient creation, could conceivably be constructed; and by extending such a curve throughout all days instead of one, the total happiness of all beings for all time would be representable.

Let us next assume an omniscient being, capable therefore of correctly forecasting the happiness curve of all beings including his own, and so constituted as to fulfil conditions 1, 2, and 3, (p. 127), whose happiness curve coincides throughout with that which represents the happiness of sentient creation for all time to come. Suppose that his forecast should show a surplus of pain. Would he prefer to live or not to live? Obviously he would prefer not to live. On the other hand, if his forecast should show a surplus of pleasure he would prefer to live. Suppose, however, he were compelled to accept life by physical necessity, but able by his own voluntary acts to determine the course of the happiness curve of sentient creation, and therefore his own, which by hypothesis remains coincident with it. If alternatives A, B, C, D, E, etc., are open to him, and he can, through his omniscience, foresee the total effect of each, and discovers that alternative C results in a curve whose integral shows a greater excess of pleasure or less excess of pain than A, B, D, E, etc., it follows from what we have discovered concerning the relation of preference to pleasure and pain, that the alternative that he will voluntarily select will be C.

We are now prepared to offer a definition, not of right and wrong, but of terms whose meaning is very similar to them. We shall call these terms *absolute right* and *absolute wrong*. By an act *absolutely right*, I shall mean that act among those at any moment possible which results in the greatest surplus of happiness. By an *absolutely wrong* act I shall mean any of the alternatives of an absolutely right act. Another way of expressing these meanings is to say that an absolutely right act is one which such an omniscient being as we have described would approve — an absolutely wrong one, one that he would not approve.

But as we are not seeking a guide for the acts of an omniscient being, it is evident that these definitions are not those we are seeking. Men are not omniscient, and can therefore never be certain which of the alternatives open to them will result in the maximum surplus of happiness. Nevertheless, though they may be unable to arrive at a *certainty*, they may establish a *presumption*. Though it is beyond our power to be certain of the effects of acts we may have reason for expectations concerning them. Probability then must serve as a guide, since certainty fails us. In truth, there are but two alternatives to the acceptance of probability as a guide. These are either to accept no guide whatever and act without any consideration of the effects of our acts, or to accept error as a guide.

It is a familiar fact, not only that men will accept pain in order to obtain pleasure of more than equivalent quantity, but that they will risk pain in order to obtain pleasure of less than equivalent quantity and the greater the presumption of pleasure, the greater the risk of pain which they will hazard.

Similarly they will forego considerable quantities of pleasure, if accepting them involves risk of too much pain. Indeed, the selection of any alternative with the object of attaining pleasure or of avoiding pain implies the estimation of probability, and while man's assurance of the results of some acts may be immensely greater than his assurance of the results of others, the difference can never be more than one of degree while he remains fallible. It is obvious that there are many ways of balancing presumptions of pleasure and pain, and some of these ways would be universally recognized as better than others. Suppose a person were offered two alternatives, A and B: A affording a presumption of much pleasure and little pain; B of much pain and little pleasure. Would common sense give us any clue as to which alternative was the better? Would it tell us that B was preferable to A, or that A and B were equally preferable? No, it would be universally conceded that A was preferable to B. If this be so, there must be some reason for such unanimity of opinion; it must be that all men have in mind, clearly or obscurely, some criterion of conduct, which, when applied to the example cited, yields an identical judgment in all minds. Is that criterion discoverable and expressible in intelligible symbols? If so, it is the duty of the analyst of common sense to discover and express it if possible. Let us make the attempt.

That operation of the mind which is involved in correctly comparing the relative promise of happiness offered by two or more alternatives I shall denominate a *Use-judgment* or *Chresyllogism,* (Gr. $\chi\rho\hat{\eta}\sigma\iota\varsigma$ = use: $\sigma\upsilon\lambda\lambda o\gamma\iota\sigma\mu\acute{o}\varsigma$ = judgment). The easiest way to reveal the nature of a use-judgment will be to treat a simple case first and then develop from it the universal law. For this purpose reference should be made to Table I, which represents one of the simplest of use-judgments. It may be explained thus:

Assume an individual — call him X — to whom units of money correspond to units of pleasure and pain; to whom, let us say, the gain of one dollar would mean a gain of one hedon-minute, a gain of two dollars a gain of two hedon-minutes, etc.; similarly the loss of one dollar would mean the loss of one hedon-minute or the gain of one pathon-minute, etc. In other words, assume that pleasure and pain can be thus expressed exactly in terms of money gained and money lost. This is not generally true, but it will make the explanation simpler to assume it in the present example

Assume now, X to be confined to the selection of seven and

USE-JUDGMENT OF SEVEN ALTERNATIVES OF TWO CONTINGENCIES OF EQUAL PROBABILITY EACH.

	Probability of		Probable surplus of		Mean surplus of		
1	2	3	4	5	6	7	8
Alternatives	Contingency 1	Contingency 2	$ Contingency 1	$ Contingency 2	$ Contingency 1	$ Contingency 2	$ Presumption of gain
A	½	½	0	-3	0	-1½	-1½
B	½	½	1	-3	½	-1½	-1
C	½	½	2	-3	1	-1½	-½
D	½	½	3	-3	1½	-1½	0
E	½	½	3	-2	1½	-1	½
F	½	½	3	-1	1½	-½	1
G	½	½	3	0	1½	0	1½

Table I.

only seven alternatives, signified by A, B, C, etc. (Column 1) each alternative consisting of the toss of a separate coin. That is, X may select any coin of the seven he pleases, but he must select one. Now a coin must fall either heads or tails — it matters not which alternative he selects, one of two contingencies is sure to occur — the coin will fall either heads or tails, and the probability of each will be one-half. Call the fall of heads, *contingency 1*, and the fall of tails *contingency 2*. Then the probability of contingency 1 will be one-half, and of contingency 2 will be one-half. (Columns 2 and 3.) Next let us make the following assumptions: In the case of alternative A, the occurrence of contingency 1 will involve a gain or loss of nothing; the occurrence of contingency 2 will involve a loss of $3.00. In the case of alternative B, the occurrence of contingency 1 will involve a gain of $1.00 and of contingency 2 a loss of $3.00, etc. Columns 4 and 5 contain these values for each alternative; they are called the *probable surpluses* of contingencies 1 and 2, respectively. A gain is expressed by a positive sign; a loss by a negative sign. If now we multiply the figures in Column 2, by the corresponding figures in Column 4, we obtain Column 6, and by the same operation on Columns 3 and 5, we obtain Column 7. These are called the *mean surpluses* of contingencies 1 and 2, respectively: their algebraic sum is contained in Column 8, and is called the *presumption of gain* (*or loss*) of alternatives A, B, C, etc. In order to understand exactly what the last three columns represent, let us consider some one alternative, say B. To say the chance of tossing heads is one-half, is to say that if the coin is thrown a great number of times, heads will turn up, on an average, once in two times. Say the coin is thrown six million times; then heads will turn up three million of those times, and tails also three million. Of course, there will be a slight percentage error, but were the number of times indefinitely increased, the error would indefinitely decrease. This being the case, it is obvious, that in six million throws X will gain three million dollars and lose nine million dollars if he accepts alternative B. To obtain the amount won and lost at each throw, on the average, we must divide by the number of throws, viz. six million. This shows that the mean amount gained per throw will be one-half a dollar; the mean amount lost will be one dollar and a half. These are the figures in Columns 6 and 7 respectively. Column 8 is the algebraic sum of these two. It shows that, on the average, X will lose one dollar on every throw. A similar

134 THE PRINCIPLES OF COMMON SENSE [Book I

USE-JUDGMENT OF SIX ALTERNATIVES OF TWO CONTINGENCIES OF UNEQUAL PROBABILITY EACH.

1	Probability of		Probable surplus of		Mean surplus of		8
Alternatives	2 Contingency 1	3 Contingency 2	4 Contingency 1 pathedon-minutes	5 Contingency 2 pathedon-minutes	6 Contingency 1 pathedon-minutes	7 Contingency 2 pathedon-minutes	Presumption of happiness pathedon-minutes
A	1/12	11/12	-2	20	-1/6	18 1/3	18 1/6
B	1/4	3/4	4	-3	1	-2 1/4	-1 1/4
C	1/5	4/5	8	8	1 3/5	6 2/5	8
D	2/15	13/15	6	-5	4/5	-4 1/3	-3 8/15
E	1/8	7/8	9	2	1 1/8	1 3/4	2 7/8
F	5/24	19/24	20	-1	4 1/6	-19/24	2 3/8

Table II.

Chap. III]   UTILITY   135

meaning is to be given to the other figures in Columns 6, 7 and 8. From these considerations it is clear that the *best* alternative of the seven, the one promising the greatest gain, is G, the next best is F, the next E, &c., A being the *worst*.

Table I is the expression of a use-judgment on the assumption that units of happiness are equivalent to units of money. Dropping this erroneous assumption, let us consider Table II which shows a slightly more complicated use-judgment, in which the probabilities of the two contingencies are unequal. In this table the surpluses are expressed in pathedon-minutes, as they should be, instead of in dollars. We may suppose the alternatives to be those offered by the fall of a die whose faces are unequal in area, so that the chance of face 1 turning up is $\frac{1}{12}$ and of not turning up therefore $\frac{11}{12}$; of face 2 turning up $\frac{1}{4}$ and of not turning up $\frac{3}{4}$, etc. The assumed surpluses of these contingencies are recorded in Columns 4 and 5. The same principles are embodied in this as in the previous use-judgment, and by the same operations we discover that alternative A is the best, C the next best, E next, and D the worst. When there are only two contingencies to an alternative, or only two are considered, we shall call the probability of that contingency whose probable surplus is algebraically the greatest, the *probability of success*, and its probable surplus, the *surplus of success;* the probability of the other contingency will then be called the *probability* of *failure* and its probable surplus the *surplus* of *failure,* etc. The grounds for this terminology are obvious; since the only reason an alternative is, in general, selected is because of the presumption which it affords of happiness, and the occurrence of that contingency which affords the most happiness would be deemed a successful result of selecting the alternative. The occurrence of the other contingency would constitute failure, of which there is always risk.

Table III shows a yet more complex use-judgment, containing three alternatives of four equally probable contingencies each. These alternatives may be considered as arising from the optional casts of three separate dies having the shape of an isohedral tetrahedron, each corresponding to an alternative. The operations are the same as in the previous example — the mean surpluses of pain and pleasure being first found by multiplying the corresponding columns together, and the algebraic sum constituting in each case the *presumption of happiness* of the corresponding alternative.

To more perfectly reveal the nature of a use-judgment Table

IV is inserted. It is the complete analysis of a single alternative containing five contingencies (Column 1). The probabilities, probable surpluses, and mean surpluses of these contingencies are given in columns 2, 3, and 4 respectively. The algebraic sum of the figures in column 4 is, of course, the presumption of happiness of the alternative (equal in this example to $-\frac{9}{10}$). Now it may be said of any contingency that it will either occur, or it will not. Call the non-occurrence of

USE-JUDGMENT OF THREE ALTERNATIVES OF FOUR CONTINGENCIES OF EQUAL PROBABILITY EACH.

1	Probability of				Probable surplus of				Mean surplus of				14
	2	3	4	5	6	7	8	9	10	11	12	13	
Alternatives	Contingency 1	Contingency 2	Contingency 3	Contingency 4	Contingency 1	Contingency 2	Contingency 3	Contingency 4	Contingency 1	Contingency 2	Contingency 3	Contingency 4	Presumption of happiness
					path.-mins.	path.-mins.	path.-mins.	path.-mins.	path.-mins.	path.-mins.	path.-mins.	path.-mins.	path.-mins.
A	¼	¼	¼	¼	1	0	-1	-2	¼	0	-¼	-½	-½
B	¼	¼	¼	¼	2	1	0	-1	½	¼	0	-¼	½
C	¼	¼	¼	¼	3	2	1	0	¾	½	¼	0	1½

Table III.

a given contingency its *anti-contingency*. This anti-contingency, of course, will have a probability, a probable surplus, and a mean surplus, (Columns 5, 6, and 7,) just as the corresponding contingency has, and as one or the other must occur, it is clear that we may calculate the presumption of happiness of any alternative by adding the mean surplus of any contingency involved, to the mean surplus of the corresponding anti-contingency; and if a use-judgment is consistent with itself, we should always obtain thereby the same result. Let us make the trial.

Obviously the probability of an anti-contingency is found by subtracting the probability of its contingency from unity. This figure is given in column 5. The mode of ascertaining its probable surplus may be explained thus: If any contingency involved in an alternative fails to occur, it must be because some one of its associated contingencies occurs. Let us assume, for example, that contingency IV fails to occur. Now contingencies are either *independent,* or they are not; that is to say, the assumption of the non-occurrence of any one, either increases the probability of each of the others in equal ratio, or it does not. Let us assume the contingencies in the present example to be independent. Then by the assumption of the non-occurrence of contingency IV, the probability of each of its associates is increased in equal ratio. Moreover, as some one of them must occur, the sum of their probabilities must be unity. To fulfil both these conditions the probability of each of the associates of contingency IV must be multiplied by the reciprocal of the probability of the anti-contingency of contingency IV, viz., by $\frac{5}{4}$. This will give the probability of each, assuming the non-occurrence of said contingency. Multiplying in each case this revised probability into the corresponding probable surplus, and adding together the four mean surpluses thus obtained, we obtain the probable surplus of the anti-contingency of contingency IV, viz. $-1\frac{7}{8}$. Multiplying this into its probability we obtain its mean surplus, viz. $-1\frac{1}{2}$, and if this be added to the mean surplus of contingency IV we obtain $-\frac{9}{10}$ as the presumption of happiness of the alternative. This is the same result as is obtained by adding together the figures in column 4. By performing these same operations in the case of the other contingencies the result is the same, and thus the consistency of the use-judgment is verified. In fact, if we substitute letters for numbers in the process we have described, and equate the several expressions obtained for the presumption of happiness, we shall get a series of identical equations, (of the form $1=1$) showing that the result is a general one. To follow the explanation we have given may prove rather tedious, but he who does so understandingly will have no difficulty thereafter in comprehending the nature of a use-judgment.

In the case of *dependent* contingencies no general rule for

COMPLETE ANALYSIS OF AN ALTERNATIVE ASSUMING INDEPENDENT CONTINGENCIES.

1	2	3	4	5	6	7	8
Contingencies	Probability of contingency	Probable surplus of contingency (pathedon-minutes)	Mean surplus of contingency (pathedon-minutes)	Probability of anti-contingency	Probable surplus of anti-contingency (pathedon-minutes)	Mean surplus of anti-contingency (pathedon-minutes)	Presumption of happiness (pathedon-minutes)
I	1/4	8	2	3/4	-3 13/15	-2 9/10	-9/10
II	1/12	-10	-5/6	11/12	-4/55	-1/15	-9/10
III	1/3	0	0	2/3	-1 7/20	-9/10	-9/10
IV	1/5	3	3/5	4/5	-1 7/8	-1 1/2	-9/10
V	2/15	-20	-2 2/3	13/15	2 1/26	1 23/30	-9/10
Presumption of happiness -9/10							

Table IV.

calculating the probable surplus can be given, because the operation will vary according to the mode of dependence. Hence alternatives involving such contingencies can only be analyzed by applying to them the theory of probabilities in the manner required by the conditions peculiar to each.

Now it is obvious that a use-judgment or chresyllogism may contain any number of alternatives, that each alternative may involve any number of contingencies, that the probability of said contingencies may be equal or unequal, that their probable surpluses may be positive or negative, yet exactly the same principle exemplified in the samples shown will be applicable in determining the relative presumption of happiness of the various alternatives exhibited thereby. Indeed, this is the method by which common sense always judges, and by the same method every man, when he acts wisely, guides his conduct; for in choosing the alternatives, or series of alternatives, which constitute his conduct, he strives at each moment of his life to select the best offered by circumstances, and he is enabled to select the best from among those offered, by a process in all respects similar to that explained. One important difference, however, must be noticed. In the hypothetical cases we have considered, the probabilities and probable surpluses are assumed to be exactly known, but in most of the alternatives offered us in life these quantities must be estimated. Not merely is the surplus of each contingency only a probable surplus, but its probability is only a *probable* probability. It is in the estimation of these quantities that knowledge is most useful. Without knowledge we are unable to estimate them at all, and hence have no guide to conduct. The greater our knowledge the more closely can they be estimated — were we omniscient, we could estimate them exactly. As knowledge rests upon belief-judgments derived from observation, the ability to judge of usefulness rests, in its final analysis, upon observation. In all the familiar deliberate acts which concern our personal interest, particularly those whose consequences promise to be of some importance, we are conscious of making estimates of the kind illustrated — attempting to approximate the pleasure and pain value, not of some one of the possible effects or contingencies of the alternatives offered, but of all the possible effects or contingencies — not of the immediate and direct contingencies alone, but of the remote and indirect contingencies as well — seeking to measure not only what we shall gain if the contingency we desire eventuates, but what we shall lose if it fails to eventuate. In fact, the more we consider partial effects to the neglect of total, the more what we do, departs from what we should or ought to do.

A *moral being* may be defined as one possessed of volition and capable of employing a use-judgment. At any and every moment in such a being's life, an indefinite number of alternatives is offered him, to each of which correspond an indefinite number of contingencies, whose probability and probable surplus must be estimated, if at all, by the inductive method. Hence the general expression for a use-judgment or chresyllogism is as follows:

Let A, B, . . . &c., be the alternatives offered, each involving an assemblage of contingencies. Let p_1 p_2 p_3 . . . p_m, &c.; p'_1 p'_2 p'_3 . . . p'_n, &c. be the several probabilities of said assemblages of contingencies respectively. Let h_1 h_2 h_3 . . . h_m, &c.; h'_1 h'_2 h'_3 . . . h'_n, &c. be the corresponding probable surpluses: then if P_A, P_B, . . . &c. represent the presumptions of happiness of the several alternatives, the following equations will be valid:

$$P_A = p_1 h_1 + p_2 h_2 + p_3 h_3 + \ldots p_m h_m.$$
$$P_B = p'_1 h'_1 + p'_2 h'_2 + p'_3 h'_3 + \ldots p'_n h'_n.$$

and so with the other alternatives. *The greater the algebraic value of the presumption of happiness, the greater the utility.* That is to say, the *degree of utility or usefulness* of an alternative is measured by its presumption of happiness.

Of course, in any actual situation in life the number of alternatives considered and the number of contingencies corresponding to each is limited. We ignore the vast bulk of possible alternatives and consider those alone which offer, or which appear to offer, the greatest presumptions of happiness.

What we have on page 80 remarked concerning a belief-judgment holds good for a use-judgment — the presumptions which determine acts must be based upon data at the time and place available. So long as a person adheres strictly to the method of common sense and employs all the data available, he has done the best he can. If then he makes mistakes it must be charged to the fallibility of human faculty and not to any error in the principles employed.

The fact that common sense has only the theory of probability to offer as a guide to human acts is frequently cited by persons who have not considered the matter as proof of the incapacity of science to provide a practical code of conduct.

"It is all very well," say they, "to talk about selecting those acts which will lead to the greatest happiness; but how are we going to know what acts will so lead?" The shallowness of this style of criticism has been already exposed and may be further exhibited by inquiring what alternative they have to offer us for the theory of probability as a guide to conduct. Not being omniscient they cannot offer us certainty; and if they offer us local intuition they must be prepared to encounter the objection that one local intuition is as good as another.

Indeed, it is clear that he who would derive the most happiness from the alternatives offered by his surroundings must employ the principle we have revealed, for what suggestible departure therefrom would afford a greater amount? It may perhaps be suggested that occasionally, when some alternative is offered involving a contingency whose probable surplus is very great, though the probability of the contingency itself is small, that such an alternative should perhaps be risked, even if some other affords a greater presumption of happiness. But those who deem such risks justifiable should not forget that the particular grounds upon which probabilities have been established are a matter of indifference in judgments of utility — it is only the *degrees* of probability which are considered. Hence, if such a risk is justified on any one occasion, it will be justified on all occasions when the relative probabilities are the same; that is, if a man is justified in departing in a specific manner from the principle of the use-judgment once, why is he not justified in departing twice under the same circumstances, and if twice why not three times; if three times, why not four times, etc.? Indeed, any departure from the principle we have laid down involves inconsistency unless the departure is governed by some principle which would require a like departure in all similar cases — and if such a principle is proposable, what is it?

I will not say that individuals do not depart from this principle — I will not say that in departing therefrom they have not sometimes been the gainers — I will say that in the total departure therefrom more has been lost than has been gained. In gambling at a regular gaming establishment, where the chances are always in favor of the establishment, many men have won — but more have lost. It would be absurd for any gambler to assert that because he had won once on a great risk that he, or any one else, could therefore safely take the risk thereafter. The principle of utility embodied in a use-judgment involves risks, but the risks are exactly apportioned to the probability of the contingencies, and of the surpluses thereof, instead of being selected fortuitously. Men may, and often do, in guiding their conduct, depart from the principle we have discussed, but they cannot do so without at the same time departing from common sense. Kant has said that whatever rule is taken as the foundation of morality it must be of universal application; and this requirement the rule imposed by a use-judgment fulfils, for it is obvious from the nature of probability that the more universally conduct is controlled by use-judgments the greater the probability that happiness will approach a maximum; and every departure therefrom diminishes said probability. Indeed, that which Laplace remarked of the mathematical theory of probability may, with equal justice, be remarked of the mathematical theory of utility — *it is common sense reduced to calculation.*

Now one who employs a use-judgment to forecast the effect of his acts on his own happiness curve alone, and whose conduct is controlled by judgments so derived, may be called an *egotist* — the lower unsocial animals are representatives of this class. One who considers his own family but ignores the rest of creation may be called an *oeciot* (*Gr.* οἰκία = family) — many animals and primitive men have attained such a stage. One whose consideration extends to his tribe or "gang" may be called a *phyliot* (Gr. φυγή = tribe). One whose acts are controlled by their presumable effect on those composing his nation is called a *patriot* — modern civilized communities have attained the patriotic stage. One who in acting considers mankind as a whole is called a *humanitarian;* and one who controls his conduct by its presumable effect upon sentient creation is called a *utilitarian.*

The meaning of the word *reason* as applicable to acts is at this stage of our exposition discoverable. A *reason* for an act is any portion of evidence, *aposteriori* or *apriori,* adapted to aid in establishing the degree of utility of said act, and is adjudged a good or a bad reason according as it tends, or does not tend, to establish a high degree of utility therefor. The word *reason,* as applied to egotistic, oeciotic, phyliotic, patriotic, humanitarian, and utilitarian acts respectively, will, from this definition, be obvious; and it is equally obvious that the terms *utility, probable surplus, mean surplus,* etc., are capable of a like variation in meaning; but as employed in this work, unless otherwise specified, they will retain their utilitarian meanings, since it is a clear comprehension of these alone which can lead us to the goal we seek — the definitions of the words *right* and *wrong.* These definitions, toward which we have been travelling so long, may now be formulated, thus:

A RIGHT ACT IS AN ACT OF MAXIMUM UTILITY — *it is that act among those at any moment possible whose presumption of happiness is a maximum.* **A WRONG ACT IS ANY ALTERNATIVE OF A RIGHT ACT**   Or, assuming $a, b, c, d, e,$ &c. express the presumptions of happiness of sentient creation corresponding to alternatives A, B, C, D, E, &c., and of these a is greater than $b,$ or $c,$ or $d,$ &c., then A is right and B, C, D, E, &c. are all of them wrong.

Thus voluntary acts are divided into two classes (1) Right, (2) Not right, or Wrong, i. e., *wrong* is equivalent to *not right,* and there is no class of acts which are neither right nor wrong, which neither should nor should not be done.

Of course it may be contended that occasionally two or more alternatives may arise the utility of which is exactly the same. Perhaps it must be admitted that such a case might occasionally occur; but it will rarely, if ever, happen in situations where the effects are of sufficient importance to justify careful deliberation, that such deliberation will fail to develop some presumption, however small, in favor of one or another alternative, and if it does so fail, it is a matter of indifference which alternative is selected.

Any act which is adapted to attain the end for the attainment of which it is selected may be called an *adaptive* act — if the end be hedonistic it is a *correct* act, but it is convenient to restrict the word *right* to that class of correct acts whose end is the utilitarian end. An adaptive act may be correct or right, but it may be neither. A correct act is adaptive, and may or may not be right. A right act is both adaptive and correct. Thus the relative meaning of these terms is made clear.

It may be objected that in practical affairs we seldom or never hear men refer to such a thing as a *presumption of happiness* or the *probable surplus* of such and such a contingency, much less do we ever perceive them casting their judgments into such forms as those we have shown as representing use-judgments. Men seem to get along very well without knowledge of this character. Neither do we hear men, when about their ordinary affairs, refer to *major premises,* or the *rules of the syllogism,* or the *inverse method of induction.* Nevertheless, as already noted, they use the inductive or common sense method as a guide to belief every hour of their lives in their familiar affairs, and they would use it in all affairs did they understand the nature of common sense. Similarly, in commonplace matters men employ use-judgments as guides to conduct, and they would employ them in all matters did they consistently adhere to common sense. Not understanding the nature of common sense any more in the one case than in the other, as soon as they leave the realm where error is subject to the constant check of immediate experience they become subject to the rule of intuitionism, the result being that their means are no longer adapted to their ends. Should a farmer be told that in carefully fertilizing his field, sowing, cultivating, and harvesting his crops, he is pursuing a correct policy, but that after the crops are harvested it makes no difference what is done with them, whether they are left in the field to rot, fed to the swine, or sent to market, he would suspect that he was not listening to common sense. But should he be told that the correct policy for a nation to pursue is to produce wealth as economically as possible, but that its mode of consumption, its disposal after being produced, is of no consequence, he would not perceive anything to criticise in the statement; in fact, had he been an early and close student of dogmatic economics he probably would be tempted to say that this truth was almost self-evident — a political axiom. He would, in other words, apply common sense to the conduct of an individual, but not to the conduct of a nation. Had he, however, understood its nature and confined his methods of distinguishing between the correct and the incorrect to those we have specified, he would have seen that common sense is as applicable to the one as to the other. Should the reader deem that in stating the case thus strongly I am indulging in exaggeration I commend to his impartial judgment the considerations with which this work hereafter deals.

But it may occur to some readers that so long as right and wrong must in minds not omniscient always include the doubt attaching to probability, that after all the safest method is — at any rate in important matters — not to select any alternative at all, but to let things take their course. The difficulty with this view is that to fail to act constitutes as deliberate a selection of an alternative as to act; it may be the right or it may be a wrong alternative, but it must be one or the other, so long as the probabilities of the effects on pleasure and pain are not in perfect equality.

This consideration leads us to some further distinctions of

importance in the theory of utility. In the last chapter it was pointed out that the word *probability,* besides signifying the measure of an expectation's validity, could be, and often was, applied to expectations of the higher degrees of validity. A similar innocuous equivocality attaches to the words *utility* or *usefulness.* Besides signifying the degree of an alternative's presumption of happiness, they may be applied to alternatives of the higher degrees of utility.

To fail to act can only mean to select that alternative which involves the minimum of activity, whether of mind or body, the presumable surplus of happiness of this alternative being, in general, as definite as that of any other. Now a *useful* act or alternative is one whose presumption of happiness is greater than the alternative of minimum activity, except when said alternative of minimum activity involves a greater presumption than any other. In this case the alternative of minimum activity is the only useful one. Any useful act to which there is an alternative more useful will be wrong; otherwise it will be right; that is of course, a right act is simply the most useful act. Any act whose presumable surplus is not greater than that of the alternative of minimum activity is called a *useless* act, except when the utility of said alternative is a maximum, in which case all other alternatives are useless. A *harmful* act or alternative is one having a negative presumption of happiness when alternatives involving a positive presumption are selectable. The meanings of the words *useful, useless,* and *harmful* as applied to objects or events will, from what is here said, be sufficiently obvious.

The foregoing definitions incidentally partake of the nature of inductions. I have sought to discover and express by them, with as high a degree of precision as possible, the meaning which the great teachers of morality in all ages and climes, consciously or unconsciously, vaguely or clearly, must have intended to convey when they formulated their rules for the guidance of mankind — at least in so far as they intended to convey any meaning capable of being made consistent with itself — for they are founded upon the only distinction in experience whose interest to mankind persists and will continue to persist throughout all countries and all history, independent alike of space and of time — the distinction between pleasure and pain. They constitute the test by which we may judge of the goodness or badness, the usefulness or uselessness, the desirability or undesirability, not only of voluntary acts, but of anything and everything which affects sentient beings. Many objections to them will doubtless occur to the reader, but I apprehend that there will be two of particular prominence. The first of these has reference to the relation of conscientious to right acts and will be fully treated in Chapter 6. The second refers to the fact that our definitions specify nothing concerning that very essential factor — the *distribution* of happiness. Justice would seem to demand that such happiness as the world may afford should be equally distributed. It is palpably unfair that one set of men should have all the pleasure and another all the pain. Bentham expressed the utilitarian doctrine by asserting that the object of voluntary acts should be the greatest happiness of the greatest number, thereby making the *number* of persons affected a factor in distinguishing right from wrong. We have asserted that right and wrong are determined only by the presumption of happiness, independent of distribution, and it remains for us to justify our definitions in the face of this objection, which will, I apprehend, be a very general one.

Let us examine, in the first place, the assumption which must be made if we accept the number affected as a critical factor in distinguishing right from wrong; and first let us inquire if there is any universally accepted rule which will tell us what the distribution of happiness should be. Should we ask a Mohammedan how happiness ought to be distributed, he would reply that the faithful followers of the prophet ought to get the bulk of it. A Chinaman would deny the right of the hated foreigner to any share in happiness. A Turk would assert that in the distribution of happiness men should be considered before women. And a Hindu would claim that it is entirely a matter of caste. Many Christians would maintain that the idolatrous heathen have no just title to share in the blessings of the elect — and with various reservations, practically all races and creeds would agree that in the distribution of happiness little or none should fall to the share of the wicked, while the righteous should get whatever the world may afford. Evidently then, there is little general agreement on the subject of distribution. All but the last mentioned view, however, may be attributed to local dogma, prohibiting any impartial judgment, as dogma always does. Perhaps an impartial judge would claim that all persons, independent of race, creed, age, sex, or character, ought to have an equal share in the pleasure and pain which the world affords; but this suggests the question — Why confine equality of distribution to persons? Have animals no claims? If not, why not? If so, should their share be the same as that of men, or less, and if less, how much less? These questions must be answered, or at least answerable, if the definitions we are discussing are to serve as a guide to conduct. Admitting that right and wrong are to be expressed in terms of pleasure and pain, a definition consistent with itself must apply to any community — or to put the matter more generally — must apply to any *system* capable of pleasure or pain. How then would a definition, involving equal distribution as an essential factor, be applied to a system consisting of various animals, men, horses, dogs, cows, hawks, crocodiles, moths and mosquitoes? Should the distribution be equal? If not, how should it be determined? Again suppose the community included no men, but animals only — how then would the definition apply? I am aware that many persons would dispose of this matter by saying that, as animals have no souls, they are entitled to no consideration, and that the pleasure or pain of animals should always be ignored if the failure to ignore it diminishes the pleasure or increases the pain of men. Such persons would probably claim that the words *right* and *wrong* have no meaning when applied to animals alone. Without arguing the question as to whether the word *soul* has any definite meaning, or without inquiring how we are to know which animals have, and which have not, souls, the question may be asked: Why should the possession or lack of possession of a soul make any difference? Pain is pain by whomsoever felt, and pleasure is pleasure. To say that a soul has anything to do with the question of right and wrong is, in effect, to say that right and wrong cannot be expressed in terms of pleasure and pain. Indeed, it is so obvious that dogma alone dictates this view of the nature of right and wrong that any effort to oppose it by reason would be superfluous.

It matters not whether the beings which feel are men, horses, toads or flies; it is the quantity of pain or pleasure produced, not the particular configuration of the body of the being who feels it, that is of consequence. If a man will, for a moment, cease to take counsel of his prejudices, he will concede that this must be so. For, if we are to declare that the shape of the body, the nature of the tissues, or the degree of intelligence, of a being, must be taken into consideration in deciding whether the pleasure or pain felt by it are worthy of estimate in the surplus of pleasure which it is our duty to increase, then we must be able to give some reason why a particular shape of body or particular degree of intelligence justifies us in ignoring the pain or pleasure associated with it. The mere statement of this condition must convince us of the futility of attempting to formulate a consistent definition of *right* which will meet it. Surely the desirability of pleasure or the undesirability of pain cannot depend upon whether they are felt by a being who has a long nose rather than a short one, black hair rather than brown, a dark skin rather than a light one, two legs rather than four, a vertebrate skeleton rather than an articulate one; nor can it depend upon whether said being is more or less proficient in mathematics, is better or worse in disputation, is capable of reasoning or incapable of it. If it does so depend, then it is in order to inquire what may be meant by the words *desirable* or *undesirable* in this connection. Certainly the definition must be very different from that which we have given; for the definition of *right* and *wrong* determines that of *desirable* and *undesirable* when those words are used without qualification. We may feel assured that should a definition of these words be formulated which would justify their use in violation of the condition noted, it would have no interest for us; it would be rather a useless definition, and refer to some inconspicuous distinction in experience. It is upon the presumable capacity of beings for pleasure and pain and upon nothing else that consideration for them should be based. If we had reason to believe that a pine plank was capable of pleasure, and if we had presented to us two alternatives and only two: (1) An act which produced in said plank one hedon-minute and (2) An act which produced in the most worthy being on earth $\frac{9}{10}$ hedon-minute, then the first alternative would be right, the second wrong; always provided that the effects specified were, in fact, the total effects.

By putting the case generally the matter will become clear. Assume a system, consisting of a series of sentient beings, A, B, C, D, E, F, &c., and suppose we have open to us two alternatives, the first involving a total surplus of happiness in the system of n hedon-hours, confined let us suppose to the beings A, B, and C, the others not being affected: the second involving a total surplus of happiness of m hedon-hours, equally distributed among all the beings. Suppose n greater than m: Which alternative is right? According to our definition there can be no doubt; the first alternative involving the greater surplus of happiness is right. By any definition including the criterion of number, which would be right? Would we insist that equality be obtained at any cost? That no matter how small m and how large n, that the alternative involving equality was right and that involving inequality was wrong? Should the totality of happiness always be sacrificed to its distribution? If not, what must the quantitative relation between n and m be which would justify us in selecting the one or the other? There is obviously no answer to this question. Hence a definition involving the criterion of number can afford no consistent guide to conduct. Indeed, even to an omniscient being it could afford no guide; because, though he might foresee perfectly the effect of all alternatives on total happiness and distribution, the definition would afford him no means of telling what relation between the two constituted the right relation. It is idle to maintain that if he were omniscient he would then, of necessity, know what the right relation was: that would be equivalent to saying that he would know what we, according to this view, do not know, viz., the meaning of the word *right,* and would be admitting, what must be admitted, that we use the word *right* and its correlative *wrong* without any meaning when we attempt to incorporate in their definition the factor of distribution.

But after all, when we examine our own minds critically, we see that the really conspicuous distinction is between quantity of pleasure and quantity of pain. To say that distribution is of importance, is merely to say that it is important what the co-ordinates of pleasurable and painful states of consciousness are; it is to say that a given pleasurable state B is desirable because it happens to be preceded by state A and succeeded by state C; while a state involving an exactly equivalent quantity of pleasure E is less desirable because preceded by state D and succeeded by state F. This is all that we assert when we assert one distribution to be more desirable than another, and, as we have seen, it would probably be impossible to give a consistent meaning to the word *desirable* when used in this connection. If the reader thinks otherwise, let him attempt to give a real, and useful, definition of the word which will include the criterion of distribution.

From what has been said it appears that examination of the mind fails to disclose any principle, independent of individual approval or disapproval, by which one distribution of pleasure and pain can be predicated as preferable to another. Even the patriot or humanitarian is not a wholly emancipated egotist. The principle thus disclosed I shall call the DILEMMA OF DIS-

TRIBUTION. Should the reader be disposed to reject the consequences of this dilemma on the ground that he is unable to approve them, I commend to him a consideration of the dilemma of intuitionism, discussed in Chapter 6.

Must we then conclude that our almost ineradicable conviction that happiness should be distributed equally among men, and that the righteous should be rewarded and the unrighteous punished, is all a delusion? Must we admit that there is no consistent meaning of the word *should* which can justify such an assertion? By no means. One of the strong claims to our confidence that the definitions we have given are those we are looking for is that, animal and human nature being constituted as they are, these practically universally admitted propositions are deducible from them. The first of these subjects is discussed in Chapter 7 and the second will be cleared up in the present chapter.

On page 127 we have implied that a day whose curve of happiness shows a surplus of pain might still be considered worth living, and that on egotistic grounds, provided it included acts or events presumed to affect the surplus of pleasure or pain of subsequent days. That is, the immediate object, purpose, or end of an act may not be its ultimate object, purpose, or end. When a farmer plants seed, he does not do it because the act is worth doing for itself. He foresees, or expects, that the effect of his act will be the growth of the wheat, its ripening in the autumn, the harvesting of the ripened grain, its threshing, grinding, etc., and finally its consumption by some being, through whose life, thus sustained, happiness may be increased, either that of him who consumes it, or that of some other being or beings influenced by him. We shall call an act thus selected because it is a presumable cause, immediate or remote, of some end desirable in itself — a *means;* that effect in the expectation of inducing which it is selected, we shall call an *ultimate end,* or simply an *end.* A *proximate end* is any effect produced by a means as one link in the chain of causation which connects said means with its end. In the above example, planting the seed is the means; the happiness to be produced is the end; the growth and ripening of the wheat are proximate ends. In the threshing, grinding, etc., other means are employed to produce other proximate ends, all with the ultimate object of producing happiness: in other words, the clean grain, the flour, the bread made from it, the life or possibility of sensation sustained by the bread, are all proximate and not ultimate ends.

These proximate ends are often themselves called means. Bread, for example, would be called a means whose proximate end is the sustaining of life, and as it will be convenient to do so, I shall extend the definition of the word *means* so as to include proximate ends, and by a *means* shall signify any cause of an ultimate end, producible or modifiable by voluntary acts. Hence, when I say that a right act is that one among two or more alternatives which is the presumable means of attaining the greatest total surplus of happiness, irrespective of other ends, I but recast the definition given on page 143 in terms of means and ends. In other words, by the very definition of the word *should*, and the only one which is at once useful, intelligible, and consistent with itself, total happiness *should* or *ought to* be the only ultimate end of voluntary acts. *No other end can justify any means, and this end justifies all means.* In truth, this statement again follows directly from definition. For by the phrase *to justify* in this connection, I mean to make consistent with justice; by *justice* I mean the quality common to just acts: and a *just* act is always a *right* act.

Means and ends then are connected with one another by the relation of cause and effect. In many cases of very general means, the means and ends are so closely related as to be mistaken for one another. Means, in fact, are continually mistaken for ends, as we shall have ample occasion to make evident. Thus many persons would claim that life was an end in itself, instead of one of the means — one of the essential conditions of happiness. Yet would a life containing no happiness in itself, or yielding none to other lives, directly or indirectly, be of any use? Would it be worth striving for as an end? If so, what meaning can be given the words *use* and *worth* when employed in such a connection?

Character is another proximate end frequently mistaken for an ultimate one. Those who fall into this error are denominated *perfectionists*. They say it is the ultimate aim of human effort to perfect human character — to develop the faculties and powers with which nature has endowed man to a point as near perfection as possible; but when they come to specific statement it is discovered that only certain parts of man's character should be developed and perfected. Generosity, honesty, benevolence, tolerance, and unselfishness in general, it appears are the characteristics to cultivate. Nature, however, has endowed us, in a greater or less degree, with certain other traits — envy, greed, dishonesty, vindictiveness, and similar varieties of selfishness. Why should we not cultivate these traits? Why not perfect ourselves in the faculty of hating or coveting or deceiving? No moralist will admit that such characteristics are worth cultivating; but why not? They are a part of our character — should they be left unperfected?

The utilitarian has no difficulty in explaining why unselfishness should be cultivated, and selfishness repressed and opposed. It is because unselfishness leads to the happiness of society and selfishness leads away from it. On this view the prevailing ideal of character is easily explainable, but on any other it is not explainable at all. The perfectionist cannot give any reason why honesty is better than dishonesty, or altruism better than egotism, except his personal preference. He has no better test of right and wrong than his private taste, backed, it may be, by the taste of the community in which he happens to live.

We might, if we pleased, enumerate every end other than happiness which mankind have proposed as ultimate, and should discover them all to be proximate, if indeed they were useful ends at all. It is a strange but only too apparent fact that moralists are dismally ignorant of what they are really seeking. Longfellow's attitude is typical:

> "Not enjoyment, and not sorrow,
> Is our destined end or way;
> But to act, that each to-morrow
> Finds us farther than to-day."

Each to-morrow should find us farther than to-day, should it? *Farther in what direction?* This is the important question, and intuitionism cannot answer it. The fact is, that enjoyment *is* our destined end or way, and moralists, poets, politicians, and platitudinarians may sound the immeasurable depths of vagueness through all eternity without discovering any other.

Before leaving the present subject there are two doctrines relating to human conduct, opposed to one another and to the utilitarian theory, which should be discussed as an incident of our exposition. These are the doctrines known as *free will* and *fatalism*. By contrasting them with the doctrine herein expounded their relation to, and violation of, common sense will become clear. Let us begin with free will.

Those who advocate the theory of free will claim that human

conduct is not subject to the law of causation — that voluntary acts are uncaused or free. Now they must mean either (1) That volition is not causally related to acts, or (2) That volition itself is uncaused. The first contention would mean that all acts are involuntary — that it is futile to tell men to act in this way or that, because even should they attempt to do so, the acts resulting would have no relation to those which they willed to do. If this theory indeed be true, our definition of right and wrong becomes meaningless, since alternatives are non-existent and hence do not admit of selection. Should we, for example, will to walk down the street some morning, we might find ourselves climbing a tree, and it would be futile to attempt voluntarily to prevent this act, however we desired to prevent it, since our volition would have no causal relation to our act or to its prohibition. On such an assumption men cannot do what they like. It is unnecessary to say that this contention not only violates the common sense theory of conduct as herein expounded, but contradicts the universal testimony of observation, that volition is causally related to action.

But perhaps those who contend that the will is free do not support the first possible interpretation of their assertion, but support the second one — that volition itself is uncaused. This contention would mean that the distinctions between voluntary and involuntary, and between right and wrong acts are real, but of no service as guides to conduct. In this case, as in the first, it would be futile to tell men to act in this way or in that, since such advice could only affect their conduct by affecting their volition; but as their volition is uncaused it cannot be affected by anything at all; hence it is quite useless for any one to advocate a guide to conduct, since no one could avail themselves of it, even if they wanted to. On this assumption men can, in general, do what they like, but they cannot, in any degree, determine that which they, or anyone else, *likes,* since this is indeterminable. Common sense, on the contrary, asserts that not only can men do what they like, (within the limits of the physically possible) but that that which they like is determinable, or subject to causation. Hence it is useful to tell men to act in this way or in that; since, if they will to guide their own conduct by the advice thus given, their volition will causally affect their motives, which, being the determinants of other volitions, will determine their acts. Under these conditions the distinction between right and wrong is capable of serving as a guide to conduct, but not otherwise.

To bring out yet more distinctly the opposition between common sense and the theory of free will let us examine the subject of punishment. The utilitarian is, in general, opposed to the infliction of pain; but punishment is painful. Does he therefore deem all punishment wrong? Certainly not. Any means which presumably results in the utilitarian end is right: hence when punishment so results it is right, but not otherwise. Therefore, pain, though never an ultimate end, may be a proximate one. It may be used as a means to the utilitarian end, and so may pleasure. In other words, the utilitarian regards punishment and reward precisely as he does any and all other means. If they tend to the end of utility they are useful; otherwise they are not. Punishment has no relation to vengeance, but is a means to the end of utility, and it seeks said end by two routes: (1) By causing pain to him who commits wrong acts it tends to prevent their repetition by the person punished, through fear of repetition of the pain. (2) By causing other persons to fear similar punishment it tends to prevent the commission of similar acts by them. The only useful purpose of punishment therefore is as a preventative. The manner in which punishment (and reward) affect conduct is explained in more detail in Chapter 9. It is perhaps unnecessary to say that the pain inflicted in punishment should be the least which will attain the end sought. From this brief explanation of the utility of punishment the utility of reward will be apparent.

Obviously the utilitarian theory of punishment presupposes that volition is subject to causation. In fact, common sense holds that character is a cause of conduct, and hence that we may infer character from conduct, just as we may infer any other familiar cause from its effect. The free will theorist claims that character is not a cause of conduct, because conduct has no cause; and hence that nothing can be inferred of a man's character from his conduct. The best acts might be those of the worst character, and the worst acts those of the best character. To punish a man for murder or any other crime, for example, would, on this assumption, accomplish no useful end, since as his conduct has no relation to his character, it would not permit us to infer that any presumption had, by his act been established that he would commit similar acts in the future; and the punishment could not be instrumental in affecting the acts of others, since such acts would be unaffectable by any cause. Under such conditions punishment might gratify vengeance, but vengeance is not a useful end.

The doctrine of free will is obviously utterly repugnant to common sense, and even those who claim that they support it, by their acts prove that they do not. Any man who attempts to affect the conduct of others through their volition by persuasion, advice, threats, or in any other manner, proves that he does not believe in the theory of free will, and as every sane man has done these things, and intends to do them again, more or less often, it follows that no sane man believes in that doctrine, though many think they do.

But, it may be objected, if the theory of free will be rejected, if all acts are determined by the law of causation, what is the use of trying to affect things — of trying to do anything? If everything is controlled by causation, human effort can better nothing, and hence all human effort is useless. This attitude of mind is what is known as *fatalism,* and there is a very general belief that between free will and fatalism there is no alternative. The generality of such a belief is one of the best evidences that the nature of common sense has never been really apprehended; for common sense not only supplies an alternative, but is itself the alternative.

The whole difficulty arises from misapprehension of the meaning of the word *useful,* just as the difficulty about the existence of the external world arises from misapprehension of the meaning of the word *existence.* Hence, the chief question of ethics, as of metaphysics, is a verbal question, and can be answered by sufficiently defining a word. The ordinarily understood meaning of the word *useful* is sufficient for some purposes, but not for this one. Let us see just how the fatalist deceives himself by not understanding his own meaning.

The utilitarian expresses by the word *usefulness* a definite quality of alternatives — a quality specified on page 145. He asserts that when men select alternatives having this quality they have performed a useful act. What then can the fatalist mean when he says the selection of such alternatives is useless? Employing the words *useful* and *useless* in the utilitarian sense, such an assertion would be a contradiction in terms. Evidently the fatalist is attempting to express something more than a contradiction. Therefore he must imply by the term *usefulness* a different quality from that implied by the utilitarian.

Now the fatalist in saying that there is no use in doing anything, in making any effort, in performing any act, must mean either (1) That all acts are equally useless, or (2) That to do nothing at all is the only useful thing to do. If it is the first meaning that the fatalist is trying to express, it is apparent that he elects to employ the word *uselessness* to express the common quality of voluntary acts, since no other meaning of the word would justify his assertion. This quality is volition, and so far as known no other, except consciousness, is universally conjoined with it. Hence involuntary acts would be the only useful ones. Of course with such a meaning of the word *useless,* the assertion of the fatalist that all voluntary acts are useless is true — but it is not interesting. It is merely saying that what is, is. On the other hand, if the fatalist means that to do nothing at all is the only useful thing to do, he must mean by a useful act the act involving minimum activity, or he must have discovered some class of experiences universally conjoined with the act of minimum activity, to the common quality of which he gives the name *usefulness*. On the first supposition, his assertion is again only a way of saying that what is, is; this would be uninteresting if true. On the second, his assertion would be interesting if true, but it would not be true. The fatalist has discovered no such class of experiences and would not pretend that he had. The fatalist, or indeed anyone who deems fatalism the only alternative of free will, is simply a confused person who thinks that by doing nothing he can escape performing a voluntary act. He forgets that the act of minimum activity, if voluntarily selected, is as much a voluntary act as any other, and if not voluntarily selected, it is not a part of conduct. In fact, so long as a being is capable of voluntary acts he must select some alternative. It is impossible for him to do otherwise. The utilitarian in classifying voluntary acts into *right, wrong, useful, useless,* etc., thereby calls attention to the fact that the selection of some will lead to greater happiness than the selection of others. If the fatalist, or anyone else, says that this distinction is a matter of indifference to him, very well — his remark calls for no response; for either he does not tell the truth, or he is incapable of pleasure and pain, and hence can no more comprehend the difference between right and wrong, than a man congenitally blind can comprehend the difference between red and green.

Fatalism indeed is not a belief; it is a mere form of words used to confound the unreflecting mind. Consistent fatalists, like consistent advocates of free will, do not exist. Indeed they could not exist long, since they would very soon die of starvation. Eating is not an act of minimum activity. To expose these sophistries which have plagued philosophers for ages, nothing is required but common sense, for common sense is as applicable to philosophy as it is to farming. It tests the meanings of the words *use, right, exist,* etc., by the same methods it would employ in the case of the words *hat,* or *house,* or *pea soup,* and however opposed to immemorial usage the requirement may be, it insists that the first class of words must have a definite meaning, just as the second class must have one, in order to be of service to mankind.

The analysis of common sense here brought to a close, I believe is sufficient for the purposes to which I design applying it. I do not pretend that it is complete. To make it so would require a work many times longer than this one. In its formulation I have followed the scientific — not the historic method. I have not endeavored to discover any universally applied criterion of meaning, of truth, or of right — indeed, I have shown that such criteria do not exist, although they ought to. Criteria common to all minds, however, *do* exist, though they are not consistently and universally applied by all minds. Such common criteria I believe I have in the foregoing examination disclosed, and upon the distinction between them and all others, have founded the distinction between *common* sense and all other varieties of sense. I do not claim that all men at all times test or have tested the intelligibility of terms by the criteria laid down in Chapter 1; that they test or have tested the truth of propositions by a belief-judgment; that they test or have tested the utility of acts by a use-judgment. I do claim that they *ought* to do so.

The main difficulty with theories of morals thus far has been that philosophers have sought a universal moral criterion when none existed. To overthrow the utilitarian doctrine it has been deemed sufficient to show that men sometimes do not act from considerations of pleasure and pain; but such a criticism no more invalidates the utilitarian criterion of morality than the demonstration that men sometimes do not reason according to the rules of the syllogism invalidates deductive logic. It is merely a reminder that there is a difference between correct and incorrect reasoning and conduct — between what ought to be, and what is. This has been long recognized in logic, but criticisms of the theory of utility like that cited, show that it has not been recognized in ethics. I make no claim that the production of happiness or the prevention of pain are the only ultimate ends which determine the acts, even of egotists. Acts may have many ultimate ends. The end may be determined solely by habit, and often is; more often it is individual happiness only which is sought, and this, as in the acts of revengeful or malicious characters, may be found in the unhappiness of others. What I do claim is that though many ends may be possible, only one may be *right*.

The criteria of intelligibility, of truth, and of utility are not *inventions;* they are *discoveries.* Philosophers can no more invent them than Newton could invent the law of gravitation. The uniformities of nature and of human nature are alike disclosed by an examination of the mind. They are uniformities of mind — indeed they could not be uniformities of anything else, since nothing else exists.

In this and the preceding chapters I have sought to establish, and elucidate by discussion, the fundamental definitions and postulates upon which the science of public and private morals must be founded, for like other sciences that of morals must rest on definitions and postulates (or axioms). It may be that with the meanings I have given the words *correct* and *incorrect, truth* and *untruth, certain* and *probable, right* and *wrong,* and the rest, the reader may take issue — it may be that he will challenge the meaning which I have given the word *meaning* itself. To this I take no exception; but I submit that if a communicable philosophy is possible at all, to these terms of fundamental import a meaning must be assignable, and, if assignable, one or more criteria must be recognized by which a meaning may be distinguished from that which is not a meaning. It is not sufficient to commence by defining our fundamental terms — we must first define *definition.* We must investigate the nature of a meaning in order that our symbols may not consist of mere sounds. Hence if the reader deems that the science of morals should rest on definitions different from those we have supplied, let him first satisfy himself what he means by a meaning. Having established his tests of a meaning, let him then define *truth* and *untruth, right* and *wrong,* &c., for himself, and submit them to the tests thus established. If by this means, definitions more suitable than those I have proposed are forthcoming, then those I have proposed should be displaced by them; but it is idle to attempt the establishment of a science or an art of morals, or even to discuss the subject, without assigning definite meanings to the fundamental terms involved. If an issue between the meanings herein set forth and others, testable and tested, may be raised, it would be time well spent to debate their respective claims to recognition; but such an issue to have any interest must be between one distinct meaning and another. It must not be between *a* meaning and *no* meaning. Such an issue may no doubt be raised, but so far as I can discover, it has not yet been raised. In the absence therefore of alternative meanings, I shall adhere to my own, trusting to future criticism to correct them if they tend to mislead.

Having now in our possession the criteria of common sense, we may proceed to examine some of the principal modes of deviation therefrom, without danger of making mere fortuitous differences of opinion the foundation of criticism. We shall not make received opinions the test of truth and right, but shall make truth and right the test of received opinions. Common sense shall be the criterion of custom, instead of custom the criterion of common sense. This procedure, though unusual, is wiser than generally believed.

CHAPTER IV.

ERROR

Judgments, whether of belief or of use, which derive their authority from any source other than common sense, are called *errors,* and *error* is their common quality. Error, or deviation from common sense, is of two classes: (1) Abnormal. (2) Normal. To varieties of the first class the names *insanity* or *eccentricity* are attached, according to their degree of deviation, and to varieties of the second class are attached various names such as *orthodoxy, piety, conservatism,* etc.

In the study of mental pathology alienists have been able to recognize insanity, or abnormal deviation from common sense, as of several distinct kinds or classes. Our analysis of common sense will enable us to classify normal deviations in a similar manner. Not that the varieties to be discussed are confined to normal error — they are common to abnormal error as well — and may all be regarded as kinds or classes of mania, of such universal extension that we may say no one in the world is entirely free from them. They are of three classes: *logomania, proteromania,* and *pathomania.* Let us discuss them briefly in order.

Logomania (Gr. λόγος = word : μανία = madness) is a consequence of the necessity which men are under of thinking in symbols, and arises from confusion in the use of those symbols. Because reasoning requires the mental manipulation of symbols, men fall into the error of supposing that the mental manipulation of symbols is reasoning. Thus they substitute the empty forms of thought for thought itself, deeming that a sound has meaning because it is articulate — they think *of,* instead of *with,* symbols. Logomania is the most universal of all forms of mania, arising as it does from a universal necessity of thought. As already shown, the questions of the existence of the external world and of free will and fatalism — the two most perplexing questions in philosophy — are purely verbal, and would never have arisen except for logomania. A few of the strongest intellects have succeeded in freeing themselves from proteromania, but none from logomania, and I may predict with confidence that whatever errors may be discovered in the present work will be due to this pervasive weakness of the human intellect, for I cannot hope to escape the infirmities which have so universally beset acuter minds.

Every variety of sophistry is fostered by logomania, and it is doubtful if other forms of mania could maintain their dominion in the normal mind were logomania dislodged, for words are as well adapted to the concealment as to the expression of truth. In all departments of human thought delusions are concealed by phrases, such as "the point of view," "the discrepancy between theory and practice," and others, by which evidence is nullified and inconsistencies reconciled. So inseparable are expressions of this character from sophistry that they may well be called *sophist's companions*.

From logomania spring the various forms of mysticism, metaphysical, theological, and political, and the low standard of comprehension pertaining thereto. A mystic deems that he understands a proposition if he is familiar with the sound of its terms. This substitution of sound for sense results in paralysis of the understanding and a love of vagueness for its own sake which may develop into a kind of pathomania. So influenced are some persons by the poetical or rhetorical dressing to their truth, that were we to express the proposition that two and two are four in sufficiently obscure and rhythmical language they would hail the effort as the inspiration of a seer. Indeed I confidently expect that a common criticism of the utilitarian ideal as herein set forth will be that it is too distinct — too definite — that quantity of happiness, considered as a magnitude — as something capable of definition and measurement, like pig iron or coal, is altogether too unworthy and vulgar an object for high-minded human beings to seek. It is the custom of the time to refer to ideals in obscure and figurative language, and if the sound value of their expression can be enhanced by giving it poetical form, they are deemed particularly worthy of respect. Should I proclaim the elevation of humanity, the regeneration of mankind, or the ennobling of the race, as the object of human endeavor, I should doubtless have no difficulty in getting people to agree with me, and general agreement would be easier to secure from the fact that no one would have any clear idea of just what it was to which he was agreeing. No doubt this system has its advantages, but if we are content with the vague lucubration thus substituted for the discussion of a common sense ideal, we must be content to leave the question of right and wrong in the chaos in which we find it, and we shall have need of all the question-begging epithets which the language can afford in order to "reconcile" contradictions and "interpret" absurdities. He who deems the value of an ideal is to be measured by its indistinctness will certainly have no sympathy for that of utilitarianism.

Logomania leads to at least one other important class of errors besides those which arise from the equivocality and avocality of terms. This class originates from a process which may be termed *verbal emasculation*. Terms which from custom or other habitual association have, in the popular mind, come to be regarded as important — as expressing some vital object of, or distinction in, experience — are used to express something of little or no importance. Thus the mind is misled by its symbols, and distinctions of no real consequence to sentient beings come to serve as guides to conduct. Sometimes terms are purposely emasculated by dishonest persons with intent to deceive, but more frequently the process is spontaneous, resulting as often as not in self-deception. Inferences in which emasculated terms are employed lead to propositions which, though true, are of no interest. Examples of emasculation will be pointed out in the next book. Hence we need not stop to illustrate the process here.

Proteromania (Gr. $\pi\rho\acute{o}\tau\epsilon\rho o\nu$ = prior: $\mu\alpha\nu\acute{\iota}\alpha$ = madness) is the name of that form of deviation from common sense which substitutes priority for reasonableness as the test of truth and right. Next to logomania it is the most universal of all forms of mania. The victim of proteromania believes that doctrine, or approves that precept which first finds lodgment in his mind. Thenceforth, it holds its place through priority of possession and reason cannot dislodge it. Thus arise both logical and ethical dogmas corresponding to deviations from a belief- and a use-judgment respectively.

So universal is this tendency that when, through the accidents of history or the conflict of opposing views, the logical or moral codes of a people are altered, it merely results in displacing one dogma by another, and this process has operated in all departments of thought, no real progress resulting, until the inductive method, by degrees gaining a foothold, has displaced dogma and substituted knowledge for ignorance. It was by such displacements of dogma that modern civilization arose.

Intuitionists, or those who distinguish the correct from the incorrect by discovering what convictions are, and what are not, in their minds are usually victims of proteromania. What they believe they call *true* — what they disbelieve they call *untrue* — what they approve they call *right* — what they disapprove they call *wrong* — and they measure probability by the *strength,* instead of by the *origin,* of their convictions. A *dogmatist* is an intuitionist whose convictions are those of his own community or some particular class thereof. Dogmatism is merely the commonest form of intuitionism. So frequently shall we have occasion to refer to this ubiquitous opponent of common sense in the following pages that further discussion of its nature at this point is superfluous.

Scarcely less general than, and closely allied to, proteromania is pathomania (Gr. πάθος = sensibility: μανία = madness), which results from the employment of emotion or sentiment as a substitute for judgment in distinguishing truth from untruth, and right from wrong. The pathomaniac will reject any principle or precept which he dislikes to believe or approve, and recognizes truth and rightness by a kind of feeling, which is only to be distinguished from the *intuition* of the proteromaniac by its emotional nature. The violation of this feeling he looks upon with horror, thus regarding morality as a kind of hysteria, instead of a branch — and the main branch — of common sense. The sophist's companions most in use by pathomaniacs usually include the words *holy, sacred, divine,* and they are fond of referring to the *higher thought* or the *spiritual life.* They are generally persons of excellent character, but their conduct fails to get the benefit thereof because they make emotion a guide, as well as a motive, to conduct. Gunpowder is an excellent means of impelling a projectile, but a poor means of guiding it. In conduct, as in shooting, the means of direction and the means of impulsion should be distinct. Emotion is not a useful guide, though it may be a useful motive, to action. Common sense is the only useful guide and to substitute for it any emotional impulse is to imitate the conduct of animals. Emotions can no more aid in distinguishing right from wrong than in distinguishing truth from untruth.

The three forms of mania discussed, combined or uncombined, are responsible for practically all, if not all, of the normal deviations from sense to which mankind are subject. Although conspicuous in every phase of human activity, the most baneful influence of these errors is that involved in the corruption which they introduce into the various codes of morals, and of public morals in particular.

It needs but the most superficial observation of the usages of society to discover that standards of public conduct are variable in a high degree. Public acts are accepted or rejected, approved or disapproved, on many distinct grounds. The determining distinction may be that between right and wrong, expedient and inexpedient, economic and uneconomic, just and unjust, Christian and unchristian, conservative and radical, or any other which circumstances may suggest. I deem it unnecessary to cite examples of the application of such standards. The editorial page of the first newspaper which the reader may take up will probably afford several. This being the case, it becomes pertinent to inquire what relation these standards bear to one another. Are the various antithetical terms we have cited merely a series of synonyms? Are the distinctions expressed by them in reality the same distinction, which, by the decree of custom has come to be expressed by terms different in sound, and with every outward and visible sign of being different in sense? If not, how is it that we may employ any one of them we please as a standard of public conduct. Suppose, for example, that a given act is admitted to be economic. Is it therefore right, expedient, just, Christian, and conservative? Or may an economic act be wrong, or unjust, or radical? Similarly, may a just act or a right one be sometimes uneconomic, unchristian, and inexpedient? If not, then it would seem that these various standards are in reality but one standard. If so, by what means shall we judge of an act or policy which is acceptable to one standard and unacceptable to others. Of course if we accept the first hypothesis, and agree that all these and other standards are in reality the same, the modes of expression alone being different, then we may dispense with all distinctions other than that between right and wrong, since the other antithetical terms which appear to imply that other standards are permissible, are but synonyms for right and wrong. If, on the other hand, we accept the second hypothesis, and admit that there are several distinct standards by which policies may be judged, by what means shall we decide between these varying standards when we find that they disagree? For example, suppose an act were economic, just, and conservative, and at the same time wrong, inexpedient, and unchristian. By what criterion could we be guided in such a dilemma? Obviously we should require a standard by which to judge of standards. Without it we should be without any guide whatever; but with it we should possess a guide which would render all other guides subordinate, since a criterion which is a standard of standards, i. e., an ultimate standard, must be one to whose decree the decree of all proximate standards must be subordinated. Hence if it be once admitted that right and wrong furnish a standard by which to judge the policies of nations or of society, it is at the same time admitted that there is no other. If it be denied, then right and wrong are completely valueless as standards, and until some other is proposed, all suggestible public acts are equally worthy of approval, any one being as good or as bad as any other. *Whatever standard men may prevail upon themselves to accept, this much is certain: it must be either one or none, for there is no middle ground.*

It would seem as if this matter ought to be plain to anyone capable of thinking clearly, but unfortunately clear thinking since the time of Bentham has been banished from ethics. Thus Professor Hyslop after discussing the several theories of conduct with characteristic confusion concludes thus:

"No one theory therefore is complete, but taken alone is one-sided, and requires the others to supply its deficiencies. This is in accord with common sense, which judges of particular cases about as described and only gets into difficulty when some theorist unjustly asks it to explain its consistency, presuming that there should be but a single simple criterion of morality, when in fact it is synthetic or complex." [1]

It may be remarked that it is a curious variety of common sense which "gets into difficulty when some theorist unjustly (?) asks it to explain its consistency." Seldom have we seen such an explicit attempt to establish, once for all, the proposition so dear to the affections of every sophist — that what is, is not. He who maintains a compound (or synthetic) standard of morality necessarily asserts that proposition. To claim that the moral value of conduct can be measured by several ultimate standards not mutually convertible is as absurd as to claim that distance can be measured not only in such mutually convertible units as feet, meters, rods or miles, but equally well in bushels, acres, tons or amperes. A properly qualified logomaniac would probably tell us that the applicability of one or

[1] Elements of Ethics, p. 395.

the other of these standards to the measurement of distance would depend upon "the point of view," since distance being something "synthetic" is to be measured by several standards, and common sense should not "unjustly" require consistency among them.

In the endeavor to reconcile the conflicting standards of public conduct a good many sophist's companions are in common use, such as *ethically considered, morally considered, economically considered*. We are told that a standard must not be carried "too far," that theories "have their limitations," and that much depends upon the "standpoint." Such phrases are futile as a means of reconciling the irreconcilable. They are but verbal disguises for a real standard of public conduct, which under varying circumstances assumes various names, and that standard is *custom*.

The examination of the human mind undertaken in Chapters 1, 2, and 3 has supplied us with a standard — the simple standard of right and wrong — and in the light of common sense so supplied, we shall examine the prevailing political dogmas which at the present time supply such standards of public conduct as are available. I shall not attempt a complete discussion of this subject, but shall confine attention to four of the main political delusions of the day. These are: First, that individuals have inalienable rights: Second, that natural laws are, or tend to be, beneficent: Third, that political economy is the science of wealth and supplies a useful guide to public conduct: Fourth, that conservatism is caution.

(1) The Declaration of Independence asserts that "all men are endowed by their Creator with certain unalienable Rights, that among these are Life, Liberty, and the pursuit of Happiness;" and the doctrine of inalienable rights, sometimes called natural rights, as laid down in the Declaration is accepted, in theory, with practical unanimity by the people of this country, and indeed the same principle is, and has been, accepted by other enlightened nations. It is commonly supposed to embody a guide to those who exercise the legislative function of government, affording them one means of distinguishing measures worthy of adoption from those unworthy. If a proposed measure alienates an inalienable right, it is, according to this doctrine, unworthy of incorporation into law. Let us see precisely what this alleged guide to national conduct is and what relation, if any, it bears to the guide afforded by the doctrine of utility.

Bentham tells us that a law is either a command or the revocation of a command. The command or revocation can be addressed only to intelligent beings, and it must either prescribe or proscribe some specific act or class of acts. If the doctrine of inalienable rights affords a guide to those charged with making the law, it must indicate some human act, or class of acts, to the prescription or proscription of which their authority does not extend. Now it is obvious that there is a class of acts which it would be entirely useless to prescribe or proscribe; those namely which are physically impossible. Can it be these to which the doctrine refers? If so, death would be a typical inalienable right of men; that is, a law forbidding it should not be passed, since it would be a physical impossibility for men to conform to such a law. It is physically impossible to prevent men from dying by law: similarly, it would be impossible to make them subsist upon a diet of sand, or sleep while supporting themselves in an upright position. There are many such inalienable rights, if by that term is meant acts which it is physically impossible to prevent or bring to pass by law. That this is not what is meant, it requires no discussion to show. What then is an inalienable right? Are the words of the Declaration inserted therein simply for the purpose of pointing out that there are certain classes of acts which are prescribed or proscribed by law, and certain others which are not; that the law, as a matter of fact, does forbid some acts and does not forbid others, and that the inalienable rights with which all men are endowed are simply those which the law in the place and at the time of the Declaration did not prohibit? If so, inalienable rights are merely legal rights; the right to commit acts not already proscribed by law. If this is all that is meant, it certainly was a waste of words to insert so palpable a proposition in the Declaration. No, this is clearly not what is referred to. An inalienable right is not a legal, but a moral right. It does not refer to what the law is, but what it ought to be. It means that there are certain acts, physically possible to human beings, which it is wrong to proscribe by law, and hence that any measure which proposes to alienate such inalienable rights is wrong. All rights not inalienable are, of course, alienable — their legal alienation would not necessarily be wrong. To determine then what rights are inalienable and what are not, we must know what we mean by *wrong*. It is this fundamental question which men have failed to sufficiently examine. The consequence of their logomania is that they have fallen into the error of inferring that individuals have inalienable rights. Let us assume for a moment that this doctrine is sound — let us trace it to its legitimate conclusion, and observe its astonishing consequences.

If inalienable rights exist they must be some particular rights. Let us assume an individual X, who possesses a legal right to commit a given act — call it A. If A is an *alienable* right it means that if in the public interest a good reason can be given for alienating such right — forbidding X by law to commit it — that it may rightfully be so alienated. If A is an *in*alienable right it means that whether in the public interest or not, whether a good reason can be given for alienating it or not, that it should not be alienated — that to alienate it by law would be wrong. That is, X has a right to commit the act A, irrespective of the consequences to the rest of the world, even if among those consequences is involved the destruction, or the permanent misery, of society. Now it may be wrong to alienate such an inalienable right, but if so, what can possibly be meant by *wrong*? Certainly the meaning cannot be that of the utilitarian.

I apprehend that to this it will be objected that inalienable rights are all of them of such a character that by no possible contingency could their preservation be antagonistic to the public interest; that it would be physically impossible for society to suffer by the failure of the law to infringe them; that, in fact, it must always be to the interest of society that they be preserved. To this objection we may reply: How do you know that by no possible contingency the securing to an individual of an inalienable right will not work harm to the community? Are you omniscient? If not, by what authority do you prejudge the matter? To admit once for all that an individual has a given inalienable right is to waive the privilege of examining each case of the exercise of that right on its own merits.

According to the utilitarian definition of right, no one can determine whether an act is right or not without considering its presumable effect upon all sentient beings to whom its effects are known to extend. Hence any doctrine which asserts, once for all, that an individual, or any aggregate of individuals not including the whole of sentient society, has "certain inalienable rights" and has them irrespective of what effect their exercise may have on the rest of society, must be irrevocably opposed to the principles of common sense as we have expounded them. But to show the complete untenability of the doctrine, let any one select a right of an individual and attempt to consistently maintain its inalienability. Take, for example, the rights mentioned in the Declaration of Independence — life, liberty, and the pursuit of happiness. Is life the inalienable right of men? Is it wrong by law to command that under given conditions men shall forfeit their lives, and to enforce that command? If so, from what definition of *wrong* is such a doctrine deducible? Wherever capital punishment is customary this inalienable right is alienated, showing that in practice the doctrine of inalienable rights is, sometimes at least, ignored. Is liberty an inalienable right? It is alienated every time a criminal or a witness is detained in jail. Is the pursuit of happiness an inalienable right? Every act prohibited by law, in the commission of which any individual might obtain happiness, alienates it. No nation could exist as a nation without alienating such rights. If the reader is inclined to object that such rights are limited by law only under certain conditions, and in the public interest, but that otherwise they remain inalienable, my reply is that this is a surrender of the whole question at issue — it is an admission that alienable and inalienable rights are precisely the same thing; for, as we have already noticed, an alienable right is one which may be alienated under certain conditions, i. e., in the public interest. If a right is inalienable, it means, if it means anything, that there are no conditions under which it may be alienated. Otherwise it is merely an alienable right and the whole doctrine obviously becomes completely valueless as a guide to law-makers. The fact is that no single specific inalienable right can be mentioned which any nation has agreed, or would agree, to consistently recognize, and if there are no specific inalienable rights, then there are none at all.

But, it may be asked, if the law-making bodies so persistently ignore the alleged inalienable rights of individuals, if it is a standard of legislative action only in name, how can it be harmful to a state which thus makes but an empty profession of abiding by it? Why should we find fault with a shadow? The difficulty is that the doctrine does supply a guide to national conduct, but it is not the guide it pretends to be. It is neither more nor less than a cloak, one of several to be discussed, beneath which lies concealed the real guide, viz., custom, to the decrees of which the theory of inalienable rights supplies the semblance of authority. To illustrate: Suppose some enterprising individual should secure title to a pass in the Rocky Mountains through which a great railroad company desired to construct a railway. Suppose he should attempt to block the railway by refusing to sell a right of way through the pass, and should claim that, as he had an inalienable right to do what he pleased with his own private property, any attempt to take it from him by right of eminent domain would be in violation of the fundamental law and the Declaration of Independence. Every one knows that no attention would be paid to his claim and that he would be forced to part with his property in the public interest. Suppose that on the same ground, viz., that of the public interest, it should be proposed to take by purchase from the railroad company or from some other company, such as a steel works or coal mining company, a title to their property and vest it in the government. How would such a proposition be received? Some men indeed would justify the act, for there is much disagreement as to the limitations of the right of property — inalienable rights are shadowy things and few there are who have the temerity to specify them; but many, and perhaps most, persons would contend that the proposal contemplated the infringement of the inalienable right of property, and that no legislature could pass a measure authorizing such an act without doing wrong. The same men who would justify taking private property in the mountain pass, deeming it but the exercise of a well recognized right of the community, would condemn taking the property of the railroad itself as an act of unjustifiable confiscation. Now why is the inalienable right of property ignored in the first instance and appealed to in the second? Merely because it is customary to alienate the property of individuals to permit the building of a railroad, but it is not customary to alienate property in railroads, mines or factories in the interest of the people. Custom is the real guide, the doctrine of inalienable rights being but a means of concealing it. Had the custom been exactly the reverse, the theory of inalienable rights would have applied equally well.

Let us put the question generally. Assume that some individual, or set of individuals, has, by some means or other, acquired the power to plunge mankind into permanent misery. Have they the right to do so? An advocate of the doctrine of inalienable rights would be compelled to answer this question in the affirmative, asserting that they had such a right, provided the means by which they acquired the power to exercise it were of a specific kind; of some kind, namely, which individuals have an inalienable right to adopt. The utilitarian would answer the question in the negative, denying that they had any such right, whatever means they might have adopted to secure their power.

It is clear that common sense as embodied in a use-judgment lends no authority to the doctrine of inalienable rights. This doctrine has, in fact, arisen from the process of the substitution of dogma. The dogma for which it is a substitute is that of the divine right of kings. The political philosophers of the eighteenth century rejected this dogma, and being unable because of their sympathies and antipathies to frame a definition of right and wrong upon which to found the science and art of government, pursued the normal course of substituting one dogma for another, in so doing taking a step in the direction of common sense; for defective as is the doctrine of inalienable rights, it is better than the dogma which preceded it. Not apprehending that rights draw their authority from the structure of the mind, they sought some other authority and while denying that the Creator had endowed kings with the divine right to rule, they made the mistake of asserting that He had "endowed men with certain inalienable rights," failing to perceive that, under favorable conditions, individuals could avail themselves of these rights to reacquire the despotic power of kings over the welfare and destiny of the people — a condition of things which is at present to be observed in process of realization. Bentham more than a century ago perceived and exposed the untenability of the doctrine we are considering, and commenting on the assertion of that doctrine in the Declaration of Independence exclaimed " Who can help lamenting that so rational a cause should be rested upon reasons so much fitter to beget objections than to remove them?"

But although the doctrine of inalienable rights is untenable, the Declaration of Independence, which asserts that doctrine, contains by implication the refutation of it; for, after proclaiming the rights of "life, liberty and the pursuit of happiness," it proceeds to affirm: "That to secure these rights, Governments are instituted among Men." That is, government is a proximate end — a means. Following this it affirms: "That, whenever any Form of Government becomes destructive of these ends, it is the Right of the People to alter or to abolish it, and to institute new Government, laying its foundation on such principles and organizing its powers in such form, as to them shall seem most likely to effect their Safety and Happiness." Here we have an expression of the theory of utility or common sense, and by means of the principle implied in it, we may rectify the error which preceded. It will be noticed that life, liberty, and the pursuit of happiness, are referred to as *ends*. It is here that the difficulty enters. They, like government, are proximate, and not ultimate, ends, and the error arises from confounding the two. Life which contains no happiness and leads to none is not an end useful or desirable, or one which it is worth while instituting any means to attain. Similarly, liberty unless it leads to happiness is useless, and equally useless is it to pursue happiness without securing it. Hence that which the Declaration affirms of the proximate end *government* may with equal propriety be affirmed of *all* proximate ends, that whenever they become destructive of the ultimate end — happiness —" it is the Right of the People to alter or to abolish" them; and to institute new means, laying their foundations on such principles as to them shall seem most likely to effect or achieve their happiness. The Declaration indeed contains by implication a refutation of the very doctrine it asserts. By the interpretation of its own words the correct doctrine is revealed, and it turns out to be the doctrine of utility. Thus in the assertion that " all men . . . are endowed . . . with certain inalienable Rights," are we to understand the expression " all men" distributively or collectively? Does it mean *any man?* or *the totality of men?* It is customary to interpret it in the first sense, and the Declaration itself, it must be admitted, lends plausibility to the view. This interpretation leads to the doctrine of individual inalienable rights which we have shown cannot be reconciled with common sense. The other interpretation, however, inevitably suggests, if it does not actually express, the doctrine of utility, for that doctrine asserts that the totality of men — i. e., society — is endowed with a right which, by definition, it is wrong to alienate — the right namely to have any and all means adopted which shall lead to the maximum output of happiness, and such means involve rights which are truly inalienable. Thus inalienable rights are not rights of *individuals,* but of *society;* not rights of *men,* but of *mankind.*

(2) Another distinction by means of which the conduct of nations — and even of individuals — is judged is that between the natural and the unnatural, and particularly between that which conforms to natural law and that which does not. We hear much said by public men and read much in newspapers about the *natural* laws of exchange, of supply and demand, &c. Platitudinarians discourse at length upon the *natural* sphere of **woman,** and physicians sagely tell us that **our** bodily ills are

due to violation of nature's laws. The implication seems to be that there is something intrinsically beneficent in nature's methods, and we are frequently told that free trade, for example, is a beneficent policy because it is the natural law of trade, while artificial restrictions on trade are baneful because they violate said natural law. Indeed, natural laws are appealed to almost as much as natural rights as guides to conduct. Before we can pronounce on the value of this standard of action we must, as in the case of inalienable rights, discover just what it refers to. According to one meaning of the word, *nature* is simply that which is, and hence all acts are natural because they are part of what is. This is clearly not the meaning implied. Again the term *natural law,* or *law of nature,* is applied by men of science to certain unvarying uniformities to be observed in the universe about us, such as the laws of gravitation, of the reflection of light, the conduction of heat, &c. It cannot be these laws which are referred to, since men have never discovered a method of violating them, and hence would require no warning not to do so. There is, I believe, but one other distinction to which the standard can refer. It is to that between the acts of nature alone, the effects which occur or would occur if man were without volition altogether, and those which are affected by the volition of man. This is certainly the distinction between the natural and the artificial; but if this is the distinction referred to, then any and every voluntary act is a violation of natural law. Those who hold to the value of the standard would probably be loth to admit that it involved any such corollary, and yet reduced to its legitimate conclusion, this is just what it involves. By an inspection of the mode in which the attempt is made to apply it, its absurdity becomes apparent.

We have only to look about us to see that it would be very poor policy to interfere with many of the practices of nature. Trees naturally grow with their roots downward and their branches upward and we should get unsatisfactory results should we attempt to make them reverse their position. Nature has decreed that men and animals shall breathe air, shall eat albuminoids, fats and carbohydrates, and shall drink water, and we should certainly come to grief should we attempt to violate her decree in these regards. It is natural for husband and wife, parent and offspring, to feel affection for one another, and very poor results would be obtained were nations to discourage this feeling or any other altruistic impulse. But there is a great difference between admitting that some of nature's practices are beneficent, and admitting that all are. Nature never kindles fires for the purpose of giving warmth to sentient beings. Should we therefore fail to heat our houses in winter? Men in a state of nature do not live in houses, and wear no clothes. Should civilized men, discarding artificiality, go and do likewise? In their wild natural state, men have no government, for government is a result of some artificial agreement and concession between men. Should government therefore be abolished? It may be called to our attention that a man who has wrecked his body and mind by the use of liquor owes his unhappiness to the violation of nature's laws, for certainly man in his natural state drinks no liquor. Yet curiously enough when an attempt is made to cure him the very physician who has been prating about "nature's laws" subjects him to artificial medicinal diet or restraint. He would not think of acting upon his precepts, and attempting to make his patient return to a true state of nature. We may see in the newspapers an account of some depraved fellow who has been caught beating his mother. It is probable that the act will be branded as unnatural, inviting us to infer that it is therefore abominably wrong. But it is not its unnaturalness which makes it wrong. Would the act be any better if it were natural? Or suppose the act remaining unnatural, the woman were so constituted that a beating was to her a source of joy — caused her pleasure instead of pain — would it still be a wrong act to beat her? Obviously not. In fact, it is clear that the distinction between natural and unnatural is of no value as a guide to conduct, and no one is, or can be, consistent in advocating it. As examination shows, it is merely another disguise for custom. In cases in which it is customary and usual to substitute the artificial for the natural, no one ever thinks of appealing to such a standard as natural law; but in cases where the custom is not sufficiently settled, those who disapprove, casting about for some grounds for disapproval, will take up with this one if none better is at hand, and proceed to prose about the violation of nature's laws. So far as this standard has anything to do with reason at all, it is the result of a "doctored" induction. It has been observed that some of nature's practices are beneficent, and by carefully disregarding those which are not, the conclusion has been reached that to conform to natural laws is better for men and nations than not to conform to them. It is the old story. The hits are counted and the misses are ignored.

(3) Closely connected by bonds of the dogmatic sanction with the error of natural beneficence are the doctrines of the prevailing or dogmatic school of political economy. Political economy is, by definition, the science of wealth, and a definition may not be disputed; hence when I affirm that political economy is not the science of wealth as it pretends to be, I have no intention of affirming that the term is not defined in the manner specified. What I do intend to affirm is that the science of which that term is the name cannot properly be termed the science of wealth — that to so term it is misleading. It might with more propriety be called the science of the production and exchange of wealth, and the prevailing school of economy has an even more restricted scope. It deals only with the subject of the production and exchange of wealth under the capitalistic system. A useful system of political economy should treat of the production and exchange of wealth as they affect human happiness. Hence it should include the science of the consumption of wealth.

From its connotation and from the claims of those who expound the science, we should be led to the belief that the term *political economy* refers to an assemblage of precepts adapted to guide the polity of nations or of society — to the economy of that which it should be the object of society to attain. Now by the accepted definition, political economy means the economy of wealth. Hence, unless the term be entirely misleading and inappropriate, wealth is that which it should be the object of society to attain, and the assemblage of precepts adapted to the economical attainment of wealth are those which should guide the polity of nations. But is wealth a primary or a secondary object of endeavor? Is it an ultimate or only a proximate end? Clearly it is but a proximate end. It has been the object of a previous chapter to show that happiness, or the total surplus of happiness, should be the only end — the only object of any voluntary act — hence in saying it is the object which society should seek to attain, we but make an immediate inference from the definition of right. *The term political economy then, as defined, is a misleading one. It should refer, not to the economy of wealth, but to the economy of happiness; and the assemblage of precepts employed to guide the polity of nations or of society should not be those adapted to the economical production of wealth, but those adapted to the economical production of happiness.* In this confusion of wealth with happiness we have another example of confounding a means with an end, and one which has led, and is leading, to dire results for mankind.

To the particular deviation from common sense involved in the employment of the economic standard we may give the name *production-madness* or *practomania* (Gr. πρακτόν = product: μανία = madness) since it regards production as an ultimate, instead of a proximate, end. It is a form of mania particularly prevalent at the present time and the prevailing commercialism is its natural consequence. Practically all the leaders of political thought in our day are more or less affected by it, and hence arises their prattle about *trade, exports, imports, commodity output,* etc.

But again we may expect some critic to object that after all the distinction between wealth and happiness is of little practical consequence, when the means and end are so closely related; for is not the richest nation the happiest nation? Our reply is that it is not necessarily the happiest — that it is not even probably the happiest. Other things being equal, that nation will be the richest — will accumulate wealth most rapidly — whose production is a maximum and whose consumption is a minimum — but will it be the happiest? Obviously not. We must first formulate the laws which reveal the general quantitative relation between happiness and wealth before we can appreciate the relation of the economy of wealth to a true political economy.

Political economy is as incapable as archæology of being usefully applied. As at present taught, it is a purely descriptive science. It may inform us what society has done, is doing, or is likely to do — but it cannot tell us what it *ought* to do — it cannot be applied — and this for a very obvious reason. An applied science is one that supplies a guide to the acts of men, and such a guide cannot be supplied unless the object of the acts is known. Before any science can be applied as a guide to the polity of nations, it must recognize and specify what it is that nations are, or should be, trying to do. This first requirement of an applied science political economy fails to meet. Hence it is incapable of being usefully applied, though it may be, and is, misapplied.

Upon the science of political economy the economic standard of public conduct is founded, and as political economy is a true science, being founded on definitions and using the inductive method, economic reasons for acts or policies have more plausibility than those derived from the standards previously discussed. Yet the economic standard becomes in practice little more than another pretext for the dominion of dogma. It adds one more apparent sanction to the control of custom. Its application is as inconsistent as that of the standards afforded by the doctrines of inalienable rights and natural beneficence. Is it right in the management of industry to throw a great number of men out of employment by the use of machinery, thus reducing the production per capita of some of the laborers to a minimum in order to make the production per capita of the remainder a maximum? Is it right to make men, women and children engage in as much productive labor per day as is consistent with preserving their power of future production? Yes, we are told these things are right because they are economic. Would it be right to put to death all old and otherwise incompetent persons incapable of producing as much wealth as they consume? No, it would be acknowledged that this would not be right. But why not? It would certainly be economic, and according to the dictum in the first case, what is economic is right. Now why is the economic standard deemed applicable in the first case and inapplicable in the second? Because it is customary to apply it to cases of the first class and not customary to apply it to cases of the second class, and that is all we can say. Hence the real standard is custom again, and the distinction between economic and uneconomic is merely a means of concealing the fact.

(4) The three standards we have examined have arisen from the confusion of means with ends. Like all standards which meet with any favor at all, they are blundering attempts to attain the utilitarian standard. It is doubtful if custom would long sanction a standard completely subversive of utility. The sanction it has accorded, and still accords, to asceticism would seem to imply that no doctrine can be too absurd for custom to endorse, but even asceticism is practised with a view to future happiness, the expectation of bliss after death being the real motive to action. The confusion of means with ends is not the only result of ignorance of the nature of common sense. One of the standards much in favor at the present time is founded on an interesting but clumsy attempt to apply a use-judgment to the affairs of nations. I refer to that standard which attempts to determine whether an act is right or wrong by discovering whether it is *conservative* or *radical*. It may distinguish the means from the end, but does not recognize the correct relation between the two.

12

Let us first consider conservatism; and contrary to the usual practice, let us first try to discover its meaning. When we are told that a given policy is conservative, what useful information is conveyed to us? What characteristics are implied by the term *conservative,* a knowledge of which can aid us in an estimate of the value of a course of conduct which possesses them? Two distinct meanings in which this term is used are detectable. According to the first, a conservative policy is one which will not materially deviate from that at the place and period pursued. According to the second, a conservative policy is a safe or cautious one. In its first meaning, therefore, conservative simply means customary, and no discussion of this meaning is required, since custom as a standard is a too familiar friend. An examination of the second meaning will reveal an interesting point in the natural history of error, for the misjudgment to be noticed is not a rare or occasional one, but is almost as common as that of mistaking a means for an end.

Now what is *caution?* It is evidently a quality of a use-judgment. Moreover it is a varying quality. There are various degrees of caution, and it will be generally conceded that there is such a thing as too much, as well as too little, caution. Just the proper amount will lie between these two. This matter is rather indefinite in most minds, but a simple illustration, showing to just what quality of a use-judgment it is convenient to refer by the term *caution,* will make it clear.

Let us suppose three alternatives of two contingencies of equal probability each, presented to a reasoning being. In alternative A, assume the probable surplus of success to be 100 pathedon-minutes, the probable surplus of failure 0, and hence the presumption of happiness 50. In alternative B, assume the surplus of success to be 1000, the surplus of failure − 500 and the presumption of happiness therefore 250. In alternative C, assume the surplus of success to be 5000, the surplus of failure − 5100, the presumption of happiness being − 50. Now according to our definition, of these alternatives B is the correct one to select; but an over-cautious person would be likely to select A; an under-cautious one to select C. The first would attempt to justify his selection by pointing out that though A does not offer as great an opportunity of happiness as offered by B, still it offers a less opportunity of unhappiness — in fact none at all. Hence in selecting it, less risk is run. The second would attempt justification of his act by pointing out that though C offers more opportunity of pain than B, it also offers more opportunity of pleasure. The risk is greater but the stake to be won is also greater. Any one who has mastered the exposition of a use-judgment given in Chapter 3 will see the obvious incorrectness of this reasoning. Comparing A and B it may be briefly stated thus: If A is the correct alternative at any one time, it will be the correct alternative at any other time, and hence will be correct every time. Suppose these same alternatives, or alternatives whose presumptions of happiness are respectively equal, are offered a great number — say 1000 times: A will then be correct every time. But we have seen that the presumption of happiness of an alternative is that quantity which will be experienced, on the average, by the selection of that alternative a great number of times. Hence by the selection of A an average of 50 hedon-minutes per selection or 50,000 hedon-minutes for 1,000 selections would be yielded; whereas by the selection of alternative B, an average of 250 hedon-minutes per selection or 250,000 hedon-minutes for 1000 selections would be yielded. To admit then that the first selection is better than the second is to admit that a smaller quantity of happiness is better than a larger quantity — a moral fallacy. The same reasoning would apply with even greater force, should we compare alternatives B and C. Hence for either an over- or under-cautious person to consistently maintain their position would simply result in the assertion of a moral fallacy; it would mean that they employ the word *better* in the very sense in which common sense employs the word *worse,* and the word *correct* in the sense in which common sense employs *incorrect.* The utilitarian is neither under- nor over-cautious, but just cautious enough; for whether a risk is too great or not, he determines by a use-judgment alone, and his selection is one which may consistently be maintained however often the same alternatives, or their equivalents, are offered. By a *cautious* act or policy then, it is convenient to mean one having the correct degree of caution, which is none other than a correct act or policy.

Now customary and cautious policies are often confounded together; so much so indeed that the same name, viz. *conservatism,* is applied to both. A man or a nation often consider themselves cautious when they are only conforming to custom. Custom is a product of tradition — caution of reason. When conservatism is a product of reason, or a mental process superficially similar to reason, it proceeds something like this: The policy pursued in the past has not given rise to any immoderate evils. Therefore, in the future it probably will not. Though we may gain little by it, we shall probably lose little by it; the probable surplus of success may be small, but that of failure is small also. This reasoning is obviously incorrect. Were it correct it would mean that every policy which at any time had become customary was thenceforward cautious. Now no one will acknowledge this: yet such reasoning seems quite acceptable to the political theorists of our day and, of course, inevitably leads to the confusion of that which is customary with that which is cautious. There is really no relation between them. A customary policy may be cautious or it may be incautious, but is generally the latter. Were a man to assume that because he had added to the horizontal extension of a block of brick houses that he could continue to add to the horizontal extension without achieving any evil results, his assumption would be a safe one, and compatible with caution, for we have no reason to believe that the building of a fortieth or fiftieth addition to the block would involve results any more evil than building the third or fourth; but were he to assume that because no evil results were evident from adding a fourth story to a three-story house, a fifth to a fourth, a sixth to a fifth, etc., that he could continue indefinitely to pursue the policy of adding to the vertical height of his building until he reached fifty, one hundred, or five hundred stories — his assumption would be an obviously unsafe one. His policy might be conservative, but would it be cautious? The first policy carried nothing within itself which made its continued practice unsafe. The second by its own operation brought about such changes in the system operated upon as to make its continued practice unsafe. In order to clearly distinguish between policies or operations having these two divergent characteristics, we shall call those which by their own operation produce changes which modify the effects of their continued operation, *accelerative* policies. Those which do not we shall call *non-accelerative*. Accelerative policies may be of two kinds: (1) Those the pursuit of which yields a progressively better result — these we may call *beneficently* accelerative. (2) Those the pursuit of which yields a progressively worse result, these we may call *maleficently* accelerative. It is clear that one kind of accelerative policy may pass into the other. Now, conservative policies may belong to either or neither of these classes, but their tendency is to become maleficently accelerative, and hence conservatism may be only another name for incaution or danger. The disregard of this distinction is obviously dangerous, but that it is disregarded we shall have occasion to uncontrovertibly demonstrate and the common confusion of the two meanings of conservatism — a confusion sufficient to cause the two qualities to be expressed by the same term — is particularly common among men of high intelligence and training.

A *radical* policy is one opposed to a conservative policy. Hence it may refer to that which is uncustomary or to that which is incautious. The first implication is the same which we have found cropping out wherever we have examined the dogmatic standards. It underlies them all. The second distinction is of little value as a criterion of public conduct, because in order to decide whether a policy which is too cautious or one which is not cautious enough is to be preferred, we must know the relative degrees of under-caution and over-caution. Radical policies are, in fact, condemned by the same shallow reasoning whereby conservative policies are approved, viz. by the confusion of customary with cautious, and hence of uncustomary with incautious policies. This removes the last vestige of value from the distinction as one worthy to serve as a guide to conduct. Knowledge of whether a proposed course of action is conservative or radical then is not worth acquiring, since such distinctions between them as are to be discovered have no particular relation to that between right and wrong.

We might, if it were necessary, examine other standards of political conduct for there are many such, some obsolete and some becoming so. At different times and places different standards prevail and they fluctuate like the fashions. One characteristic, however, is common to them all — they never are and never have been consistently practised. If we inquire why, if natural processes are beneficent, we do not leave everything to nature, or why, if the economic standard is a valid one, we do not judge all public policies thereby, or why, if conservatism furnishes a guide to conduct, any departure from it is approved, we shall be told that none of these criteria must be applied too rigorously — they must not be carried " too far." But how far is " too far," and how far is " just far enough? " We shall doubtless be told that common sense furnishes the answer to such questions; but if common sense is competent to mark the limit of authority of these standards, is it not competent to displace them? If they do not derive their authority from common sense, from what do they derive it? And if they do, why are they substituted for it? Why do we need to know whether an act or policy is just, or economic, or expedient? Why is it not sufficient if we know that it is *right,* for whatever is right must conform to the dicta of common sense. If to this it is replied that the dicta of common sense are not sufficiently definite to constitute a guide to public policies, then we may inquire how it comes about that they are sufficiently definite to mark the limits beyond which the more definite standards are invalid? The fact is that common sense holds a painfully subordinate place as a determinant of these standards. A very little observation serves to make plain that in the minds of men, carrying a principle of conduct " too far " means carrying it farther than they approve of carrying it, or farther than it is customary to carry it, and carrying it " just far enough " means carrying it just as far as they approve of carrying it, or as it is customarily carried. Custom is the real guide back of these varying rules, though it is custom tempered by common sense.

But, it may be objected, after all, is not custom an acceptable substitute for common sense? Do not customs originate in the experiences of a people? Are they not the result of the teachings of experience? Are they not indeed the embodiments of common sense? To judge by the uniformity with which traditions are substituted for reasons, it would appear that such views as these are widely accepted; and yet who is there who will admit that any customs except those of his own people and time are the embodiments of common sense? Few persons are in a position to judge impartially of the customs of their own country, but the slightest inspection of the customs of other times and peoples will convince anyone that if customs are derived from experience, they certainly are not derived by the scientific method. Induction has been rather a check than a guide. Custom, indeed, can never take the place of reason: *there is no substitute for common sense,* and we have already demonstrated that the common standards of political action are not only irreconcilable with common sense, but with one another — since to apply any of them consistently means to exclude the application of any other, and to attempt any reconciliation by talking about carrying a principle " too far " or " the disagreement of theory and practice," is merely begging the question. It is the plainest logomania.

Crude as are the political standards we have examined, the dogmatic sanction has made them acceptable to men of trained intelligence who would not think of applying such rules in their business, or in the common affairs of life. Even men of science who deem themselves weaned from dogma, and who smile at the solemn " reaffirmations " of belief in Adam and Eve, Noah's Ark, etc., which theological conclaves occasionally indulge in, accept these political traditions as unreservedly as a person of confirmed orthodoxy accepts the teachings of Genesis. Let such as these examine their own minds and reflect on the political faith they find there. If they will but apply to it the test of reason, they will discover that they are cherishing delusions as crude, and in practice more baneful, than those they deride, only their superstitions happen to be political instead of theological. Let them pluck out the dogmatic beam from their own eye, and they will then be better able to perceive the dogmatic mote which is in their neighbor's eye.

Criticism, however, is easier than creation, and destruction simpler than construction. We have in this chapter employed the standard of common sense in its destructive capacity. In the next Book it will be employed in its constructive capacity.

We have at this stage cleared away some of the ranker dogmatic growths which, through the progress of the centuries, have flourished in the rich mould of the world's ignorance, and on the less obstructed ground thus prepared may proceed to rear upon the foundation of common sense, already laid, the structure of the economy of happiness; attempting no elaboration of detail, but confining our efforts to riveting the skeleton work, so that it may, if possible, remain unshaken by the wholesome gales of criticism. More fortunate than some preceding architects of the social structure, we have before us a definite plan of procedure. At the very beginning, we know just what we propose to do.

That which society should seek to attain, the maximum surplus of happiness, may be referred to by different names according to the relation in which we think of it, e. g. *the utilitarian end*, the *end* or *object of utility*, of *society* or of *justice*, and so forth. It is in the nature of a perfectly definite magnitude. Quantities of pain or pleasure may be regarded as magnitudes having the same definiteness as tons of pig iron, barrels of sugar, bushels of wheat, yards of cotton, or pounds of wool; and as political economy seeks to ascertain the conditions under which these commodities may be produced with the greatest efficiency — so the economy of happiness seeks to ascertain the conditions under which happiness, regarded as a commodity, may be produced with the greatest efficiency — how the maximum output of happiness may be achieved with the means available. In order to ascertain what these conditions are, we need to proceed as any manufacturer trained to his business would proceed, were he endeavoring to ascertain how he could most economically produce beer, or molasses, or oil, or tacks. He would satisfy himself by the inductive or common sense method what laws and resources of nature and of human nature were available under conditions as he found them, and the means thus available he would, to the best of his ability, adapt to his ends. Our problem is a similar one, and we shall adopt similar means to solve it.

BOOK II
THE TECHNOLOGY OF HAPPINESS
PART ONE — THEORETICAL

CHAPTER V

THE FACTORS OF HAPPINESS

A criterion of conduct, the goal of all systems of intuitional ethics, is but the starting point of the ethics of common sense. The popular judgment that philosophy has no relation to the practical affairs of life is only too well justified by much that passes under that name, but it will be our aim hereinafter to prove that such a judgment is entirely fallacious when applied to the philosophy of common sense. An ethical system which cannot be applied is a poor substitute for none at all. A science is concerned with knowing — an art with doing; but in order to do to any purpose we must first know what to do. Hence, arts are, or ought to be, founded upon sciences. Logic is the science of sciences — ethics is the art of arts — and common sense founds the art of arts upon the science of sciences. It founds ethics upon logic. The common sense criterion of conduct has been formulated in the first book. The next step is to discover how it may be employed as a guide to conduct, and that step will be undertaken in this and the following book.

The end we aim at is the maximum output of happiness. How shall we attain it? Now the mode of achieving the output we seek must depend upon the means available for achieving it, and these means consist of those portions of animate and inaminate creation affectable directly or indirectly by our acts. Therefore, our next task must be to examine the possibilities thus provided in order that we may learn how to adapt them to our ends. The particular mode of operation required will depend upon the structure and properties of the system through which we must work; namely, upon the laws of nature and of human nature as they are revealed to us by experience. Were these laws different from what they are, the technology of happiness would be different from that herein to be expounded; and no doubt, means far better adapted to the end of utility than those provided us by nature, may be imagined. But we must take things as they are. The problem before us is, not how the output of happiness might be made a maximum were a perfect apparatus at hand, but how it may be made a maximum with the means actually available. In order to make an effective examination of the working substance of our system, attention will henceforth be confined to humanitarianism or patriotism as those terms are defined on page 142, since by this means the mode which we shall propose of increasing the totality of happiness may be made clearer; and in the end the surest means of advancing the utilitarian cause, will be to advance that of humanity, since it is by the intelligent acts of man alone, if by any means, that right may be made to reign throughout the sentient world. I shall then assume, for the sake of simplicity, that man is the only sentient being whose happiness may be affected by voluntary acts, and by a right act shall generally mean that act among those physically possible, presumably resulting in the greatest surplus of happiness among men, and by a wrong act shall mean any alternative of a right act. Occasionally, however, I may use the terms in their patriotic sense, making the assumption that the only sentient beings in existence, or to be considered, are those of a given nation.

We propose then, to attempt the foundation of the economic policy of society upon a distinction no less simple and fundamental than that between right and wrong, nor should any insuperable difficulty be encountered in such an attempt. The distinction between them being understood with sufficient precision, we may proceed with the same confidence that we should in solving a problem in physics or chemistry, knowing beforehand what goal we seek and adapting the available knowledge of the age, so far as we may command it, to the attainment of that goal: but we could not have made the first step had we failed to take the not inconsiderable trouble to ascertain in just what direction we desired to proceed. The science of trigonometry and its applications in surveying, navigation, mechanics, etc., could not have proceeded far, had our knowledge of what was meant by a triangle been confined to realizing that it had some relation or other to a plane figure, and that three straight lines played some sort of conspicuous part in its make-up. Similarly, knowledge that the distinction between right and wrong bears some relation or other to pleasure and pain, and that the pleasure and pain to be considered is not alone that experienced, or to be experienced, by ourselves is not sufficiently distinct to serve as the basis upon which definite principles or policies may be founded. Before clear thinking about our experiences can be attained, words possessing clear meanings with which to think and to communicate thought must be devised. Having attempted to give the words *right* and *wrong* the required clearness, we shall seek to found upon the distinction in experience which they express, the principles of the economy of happiness.

If there existed a being whose happiness curve at the present time coincided with, and was in the future certain to coincide with, that representing the happiness of humanity (See p. 129) it might with propriety be said that the interests of that being were the interests of humanity or of society. Let us assume the existence of such a being and let us call her Justice. When referring to this personification of justice we shall use a capital letter to distinguish the word from that used in the ordinary signification. Let us further assume (1) That no way of altering her presumable future curve of happiness is possible, save that of altering the curve of happiness of humanity with which her own, by hypothesis, is and remains coincident. (2) That the society she has to deal with is the society of to-day, i. e. that she is offered the same materials to work with, the same resources of nature and of human nature that are available to the statesman. (3) That she is a perfect egotist and so well aware of her own interest as never to be influenced by the location, but solely by the quantities of pain or pleasure to be experienced. The question for the lover of justice to decide is: What are the acts or policies which Justice would presumably approve? What would she do, or desire done, under the circumstances in which we find ourselves placed? Her acts, of course, would be just acts, and a just act is a right one.

In order more clearly to apprehend the manner in which Justice should go about attaining the maximum of happiness which terrestrial conditions may afford, let us first consider a more familiar case. Suppose an engineer who had at his disposal a limited domain affording coal and water, were required to generate the maximum quantity of steam which the available resources of the domain would permit. How would he proceed? He would, to begin with, ascertain the conditions or factors, upon which the production of steam depends. He would find first, that a boiler is required as a steam-generating agency or mechanism; second, that said boiler must be furnished with a sufficient amount of coal to generate the steam, and third, that a sufficient number of boilers must be provided to consume the available output of coal. To obtain the maximum generation of steam with a given output of coal, i. e. to generate steam with the maximum economy then, three factors must be considered: (1) The efficiency of conversion of the boiler. (2) The efficiency of adaptation of the coal supply to the capacity of the boiler. (3) The number of boilers required to consume the output with maximum efficiency per boiler.

Let us assume for the sake of clearness that there are only three types of boiler from which to choose. Suppose when working at their best they have efficiencies of conversion as follows: type (a) generates 8 pounds of steam per pound of coal: type (b) 12 pounds of steam per pound of coal: type (c) 10 pounds of steam per pound of coal. Type (b) then is evidently the boiler of highest efficiency — that is, its conversion of the potentiality of steam generation possessed by the coal into an actuality is the highest, and it is therefore the one to select. It is next necessary to ascertain under what conditions this type of boiler attains its maximum efficiency of adaptation. Let us suppose by experiment our engineer ascertains that it is most efficient when consuming 10 tons of coal per day. That if, on the one hand, it is given any less, the greater relative loss of heat by radiation diminishes its efficiency, and if, on the other hand, it is given any more, some of the available heat is not absorbed in the boiler but passes with the flue gases up the chimney, and thus again diminishes its efficiency. It is clear then that a wise engineer — one who understands how to adapt his means to his end — will supply this type of boiler just 10 tons of coal per day. If now we suppose the available output of coal from the given domain to be 10,000 tons per day, it is clear that the number of boilers required will be 1,000.

In a manner very similar to that whereby the engineer in the foregoing example determines the factors upon which depends the maximum production of steam, Justice must seek to determine the factors upon which depends the maximum production of happiness. To simplify matters, suppose she has at her disposal, a limited portion of the earth's surface, having average natural resources, and suppose it to be uninhabited. Her problem is to so utilize the available resources of the domain as to produce the greatest surplus of happiness of which it is capable — the maximum surplus of hedon-hours per day or year. In attacking it she must, to begin with, distinguish the factors of happiness production as the engineer distinguished the factors of steam production. She will find, as he did, that there are three: First: just as a boiler is required to utilize the potential energy of coal in the production of steam, so sentient beings are required to convert the potentiality of happiness resident in a given land area into actual happiness, and just as the engineer's first care is to select a boiler having maximum efficiency of conversion, so the first care of Justice should be to populate the domain over which she has jurisdiction with beings capable of utilizing the available resources in the production of happiness, in a manner which will insure the maximum efficiency of conversion. Second: following the analogy of steam engineering practice, the policy of Justice must be to insure such a relation of each sentient being to its environment that in the consumption of the resources available the greatest efficiency of adaptation of which the beings are capable, will be attained. In this way she will secure the maximum efficiency per capita. Third: she must so adapt the number of beings to the resources available that the efficiency per capita will be maintained a maximum. By the practice of such a policy she will so utilize the available resources as to produce by their consumption the maximum quantity of happiness which they are capable of producing, and having done this she will have accomplished all that under the given conditions it is possible to accomplish. She will have done *right*.

If the arts did not advance, if the efficiency of boilers and of the methods of coal mining remained always the same, an engineer in solving the problem we have discussed, would need to consider none but the factors of available resources, efficiency of plant, and coal supply of same, and number of plants best adapted to maintain said efficiency, but in the world as we know it this is not true. The arts continually advance. Hence the available resources may be made to increase by the use of improved machinery, the efficiency of plant may be augmented by similar improvements in the design of the boiler, or in burning or handling the coal, and in this way the numbers adapted to maintain maximum efficiency must be readjusted. Hence the engineer requires a knowledge not only of the present condition of the arts, but of the methods whereby they may be advanced, for were he ignorant of such methods and did he fail to apply them to the improvement of his coal mining and steam plants, he clearly could not obtain the maximum quantity of steam which the available coal is capable of yielding. In other words, it is a part of his duty to know how the conditions of steam production can be changed for the better.

Similarly, Justice in addition to a knowledge of the present condition of the art of producing happiness, must, in order to attain her end, know how said art may be advanced — how the conditions of producing happiness may be changed for the better.

In Chapters 6, 7 and 8, we shall consider in order the three factors of happiness. (1) The sentient being or happiness-producing agent. (2) The adaptation of said agent to his environment. (3) The number of said agents. In the first, we shall consider the factors upon which efficiency in the production of happiness depend, so far as they relate to the agent himself, and the conditions best adapted to increase the efficiency or capacity of sentient beings as happiness-producing mechanisms. In the second, we shall consider how the environment of sentient beings may be so adapted to them as to result in the maximum efficiency of production of happiness per capita. In the third, we shall consider how the number of beings must be related to their capacity for happiness, and the adjustment of the environment to that capacity, in order that the efficiency per capita shall be maintained a maximum. If we are successful in revealing in this discussion what the factors of happiness are, how they are related to one another, and by what means the present methods of happiness-production may be altered for the better, then we shall have established the grounds of a code of political morality related to the object which it is designed to achieve, viz., *justice,* in a manner precisely similar to that by which the Ten Commandments or the Golden Rule are related to the same object, the only difference being in the mode of expression. The precepts of most moral systems have always been so worded as to be most obviously applicable to private morality. The precepts of utility which I shall hereafter formulate will be so expressed as to apply to public morality, but the object of both is, or should be, the same, namely, to increase the totality of happiness. And just as adherence to the former are but proximate ends, generally but not universally to be sought, so adherence to the latter are proximate ends of general but not universal desirability. They constitute the first and fundamental approximations to an ideal system, to be attained only by a formulation of their exceptions into subsidiary policies, and the formulation of the exceptions to these exceptions again into policies of yet lower orders, until by successive approximations, a system adapted to achieve the desired end, in a degree limited only by the knowledge of mankind, may be realized.

This process of successive approximation to secure an ideal of justice is best exemplified in the law. There is first laid down a very general rule of law to guide the decisions of courts: the exceptions to this rule are then themselves formulated into subsidiary rules; the exceptions to these exceptions are again systematized into rules, and so on, until the law becomes a vast network of rules, and their successive exceptions, each in itself subject to rule, the attempt being to make the law sufficiently definite to apply to any particular case which may arise. Were the law based on the principle of utility it would constitute the utilitarian code of morals of which we are in search, but strangely enough the law seeks to attain justice without asking what justice is. It nowhere defines, or seeks to define, justice, and yet if justice is its object, this should be its first task, and if justice is not its object, what excuse has it for being? This failure to found its precepts on definition distinguishes the law from a true science. The law uses the scientific method very largely to test the consistency of conclusions with one another, and with their premises, but with the premises upon which the whole fabric rests it has no concern. It never examines its premises, which, as is well known, are but the crystallized customs of former generations, customs depending upon the whims of sovereigns, the superstitions of the vulgar, and the accidents of history. That it so notoriously fails to attain justice then is only what, with perfect confidence, might have been predicted from a knowledge of its premises. It is, in fact, a science superimposed upon a mass of dogmas and hopelessly infected by them. No amount of consistency between premises and conclusions can ever compensate for an invalid premise. If we start an arithmetical problem by assuming that four times five is twenty-eight, no degree of rigor in adherence to the multiplication table thereafter can compensate for the error. Had astronomy accepted as a permanent premise the dictum of Kepler that the planets are guided in their orbits by spirits, it would have remained but a branch of astrology to this day. Had mathematics been founded upon the mysticism of Pythagoras concerning the occult properties of number, algebra and geometry would be where theology and politics are now.

The schoolmen or pseudo-philosophers of the Middle Ages followed the legal methods of to-day — that is, they insisted that their premises and conclusions should be logically related, but the premises themselves were left to chance — to whatever the prevailing traditions sanctioned. The jurisprudence of our day is similarly pseudo-philosophical. Law, in short, is applied scholasticism mitigated by inconsistency.

The science which treats of the economy of happiness is, or should be, an applied science — indeed its whole value is in its application, and in the effort which we have made to found it upon definitions rather than dogmas, those which constitute its principal grounds, those, namely, of *right* and *wrong,* express a distinction in experience than which none is more universally conspicuous or more generally conceded to be that upon which the policy of nations should be founded; for even the dogmatic economist would have to concede, if the question were plainly put to him, that the only use of wealth is to augment pleasure or to diminish pain. But a discussion of the economics of happiness would be of little service if it did not advance beyond definitions. To say that a nation or society should do that which presumably will result in the maximum surplus of happiness would be of little use. What society wants to know is — what can we do, how can we proceed, to attain that maximum surplus? What rules or precepts are deducible from the fundamental definitions, which are adapted to guide the policy of nations or of society? Such rules, or at least the more fundamental of them, we shall attempt to formulate; but it must be understood that they are general and not universal rules, and therefore any single or scattering exceptions to them which may be cited cannot invalidate them. When I assert that the totality of happiness would be increased by an equal distribution of wealth, for example, I do not intend to assert that no particular case of equalization could be discovered or imagined which would not increase that totality. On the contrary, there are exceptions to the rule, and this fact we shall not ignore. If the objection is made to this that nations cannot afford to found their policies upon mere general rules, we may reply that he who thinks that any nation does otherwise is profoundly ignorant of the customs of nations. Indeed, that nation has yet to be numbered among existent states whose policy is not based more upon dogma than utility — upon tradition than reason. There is, in fact, but one universal precept peculiar to our subject, and that is the one upon which all others are founded, viz., do that which will most increase the total surplus of happiness; namely, do *right*. But even with this paucity of universal precepts it possesses an advantage over current political economy, for that science has not a single universal precept peculiar to it. When political economists tell us that free trade, for example, increases the wealth of nations, they do not mean to assert that we could not discover or imagine a single exception — a single combination of circumstances under which a restriction upon the exchange of commodities between men or nations would result in no loss of wealth — that would be a mere absurdity, contradicted by their own theories of taxation. They merely mean that, as a general thing, it will increase the wealth of nations, because it will tend to confine the production of each commodity to the place and circumstances under which it will be most economically produced, and hence (so they tell us) free trade should be a policy adopted by nations and by society.

Indeed, it may be said that in the formulation of rules and precepts for the guidance of individuals or of society what we gain in definiteness, we lose in generality. To say that a man should be permitted to do as he pleases with his own property is not so general a rule as to say that justice should be done to all men, but it is much more definite. It serves better as a direct guide to conduct, because it seeks to specify how justice may be done in a particular and recognizable class of cases, and we may tell by observation in any particular case whether it is or is not done; but if the law said nothing more specific than that justice should be done, judges would be at a loss how to act, for they would not have the means of knowing, in particular cases, what the law considered justice and what it did not, and it is always in particular cases that they are called upon to decide.

Having taken the precaution thus to avow our intention of establishing only general precepts, scattering exceptions to which do not constitute an invalidation, we may proceed to a discussion of the first factor of happiness.

CHAPTER VI

THE FIRST FACTOR OF HAPPINESS

If happiness is to be produced in the world as at present constituted, it must be through the agency of sentient beings. In order to convert whatever latent possibilities of happiness the world may afford into actual happiness the first requirement is a happiness-producing mechanism, and the only known mechanisms which meet the requirement are those afforded by such terrestrial organisms as possess sentiency.

In this work we have deemed it best to ignore all beings except human beings. The first question which suggests itself then, is, what kind of human beings are best adapted to convert the potentialities of happiness afforded by the world into happiness; what characteristics or combinations of characteristics make man an efficient agent for converting potential into actual happiness? Upon what traits does efficiency of conversion depend? The terms usually employed to distinguish between the various mental or moral characteristics of human beings are, in general, rather loose and inaccurate. Fortunately we shall have no occasion to give them any such increase in precision as was necessary in the case of the terms *right* and *wrong,* because their implications are sufficiently familiar for the purposes to which we shall have occasion to apply them.

Were men always isolated from their fellow men the characteristics required in them as agents of happiness would be different from what they are; but man as he is, and is likely to remain, is a member of society, so that it is necessary to consider him as a factor of happiness in a double — in a primary and secondary — capacity. Each human being is, in the first place, in his own person, the immediate sentient agent, the happiness-producing mechanism, in whose sensorium the finished product of all successful human effort — happiness — is finally turned out. In the second place, he is a part, and an important part, of the environment of other happiness-producing mechanisms. The characteristics which make man an efficient agent in his primary capacity are not necessarily identical with those upon which efficiency in his secondary capacity depends, yet so intimately is the welfare of each being bound up with that of his fellow beings that no hard and fast classification can be constructed. A rough division, however, is possible, and we may, in the first place, consider briefly the elements required to insure efficiency in man's primary capacity, noting the more important of them, of which only two require mention.

The first of them is *health,* and so well is its importance recognized that no discussion of it will be necessary. The second is what may be termed *adjustability,* itself a function of three separate characteristics. (a) Simplicity of taste — the ability to obtain pleasure from simple things, requiring little or no labor to attain. (b) Variety of taste — the ability to obtain pleasure from many different things. (c) Adaptability of taste — the ability to modify tastes or needs to meet the exigencies of life, including proficience in the art of excluding painful thoughts or feelings from the attention and substituting for them thoughts or feelings which are pleasurable, or at least less painful. A sufficient development of the third element would dispense with the need of the first two.

In the second place, we may touch upon two elements which affect man's efficiency in both his primary and secondary capacities. The first is *intelligence. Intelligence* or *intellectuality* are names commonly given to two faculties closely related to one another — the power to reason — to use common sense — and the power to express. Power of expression is essential to reason — or at least to any high development thereof — but reason is not essential to power of expression. Poets generally owe their reputation to their power of expression, but they are commonly poor reasoners, though often good observers. Their faculty is an intellectual one, but their immediate object is very different from that of reason. The immediate aim of reason is to attain truth and its ideal mode of expression is the mathematical. The immediate aim of poetry or poetic literature is to arouse emotion and its ideal mode of expression is the musical. Reason utilizes the sense of words, poetry primarily their sound, though the ultimate aim of both is, or ought to be, the same — viz., utility. Sometimes the attempt is made to combine the functions of reason and poetry, and it is generally a failure, though some conspicuous exceptions are known. It is exceedingly dangerous to attempt the expression of such truths as may determine acts in poetic language, for so adorned, untruth is too often mistaken for truth, and wrong for right. Feeling is thus made a guide to action, when its only proper function is to stimulate it, and the inevitable result is the encouragement of pathomania.

Reason or rationality is so obviously one of the co-essentials of efficiency in man as an agent of happiness that it would be a waste of time to urge the point. Without it he would have no guide to conduct. It has always been held, and with justice, that in the high development of his reason, man is to be distinguished from the brute more than ly any other characteristic.

The second element to be noticed in this division is *will*. By *will* is to be understood that power by which a thinking being rules his impulses — by which man overcomes himself. Selfishness is the dominant trait of character in all organisms. Egotistic impulses in most men prevail and very largely determine conduct. In the interest of the totality of happiness these impulses should be, as far as possible, superseded by altruistic ones. There are but two modes whereby the power of self-interest to control individual conduct may be weakened: (1) By weakening the impulses themselves. (2) By strengthening that which may nullify them. Hence the value of altruism on the one hand, and will power on the other. Stubbornness or obstinacy is often mistaken for will power — it generally signifies the lack of it. Obstinacy is merely a strong egotistic impulse. Will is the power which, if possessed, may serve to overcome it. Determination or persistence in seeking an end may signify will power or it may not. Determination in the pursuit of principle is will; in obedience to impulse it is not. Impulse is not always egotistic — it is sometimes altrustic, as in impulses arising from sympathy or gratitude, but will is the power by which all impulses, egotistic or altruistic, are governed, and it should be exerted in accordance with the dictum of principle alone.

In the third place, may be mentioned an element which affects man's efficiency, for the most part, in his secondary capacity alone, viz., *altruism*. It is notorious that selfish people not only make others unhappy, but are frequently unhappy themselves. *Unselfishness* or *altruism* implies the absence or slight development of traits like dishonesty, hatred, vindictiveness, treachery, cupidity, and peevishness, and the presence or high development of traits like honesty, generosity, benevolence, magnanimity, and good nature. It would be superfluous to make any detailed enumeration, or to demonstrate that a community in which altruism prevails is happier than one whose members are egotists. Without mutual concession society could not exist. Courtesy is but an expression of altruism and in the conventionalized courtesy known as manners we find a code of conduct which, in a narrow sphere, recognizes the claim of quantity of happiness over distribution. Even among barbarous nations this claim is recognized in the practice of hospitality. Virtues have almost universally the quality of altruism. Vices as universally the quality of egotism. The former are elements of efficiency — the latter of inefficiency of conversion. The elements of will and altruism constitute *good character;* which for brevity we may denominate *character.*

Health, adjustability, reason, will, and altruism, then, being the traits most desirable in human beings, we may next ask by what means the development of health, adjustability, reason, will, and altruism may be promoted. If efficiency of conversion depends upon these traits, upon what do these traits depend? Is it possible by voluntary acts to modify the physical, mental, and moral characteristics of man? If so, by what means may we promote the development of traits which increase efficiency and impede the development of those which increase inefficiency? How may we increase intelligence and virtue and decrease, or eradicate, unintelligence and vice? Obviously the traits of human beings are effects of some cause or causes. If so, we must modify them, if at all, by modifying their causes. What then are their causes?

The characteristics of man, physical, mental, and moral, are the effects of two causes or two classes of causes: they are the product of two factors: *inheritance* and *experience.* By the co-operation of these causes the characteristics of every individual are completely determined. A Newton or a Socrates was what he was because his inheritance and experience were what they were. The vilest criminal in the penitentiary is what he is because his inheritance and experience were what they were. To deny it is to deny the law of causation.

By the *inheritance* of an individual I refer to the sum of the characteristics inherited by him from his ancestors, immediate and remote, and indefinitely transmissible — though not necessarily transmitted — to his descendants. By the *education* of an individual I refer to any and all means voluntarily employed to determine his individual characteristics by determining his experiences. To voluntarily cause an individual to have a given experience, or to avoid a given experience, for the purpose of affecting his efficiency of conversion — or for any other purpose — is to employ a means of education. Hence to secure any change in the characteristics of a human being, either for better or worse, we must affect either his inheritance, or his education, or both. We may now ask what kind of inheritance and what kind of education will most increase man's efficiency? To answer this question requires some consideration of those subjects, and I shall discuss inheritance first.

The inheritance of any organism depends upon the characters, or rather a certain class of the characters, of the organisms from which it sprung — its ancestors — and as we have good reason for disbelieving in spontaneous generation, we may say that all organisms have ancestors. It is a fact too familiar to require citation that the offspring resembles its parent. The offspring of cattle are cattle; of horses, horses; of dogs, dogs; and of men, men. Moreover, the offspring of a particular variety of cattle are, in general, of the same variety, of a particular style of horse, of the same style, and of a particular breed of dog, of the same breed. Indeed, it is by availing themselves of this fact that breeders are able to obtain new varieties of these animals and to keep the breeds so obtained pure. With such particularity does inheritance act that it sometimes happens that particular markings or other characters consisting of a very complex aggregate are transmitted from parent to offspring intact, and the subtle resemblances of people to their relatives — sometimes remote relatives — are evidences of the remarkable power of inheritance to preserve and reproduce very complexly related morphological aggregates.

It should be noticed, however, that although the offspring resembles the parent he never exactly resembles him, nor does one individual ever exactly resemble another, even in the case of twins. Darwin says "Some authors have gone so far as to maintain that the production of slight differences is as much a necessary function of the powers of generation as the production of offspring like their parents," and Weismann contends that the differentiation of the sexes is but a means employed by nature to multiply variations and thus increase the probability of producing favorable ones. In other words, organisms vary, some having one set of characters more conspicuously developed, others having others, nor is man any exception to this organic law. There are many varieties of men, Caucasians, Ethiopians, Mongolians, etc., and of these varieties there are many sub-varieties, such as, among the Caucasians, the Teutons, the Celts, the Gallic race, etc., and among these sub-varieties there are an indefinite number of minor sub-divisions and each of these divisions and sub-divisions tends to perpetuate its own characteristics. Moreover the laws of inheritance apply as uniformly to mental and moral characteristics as they do to physical ones. The mind of an oyster is never by any accident as highly developed as that of a normal dog, nor is that of a dog so highly developed as that of a normal man, and this is obviously because the mind of an animal resembles the mind of its parents. Furthermore the resemblances extend to characters as particularate, as specific, as complexly related, in mental as in physical inheritances. The offspring of a man of congenitally weak character or intelligence will tend to be weak in the same particulars, while the offspring of a man of congenitally strong character or intelligence will tend to be strong in character or intelligence likewise; just as the offspring of a small man tend to be small and of a tall man tend to be tall. There is always considerable variation even in the same family, however, and hence weak parents will occasionally produce fairly strong offspring and small parents fairly tall ones. It would seem then that the way to obtain an individual or a community having inheritances adapted to make them efficient is to select for them ancestors who are efficient — in order to breed an efficient race, we must breed from an efficient stock. But are efficient stocks like poets, born not made, or may a more efficient stock be created from a less efficient one; and if so, how?

Two methods for producing improved stocks have been proposed. (1) By *selection*. (2) By *education*. The first method has been much practised, though not upon men, and is in fact that whereby breeders have produced the manifold varieties of domesticated animals and plants so familiar to everyone. The method is simplicity itself. The farmer or breeder makes up his mind what characters it is desirable to perpetuate in a particular kind of animal or plant, and then systematically breeds from individuals which are found to possess the desirable characters in the most marked degree. By thus *selecting* the parents he determines the characteristics of the offspring. Every farmer selects his seed from the best specimens of corn, or pumpkins, or wheat, or cabbage, which his crops yield, and in grafting his fruit trees he selects scions from good stock. Similarly in breeding his horses, cows, pigs, chickens, or pigeons, he selects the best individuals from among his flocks. In this way domestic animals and plants are continually improved and are to-day, in general, considerably in advance of those of a century or even of a generation ago. It is extraordinary what results have been attained by breeders. The progressive lowering of the running and trotting records has been due to the continual improvement of race-horses by breeding. The vast variety of dogs ranging from the little black and tan terrier to the great Dane illustrate what may be accomplished by selection. The Japanese, according to Weismann, have increased the length of the tail of a certain kind of cock from normal proportions to six feet or more, and when we are told that the cabbage, cauliflower, brussels sprouts, and kale are all varieties of the same plant, we may realize the possibilities of modification possessed by organisms. Of the great economic importance of selective breeding, we may get some idea from the following extract taken from the report of Willet M. Hays in the Year Book of the U. S. Department of Agriculture for 1901:

"Those who have earnestly and intelligently undertaken the improvement of any plant for a period of ten or twenty years, and have observed the past improvement in animal breeding, are unanimous in their belief that 10 per cent additional can be secured in twenty years by a further improvement through plant and animal breeding alone. This would result in ten years in a total increase equal to the value of all the crops grown in one year, representing at least $3,000,000,000 additional wealth to the world. All this could be secured at a cost of less than 1 per cent of its value, or $30,000,000, and the chances are that most of the increased values secured would not cost one-tenth of 1 per cent of their worth. . . .

"Examples of past achievement, whether by private plant breeders, by seed firms, or by agencies acting for the State and Nation, make the foregoing statements seem conservative as a basis for action. The sugar in sugar beets was increased more than 100 per cent in the last century by means of rigid selection systematically and scientifically carried out on a large and practical scale by European seed growers. . . . The farmers of America having been compelled to take in the hand each ear of corn while husking, have annually chosen the largest and best-formed ears from among the many thousands. This has resulted in the most extensive breeding experiment ever carried out, and the yield of corn is probably 20 per cent greater than it would have been without this selection. . . .

"The Minnesta experiment station by six years of selection produced varieties of flax 32 inches tall from varieties only 26 inches tall, increasing the length of the fiber more than 20 per cent. . . .

"The achievements in animal breeding also include profound structural changes, the full significance of which is not generally recognized. . . .

"The production of the Poland China, the Tamworth, and other breeds of hogs with very distinctive features shows that this species is mobile in the hands of men trained in the science and art of breed formation. . . .

"Some experiment stations have demonstrated the vast difference in the ability of individual cows to produce milk products cheaply from a given amount of food. Some cows do not pay their board; others produce values equal to two or three times the cost of their food; while such animals as the famous Jersey sire, Stoke Pogis, illustrate how an occasional dairy animal has the wonderfully important ability of impressing strong dairy quality upon all his or her progeny. . . .

". . . Chicken raisers have added to or substracted from the size, and changed the form, of the wattles of their pets almost at will. Pigeon fanciers have developed from wild species most fantastic forms, producing changes far more profound than that of changing some of the families of beef cattle so as to double their milk-giving capacity without seriously reducing their value for beef production. To add 25 per cent to the lean meat on hogs of a particular breed will not require greater changes in these animals than have been wrought in some varieties of pigeons."

"While many kinds of domesticated plants and animals have been so materially improved by breeding that the wealth of the world and the pleasure of living are greatly increased, only a start has been made in accomplishing that which is possible. The greatest achievements in the few lines illustrate what may be accomplished in the many lines. The extensive application of the scientific business principles of plant and animal improvement in the breeding of sugar beets, wheat, trotting horses, and dairy cattle illustrate how the same principles, with modifications to suit the species and the purpose, may be applied to improving other species that they may better suit our needs. And the best plans yet may be greatly improved."

Man, of course, has never been improved by deliberate breeding, but he is as susceptible of improvement as any other organism. Indeed, so far as concerns his mental powers, he is, or should be, more susceptible than any other animal. It is an old observation among biologists that, in general, the characters of greatest antiquity are the least variable, while those of latest acquisition are the most variable. The tendency to possess a vertebral column has been transmitted to man through a line of progenitors extending back to the lower fishes, and the tendency to the possession of four limbs dates from about the same phylogenetic period: hence it would be practically impossible to breed from men a race of beings devoid of these structures. On the other hand, the possession of reason — of a highly developed intellect — is an acquisition of the geological yesterday. Fish are found as far back as the Upper Silurian Period, while man as *homo sapiens* — as a being possessed of reason — probably does not antedate the Glacial Period. The former period is at least a hundred times as remote as the latter. Hence, as might have been expected, we find man's mental capacity the most variable of all his characteristics. Between the intellect of a Newton or an Aristotle and that of a Hottentot there is probably a greater discrepancy than between that of a Hottentot and that of a horse; and the ability to learn and to reason among the rank and file of men is far more variable, for example, than the length of their arms, or legs, or noses. Their mental stature is more variable than their physical. Now the ease with which a character may, by selection, be made to depart from the normal, will obviously depend upon its tendency to deviate from the normal in individual cases, i. e., upon its variability. By breeding from idiotic or feeble-minded human beings it would be easy to obtain a race whose grade of intelligence was on a par with that of sheep. In a corresponding manner, by repeatedly selecting from those of the highest intellectual power, a race of men could probably be produced as much superior to the average man in intellect as the average man is superior to a sheep. If a physical structure like the tail of a cock can be increased twentyfold in size, why may not a faculty like that of the intellect be increased twentyfold in power?

So many persons appear to believe that intellectual pre-eminence is, in marked contrast to all other characteristics, non-transmissible, that it will be well to quote at this point the views of Francis Galton, whose investigations of the matter have probably been more extended and careful than those of any other authority. He says:

"A remarkable misapprehension appears to be current as to the fact of the transmission of talent by inheritance. It is commonly asserted that the children of eminent men are stupid; that where great power of intellect seems to have been inherited, it has descended through the mother's side; and that one son commonly runs away with the talent of a whole family. My own inquiries have led me to a diametrically opposite conclusion. I find that talent is transmitted by inheritance in a very remarkable degree; and that whole families of persons of talent are more common than those in which one member only is possessed of it. I justify my conclusions by the statistics I now proceed to adduce, which I believe are sufficient to command conviction."[1]

I cannot conveniently quote the statistics here, but must refer the reader to the original article. Concerning another common fallacy, Galton remarks:

"There has been a popular belief that men of great intellectual eminence are usually of feeble constitution, and of a dry and cold disposition. There may be such instances, but I believe the general rule to be exactly the opposite. Such men, so far as my observation and reading extend, are usually more manly and genial than the average, and by the aid of these very qualities they obtain a recognized ascendancy. It is a great and common mistake to suppose that high intellectual powers are commonly associated with puny frames and small physical strength. . . . Most great men are vigorous animals with exuberant powers and extreme devotion to a cause. There is no reason to suppose that, in breeding for the highest order of intellect, we should produce a sterile or a feeble race."[2]

If the reader finds that his own mind is occupied by the idea that men of talent lack the power of transmitting their characteristics I commend to him an examination of Galton's work on Hereditary Genius, where he may find ample evidence to dispel the error.

Obviously the other factors of efficiency, particularly health, altruism, and will, are transmitted with the same freedom as intellect and hence these qualities may be cumulatively intensified in the same manner.

In a later paper on "The Possible Improvement of the Human Breed under the Existing Conditions of Law and Sentiment" Galton points out of what vast advantage to a nation the deliberate improvement of its stock would be, considered merely as an investment, and he proposes means, which he deems practicable, of attaining such an end. The means which he proposes are set forth at length in the paper referred to. Their character may be inferred from the following quotation:

"The possibility of improving the race of a nation depends on the power of increasing the productivity of the best stock. This

[1] Macmillan's Magazine; June, 1865, p. 157.
[2] Ibid: p. 164.

is far more important than that of repressing the productivity of the worst. They both raise the average, the latter by reducing the undesirables, the former by increasing those who will become the lights of the nation. It is therefore all important to prove that favor to selected individuals might so increase their productivity as to warrant the expenditure in money and care that would be necessitated. An enthusiasm to improve the race would probably express itself by granting diplomas to a select class of young men and women, by encouraging their intermarriages, by hastening the time of marriage of women of that high class, and by provision for rearing children healthily. The means that might be employed to compass these ends are dowries, especially for those to whom moderate sums are important, assured help in emergencies during the early years of married life, healthy homes, the pressure of public opinion, honors, and above all the introduction of motives of religious or quasi-religious character. Indeed, an enthusiasm to improve the race is so noble in its aim that it might well give rise to the sense of a religious obligation. In other lands there are abundant instances in which religious motives make early marriages a matter of custom and continued celibacy to be regarded as a disgrace, if not a crime. The customs of the Hindoos, also of the Jews, especially in ancient times, bear this out. In all costly civilizations there is a tendency to shrink from marriage on prudential grounds. It would, however, be possible so to alter the conditions of life that the most prudent course for an X-class person [1] should lie exactly opposite to its present direction, for he or she might find that there were advantages and not disadvantages in early marriage, and that the most prudent course was to follow their natural instincts."

Much ignorance and prejudice must be cleared away before methods of the character suggested can be introduced into even the most civilized of modern states. Other means of promoting the cause of humanity, of increasing the total happiness, such as those represented in the advancement of science and art, of invention and government, fade into insignificance when compared with what might be accomplished were men bred for efficiency as happiness-producing agents, as domestic animals and plants are bred for efficiency as agents in the production of wealth. Nothing could so augment the power of the sentient world to produce happiness as thus to increase the efficiency of the sentient agent itself. Were Justice ever to find herself in a position to breed men in some such manner as that suggested by Galton, her prospects might be compared to that of an engineer who having been, by the backward condition of the arts,

[1] X represents the highest class in Galton's system of classification.

compelled to generate steam in an earthenware retort, finds himself in a position to utilize a modern tubular-boiler. Under present conditions I fear that any attempt to improve, in civilized communities, upon the traditional method of breeding the human race — a method identical with that which woodchucks, rabbits, crows, turtles, and all wild animals follow — would be as unsuccessful as an attempt to establish a society for the prevention of cruelty to animals among Fiji Islanders. Nevertheless, should a nation finally arrive at a stage of civilization sufficiently advanced to permit the adoption of improved methods, it would, in a few generations, dominate the earth and subjugate the rest of the human race with an ease as great as — but with a humanity, let us hope, greater than — that with which men have subjugated the domesticated species of animals. For the present the restriction which the state puts upon the propagation of idiots and the more obtrusively feeble-minded, by confining them in institutions, is as much as we may expect to be done in the way of improving the human breed by selection.

This brings us to the second proposed method, the method of improvement by education. In its employment we might perhaps proceed thus: Taking the individuals of an inefficient or poor stock while young, we might educate them, cultivate their minds, train their morals, etc., and so convert them into efficient individuals; their offspring, springing from the individuals thus improved, would tend to inherit the characters thus superimposed upon their parents. By repeating the operation with succeeding generations a poor stock might, by this means, be converted into a good one, an inefficient race into an efficient one. Let us examine the theory of this suggested method.

The traits, qualities, or characters of an individual man (or other organism) may be divided into two classes: (1) Those with which he was born, or which would have been developed in him by the simple process of growth, independent of the particular circumstances of his environment or experience; such characters as the color of his hair, and eyes, the shape of his nose, or ears or fingers, his stature, or such mental characters as were inherited. These are called *spontaneous* characters, or variations. (2) Those which have been imposed or engrafted upon the individual during his lifetime; those which he has acquired from contact with the environment, or which have become a part of him because of his particular experience. In other words, those which he did not inherit. Such characters include the enlargement of muscular tissues due to exercise, the modifications in various organs due to disease or immoderate stimulation, callouses, scars, or other mutilations, and all those physical or mental characters acquired by education. These are called *acquired* characters. Weismann characterizes them thus:

"By *acquired* characters I mean those which are not performed in the germ, but which arise only through special influences affecting the body or individual parts of it. They are due to the reaction of these parts to any external influences apart from the necessary conditions for development. I have called them '*somatogenic*' characters, because they are produced by the reaction of the body or soma, and I contrast them with the '*blastogenic*' characters of an individual, or those which originate solely in the primary constituents of the germ ('Keimesanlagen')."[1]

The question we are considering may now be stated in the form: Are acquired characters inheritable, or are they not?

Let us first clear up a possible source of confusion as to the meaning of our terms. Just above I have said that the acquired characters of an individual are those which he did not inherit. It might seem from this statement that I have begged the question under examination in my definition. This is a mistake. By the acquired characters of a given individual I certainly do mean those which he did not inherit from his ancestors, but this definition does not imply that therefore his descendants cannot inherit them from him. That is a question which, of course, cannot be settled by a definition, but only by evidence. To state the case more clearly:

A, B, and C are three individuals, A is the father of B, and B the father of C. B has certain characters — x, y, z, &c., which he did not inherit from A or from any other ancestor, immediate or remote. Are the characters x, y, z, &c., inheritable by C or any of his descendants? This question is a perfectly unambiguous one. Is it susceptible of an unambiguous answer?

Obviously a question thus proposed is one which can be answered only by an appeal to experience — by an examination of organic nature. It is a subject which, for about a score of years, has been much discussed by naturalists. It must be settled, if at all, by the inductive method; and three hypotheses are possible:

[1] August Weismann: "The Germ-Plasm"; translated by W. Newton Parker and Harriet Ronnfeldt, 1893 — p. 392.

Chap. VI]   FIRST FACTOR OF HAPPINESS   209

(1) All acquired characters are inheritable.
(2) Some acquired characters are inheritable and some are not.
(3) No acquired characters are inheritable.

Of the classification of acquired characters Weismann remarks:

"Somatogenic variations may be classified according to their origin into three categories,—viz., *injuries, functional variations,* and variations depending on the so-called *'influences of environment,'*—which include mainly climatic variations." [1]

Of course, if acquired characters are inheritable we should expect to find that they are inherited; and if all acquired characters are inheritable we should expect to be unable to mention any class of such characters, instances of the inheritance of which could not be cited. Can such a class be mentioned? To this the reply is unreservedly — yes. Thousands, if not millions, of certain kinds of acquired characters are known, no instance of the inheritance of which has ever been observed. These are injuries or mutilations. Millions of men and animals have been mutilated in one way and another; legs, arms, ears, teeth, fingers, and many other parts of the body have been removed by accident or design, but though the organisms thus mutilated have frequently bred after the mutilation, the offspring are never mutilated, but are as sound as those born of unmutilated parents. Similarly, all kinds of scars, including those made by smallpox or ulcers, callouses or malformations of parts of the body due to accident or illnesses like rheumatism or paralysis, are never inherited. The Chinese women of the higher classes have deliberately deformed their feet from time immemorial, yet the feet of Chinese infants of both sexes are as perfect as those of any other race, and the deforming process has to be repeated in the case of each individual. The so-called Flat-head Indians have a custom of binding a piece of wood against the forehead of their infants so as to deform the head in a particular manner, and this custom has been religiously observed for many generations, but the malformed head thus acquired is never inherited. Weismann, who more than any other man, living or dead, has thrown light on this important question, tried the experiment of cutting off the tails of a succession of generations of rats, but

[1] Ibid: p. 393.
14

the tails of the later generations were just as long as those of the earlier ones. Innumerable instances of mutilation and malformation acquired during the lifetime of individuals, not only of men, but of dogs, cattle, and even of all kinds of plants, have been observed, but in no organism whatever, so far as the records of science are able to reveal, has a single instance of the inheritance of such an acquired character been observed. This evidence — and it might be indefinitely extended — obviously disposes of the first hypothesis. It is overwhelmingly improbable that all acquired characters are inheritable, and the most we can say is that some are and some are not. But are we able to say even this — have we any evidence that any kind of acquired characters are inherited? All we can do is to appeal to experience again.

When Charles Darwin began studying the subject of evolution in the first half of the last century there was already extant a theory of inheritance which sought to explain the transmutation of organisms by postulating the inheritance of acquired characters. This was the theory of Jean Baptiste Lamark, a French naturalist, who promulgated his theory in the latter part of the 18th century. His view was, in brief, that the various habits of animals caused them to use certain portions of their bodies more than other portions. By such disparity of employment certain parts were strengthened and other parts were left weak, and the effects thus induced by habit were inherited by the offspring. They, in turn, adopting the habits of their ancestors, strengthened the same parts and left unstrengthened the same parts as did their parents, so that their offspring in turn, inheriting this re-enforced disparity between the parts used and the parts disused, departed still more from the original type than their parents did, and in this manner were accumulated characters due to the habits of organisms which, in time, became sufficiently emphasized to have changed one species into another. Thus he accounted for the web-feet of water-fowl by the stimulus afforded by the continual effort to spread the toes in swimming on the part of the non-web-footed ancestors of water-fowl, and the long neck of the giraffe he explained by the habit which its ancestors had of continually stretching their necks upward to feed on the foliage of trees, as giraffes are known to do. This constant effort gradually stretched the tissues of the neck, and the effect being inherited and accumulated during many generations, the long neck of the giraffe finally resulted.

The elements of plausibility in this theory appealed to Darwin and he adopted it, incorporating it with his own theories of natural and sexual selection as one of the factors of evolution; and Herbert Spencer, before the appearance of Darwin's work on the Origin of Species, adopted the doctrine of Lamark and made it the foundation of his whole theory of organic evolution. It is probably to the influence of Spencer more than to any other cause that the opinion that acquired characters are inheritable still prevails. As we hope to show, the opinion is entirely fallacious. Its antecedent probability, however, appears to be strong until the evidence is critically examined. Darwin and his immediate disciples believed that by the inherited effects of use or disuse of organs — what Weismann terms "functional variations" — parts of the body could be made to increase or diminish in size, or even to entirely disappear. In particular the so-called *rudimentary* organs were explained on this ground. More than one hundred such organs occur in the body of man, for instance, of which the vermiform appendix, the tonsils, and the eustachian tubes are examples. They are useless or worse than useless in man, but in him they are but the rudiments of organs once useful and functioning in some of his animal ancestors. The rudiments of the muscles which in animals serve to move the ears, and which in such animals as the horse are utilized to shake the muscles of the shoulder in order to drive off flies, have been found in man. In some men these muscles are not completely rudimentary. Now, that such organs have become rudimentary there can be little doubt. But did they become so because of disuse, as the Lamarkians claim? If so — if disuse causes an organ or tissue to progressively dwindle from generation to generation — then we ought to observe that all parts of an organism thus disused tend to dwindle. Do we observe this? By no means — nothing of the kind is observed, though there would be ample opportunity to observe it, did it occur. The Lamarkian theory, in fact, explains too much. The bones of the human body, or at any rate some of them, may be said to be perpetually in disuse, if the mere failure to perform some active function is disuse, and this is what the Lamarkians must mean by that term in explaining how organs become rudimentary. The bones of the head for example; do they fulfil any function more active than a disused muscle? Yet they do not seem to tend to become rudimentary in either animals or man. A great many muscles in the human body are seldom if ever used, yet there is no evidence that they are progressively dwindling. If use progressively enlarges an organ and disuse progressively diminishes it, we should get an astounding condition of things in the human body, not to speak of animals. Such glands as those of the stomach, liver, etc., which are actively secreting during a large part of the life of every individual would become larger and larger in each succeeding generation, while the tear glands would tend to dwindle and disappear. The muscles of the heart and diaphragm which are in perpetual activity during every moment of an animal's life would tend to increase in size until the body could no longer contain them, for, according to the Lamarkians, the effects of use and disuse are cumulative. The relative sizes of the leg and jaw muscles which are used a great deal and of the abdominal muscles which are used very little, ought to exhibit greater and greater disparity, while such organs as the outer ear or the finger nails ought to disappear because they are incapable of any more active use than a rudimentary organ. None of these effects are observed and yet if the theory is sound they all ought to be. But it may be contended that nature automatically regulates inheritance in such a manner that after reaching a certain size further effects of the use of an organ are no longer inherited, and, on the other hand, that after an organ has dwindled to a certain irreducible minimum the effects of disuse are no longer inherited. This would be perfectly consistent with the proposition that some acquired characters are inheritable. But if nature does thus limit the inheritability of acquired characters it is obvious that disuse can never cause an organ to completely disappear as is claimed. On the other hand, if use can cause a giraffe's neck to be lengthened in the extraordinary degree observed, why should not the muscles of the heart in practically all animals enlarge in a similar abnormal manner in a degree greater than is required for them to perform their functions? Surely it is not because their use is less constant and long continued. It may be said that such a tendency would be perpetually checked by the intervention of natural selection, which would kill off such individuals as inherited hearts so large as to be disadvantageous, but unless the inheritance of acquired characters is merely a rare and occasional event, not a few but all animals would thus inherit abnormal hearts or other organs which in the life of their ancestors had been in constant use. Thus from a consideration of injuries and functional variations among physical characters it is obvious that a considerable presumption against the theory of the inheritance of acquired characters may be established.

But it is only when we examine the evidence afforded by mental characters that the presumption against such a theory becomes so strong as to put the matter beyond any considerable doubt. Here the opportunity for observation is vast, and the complete absence of a single unmistakable case of the inheritance of an acquired character is most significant. If acquired mental characters are inheritable, surely we ought to find at least one unmistakable case of this inheritance among the millions which have been examined. But not one appears. Romanes, a prominent supporter of the Lamarkian theory, in discussing the development of the fear of man among animals on uninhabited islands soon after man's appearance among them, attributes it to what he calls "inherited memory." It is clear that the development of such fear can easily be explained on other grounds. The communication of ideas among animals has frequently been observed by naturalists and the explanation of the phenomenon on the ground that the various animals communicated the fears generated in them by man to their offspring would be sufficient to account for it, without postulating such an extraordinary hypothesis as an inherited memory which, in one generation, nullifies the effects of the inherited memories of thousands or millions of generations which preceded it. But let us examine this hypothesis of inherited memories and observe the result of attempting to verify it.

In the first place, can the reader remember a single event which occurred in the life of his father or mother or any of his other ancestors before he was born, or does he know, or has he ever heard of anyone who can? If memories can be inherited, as Romanes claims, there should be many persons now living who could remember the Revolutionary War, or the events attending the settling of Plymouth Colony, or some which occurred in the reign of Henry VIII. In fact, people should occasionally be found who could remember the battle of Hastings, or even the invasion of Britain by Cæsar, and in Egypt we ought to find here and there a native who could remember the building of the Pyramids. It is needless to say that such persons are not to be found.

Were memories, or educative effects in general, inheritable it would not be necessary for us to support schools to instruct youths in reading, writing, and arithmetic. Such knowledge would generally have been inherited from their ancestors, and thus by instructing a few generations in these or other useful branches, we could thereafter dispense with the necessity of further instruction in them. Experience, however, teaches us that if there is any inherited knowledge of this kind, much searching does not suffice to discover it. But consider the evidence furnished by language. Not one, but all the ancestors of many children born in the present generation back for at least several centuries have habitually spoken the English language, yet every child has to be taught the language, and not one has ever been known who came to a knowledge of it without being taught. Surely if an acquired character can be inherited language ought to be, for its use is not occasional and confined to one or a few persons, but habitual and universal. As we find that it has not been inherited in the past, we are forced to the conclusion that it will not be inherited in the future, that in truth it is not inheritable; and the same can be said of any and every mental character which has been brought to the test.

It may be contended, perhaps, that no expectation is to be cherished of the inheritance of a knowledge of the actual words of a language or of any specific knowledge, but that education or habit merely strengthens the particular mental powers brought into activity by them, so that the offspring of a man trained, let us say, in reasoning would be able to acquire the habit of reasoning more readily than he would have done had his parent not exercised that power in the years preceding his birth. In other words, though he might not inherit an actual acquirement, he might inherit a tendency to its acquisition. This is a possible hypothesis — indeed it is a plausible one. The question is, has it been verified — or is it verifiable? Can we test it? Can one or more expectations be adduced from it which may be compared with observation? I am aware that practically everyone believes that the hypothesis is amply verified by experience and the mental and moral traits of individuals and races alike are continually explained as the inherited effects of the habits of their ancestors. Indeed this explanation is so habitually resorted to that many persons appear to believe that no other can be suggested, an assumption which I shall presently show is quite unwarranted. Fortunately, there is one class of cases by which the assumption may be brought to a critical test, which furnishes, in fact, an *experimentum crucis*.

If habit can be transmitted from parent to offspring in such a way that the offspring's power to acquire a given habit depends upon the degree in which the parent practised it, then we should be able to predict that a child whose ancestors had habitually spoken the English language would acquire that language more readily than one whose ancestors had habitually spoken the French language, and similarly a French child would learn the French language much more readily than an English child would. Here is a deduction from the hypothesis which may be readily tested. Does it verify the hypothesis? No, it refutes it. A French child brought up from infancy in England acquires the English language as readily and rapidly as an English child does. Moreover it speaks the language without the slightest accent, provided of course, it is taught by those who have no accent; thus showing that it has not even a faint *tendency* to inherit the French language, and furthermore if it is subsequently taken to France it acquires the French language with as great difficulty as though it were an English child, and speaks it with an English accent quite as strong. Obviously, thousands of cases similar to this have been observed of children brought up in foreign countries, and no evidence to show that they inherit even a tendency to their own language has, so far as I am aware, ever been adduced. Had such a case occurred, it would almost certainly have been proclaimed, for the Neo-Lamarkians have moved heaven and earth to find one solitary case of the unmistakable inheritance of an acquired character, and they have failed. They have, however, discovered many doubtful cases, that is, cases of inheritance which at first sight appear to be due to the Lamarkian factor, but on examination are found to be susceptible of another explanation. They point out that men who have spent their lives in the study of music, or mathematics, or literature, or even politics or war, and become eminent therein, have, more frequently than would have occurred by chance, had children who inherited their talents and who became eminent likewise. The observation in these cases is correct, but the inference is incorrect. Such talents do run in families, but it is spontaneous, not acquired characters, which are inherited, a predisposition, not a habit. If a man devotes his life to music, it is obviously because he has a natural inclination to do so, an inclination as little due to inherited habit as the shape of his nose or the color of his hair, and hence as inheritable as these. It is this natural inclination or predisposition which is inherited and we have good reason to believe that the offspring of a musician would have been just as musical had the parent never touched a piano or never seen a bar of music. Indeed, most of the men who have attained eminence in any art or calling have sprung from parents who did not habitually practise the art or calling before them, although when a person does thus develop peculiar powers it is exceedingly probable that among his immediate ancestors one at least could have been found who, had occasion arisen, would have developed them likewise; just as when we see a very tall man we have reason to expect that, should we search his immediate ancestry, at least one tall man or woman would be found among them. Those who so confidently adopt the Lamarkian explanation of inherited habit appear to ignore the obvious inference that if the ancestors of an individual or race deliberately adopted some habit of mind, which can only mean a habit of centering the attention upon some particular idea or group of ideas, that they adopted it because of a previous predilection or predisposition on their part to centre their attention on that particular idea or group of ideas rather than on others; thus, instead of the habit being the cause of the mental trait, the mental trait was the cause of the habit; and that which was inherited was not the habit, but rather the predisposition that caused it. At any rate, this hypothesis would as completely explain the facts as the other.

Having thus discussed briefly the subject of injuries, and of functional variations, let us as briefly consider those influences which Weismann classes as "climatic." They include all direct effects of the environment, such as temperature, nutrition, presence or absence of specific reagents in the system, diseases, etc. They cannot be classed as injuries, or as effects of use or disuse of parts.

It has been observed in the case of some butterflies, notably *Polyommatus phlœas* belonging to the family *lycœnidœ,* that the color of certain parts of the body depends upon the temperature at which the change from the larval to the mature stage takes place, and that furthermore the effects thus induced directly by the environment are transmissible. Bees by varying the kind and degree of nutriment furnished to the pupæ can cause them to develop into queens, drones, or workers, at will, and an Austrian physician, Dr. Schenk, has claimed that by a somewhat similar variation of nutrition in the case of breeding women he can determine the sex of their offspring.

The hereditary transmission of diseases has always been cited by the Neo-Lamarkians as furnishing evidence to prove their contention; for a disease is certainly an acquired character and

Chap. VI] FIRST FACTOR OF HAPPINESS 217

some diseases may as certainly be transmitted. The experiments of Dr. Brown-Sequard in particular are referred to, who produced epilepsy in guinea pigs by a lesion of the spinal cord, which artificially induced disease was transmitted. The phenomena are, however, susceptible of another and more plausible explanation, as the following extract from Weismann will suffice to make clear:

"There is no doubt that some diseases are passed on from one generation to another. All such cases are not, however, connected with heredity, and many of them are in all probability to be explained as the result of infection of the parental germ-cell with microscopic parasites, and ought consequently to be described as *infections of the germ.*

"In man such a transference of disease has only definitely been proved to occur in the case of syphilis. The father, as well as the mother, is capable of transmitting this disease to the embryo, and the only possible explanation of this fact is, therefore, that the specific bacteria of syphilis can be transmitted by the spermatozoon. Amongst the lower animals the 'pebrine' of the silkworm is an example, which has been well known for several decades, of the transference of a fatal disease from one generation to another through the egg: . . .

"As we now know that many diseases of man and other mammals are due to such low forms of parasites, it is natural to suppose that the transmission of such diseases results from infection of the germ-cell with microbes, and not from inheritance in the true sense of the word — that is, from the transmission of an anomalous state of the germ-plasm itself.

"I have elsewhere attempted to trace the 'heredity' of 'epilepsy,' produced artificially in guinea-pigs, by supposing that in this case a similar process occurs. The slow development of this form of 'epilepsy' resulting from an injury to the spinal cord or one of the larger nerves, seems to me, indeed, to support the conclusion that its symptoms, which resemble those of true epilepsy, are due to the migration of microbes, which advance from the injured part along the nerves in a centripetal direction until they reach the brain, where they set up the state of irritation characteristic of the disease. The great inconstancy of the symptoms, and the variety of forms of nervous diseases which the offspring exhibit, also indicate that a true heredity is not concerned in the process, and that the transmission is in this case due to infection of the germ with the microbes by which the case is induced.

"The 'transmisson' of carcinoma might be accounted for in a similar way,— if, as has recently been supposed, this disease is really due to microbes.

"It is, however, also conceivable that both causes — the transmission of abnormal predispositions and infection of the germ — might combine to bring about the transference of a disease from one generation to another. Without desiring to encroach upon the domain of pathology, I am inclined to suppose that this is the case as regards 'hereditary' tuberculosis: there is no doubt about the occurrence of a 'tuberculous habit'— that is, a certain complication of structural peculiarities which is commonly connected with the disease, such as a narrowness of the chest, for instance. These peculiarities must result from the structure of the germ-plasm, in which a definite variation of certain determinants and groups of determinants must have taken place, and they are therefore certainly transmissible. The disease itself, however, is not due to this 'habit,' but is caused by the presence of specific parasites, the tubercle-bacilli, which have a harmful effect upon the various living tissues. They may be introduced artificially into the blood, and then produce the disease even in perfectly normal individuals. They may, moreover, enter the body 'spontaneously,' e. g., by some natural means, and will then also give rise to the disease. But in the latter case the probability of infection seems largely to depend upon the susceptibility or power of resistance of the individual, and at the present day pathologists are of opinion that persons exhibiting the 'tuberculous habit' already referred to have a much slighter power of resistance to the parasites which have passed into the body than strongly-built people. The inheritance of the disease would accordingly depend on the transmission of a constitution very liable to infection.

"Without wishing to deny the existence of such a predisposition to infection, I do not believe that the transmission of tuberculosis is due merely to the inheritance of a greater degree of susceptibility. A large number of facts seem to me, on the contrary, to support the view that *infection of the germ plays the chief part* in the process." [1]

Concerning the alleged inheritance of drunkenness, Weismann says:

"It has often been supposed that drunkenness of the parents at the time of conception may have harmful effect on the nature of the offspring. The child is said to be born in a weak bodily and mental condition, and inclined to idiocy, or even to madness, etc., although the parents may be quite normal both physically and mentally.

"Cases certainly exist in which drunken parents have given rise to a completely normal child, although this is not a convincing proof against the above-named view; and in spite of the fact that most, or perhaps even all, the statements with regard to the inju-

[1] Ibid: p. 387.

rious effects on the offspring will not bear a very close criticism, I am unwilling to entirely deny the *possibility* that a harmful influence may be exerted in such cases. These, however, have nothing to do with heredity, but are concerned with an *affection of the germ by means of an external influence.*

"The experiments of the brothers Hertwig show that the development of the fertilized egg in lower animals may be considerably retarded by the action of various chemical substances, such as chloral, quinine, and morphia; and we also know that the ova of sea-urchins, if kept too long in the sea-water before being fertilized, tend to lose their vital energy, and consequently many spermatozoa, instead of a single one, are likely to enter each of them. A similar result may follow from the effects of the above-mentioned chemical reagents, and in both cases an abnormal development of the egg, such as a duplication of parts may be the consequence.

"It does not appear to me impossible that an intermixture of alcohol with the blood of the parents may produce similiar effects on the ovum and sperm-cell. According to the relative quantity of alcohol, either an exciting or a depressing influence might be exerted, either of which would lead to abnormal development." [1]

It appears from these extracts that the effects produced directly on the germ by its environment can scarcely be classed as inheritances. Infection is not inheritance, and the direct effects of environment, not due to infection, may be distinguished from inheritance by a fundamental difference in character which may be brought out as follows: Inheritance is always detectable by the resemblance existing between one or more characters of an individual and corresponding characters occurring in one or more of its ancestors. If a father has red hair and his son black hair, it would not be said that the son inherited the color of his hair from his father, would it? Certainly not. There is no resemblance between the color of the father's hair and that of the son, and resemblance is necessary for the detection of inheritance. Between two characters, one of which is said to be inherited from the other there is a causal connection. Weismann has made it appear probable that the relation is not that between cause and effect, but rather between effects of a common cause. Into his theory we need not enter. The universal relation which holds in all true inheritances, however, is, that between the characters thus causally related there is a resemblance. The case is very different with characters caused by peculiarities of environment. There is

[1] Ibid: p. 386.

no detectable resemblance between a high temperature and a dark color which appear to stand in the relation of cause and effect in the case of the experiments cited on *Polyommatus phlœas,* and as to the determination of sex by the variation of the food supply in bees, and perhaps in human beings, in what sense can masculinity or femininity be said to resemble any particular kind or degree of nutriment? There is no resemblance to be detected between the characters thus causally related. Indeed, the characters due to the direct action of the environment should be classed as effects due to prenatal experience, rather than inheritance. It may be asked how an individual can have an experience before he has even begun to exist? He does not, but that from which he arises does. An individual may be said to begin to exist at the moment of fertilization of the ovum by the spermatozoon, but before fertilization these sexual elements, from the conjunction of which the individual originates, may, and do, undergo experiences — that is, are acted upon by their environment, and the effect of such experiences may persist in the organism and may even become inheritable; but so far as is known, it is only experiences of the germ itself which can thus give rise to inheritable characters. Somatogenic experiences have no inheritable effects. That all the so-called climatic effects should be classed as results of experience rather than of inheritance is clearly seen when we consider that they, in common with all the experiences of an individual, exhibit no resemblance to that with which they are causally connected, whereas inheritances do. A man who inherits a Roman nose inherits it from some one whose nose resembled his, but when a man's nose is broken by the impact of a stone, it cannot be said that the nose thereafter resembles the stone.

But whether we care to call the transmitted effects of "climatic" influences inheritances or results of prenatal experience, it is equally obvious that they can have no influence in changing an inefficient stock into an efficient one by education, because the effect in this class of cases has no resemblance to the cause. Hence the influence of the education of a parent on his offspring would be as likely to make that offspring less intelligent as it would to make him more intelligent, and it might have more influence on the faculty of digestion than on that of thought.

Thus from an examination of the three classes of acquired characters *injuries* or *mutilations, functional variations,* and *climatic* or *environmental* effects, we are led to the conclusion that characters acquired by the individual, that is, the somatic individual, are not transmissible, though such as are directly imposed upon the germ may be; and this latter fact often gives rise to the belief that the experiences of a somatic individual are inheritable. Obviously it is the possible transmissibility of the experiences of the somatic individual which is of interest to us, and the reasoning whereby we conclude that they are not transmissible may be summarized thus:

If acquired characters are inheritable, the inheritance of some unmistakable acquired character would be observed.

The inheritance of an unmistakable acquired character has not been observed.

Therefore acquired characters are not inheritable.

This is a hypothetical syllogism, such as that whereby all hypotheses are tested. By an examination of the corresponding syllogism whereby the hypothesis of universal gravitation is tested we shall find that the grounds upon which the two hypotheses are established are similar. Of course, neither syllogism establishes more than a probable conclusion.

If gravitation were not universal, one or more unmistakable instances of a material body devoid of gravitation would have been observed.

No instances of a material body devoid of gravitation have been observed.

Therefore gravitation is universal.

The minor premise in each of the above syllogisms is merely a record of experience. The justification for the assertion of the major premise rests upon the grounds we have for believing that the instances observed are fair samples of the instances observable. In the case of gravitation this is generally conceded. Many billions of billions of bodies have been tested as to their property of gravitation and none have been found devoid of that property; a vastly greater number exist which have not been tested — which, indeed, are not testable — such as the bulk of the rocks below the surface of the earth, any fragment of which *might* turn out to be without weight; nevertheless, the instances observed are considered fair samples of the instances observable, and if bodies devoid of gravitation exist, they must at any rate be very rare, or they would almost certainly have been observed, considering the great extension of the range of observation. Euler's remark that " although he had never made trial of the stones which compose the church of Magdeburg, yet he had not the least doubt that all of them were heavy and would fall if unsupported" illustrates our point, that we judge of the untestable cases by the testable ones — of the unobserved by the observed.

On precisely similar grounds the non-inheritability of acquired characters is established. Acquired characters may be divided into (1) Those whose inheritability is testable. (2) Those whose inheritability is not testable. The confidence with which our major premise may be asserted depends upon how fair a sample the instances belonging to the first class are of those belonging to the second. Nor does the fairness of the sample depend on the numerical proportion between the two. This we have pointed out in Chapter 2, but for the sake of clearness will illustrate its application to the induction we are considering. If we are drawing balls from a huge ballot box, containing say 10,000,000 balls, half of which are white and half of which are black, we need not draw the whole 10,000,000 balls in order to get a good idea of the relative proportion between white and black balls, provided the balls are mixed and not segregated. After we have drawn fifty or one hundred we shall be able to draw a fairly good conclusion. If, however, we have independent reasons for believing that the balls are segregated, that is, that the balls drawn are not a fair sample of those not drawn, then our conclusion will be vitiated. Suppose instances of inheritable acquired characters to be represented by black balls and instances of non-inheritable acquired characters to be represented by white balls. Then from the great ballot box of nature it is found that we draw nothing but white balls, and we draw millions of them. Therefore we conclude that the ballot box contains white balls only, though we have no means of making our conclusion other than probable. It may be that the balls are so unequally distributed that about the particular parts of the ballot box from which we are able to draw, white balls only are congregated, but until some reason is given for thinking this we are entitled to believe that the sample drawn is a fair one. The instances of acquired characters which are testable and have been tested include mental as well as physical characters, injuries, functional variations, and environmental effects, yet among them not a single unmistakable case of inheritance is to be observed. This, of course, is too significant to be ignored, and forces us to the conclusion that if nature can and does produce inheritable acquired characters she at any rate carefully confines them to the class of non-testable characters; so carefully indeed that by no oversight is one included among the millions of testable cases. Such an assumption is extremely improbable and until some reason is given for making it we are not entitled to do so. The burden of proof is upon those who make the assumption.

Thus the second hypothesis (p. 209) is disposed of, and as the third is our only alternative we are forced to admit it and to conclude that *no acquired characters are inheritable.*

Before leaving this subject I desire to emphasize one point. In order to prove the inheritance of an acquired character it is necessary to establish by observation the truth of two propositions. (1) That a given individual A has a given characteristic b which was *unmistakably* acquired, and not inherited by him. (2) That the characteristic b appeared in one or more of the offspring of A. A very few observations of this character — sufficient to convince us that they were not mere coincidences — would establish the Lamarkian contention. Many persons think they know of such observations; but if they will carefully test them they will, I feel assured, find that they fail to fulfil condition (1). The character inherited must be *unmistakably* an acquired one — if there is doubt about the matter it is clear that the conditions required for proof are not fulfilled.

I have thus examined the subject of the inheritability of acquired characters at considerable length for two reasons: first because the conclusion arrived at has immediate application to the most vital problems now before the American people, and particularly vital to their posterity: and second because the practically universal belief is directly contrary to that which the evidence establishes. It is a very general conviction, and one almost ineradicable, that an inferior race may be converted into a superior one by changing its surroundings, and particularly by the influence of education. A fair sample of the prevailing opinion is that expressed by Jacob Riis in the "Battle with the Slum," in which he says "You have got your boy and the heredity of the next one when you can order his setting." The fact is "his setting" can, and obviously does, influence the boy, but it has not one iota of influence on the heredity of the next one, and as we shall presently show, it is fortunate for the human race that it has not. The individual may be elevated by education but not the race. If, for example, we assume that the negro race is an inferior one — is congenitally deficient in intelligence and character as compared with the white race (I do not assert that it is, but simply assume it for the sake of illustration) — then the conclusion we have established entitles us to predict that unless some other means than mere changed environment, including education, is adopted, that it will permanently remain congenitally deficient in intelligence and character; that the negro child born after ten or one hundred or one thousand generations of education will start from exactly the same point as the child whose ancestors received no education at all. I am aware that this assertion will be emphatically denied and that the advance in civilization of various races will be adduced as evidence that it is unfounded. The assertion, however, rests upon the evidence we have cited in the foregoing discussion, and is entirely unshaken by the advance of any community in civilization, whether such advance is material merely or moral and mental likewise. For in such an advance, the individuals of each succeeding generation are educated better than those of the preceding generation; knowledge continually accumulates and as a result the arts continually advance, but the race remains stationary; that is, the congenital characteristics, the intellectual and moral capacity or efficiency of the race is not altered. The average individual of one generation may, after he has been educated, be an improvement upon the average individual of the generation preceding, but this is simply because he has been better educated, mentally and morally, not because his capacity for education or improvement, his potentiality for cultivation, is any greater. The level of intelligence and character from which he starts is exactly the same as that of his ancestors of a thousand years before. The effects of education and inheritance are continually confused, and hence the effects due to an improved education are continually attributed to an improved inheritance. As well might an engineer infer that he had improved the quality of his engine and boiler from the observation that when he used better coal he obtained a better efficiency. As well might a farmer infer that he had produced an improved variety of corn from the observation that on sowing the same seed in soil better and better fertilized he obtained a better and better crop.

But, it may be objected, what difference does it make if we can continually improve individuals by bringing them up in continually improved surroundings, why should we care at what level they start? What we desire to obtain is individuals of intelligence and character — efficient individuals — we do not care how we get them. The reply to the criticism implied in this observation is that although by ignoring congenital capacity, and continually improving education we can get a continually improving assemblage of individuals, yet the assemblage of individuals so obtained will not be nearly so efficient, will not be nearly equal in intelligence and character to those who might be obtained if we considered *both* factors of the problem — inheritance and education — race and training. The greater the congenital capacity, the higher the level from which an individual starts, the more will any given amount of education accomplish. We might spend six hours a day for twenty years in educating a born dullard and never do more perhaps than make him fit for the duties say of a shipping clerk, whereas one-tenth the same amount of educational effort expended on the mind of a Newton, a Faraday, or a Lincoln, would convert it into a mighty engine for the advancement of mankind. He would be a shallow engineer who inferred that because he had prospects of a continually improving quality of coal that therefore nothing was to be gained by improving the efficiency of his boiler, upon which its capacity for converting the energy of the coal into steam depends. He would be a shallow farmer who concluded that because he had prospects of a progressively improving quality of fertilizer that therefore it made no difference what kind of corn he planted — whether a variety yielding forty bushels to the acre or one yielding only twenty bushels under the same conditions. It is not by improvements in fertilizers and methods of cultivation alone that agriculture advances, but by improvement in breeds and to improve a breed fertilization and cultivation of the soil is of no value.

Having thus discussed the possible means of advancing a stock — of increasing its efficiency of conversion by inheritance — we must consider what means are adapted to deteriorate it — to diminish its efficiency — for both in wild and domesticated organisms retrogression is to be observed as well as improvement, and it is as important to prevent the first as to promote the second. We have seen that races may be improved by the method of selection, but not by that of education. By the same evidence we may infer that deterioration may result from selection, but that from education (with one class of exceptions) we have nothing to fear. Let us take up the latter topic first and see just what education can and cannot do to deteriorate a race.

And first, as to injuries. We cannot produce a mutilated or deformed breed by mutilating or deforming their parents: second, as to functional variations, we cannot make a race weak physically by preventing their progenitors from exercising their bodies, or weak mentally by withholding from said progenitors the means of education: neither can the results of immoral practices (unless they have certain secondary effects to be discussed presently) or of acquired infirmities of will be visited by the parent upon its offspring through inheritance. Many persons perceive that by means of the alleged power of modifying breeds by the inheritance of acquired characters mankind might be indefinitely and rapidly elevated mentally, morally, and physically, but they appear not to perceive that had such a power been in operation throughout history the human race would, by this time, have been in such a condition of mental and moral degeneration as to offer but a poor subject for improvement. If the use of the intellectual faculties can elevate a race mentally, their disuse can deteriorate it mentally: if the habitual exercise of will power, self-control, and virtue can raise a race morally, the habitual practice of self-indulgence and vice can lower it morally. If civilization can advance a race by inheritance, savagery can retrograde it by the same means. Most races have never known any civilization; hence if barbarous practices have a deteriorating effect on breeds most races have been deteriorating ever since the human breed originated, and the men of to-day must be fearfully degenerate compared with those of twenty thousand years ago, for the baleful effects of their "setting" have been accumulating for six hundred generations. Hence to bring the members of these races back to the condition in which they were twenty thousand years ago we must, according to the Lamarkians, by the inherited effects of an improved "setting" nullify the accumulated degeneracy of six hundred generations. The prospect is not encouraging. Even the most civilized races are but partially and recently emerged from barbarism, and hence they are, as far as the alleged inherited effects of their improved condition goes, in practically the same position as their savage contemporaries. What are a few centuries of civilization to ten thousand or one hundred thousand years of savagery? Fortunately for the human race, however, acquired characters are not inherited, and barbarism through lack of education has involved no race degeneracy, as civilization through education can involve no race improvement.

When the third class of acquired characters, climatic effects, or those induced directly by the environment, are examined, a means of deterioration is discovered. Any diseased or morbid physical condition, whether the result of accident or of vicious or unhealthy practices, which disseminates through the system of the parent that which may infect or poison the germ-plasm itself will probably result in a diseased or enfeebled issue, and a race whose habits are such as to foster infectious diseases or alcoholism will inevitably deteriorate; but that these effects are not inheritances, but due to prenatal experience is made clear by one test, viz., that they are not indefinitely transmissible. If, for example, a parent A acquires an infectious disease which he transmits to his offspring B, and B by wholesome living or other means rids himself of that disease before himself breeding, then his offspring C will not inherit the disease, nor will there be any tendency to it in any of the offspring of C, immediate or remote. This, of course, is not true of predispositions to disease, or of any spontaneous characteristic. Supernumerary digits, for instance, whether amputated or not, are indefinitely transmissible, and their complete absence in one generation does not insure their absence in subsequent generations. Thus the transmission of "climatic" effects is further to be distinguished from inheritance.

When we turn from the method of education to that of selection we find a potent agent of race degeneration. It is, in fact, much easier to breed an inferior race by selection than a superior one; and in modern society there are a number of causes in constant operation which are steadily deteriorating the breed of all civilized communities. Uncivilized communities are also subject to some degenerating influences, but these are counteracted by influences of an opposite tendency. So far as I have knowledge no cause of race elevation is put in operation by civilization, while those contrary in tendency are fostered by it. At the same time it eradicates those causes which in savage society tend to prevent degeneracy. No peril which threatens the human race is so grave as that of degeneracy; yet those in power, who alone are in a position to do anything to check its progress, are ignorant of the whole matter. I know of no more lucid exposition of this subject than that contained in President Jordan's brief essay entitled "The Blood of the Nation." The object of the essay is to show that while it is true that the "blood of a nation determines its history," it is equally true that the "history of a nation determines its blood." Any nation whose history sets agencies in operation which result in the selection of the inefficient must shortly become degenerate. The philosophers of history are fond of telling us that nations, like individuals, must inevitably decline and die, and vaguely imagining that it is so much a part of the eternal order of things as to be uncaused and inscrutable, they usually make no effort to discover the cause of the phenomenon. But like other effects it has a cause, and a slight examination of the history of great nations reveals it. Civilization sows the seeds of its own destruction by inducing racial decay. It suspends the natural selection which among savages neutralizes the tendency to decay, and in its place substitutes agencies which hasten the nation to its doom. These agencies are not always the same, but they all operate in the same manner — they result in the selection of the inefficient and incapable of each generation to be the breeders of the next. As President Jordan says:

"A race of men or a herd of cattle are governed by the same laws of selection. Those who survive inherit the traits of their own actual ancestry. In the herd of cattle, to destroy the strongest bulls, the fairest cows, the most promising calves, is to allow those not strong nor fair nor promising to become the parents of the coming herd. Under this influence the herd will deteriorate, although the individuals of the inferior herd are no worse than their own actual parents. Such a process is called race degeneration, and it is the only race degeneration known in the history of cattle or men. The scrawny, lean, infertile herd is the natural offspring of the same type of parents."

Spain, the greatest nation of mediæval Europe, bred a degenerate race because the best of her breed either entered the celibate clergy and left no posterity, or were killed or driven from the country by the Inquisition because they had the ability to think for themselves. Hence the mediocrities and clowns were left to become the parents of the succeeding generations, and Spain, after the Reformation, was rapidly shorn of her power because she could not furnish the men capable of retaining it. A similar cause has had a similar effect in other Latin nations.

War is a potent cause of degeneracy in all nations which encourage the best of their breed to enlist. Warlike nations rapidly decay, for if the best are killed in large numbers the inferior residue will furnish the characteristics of the succeeding generation. This cannot be continued long without producing a nation of incapables. Jordan brings out this point with power:

"Greece died because the men who made her glory had all passed away and left none of their kin and therefore none of their kind. ' 'Tis Greece, but living Greece no more' ; for the Greek of to-day, for the most part, never came from the loins of Leonidas or Miltiades. He is the son of the stable-boys and scullions and slaves of the day of her glory, those of whom imperial Greece could make no use in her conquest of Asia." . . .

"Why did Rome fall? It was not because untrained hordes were stronger than disciplined legions. It was not that she grew proud, luxurious, corrupt, and thereby gained a legacy of physical weakness. We read of her wealth, her extravagance, her indolence and vice; but all this caused only the downfall of the enervated, the vicious, and the indolent. The Roman legions did not riot in wealth. The Roman generals were not all entangled in the wiles of Cleopatra."

"'The Roman Empire,' says Seeley, 'perished for want of men.' You will find this fact on the pages of every history, though few have pointed out war as the final and necessary cause of the Roman downfall. In his recent noble history of the 'Downfall of the Ancient World' ('Der Untergang der Antiken Welt,' 1897), Professor Otto Seeck of Greifeswald, makes this fact very apparent. The cause of the fall of Rome is found in the 'extinction of the best' ('Die Ausrottung der Besten'), and all that remains to the historian is to give the details of this extermination. He says, 'In Greece a wealth of spiritual power went down in the suicidal wars.' In Rome 'Marius and Cinna slew the aristocrats by hundreds and thousands. Sulla destroyed no less thoroughly the democrats, and whatever of noble blood survived fell as an offering to the proscription of the triumvirate.' 'The Romans had less of spontaneous power to lose than the Greeks, and so desolation came to them all the sooner. He who was bold enough to rise politically was almost without exception thrown to the ground. *Only, cowards remained, and from their brood came forward the new generations.* Cowardice showed iself in lack of originality and slavish following of masters and traditions.' Had the Romans been still alive, the Romans of the old republic, neither inside nor outside forces could have worked the fall of Rome."

The fearful mortality of the American Civil War left the Americans a poorer race; for the best of both sections were sacrificed and for such a loss no amount of advancement in the arts and education can compensate. It means a permanent loss of efficiency in the race which peoples North America and in their posterity forever.

Civilization supplies other means of race deterioration and some of them are discussed by President Jordan, but the most potent of all, so far as the modern ideal of civilization is concerned, he completely ignores. As it will be more appropriately discussed in connection with its causes (p. 373) I shall not consider it here.

So much for inheritance as a means of altering for better or worse the individual efficiency of a nation or of society. It is at once the most potent for good or for ill of all the determinants of happiness. Whether society will ever sufficiently advance to appreciate and act upon the knowledge of the subject already available, time alone will determine, but there is strong reason to hope that it will. Already sufficient knowledge concerning heredity has been accumulated to insure to the nation which will but act upon it, not only immunity from decay and death, but the moral, material, and political supremacy of the earth.

The second method of altering the efficiency of the individual for the better (or worse) is by education. We have already seen that as a means of altering a race education is powerless, but as a means of altering the individual it is potent. I have no intention of entering into a detailed discussion of the subject at this point, but shall confine myself to some of the fundamental principles of education, as they are deducible from the theory of utility. Useful education is simply a means of increasing the efficiency of individuals as agents for the conversion of potential into actual happiness — of converting terrestrial resources to useful purposes. It may modify individuals physically, mentally, and morally.

The discussion of physical education need not detain us long. As good health is the most vital of purely physical characteristics, the means best adapted to maintain it, as fast as these are discovered by the study of hygiene and medicine, should become a matter of common knowledge. I do not mean that all mankind should study medicine, but that an understanding of the laws of health should be generally diffused. If everyone, for example, were forewarned concerning the ease with which evil habits — such as the drinking habit — are acquirable by human beings, it would be a factor in preventing such evils. A public knowledge of the utility of quarantining contagious diseases and of taking other measures for maintaining the health of a community is also desirable.

The degree in which physical training should enter into the education of youth is a matter of detail not suitable for discussion here. That some training, and deliberate training, should be had is now generally acknowledged, but to permit it to monopolize attention to the exclusion of other training, as among the Greeks, is short-sighted policy. Modern communities, nevertheless, might profit by the Greek example. Were means adopted to stimulate interest in athletics among the youth of great cities by organizing contests in which all could compete, it would divert much attention and energy now devoted to the acquisition of vices and the commission of crimes. It would serve as a stepping stone to better things and would be well adapted to enlist the interest of those whose opportunities have been so restricted as to afford scant resources for intellectual enjoyment.

As a means of cultivating the mind education has two immediate aims. (1) To supply information. (2) To train the faculties. These functions are co-essential. Educators deem the second one paramount, because a trained faculty has a wider application than all but the most fundamental and universal of information. A musician trained in his art can apply his skill to any particular piece of, or occasion for, music which the exigencies of his vocation may demand, whereas a routine knowledge of even a vast number of musical compositions would not confer such a power. A trained observer can apply his powers wherever the faculty of observation may be exercised. A man whose powers of reasoning have been cultivated can make inferences as well in one department of knowledge as in another, provided his intuitionism is equally distributed. Mere information, however extended, cannot provide the means of dealing with the new and involved exigencies which life presents and by which men's acts, for better or worse, must be determined. Hence the effort of deliberate education is, or should be, directed more to the training of man's faculties than to the acquisition of varied information. Certain vital and fundamental information, however, must be, and is, supplied. The more men specialize, the more information they require in their speciality, and as knowledge increases, specialization becomes more and more a necessity.

Although it is desirable that a man's education should be in progress throughout life, and in alert minds it generally is, it must be and is recognized that the earlier portion of life is that in which systematic education is desirable. There are two principal reasons for this. The first is particularly obvious. Since the efficiency induced by education is only that of an individual lifetime, the earlier that efficiency is developed the greater will be the proportional part of life during which it is effective. The second reason is but little less obvious than the first. The capacity to acquire information and to mould the faculties is, in general, greater during youth than in maturity. Hence educational effort is more effective at that period. The capacity to acquire beliefs and habits of thought is particularly great in youth and in some minds is practically confined to that period of life. Professor James remarks:

"Outside of their own business the ideas gained by men before they are twenty-five are practically the only ideas they shall have in their lives. They *cannot* get anything new. Disinterested curiosity is passed, the mental grooves and channels set, the power of assimilation gone." [1]

The significance of the characteristic of human nature here mentioned, in all its vast consequences to the race, we shall discuss presently.

After the acquisition of certain fundamental branches — the notation of knowledge — reading, writing, and some others, the course of systematic education separates into two rather distinct lines of effort — into *academic* and *technical* education. The first seeks to supply men with the means of utilizing their time in the production of happiness by cultivating their musical, artistic, literary, or other tastes, by the indulgence of which happiness is directly produced. The second seeks to supply the means of utilizing time in the production of means to happiness by training men in law, medicine, engineering, etc. By the application of knowledge so acquired the terrestrial conditions essential to the maintenance of happiness are secured. Academic education is concerned primarily with the fine arts; technical education with the so-called useful arts. The restriction of the designation *useful* to the arts concerned in the production of wealth well illustrates the prevailing confusion as to the nature of usefulness. The fine arts are, in fact, more immediately useful than the useful arts, since they produce happiness directly, while the useful arts produce it indirectly if at all, and we shall hereafter give reasons for believing that, as society is at present constituted, they fail to subserve any immediate useful end whatever.

Academic education, of course, should increase man's efficiency, both in his primary and secondary capacity. It should, in the first place, seek to promote the simplicity and variety of his tastes by increasing his sensitiveness to the possibilities of

[1] Principles of Psychology, Vol. 2, p. 402.

happiness in his surroundings, by opening his mind to the beauties of nature and of art, by giving him access through literature to companionship with the great minds of the past and present, by revealing to him the intrinsically interesting character of the animate and inanimate world of which he is a portion. To a responsive mind more pleasure will be yielded by the exploration of a rocky pasture than will be derived by an insensate one from contemplation of all the wonders of the earth. Academic education should seek to so increase man's mental resources as to make him a pleasant companion to himself. If companionable to himself he generally will not fail to be companionable to others, and thus by adding to the possibilities of happiness in the surroundings of others he will augment their happiness, and through sympathy his own.

One defect in modern academic training is particularly conspicuous — a defect which, by sheer force of inertia, persists, though recognized and condemned by numerous critics on both sides of the Atlantic. I refer to the study of dead languages in secondary schools and as a part of the regular curriculum in colleges. Had educators a clear, instead of a vague, idea of the function of education they would see that the time now occupied in attempting to teach Latin and Greek could be utilized to far greater advantage in the acquisition of other knowledge now neglected. But the end they seek is not clear, hence they cannot determine their course by a deliberate adaptation of means to attain it, but are compelled to drift along in the direction determined by tradition, seeking and failing to attain the ideal of a past age. It is a clear case of control by dogma. Latin was in the past the language of the learned world. All the scholars of the Middle Ages and even of later times used it. Hence in the past, book knowledge was inaccessible to him who was ignorant of the language. But a couple of centuries ago things began to change, translations were made and scholars begun writing in modern tongues: the ideal of education, however, did not change much. The tool of the scholar became the bauble of the pedant. Men were deemed deep who uttered platitudes in Latin, though no one ever found what they said in modern tongues worth alluding to; and the shallowest conversation, if embellished with classic quotations, was considered profound. The ability to compose bad Latin hexameters was of more importance in the colleges than any amount of scientific knowledge. Sydney Smith's comments on this curious symptom of dogmatism are amusing:

"A learned man! — a scholar! — a man of erudition! Upon whom are these epithets of approbation bestowed? Are they given to men acquainted with the science of government? thoroughly masters of the geographical and commercial relations of Europe? to men who know the properties of bodies, and their action upon each other? No: this is not learning; it is chemistry, or political economy — not learning. The distinguishing abstract term, the epithet of Scholar, is reserved for him who writes on the Æolic reduplication, and is familiar with the Syllburgian method of arranging defectives in ω and μ. The picture which a young Englishman, addicted to the pursuit of knowledge, draws,— his *beau ideal* of human nature — his top and consummation of man's powers — is a knowledge of the Greek language. His object is not to reason, to imagine, or to invent; but to conjugate, decline, and derive. The situations of imaginary glory which he draws for himself, are the detection of an anapæst in the wrong place, or the restoration of a dative case which Cranzius had passed over, and the never-dying Ernesti failed to observe."

Conditions have improved since this was written, but in the higher institutions of learning the old ideal survives. The requirement of Latin or Greek in the colleges forces the preparatory schools to teach them. Thus, during a course lasting several years, the student's attention is monopolized by studies which will never be of any use, and which as a means of mental discipline have not nearly the value of others now neglected. The claim made is that these studies are a necessary preparation for the humanities — that the great classics of antiquity which are profaned by translation are thus rendered accessible to the student. Were this claim just, it would be some excuse for the system, but experience proves it preposterous. Less than one out of a hundred of those who go through the years of preparation ever acquire sufficient proficiency to appreciate the literary value of Homer, Sophocles, Virgil or Horace. Students may labor through book after book of the Iliad or Eneid with the help of grammar and dictionary, but their attention is so centered upon syntax that poetry is excluded. These works are about as much appreciated by the school boy who reads them as a part of his daily task, as Shakespeare would be by a child in the third reader, compelled to wade through Hamlet by the aid of "ponies" in words of one syllable. Indeed, the effect of so-called "classical" training is more often than not to create a genuine distaste for the classics by associating them in the student's mind with unprofitable drudgery, and at the end of his course he is usually prepared to echo with enthusiasm the parting salutation of Byron: "Then, farewell, Horace, whom I hated so!"

When we turn from academic to technical education we find no such dominance of dogma. This is because it is a thing of recent development and has no traditions to retard it. As the useful arts are founded upon science, technical education is scientific, and though much of the information imparted has no popular interest and does not pretend to have, its value as mental training is much greater than the study of languages, or even of history. Hence technical education attains its immediate end with a much greater degree of success than academic. The present work claims to be a contribution to technology. Its aim is to show how the production of happiness, considered as an art whose practice and promotion should be the sole object of society, may be founded upon the inductive or common-sense method, just as at the present time the art of producing cotton fabrics or sulphuric acid or glass-ware is founded upon that method. It seeks to supply a technology of happiness of which all other branches of technology are, or rather should be, but tributaries. Unless these tributaries flow to a common end, and that end the totality of happiness, they, and the arts founded upon them, become useless and valueless — indeed, as we shall have occasion to show, they may become harmful. To lose sight of this is to lose sight of the whole object of industry, of art, and of the technology upon which they are founded. Technical education is adapted more to the increase of a man's efficiency in his secondary capacity than in his primary, because the applications of technical knowledge are of a nature to affect the welfare of society as a whole; but in a measure it is useful in both capacities.

In what degree the moral elements in man, *will* and *altruism*, may be cultivated is a matter of speculation. No systematic effort to accomplish either object has ever been undertaken. Will has been completely neglected, though its deliberate cultivation, if as effective as with the faculty of reasoning, would result in extraordinary benefits. In the first place, it would increase man's capacity to deliberately choose the right, for it takes will power to select alternatives opposed to self-interest; and yet these are often right. In the second place, it would afford him the assurance that his determination was sufficient to go through with difficult tasks from which men, conscious of feeble will power, would shrink; and this is often useful, for undertakings hard and painful in their inception may result in ultimate benefits which more than compensate for the evils involved. In the third place, it would supply the best foundation for what we have referred to as *adaptibility*, the third factor of adjustability — the capacity to adapt our desires to our ability to satisfy them. Men may achieve happiness by either getting what they want, or wanting what they get; desires may be gratified by adapting the conditions to the desires, or the desires to the conditions To do the second requires will — hence man's first impulse is to do the first; but the second would as frequently, or more frequently, be the better alternative were man's faculties educated as they perhaps might be. Adaptability is the essence of stoicism, and Marcus Aurelius clearly portrays the attitude of mind which that school of philosophers cultivated:

"Is it not better to use what is in thy power like a free man than to desire in a slavish and abject way what is not in thy power? And who has told thee that the gods do not aid us, even in the things which are in our power? Begin then to pray for such things, and thou wilt see. One man prays thus: How shall I be able to possess that woman? Do thou pray thus: How shall I not desire to possess her? Another prays thus: How shall I be released from this? Pray thou: How shall I not desire to be released? Another thus: How shall I not lose my little son? Thou thus: How shall I not be afraid to lose him? In fine, turn thy prayers this way, and see what comes?"

When no benefit can accrue from keeping the attention upon a subject, it is clearly best to deliberately exclude it from the mind, centering the attention upon some subject from which benefit *can* accrue. The philosophy of adaptability has never been better expressed than in the familiar dilemma of Mother Goose:

"For every evil under the sun
There is a remedy, or there is **none**.
If there be one, try and find it,
If there be none, never mind it."

Had sentient beings sufficient control over attention, were desire entirely a matter of volition, other factors of happiness would require little discussion. Enjoyment could be had from any occupation simply by taking thought, and all pain, and with it all evil, would be at an end. Men could be happy on the rack or at the stake. Under such circumstances happiness would be independent of external conditions. While means of realizing such a state of things have never been proposed, there is no doubt that a consistent training of the will would render man far less the sport of circumstances than he is. The education of the Stoics involved such training, but it has no counterpart in modern education — a defect which educators should strive to correct.

Rather more attention is paid to the cultivation of altruism than of will. The most potent factors in our country for the stimulation of altruism are the home, or other habitual association, and in a less degree the church and the school. In the majority of homes children from their earliest years are taught courtesy and the church reinforces this teaching by inculcating the moral code of Christianity — which in its simplicity is an ideally altruistic code. But it is a matter of familiar experience that altruism may be taught more effectively by example than by precept. Hence it is of little use for parents who practise discourtesy to attempt by precept to instil courtesy into their children, and it is equally ineffective for ministers to preach the Golden Rule and then fail to practise it. Altruism between man and man is so easily distinguished from egotism that little mental effort is required to acquire a knowledge of the distinction. It is this fact which so frequently helps to deceive men into thinking that everyone knows the difference between right and wrong. In the simple everyday relations between man and man the difference between right and wrong is indeed practically identical with that between individual altruism and egotism, but in the more complex affairs which involve the policy of states right may not so easily be distinguished from wrong. A far more thorough knowledge of the relations between men and their environment — animate and inanimate — is required, and intuitionism is not adapted to reveal it. When dealing with such affairs, to be practical we must first be profound.

In private morality there is little need of multiplying explanations or precepts, and much need of cultivating an altruistic habit. Naturally, a system of moral discipline, of punishments and rewards, whereby the powerful impulses of self-interest are utilized is almost essential to the successful formation of such a habit — but such a system would operate automatically in a community which consistently practised altruism, and a child brought up therein would acquire the habit without the necessity of precept, simply by imitation.

The public approval involved in conformity to, and the disapproval involved in departure from, the prevailing practice would be sufficient discipline for all save those most powerfully predisposed to egotism. For them a sterner discipline would be required, a discipline which could hardly be classed as a branch of education, though not without educative features.

Of the characteristics of home life best adapted to promote altruism there is little need to speak. It is a well worn subject. Example is the most powerful instrument of instruction. Discipline, when required, should be consistent. When breaches of the adopted code invariably and promptly meet with punishment, the necessity for punishment may be almost dispensed with. On the other hand, an inconsistent and lax discipline fails to accomplish its object, though it involves, in the end, more punishment than strict discipline. This rule holds as well for a community as for a family. The most merciful discipline is the strictest, though strict discipline does not imply a restricted code of conduct. Neither in the family nor in the community should punishment be dictated by passion. Discipline is an instrument of Justice and Justice cannot accept emotion of any kind as a guide.

It is a common opinion that the function of the church as a factor in moral education is a subject excluded from the sphere of science, and not adapted to treatment by the scientific method. Such an opinion must be erroneous, for whatever is excluded from science is excluded from common sense, since the methods of the two are identical. Conduct not controlled by common sense is fortuitously controlled, and codes of morals, like codes of belief, left to the whims of intuitionism, whether of individuals or of communities, are left to chance. The church attempts to provide for the guidance of mankind two systems, more or less associated with one another: (1) A system of morality. (2) A system of cosmology, usually called theology. The first claims to inform us concerning the rightness and wrongness of conduct. The second claims to inform us concerning the truth or untruth of propositions — particularly of certain propositions respecting the origin, history, and destiny of the universe, and of man as one of the sentient beings inhabiting it; and, moreover, the church claims that its system of morality is deducible from its system of cosmology. It claims that because the universe and man had a particular origin and history, and will have a particular destiny, that certain kinds of conduct are right and certain other kinds wrong. Thus arises the prevailing theological system of morals, founded upon a series of syllogisms of the following form: Acts which God approves are right: acts which He disapproves are wrong. He approves the class of acts A and disapproves the class of acts B. Therefore A is right and B is wrong. The data for establishing the minor premises are derived from Holy Writ, which is a product of revelation. This statement of the theological foundation of morality, I believe, is correct so far as theology supplies any specifiable foundation. To be sure, among the different sects there is disagreement as to what is signified by certain expressions occurring in Scripture; hence there is some divergence in the various moral codes, but the essential part of the system is the major premise — the theological definition of right and wrong. We have already suggested why science must reject this definition. In connection with the subject of education some further discussion is almost imperative.

In order to contrast the theological with the utilitarian foundation of morality, let us state the latter in the same form, thus: Acts which presumably result in the maximum surplus of happiness are right: those which do not are wrong. The class of acts A presumably results in the maximum surplus of happiness; the class of acts B does not. Therefore A is right and B is wrong. A glance shows that these two systems are irreconcilable. The first asserts the approval of God to be the criterion of right: the other asserts the surplus of happiness to be the criterion. Of course, could it be shown that God and a utilitarian Justice approve the same acts the two codes would become identical, but this would only be an accident. It so happens, however, that this accident occurs so far as relates to many, and the most important classes, of acts. Both the Christian and the utilitarian code advocate altruism, which suggests that the former is, in reality, the latter somewhat disguised and mixed up with various extraneous doctrines; since, if the surplus of happiness is not the criterion of right and wrong, no reason why altruism should be deemed right and egotism wrong can be suggested. The theologian may claim that, as the Christian God is a beneficent one, He approves (in general) those acts which result in the greatest surplus of happiness; but such a claim is little more than an admission that it is this surplus which is the real criterion. The theologian claims that should His approval be reversed, right and wrong would be reversed. The utilitarian claims that they would remain as before. Had Christ directed us to do unto others as we would *not* that they do unto us, the consistent Christian would be compelled to accept this inversion of the Golden Rule as his guide, because he judges of the value of the precept by the authority from which it proceeds. The utilitarian, on the other hand, would reject any inversion of the Golden Rule from whatever source proceeding, since he deems right and wrong independent of all authority. The sum of two and two is independent of what any being, whether man or God, believes about it; and the distinction between right and wrong is equally independent of how any being, whether man or God, feels about it, nor does the fact that right must always involve probability make any difference; since the only way we may avoid acting upon that alternative whose presumption of happiness is a maximum is to act upon one whose presumption of happiness is less than a maximum. Anything which alters the presumption of happiness of an alternative can alter the rightness of an alternative, but nothing else can. Right is not a mere matter of taste, whether the taste be that of God or man. If God could make two and two equal five by thinking so the theological definition of right and wrong would have some foundation; at present it has none but accident

The observed similarity between the Christian and the utilitarian codes of morals leads to rather a curious result. The dictum of science respecting the teaching of the church is that its system of cosmology or theology is incorrect; that its system of morality is correct; at least so far as that essential part which advocates altruism is concerned. Hence the function of the church should be to teach morality, but not theology; and as morality is taught better by example than by precept, it should devote its energies and resources more to deeds than to words; to practice rather than to preaching; and this, I believe, it is doing more and more. Hence there is reason to believe that the church to-day is a more beneficent factor in society than it has ever been before; but it is not preaching which makes it beneficent. Preachers too often give their hearers mere husks, forever dwelling upon precepts which everyone recognizes, but upon which there is no need to dwell. Preachers seldom tell us anything new. But when ministers and church members go about doing good, causing pleasure and relieving pain, in short, increasing the surplus of happiness, their practice of altruism has an educative effect which discounts a world of preaching. Could the church, by the united effect of example and moral discipline, substitute altruism for egotism in the personal relations of men; could it so extend the practice of courtesy as to make men habitually find their own happiness in the happiness of others — could it convert altruism into a habit as egotism now is — it would make the achievements of science appear insignificant; for though science must be credited with having created civilization, it has not as yet applied civilization to a beneficent purpose. Whatever beneficent effects civilization has thus far had have been incidental rather than deliberate, for society seems not to realize that civilization, like everything else, is useless except as a means to happiness. Hence it often defeats its only useful end.

The church then as a factor in moral education is a beneficent one. Its code of morality is essentially that of utility, but it restricts that code too much to personal and immediate relations. The utilitarian doctrine teaches that in considering the effect of our acts upon happiness we must consider the remote as well as the immediate effects. The Golden Rule is as applicable as between one nation and another, or one generation and another, as it is between one man and another. To teach men to do unto others as they would that others would do unto them is not sufficient. Unless our view of the nature of right is at fault, it is equally obligatory that we, as a nation, do unto other nations as we would that other nations do unto us, and that we, as a generation, do unto our posterity as we would that our ancestors had done unto theirs. This latter extension of the Golden Rule is the most important of all; for the interests of posterity are immeasurably greater than those of any single generation and those interests are largely in our hands. Thus, as a factor in education, the church, so long as it confines itself to the teaching of morality and the inculcation of habitual altruism, is an immensely useful influence. The effect upon education of its theological teaching is precisely the reverse. In the first seventeen centuries of the Christian Era the influence of theology was probably the most baneful influence to which humanity was subject. The period of complete theological control is universally denominated the *Dark Ages*. Despite the most powerful opposition of the church — an opposition whose instruments were the thumb-screw, the rack, and the stake — science broke the bonds of intellectual slavery which had kept a world in darkness and created modern civilization, and in so doing converted the church from a harmful into a useful institution. This was accomplished by the progressive elimination of theology, beginning at the time of the Reformation, and

16

continuing to the present day. When the cosmological system of the church has been completely eliminated, and her moral system extended so as to apply to sentiency present and future, the task of science in this direction will have been completed. In our country the first part of this task is almost done. With an exception hereafter to be noticed, theological dogmas are all but innocuous. The belief in them has lapsed into little more than a meaningless form. Men in our day instead of believing a creed merely approve a formula; assenting not to the truth, but to the sound, of propositions.

But if the work of science in dispelling *theological* dogmas is almost done, its work in dispelling *political* dogmas has little more than begun. As theological dogma kept the ancient world in intellectual bondage, political dogma keeps the modern world in industrial bondage. The overthrow of political dogma, however, will be much more rapid than was that of theological dogma. With the advance of education, common sense has infected the people too deeply. Dogmatism may seem rampant now, but it is mild compared with what it was once. Nevertheless the advance of civilization and the vastly increased power of supporting population which the earth in consequence affords makes the dogmatism of to-day dangerous in the highest degree. We shall make this plainer in a later chapter. For the present it is sufficient to assert that education has no function so important in the modern world as to free the minds of men from dogma. Yet dogma is itself the product of education; for education, like inheritance, may be applied to diminish, as well as to increase, efficiency. As inheritance may result in deterioration as well as in advancement, so education may be adapted to darken the mind as well as to enlighten it. Superstition no less than knowledge may be a product of education. In a discussion of education then, as a factor of efficiency, no more essential task may be undertaken than that of distinguishing between common sense and dogmatism. In order to do this, however, we must first know the nature of common sense. We have in Book I revealed it, and we shall therefore have little difficulty in distinguishing it from that of dogmatism. While in the discussion to follow I shall refer specifically to dogmatism, it should not be forgotten that my remarks apply almost equally well to intuitionism in general. Proteromania is not the only, though it is the usual, cause of intuitionism. Pathomania, and even unadulterated logomania, are also occasional causes.

CHAP. VI] FIRST FACTOR OF HAPPINESS 243

In our consideration of the nature of truth and of right, it appeared that judgments might conveniently be classified as follows:

Judgments
(1) Of belief.
    (a) Peithosyllogisms.
    (b) Other judgments.
(2) Of use.
    (c) Chresyllogisms.
    (d) Other judgments.

Furthermore we found it convenient to have words which would distinguish judgments of class (a) from those of class (b), and of class (c) from class (d). Hence judgments of classes (a) and (c) we denominated *correct* judgments; those of classes (b) and (d) we denominated *incorrect* or *erroneous* judgments. We asserted further that judgments of classes (a) and (c) were those generally applied by men, and even by animals, to their common affairs — to those matters with which experience made them most familiar, such as eating, going from place to place, avoiding danger, and gratifying their desires; and that they were independent of time and place, common to men in all parts of the world, and in all periods of history, employed alike by the American, the Chinaman, or the South Sea Islander, by the man of the Palaeolithic Age, the ancient Egyptian and the modern European. Hence to judgments of these classes we deemed the name *common sense* judgments appropriate, since they are the only kinds of judgments common to all men. Indeed, should a community suddenly be called into being which, in those matters affecting their very existence, employed judgments of classes (b) and (d) they would speedily become extinct. Common sense in these matters is essential to existence. Happiness, however, is not essential to existence. Hence men, though employing common sense sufficiently to exist, may fail to employ it sufficiently to exist happily. It is this failure which an analysis of common sense should permit us to avoid.

The mind of a child has been compared to a blank sheet of paper upon which may be written whatever those who have access to the mind care to write and the chances are that what is there first written will remain indelible, provided it is not something which the most immediate experience will rub out. A child's mind is " wax to receive and marble to retain." Should we attempt to record there that fire will not burn or that water is not wet the record would not long survive; but should we record that the sound of thunder is due to the impact of Thor's hammer, or that whatever a certain book says is true, or that the earth is flat, or that the moon is made of green cheese, it would become a matter of difficulty in later life to eradicate these impressions, and in many minds it would be impossible, however overwhelming the evidence to the contrary. Of course, such impressions are not usually made by one communication — by a single assertion of a proposition — but by much reiteration, and by surrounding the growing child with people who continually echo the beliefs or sentiments which it is desired to record. Occasionally we encounter minds so dogmatic that one communication will make an ineradicable impression. We are all familiar with the man or woman who, having heard casually that snakes sting with their tails, or that Bacon wrote Shakespeare, or that Patagonians are ten feet high, will maintain the proposition with a confidence which in persons of ordinarily open mind would only be born of much experience or much reiteration.

Now what is the cause of this peculiar and vital characteristic of human nature? It is because beliefs, like other bodily and mental acts, are matters of habit and subject to the laws of habit. No one, perhaps, has discussed the psychology of this subject with more lucidity and thoroughness than Professor William James, and from his discussion the cause we are seeking will be, in detail, revealed. His fundamental proposition is "that the phenomena of habit in living beings are due to the plasticity of the organic materials of which their bodies are composed." Proceeding, he says:

"But the philosophy of habit is thus in the first instance, a chapter in physics rather than in physiology or psychology. That it is at bottom a physical principle is admitted by all good recent writers on the subject. They call attention to analogues of acquired habits exhibited by dead matter. Thus, M. Leon Dumont, whose essay on habit is perhaps the most philosophical account yet published, writes:

"'Every one knows how a garment after having been worn a certain time, clings to the shape of the body better than when it was new; there has been a change in the tissue, and this change is a new habit of cohesion. A lock works better after being used some time; at the outset more force was required to overcome certain roughnesses in the mechanism. The overcoming of their resistance is a phenomenon of habituation. It costs less trouble to fold a paper when it has been folded already. This saving of trouble is due to the essential nature of habit, which brings it about that to reproduce the effect, a less amount of the outward cause is required. The sounds of a violin improve by use in the hands of an able artist, because the fibres of the wood at last contract habits of vibration conformed to harmonic relations. This is what gives such inestimable value to instruments that have belonged to great masters. Water, in flowing, hollows out for itself a channel, which grows broader and deeper, and, after having ceased to flow, it resumes, when it flows again, the path traced by itself before. Just so, the impressions of outer objects fashion for themselves in the nervous system more and more appropriate paths, and these vital phenomena recur under similar excitements from without, when they have been interrupted a certain time.' . . .

" Can we now form a notion of what the inward physical changes may be like, in organs whose habits have thus struck into new paths? In other words, can we say just what mechanical facts the expression ' change of habit' covers when it is applied to a nervous system? Certainly we cannot in anything like a minute or definite way. But our usual scientific custom of interpreting hidden molecular events after the analogy of visible massive ones enables us to frame easily an abstract and general scheme of processes which the physical changes in question *may* be like. And when once the possibility of *some* kind of mechanical interpretation is established, Mechanical Science, in her present mood, will not hesitate to set her brand of ownership upon the matter, feeling sure that it is only a question of time when the exact mechanical explanation of the case shall be found out.

" If habits are due to the plasticity of materials to outward agents, we can immediately see to what outward influences, if to any, the brain-matter is plastic. Not to mechanical pressures, not to thermal changes, not to any of the forces to which all the other organs of our body are exposed; for nature has carefully shut up our brain and spinal cord in bony boxes, where no influences of this sort can get at them. She has floated them in fluid so that only the severest shocks can give them a concussion, and blanketed and wrapped them about in an altogether exceptional way. The only impressions that can be made upon them are through the blood, on the one hand, and through the sensory nerve-roots, on the other; and it is to the infinitely attenuated currents that pour in through these latter channels that the hemispherical cortex shows itself to be so peculiarly susceptible. The currents, once in, must find a way out. In getting out, they leave their traces in the paths which they take. The only thing they *can* do in short, is to deepen old paths or to make new ones; and the whole plasticity of the brain sums itself up in two words when we call it an organ in which currents pouring in from the sense-organs make with extreme facility paths which do not easily disappear. For, of course, a simple habit, like every other nervous event — the habit of snuffling, for example, or of putting one's hands into one's pockets, or of biting one's nails — is, mechanically, nothing but a reflex discharge; and its anatomical substratum must be a path in the system. . . .

"For the entire nervous system *is* nothing but a system of paths between a sensory terminus *a quo* and a muscular, glandular, or other terminus *ad quem*. A path once traversed by a nerve-current might be expected to follow the law of most of the paths we know, and to be scooped out and made more permeable than before; and this ought to be repeated with each new passage of the current. Whatever obstructions may have kept it at first from being a path should then, little by little, and more and more, be swept out of the way, until at last it might become a natural drainage-channel. This is what happens where either solids or liquids pass over a path; there seems no reason why it should not happen where the thing that passes is a mere wave of rearrangement in matter that does not displace itself, but merely changes chemically or turns itself around in place, or vibrates across the line. The most plausible view of the nerve-current makes it out to be the passage of some such wave of rearrangement as this. If only a part of the matter of the path were to 'rearrange' itself, the neighboring parts remaining inert, it is easy to see how their inertness might oppose a friction which it would take many waves of rearrangement to break down and overcome. If we call the path itself the 'organ,' and the wave of rearrangement the 'function,' then it is obviously a case for repeating the celebrated French formula of '*La fonction fait l'organe.*'

"So nothing is easier than to imagine how, when a current once has traversed a path, it should traverse it more readily still a second time."[1]

Here, then, we have the origin of dogma. Suppose to a person — call him X — whose brain is plastic, we utter the proposition — A is B. If prior to hearing this utterance X has entertained no expectations about the relation of A to B, a path of nervous discharge will be improvised within his brain corresponding to the expectation A is B. If the proposition is repeated often in X's presence this path will be deepened, and the ease with which subsequent discharges therethrough take place will be increased. After the path has been once established, suppose X is informed that A is not B. What happens? The expectation which relates A to B has taken a path which we may call the *is* or affirmative path — hence conforming to the law of habit, it will continue to take the path. That is, a person in whose brain the expectation A is B

[1] Principles of Psychology, Vol. 1, pp. 105–109.

has once been thoroughly registered will refuse to accept the proposition A is not B. The reasonableness of the proposition will not affect the matter, because the channel connecting A and B has been established on the *is* circuit, and if it has been sufficiently deepened no other channel can thereafter be established connecting A and B.

It is a fact worthy of meditation that the circuits of nervous discharge established in the minds of men by means other than those of common sense are the greatest obstacles to their happiness. More difficult to combat than the physical barriers which nature opposes to its progress, these insidious enemies of the race continually sway society from one course of folly to another. Many, if not most, of the horrors of history have arisen — not from any necessary obstacles encountered in the external and inanimate world — but from imperfections in the constitution of men's cerebral tissues, which, structurally considered, are insignificant. The greatest foe of man is, in fact, located in the nerve substance of his brain; and the emancipation of the race from misery can be achieved only by overcoming an enemy thus entrenched in the very structure of its victim's nervous system.

The tissues of the brain, which in youth are plastic and easily moulded, progressively harden as age advances, like the other tissues of the body. As the brain hardens the impressions which have been made upon it in youth, whatever they are, tend to become fixed and with difficulty alterable. The process may be compared to the hardening or setting of cement, which when freshly mixed is plastic and easily moulded to any form desired, but which gradually hardens, losing its plasticity and congealing into an unalterable rock-like mass the form impressed upon it while plastic. To this may be traced the extraordinary prevalence of dogma in old persons. The progressive loss of plasticity by the brain, and hence by the mind, causes convictions once entertained to become ineradicable. Indeed, the original impressions may be so deep and the hardening process so complete, as to give rise to local ineradicable intuitions, indistinguishable from universal ineradicable intuitions, or laws of thought. Almost any piece of nonsense may be converted into a local intuition by early and persistent inculcation.

But if the fortuitous establishment and fixation of discharge channels accounts for dogmatism, what accounts for common sense? A slight inspection will reveal it. Dogmatism, as we have seen, is generally derived from testimony; but observation can generate expectations as well as testimony, and when it does so, it generates them in conformity with the laws of induction already discussed The reason for this we may plausibly seek in the theory of natural selection discussed in Chapter 11. The higher animals being exposed to a much greater variety of environmental conditions than the lower, a much wider variation in the mode of reacting, so as to adjust themselves to those conditions, is required of them. If a nervous structure capable of making such variable response is not developed the animals perish, because they are unable to adapt their means to the end of preserving their life. Hence only those survive in which the appropriate nervous structure *is* developed. Now expectations generate actions, and any nervous structure which generates expectations from experience in any other manner than that formulated in our discussion of induction will fail to make the resulting actions appropriate to the maintenance of life. Hence, in the essential details of life, the inductive method is followed, and the paths of nervous discharge determined by common sense alone are those which have been built into the nervous structure of the higher animals by the process of natural selection. Hence they are not fortuitous, but derived from universal experience: not by the actual inheritance of experience, but by the survival of those organisms alone which developed nervous structures adapted to profit by it in the degree required for survival.

In its primitive form the process of adapting an animal's means to its ends is purely automatic — a mere reflex action. It is then known as *instinct*. In the higher animals, and conspicuously in man, instinct develops into voluntary adaptation based upon expectations generated by experience. It is then called *reasoning*. If the common processes by which experience generates expectations are analyzed they will be found to consist of the inductive and deductive operations expounded in Chapter 2, the mathematical expression of which is a peithosyllogism, and the necessary foundations of which are three universal intuitions, viz., the law of contradiction, and the two inductive postulates — those of existence, and of the uniformity of nature. Analysis of the common operation by which expectations generate voluntary acts leads to the discovery of the chresyllogism, the application of which to the determination of the presumption of happiness of alternative acts results in the theory of utility. The nature of the sensations of pleasure and pain themselves, as well as our inability to discover any one specifiable distribution of those sensations in space or time of more significance to sentient creation than any other, leads to the discovery of the principle of preference and the dilemma of distribution as the only foundations of a consistent application of a chresyllogism; that is, any other foundations would substitute local for universal considerations, and thus lead to inconsistency. *Hence utilitarianism is the common sense system of morals,* founded as it is upon the only consistent application of the common operations of the mind to the conduct of moral beings.

Why nature, whenever she produces beings capable of adapting means to ends, always requires of them the same mental operations we cannot tell, nor can we tell why no other operations can lead to knowledge. It is all a part of that profoundly significant unity of creation which excites our curiosity without satisfying it. All we can say is that the common mind revealed to us as the universe, is so constituted that through these common processes, and apparently through no others, it is able to comprehend, and may eventually direct, itself. What agencies sentient nature may succeed in creating through which to achieve her end — which can scarcely be other than universal happiness — we do not know; but if we assume that man, however feeble his present powers, is destined to become such an agent, then it is his obvious duty ceaselessly to seek said end by means of that common sense with which nature through her inscrutable operations has endowed every moral being, and in the absence of which all seeking is in vain.

The examination we have made of the origin of judgments derived from common sense and from dogma respectively, reveals the universal distinction between the two. *The first derive their authority from the original structure or constitution of the mind — the second from its previous history.* The first owe their acceptance to their *reasonableness* — the second to their *priority.* The first are functions of previous history at all, because the rational faculty can pronounce judgment only on such experience as is brought to its attention, and this varies in each individual. Otherwise it is independent of previous history. The second depends upon memory alone and is independent of the rational faculty. Hence a dogma can only be valid by accident.

If, as we infer, the inductive method of arriving at judgments results from the constitution of the mind, while the dogmatic method results from its previous history, we should expect to find the first method universal and inheritable, the second local and uninheritable; and this is precisely what we do find. As already noticed, sentient beings in all parts of the earth and in all periods of history use, and have used, the method of common sense in their daily life. An animal left to himself spontaneously adopts it in controlling his acts. It does not have to be acquired, and in fact, so far as it applies to the most essential affairs of life, it cannot be eradicated by education. Hence it is not only universal but inheritable, i. e., independent of education. That dogmas are local is, on the other hand, a matter of familiar observation. Each locality, each period of history, has its own dogmas; those peculiar to a given place at a given time being determined by various accidents, for it is as true of communities as of individuals, that their dogmas are due to their previous history. Moreover, dogmas are uninheritable. A child assumes the opinions and customs of the community in which he is brought up; not those cherished and practised by his ancestors, unless indeed they happen to be the same. A Christian child, if brought up by Mohammedans, will be a Mohammedan, if by Buddhists, a Buddhist, etc. The dogmas of his ancestors, being acquired characters, are not transmitted, nor is there even a tendency to their transmission. No dogmatic sect which fails to provide means of establishing the appropriate discharge channels in the brains of each generation as it arises can long maintain itself. This precaution once taken, any sect, whether its doctrines be true, false, good, bad, or indifferent, may be indefinitely maintained through the laws of mental habit.

From these considerations it is perhaps clearer why conscience as an arbiter of right and wrong is of no value. That which the conscience of a given individual approves or disapproves is determined by his previous history: this in turn is usually determined by the previous history of the community of which he is a member, for it is the approval or disapproval common to his community or some part of it which, in general, determines his. Hence to leave the determination of right and wrong to conscience is to leave it to the accidents of history. As Montaigne remarks: "The laws of conscience, which we pretend to be derived from nature, proceed from custom." Two thousand years ago the same observation was made by Herodotus:

"If any one should propose to all men to select the best institutions of all that exist, each, after considering them all, would choose their own; so certain is it that each thinks his own institutions by far the best. . . . That all men are of this mind respecting their own institutions may be inferred from many and various proofs, and among them by the following. Darius having summoned some Greeks under his sway, who were present, asked them 'for what sum they would feed upon the dead bodies of their parents.' They answered that they would not do it for any sum. Darius afterward having summoned some of the Indians called Callatians, who are accustomed to eat their parents, asked them, in the presence of the Greeks, and who were informed of what was said by an interpreter, 'for what sum they would consent to burn their fathers when they die'; but they, making loud exclamations, begged he would speak words of good omen. Such, then, is the effect of custom; and Pindar appears to me to have said rightly, 'That custom is the king of all men'"[1]

The discussion in Chapter 4 of the dogmatic standards suffices to show that in political affairs custom is to-day as much the "king of all men" as in the days of Pindar. Proteromania is as universal as the laws of habit which cause it.

The real relation of that which is conscientious to that which is right or to that which is useful is now obvious. Conscience, when it has any use at all, is merely a means of increasing the surplus of happiness. It is a kind of habit fostered in youth, a predisposition to conform to the precepts of some particular code of morals. Whether it is useful or not *will depend upon the code of morals.* A conscientious act may or may not be a right act. The Thugs in strangling their victims, the officers of the Inquisition in burning heretics, Charles IX in ordering the massacre of St. Bartholomew, were probably committing *conscientious* acts, but were they for that reason *right* acts? If so, to assert that any given act is right may be true, but it will not be interesting. We are, in fact, entitled to an answer to the inquiry — What acts *ought* conscience to approve and what acts *ought* it not to approve? In the definitions of *right* and *wrong* heretofore given we have the means of supplying an answer to that inquiry, and at the same time of affording an explanation of the fact (noted on page 120) that the distinction between acts which should be, and those which should not be committed, when said acts affect the interests of him who commits them only, carries with it no notion of moral obligation fulfilled or violated. As has been more than once remarked, the all but universal impulse of organisms, including man, is to act egotistically. But the difference between right acts and wrong ones is not a difference concerned with one individual, but with all

[1] Thalia.

individuals whom any of the alternatives possible may affect. Therefore to induce an individual who is a member of society to do right, we must emphasize his duty to others, since the emphasis of his impulses is upon his duty to himself. Moral precepts do not need to emphasize a man's duty to himself — self-interest can be trusted to take care of that — and as moral obligations are associated with, or imposed by, moral precepts, they become associated only with the distinction between right and wrong as it concern others, and the distinction between what should be and what should not be done, when a man's acts concern himself alone therefore, carries with it no sense of moral obligation fulfilled or violated.

Suppose, however, that we should found a code of morality on the utilitarian doctrine. Such a code would embody but one universal precept: "Do that which presumably will result in the greatest surplus of happiness." Should a community adopt this as its code, and train the conscience of youth to conform to it, then a right act would always be a conscientious act, a wrong act an unconscientious one. On the other hand, should a code of morality be embodied in the precept "Do that which presumably will result in the greatest surplus of unhappiness"— a conscientious act would always be a wrong act, and it would only be an unconscientious act which could by any possibility be right. According as a code of morality tends to approximate to the utilitarian code, conscience will be desirable and the more conscientious people are, the better: according as it approximates to the anti-utilitarian code, conscience will be undesirable, and the less conscientious people are, the better. Most, and probably all, codes of morality approximate more or less closely to the utilitarian, and the Christian code as embodied in the Golden Rule expresses the utilitarian code in language adapted to the comprehension of the untutored mind. Therefore, conscience has come to be confounded with the end which it is the principal purpose of conscience to promote. *Conscience is, in fact, a test of character and not of conduct.* The conscientiousness or unconscientiousness of an act is a function of him who commits it only. Its rightness or wrongness is a function of its total effect on pleasure and pain. An individual completely isolated from other sentient beings, one whose acts could affect none but himself, would, according to our definition, be doing right only when he acted egotistically; it would be his duty to be as happy as possible, since only by so doing could he increase the total surplus of happiness. It is solely because his acts affect the happiness of other beings that man should ever be called upon to deny himself; for it is obvious that if he sought the interests of himself alone, he would only too often increase his own happiness at the cost of that of others, and if in so doing he diminished the happiness of others by an amount greater than that by which he increased his own, he would be committing a wrong act — provided, of course, that he was not forced to do so by lack of better alternatives.

The theory herein criticized, that right and wrong may be distinguished by a moral faculty or conscience, I have called *intuitionism*. Bentham calls it *the theory of sympathy and antipathy,* and comments upon it thus:

"By the principle of sympathy and antipathy, I mean that principle which approves of or disapproves of certain actions, not on account of their tending to augment the happiness, nor yet on account of their tending to diminish the happiness of the party whose interest is in question, but merely because a man finds himself disposed to approve or disapprove of them: holding up that approbation or disapprobation as a sufficient reason for itself, and disclaiming the necessity of looking out for any extrinsic ground. Thus far in the general department of morals: and in the particular department of politics, measuring out the quantum (as well as determining the ground) of punishment, by the degree of the disapprobation.

"It is manifest, that this is rather a principle in name than in reality: it is not a positive principle of itself, so much as a term employed to signify the negation of all principle. What one expects to find in a principle is something that points out some external consideration, as a means of warranting and guiding the internal sentiments of approbation and disapprobation: this expectation is but ill fulfilled by a proposition, which does neither more nor less than hold up each of those sentiments as a ground and standard for itself.

"In looking over the catalogue of human actions (says a partizan of this principle) in order to determine which of them are to be marked with the seal of disapprobation, you need but to take counsel of your own feelings: whatever you find in yourself a propensity to condemn, is wrong for that very reason. For the same reason it is also meet for punishment: in what proportion it is adverse to utility, or whether it be adverse to utility at all, is a matter that makes no difference. In that same *proportion* also it is meet for punishment: if you hate much, punish much: if you hate little, punish little: punish as you hate. If you hate not at all, punish not at all: the fine feelings of the soul are not to be overborne and tyrannized by the harsh and rugged dictates of political utility.

"The various systems that have been formed concerning the standard of right and wrong, may all be reduced to the principle of sympathy and antipathy. One account may serve for all of them. They consist all of them in so many contrivances for avoiding the obligation of appealing to any external standard, and for prevailing upon the reader to accept of the author's sentiment or opinion as a reason for itself. The phrases different, but the principle the same." [1]

In these words, penned more than a century ago, Bentham exposed the folly of intuitionism. That an exposure so clear should have been ignored by later writers shows that the human mind finds it as difficult to comprehend that which is too simple, as that which is too complex, for nothing can be simpler than the universal moral fallacy here referred to; yet there is no evidence that its significance is anywhere comprehended. Hence I deem it wise at this point to essay the task of discussing more fully a matter so vital. I believe nothing more worthy of comprehension can be suggested to human beings in the present condition of their mental habits. Certainly nothing so important is treated in this work. Let us attempt then to make it even plainer than Bentham made it.

Human acts may be classified in an indefinite number of ways. To two of these ways I desire to call attention. First, they may be divided into (a) Those which are approved by a given individual or individuals. (b) Those which are not. Second, they may be divided into (c) Those which at the time of their commission afford the maximum presumption of happiness. (d) Those which do not. The first distinction is that which intuitionism expresses by means of the words *right* and *wrong*. The second is that which utilitarianism expresses by the same words. Let us examine the intuitional distinction.

We have already shown that an individual's or a community's approval and disapproval is not a test of anything but the influences to which his or its mind happened to be exposed during the period of plasticity; hence it is valueless as a test of anything worthy to be a guide to conduct. Moreover, if, ignoring this fact, we attempt to make approval the test of right and disapproval the test of wrong, we are led into a contradiction, because if approval is the test of right, then anything which is approved must be right, since it meets the test of right, but the same acts that are approved by some individuals are disap-

[1] Principles of Morals and Legislation.

proved by others. Hence some acts must be both right and wrong since they meet both tests, and as wrong acts are of the class *not right* acts, it follows that some acts are both right and not right — that what is, is not. To this contradiction as the first horn of the dilemma, or to the use of the terms *right* and *wrong* in an emasculated and inconsequential meaning as the second, every intuitionist is forced. If he attempts to escape the first horn by maintaining that approval and disapproval *constitute* right and wrong respectively, he is impaled upon the second, and finds himself proposing an immaterial distinction in experience as a guide to conduct. If he attempts to escape the second horn by maintaining that approval and disapproval are the *tests* of right and wrong respectively, he is impaled upon the first, and finds himself uttering a contradiction. We may call this the **Dilemma of Intuitionism.** As Bentham says, every moral code which has ever been proposed, with the exception of utilitarianism, is intuitional, *the difference being one of phraseology alone;* for however much men may refer their moral precepts to this or that authority, natural or supernatural, their own approval thereof is the real test, as is made evident by the fact that they promptly reject any precept which they disapprove. This is notoriously true of all theological systems, in which the approval of God is obviously governed by that of man, although the imputation is the reverse. In the progress of Christendom from barbarism, for example, men never discovered that God disapproved a practice until after the discovery that it met with their own disapproval. Nor are those who, rejecting all supernatural authority, seek to formulate a code of morals upon some local intuitive principle, in any better position, since in the end they can only succeed in classifying their own approbations and disapprobations.

It is commonly supposed that the dilemma of intuitionism may be escaped by the use of various sophists' companions. Among those much used for this purpose are the terms "absolute right" and "relative right," with meanings apparently about equivalent to "absolute x" and "relative x." The arguments based upon this supposed distinction are purely verbal. Another familiar mode of escaping the dilemma is through the contention that approval is not the test of right (sometimes the term "absolute right" is used here) but is the test of what each individual *believes* to be right. Even were such a truism pertinent it would contribute nothing to the solution of the difficulty, since "what a person believes to be right" is a phrase exactly equivalent in meaning to "what a person approves." Obviously then, everyone must approve what he believes to be right, because he must approve what he approves.

If now we turn to the distinction in experience which the utilitarian expresses by the words *right* and *wrong*, we see at once that the terms so applied, at any rate, are not emasculated. About the importance of the distinction there can be no question. But can we give a reason why this distinction should be made the basis of a guide to conduct? No we cannot; but it is clear that it would be equally impossible to give a reason why any distinction suggestible should be a guide, since without first establishing some distinction as the foundation of a guide to conduct, a *reason* for doing anything does not exist. Without such a foundation the word *reason*, as applied to an act, is meaningless. If we consider the related case of the foundation of logic this will become clear. We cannot give any reason for making the principle of the uniformity of nature the foundation of inductive logic. Other foundations are proposable and they might be adopted as guides to expectation. If a direct appeal to experience does not convince a man that a useful system of inductive logic requires the postulate of the uniformity of nature, there is certainly no way of proving that it does, since the postulate would be the foundation of the proof; and this difficulty would be encountered whatever postulate was made. Similarly, no reason why the utilitarian classification of human acts should be made the foundation of morals can be given. It would be almost like trying to give a reason why what is, is. That which prompts us to make it the foundation of morality may, however, be discovered by an operation no more complex than an examination of our own minds, an operation which if executed without prejudice will convince us that an act which gives no being pleasure and saves no being pain, directly or indirectly, immediately or remotely, is of no interest to sentient beings, now or hereafter; but *why* it is of no interest, it would be at once impossible and unnecessary to explain.

It is very easy to fall into the error of supposing that utilitarianism is itself but one disguise for intuitionism, the notion being that it is the very common and natural approval of pleasure and disapproval of pain which is the real foundation. A glance at the contrasted distinctions on page 254, however, will dispel this mistake. The two bases of classification there enumerated are entirely independent and either could exist were the other incapable of existence. If, like some ascetics, everyone disapproved pleasure and approved pain, it would not alter the importance of the utilitarian distinction in the slightest degree. It is because pleasure and pain *are what they are,* not because they are *approved or disapproved,* that the distinction is one of consequence.

It would be perfectly possible to divide human acts into (1) Those which presumably result in the maximum production of sawdust. (2) Those which do not: to name the first class of acts *right,* and the second class *wrong* — and upon the distinction thus made to propose the foundation of a system of morals. Such a foundation would result in neither an intuitional nor a utilitarian system, but in a *sawdust* system. It would be of little interest to sentient beings, yet history records many intuitional codes of morals, or portions thereof, having no more utility in them than a sawdust code — indeed the *im*moral codes of asceticism have less.

Although an indefinite number of alternatives to both intuitionism and utilitarianism might be suggested, it happens that none ever has been. Hence we may say that at present utilitarianism is the only alternative to intuitionism and between the two every man may take his choice. It scarcely seems possible that any one who values his own influence upon the sentient world which surrounds him can accept intuitionism when once its real nature has been revealed.

But if we do not admit that approval and disapproval determine right and wrong, we must be prepared to find certain right acts which we disapprove and certain wrong ones which we approve, for, as our approval and disapproval has been largely determined by the accidents of history, it would indeed be extraordinary if we alone among the millions of mankind had escaped all taint of the dogmatic sanction. Are we not continually condemning our fellow men for disapproving the right or approving the wrong? If we are merely calling attention to the fact that they happen to approve what we happen to disapprove, the matter is of slight consequence. If we are calling attention to anything more than this, then we cannot expect to escape a defect so prevalent as that of approving wrong and disapproving right. Hence, not only should we expect to find that we have this defect, but should be suspicious of ourselves if we find that we have not, since, if that which meets our approval coincides completely with that which is right, it is clear that it has come about through our confounding of the two ideas. If not, how comes it that the coincidence is complete?

17

The fact is that their own approval and disapproval is all that men generally have in mind when they speak of right and wrong. Yet should we ask a man if he could give a reason why a particular act, a lie for instance, is wrong, he would feel confident that he could. He would say that a particular lie is wrong because all lies are wrong; but this is clearly not a reason; it is merely asserting that he disapproves each act of a class of acts which he disapproves. Should he say it is wrong because it is generally or universally conceded to be so, he would still not be citing a reason, since he would but be substituting as a criterion the disapproval of several persons for the disapproval of one. He would but appeal from conscience to custom. There is an element of strangeness that in an age so enlightened as ours the most vital of all man's interests should thus be determined so largely by the merest accident. We accept the prevailing code of morals as we accept the prevailing mode of dress — because it happens to prevail. We reject the code of morals of ancient Greece as we reject its costume — because it does not happen to prevail. Fashion, to paraphrase Saxe, "shapes alike our consciences and coats." Why do we look with horror and protest on a bull fight in which a few animals are made to suffer for an hour or two, while we look with complacence and resignation on a system, and a preventable system, by which millions of human beings pass their lives in toil and misery and want, in order that the few in spending what the many have earned, may add novelty to their indulgence and perhaps variety to their vice? The answer is easy to give. It is because we are not accustomed to the one, and we are to the other. It is customary to condemn the one and condone the other. This is enough for the dogmatist. A bull fight is wrong. The preventable perpetuation of poverty is not.

Nor is the fundamental error as to the foundation of morality implied in the theory of sympathy and antipathy confined to the unthinking part of the community. With the single exception of Bentham, every prominent writer on ethics, so far as I know, has fallen into it. If we observe the process they employ, we shall find that they systematically exclude from the class of right acts all acts which they disapprove, and from that of wrong acts all those which they approve, without inquiring as to the origin of the approval and disapproval. To thus bring all acts to the test of their approval is to beg the whole question and *assume the very criterion which they profess to seek*. No wonder they have made no progress in two thousand years. They will make no progress in two thousand or twenty thousand years more unless they are prepared to say to themselves: "I, like my fellows, owe many of my beliefs, preferences, and antipathies to my education. My education is determined by the previous history of the community in which I was brought up and is a function of the accidents thereof. Right and wrong are not functions of the previous history of any community. Therefore, I must expect to find among right acts some which are repugnant to me and which I disapprove and among wrong acts some which attract me and which I approve. If I reject the approval and disapproval of others as a guide to conduct, I must, to be consistent, reject my own." This impartial and reasonable attitude of mind must be assumed before men can advance one step toward the solution of the ethical problem; for right and wrong cannot be determined by what this or that individual, or assemblage of individuals, approves or disapproves — but by what Justice, who has no local sympathies or antipathies, would approve or disapprove. It is clearly absurd to test right and wrong by our approval and disapproval. We should reverse the process — first ascertain the difference between right and wrong, and then test our approval and disapproval by it. *Let us not make conscience our guide to right and wrong. Let us make right and wrong our guide to conscience.* We may then follow its behests without fear that our acts are controlled by the accidents of our education.

Now there is but one thing which all sentient beings in all times have desired, and will always desire, to secure — and that is happiness — and there is but one thing which they as universally desire, and will desire, to avoid — and that is unhappiness. Hence to strive for anything except securing the one and avoiding the other as an ultimate end, is to strive for what transient and local influences alone have caused us to approve. The difference between all other proposable ends and that of utility is the difference between a passing and a permanent ideal. To seek to establish among men the approval of any act which has no relation to happiness as an end, is to seek the approval of that which will no more meet with the interest or approval of our posterity than the Callatian obligation of eating our sires meets with ours. But could we establish the ideal of increasing the totality of happiness irrespective of its distribution in space or time, we could be sure that our efforts would have no mere passing effects, but would be of interest to sentient beings so long as pleasure and pain remain perceptible.

Custom to-day is in undisputed control of morality, but this cannot always continue. Common sense, which has already conquered so many of the domains of dogma, will conquer that of morals. Education, which is the cause of this universal moral disease, will also be its cure.

Though most conspicuous in moral issues, intuitionism is by no means confined to them. It is as common for men to test truth and untruth by their belief and disbelief as to test right and wrong by their approval and disapproval. Such an inversion of common sense though extremely injurious in the domain of logic is even more injurious in that of ethics, because of its more immediate relation to conduct.

It has often been observed and deplored that our civilization is a material one — that it does not extend to many of the affairs upon which the welfare of men most conspicuously depends. If the various domains of knowledge whose advancement has undeniably produced civilization be examined, it will be found that they are those in which the inductive method has displaced the dogmatic, and the advancement is, in general, proportional to the degree of this displacement. It is in the knowledge of material things that the inductive method has most completely dispossessed the dogmatic, and hence it is in such domains that knowledge has advanced. Civilization being the product of science has therefore advanced most conspicuously upon materialistic lines. During the reign of dogma, which was undisputed during the Dark Ages, civilization was dormant. When the inductive method shall have completely dispossessed the dogmatic in all domains of knowledge and conduct, as we have reason to hope that in a generation or two it will do, civilization will cease to be materialistic only, and our knowledge of the moral world, and the policies founded upon that knowledge, will leap forward with the same freedom as that which the stimulus of the inductive method gave, and still gives, to our knowledge of the material world.

Indeed, such gains as have been made in morals since the Reformation, and they have by no means been inconsiderable, have been due to the steady encroachment of the utilitarian or common sense code of morals upon the dogmatic; as is evidenced by the fact that whenever men point to the moral advances which have taken place since the Dark Ages, they always point to the advancement of those agencies whose tendency is to increase the happiness and decrease the unhappiness of the world. Were happiness not the end of morality such advancement, of course, would be no evidence of the advancement of morality. It is only because mediævalism survives longer in the moral than in the material realm that civilization remains one-sided.

The so-called warfare between religion and science is but one manifestation of the opposition between the mediæval and the modern method of distinguishing truth from untruth and right from wrong; it is but a special case of the warfare between intuitionism and common sense. Wherever the old method survives a struggle is bound to occur as soon as the new one begins to encroach upon it. The old method gave us astrology — the new one gives us astronomy; the old method gave us alchemy — the new one gives us chemistry; the old method gave us Genesis — the new one gives us geology; the old method in mathematics, in medicine, in biology, in physics, substituted mysticism for knowledge; the new one in all these subjects has substituted knowledge for mysticism, and it will not stop there. The old method has given us the politics of commerce — the new one will give us the politics of utility; the old method has given us the moral code of asceticism — the new one will give us the moral code of happiness.

We have thus dilated with some reiteration and at considerable length upon the natural history of dogma because in a discussion of education as a factor of efficiency it is fundamental. *The educative effect of a clear comprehension of the dilemma of intuitionism is greater and more broadening than that of a college education, since at one stroke it abolishes proteromania, pathomania, and much of logomania.* The mind which once masters it is emancipated. To the philosophical educator the protection of the developing mind from abuse of its plasticity is of paramount interest. The experience of history and of every-day life tells us that dogmatism is to be avoided like a pestilence — it is a mental and moral disease, and should be treated as such. Is it the prevailing practice so to treat it? By no means. Long before the youthful mind has developed judgment sufficient to render it immune, it is deliberately infected by the dogmas, theological and political, at the time and place prevailing. These dogmas thereafter hold their own against common sense, for, owing their sanction to their priority of occupation and not to their reasonableness, they cannot be dislodged by a demonstration of their unreasonableness. Thus all kinds of superstitions, harmless and harmful, are perpetuated for generations, some being peculiar to certain localities, others spreading like a contagion to all parts of the earth. So persistent are these constantly cultivated errors, that did we not observe the process of perpetuation by education, we should be tempted to believe that they were transmitted by inheritance. Were it possible to check for a single generation the inculcation of the multitude of dogmas which are now assiduously cultivated throughout the world, they would at once become of no more human interest than the myths of the ancient Egyptians. While this method of education prevails there is no safety for the human race, for should a dominant part of society become by any means infected by dogmas destructive of happiness — such as the doctrines of the ascetics — they might readily spread them throughout the world and perpetuate them to a remote posterity. Each generation would register the dogmas it had received from its predecessor on the sensitive mind of its youth, there to become fixed by the operation of the law of diminishing plasticity, and thus a world might become permanently plunged in misery from an infection starting perhaps in the mind of a single imbecile or fanatic. History shows us examples of such cases, too numerous to mention, none of which perhaps have become universal, because in the past there has happily been no ready means of universal contagion. With modern methods of communication extended to all parts of the world, a contagion once started might become universal if the advance of science fails to develop a method of inoculation which will render the mind immune to dogmatic infection.

Such a method would simply consist in inoculating the youthful mind with common sense instead of with dogma. Very young children could not, of course, grasp the principles of common sense, but if we were content to leave their minds open until prepared so to do, no harm would result from delay. A knowledge of the exact distinction between truth and untruth, correct and incorrect, right and wrong, and proficiency in the application of such knowledge to the affairs of society, should be possessed by every youth educated in a civilized community. These terms would not then be employed in speech or thought merely to distinguish what is customary from what is not customary. The most narrowing influence to which the modern mind, educated or uneducated, is now subject would be at once removed. Men with such knowledge would be immune to sophistry whether suggested by their own or other minds, and even such as were deficient in information would, in general, be prepared to better adapt their means to their ends than the best educated under the present system; for an undogmatic fool is better equipped to deal with practical affairs than a dogmatic sage. It is not sufficient to prescribe the method of science for this or that department of knowledge; it should be impressed upon the student's mind that there is no other correct method — that the very distinction between *correct* and *incorrect* judgments is that between those which are determined by the method of science and those which are not. If a single avenue of knowledge is left unguarded, there dogma will enter. Most men apply the method of science to those branches to which it is customary to apply it, but withhold it from those from which it is customary to withhold it. Few would withhold the scientific method from chemistry; but fewer still would apply it to politics. Newton, whose name stands first among the masters of science, wrote treatises on theology, but he did not apply to them the method of science. His Principia is probably the most famous of scientific works, but his Lexicon Propheticum has no rank in literature and few have ever heard of it. Had he applied the method of the latter work to the former, the name of Newton would have been known only to a few antiquarians. Had he applied the method of the former to the latter, he would have been as famous for his abolition of theology as for his discovery of gravitation. Indeed, the domain in which dogma prevails is itself determined by dogma — the limits of the authority of custom are themselves subject to custom — and hence it comes about that not only do dogmatists deviate into common sense, but men of science deviate into dogma.

Thus to guard against dogmatism open-mindedness should be inculcated, not in one branch of knowledge, but in all branches. In our examination of the nature of knowledge we showed that certainty is confined to the laws of thought. Hence all other knowledge may be subject to correction and every hypothesis is a provisional hypothesis. As knowledge advances, therefore, science is continually abandoning old hypotheses and adopting new ones; but this does not mean that all her former views were defective, but simply that some of them were. For example, all the discoveries of Euclid in geometry, most of those of Archimedes in physics, and some of those of Hipparchus in astronomy, have stood the test of twenty centuries. The readjustment of knowledge is the life of science; it is the death of dogma. When the facts do not agree with the theory, science rejects the theory; dogma rejects the facts. Hence he who would consistently practise common sense must keep his mind open even to the point of questioning the method of science itself. The very methods we have considered of distinguishing expectations which will, from those which will not, be fulfilled and of distinguishing useful acts from those not useful, must be regarded as open to debate. No man is omniscient. Hence logicians may have erred even in those matters upon which all agree. To be sure it is not likely, but the possibility should always be entertained.

This attitude is the only antidote to dogmatism, and the mind once thoroughly inoculated with it will be as immune as a mind subject to the laws of habit can be. It is difficult to overestimate its importance in education. Nevertheless, it has one disadvantage. It destroys the beneficent with the baneful dogmas. Truth, like everything else, is useful only so far as it increases the totality of happiness; but many have made of truth an idol and deem it an ultimate end in itself. Scientific men are particularly prone to this mistake, and the more philosophic among them, like Clifford and Huxley, speak of the duty, or sometimes of the "sacred" duty, of testing all beliefs by the inductive method. We have seen that such a duty relates only to beliefs which determine acts. Among theological dogmas there are many which will not stand the test of the inductive method, and yet it would be far from useful to destroy them.

"The fear o' hell's a hangman's whip
To haud the wretch in order;"

Yet it is a useful whip for those whose egotism is unrestrained by other considerations, and the extinction of the belief in hell which the advance of knowledge is now so rapidly accomplishing, is by no means an unmixed blessing. Among a considerable proportion of society a real belief in a real hell would be a beneficent dogma, though it would be wise to mitigate some of the traditional fervor of the region. The belief in immortality and the hope of future happiness founded thereon may or may not stand the test of the inductive method; but so long as it does not lead to asceticism or other forms of harmful fanaticism, it is not the province of common sense to attempt its destruction. It is of no interest to inquire whether such an attempt would be successful or not; it is sufficient that it would be wrong. Indeed, so long as men make no attempt to guide their conduct by ecclesiastical cosmology common sense need seek no quarrel with it. There are too many real foes to fight. It was only because it permitted its dogmas to govern its acts that the church was an agent of evil in mediæval times. The practice in this country is now all but extinct. We have already shown that the Christian code of morals is founded, not on Christian cosmology, but on common sense. Hence the only surviving good of theology is that involved in its beneficent dogmas. Those who would destroy them because they are dogmas commit the very error they condemn. Observing that dogmas when factors in determining conduct are injurious, they conclude that injuriousness is an essential quality of dogmas. Hence they are intolerant of them and become dogmatic on the subject of dogmatism. They set up truth as a fetish just as others by similar bad reasoning set up conscientiousness, or character, or beauty, or wealth, or even money, as a fetish. They mistake the means for the end. He who would be consistent with himself cannot thus have a compound standard. Use-judgments alone can inform us concerning the usefulness or lack of usefulness of acts. Dogmas are beneficent if they lead to a surplus of happiness; otherwise they are not. A fool's paradise is better than a sage's purgatory, and it is sound philosophy which holds that "when ignorance is bliss, 'tis folly to be wise."

But because ignorance occasionally is bliss, it would be folly to encourage ignorance; for ignorance is much more often not bliss, nor a means to it. If, then, an education in common sense would destroy beneficent as well as baneful dogmas, we may deplore it, but it can scarcely furnish a reason for the suppression of common sense. To so infer would indicate a very defective sense of proportion. Dogmatism is so dangerous, and in general so harmful, that we must be ready to make great sacrifices to eliminate it as a determinant of conduct. *To do so is the primary province of education.* I have attempted to show that it is dogmatism combined with logomania which prevents men from understanding the nature of right and wrong itself, and is the chief cause of the confusion in the understanding and application of those terms. I shall in the following chapters attempt to show that it is dogmatism which stands between man and his own happiness — that the world could be converted from unhappiness to happiness by the simple elimination of dogma, which now prevents men from perceiving, not only the interests of society as a whole, but of each man individually. Perhaps in this attempt I shall fail to carry conviction, but if so, I shall take care that the failure is not due to any abandonment of common sense.

CHAPTER VII

THE SECOND FACTOR OF HAPPINESS

In the foregoing chapter have been in some degree considered what qualities of individual minds contribute to happiness. In the present one will be considered the relation which the environment — that part of mind common to normal individuals — should bear to them, in order to contribute to the same end. The problem presented to Justice of how to adjust the environment of men so that in its reaction upon them it will generate happiness with maximum efficiency is essentially the problem of the engineer who is required to adjust the fuel supply and other conditions of steam generation to his boilers, so as to generate steam with maximum efficiency. We shall therefore approach the problem as though it were one in steam engineering, nor shall we abandon the method of common sense in dealing with it merely because it is a problem of greater complexity than is presented to the engineer.

In order, however, that the object of Justice may be in any degree attainable, it is clear that not only must there be a causal relation between a given condition of man's environment and his happiness, but it must be a recognizable one. In order to select those conditions which will, and reject those which will not, increase happiness or decrease unhappiness, we must be able to distinguish them from those which will have an opposite effect. Can experience supply the means of thus distinguishing? There is a large class of persons who in effect deny that it can. They have something like this to say: "The world cannot be made happy by attempting to create external conditions of happiness. Happiness is within ourselves. One man's meat is another man's poison. Men's tastes and needs differ so that we cannot lay down any rules by which the environment may be made to conform to them, for by changing the conditions so as to produce greater happiness in one, we may produce less in another; so it is best to do nothing at all." I believe we are all familiar with such fatalistic rejoinders to any proposal which seeks to increase joy or diminish misery by changes in the external world. We may admit, and have admitted, that happiness is partly within ourselves — that the first factor of happiness involves the qualities of the individual, and we may further admit that an attempt to discover means of gratifying every desire which by any member of the present or future generations might be felt, would be quite futile. But is it not possible to discover some causal relations between human environment and happiness so general in their application as to make the presumable total surplus greater by acting upon them than by ignoring them? If so, then the conditions which determine useful acts are thereby fulfilled and it will be more useful to act upon our knowledge of such relations than not to act upon it. That is, it will be of use to consider the second factor of happiness, viz., the adjustment of external conditions, as something which may be changed for the better. Can any such general relations be cited? Let us see. Out of 1,000 men, how many would enjoy being boiled in oil? Answer: 0. How many would prefer health to sickness? Answer: At least 999, probably more. How many would prefer riches to poverty? At least 990, probably more. How many would prefer consuming $10,000 worth of wealth to producing it? At least 980, probably more. If it is admitted that these answers are correct, then it is admitted that there are general rules concerning the relation of man and his environment which it is better to observe than to ignore. This much being acknowledged, our next step is to attempt to discover them.

Could all individuals be so modified by inheritance and education as to attain perfect adaptability, the questions discussed in this chapter would be of no human interest. It would only be necessary to consider what means would be best adapted to maintaining the greatest population, for a perfectly adapted individual would be one capable of being as happy as his capacity for happiness would permit, irrespective of external conditions. Such a being would be independent of his environment and no adjustments other than those for the mere maintenance of sentiency, that is of life, would be required to secure maximum efficiency. On the other hand, were external conditions always perfectly adapted to the desires of individuals, could all persons gratify their wants by merely wishing or commanding that they be gratified, were they in the position of Aladdin with his lamp, it would be equally unnecessary to seek the conditions of maximum efficiency of adaptation — mere existence would supply them. Perfect adaptability by either means, however, cannot be attained. Men cannot in every contingency adapt their desires to their means of attainment, or adapt the means of attainment to their desires. Hence the question of improving the adjustment of man and his environment — of adapting his means of attainment to his desires and *vice versa,* becomes of human interest.

A clear comprehension of this subject requires that we establish the foundations of a nomenclature adapted to its expression. Hence the immediate object of our attention must be the differentiation of a number of important objects of experience into classes; and the selection of suitable terms by which to designate them. This essential digression being disposed of, we may return to the consideration of the laws of nature and of human nature upon which efficiency of adaptation depends, with an increased power of comprehending them.

As long as a being is capable of voluntary acts he must commit them. Whether his attitude be active or passive, whether he directs his body or mind to active effort or abstains therefrom, so long as his mental or physical state is voluntarily assumed, he commits a voluntary act. Inaction, if the result of volition, is as much a voluntary act as action. Hence we may say that the waking life of a human being consists of a succession of voluntary acts. The exceptions to this dictum are too infrequent to merit discussion.

Voluntary acts may be divided into (1) *Useful.* (2) *Useless.* It is scarcely necessary to remark that the only interest men can have in the second class of acts is that implied in acquiring means of avoiding them. Useful acts may be divided into (1) *Consumptive* acts, or those whose immediate result is designed to be an increase of happiness, or a decrease of unhappiness. (2) *Productive* acts, or those whose more or less remote result is designed to be an increase of happiness or decrease of unhappiness. Another name for productive acts is *labor.* Between the consumptive act of an individual and the alteration of happiness it is designed to effect, there intervenes no other voluntary act. Consumptive acts may be divided into (1) Those designed to affect the individual committing them, *egotistic* consumption. (2) Those designed to affect one or more other individuals, *altruistic* consumption. By the word *consumption* I shall, in general, refer to egotistic consumption. The submission by one individual to the acts of altruistic consumption of another, is an act of egotistic consumption. Consumptive acts furthermore may be divided into (1) Those designed to result in a surplus of happiness, *positive* consumption; (2) Those designed to result in a surplus of unhappiness, though less in quantity than that involved in inaction — *negative* consumption. They may also be *both* egotistic and altruistic, and *both* positive and negative. Productive acts differ from consumptive in their greater remoteness from their end. One or more voluntary acts intervene between them and the effect upon happiness which they are designed to achieve. Hence they are less likely to attain their end than consumptive acts and the less likely the more remote they are. The immediate aim of consumptive acts is an ultimate end, that of productive acts is a proximate end. One produces an end, the other a means. The relation between consumptive and productive acts may be compared to that between the last operation of a process involving a succession of operations, and the first operations. In the making of cotton cloth, the weaving would correspond to a consumptive act, the planting, cultivating, harvesting, ginning, baling, and spinning of the cotton would correspond to productive acts. Productive, like consumptive, acts may be *egotistic, altruistic, positive* and *negative,* and likewise may be similarly combined. They may also be divided into (1) *Pleasant,* (2) *Unpleasant,* according as their immediate effect is pleasurable or not pleasurable. Pleasant productive acts are distinguished from positive consumptive ones by the fact that in the one, pleasure is incidental to the act, in the other, it is the object thereof.

Examples of consumptive acts are such acts as listening to music, looking at a play, smoking, playing games, travelling for pleasure (involving, of course, some productive acts), reading stories or poetry, taking medicine, etc. Examples of productive acts are sawing wood, driving a locomotive, painting a house, dressing, peddling groceries, digging potatoes, forging horseshoes, etc.

Productive and consumptive acts are designed to satisfy desires. Without inquiring as to how many kinds of desire may exist, two of import in utility may be distinguished — the desire to attain pleasure, and the desire to avoid pain. A desire the gratification of which results in a surplus of pleasure, we shall call a *taste;* one the failure to gratify which results in a surplus of pain, we shall call a *need.* Desires may also be both tastes *and* needs. Any means, other than an act, which may be employed to attain a surplus of pleasure, we shall call a *positive desideratum.* Any means, other than an act, which may be employed to avoid a surplus of pain, we shall call a *negative desideratum*. Desiderata may be either *external* or *internal*. Anything about us which may be put to a useful purpose is an example of an external desideratum. External desiderata may be divided into *material* and *non-material;* the first being material objects or combinations of the same; the second being functions of the relative positions or motions of material objects, comprising force and energy. Material desiderata whose quantity is sufficiently restricted to give them a value in exchange, that is, to make men willing to sacrifice something to obtain them, constitute *wealth*. We shall frequently use the word *wealth* as if it was equivalent to *desiderata,* because it is more familiar and will result in no misunderstanding. Character, intellect, capacity for pleasure, education, etc., constitute internal desiderata.

Now among external desiderata there are some which need little or no adjustment in order to satisfy desires or wants — they require no productive acts — no labor — to adapt them to consumption; there are others which do. It is important to distinguish between these. Any external desideratum which, when unmodified except in locality, may be employed in consumptive acts, we shall call a *complete* desideratum. All other external desiderata we shall call *incomplete*. The visible heavenly bodies, air, water, scenes of natural beauty, the pleasing fruits and flowers produced spontaneously by nature, are examples of *natural complete desiderata*. Tobacco, confectionery, perfumes, pictures, interesting books, musical sounds, etc., are examples of *artificial complete desiderata*. Iron ore, coal, winds, water-powers and raw materials and natural powers in general are examples of *natural incomplete desiderata*. Pig iron, copper wire, bricks, boards, machinery, factories, and means and elaborated materials of production in general are examples of *artificial incomplete desiderata*. Two points regarding the classification of external desiderata into complete and incomplete must be noticed. First, the distinction between them is not sharp because almost any object might, under unusual circumstances, be utilized directly in consumption and hence be classified as a complete desideratum. Second, it should be noticed that most complete desiderata may be employed for other purposes than immediate consumption. Water, for example, may be used in all sorts of productive processes, and even the stars or some of them are useful in determining direction or position at sea. Thus we see that incomplete desiderata are not utilizable exclusively in production, nor complete desiderata in consumption.

Productive acts may be *internal* or *external*. Thought for the purpose of adapting means to ends is an example of internal productivity. External production is either: (1) *Localization,* the alteration of the position of material bodies or substances with relation to the earth; or (2) *Manipulation,* the alteration of the position of material bodies or substances with relation to other bodies or substances. Transportation industries afford examples of localization; manufacturing industries, of manipulation. One degree of localization which may be called *perfect* is not a productive but a consumptive act. In the perfect localization of a complete desideratum, the organization of some sentient being is, without further intervention of volition, affected beneficially. An apple is a complete desideratum. It is perfectly localized when it is bitten, and not until then. Thus any act which causes a complete desideratum to act upon the sensorium of a sentient being is an act of perfect localization. It is most often accomplished by changing the location of the desideratum, or the being, but not always. To open a door separating a person from a source of harmonious sounds would result in perfect localization. A desideratum so localized as to be available for consumption through some simple act of an individual, such as a movement of the arm, taking a few steps, etc., we shall call *adequately* localized.

As the whole of man's waking life is occupied in acts which are either productive, consumptive, or neither, we may conveniently assign names to the fractions of an individual's or a community's life, occupied in these three ways respectively. The ratio of that portion of life spent in production to the total waking life may be called the *producing ratio;* the ratio of that portion spent in consumption to the total waking life may be called the *consuming ratio;* the ratio of that portion spent in neither may be called the *wasted ratio.* It should not be forgotten that productive and consumptive acts may be really, if not nominally, wasted if any method other than that of common sense is employed in adapting them to their end, for though they are *designed* for a useful purpose, they may — and often do — fail in their design, and this occurs most often through the use of some substitute for common sense.

Having now established a sufficient nomenclature to enable us to discuss the subject in hand with clearness, we may proceed to develop the principles upon which depend efficiency of adaptation, free from any serious risk of ambiguity.

Neglecting the rare cases of involuntary happiness, *the happiness curve of an individual can never be on the positive side of the X axis except when he is engaged in positive consumption, or pleasant production.* It would seem to be most economical then for men to confine themselves to positive consumption and pleasant production, and to avoid all unpleasant productive and negative consumptive acts. Should they attempt to do this, however, they would develop a policy of maleficent acceleration, and would soon encounter a situation which, among its alternatives, afforded none that were positively consumptive or pleasantly productive, although affording millions that were not. The world, as we know it, requires too much preliminary adjustment — its desiderata are too incomplete and the labor required to make them complete is too unpleasant to permit of such perpetual happiness. Since unpleasant labor and negative consumption then cannot be altogether abolished, it is next of interest to inquire how they may be minimized; and in order to lead up to the inquiry, let us develop a fundamental rule of conduct, governing the relation between production and consumption which individuals, consulting only their own interest and using common sense, habitually employ. Suppose a sensible individual to have offered him an alternative involving A units of pleasure, to be attained by first employing means involving more than the equivalent of pain, or by the sacrifice of more than A units of pleasure. Would he regard it as an opportunity of any value? Would he consider it preferable to an alternative which offered no pleasure whatever? Obviously not? Or would he, in general, adopt any alternative which promised relief from a given quantity of pain only by the employment of means involving a still greater quantity? Clearly not, unless he was in the predicament of having no better alternative. The principle here involved determines our decisions in scores of every-day acts. It tells us whether it is worth while to go down stairs after a drink of water or not, whether it is worth the trouble to dress for a given entertainment or not, whether it will pay to part with twenty-five cents for a cigar or not. Now has this simple rule of individual conduct ever been proposed as worthy to govern the conduct of a nation? If nations are guided by the same rules of common sense that guide individuals it would be too much of a commonplace to require proposal; and indeed we must admit that it sometimes does guide the affairs of nations. Yet it has never been definitely laid down as a rule of action, and a large proportion of the acts of all communities are at variance with it. As applied to the problem under discussion, the rule may be expressed thus: If the consumption of a desideratum produces a quantity of pleasure or saves a quantity of pain less than equivalent to the quantity of pain involved in its production, the production of the desideratum is unjust and should be avoided. A nation guided by this principle or deliberately recognizing it as a worthy guide, would thereby be adopting a rule of common sense universally recognized and applied in every-day life. I shall call this the *rule of self-support*. It should be the effort of all sensible communities to dispense with activities which are not self-supporting. What may be called the *margin of self-support* is determinable thus: Suppose one and the same individual to experience the total effect on happiness involved in the production and consumption of a given desideratum. He would judge as to whether the whole operation was worth while, that is, were self-supporting, by the rule just mentioned. If it were self-supporting, the margin of self-support would be the happiness equivalent of the quantity of pain he would suffer, and no more, rather than forego the operation; if it were not, the margin whereby it failed of self-support would be the unhappiness equivalent of the quantity of pleasure it would require, and no more, to induce him to undergo the operation. The first is a *positive,* the last a *negative* margin of self-support. The larger the margin can be made (algebraically) in the case of any operation or industry the better — for the greater the quantity of pain that an individual would be willing to suffer rather than forego the pleasure involved in the production and consumption of a given desideratum, the greater, of course, would be the happiness value of producing and consuming it.

The value or desirability of happiness not being a function of its distribution, the margin of self-support of a given productive and consumptive operation is not altered because the productive portion is confined to one set of men and the consumptive to another. It matters not whether A produces and A consumes, or whether A produces and B consumes. It is the total effect on happiness which is of consequence. Hence the mode specified of determining the margin of self-support is applicable to communities where the producer and consumer of a given desideratum are not necessarily one and the same individual. Now, as all useful acts consist either in producing

18

or consuming desiderata, internal or external, it is clear that if we can discover the means of making the margin of self-support of acts or aggregates of acts approach a maximum, we shall have discovered the means of making the output of happiness approach a maximum, which is the object of our search. These means must consist either in the modification of individuals or in the modification of their environment. We have in Chapter 6 partially discussed the first subject, and may now with such system as is attainable, examine the second.

In the following discussion we shall assume that factors (1) and (3) — the efficiency of conversion of the sentient agent, and the number of agents, remain constant, in order that the effect of variation in the second factor alone may be studied. Useful acts then being either productive or consumptive, their total effect upon happiness is that of the surplus of pain or pleasure of production plus the surplus of pain or pleasure of consumption. Call the first the *surplus of production,* the second the *surplus of consumption.* The first will then be equal to the duration of production multiplied by its average intensity. The second to the duration of consumption multiplied by its average intensity. Hence the margin of self-support of a combined productive and consumptive act or industry, or the assemblage of such combined acts or industries comprised in all useful acts may be, in general, increased:

(1) By increasing algebraically the average intensity of productive acts.

(2) By increasing the duration of productive acts, if the intensity is positive.

(3) By diminishing the duration of productive acts, if the intensity is negative.

(4) By increasing algebraically the average intensity of consumptive acts.

(5) By increasing the duration of consumptive acts, if the intensity is positive.

(6) By diminishing the duration of consumptive acts, if the intensity is negative.

While an algebraic increase in intensity will always increase the margin of self-support, alteration in duration in the directions specified might not always do so. The relative duration of production and consumption should depend upon their relative intensities. The mode of determining the most economic ratio between them will be indicated presently.

Chap. VII]   SECOND FACTOR OF HAPPINESS   275

It is clear that by appropriate changes in the first factor of happiness, the sentient agent, the margin of self-support may be increased in any or all of the six modes specified, and the employment of educational or hereditary influences to effect such changes are special cases of productive acts. I shall postpone consideration of the effect of specific changes in the first factor to the next chapter, confining attention for the present to the effect of changes in the second factor, and let us first concern ourselves with production.

There are open to every normal individual innumerable alternatives which are painful, to every one which is pleasurable. With an ordinary hammer there are an indefinite number of ways in which a man can inflict pain, and intense pain, directly on himself and others, whereas the modes of using a hammer whereby pleasure may be produced are as indefinitely restricted, and the effect is indirect and remote. It is unnecessary to multiply examples. Voluntary acts unless especially designed to produce pleasure are not at all likely to produce it. A random act, without any particular design, is exceedingly unlikely to produce pleasure either directly or indirectly, and hence we should expect that acts designed to produce a surplus of pleasure indirectly, namely, acts whose immediate object is a proximate end, would probably not result in the immediate production of an ultimate one. In other words, labor is *apriori* not likely to be pleasant. Not being especially designed to produce pleasure immediately, productive acts are not likely to so produce it. The antecedent probability thus established is amply confirmed by *aposteriori* evidence. We have but to look about us to find that labor is generally an unpleasant operation — that its intensity is more often negative than not — sometimes it is strongly negative — more often moderately so — frequently it is almost indifferent — less frequently it is positive — occasionally it is strongly positive; but the vital fact must be recognized that most labor is unpleasant. During the working hours of an average individual the curve of happiness of that individual is usually below the X axis — more pain is experienced than pleasure, using the word *pain* as exemplified on page 105. A purely productive life would not be worth living — to him who lived it oblivion would be preferable. That such is the opinion of mankind is clearly seen from their expressions and acts. Inquire of an average man whether he would desire to live again that portion of his life which consisted of productive acts alone, leaving out all the consumptive ones, and his answer will invariably be a negative one — usually an emphatic negative — which is but a mode of testifying that the productive portion of life affords no surplus of happiness. The phrase "labor in vain" is a common one, but no one speaks of taking pleasure in vain. An act which causes an increase in the totality of happiness — a successfully consumptive act — can never be in vain, but a productive act can be, and often is.

Theologians tell us that work is a curse imposed on man as a consequence of the original sin of Adam — they represent Heaven as a place where there is no labor. The continual effort of man is to devise means of dispensing with the necessity of work. The development of labor-saving machinery is deemed a worthy object of effort. Where men are freed from the necessity of work by acquiring wealth they either cease to work systematically or confine themselves to certain kinds of work which are pleasant. No one ever heard of men, in any industry, striking for more hours of labor, except in certain rare cases where longer hours have meant more pay. Wherever we turn, the unpleasantness of average labor becomes apparent. If work were a pleasant occupation, as some worthy speculators would have us believe, it would be easy for everyone to be happy. Every house could be equipped with a treadmill, or some equivalent device, to which the members of the family could resort when in search of recreation. There is no demand for such devices, even among those who inform us that work is joyful. Hence we must be sceptical of him who avers that labor is a good in itself, for were this so, the kind of labor would be a matter of indifference. Mill remarks:

"It is necessary to include in the idea, (of labor) not solely the exertion itself, but all feelings of a disagreeable kind, all bodily inconvenience or mental annoyance, connected with the employment of one's thoughts, or muscles, or both, in a particular occupation." [1]

Thus the unpleasant character of average labor is a postulate of political economy.

In fact, most of the work which has to be done in the world is a dismal bore, and the attempt by men, women, and children to avoid it is perfectly natural. It would be unnecessary to dwell on the unpleasant character of average labor were it not that the subject is badly confused by sincere but superficial moral-

[1] Principles of Political Economy; Book I, Chap. 1.

ists. They preach perpetually on the virtue of work and the vice of leisure. They exhort men to labor long and faithfully and they have words of particular opprobrium for him who does not — such as shirk, or loafer. The continual necessity which these moralists deem themselves under to exhort men to work is but another evidence that there is disinclination to do it, and there would be no such general disinclination if work really gave pleasure. So successfully, however, has this school of morality wrought upon the conscience of the people that a vast number of men deem labor a duty — just as the Puritans of two hundred years ago deemed all sorts of unhappiness a duty, and most sorts of happiness a sin — just as the ascetics of the Middle Ages deemed it their duty to mortify the flesh and renounce the world and all its pleasures. The modern school of morality which indiscriminately urges the duty of work is a direct descendant of the ascetic school which urged the duty of unhappiness. No one who clearly understands the difference between right and wrong can indorse the morality of those who make of toil a fetish and deem it an end in itself. Work, like anything else, is only useful or moral in the degree that it contributes to the surplus of happiness. The only duty which men have to perform productive acts is that involved in the obligation to achieve consumptive ones. Production is moral only because it leads to consumption. It certainly is a sign of nobility of character for a man to be willing to spend his life in labor for others, and the very characteristic by which we recognize its nobility proves that there is a duty to refrain from work as well as a duty to work. His nobility consists in being willing to produce that others may in that degree dispense with production; his willingness to forego consumption enables others to consume in a greater degree. The fact that this is recognized as an altruistic act, but confirms our claim that labor is generally deemed unpleasant. Indeed, were this not so, it is clear that it would be no sign of altruism to work for others — the shirk would be the typical altruist, since if labor is pleasant, he who foregoes it by shifting it upon others is doing them a service. Suppose everyone, desiring to be altruistic, did, in fact, labor continually for others. Suppose that A labored continually that B, C, and D, might reap the reward of his labor; B labored continually that A, C, and D, might reap the reward, and so with the rest. It is clear that the labor of all would be wasted, since none would have permitted himself time to consume that which the others had made available for his consumption. I shall, in fact, hereafter prove that not only is it the duty of every man to spend a part of his time in production, but it is equally his duty to spend a part in consumption, and most important of all, it is his duty to continually increase the duration of consumption at the expense of that of production. Men have but one life to live: if they are not happy, they may, to be sure, be economic factors in society from the happiness they cause others, but the unhappiness of the average man would involve the failure of society in its only useful object. His duty to play is, if anything, more imperative than his duty to work. The old hymn exhorts us to "Work, for the night is coming when man's work is done." The exhortation of the utilitarian moralist should be "Play, for the night is coming when man's play is done."

All desiderata save those which nature supplies gratis may be produced only by the expenditure of labor. The happiness value of the labor required to produce a given desideratum we shall call its *labor cost,* and shall measure that cost by the amount of pleasure or pain involved in it. Thus the labor cost of a desideratum is found by multiplying the average intensity of pleasure or pain of the operations required to produce it by the duration of said operations. As labor is generally unpleasant, labor cost is most conveniently measured in pathon-minutes or hours. Hence a positive labor cost will indicate a negative amount of happiness, and a negative labor cost a positive amount.

The change which labor accomplishes — its product or amount of production, on the other hand, is determined by the initial and final states of the system operated upon, and is independent of the mode by which the change has been brought about. Thus to convert a ton of iron ore into an equivalent of pig iron is a definite amount of production and is the same amount whatever the means employed to effect it — whether involving much labor cost or little.

No general method of measuring production, except in terms of labor cost, however, has ever been suggested. We might say that the production of 1,000 bushels of oats was a thousand times the production of one bushel; but when different desiderata are compared, labor cost is the only useful common measure. Unless such a measure is employed we cannot assign any meaning to the statement that one amount of production is greater or less than another. Nevertheless at any given place and time a relation between any given amount of production and its

Chap. VII]   SECOND FACTOR OF HAPPINESS   279

labor cost must obtain; and it is of particular interest to compare this relation at different times, since it measures the advance of the productive arts. Hence the *amount* of a given production I shall measure by the labor cost required to achieve the change from the given initial to the given final state *in a specified condition of the efficiency of conversion and of the productive arts*. This enables us to define the term *efficiency of production*. It is the ratio of a given production to its labor cost, being directly proportional to the amount of production, and inversely proportional to the labor cost. By the *productive power or capacity* of a given individual or assemblage thereof, I mean the amount of production achievable by him or them in a given time: i. e., the rate of production of desiderata. *The amount of production required in the creation of wealth is the measure of the amount of wealth so created.* Were it necessary, a unit of production might be established by fixing the labor cost under specified conditions of some particular product as a standard, but as no such unit is required, none will be established.

Let us next examine the uniformities discoverable in nature and human nature which affect the efficiency of production. One fact is universally acknowledged. Monotonous labor is more unpleasant than varied labor. The continued repetition of a series of productive acts is usually disagreeable and progressively so. Varied labor is less unpleasant and is, in truth, frequently pleasant, particularly at first, but the pleasure of successive acts, exclusively productive, continually dwindles; at least such is its normal course. This diminishing return in pleasure to reiterated stimulus we may call the *law of fatigue*. It is by no means confined to productive acts. Its operation in extreme cases is conspicuously painful, and is most marked in monotonous occupations where the stimulus is continually applied to the same set of nerves. The law of fatigue may be expressed graphically, as in the accompanying diagram, (Fig. 7), the abscissae representing duration, the ordinates intensity. (1) Represents a normal and maintained pleasant productive operation: (2) An operation which, in its earlier stages, is pleasant, but in which the pleasure is not maintained: (3) Represents what may perhaps be considered a normal productive operation: (4) A purely unpleasant operation. (1) and (2) represent varied operations and would be typical of the fine arts: (3) and (4) monotonous operations typical of the useful arts, so called.

The fatigue curves of most productive operations tend to

become asymptotes to a line parallel with the X axis and below it, that is, they continually approach and continually become more nearly parallel to such a line. Obviously the curves shown are only typical; they merely illustrate the type of curve which the law of fatigue produces. The curves of productive operations have many different initial points, and vary much in steepness and curvature. Many circumstances, too, may make them depart from the normal, but these do not concern us. What does concern us is that the law of fatigue is a *law of*

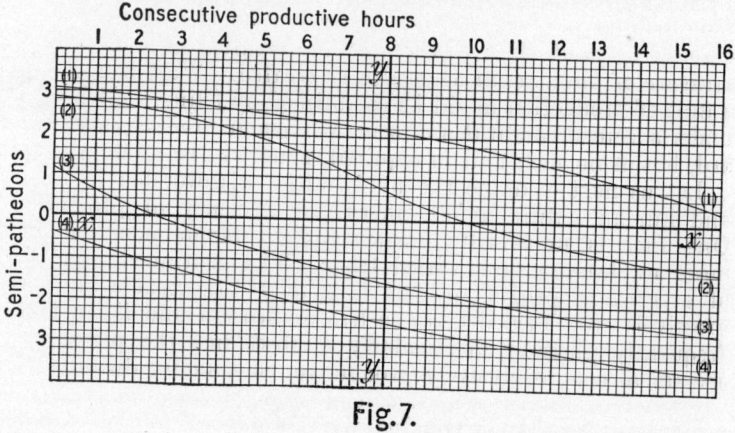

FATIGUE CURVES OF PRODUCTION.

Fig. 7.

human nature, not accidental, occasional, or varying materially with the history of the individual, and hence if we would discover the economics of happiness, we cannot ignore it.

We come next to the consideration of two laws, partly of human nature, partly of nature, which are of profound significance in the economy of production. They are both laws of decreasing returns to labor. The first I shall call the *law of diminishing returns*. It holds a conspicuous place in political economy, and is the result of two conditions: (1) The resources of nature are in very various degrees adapted to the requirements of man. Some portions require much less adjustment than others to satisfy his ends, whether those ends be right, correct, or merely adaptive. (2) Man, in general, will adapt those portions of the available resources to his ends which are most easily adapted, whose adjustment requires the least labor. The consequence of these two conditions is that, in the development of the resources of a country, those which are most easily accessible and which require least adaptation, are utilized first; those less accessible and requiring more adaptation, being left to future utilization. The richest soils and mines are developed and exhausted first, the best timber lands cleared, the most valuable fur-bearing or other animals exterminated. Thus progressively less well-adapted resources have, in the course of history, to be utilized, and were there no offset to this diminishing return of nature, it would become progressively more difficult for man to adjust the available resources to his end, and it would require progressively greater labor to adapt desiderata so as to produce the same possibilities of consumption. There are many modes by which the return from a given quantity of labor may be diminished besides that we have mentioned. Any sort of bad management in industry can accomplish it. To the result of one kind of bad management I shall confine the term *law of dwindling returns of labor,* to the result namely of the bad distribution of labor. Economists generally discuss this law in its relation to agricultural operations, but it is not confined to such, though it is true that in agricultural industries the law of diminishing returns stimulates the operation of the law of dwindling returns. I shall not discuss it here since it is sufficiently explained on page 316.

As all economists recognize, there exists an offset to the law of diminishing returns which may be called *the law of increasing returns.* Its characteristics are easily made manifest. Suppose two men, A and B, start to mow a field one acre in extent, A equipped with a scythe, B with a mowing machine. The object of both is to convert the incomplete desideratum of the standing grass into the less incomplete desideratum of mown grass. Let us, for the sake of simplicity, call the intensity of labor the same for both A and B. Normally the surplus of production is negative. It is not fun to mow the acre in either manner. Neither A nor B on finishing his mowing would feel gratified to see the grass standing again, thus offering another opportunity for them to mow it. Now it will take A with his scythe about ten hours to mow the field, whereas B with his mowing machine can do it in one hour. Hence the same amount of production is accomplished with less labor by B's method than by A's; the intensity of labor being the same, but the duration being less for B than for A. What has caused this difference? Simply the employment by B of better or more improved machinery than that employed by A. Now a similar result is obtained by the use of labor-saving machinery in all arts in which it is introduced. For cultivating the ground a sharp stick is better than the unaided hand, a spade is an improvement on a sharp stick, an ordinary plow is an improvement on a spade, a sulky plow better than an ordinary one, and a steam plow better than a sulky plow. Examples might be indefinitely multiplied. In our day machinery is applied in most, if not all, productive processes. The adjustment of the environment to the requirements of man is largely accomplished by its help, and in all arts the same result is accomplished — the productive power per capita is continually increased. This law of increasing returns is obviously a direct offset to the law of diminishing returns, the one acting to increase, the other to diminish, the productive power per capita. The more rapidly the resources of a country are exploited, the more is the law of diminishing returns stimulated into operation and the more will the productive power per capita diminish. The more rapidly labor-saving machinery is introduced into production, the more will the law of diminishing returns be nullified and the more will the productive power per capita increase. On the relative rate of speed of these two opposing developments the productive power per capita at a given time will depend.

It is worth remarking at this point that whereas in every country the law of diminishing returns is, and during the period of its habitation always has been and always will be, in operation, the law of increasing returns is only in operation where men deliberately use their brains to devise improvements in the productive arts — where they employ their common sense to better adapt their means to their ends, proximate or ultimate. The better equipped they are then with common sense and with the means of knowledge, theoretical and applied, which the operation of common sense supplies, the more rapidly will their productive power per capita increase. In other words, the law of increasing returns results from the application of science, and the degree in which it affects the industries and the productive power of a country for the better, is directly proportional to the degree of development of science in that country. To effect the most simple and primitive or the most complex and modern improvements in the arts the same mental processes are employed, viz., observation, and inference. When a monkey uses a stone or a club to knock cocoanuts from a tree, he uses

the same kind of mental operation which is employed by a
Watt, a Stephenson, a Bessemer, or an Edison in devising the
ingenious improvements in the arts which have made these inventors famous; and the same kind, indeed, which a Newton, a Galileo, a Faraday, or a Kelvin uses in discovering the
great uniformities of nature upon which the progress of applied science depends. The monkey, the inventor, and the
scientific explorer or discoverer, employ the same method, viz.,
common sense; for science, as we have already observed, is
merely consistent common sense. The monkey would never
have used the stone to save himself labor had he not known
something of the laws of gravitation and momentum, though
he had no name for either. Similarly, Watt would never have
invented the steam engine had he been ignorant of the laws
of gaseous expansion, nor would modern electrical inventions
have been possible without a knowledge of the laws of electro-
dynamics discovered by Ampere and Faraday. To apply these
laws, or any others, in the arts it is first essential to determine
what we desire to accomplish, and second to apply the knowledge made available by science to its accomplishment.

It will be of service before proceeding further to more clearly
define a *machine*. A printing press, a locomotive, a derrick, are
generally recognized as machines; but is a shovel a machine, is
a tooth-pick a machine, are buildings, stove-pipes, bolts and
barrels machines? It will be convenient to class them as such,
as will appear from the following distinction.

In the production of external desiderata, whether it be by
manipulation or localization, we may distinguish between that
which is manipulated or localized, and that through the agency
of which the manipulation or localization is accomplished. The
first I shall call the *material,* the second the *machinery* of production. Together they constitute the *means* of production.
The first may be almost any material object, mineral, animal,
or vegetable, and often consists of the unchanged or raw material of the earth itself. The second includes any means, not
essential to all production, by which to effect the manipulation
or localization of the first. We shall not class the human body
with machines, since it must, immediately or remotely, always
take part in production, and for the same reason, we shall not
class the earth or the forces of nature as machines. But if a
tool or instrument, such as those already cited, is used, then a
means not essential to all labor is employed, and such tool or
instrument is a *machine* whether it be as simple as a stick used

as a lever or as complex as a marine engine. It must not be inferred, however, that the only machinery employed in production is that which is visible and tangible. It makes a difference where, by whom, how continuously, and with what relation to other processes, men's acts are performed. The rules, policies, or plans according to which these things are determined is a part of the machinery of production. The policy of the division of labor is such a part. The principle by whose operation the place and functions of each man in a productive establishment are determined is such a part. In short, the organization of industry is a part of the mechanism of production. Human language itself is a species of machinery. A *machine* then is any means of production, exclusive of the materials thereof, the human body, the earth, and the forces of nature. This definition may appear somewhat loose; but for the purpose we have in view, it is sufficient. If flaws may be found in it I believe they will not be such as to invalidate any conclusion we may draw. Machines may be divided into *material* and *non-material,* according as they are material objects or not. They may be employed directly or indirectly in the production of either internal or external desiderata.

Before proceeding with the subject of machinery it will be well to point out that the development of a country does not necessarily result in the progressive depletion of its resources. There is a variety of development the effect of which is to produce machinery by which the resources of a country may be made available. Examples of such development are the construction of roads, bridges, railroads, and irrigation works, the improvement of water powers and harbors by dredging, breakwater construction, etc., and the clearing of land of stones and forest for purposes of cultivation. This kind of development may be called *preparatory* development in distinction to that by which the resources of a country are caused to diminish, which may be called *final* development. The object of preparatory development is the construction of a machine, for a road or an irrigation reservoir is a kind of machine, and a cleared field may be put in the same category, since it is a portion of the earth artificially prepared for productive purposes. Incidentally, of course, preparatory development may — in fact must — involve some final development, since stone must be quarried to build roads and dams, and food and coal utilized by the men and prime motors employed in their construction. Indeed, the clearing of land, if carried too far, may convert this incidental effect into a primary one. There comes a time in the clearing of a country when the destruction of forests to produce arable land results in more loss than gain; for lumber itself is a crop and destruction is not the best mode of harvesting it. Hence the progressive clearing of forests may be transformed from a useful into a maleficently accelerative policy. By comparing the two kinds of development, it becomes clear that preparatory development is an application of the law of increasing returns, and that it is only final development which sets in operation the law of diminishing returns.

We have ascertained that the law of increasing returns operates to diminish the duration of labor required to accomplish a given amount of adjustment. What is its effect upon intensity? Does the introduction of machinery make production more, or less, pleasant? In agricultural and certain other pursuits, where it relieves men of severe muscular effort, it usually diminishes the intensity of pain involved in production, but in a majority of cases it has the opposite effect. This is particularly true of manufacturing operations which absorb more and more of the world's labor.

In the primitive condition of production, each man or family obtained the food, the skins for clothing, the wood for burning, and the materials for building the rude shelters which served primitive men for dwellings, with his or their own hands. All that each family required was produced by the family, and no exchange of products took place. This condition is to be observed among animals and is called *individualistic* or *individualized* production.

As the ingenuity of men resulted in the invention of new articles of use, however, certain individuals confined their attention more and more to the production of some one article, some perhaps making bows and arrows, others making no bows and arrows, but utilizing those made by their fellows in the chase; still others confining their attention to making clothes or pottery, etc. As soon as such a division of production had taken place, exchange arose, for each family no longer satisfied all its own requirements by its own activities, but only a part of them. To supply the deficiency it produced more of certain articles than for its *own* purposes were required, and exchanged the surplus for articles which it did not produce, but which other individuals produced in quantities greater than were required for *their* use. Thus the bow-maker exchanged his bows with the hunters of the vicinity for game procured by them, the maker of clothing similarly exchanged his product for food or other desiderata, and thus trade or commerce arose, and by slow stages developed into the vast and complex system of local and international exchange which to-day occupies so much of the world's attention. I do not propose to trace the course of this development or to comment on the rise of the system of exchange through the medium of money, or the credit system — all this is sufficiently discussed in any political economy. What I do desire is to trace the effects of this system upon the introduction of machinery and the intensity of labor. The division of labor which gave rise to exchange is, in modern industries, pushed to extremes. Instead of confining their attention to the making of one article, the operatives in modern factories make but a small portion thereof, the co-operative labor of many such operatives, each performing a separate function, being required to produce the finished article. Production which thus requires the co-operation of a number of persons is known as *socialistic* or *socialized* production.

It is found that by this method the same number of operatives can produce far more in a given time than if each operative carries on a succession of operations resulting in the production of a completed commodity, as in the more primitive methods of manufacture; methods which survive in some kinds of production to-day. Blacksmiths, cabinet makers, and masons, for example, employ the more primitive methods and so do small farmers and fishermen. Less than three generations ago, clothing, bedding, table linen, etc., was spun and woven at home, the women of the household starting with the raw material and carrying it through a succession of operations to the completed coat, or sheet, or table cloth. To-day the same operations are carried on with far less labor by a series of complex machines, spinners, looms, etc., each kind of machine being attended by an operative who confines his attention to one or more machines of that one kind. The machines are usually power driven and largely automatic, the duty of the operatives being merely the feeding of the machines or the periodic pressing of a lever or pulling of a cord. Thus the operatives may almost be said to be employed by the machines rather than to employ them; they may, indeed, be compared to a part of the machine, a cog or cam whose almost automatic action has not as yet been sufficiently simulated by a mechanical device to dispense with the services of the human hand and brain. Continually, however, these gaps in the perfect self-sufficiency of the mechanism are filled by the progress of invention and the successive operations of production are performed by gigantic automata which do everything but think. The result is that modern production is generally exceedingly monotonous, involving little muscular, but great nervous, strain, and as all productive operations tend to become increasingly automatic and self-regulating, productive labor tends, in most industries, to become increasingly monotonous and the pain involved of greater intensity. Division of labor then, and the introduction of machinery, while they diminish the duration required for a given amount of production, increase the intensity of a given duration of labor.

Thus the introduction of machinery into industry tends to modify another factor of productive efficiency — the skill and interest with which men labor. Other things being equal, the efficiency of production is a direct function of these. Production by machinery tends to dispense with the need of the first and to diminish the second; the former being a good, the latter a bad effect. The less skill required of a laborer, the greater the chance that such as is required will be supplied, and the less labor will be needed to acquire capacity for production. The less interested a laborer is in his work, the less likely is he to apply the skill he possesses, and the speed of production, as well as the quality of the product both suffer. Hence independent of its effect upon productive intensity, loss of interest tends to inefficiency of production.

Let us now define a *labor-saving machine*. We have shown that labor should be measured by duration times intensity. Is this true of labor with a machine? It is, but the labor involved in producing and maintaining the machine must be considered in the calculation. Suppose a man who owns a spade has an acre of ground to turn over. Suppose in order to save himself labor, he constructs a crude plow for the purpose which is worn out after turning over the acre. Ignoring the labor involved by the horses which draw the plow, if the labor of making it plus the labor of turning over the acre therewith is greater than that of turning it over with the spade, it is clear that no labor is saved by the production and use of the plow. It is not a labor-saving machine. Suppose, however, the plow, though costing the same labor to make, has been well enough made to plow one hundred acres before wearing out. It will then be necessary to add to the labor of plowing the field but $\frac{1}{100}$ the labor involved in making the plow, and this, if it is less than that of spading an acre, as it obviously will be, will constitute the plow a labor-saving machine. It is clear that all repairs made on the plow will have to be calculated in the total. Now it makes no difference whether A makes the machine and A uses it, or whether A, B, and C make the machine and D, E, and F use it; the same rule applies. The labor cost of a given amount of production by the employment of a given machine M is measured by the sum of three terms: (1) The labor involved in designing and making M — the initial cost I, multiplied by a coefficient (k) representing the fraction which the given amount of production is of the total amount of which the machine is capable. (2) The total labor cost of repairs R, multiplied by a fractional coefficient (p) indicating the proportion of the total repairs to be credited to the given amount of production. (3) The labor cost L of operating the machine during said production. Calling the labor cost L.C. and expressing the proposition in mathematical form, we have:

$$L.C. = (k)I + (p)R + L$$

If this quantity is less than that required had M not been used, then M is a labor-saving machine — otherwise, it is not. It is evident that the machine M may have been produced by the use of other machines M_1, M_2, M_3, etc., and the term L.C. must in each case be calculated in precisely the same manner as the labor cost is calculated in any other instance of production. These machines in turn may have been made by the aid of other machines, and thus it becomes clear that the labor cost of any item of modern production contains sums which must be credited to some of the earliest machines made by the hand of man; but after going back in this manner a very little distance the sums to be credited to earlier machines become negligibly small. For convenience, we may call the term $(k)I$ the *first* term, the term $(p)R$ the *second* term, and the term L the *third* term, of the labor cost L.C. Many products cannot be made at all without the use of machinery. The first machine for making these products is, in that case, of course, labor-saving, whatever the labor cost. In modern industry, it frequently happens that, owing to the development of the arts, old machines are replaced by improved types long before they are worn out. In this contingency, the total productive capacity will be, not the productive capacity before wearing out, but the capacity before being replaced.

We may now direct attention to a distinction of vital import in the economy of happiness — that between the *sentient* and *non-sentient* factors of production. When a man employs a machine in a productive operation, two factors are combined to produce the result, the man and the machine. The first is the *sentient,* the second, the *non-sentient* factor of production. The labor cost of such an operation must be calculated as in all other cases, namely, by the equation above given.

The first two terms (k)I and (p)R are the terms of the non-sentient, the third term L of the sentient factor. When a labor-saving machine is introduced into production, the first two terms may or may not be increased, but the third term is diminished, and diminished in such a degree that the sum of the three terms is less than before. If the last condition is not fulfilled the machine is not a labor-saving one, and is not an economic factor in production however efficient it may be in other respects.

In the preceding brief discussion of the economics of production, three points appear clearly: (1) Average labor is unpleasant. (2) Machinery does not diminish the intensity of its unpleasantness, but (3) May diminish its duration without decrease, and even with increase, in the productive power per capita.

Thus machinery *may* be employed to save labor, but it does not follow that it *must* be. It is a means of increasing the efficiency of production; that is, of increasing the ratio between a given amount of production and its labor cost, and this may obviously be accomplished in a variety of ways, three of which are of interest to the economist: (1) The amount of production may remain constant and the labor cost decrease. (2) The labor cost may remain constant and the amount of production increase. (3) The labor cost may decrease and the amount of production increase. To the question of which of these three policies it is most economic for society to adopt — of which will most increase the margin of self-support — we shall return when better prepared to decide. Such preparation requires an understanding of the object of production — consumption.

The intelligent understanding of consumption requires that a current delusion be dissipated at the outset of our discussion. Dogmatic political economy has only an incidental interest in consumption, whereas real political economy has a cardinal interest in it. The dogmatic economist regards that labor only as productive which results in the production of wealth, and the destruction or dissipation of wealth by men in the attainment of ends — whether useful or useless — he calls consumption. Here is a case of verbal emasculation, and it affords an impressive example of the baneful results of that variety of logomania. Compare this immaterial distinction of the dogmatic economist with that which has been made in the present work between production and consumption. Which is the more likely to be of service in expressing propositions of interest to sentient beings? Important terms should express important objects of, or distinctions in, experience. By ignoring this maxim of common sense and giving unimportant meanings to their fundamental terms, economists are, at the outset, beset by the danger of promulgating propositions, true perhaps, but of slight human interest, and observation proves that it is a danger they have been unable to avoid. By substituting such immaterial propositions for material ones as a guide to the conduct of society, they have hopelessly deflected the thought and policies of modern states from the path of common sense into that of practomania — from utility into commercialism. Let us trace their mode of accomplishing this.

After making their arbitrary distinction between production and consumption they proceed to distinguish between productive and unproductive consumption. Thus, Mill says:

"The distinction of Productive and Unproductive is applicable to consumption as well as to labour. All the members of the community are not labourers, but all are consumers, and consume either unproductively or productively. Whoever contributes nothing directly or indirectly, to production, is an unproductive consumer. The only productive consumers are productive labourers; the labour of direction being of course included, as well as that of execution. But the consumption even of productive labourers is not all of it productive consumption. There is unproductive consumption by productive consumers. What they consume in keeping up or improving their health, strength, and capacities of work, or in rearing other productive labourers to succeed them is productive consumption. But consumption on pleasures or luxuries, whether by the idle or by the industrious, since production is neither its object nor is in any way advanced by it, must be reckoned unproductive; with a reservation perhaps of a certain quantum of enjoyment which may be classed among necessaries, since anything short of it would not be consistent with the greatest efficiency of labour. That alone is productive consumption, which goes to maintain and increase the productive powers of the community; either those residing in its soil, in its materials, in the number and efficiency of its instruments of production, or in its people."[1]

[1] Principles of Political Economy; Book I.

After dwelling upon unproductive consumption and the labor required to make it possible, he proceeds:

"We see, however, by this, that there is a distinction, more important to the wealth of a community than even that between productive and unproductive labour; the distinction, namely, between labour for the supply of productive, and for the supply of unproductive, consumption; between labour employed in keeping up or in adding to the productive resources of the country, and that which is employed otherwise. Of the produce of the country, a part only is destined to be consumed productively; the remainder supplies the unproductive consumption of producers, and the entire consumption of the unproductive classes. Suppose that the proportion of the annual produce applied to the first purpose amounts to half; then one-half the productive labourers of the country are all that are employed in the operations on which the permanent wealth of the country depends. The other half are occupied from year to year and from generation to generation in producing things which are consumed and disappear without return; and whatever this half consume is as completely lost, as to any permanent effect on the national resources as if it were consumed unproductively." [1]

It is here that Mill slips into his own and the reader's mind the confusion which renders the science of economics so dangerous, for all dogmatic economists from Adam Smith to the present time make the same error. Mill speaks of "a distinction more important to the wealth of a community than even that between productive and unproductive labor." What does he mean by "important to the wealth of a community?" The latter part of the quotation shows that he means "important to the accumulation of a community's wealth," and his whole work, as well as that of other economists, shows that it is deemed the proper policy of a community to accumulate wealth as rapidly as possible. This requires that production be made a maximum and consumption a minimum. In other words typical economists confuse *productive* with *useful* and *unproductive* with *useless,* and infer that men should consume only in order that they may produce, instead of producing in order that they may consume. Economists, of course, do not explicitly maintain this. On the contrary, in words, they disavow the doctrine. Thus Mill utters this pregnant truth:

[1] Ibid.

"It would be a great error to regret the large proportion of the annual produce, which in an opulent country goes to supply unproductive consumption. It would be to lament that the community has so much to spare from its necessities, for its pleasures and for all higher uses. This portion of the produce is the fund from which all the wants of the community, other than that of mere living, are provided for; the measure of its means of enjoyment, and of its power of accomplishing all purposes not productive. That so great a surplus should be available for such purposes, and that it should be applied to them, can only be a subject of congratulation. The things to be regretted, and which are not incapable of being remedied, are the prodigious inequality with which this surplus is distributed, the little worth of the objects to which the greater part of it is devoted, and the large share which falls to the lot of persons who render no equivalent service in return." [1]

Had Mill followed up this suggestion and sought means whereby wealth might be applied economically in the production of happiness, suggesting some remedy for the "prodigious inequality" which he observed, his words would have had more force. But he does nothing of the kind. He proceeds on the implication that productive and useful acts are identical instead of on its explicit disavowal, and modern writers of his school follow in his steps. They all proceed on the assumption that the distinction between productive and unproductive labor and consumption is important, not only to the wealth of a community, but to the community itself. The fact is, that it is not. Of course, economists, if it affords them amusement, are entitled to point out that labor may be divided into two classes, productive and unproductive, just as anthropologists are entitled to point out that mankind may be divided into two classes, the bewhiskered and the unbewhiskered. Both asseverations, however, are of that class of propositions which are uninteresting, if true. The harm comes in confusing the distinction between productive and unproductive, with that between useful and useless.

It has already been observed that a purely productive existence is not self-supporting; that it involves an output of more pain than of pleasure. Unless the intensity of consumption then is considerable, it is impossible in a world in which men devote the majority of their waking hours to production, to make their average acts self-supporting, or worth while. In such a world life is not worth living, and were it not for the fear of death

[1] Ibid.

men would not consent to live in perpetual production. The definite integral of happiness for an average productive day is negative. Under these conditions it is clear that practomania is an exceedingly dangerous deviation from common sense — a deviation which society can ill afford to tolerate.

Let us suppose a steam-engineer to have practomania. Suppose by burning his coal with maximum efficiency of adaptation he can produce twelve pounds of steam per pound of coal; steam is what he seeks, and hence he desires a surplus of it, but he must use some of it in mining and hoisting his coal. Let us assume that he has machinery whereby by the use of one pound of steam he can mine one pound of coal. By consuming this one pound economically in his boilers he can produce twelve pounds of steam, which gives him a surplus of eleven pounds of steam for every pound of coal mined. But if he has practomania, he will not do this. He will reason thus: "In order to produce steam, coal must be mined, and the more coal the more steam. Hence I must produce all the coal possible; this may be accomplished best by utilizing all the steam I generate in the mining of coal." By this method he would, of course, obtain a great accumulation of coal, and if he burned it economically this accumulation would continually increase; suppose, however, he paid no attention to the economy of consumption, but so fed the coal to the boilers that some obtained much more than that required for maximum efficiency and some much less. It is clear that in this way he would obtain a wretched efficiency of adaptation and would get neither a surplus of steam nor an accumulation of coal. In fact, he might get a deficit of steam, and have to buy it from some other producer in order to get enough to mine his coal. Hence an engineer with practomania would not only fail to make his steam plant self-supporting — he might achieve a negative margin of self-support — that is, a deficit. What would be thought of such an engineer? Would anyone say he used common sense in his business? Would Justice imitate him in directing the affairs of society whose business is the production of happiness? Not if she had common sense. Political economists, however, invite us to adopt just such a policy. So far as they consider happiness as an end at all they reason like the mad engineer. In order to produce happiness, wealth must be produced, and the more wealth the more happiness. Hence we must produce all the wealth possible; this may be accomplished by employing all our leisure or potentiality of happiness in the production of wealth. By this method, wealth may be accumulated most rapidly. Yes, but how are we to get a surplus of happiness by this method? Can we afford to pay no attention to the economy of consumption of wealth? Economists, by completely ignoring the economy of consumption, leave us to infer that we can.

Every business man knows that to permit productive machinery to stand idle when it might be employed in production is an uneconomic policy. Suppose those who at present are chiefly instrumental in guiding the affairs of society, the statesmen and economists of our day, should regard themselves as the managers for, or representatives of, Justice on earth; responsible to her for the just management of the machinery of happiness provided by terrestrial conditions. What excuse could they offer for permitting the happiness producing mechanisms — the sentient beings of the earth — to stand idle so large a part of the time — idle, that is, so far as the production of happiness is concerned? Would they have a better excuse than the mad engineer for allowing the machinery in their charge to consume most of its time in producing something other than that which it is its object to produce; and if they offered ignorance as an excuse — what excuse would they offer for ignorance? Why do they not inform themselves of what the end of Justice is, before they attempt to seek it. Would they be guilty of such a travesty in any of the common affairs of life? If not, can they offer any excuse for their omission, save that custom has seduced them from common sense?

We have seen that the margin of self-support of an act may be increased by one or more of three effects upon consumption: (1) By increasing its intensity algebraically. (2) By increasing its duration if positive. (3) By diminishing its duration if negative. Let us consider positive consumption first.

As in the case of production, consumption may be monotonous or varied. A case of monotonous consumption is represented in Fig. 8, (2). It resembles the similar curve of production, but, of course, it ranges much higher. The curve shown is merely typical — some curves would be steeper — others would cross the X axis; nor is such a thing inconsistent with acts of positive consumption, since such acts are merely those *designed* to produce happiness — they may fail in their design. Curve (2) simply illustrates what is familiar to everyone, that successive repetitions of the same cause of happiness normally result in a progressively diminishing amount of happiness. Satiation is approached relatively rapidly — we tire of things. This is true whether the cause continually excites the sight, the hearing, the taste, the smell, the touch, or even thought or emotion. Examples will occur to anyone. The characteristic of human nature expressed by this curve is generally referred to in the familiar observation that pleasure palls. Of course, it is not pleasure, but consumptive acts, which pall. Pleasure is always pleasurable; but the reiteration of the same cause of pleasure does not continue to produce the same pleasurable effect. This is what people mean when they say they are tired of pleasure — they are not tired of pleasure, but of a particular cause of it. If they abandon a certain cause of pleasure for one normally perhaps a

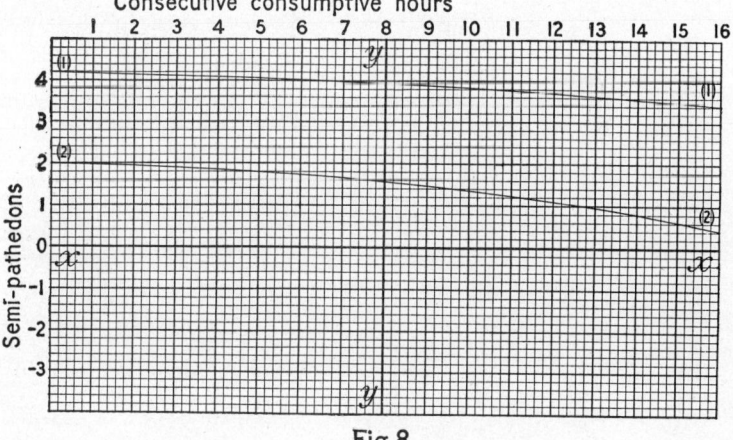

FATIGUE CURVES OF CONSUMPTION.

Fig. 8.

cause of pain, it is commonly because, under the particular circumstances, the second cause gives them more pleasure than the first, though normally the reverse is true.

When the causes of pleasure are varied — when different kinds of pleasure succeed one another, instead of the same kind, the diminishing return in pleasure is less marked. Satiation is approached less rapidly. Curve (1) in Fig. 8 represents such a succession of consumptive acts, though the intensity is too great to be typical.

Of course, a succession of pleasures might produce all sorts of fluctuations in a curve. That shown is intended to represent simply the effect of a succession of varied positive consumptive acts, which, if experienced separately, would produce the same average intensity of pleasure. It is intended to express the fact that even varied pleasures pall, though less rapidly than monotonous ones. Indeed, it is a familiar observation that we appreciate pleasure more keenly after a period of indifference, or of pain. Here again we mean that the same act or cause will produce more pleasure when preceded by pain than when preceded by pleasure. We appreciate the *cause* more keenly — not the *pleasure* more keenly. It would be absurd to say that the same pleasure gives us more or less pleasure than it gives. This would be a contradiction, since it would be saying a pleasure was greater or less than itself. What we mean is that the same cause of pleasure yields more pleasure in the first case than in the second. The characteristic of human nature thus expressed has led some philosophers to a very absurd doctrine — the doctrine, namely, that pleasure is impossible without pain, or pain without pleasure. They tell us that the one is recognized simply by contrast with the other. Were this true it would be impossible to experience either, for when should we begin? A newly born infant could feel no pain because it had not already felt pleasure; it could feel no pleasure because it had not already felt pain. Thus it could not begin to feel either. Therefore, it could never feel either. The notion that scalding water would not hurt a person who had not felt pleasure is a highly speculative one. Despite the absurdity of the doctrine, there are not wanting those who maintain the beneficence of pain on the ground that without it we could have no pleasure, and thus convince themselves that the way to escape being miserable is to be miserable.

Another doctrine allied to this one is that known as the law of compensation — the notion that by some occult process or other, the pain and pleasure in the life of each individual balance one another, and the same surplus of happiness — positive or negative — is attained, however we may attempt to alter it. This is a famous view of Emerson, though true to the idealism of obscurity, he does not state it thus definitely. He seems to regard it as a sort of law of nature and attempts to establish it by the inductive method, handling that method much as a hod-carrier would handle a scalpel. That compensation is frequently to be observed in the world there is no need to deny, but that it is universal, or even common, there is no reason to believe. The doctrine simply leads to fatalism, for if such an inexorable relation between pleasure and pain exists, then, indeed, it is useless for man to attempt the betterment of his own condition or that of his fellows; for should he succeed in eliminating a certain amount of pain, he would, perforce, have eliminated its equivalent of pleasure at the same time, and should he succeed in producing a given amount of pleasure, it would be of no service, since in so doing, he must produce its equivalent of pain. Fortunately we do not need to regard these speculations seriously — they are not derived from experience, but have been suggested by the general effect of pain in increasing our sensitiveness to pleasurable stimuli, and the corresponding effect of pleasure in increasing our sensitiveness to painful stimuli.

The two laws, or rather two examples of the same law, we have noticed, may be called the *fatigue laws of monotonous and varied consumption* respectively; they correspond closely to the similar laws of fatigue of production, and, indeed, result from the same characteristic of the nervous system — a decreasingly pleasurable, or increasingly painful, reaction to successive stimuli, the change being more rapid in the case of similar than of dissimilar stimuli.

When we approach negative consumption, matters are not so simple and there are no laws of production corresponding, since negative production could only mean destruction — a process of maladjustment instead of adjustment, retarding instead of promoting the production of complete desiderata; and hence not normally useful at all. So long as men have needs, however, negative consumption will be useful.

The first point we should observe is that man's capacity for pain is much greater than his capacity for pleasure — that he can experience intensities of pain to which no intensity of pleasure of which he is capable are equivalent. For example, what intensity of pleasure, lasting say for one minute, would a person be willing to exchange for the pain involved in having his hand held in boiling water for one minute. It is doubtful whether a duration of one thousand or even several thousand minutes of the most intense pleasure of which he is capable would be equivalent to one minute of such pain. This means that man is at least several thousand times more capable of pain than of pleasure. It would, perhaps, be fruitless to seek a reason for this unfortunate difference in capacity, but we may incidentally direct the attention of those who think they see evidences of beneficence in the operations of nature to a consideration suggested by it. As already remarked, it is a fact open to the observation of anyone that there are normally many thousands of ways in which a man can produce pain in himself or others to one in which he can produce pleasure. The average intensity of pain which he can produce being thousands of times greater than the average intensity of pleasure, his opportunity for pain is thus not only thousands but *millions* of times greater than his opportunity for pleasure, and a disproportion the same in kind, but probably less in degree, obtains among other sentient beings. Can we appropriately call a universe in which such a condition obtains beneficent? Can we perceive beneficence immanent in its design? If so, what term should we apply to a universe where the capacities of sentient beings for pleasure and pain were reversed? Where man's opportunity for pleasure was millions of times his opportunity for pain? Where it was as easy to produce pleasure and as difficult to produce pain as in our world it is to do the reverse? Would it not be more appropriate to say that in *such* a universe beneficence was immanent, and if so, how can we withhold the term *maleficent* from a universe in which these obviously beneficent relations are reversed? We do not propose to speculate on this matter, since speculation would lead nowhere, but we commend it to the attention of those who claim that the universe and its laws are intrinsically beneficent.

In a succession of long-continued painful stimuli the same effects of fatigue are often to be observed as result from the application of pleasurable stimuli. Long continuance of pain results in numbness or insensitiveness more or less marked, and this is particularly so of monotonous pain. The fatigue effects of pain are not so uniform as those of pleasure, however. Continuous pain, whether monotonous or varied, may induce secondary nervous effects, which result in marked intensification more than counterbalancing the effects of numbness, and these secondary effects may fluctuate in any degree. Two effects unknown in the case of pleasurable sensations may be noticed, resulting directly from man's greater capacity for pain than for pleasure. Severe pain may, and if sufficiently severe, in fact does, lead to unconsciousness, thus curing itself, and severe pain long continued may result in destructive changes in the nervous system, which permanently affect the sensitiveness or capacity of the organism for either pain or pleasure. When the elastic limit of the system has been passed complete recovery is impossible. Insanity, resulting from long illness, or intense grief, or fear, is an example of this effect. A discussion of these phenomena

CHAP. VII] SECOND FACTOR OF HAPPINESS 299

would, however, be out of place here. To the science of medicine, whose application consists in considerable part in acts of negative altruistic consumption, such matters are of importance, but in the formulation of political precepts only the most universal or marked features may be considered.

Two other characteristics of human nature should be mentioned here. The effect of pleasure and pain on memories and expectations. It is not always, but it is usually, true that pleasant experiences are those which it gives most pleasure to recall, whereas painful experiences are painful to recall. Hence the retrospective effect of pleasurable acts is an *increase* — of painful acts a *decrease* in pleasure. This same result is much more marked when we come to anticipatory effects. The anticipation of pleasure is itself a pleasure, often greater in truth than the realization, and the same may be said of pain. These anticipatory effects should not be disregarded in estimating the presumable surplus of happiness to be derived from a given experience. Indeed, no small proportion of the total happiness experienced by mankind is that of anticipation, though realization by no means always follows. Nevertheless, exclusive of the effects of disappointment, such pleasurable anticipations, whether fulfilled or not, are an unmitigated benefit, and were mankind denied the pleasure they afford the total surplus would be much smaller than it is. Offsetting these pleasurable anticipations are painful ones. Anxiety and dejection concerning the future constitute no small part of the sum total of the misery of the human race.

By the *efficiency of consumption* I mean the ratio of the happiness produced by a given amount of wealth to the amount of production required to complete it: so that the efficiency of consumption varies directly as the quantity of happiness and inversely as the production necessary to cause it. By the *consumptive power or capacity* of a given individual, or assemblage thereof, I mean the amount of happiness achievable by him or them by the consumption of a given amount of wealth in a given time: i. e., the rate of production of happiness.

The distinctions we have discussed and the principles we have undertaken to establish (for so obvious are they that to point them out is to establish them) will be of most service as guides to political conduct if applied to the determination of the value of an individual life as a means of contributing to the output of happiness of society. Therefore we must next inquire under what conditions the life of an individual is self-supporting and by what laws the margin of self-support is governed. It may not be denied that it is of more importance that *acts* should be self-supporting than that *lives* should be. Acts which are not self-supporting cannot yield happiness, but lives not self-supporting may. The life of an individual which shows a negative surplus may still be a useful life on account of service done to others — and on the other hand, the life of an individual which shows a positive surplus may be an injurious life on account of disservice done to others. The acts of the first are self-supporting though the life is not — the life of the second is self-supporting though the acts are not. It is nevertheless clear that if we consider an average individual — a fair sample of a community — that his life must be self-supporting, or the community will yield a deficit instead of a surplus of happiness. Individuals may be average in many differing respects. If the total surplus of happiness of a community for a given period be divided by the number of members in the community, the resulting surplus will be that of the average member for that period, and it is an individual having this surplus to whom I refer when I speak of an *average individual*. Strictly speaking, such an individual is an ideal one: the happiness curve of no specifiable member of the community will coincide with that of such an average individual, but the average integral of happiness of all curves will coincide with its integral. A community whose average member produces a negative surplus (unless it is the means of giving rise to one which produces a positive surplus) is entirely useless — less useful, in fact, than none at all. A community of trees or stones would yield a preferable output; since at least it would not be negative. If we multiply the margin of self-support, over any period, of the average member of a community by the number of members, we shall obtain the total output for that period, and it is to make the total output of society, which includes all communities, a maximum, which is or should be the object of all acts, whether of individuals or aggregates of individuals, whether of men or of nations. The problem before us may now be stated thus: Assuming the first and third factors of happiness to remain constant, how may the environment be adjusted to the average individual, so as to make the margin of self-support of his life a maximum? Or, if we please, we may take the average family as our unit instead of the average individual, and the reasoning which follows concerning the average individual may, without essential change, be applied to the average family as well.

SECOND FACTOR OF HAPPINESS

Now a day consists of just twenty-four hours and, on the average, eight of these hours are spent in sleep. This means that whatever happiness is to be turned out by the average individual in an average day must be during the sixteen hours of his waking life. This waking life must consist of voluntary acts and they all must belong in one of three classes. They are either (1) Productive, (2) Consumptive, or (3) Neither. The third class of course are useless. Hence they should always be avoided: that is, life should be confined to productive and consumptive acts exclusively. The problem thus narrows itself to the determination of how life should be divided between these two classes of acts. This is a function of four magnitudes: (1) The productive efficiency. (2) The productive capacity. (3) The consumptive efficiency. (4) The consumptive capacity. We have already discussed separately the chief laws of nature and of human nature which affect these magnitudes: we shall now apply them to the case of the average individual and ascertain their aggregate effect upon his output of happiness per day.

For this purpose let us inquire first how happy an average individual would be who consumed no wealth at all per day. The answer is easy. He would be neither happy nor unhappy — he would be dead. There is a minimum rate of consumption for an average individual below which he cannot go and continue to live. Suppose he consumed at this minimum rate, would he be happy? Obviously not. He would be on the verge of starvation, would have just enough clothes and shelter to keep him alive, and would be in almost perpetual and very keen misery. Suppose now we increase his rate of consumption by equal increments. Suppose, to fix our ideas, the minimum consumption to be at the rate of $50.00 per year and we add successively increments of $10.00 a year. Will his misery be diminished in equal degree for each increment? No, the first increment will diminish it more than the second, the second more than the third, the third more than the fourth, etc. If we continue adding increments we shall gradually increase his opportunity for satisfying his needs, and when the more imperative of these are satisfied, he will begin to gratify the least expensive of his tastes. A point will finally be reached when the definite integral of happiness for an average day will be zero, and at that point he will no longer produce a negative surplus. From this point henceforward each increment of rate of consumption will lead to an increased positive surplus of happiness, but the laws of his nature will still operate to make the return of happiness for each successive equal increment of consumptive rate less than that yielded by the preceding increment. The time will eventually come when an increment of consumption will yield a very small return in increased happiness — in other words. it will take a great increase in the rate of wealth consumption to effect a moderate increase in the rate of happiness production. This general tendency to a diminishing return may be illustrated by comparing the effects of adding a dollar a day to the wages of a man who already receives a dollar a day, and adding the same amount to the salary of one who already receives a hundred dollars a day. The return in increased happiness or decreased unhappiness would be much greater in the first than in the second case. Or, suppose we diminish the wages of both by fifty cents a day. Is it not obvious that the happiness of the first will be diminished by an amount hundreds if not thousands of times greater than that of the second? The second has his income diminished by only one-half of one per cent; the first by fifty per cent — yet the actual amount of diminution is the same in both cases, viz., fifty cents.

The law here referred to is so important that we can well afford to take some trouble in rendering it as exact as our knowledge of the subject will permit, but before proceeding, it may be noted that at present it will be best to confine attention to hypothetical rather than actual conditions, because by thus dealing with definite, though ideal, data we shall be able to more clearly apprehend the essential relations between happiness and the available means of attaining it than we could by an immediate discussion of the subject in all its actual complexity and consequent confusion. In adopting this course, we are but applying the method used in the preliminary exposition of any science. Thus every work on theoretical mechanics is engaged in the discussion of the properties of perfectly rigid or elastic bodies, frictionless surfaces, etc., although such things are never found in nature. Nevertheless the theorems established by a discussion of these ideal cases are essential in applied mechanics, and were they uncomprehended, little insight into the subject of mechanics, theoretical or applied, could ever be obtained. In a similar manner, if we can once establish the essential principles of political utility by a discussion of ideal cases, we shall have little difficulty in applying them in actual cases. For the sake of dealing with definite data, therefore, we shall consider a hypothetical community, the required knowledge of which we may assume. We shall assume the average labor intensity in the community to be 2.5 pathon-minutes per hour — thus during an average hour of labor, the average intensity of pain experienced is $\frac{1}{24}$ pathon; and we shall further assume that the average efficiency of conversion and the condition of the arts are such that the labor cost of any given production measures the amount of that production. We shall assume the average member of this community to live in such an environment, and to have an efficiency of conversion such, that his consumption per hour of the desiderata produced by 2 minutes labor of average intensity will just suffice to keep him alive. We shall assume that the relation of his rate of consumption to its return in happiness is such that if the labor cost required to produce the desiderata consumed in one average consuming hour be represented by abscissae, and the definite integral of happiness for that hour be represented by ordinates, that Fig. 9 will represent the relation between the rate of consumption of wealth and the return in happiness resulting therefrom. That is, *this curve will show how the consumptive power varies with the consumptive rate.* Now, in every community at a particular period there must be some average labor cost of wealth production, and there must be some average rate of happiness output resulting from the consumption of wealth so produced; hence there must be some definite relation between the two. I ask the reader to inspect Fig. 9 with care and decide whether in general form he believes it to fairly represent the relation as it actually exists in normal communities, or whether some very dissimilar curve would represent it more fairly. If it is acknowledged that this is as fair a representation as our ignorance will permit us to attain, then we may justly claim that the conclusions we draw from the hypothetical relation expressed by it may with propriety be applied to actual communities, on the principle that an approximate solution of a problem is better than none at all. We must either accept and act upon the most probable relation suggestible, or we must accept and act upon some relation less probable, nor can we escape the dilemma by inaction, since this is but a special case of action. Once acknowledge that we have here a substantially correct expression of the relation sought, and we shall be prepared to reveal relationships of far-reaching import, for the curve in question represents the simple logarithmic function: $y = \log_{1.2} x$. 1.2 is selected as a base, because the corresponding curve is a convenient one by which to illustrate the appropriate relations.

304 TECHNOLOGY OF HAPPINESS — PART I [Book II

At this point I must beg the non-mathematical reader not to grow impatient. The relation assumed is merely for the sake of definiteness. The law expressed by the above equation is one which satisfies the conditions postulated as determining the relation between given successive increments of happiness, and the

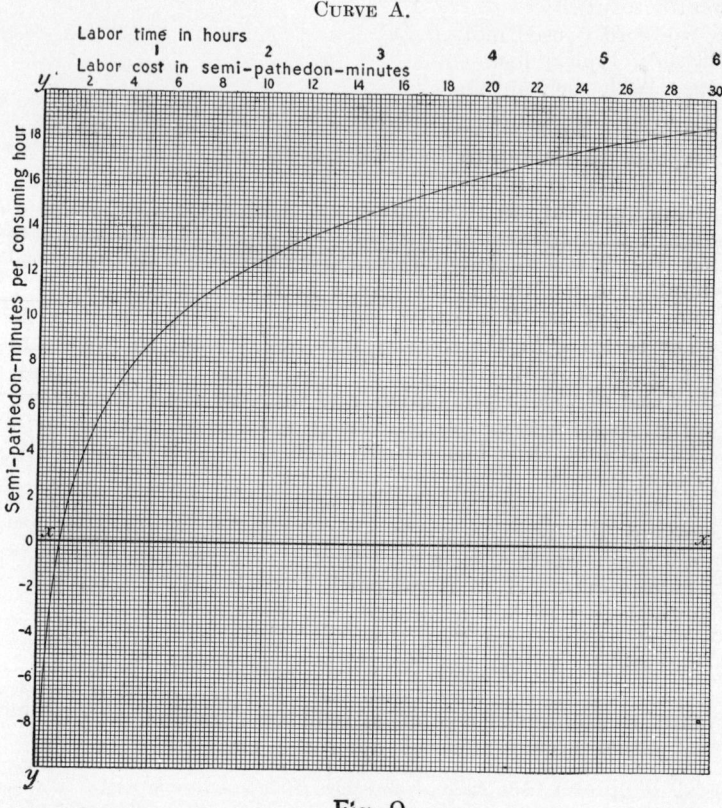

Fig. 9.

equal increments of rate of consumption of which they are functions, viz., that equal increments of consumptive rate produce (algebraically) diminishing increments of happiness, positive or negative. We, of course, have no warrant for asserting that in any actual community the exact relation between these increments is that represented by the logarithmic function cited. All we can say is that the two resemble one another sufficiently for our purpose. The figure represents the relation we are considering as clearly to the non-mathematical as to the mathematical reader, and if carefully inspected will, in connection with Figs. 10 and 11, serve to make definite the whole subject of the relation of the production and consumption of wealth to utility.

No word is used more by economists than the word "utility," yet with typical logomania they never give it a definite meaning. With such an omission how can they hope to construct a useful science of wealth? Indeed, without an understanding of the relations about to be explained, they can no more comprehend the relation of wealth to utility than a mill manager who does not know the utility of yarn can comprehend the relation of spinning to weaving, or an engineer who does not know the utility of coal can comprehend the relation of its production to its consumption.

The law expressed by Curve A we shall call the *Law of Diminishing Returns of Happiness*. Distances along the X axis represent the labor cost of the desiderata whose consumption in one hour produces the surplus of happiness represented by corresponding distances along the Y axis. Both are expressed in semi-pathedon-minutes, but it must not be forgotten that labor cost is negative in sign (See p. 278), and as we have assumed it to be 2.5 pathon-minutes per hour, it is obvious that 5 divisions on the diagram represent one hour of average labor. A unit one-half that established in Chapter 3 is employed here because it happens to be convenient. To convert quantities of happiness expressed in this unit into quantities expressed in pathedon-minutes, we need but divide by two.

It is clear that the happiness derived from the consumption of wealth is not a function of the unhappiness involved in producing it. The pleasure derived from smoking a cigar is the same whether the cigar is made by a machine or by the hand labor of tired women. The relation brought out in Curve A is one between happiness and rate of wealth consumption, and labor cost is involved only because we measure amount of wealth by amount of production, i. e., in terms of the labor cost required to produce it. But as wealth to be consumed must first be produced it is obvious that in estimating the total effect of wealth upon happiness, we cannot confine ourselves to the effect of its consumption — we must not ignore the effect upon happiness of its production — that is, we must, in our estimate, consider the

20

total — not the *partial* — effect. Curve A shows the relation between happiness and *consumption;* what we want is an expression of the relation between happiness and *production and consumption*. In order more clearly to reveal this relationship, we shall derive from Curve A a second curve by subtracting from each successive value of y the corresponding value of x. Thus we derive Curve B whose equation is $w = \log_{1.2} x - x$. The significance of this curve becomes apparent by a consideration of the mode of its derivation. Any point (p) on Curve A fixes one abscissa and one ordinate; it represents two things: (1) A consumption of wealth per hour — always positive. (2) A surplus of happiness — positive or negative. Now a consumption of wealth involves a production of wealth, and production involves labor, and labor involves labor cost. Hence the total effect of the acts whose consumptive effect is represented by the ordinate at point p will be made up of said consumptive effect and the productive cause or labor cost in the absence of which the consumption would have been impossible. Average labor cost being negative, the total effect on happiness must, in general, be less than the consumptive effect, and less by the exact amount of the labor cost expended in producing the desiderata whose consumption results in the surplus y. Hence the total effect is $y - x$. Thus the ordinate y of any point on Curve A becomes equal to $y - x$ on Curve B.

Four points on this curve are of especial significance: (1) *a,* the point of minimum consumption — the point at which life is just sustained, with a resulting output of -10 pathedon-minutes per consuming hour. (2) *b,* the minimum point of self-support, or the point at which combined production and consumption is just self-supporting. (3) *c,* the point of apparent maximum efficiency, or the point at which the margin of self-support is a maximum, provided the relation between the producing and consuming ratio indicated in the curve, is maintained. (4) *d,* the maximum point of self-support, or the point beyond which combined production and consumption is no longer self-supporting on account of the negative integral resulting from production exceeding the positive integral resulting from consumption.

The consuming ratio is fixed by the law of diminishing returns of happiness in conformity with the following principles. If a community, avoiding useless acts, divides its time between production and consumption, and consumes at the rate denoted by *c,* then it must produce at the rate required to sustain that

CHAP. VII] SECOND FACTOR OF HAPPINESS 307

rate of consumption. That is, for every hour of consumption, about one hour and six minutes of production will be required. This fixes the producing ratio at .523, and the consuming ratio therefore at .477.

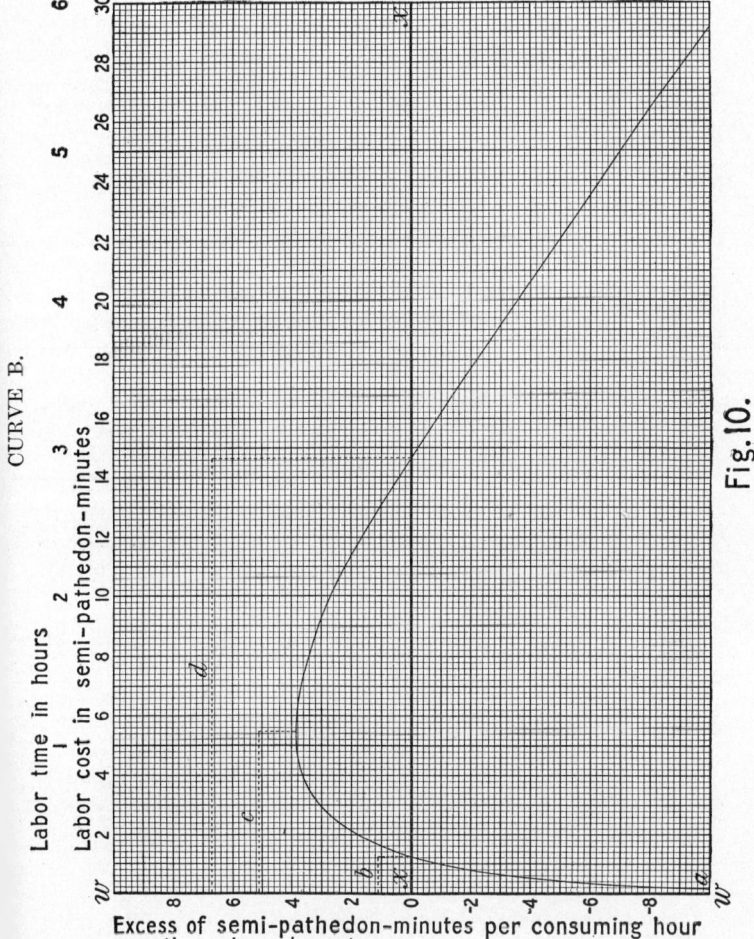

Fig. 10.

The production and consumption of wealth by the average individual between the points a and b and from d onwards is not only useless as a completed process, it is harmful, and at points near *a* and far beyond *d,* exceedingly harmful. A community whose average member produces and consumes wealth under such circumstances will be a useless community — it will produce less happiness than no community at all. The sum total of life in such a community will not be worth living; the sum of its acts will not be self-supporting. It is equally obvious that the production and consumption of wealth between the points *b* and *d will* be self-supporting, and the life of a community whose average member consumes between these points will be worth living. The zone between *a* and *b* I shall call the *zone of underconsumption.* That beyond *d,* the *zone of overconsumption.* That between *b* and *d,* the *zone of self-support.*

We may calculate the daily or yearly output of happiness of a hypothetical individual consuming at maximum efficiency from Curve B, on the assumption that the margin of self-support, which is *apparently* a maximum at the point *c,* is *really* a maximum there. Doing this we discover that, on the assumption of sixteen hours of sentience per day, the daily output will be about 14.6 hedon-minutes, and the yearly output about 5,329 hedon-minutes. But this calculation assumes that, under the conditions postulated, a consuming ratio of .477 is the best, and there is no warrant for this assumption. Is it not possible that by diminishing the rate of consumption we could so increase the duration of consumption which it would take a given labor cost to supply, that it would more than offset the loss in intensity? It is clear that such a result could not be obtained by *increasing* the rate of consumption, since this would diminish the duration which a given labor cost could supply, and we know from the law of diminishing returns, that for each successive increment of consumptive rate the corresponding increment of happiness is increased in less proportion. Hence by increasing the consumptive rate we should get a diminished, instead of an increased, return. Suppose, however, we *diminish* the consumptive rate. If this will increase the daily average output, then it is certain that the real point of maximum efficiency will be found somewhere between *b* and *c.* Can we ascertain just where in our hypothetical case? Yes, this may be ascertained; but first it will be necessary to consider a separate problem, that namely, of the effect upon happiness of the *distribution* of productive and consumptive acts.

Assume two individuals A and B, of average productive and consumptive capacity, who between them are to produce and

CHAP. VII] SECOND FACTOR OF HAPPINESS 309

consume all the wealth of a given domain. Assume the efficiency of production and consumption to be such that the point of apparent maximum efficiency is attained when the wealth produced in one hour is consumed in one hour. Assume that both A and B sleep eight hours of the twenty-four, thus leaving sixteen hours in which all production and consumption must be accomplished. Assume all the production to be assigned to A and all the consumption to B. (For the sake of simplicity we shall assume this, although, of course, B must consume some of the time in order to live.) Under these conditions, A labors sixteen hours a day and B has sixteen hours a day of leisure in which to consume the wealth produced by A. Thus it would seem to be possible, perhaps, to attain good economy, because the wealth produced in sixteen hours will be consumed in sixteen hours, that is, the wealth produced in one hour will be consumed in one hour, which would seem to satisfy the requirement of consumption at the point of apparent maximum efficiency. Were production and consumption non-accelerative operations this arrangement might give the desired result. If, for example, the intensity of production is and remains two pathon-minutes per hour and the intensity of consumption is and remains four hedon-minutes per hour, we could represent A's curve of happiness by a straight line 2 units below the X axis, and B's by a straight line 4 units above. A's daily deficit would thus be 32 pathedon-minutes and B's daily surplus would be 64 pathedon-minutes, the combined surplus being 32 pathedon-minutes. But both production and consumption are accelerative operations, as has already been made manifest in our discussion of the effects of fatigue. The "average labor cost" referred to in Figs. 9 and 10 is the average under given conditions of distribution of leisure, and it will be convenient to consider these conditions the most favorable ones. Under the conditions assumed in our example, both the average labor cost and the average happiness per hour of consumption will be changed, the first increasing, the second decreasing. Assuming the effects of fatigue alone to be operative, the happiness curves of A and B will be something like those shown in Figures 7 and 8, No. 4 in Fig. 7 (p. 280) perhaps representing A's curve, and No. 2 in Fig. 8 (p. 295) representing B's.

Thus it is clear that if the laws of fatigue alone determine the (negative) acceleration of the return in happiness from production and consumption, that the most economic policy to adopt in order to achieve the greatest surplus of happiness will be to make A and B share equally in production and consumption, each producing for eight hours and consuming for eight hours. In addition to the effects of fatigue, however, there are three other factors which must be considered as affecting the problem: (1) (*a*) The effect of labor in increasing the efficiency of subsequent consumption, and (*b*) The effect of consumption in decreasing the labor cost of subsequent production. The first is only effective when labor is not excessive. Long and continuous labor has the opposite effect, and induces such fatigue that the laborer is rendered almost incapable of any intensity of positive consumption beyond that involved in resting. Moderate labor increases the intensity of consumption. Immoderate labor decreases it. Hence this factor affords a double reason for an equal distribution of leisure. Consumption, on the other hand, breeds more than the normal distaste for production only when too continuous, and the effect is merely temporary. (2) The effects of retrospection and anticipation — particularly the latter. (3) The effect of duration of production in progressively decreasing the output of wealth per unit of time. It is notorious that a laborer cannot produce ten times as much in ten hours as he can in one hour; the effect of fatigue, indeed, is not only to increase the labor intensity of each succeeding hour, but to diminish the output of wealth in a similar manner, thus diminishing the efficiency of production in two ways: by decreasing the numerator and increasing the denominator. It is superfluous to comment upon the effect of these characteristics of human nature on the principle we have mentioned. Although exceptional instances might be adduced, it is obvious that, in general, the influence of all of these factors serves only to render the contrast between the two cases of distribution of leisure more emphatic. The existence of these human attributes furnishes additional reason for belief that, under the conditions specified, an equal distribution of production and consumption is the most economic distribution, and hence that *units of average productive and consumptive capacity should produce the equivalent of what they consume;* that is, the labor cost of the desiderata consumed should be equal to that of the desiderata produced. Individuals or aggregates thereof who produce the equivalent of what they consume we shall call *self-sufficing or self-sufficient.* As production is not a spontaneous operation, society must, as a whole, be self-sufficient. Equality in the distribution of production and consumption is just, however, only on the assumption that productive and con-

CHAP. VII] SECOND FACTOR OF HAPPINESS 311

sumptive capacity is equal. Individuals are not, in general, convenient units of equal productive and consumptive capacity — children, for example, have generally a less productive and greater consumptive capacity than mature persons, and hence, on this ground alone, should have a greater consuming and a less producing ratio. The same thing may be said of old persons, though it may be a matter of doubt whether their consumptive capacity is greater than the average. A family constitutes the most convenient unit of average productive and consumptive capacity. Hence it may be taken as a general rule of political conduct that families should be self-sufficient. Marked deviation from this rule is exceedingly uneconomic. It leads to the division of society into two classes — a laboring, and a leisure class — the first producing more than they consume in order that the second may consume more than they produce; the first consuming in the zone of underconsumption in order that the second may consume in the zone of overconsumption; the first submitting to a consuming ratio too low in order that the second may enjoy one that is too high. The contrast between self-sufficiency and the lack of it becomes vastly greater when say five million persons produce what fifty thousand consume than in the very mild case of inequality considered in our example, in which one person produces what one other consumes.

Let us now return to the question proposed on page 308. If we assume that our units are self-sufficient, the question is theoretically answerable, but not otherwise. Indeed, we were able to calculate the daily or yearly output of happiness from Curve B. only by tacitly making this assumption. In the following solution we shall confine our reasoning to an average individual in order to make the explanation uniform with that of Curve B., but it more appropriately applies to an average family.

The abscissae of the B curve (Fig. 10) represent both labor cost and labor time, the unit of the second being equal to five units of the first as measured along the X axis. As each individual produces the equivalent of what he consumes, and as his waking life is divided between production and consumption, the wealth produced during his hours of production must be equivalent to that consumed during his hours of consumption. His total output of happiness for any sample period of time then will be that produced during the producing portion plus that produced during the consuming portion. Let T be such a sample period; then for the condition represented by any point p on the B curve, the consuming ratio will be $\frac{5}{x+5}$, the producing ratio will therefore be $\frac{x}{x+5}$. The consuming period will then be $\frac{5T}{x+5}$ hours, the producing period $\frac{xT}{x+5}$ hours. The intensity for the consuming period will be $\frac{\log_{1.2} x}{2}$ pathedon-minutes per hour, and for the producing period will be -2.5 pathedon-minutes per hour, or the output for the consuming period will be $2.5T \left[\frac{\log_{1.2} x}{x+5} \right]$, and for the producing period will be $-2.5T \left[\frac{x}{x+5} \right]$. The total effect therefore will be the sum of these, or $2.5T \left[\frac{\log_{1.2} x - x}{x+5} \right]$ pathedon-minutes. That is, for any sample period T there will be a multiplier $2.5 \frac{\log_{1.2} x - x}{x+5}$ which multiplied into T expressed in hours, will show the surplus or deficit during that period. Let us call this multiplier z; then expressing the result in semi-pathedon-minutes, instead of pathedon-minutes, we have:

$$z = \frac{\log_{1.2} x - x}{.2(x+5)}.$$

Plotting this equation we obtain Curve C (Fig. 11).

The abscissae indicate: (1) Labor time, five divisions being equal to an hour, and (2) Labor cost, two divisions being equal to a pathon-minute. The ordinates indicate the average output per hour of sentient life, assuming the wealth produced in x hours is consumed in one hour, and that life is divided between production and consumption. Each point on the curve therefore expresses a particular consuming ratio. Thus to discover the surplus during any period having a given consuming ratio, we need only multiply it, expressed in hours, by the ordinate corresponding to the given consuming ratio. The result will be the total surplus or deficit for the period. The curve indicates clearly the points of minimum consumption, and minimum and maximum self-support, and these are situated as in Curve B, but it needs but a glance to make plain that the point of maximum efficiency has receded and is now at about the point $x = 3.8$ instead of at $x = 5.48$: thus the intensity per consuming

CHAP. VII] SECOND FACTOR OF HAPPINESS 313

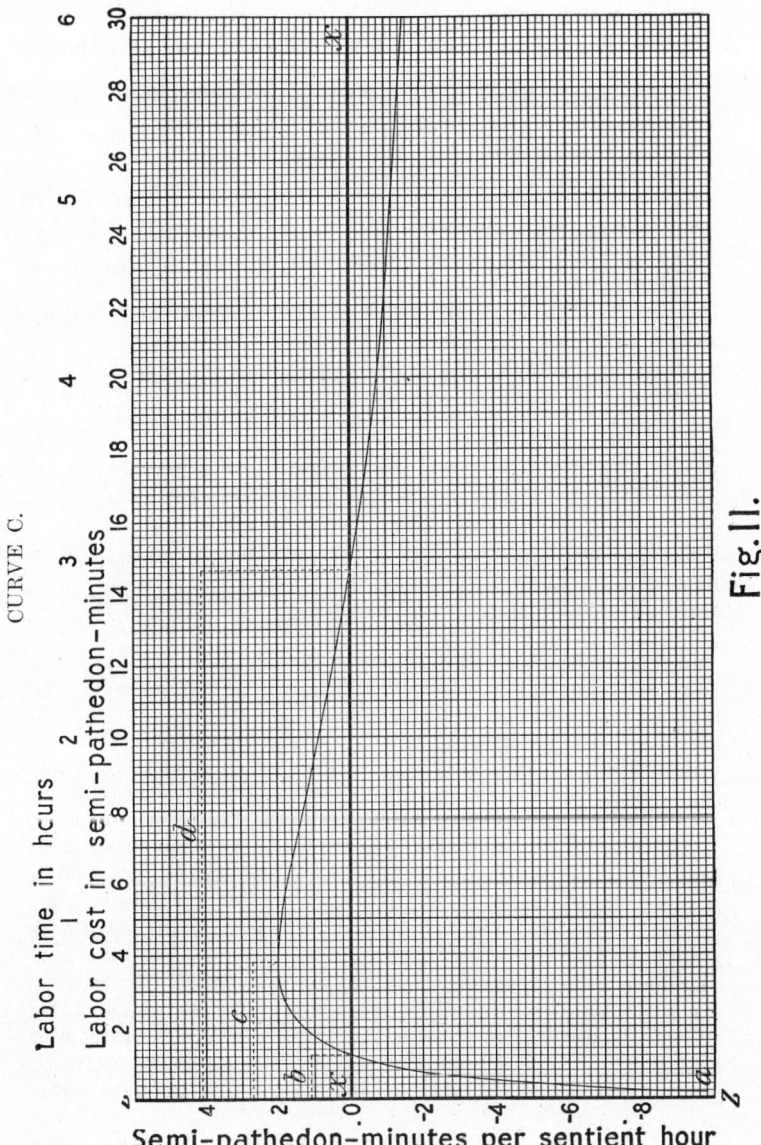

Fig. 11.

hour has fallen from 9.30 to 7.28 semi-pathedon-minutes per hour, but the consuming ratio has risen from .477 to .570. The point $x = 3.8$ then is the point of *real* maximum efficiency of adaptation — the point at which the margin of self-support is a maximum — and the corresponding rate of consumption per capita per hour is obviously the just one for the community in question as a whole — it is the rate which Justice would seek to attain.

Calculating the output of happiness for an individual consuming at the point of real maximum efficiency, we find it is 16 hedon-minutes per day, or 5,840 hedon-minutes per year, as compared with 14.6 hedon-minutes per day, and 5,329 hedon-minutes per year when calculated from the point of apparent maximum efficiency — a gain of nearly ten per cent.

Efficiency of consumption has been defined as the ratio of the happiness value resulting from the consumption of given desiderata to the amount of production which they represent. Measuring production in positive units, the maximum efficiency of consumption in the example before us will be 1.94. If we select any other point in the zone of self-support, this ratio will be positive and greater than 1, the greater ratio showing the better efficiency. In the zone of underconsumption it will be negative the greater ratio showing the poorer efficiency; in the zone of overconsumption it will be positive and less than 1, the less ratio showing the poorer efficiency.

The accuracy of Curve C. will, of course, be less at points far removed from the point of maximum efficiency than at points near to it, because the intensity of labor, assumed for purposes of simplicity to be a constant, would, in fact, be greater than said constant at points to the right of c, and slightly less at points between b and c. At points near a the labor cost of production would obviously be very high — not from the intrinsic unpleasantness of labor — but from the physical and mental suffering incident to defective consumption. For the proximate solution which we seek, these sources of inaccuracy may be neglected.

It goes without saying that the same amount of wealth can be consumed in an indefinite number of ways. 1,000 persons consuming wealth at a rate per capita corresponding to the point $x = .38$ and 10 consuming at the point $x = 38$. would consume the same amount of wealth as 100 at the point of maximum efficiency, but while in the first case the production and consumption would result in a deficit of 42,560 pathedon-

CHAP. VII]   SECOND FACTOR OF HAPPINESS   315

minutes per day, in the second in a deficit of 150 pathedon-minutes per day, it would in the third case result in a surplus of 1,600 pathedon-minutes per day. Indeed any departure from the point of maximum efficiency must be in some degree uneconomic, i. e., unjust.

Curve C is particularly useful as a means of illustrating the importance in the economics of happiness of adjusting the producing to the consuming ratio. In the absence of such adjustment the very highest efficiencies of production and consumption are futile, since these efficiencies take no account of the relation of happiness to the great independent variable — *time*. The quotient of the consuming by the producing ratio I shall denominate the *indicative ratio,* because its magnitude is an index of the position of an industrial community in the scale of civilization. It is an exponent of the degree in which common sense governs the conduct of the body politic. So long as average labor remains unpleasant, low values of the indicative ratio practically preclude a positive surplus of happiness.

If we assume a community whose average intensity of labor is q, then in order to attain to self-support, the average intensity of consumption for an indicative ratio of $\frac{1}{7}$ must be $7\,q$, of $\frac{1}{3}$ must be $3\,q$, of 1 must be q, of 3 must be $\frac{1}{3}\,q$, etc.; and even such relations as these hold good only under the most favorable assumption — the assumption, namely, that the wasted ratio is zero. As consumption is in large part negative, it is clear that, with low indicative ratios, there is little prospect of self-supporting communities. With the poor efficiency of conversion to be found in typical communities of our time, a systematic working day of eight hours effectively precludes any prospect of self-support, since it requires an intensity of consumption more than equivalent to that of production — in fact, considerably more, since the actual duration of production is necessarily in excess of that of the systematic production included in the working day. In every industrial community in the world, the average intensity of consumption, with the exception of eating hours, is slight, if not negative.

In closing this chapter we must point out the vital bearing of the doctrines here advanced upon the general belief that justice demands some sort of equality in the distribution of happiness. Attention was called to this belief on page 146, and if we are correct in our technology the view is well founded. It is simply a recognition of the law of diminishing returns of happiness. This law is strictly comparable to the law of dwindling returns of labor (p. 281). If we have the labor of 100 men available, a greater crop can be raised if we apply that labor to 100 acres than if we confine it to one, for though the labor of 100 men on one acre will result in a greater crop than the labor of one on the same area, it will by no means be greater in the ratio of 100 to 1: whereas if the labor of the 100 is distributed over 100 acres, the return will be greater in the ratio of 100 to 1. Similarly the return in happiness from the consumption of say $1,000,000 worth of wealth in a year will be greater if it is distributed among 100 persons than if it is all consumed by one, although the consumption by that one, of the whole $1,000,000, will result in greater happiness than the consumption of $\frac{1}{100}$ of that amount. On the other hand, the labor of 100 men may be too much dispersed as well as too much restricted. Were 100 men required to cultivate 10,000 acres, the attempt would result in little or no return, since they could not cover so much ground and do the work required with sufficient thoroughness to make their labor self-supporting. The crop would necessarily be so neglected as to be worth less than the cost of cultivation. Under such circumstances a deficit would be realized. Similarly were the consumption of $1,000,000 worth of wealth in one year distributed among 10,000 persons, it would be too much dispersed to be self-supporting and would force the whole community into the zone of underconsumption. Such a community would be worse than none, since its output would be negative. It is unnecessary to dwell further upon these obvious relations. There is the best of justification for the all but universal conviction that happiness should be equally distributed, since its unequal distribution means, in general, the unequal distribution of its causes, and this in turn involves bad efficiency and a consequent diminished return of happiness. It is wealth — opportunity for happiness — which should be equally distributed, since any other distribution will result in a diminished surplus of happiness, and only that alternative among those physically possible can be right which will presumably result in the greatest surplus of happiness. Hence unequal distribution must, in general, be wrong. Thus the theory of utility founds the doctrine of equal opportunity and equal distribution of wealth upon something more substantial than a *sentiment* — it founds it upon a *reason*. The doctrine is directly deducible from the definition of right and the principle of diminishing returns of happiness.

The foregoing discussion of the relation between production

and consumption is perhaps rather involved, but its bearing upon the economy of happiness is too vital to admit of superficial treatment. Were human beings not subject to the law of diminishing returns of happiness, the relation of wealth to utility would not be what it is. No reason would be assignable for an equal distribution of wealth or of leisure or for any other distribution, and to sacrifice the interest of all to the interest of one would be as consistent with utility as to sacrifice the interest of one to the interest of all.

In essaying the solution of the problem presented in this chapter the methods of technology have been adhered to. Should we care to carry out the analogy in detail it would not be difficult to demonstrate that the equations herein applied to human beings would be equally applicable to steam boilers, provided the relation of said boilers to steam generation was the same as that of human beings to happiness generation. I am aware that in this mode of treating an essentially moral question many critics will find a deplorable deficiency of vagueness. They will shake their heads wisely and declare that happiness cannot be measured with rule and compass, that morals and mathematics will not mix, that " you cannot treat these matters in that way, don't you know." This unspecific style of criticism is more familiar than convincing. The happiness that men crave is something more than a *word* adapted to serve as the subject or predicate of a platitude. It is a definite *sensation,* not to be mistaken for any other — a sensation to be experienced only during the sentient hours of life and the conditions of its generation during those hours cannot be too searchingly investigated. Where I could apply mathematical modes of expression to render these conditions less indefinite, I have applied them — where I could not, I have not done so. In adopting this procedure I have endeavored to operate in the clear light of common sense, attaining as great a degree of precision as possible. My only regret is that thus far I have been unable to attain a greater degree. It is with deliberate intent that I have aimed to avoid the obscurity pervading the fog-bank of intuitionism wherein the truth-seeker is doomed to wander in eternal circles, knowing neither where he is nor whither he is going.

CHAPTER VIII

THE THIRD FACTOR OF HAPPINESS

As the most marked feature of modern industrial states is their defective economy of consumption, there can be little doubt that the most strictly economic policy they could pursue would be curtailment of final development to a point where the rate of consumption is as low as is consistent with preserving the productive capacity of the community unimpaired; and the immediate employment of all the productive powers available in constructing and applying an economic system of consumption and bringing it to a high order of efficiency. The main feature of such a policy would be the diversion of human effort from final development of the country to initial development of the human mind — so far as possible from agriculture, mining, and manufacturing, to education, and breeding, since the most fruitful of all natural resources in any nation are the human beings who compose it, and the development thereof supplies no stimulus to the law of diminishing returns of labor. Simultaneously, preparatory development and improvement of the arts should be promoted, and as the foundation of all useful arts, the knowledge of nature and her powers should be advanced through the organized, instead of the unorganized, efforts of science. After an economic system of consumption was once devised, put in operation, and brought to a high degree of perfection, it would then be time to proceed with the development of the material resources of the country, with the assurance that they would be put to a useful purpose — that in their dissipation and depletion happiness would be produced — that society would have something to show for the exhausted mines and diminished fertility of the domain it occupied. Much the same situation as faces Justice to-day would face the steam-engineer whose boilers had a poor efficiency of conversion and poorer efficiency of adaptation. His policy would be to reduce to a minimum the development of his coal mines and to concentrate all his energies on the problem of securing economy in the consumption of his coal through improvements in the efficiencies of conversion and of adaptation. This once accomplished, he could proceed with the development of his mines with the assurance that the steam he produced would be worth more than the coal he consumed — that he would have something to show for his disappearing coal supply. I shall hereafter submit reasons for believing that modern industrial states with their present provision for consumption produce a heavy deficit of happiness — that the sum of their activities is not self-supporting — and hence that every ton of coal, iron, and copper taken from their mines, every pound of phosphorus, potassium, and nitrogen extracted from their soil by agricultural operations is worse than wasted, or at any rate will be so, unless the communities now existing can develop sufficient intelligence to devise and apply a system of consumption which shall lift their posterity into the zone of self-support. Every dollar's worth by which the natural resources of the earth are at present diminished by final development means the destruction of just so much potentiality of happiness — a potentiality which, in the future, with improved economy of consumption, could be converted into an actuality. Hence the duty of every intelligent state to retard the development of its material resources as much as possible, and divert the energies employed in developing them to the development of the human mind and character, and the construction of an economic system of consumption.

To carry out this policy with maximum effect, however, would require considerable self-sacrifice on the part of the present generation; it would involve a denial of consumption on their part that their posterity might have the more to consume. It is doubtful if human nature affords the motive power for consistently pursuing such a policy — hence my endeavor is to ascertain the conditions under which a developing society may attain a state approximating to the maximum happiness for the stages of development it successively attains, and this indeed will not differ very much from the policy first suggested; since the application in practice of an improved and improving system of consumption can only be secured by careful effort and patient experiment. In order to develop in detail an economic mode of applying labor in the production of happiness, we must actually apply it in order to observe how it works; just as in the perfection of any other mechanism for accomplishing a desired result, we must test it by continued trial. Nevertheless the superior claim of posterity to consideration should never be ignored.

If a given population occupying a definite land area attains a condition of maximum efficiency of adaptation, it cannot maintain that condition — that is, it cannot maintain the same output of happiness per capita per day, if the efficiency of production remains stationary. This is owing to the effect of the law of diminishing returns of labor upon the labor cost of desiderata; in other words, to maintain the same number at the same rate of happiness per capita, an increase in efficiency of production is required. Let us call this the *essential* increase. Its magnitude is directly proportional to the population and inversely proportional to the natural resources of the area occupied; thus, it is roughly proportional to the density of population.

Let us assume a community consisting of 10,000,000 members which has attained a condition of maximum efficiency of adaptation and maintains the essential increase in efficiency of production, and the average member of which possesses an efficiency of conversion such that Fig. 9 (p. 304) represents the law of diminishing returns of happiness for that community. Assuming an average sentient day of sixteen hours, the output of happiness per year is 5,840 pathedon-minutes per capita, or for the whole community, 973,000,000 hedon-hours. Let us call this community the *sample community,* and the condition of output here specified the *initial condition.* To be sure, no actually existing community has attained conditions of efficiency even approaching this; but nevertheless it may be used for purposes of illustration.

On page 191, Chapter 5, where the problem of the technology of happiness is formulated, we have pointed out that the third factor of happiness is number. Let us consider the effect on the sample community of varying this factor alone. Owing to the laws of diminishing and dwindling returns, the labor cost of desiderata will increase with increasing population, and decrease with decreasing population. In a new community of low density of population there will be little or no increase at first, because of the abundance of land of practically equal fertility, but as the lands are occupied, and poorer and poorer soils are brought under cultivation, while the better ones are progressively exhausted, the increase in labor cost will accelerate faster than the population increases The increase of labor cost is due to an increase in the time required to effect a given production. It is not, in general, due to any increase in the intensity of labor cost, except as that intensity is in-

CHAP. VIII] THIRD FACTOR OF HAPPINESS

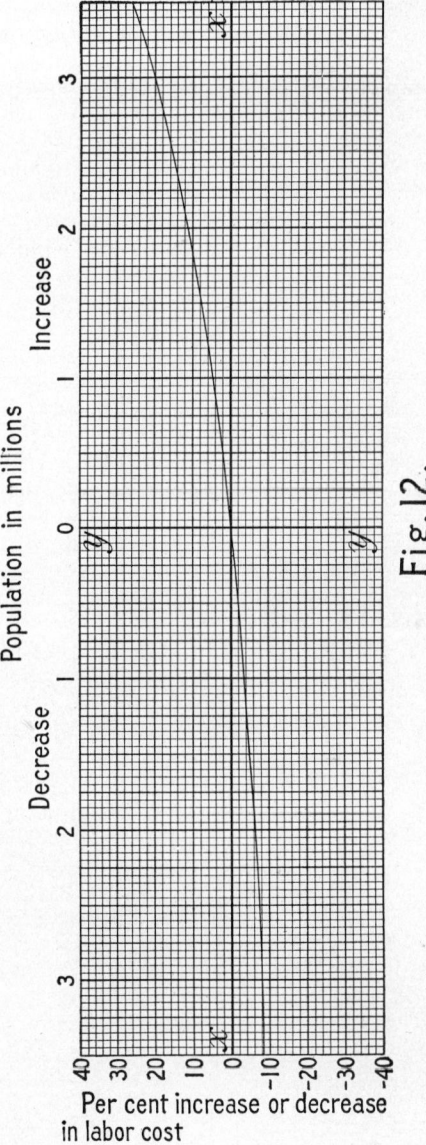

Fig. 12.

21

creased by an increase in duration. While data for determining just what the increase is, or would be, for any actual community, are wanting, the general law is known, and for the sample community may be represented by Fig. 12. Abscissae represent increase or decrease in population, each division corresponding to a population of 250,000; 0 representing the population of the sample community, viz., 10,000,000. Ordinates represent per cent increase or decrease in labor cost with increase or decrease of population. By the use of this curve in conjunction with Figs. 13 and 14, the effect on the rate of happiness output of any increase or decrease of population may be determined. Thus an increase of 10% in the average labor cost of production will be induced by an increase in the population of 1,850,000; this will alter Curve C to the form shown in Fig. 13. At the point of maximum efficiency the average output will be reduced to 13.7 hedon-minutes per day. But as the population will now be 11,850,000, the total output for the year becomes 988,000,000 hedon-hours, as compared with 973,000,000 for a population of 10,000,000. If, however, the population is increased, so as to increase the labor cost of production to 20%, as will result from an increase of 3,000,000, Curve C will take the form shown in Fig. 14 and the maximum output per capita per day will then become 11.6 hedon-minutes, and the total output per year for the increased population will be 917,000,000 hedon-hours, a diminution of 56,000,000 hedon-hours. Between these two points a relation between the increase in total output due to increased population, and the decrease in output per capita due to diminished returns to labor exists, which will give a maximum output for the assumed community. Were it worth while, a method could be given for discovering it, but as the figures we have been citing are for illustrative purposes merely, it would only add confusion to undertake the process. The population giving maximum output in the case we have been discussing would obviously be about 12,000,000. A population thus adjusted to its means of happiness, so as to produce a maximum output thereof, we shall say is in *beneficent equilibrium*. Any increase or decrease of its numbers will result in a diminished output of happiness.

Clearly, for a community at a given stage of efficiency of conversion and adaptation there is some particular population whose number is better adapted than any other to the available resources. The number which would be best adapted to the island of Sicily, for example, would not be the same as that best

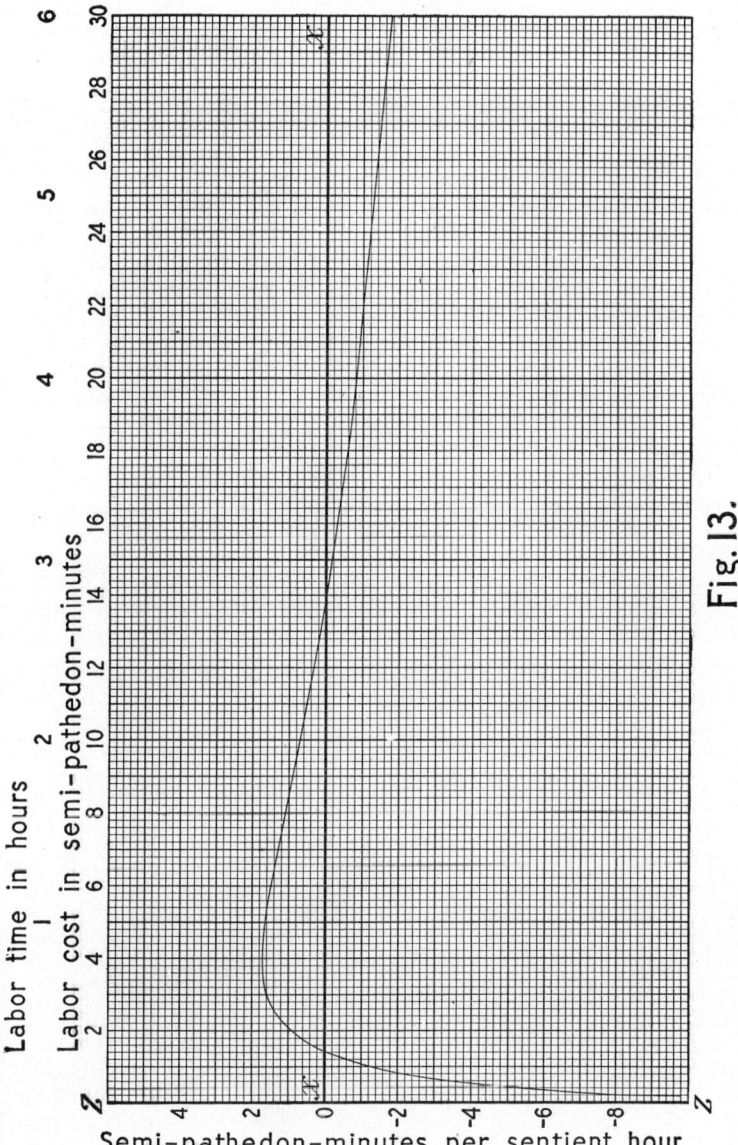

Fig. 13.

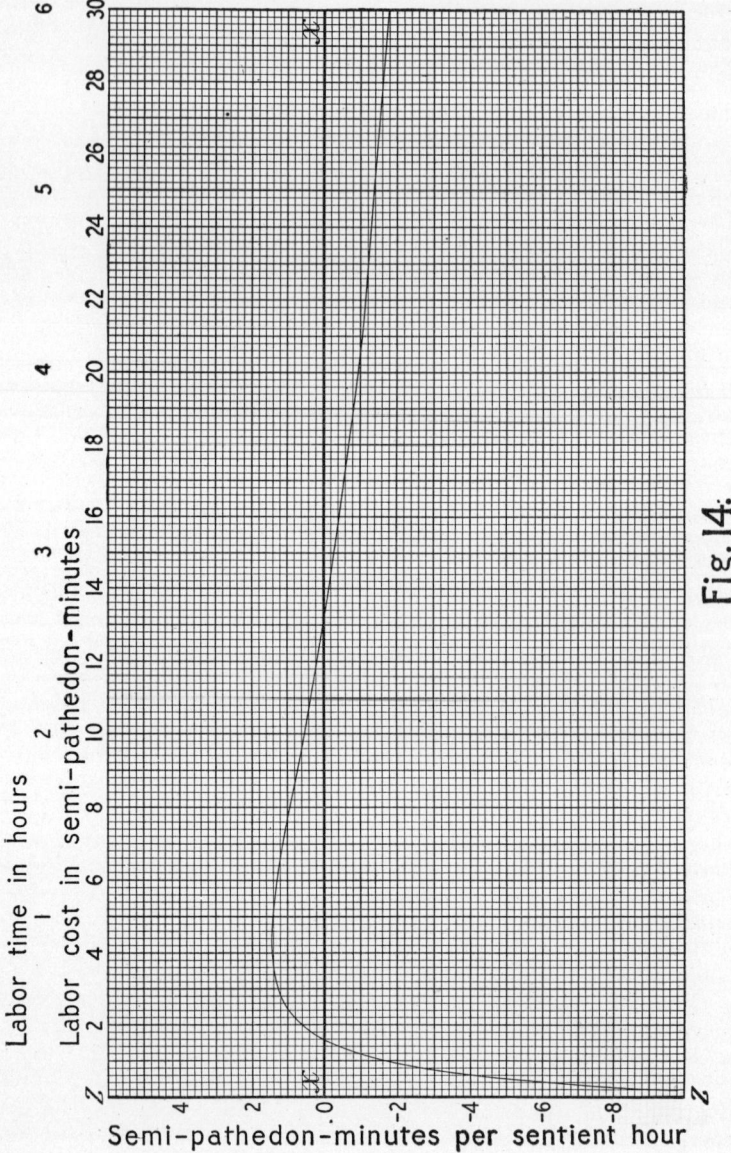

Fig. 14.

adapted to the continent of Europe. If this be so, it is because there is some relation between a given environment and the number of sentient agents it is best adapted to support in a condition to afford the greatest happiness. If it is admitted that there is some ratio between the number of members of a community and the resources thereof better adapted to the production of happiness than any other, then it may be inquired what determines that ratio if the principle we have propounded does not? If it is denied, then there is no reason why the population of a continent should be greater than that of a county. In a community wherein the distribution of wealth is unequal and extremes of wealth and poverty exist, no rule as to the number of the population can be given, since the first approximation to an economic system of happiness manufacture has not been attained. It would be like trying to determine the proper number of boilers to consume a given coal output when the distribution of coal to the boilers is indeterminate and unequal. The chances are that the best number of boilers would be none, since a system which would leave the matter of coal distribution to chance would almost certainly yield a deficit. For a similar reason, if the distribution of wealth in a community is indeterminate and left to chance, it is probable that the less the number of members of that community the better — none at all being the best — since a deficit of happiness will almost certainly result.

The increase in curvature of the curve shown in Fig. 12 makes it unnecessary to expend much time in explaining the effect of too great an increase in the population. Increase in the density of a population, resulting, as it must, in an augmented intensiveness of cultivation of the soil, acceleratively stimulates the laws of diminishing and dwindling returns of labor, the zone of self-support progressively dwindles (compare Fig. 13 with Fig. 14) and finally disappears and the permanent underconsumption or impoverishment of the community is the inevitable result. The evils of over-population will be discussed in Book III and need not be further considered here.

Obviously anything resulting in an increase in efficiency of production (beyond the essential increase) or of consumption, will require an increase in population to a new point of beneficent equilibrium as a condition essential to the maximum production of happiness. Increase in these efficiencies may be accomplished by adapting external conditions to desires, or by adapting desires to external conditions. There is no necessity of discussing each case separately, since the effect on the third factor is the same in both; therefore, as an example of the relation between increase in the efficiency of production or consumption, and number of population, it will suffice to examine the manner in which an increase in the efficiency of conversion operates.

In this treatment we shall, for simplicity, regard increase in the efficiency of conversion as essentially a process of developing *health* and *adjustability*. The utility of these primary qualities is obvious, once the nature of utility has been disclosed. Their development by inheritance and education acts in two ways. (1) To diminish the labor cost of a given amount of production by diminishing its intensity; (2) To increase the happiness output of a given amount of consumption, (a) by diminishing the proportion and intensity of negative consumption, and (b) by increasing the intensity of positive consumption.

All moralists claim that labor ought to be pleasant, and no view can be sounder. If both production and consumption could be made positive, it is clear that the happiness output of a community would be vastly increased, and if productive could be made pleasanter than consumptive acts, the indicative ratio could be indefinitely diminished. Unfortunately however, the advantages of pleasant labor are more clearly perceptible than the means of attaining it, though such means as are available should be employed. In this regard the advice of the utilitarian is — " If possible make a pleasure of business, but by all means make a business of pleasure."

The more needs a man or nation has the more labor will be required to satisfy them; the greater will be the proportion of consumptive acts merely negative, and the greater will be the unhappiness if they are left unsatisfied. Could men dispense with the necessity of eating, the cultivation of wheat and potatoes, and many other agricultural operations would become useless, and could be done away with; and could they get along just as well without clothing, the raising of cotton and wool, etc., with their attendant manufacturing operations would be superfluous. To dispense with needs is one of the best means of increasing the efficiency of conversion of men or of nations. This being so, it is evident that simple tastes are better than any others. A nation whose tastes are of the simplest can, other things being equal, dispense in greatest proportion with the most universal of needs — the need of labor. It is for this reason that luxurious tastes are so uneconomic. A nation whose wealth is so ill distributed as to create a demand for luxuries of high labor cost, is organized uneconomically — the production of such luxuries is a waste of labor, and the conditions which involve such production are unjust. The production of one expensive diamond may represent the severe labor of several lifetimes, yet its power of producing happiness is very slight. Its labor cost is millions of times its happiness value. Had the same amount of labor cost been expended in producing toys for children, for example, the result would probably be to cause as much happiness to each of thousands of human beings as by the production of the diamond was caused to one. Such industries as diamond mining can never be self-supporting. They are hopelessly uneconomic.

Yet expensive luxuries are not necessarily uneconomic. Great works of art, for instance, such as pictures and statues, are expensive but economic. Their money cost may be high but their labor cost is little or nothing, because the work of the artist is pleasant. Works of art, however, should not be hoarded in private collections where they can be enjoyed only by the few. They should be placed in public places where they may educate and edify the multitude. So placed, they are among the most economic of products, because their labor cost is negative, and the consumptive acts which they make possible do not destroy them. They are at once of great permanence and of less than no labor cost. The average labor cost of all products of the fine arts is negative. This is one factor of their high utility.

The most useful classes of tastes are among the most simple. The pleasures of childhood are first among these — they should be perpetuated as long as possible. There are few permanent sources of happiness greater than that proceeding from a taste for the companionship of nature, and the labor cost required to gratify it is no more than is required to obtain the necessary leisure. Literature, and the cultivation of taste to enjoy it, the opportunity for thought, and the mental training which makes it a source of pleasure, health, friends, a congenial occupation, and freedom from worry, are all that men of economic tastes require, to be happy. Expensive clothes, houses, yachts, estates, or jewelry are unnecessary. Another reason why simple tastes should be cultivated is that tastes, once acquired, tend to become needs, and as expensive tastes are those the opportunity for gratifying which it is easiest to lose, it is the more incautious to acquire them. Sometimes this tendency of tastes to become needs is advanced as a reason why opportunity for acquiring new tastes should be altogether denied certain large classes of the community, e. g. the working classes. Such opportunity, it is maintained, would but increase dissatisfaction and discontent; but such a doctrine is self-destructive — consistently pursued it would mean that mankind should aim to dispense with tastes as well as with needs, for thereby they would insure contentment. By such means complete contentment could indeed be approached, but the same end could be much better attained by the annihilation of the race. No taste would then go ungratified, nor any need neglected, for tastes as well as needs, would no longer exist. A community of stones is perfectly contented. Contentment is a more useful end than a surplus of pain, but it is a less useful one than a surplus of pleasure. There is certainly no use in cultivating tastes unless they can be gratified, and by stoicism or otherwise effort should be made to prevent them from becoming needs, but the principle here mentioned should determine the rate at which tastes may safely be acquired with the progress of society, rather than the interdiction of their acquisition altogether.

Variety of taste is essential to a high output of happiness as well as simplicity, but not for the same reason. It may be apprehended that these qualities are opposed, as a great variety of tastes requires a corresponding variety of desiderata to satisfy them. Variety of taste is required, however, because of the effects of fatigue in diminishing the return from a succession of similar stimuli. As long as a taste is not at the same time a need, the absence of the means of gratifying it causes no pain. The more varied our tastes, the more likely are we to find something in every situation which will appeal to them, particularly if, at the same time, they are simple.

The possession of many tastes which are not at the same time needs and the possession of few needs constitutes adaptability, since these are qualities of mind which enable men to adapt themselves well to their surroundings — hence requiring less adaptation of their surroundings to them. The ideal case would be that which required no adaptation of the surroundings at all.

As the development of health and adjustability serves to increase the efficiency of production and of consumption, and as the third factor of happiness should be a function of these, it follows that the population of a country should be a function of the average efficiency of conversion of its inhabitants, increasing with said efficiency, and decreasing with it. By reference to the hypothetical community we have previously discussed, this relation may be expressed with great definiteness. Assume the average member of the sample community to have so increased his efficiency of conversion that the labor cost of a given amount of production is diminished 20% and the happiness resulting from a given rate of consumption is increased 20%. By making the proper calculations we discover that, under these conditions a population of 10,000,000 maintained at the point of maximum efficiency would yield happiness at the rate of about 330,000,000 hedon-minutes per day, or about 2,000,000,000 hedon-hours per year, as compared with 973,000,000 hedon-hours per year when possessed of a poorer efficiency of conversion. But an even greater output could be produced by an increase of the population to a new point of beneficent equilibrium in conformity with the principle of readjustment already discussed, the output per capita diminishing, but the total output increasing, and it is obvious that with increased efficiency of conversion the increase in population will be greater than in the case already cited (p. 322) before the point of beneficent equilibrium is attained.

A rate of happiness greater still would be temporarily obtainable by diminishing the indicative ratio in some degree, thereby increasing the production per capita and permitting of a still larger population. Such a course would diminish the rate of happiness per capita, but if the diminution of the indicative ratio did not exceed a certain critical value, the increase in numbers would more than compensate therefor. What the critical value would be, would, of course, be a function of the precise forms of the curves of diminishing returns of happiness and of labor. It would indeed be calculable on the assumptions already made, but the calculation would be tedious and unprofitable. Moreover, the practice of such a policy by society would, in the end, be uneconomic, since the object of society is not the greatest immediate output of happiness possible, but the greatest total output, and to secure this it is better that the happiness per capita should augment at the expense of number than that number should augment at the expense of happiness per capita, since increase in number involves stimulation of the law of diminishing returns of labor, and consequent dissipation of natural resources at an unnecessarily reduced efficiency of consumption. Husbandry of nature's resources and not their hasty development is the only sensible policy for society to pursue, since it results in a higher rate of happiness per capita for the present generation, and insures to posterity a greater output.

In Book I we set ourselves the task of ascertaining exactly what the object of society ought to be. Satisfying ourselves that this object was the maximum output of happiness, our next task was to ascertain upon what uniformities of nature and of human nature the production of happiness depends, for until this is cleared up, it is obvious that we cannot apply our knowledge of society's object to any useful purpose. In the present book our attention has been occupied with ascertaining the most general and vital of such characteristics. Starting with the proposition that the happiness of society is a function of three factors: (1) The sentient agent: (2) The environment of said agent: (3) The number of said agents — we have endeavored by a discussion of the various elements of which these factors themselves are functions to discover a test, or series of tests, by which the polity of society could be judged and directed. Although the subject is complex, and in proceeding from the universal proposition that society should do what will presumably result in the maximum surplus of happiness to the determination of what policies will so result, we have inevitably lost something in generality, yet we have gained in definiteness sufficiently to enable us to formulate general rules for the guidance of society — rules which will remain valid as long as the laws of nature and of human nature upon which they are founded remain what they are. It is undeniable that the policy of society should be determined by the structure of the human mind, and the laws of its environment. If these, or either of them, were different from what they are, then the policy of society should be different from what, under present conditions, it should be.

Society's object in existence then being the production of happiness, it at once follows that all the acts of men ought to be directed to that object. Happiness must be attained either directly or indirectly. The immediate object of men's acts therefore should be either *happiness* or *the means to happiness* — either *consumption* or *production*. But in their attempts to attain these objects men may meet with very various degrees of success — they may produce and consume with very varying degrees of economy. As production is necessary to consumption, men's time must be divided between the two, but the ratio in which they are divided (the indicative ratio) should depend upon the relation between the productive and consumptive efficiencies and capacities. It should increase as productive capacity, productive intensity, and consumptive capacity increase, and decrease as they decrease. Hence, though the efficiencies and capacities of production and consumption cannot be too great, the indicative ratio *can* be too great.

The adjustment of the indicative ratio to the efficiencies and capacities of production and consumption in such a manner as to maintain the happiness per capita a maximum, as illustrated in the last chapter, I shall denominate the *primary adjustment.* The adjustment of a population to its available resources in such a manner as to maintain it at the point of beneficent equilibrium, as illustrated in the present chapter, I shall denominate the *secondary adjustment.* The determinants of these adjustments are the efficiencies and capacities of production and consumption; but what are the determinants of these efficiencies and capacities? Our examination of the factors of happiness enables us to enumerate them.

In the first place there are two which affect *both* efficiencies and capacities. These are: (1) The quality of the sentient agent, that is, his intelligence and character. (2) The health and adjustability of the sentient agent. In the second place there are three which primarily affect the efficiency and capacity of production: (3) The availability of natural resources. (4) The employment of machinery, material and social, in production. (5) The skill and interest of the employers of said machinery. In the third place there is one which primarily affects the efficiency and capacity of consumption: (6) The distribution of wealth and leisure. If to these we add (7) The primary adjustment, and (8) The secondary adjustment, we shall have enumerated what may be called the *Eight Elements of Happiness.*

We do not pretend to assert that these are mutually independent or mutually exclusive elements. Indeed each is, in greater or less degree, a function of every other. They are simply convenient criteria by means of which any proposed social system may be tested. In the present condition of society, the departure of the social system from the ideal of utility is too great to require any refinement in the means of measuring it. It would be like weighing coal for domestic purposes with a chemical balance. For our present purpose it is sufficient to know that a just social system should fulfil the following eight requirements: (1) It should promote the development of a high quality of sentient agent. (2) It should promote the adjustability and health of said agent. (3) It should husband natural resources while the efficiency of consumption is low. (4) It should promote the employment of machinery in production as a substitute for men. (5) It should stimulate the skill and interest applied to the employment of said machinery. (6) It should promote the equality of distribution of wealth and leisure. (7) It should tend to maintain the indicative ratio at the point of maximum efficiency per capita. (8) It should tend to maintain the population at the point of beneficent equilibrium.

In the degree in which a system fulfils these conditions it is good; in the degree in which it fails to fulfil them it is bad. Thus we are provided with a proximate means, free from intuitionism, of testing whatever social systems men have proposed, or may propose, and we should proceed to the task of so testing at once were it not that a prolific source of confusion needs first to be cleared away. I refer to the general misunderstanding of the meaning of *liberty*. There is no word so dear to the political mystic, and to ask what it means may not be conventional, but as our subject requires it, I shall waive convention and devote a chapter to the examination of its meaning. Such an examination will serve to verify in a general way the criteria of the social system which have been laid down in this chapter, and incidentally to develop an auxiliary criterion — the adaptive principle (p. 341) — applicable to all systems which men are likely to devise anterior to the abolition of their egotism.

CHAPTER IX

LIBERTY

Liberty is a matter much discussed in our country and we deem ourselves highly appreciative of it. In reality we have no adequate apprehension of the value of genuine liberty — otherwise we should not be content to possess so little. We read a good deal in the newspapers about civil, personal, or individual liberty, and how jealous we should be about permitting the government to restrict it, and we are led to the belief that it is something which the community, acting in its collective capacity, can diminish but cannot increase. Those who use the word *liberty* apparently confuse several different things together under the same name, and even Mill has written a long and interesting essay on liberty without telling us what it is. Demagogues frequently employ the *term* as a means of inducing the community to forego the *thing;* and it is equalled by few of the resources of our language as an instrument of political logomania. Some attempts have indeed been made to dissipate the equivocality of the term. Analytical commentators have done mankind the service of pointing out that there exists a critical distinction between *liberty* and *license,* the former being a species of freedom which they approve, the latter one which they disapprove. Without questioning the value of this profound distinction, I shall attempt an analysis less intuitionistic.

By noticing the connection in which the word is used, it becomes clear that liberty has to do with the power of choosing alternatives and that it is something, or several things, capable of varying in degree — of being greater or less. Can it refer to the *number* of alternatives? At any given moment a person of normal faculties has an indefinite number of alternatives among which to select. He can, for example, move his arms, his legs, his fingers, or his head, in an indefinite number of ways. Most of these alternatives would be useless, however, and it would be of slight service to measure liberty by their number. Does it refer to the number of *useful* alternatives? Suppose A capable of selecting 150 alternatives which have some presumption of usefulness to himself, and B 100. Can we say A has more liberty than B, or is there doubt? I apprehend most men will feel some hesitation in pronouncing an opinion on this point. If so, it will confirm my statement that there is no very definite implication to the word as commonly employed. Now A has more of something than B, and as it may be convenient to refer to that something, we shall give it a name. Let us call it *nominal liberty*. The nominal liberty of an individual at any moment then is the number of alternatives useful to him which it is possible for him to select at that moment. Let us see if we can find another kind of liberty. Suppose at some particular time, A to have a nominal liberty of x and B of $\frac{x}{10}$; thus, A's nominal liberty is ten times B's. Suppose further that A's best alternative, namely, the one promising the greatest excess of happiness, yields a presumable surplus of y, and that B's best alternative yields a surplus of 10 y. Which has the greater liberty? A's nominal liberty is ten times that of B; yet there is no doubt that any normal human being would prefer B's liberty to A's. B, indeed, has less nominal liberty than A, but he has more of another kind of liberty. We shall call this *real liberty*. The real liberty of an individual at any moment, then, is the presumable surplus of happiness of the best alternative which it is possible for him to select at that moment. It may be positive or negative. It is assumed, of course, that the presumable surplus is to be determined by the common sense of the individual applied to the data in his own possession. Now the kind of liberty that is of interest to normal mortals is not nominal but real liberty. This is the kind that men cannot have in too high a degree. Any one would prefer a situation in which he had but one alternative, and that a good one, to one which offered 10,000 if they were all evil. There are at all times a thousand ways of securing pain to one of securing pleasure. If pain were what men desired they would have no difficulty in getting all they wanted. At no cost whatever anyone can secure a quantity of pain whose equivalent of pleasure cannot be purchased with all the money in the world.

The value to any individual of any particular period of time, as a day or a month, is the presumable surplus of happiness which would be yielded to that individual by selecting the presumably best alternatives offered at each moment during the period. We shall call this the *opportunity* of, or offered by, that period. It is *positive* or *negative,* according as the surplus offered is positive or negative. Probably no one has ever taken complete advantage of his opportunity for even so short a period as one day. Frequently the bulk of the best alternatives over considerable periods will consist, not in physical acts, but simply in thought, for more can be accomplished by even a little well-considered action than by a great deal that is ill considered. The *average opportunity* of an individual during any period of time is the opportunity of that period divided by the duration of the period. It is this quantity which we shall refer to as the *real liberty* or simply the *liberty* of an individual, and if no period is specified, the lifetime of the individual is to be understood. Now opportunity is to be expressed in terms of quantity of pleasure or pain. Hence if we express liberty by L and suppose the opportunity during time T to be Q, we shall have:

$L = \dfrac{Q}{T}$ — that is, liberty varies directly as the opportunity and inversely as the time over which that opportunity is distributed. Suppose the liberty of an individual were ten hedon-minutes per hour. By distributing the ten hedon-minutes over 100 hours, we should have decreased his liberty one hundred times, whereas by increasing his opportunity (Q) in one hour to 1,000 hedon-minutes, we should have increased it one hundred times. Q in the foregoing equation is expressive of an intensity of pleasure or pain multiplied by a duration. Suppose we express the duration by T; there will then be an intensity, call it X, which, multiplied by T, will equal Q, or $X \times T = Q$. Substituting in the above equation we have:

$L = \dfrac{X \times T}{T}$, or $L = X$. Hence L is expressible in terms of intensity of pleasure or pain, and a glance at the equation will show that it expresses the average intensity of pleasure or pain which the individual in question would presumably have experienced had he always selected the best alternatives open to him. For short periods of time this equation might be misleading, since the best alternatives are often those which require future action to bring to fruition, and it would be difficult to formulate other than an arbitrary rule which would determine what proportion of the presumable surplus resulting from a compound act should be attributed to some short period which included a portion of that act. When we consider a lifetime, however, this difficulty disappears, since it includes all the acts of an individual as well as all the pleasure or pain he is capable of experiencing. The lifetime involved is, of course, the presumable lifetime, assuming the invariable selection of the best alternatives. If T represents such a lifetime, the intensity X, which is the measure of the real liberty, will invariably be algebraically greater than that actually experienced, for in any considerable period it is practically impossible that a combination of accidents should yield greater happiness to an individual than strict adherence to common sense would yield.

We are now prepared to consider an important question, viz., what conditions are essential to real liberty. It is apparently a general impression that these consist exclusively of such conditions as include the physical possibility of selecting alternatives. This is an error. We have seen that liberty is but a name for the happiness value of opportunity per unit of time. He who in any given period of time has the greatest opportunity of happiness has the greatest real liberty for that period. If we discover the essentials of opportunity then we shall discover the essentials of liberty. We may best learn them by considering a concrete case, as follows: Let us suppose that a large uncut diamond is lying in a road and that an individual of normal common sense observes it. Let us first suppose that he is ignorant of one, or both, of the following propositions: (1) The object before me is a diamond. (2) Diamonds may be exchanged for money or other useful things; that is, things which serve to produce happiness or prevent pain. Let us call these, *facts (1) and (2)*. If he is ignorant of either of these facts, it must be because he has never had presented to him the observations from which they might be inferred by a person of normal common sense. The question is, does the observation of the diamond increase his opportunity for happiness? It does not, because in the absence of the information above noted, he would be as likely to possess himself of any other stone in the road as of the diamond. It would be physically possible for him to pick up the diamond, but if he did pick it up and dispose of it to advantage it would only be by accident, since one essential condition for establishing a presumption of happiness would be absent. Second, suppose that he has had presented to him the observations from which a person of normal common sense would infer facts (1) and (2), but that his common sense has been impaired, as for instance by dogma, so that he employs some substitute for common sense as a means of inference. Does the observation of the diamond increase his opportunity for happiness? It does not, because the impairment of his reasoning powers would prevent his deriving facts (1) and (2) from the observations presented, or of making the necessary deduction from them, even if he could make the preliminary inference. Hence he would be as likely to possess himself of any other stone as the diamond, and it would only be by accident that he could derive advantage from its presence. Thus, a second essential condition of establishing a presumption is absent in this case. Therefore the first two co-essentials are those required for establishing presumptions. We have remarked in Chapter 2 that expectations are derived from observations by inference, and in Chapter 3 that acts are guided by expectations. Hence in the absence of either the requisite observations or inferences there is no guide to action, and in the absence of a guide one act is as probable as another. To any being incapable of establishing a presumption, whether it is a tree, a beetle, an infant, or an idiot, opportunity is impossible. Third, suppose an individual who has had presented to him the observations necessary for inferring facts (1) and (2) and is also possessed of normal common sense, to be passing along the road, but that there is no diamond there to observe. Obviously he has no more opportunity than the first two individuals had, because the external condition of opportunity — the physical possibility of possessing himself of a diamond which was present in their cases is absent in his. Hence a third condition of opportunity is absent in this case.

Suppose now these three conditions all to be present. It is clear that an opportunity is present. Propositions (1) and (2) would lead to the conclusion: "This object may be exchanged for money or other useful things." This in turn would lead immediately to a use-judgment, indicating that to pick up the diamond would presumably lead to greater happiness than not to pick it up; and this, in turn, would lead to the act of picking up the diamond. The means would have been adapted to the end, and the opportunity would thus have been accepted, whereas in the absence of either the appropriate observations, the appropriate inferences, or of the presence of the diamond, the act of picking it up either would have been physically impossible, or could have occurred only as the result of chance.

There are thus three co-essentials of opportunity and hence of liberty. Two inhere in the sentient agent and one in the environment. The co-essentials are: (1) *Experience of the requisite observations from which to infer.* (2) *Capacity for inference, or the ability to correctly convert observations into expectations.* (3) *Physical possibility of acting upon the expectations inferred.* We shall call these the *first, second* and *third essentials* of liberty, respectively. The physical possibility of an alternative is merely a potential opportunity. Hence to provide an individual or a community with the third essential of liberty may or may not increase its real liberty. The world furnishes to men the first and third essentials of opportunity for happiness, but this opportunity must remain a potential one until they have acquired the second essential. It is men's intuitionism that enslaves them, for " where there is no vision the people perish."

The liberty of an individual may be expressed in terms of intensity of pain or pleasure — of quantity of happiness, positive or negative, per unit of time. If the sum of the liberties so expressed of all the members of the community be divided by the number of members in the community, the result is an expression of the liberty of the community which is also the liberty of the average individual in the community. Its co-essentials are obviously those of individual liberty.

So much then for the co-essentials of real liberty, individual and social. They are the necessary conditions of any or all liberty. Without them opportunity is as impossible to a man as to a fence post. The degree in which an individual or a community profits by his or its liberty will, however, depend upon other factors.

A number of objections will probably occur to the reader against this treatment of liberty. Men's preference is frequently determined by motives of distribution in time instead of quantity of happiness. Hence if real liberty is to be measured by preference alone, we should consider this fact. We might, if we pleased, discover another variety of liberty by taking mere preference, instead of *correct* preference as a measure, but it would not lead us to any useful distinction. To add to any set of alternatives, whether including a high or low degree of real liberty, the possibility of another whose presumption of happiness is less than one already available would not, in general, be useful. Another objection to be expected is that preference is frequently governed by a desire for the good of others and not that of ourselves alone. This is true, and by examining the matter we could distinguish several other varieties of liberty; but for the purpose of political discussion these varieties would not be of much service. It is not such varieties that are restricted, or against the restriction of which protest is made; or if restricted, the restriction is but incidental to that upon real liberty as already defined. A positive degree of real liberty is a necessary, but not a sufficient, condition of happiness, and it is primarily for real liberty, or rather for the happiness of which it is a necessary condition, that men in all ages have suffered and striven, and when this kind of liberty shall have become a maximum, the conditions for all other useful kinds will have been attained, or will be easily attainable.

It will next be useful to distinguish another kind of liberty. Human nature is ruled by two forces. Self-interest and custom; the first is fixed, the second variable. In order to determine the acts of individuals, one or both of these forces must be employed, for these are practically the only forces competent to control human conduct. It is probable that all motives may be classed as of *self-interest* or as of *custom;* conscience, as already demonstrated, being itself of the latter class. Hence he who would control the acts of men for the benefit of society must employ these forces of human nature or fail to accomplish his object, just as he who would produce changes in the external world must employ the forces of nature inherent in gravitation, heat, chemical affinity, etc., or fail to accomplish his object. Many of the restraints upon liberty required for the well-being of society are imposed by custom; those which custom fails to impose, however, must, if imposed at all, depend upon the force of self-interest, and the mechanism whereby this force is employed to accomplish the object of society is that of law.

A law is a command issued to one or more persons by some person, or persons, presumably possessing the power required to execute it. It is universally recognized that laws restrict liberty, real or nominal. Let us see how they do it; and first in the case of individual liberty. Is it by altering one or more of the co-essentials of liberty? No, the co-essentials of liberty are unaltered by law. We have seen that the value of opportunity is measured by the presumable surplus of happiness it offers. The legal restriction of liberty is effected by altering its presumable surplus, not by abolishing the physical possibility of the act which leads to it, though such abolition is a frequent result of the *execution* of the law. The surplus may be either increased or decreased by law. Consider, as an example, a case in which it is decreased (as in a law prohibiting burglary). Among the alternatives physically possible to men is that of breaking and entering houses for the purpose of appropriating the goods of others. Suppose no law against it existed. Men, not restrained by conscience or custom would often be tempted to select such alternatives because of the presumable surplus of happiness resulting to themselves from such a selection. A law against burglary does not make burglary a physical impossibility, but it decreases the temptation to burglary in frequency and strength, diminishing the presumable surplus resulting from the act, by fixing a penalty for those who select it. This it does by its effect upon the appropriate use-judgment, for the mean surplus of failure is obviously diminished (algebraically) by the threat to execute the law and apply the penalty, because the probability of failure is increased, and its probable surplus diminished (algebraically) thereby. This, in turn, diminishes the presumption of happiness, and as a use-judgment is a normal operation of the mind, the frequency of burglary is diminished, and thus the object of the law accomplished. If we are correct in this analysis of the mode in which laws operate in the attainment of their ends, we should expect to find: (1) That the effectiveness of a law is proportional to (a) the severity of its penalty, (b) the probability of its execution, and (c) the degree of real liberty in the community affected, that is, upon the happiness value of the alternatives to illegal acts: and (2) That penalties do not apply to beings presumably incapable of applying a use-judgment to the acts prohibited. The expectations thus specified are fulfilled by experience. First, other things being equal, laws are most effective (a) when their penalties are severe rather than slight, (b) when their enforcement is strict rather than lax, (c) among the happier classes whose opportunity is positive, rather than among the more miserable classes whose opportunity is negative. Second, penalties are not applied to children whose minds are undeveloped, or to insane persons whose minds are abnormal.

If we examine the operation of law in establishing departments of government, courts, schools, etc., we shall find that it proceeds in the same manner, only in this case it aims to cause the selection of acts instead of preventing their selection. Hence it increases the mean surplus of success of alternatives which it desires selected, and consequently the presumption of happiness of such alternatives. This is done by the offer of reward, either in the form of money or honor, generally the former. Now this mode of operation of law is universal. It has not changed throughout history and is common to all countries alike. Thus it is strongly confirmatory of the claim advanced in Chapter 6 that a use-judgment is a mental operation dependent upon the structure of the mind and not upon its previous history. The principle recognized in the utilization of the omnipresent motive of self-interest in the manner thus specified is so universally adapted to its end that I shall call it *the adaptive principle*. It is doubtful whether a social system which aims to control any large section of society can succeed without appealing to it; that is, a system which does not make it to the self-interest of the individual members of society to seek the end of utility, or does not make them cognizant of the fact that it is to their self-interest, is not at all likely to achieve that end. The adaptive principle may be applied positively or negatively. It is *positive* when the act is induced by the promise of pleasure: *negative* when induced by the promise of pain. It is obvious that the positive adaptive principle should be employed in preference to the negative whenever practical. In other words, when using pleasure and pain as means, it is more economic to use pleasure than pain. In many cases, however, this is not practicable, for obvious reasons, and hence the negative adaptive principle has to be applied.

We are now prepared to inquire what legal liberty is, and to discover its relation to real liberty. Every restraint imposed by law affects one or more of the alternatives open to members of society, but they are not always useful alternatives even in the absence of law. Hence we shall regard the legal restraint of a community as proportional to the number of alternatives of the average individual upon which the law imposes restraint. Legal liberty is inversely proportional to legal restraint. Hence if L_1 is the legal liberty of a community and R_1 its legal restraint, then $L_1 = \dfrac{1}{R_1}$ — or, legal liberty is expressed by the reciprocal of legal restraint. Suppose an individual whose acts do not affect, and are not otherwise affected by, the acts of others to have his opportunity, and hence his real liberty, restricted by law in the manner already specified. That his real liberty may thereby be diminished is obvious. If any act which at any time might, in the absence of law, have been the best open to him, is prohibited, his liberty is thereby diminished. Such a person would be oppressed by law. Would there be any means whereby the liberty of such an individual might be increased by law? It seems so.

In the third chapter we have pointed out that alternatives are often selected from considerations of distribution in time instead of quantity. It is true that acts so determined involve a moral fallacy, but still they may be prevented if the quantity of pain involved, relatively remote though it be, is made large enough, just as a logical fallacy may be prevented by strong evidence when it would be committed if weak evidence alone were presented. Now the commission of such a moral fallacy would involve a diminution of real liberty for it would interfere with future opportunity. Hence a law which prevented it would increase real liberty. Thus, consider an individual the indulgence of whose impulse to drink to excess and ruin his health and prospects is preventable and prevented by his fear of the penalty of a prohibitory law. The real liberty of such an individual is increased by said law, and in civilized communities many laws are directed against acts which harm primarily the acting individual himself. Such laws may be called *paternalistic,* and the principle involved *paternalism.* Prohibitory and compulsory education laws are paternalistic, since he who violates them usually harms himself more than he does others. Were we to restrict the term *paternalism* to laws restraining acts which affect the liberty of absolutely no one but him who commits them, it would apply to no possible class of laws either enacted or enactable, since the interests of human beings are so bound up with one another that it is probably impossible to discover any considerable class of acts which affect the liberty of him alone who commits them.

The frequency with which a man interferes with his own liberty, however, will, in the absence of restraint, be far less than that with which he will interfere with the liberty of others. Hence in a community where the acts of individuals affect, and are affected by, the acts of others, the number of ways in which law can increase liberty is augmented in greater measure than the number of ways in which it can diminish it. When applied to society the law may increase liberty, not only by restraining the exercise of incorrect judgments, but by restraining that of correct but egotistic judgments. By curtailing some kinds of opportunity in some, or perhaps all, members of society, the liberty of society, namely, the liberty of the average individual, may increase. Hence, if laws are determined by common sense, the greater the number of legal restrictions, the more is real liberty increased, i. e., as legal liberty diminishes, real liberty increases. Whence, then, comes the general notion that laws tend to diminish liberty, a notion which may be amply justified by an appeal to experience? The answer is simple: it is because laws in the past have usually not been dictated by common sense, or have not been designed to accomplish the object of utility. Bad laws may be divided into three classes: (1) Those which seek no good end: (2) Those which seek a good end, but abandon common sense as a means of attaining it: (3) Those which seek a good end, and adhere to common sense, but owing to lack of the requisite knowledge, fail to attain their end. Most bad laws belong to the first two classes. The reasons for this are two in number. First, because the interests of those who in the past have enacted laws, have not been similar to the interests of the community. Second, because it has not been customary to apply common sense to political conduct.

The English political philosophers of the 19th century (the school of Mill and Spencer, of which the editors, teachers, and politicians of to-day are supporters) lay particular emphasis on the power and the tendency of law to diminish liberty. They contend that the less law the better, and that the interference of government in anything but the protection of life and property, and in a few other scattering cases, is unwarranted meddling on the part of the state. They claim to have discovered that the best policy for a state (except in certain cases in which they discover that they approve action) is inaction. Hence the name *laissez faire* or *let alone* which is applied to their school of political economy, a school whose dogmas are conscientiously inculcated in the universities. It may with propriety be called the school of *drift,* since it advises all nations to drift wherever the unrestrained forces of society tend to take them, making no effort to restrict the course of nature by law. The *laissez faire* policy is merely fatalism applied to the conduct of society and applied as inconsistently as individual fatalism always is. There is, however, a school of consistent fatalism. It is called *anarchy,* though this term has often been otherwise applied. It teaches that government should not meddle in anything; that there should in fact be no government, and is merely the *laissez faire* system pushed to its legitimate conclusion; for if " the less government the better " as political dogmatists are fond of telling us, then the best government is none at all, and the anarchists are right; at any rate they are consistent with themselves. The *laissez faire* economist is simply an inconsistent anarchist, and though he has produced many volumes to show that there are certain matters which, in the nature of things, are and must eternally be, outside the function of the state to regulate, he has failed to make his point. Not that it can be denied that there may be such matters. It would take omniscience to decide whether there were or were not. No universal rule has ever been consistently maintained by which those things to which the functions of government extend may be perfectly distinguished from those to which they do not, yet the effort to find and apply such a rule is continually made by the economists of the school of drift, even after its non-existence is acknowledged. Thus, Mill says:

" When those who have been called the *laissez faire* school have attempted any definite limitation of the province of government, they have usually restricted it to the protection of person and property against force and fraud; a definition to which neither they nor any one else can deliberately adhere, since it excludes some of the most indispensable, and unanimously recognized, of the duties of government.

" Without professing to entirely supply this deficiency of a general theory, on a question which does not, as I conceive, admit of any universal solution, I shall attempt to afford some little aid towards the resolution of this class of questions as they arise, by examining, in the most general point of view in which the subject can be considered, what are the advantages, and what the evils or inconveniences, of government interference." [1]

This sounds modest, but in his Essay on Liberty, Mill propounds just such a rule as he claims does not exist:

" The object of this Essay is to assert one very simple principle, as entitled to govern absolutely the dealings of society with the individual in the way of compulsion and control, whether the means used be physical force in the form of legal penalties, or the moral coercion of public opinion. The principle is that the sole end for which mankind are warranted, individually or collectively, in interfering with the liberty of action of any of their number, is self-protection. That the only purpose for which power can be rightfully exercised over any member of a civilized community, against his will, is to prevent harm to others. His own good, either physical or moral, is not a sufficient warrant. He cannot rightfully be compelled to do or forbear because it will be better for him to do so, because it will make him happier, because, in the opinion of others, to do so would be wise or even right." [2]

Mill here ignores the fact, already alluded to, that no considerable class of acts can be named which may not interfere with the interests of others, and this omission is characteristic of

[1] Political Economy; Chap. 9.
[2] Essay on Liberty; Chap. 1.

his school. But even assuming that the kind of paternalism that Mill has in mind can exist, his doctrine is not sound, and he is forced to qualify it immediately. Thus, he says:

"It is, perhaps, hardly necessary to say that this doctrine is meant to apply only to human beings in the maturity of their faculties. We are not speaking of children, or of young persons below the age which the law may fix as that of manhood or womanhood. Those who are still in a state to require being taken care of by others, must be protected against their own actions as well as against external injury. For the same reason, we may leave out of consideration those backward states of society in which the race itself may be considered as in its nonage. The early difficulties in the way of spontaneous progress are so great, that there is seldom any choice of means for overcoming them; and a ruler full of the spirit of improvement is warranted in the use of any expedient that will attain an end, perhaps otherwise unattainable. Despotism is a legitimate mode of government in dealing with barbarians, provided the end be their improvement, and the means justified by actually effecting that end. Liberty, as a principle, has no application to any state of things anterior to the time when mankind have become capable of being improved by free and equal discussion. Until then, there is nothing for them but implicit obedience to an Akbar or a Charlemagne, if they are so fortunate as to find one."[1]

Whether we agree or disagree with the general applicability of these principles, it is clear from the indefinite nature of its exceptions that here is no universal rule. Were it worth while to do so, we could show that in attempting to formulate and apply such rules as the above, political philosophers inevitably contradict themselves, but in our discussion of inalienable rights, we have by implication shown this. The attempt to put hard and fast limits upon the application of law to individuals is merely the assertion of the doctrine that individuals have inalienable rights. Of course, if it could once be shown that a particular class of acts of individuals could not possibly interfere with the real liberty either of themselves or others, we should have discovered a class of acts which we could forever banish from among those which the law could rightfully restrict. This is clear from the relation of liberty to utility. The difficulty is that it would take omniscience to show such a thing. Hence, we must rest content with general rules.

Now, what is the attitude of the utilitarian on this matter of

[1] Ibid., Chap. 1.

individual liberty so called? Can he propound a rule by which to set any limits on the rightful restraint of society upon its own members? None, except that by which the rightfulness of any restraint at all is itself established, viz., the definition of utility itself which is, of course, universal and certain. Governments should restrain individual liberty by law when it will presumably result in a greater surplus of happiness than not to restrain it. Otherwise they should not. This rule may be indefinite, but it is correct. All other universal rules may be definite, but they are incorrect. Some persons may deem such a rule as this so incontrovertible that no one would be so absurd as to deny it, yet anyone who attempts to establish any other universal rule does deny it. For, suppose such a rule to be established and call it rule A. Then rule A is either inferrible from the rule of utility as given, or it is not. If it is, of course, it tells us no more than we could ourselves infer from the rule. If it is not, its authority must be derived from some source other than utility; hence it implies the existence of some other source, and this controverts the universality of the rule.

We may render the rule we have given somewhat more definite by considering the universal utility of restricting all human acts to productive and consumptive ones.

In production, economy is best attained by restricting the acts of the laborer to specific operations, having a definite succession, determined not by his immediate choice, but by the requirements of his task, said acts being performed with relation to the correlated and predetermined acts of others. In consumption, on the other hand, economy is best attained by the absence of restriction to specific acts or operations, permitting these to be determined by the immediate desires or impulses of the moment. In both cases the acts should be governed by, or adapted to, the end sought, but the ends of production are *proximate;* those of consumption are *ultimate.* In young, or otherwise irresponsible persons, consumptive acts may — in fact must — be more or less restricted to prevent harmful reactions upon the individual committing them, but in mature and responsible persons, restrictions should, in general, be imposed upon consumption only to prevent harmful reaction upon others. With these exceptions, the ends of consumption, i. e., egotistic consumption, may best be attained by leaving the individual to follow his own impulses. It would be absurd, for example, to attempt the production of happiness by prescribing that everyone in a community should eat certain kinds of food, keep certain definite hours, read certain books, play certain games, go to see prescribed plays at prescribed periods. Tastes vary too much to make such restrictions economic, though in production analogous rules are necessary. The best judge of the adaptability of productive acts to their end is he who is in the most advantageous position to observe and compare the amount of production resulting from a given amount of labor. This will, in general, be the director or controller of the given productive operations. The best judge of the adaptability of consumptive acts to their end, on the other hand, is, in general, the individual affected by them. Freedom is thus more essential in consumption than in production. What men desire, however, is liberty to consume, or if they desire liberty to produce, it is only because their consumption is dependent upon their production. Liberty to dispense with production is everywhere more desired than liberty to produce, and such liberty can be achieved only by increasing the productive capacity; this in turn requires the division and co-operation — that is, the socialization of labor. Hence *to obtain the maximum amount of real liberty and the best economy in the production of happiness, it is essential to secure socialism in production while preserving individualism in consumption.*

Now, by what means do the advocates of drift seek to establish the criteria by which we may judge when individual liberty may be restrained by law and when it may not. Inspection shows that a single method is adopted. A greater or less number of instances in which individual liberty has been restrained in a manner to cause distress and increase misery are cited and the conclusion drawn therefrom that the restraint of individual liberty is therefore always a bad thing. Unless we have mistaken the nature of common sense, we should, in order to reason from *aposteriori* grounds concerning the effect of governmental action in increasing or decreasing real liberty, seek data of the following classes: (1) A fair sample of the effect of government action in increasing the real liberty of communities: (2) A fair sample of the effect of action in diminishing it: (3) A fair sample of the effect of inaction in increasing said liberty: (4) A fair sample of the effect of inaction in diminishing it. Only from such data could we formulate even a general rule as to the effect of the action of government on the real liberty of communities, and even then we should have no means of telling whether action was preferable to inaction in particular cases. Data of the kind designated in class (2) is that to which advocates of the current policy of drift almost exclusively confine themselves, and their examples are largely drawn from the acts of monarchical governments whose function has never been deemed the promotion of happiness. Such a one-sided mode of induction can have little value. It is doubtful if experience furnishes the means of formulating a law which can furnish any useful relation between governmental inactivity and desirability. Certainly none has yet been formulated. Each proposed policy should be judged solely on its own merits, and that which is most useful adopted; that which is not, rejected. Neither action nor inaction have any necessary relation to utility.

In our day the doctrine of *let alone* is little more than another buttress of custom, for restrictions of individual liberty which have become traditional are seldom assailed. The institution of property is such a restriction, and the genuine anarchist, more consistent than his conventionalized prototype, assails this as he does all restrictions. The institution of property is a product of custom, more or less tempered by common sense. Private property in material objects consists in certain legal restrictions whereby the control and disposal of such objects is confined, in a greater or less degree, to one or a few persons. The degree of control varies a great deal, so that the term *property* is not very definite. Property is founded upon legal prohibitions, upon restrictions of individual liberty, for the control and disposal of a material object can be confined to its owner, only by denying like control and disposal to all others. That opportunity is thus forfeited by some or many among those others is obvious. Hence liberty is restricted by the laws which establish private property. But the important question is as to the total effect of such restriction. Is the real liberty of the community increased or diminished by it? The answer is that it is sometimes increased and sometimes diminished. The legal title to a house and its contents by an individual restrains all other individuals from entering the house and making use of its contents in the manner open to the owner, and if this was the only effect of granting legal title to houses, the liberty of the community would be diminished by property in houses. But it is not the only effect. The real liberty of the owner of the house is increased by the security granted by law. He is not compelled to protect himself from dispossession and despoilment by others; thus he can avail himself of much opportunity which otherwise would not be open to him. He is at liberty to leave his house, protected by law, and seek pleasure and profit elsewhere. He is at liberty to sleep undisturbed at night, and to anticipate unchallenged enjoyment of his house in the future. He is at liberty to feel the peace of security instead of the alarm of insecurity. It is true that the same restriction which thus adds to his opportunity also substracts from it whatever opportunity would be yielded by despoiling and dispossessing his neighbor, but for the average man much more opportunity is gained than is lost by this restriction, and thus legal restraint has caused real liberty to increase. On the other hand, consider a case of the effect of private ownership on the agricultural population of Great Britain, as brought out by Marx. In this case the legal restraint involved in the institution of property diminished the liberty of the community. The first kind of private property is useful — the second is not.

" The last process of wholesale expropriation of the agricultural population from the soil is, finally, the so-called clearing of estates, i. e., the sweeping men off them. All the English methods hitherto considered culminated in 'clearing.' As we saw in the picture of modern conditions given in a former chapter, where there are no more independent peasants to get rid of, the 'clearing' of cottages begins; so that the agricultural laborers do not find on the soil cultivated by them even the spot necessary for their own housing. But what 'clearing of estates' really and properly signifies, we learn only in the promised land of modern romance, the Highlands of Scotland. There the process is distinguished by its systematic character, by the magnitude of the scale on which it is carried out at one blow (in Ireland landlords have gone to the length of sweeping away several villages at once; in Scotland areas as large as German principalities are dealt with), finally by the peculiar form of property, under which the embezzled lands were held.

. . . As an example of the method obtaining in the 19th century, the 'clearing' made by the Duchess of Sutherland will suffice here. This person, well instructed in economy, resolved, on entering upon her government, to effect a radical cure, and to turn the whole country, whose population had already been by earlier processes of the like kind, reduced to 15,000, into a sheepwalk. From 1814 to 1820 these 15,000 inhabitants, about 3,000 families, were systematically hunted and rooted out. All their villages were destroyed and burnt, all their fields turned into pasturage. British soldiers enforced this eviction, and came to blows with the inhabitants. One old woman was burnt to death in the flames of the hut, which she refused to leave. Thus this fine lady appropriated 794,000 acres of land that had from time immemorial belonged to the clan. She assigned to the expelled inhabitants about 6,000 acres on the sea-shore — 2 acres per family. The 6,000 acres had until this time lain waste, and brought in no income to their owners. The Duchess, in the nobility of her heart, actually went so far as to let these at an average rent of 2s. 6d. per acre to the clansmen, who for centuries had shed their blood for her family. The whole of the stolen clan-land she divided into 29 great sheep-farms, each inhabited by a single family, for the most part imported English farm-servants. In the year 1835 the 15,000 Gaels were already replaced by 131,000 sheep. The remnant of the aborigines flung on the sea-shore, tried to live by catching fish. They became amphibious, and lived as an English author says, half on land and half on water, and withal only half on both.

"But the brave Gaels must expiate yet more bitterly their idolatry, romantic and of the mountains, for the 'great men' of the clan. The smell of their fish rose to the noses of the great men. They scented some profit in it, and let the sea-shore to the great fishmongers of London. For the second time the Gaels were hunted out." [1]

It is not my purpose here to discuss the legitimate limits of the restriction of individual liberty involved in the institution of property. That there are limits, and that they are at the present day exceeded, resulting in a decrease of the real liberty of the community, is obvious. I discuss property at this point at all, principally to show that it is simply an expedient to restrict individual liberty, and may be used either to increase or diminish the real liberty of the average individual. There is nothing "inalienable" in a property right any more than in any other right, and property in this or that object should be conferred or withheld in strict conformity with the rule of common sense. When it is more useful to confer it than not, then confer it; when it is not, do not; and in its dogma free applications, the law follows this rule admirably, as in the following example:

An individual A, by paying a certain sum and observing certain legal forms, acquires property in certain lands in a certain city. His title prohibits the trespass of others upon his domain without his consent. This constitutes a restriction upon the liberty of some among those thus prohibited from trespass. The interests of the city require that a street be cut through the land owned by A. Therefore, the city alienates his property rights, removes the restriction upon the liberty of others, and restricts the liberty of A by denying him the opportunity involved in those rights. Thus the land becomes public property and is open to the use of everyone. But suppose that some organization desires to parade through the street and obtains a

[1] Capital, p. 752.

permit for that purpose. During the parade the street is no longer open to everybody. Vehicles cannot pass through it, and its use is by law confined to certain individuals. Thus the right of the public in their street is alienated. Suppose now, that a fire breaks out in the vicinity and that to reach it the fire engines must traverse the street occupied by the parade. The exclusive right to the street by the paraders is at once alienated and the engine permitted to pass. Thus the law successively grants exclusive control over a piece of land, then withdraws it, grants it again, and again withdraws it, according as it is useful or not useful to do so. This is common sense. In such a case no question is raised about inalienable rights or the restriction of individual liberty, because these applications of common sense happen to be customary. Now, precisely the principle which governs in this case should govern in all cases, and property in one thing or another should be granted or withheld in strict conformity to the principle of utility. All we should ask is: Is it presumably more useful to do it than not to do it? This once answered by a direct appeal to experience, such questions as "Is it conservative?" "Is it economic?" "Does it deny an inalienable right?" "Does it restrict individual liberty?" "Does it set a dangerous precedent?" require no consideration, since the answers to any or all of them would be derived from data which, if pertinent, could be applied directly in deciding the question of utility. We shall later encounter instances in which this simple rule of utility is notoriously ignored.

Closely connected with the subject of legal liberty is that of legal right and the relation of legal to moral rights among men. There is no disagreement about the nature of a legal right. It is simply any alternative not prohibited by law. But what is a moral right? The literature of politics teems with loose assertions about the "rights of the people," or this or that class among them — such as the "rights of capital," "the rights of labor," etc., and that which is referred to is evidently seldom a legal right. The failure of men to come to any agreement as to what constitutes a moral right is but one consequence of leaving the word *right* undefined. The moral rights about which orators declaim are generally determined by the customs into which communities happen to drift in the course of their history. A privilege if customary is deemed a right. Yet men cannot help perceiving that these rights founded upon custom are often opposed to common sense, and many of them have been abolished.

When the common sense standard of right clashes with the standard set by custom, there is always indignant protest from those whose privileges are threatened. Thus King John when forced to sign the Magna Charta was convinced that his "rights" were being wickedly taken from him. Throughout history whenever by statute, revolution, or otherwise, any form of parasitism of one class upon another, sanctioned by custom, has been eliminated, the parasitic class has always complained that their "rights" have been invaded, and the same notion about the nature of a moral right is as prevalent to-day as it always has been. It is wholly unacceptable to common sense.

But common sense once accepted as a guide, matters become very simple. No man has a moral right to do wrong, which is but to say that no man has a moral right to choose any alternative but that which will presumably result in the maximum surplus of happiness. Hence *moral rights* are simply right alternatives, and no others. *Rights* are identical with *duties*. A use-judgment alone can determine them, and they are not products of custom. If the reader is not satisfied with this definition, let him attempt to frame one for himself. It is difficult to see how any other useful definition can be framed without implying that right is wrong.

Now, it is the duty of society in its quest after the maximum output of happiness to restrict the acts of men, so far as is possible, to right acts. As will appear presently, governments are, or should be, mechanisms whereby a community is enabled to act as a unit; hence the legal restraints imposed by governments should simply be those which tend to confine the acts of men to right acts. In short, it is the function of government, first to convert moral into legal rights by the enactment of laws — this is the function of the legislative department; second, to administer said laws in specific cases — this is the function of the judiciary department; third, to carry out the laws as administered — this is the function of the executive department. The sphere of governmental activities cannot be justly restricted by any artificial or traditional distinctions between those things which a government can do, and those things which it cannot do. Every such distinction is purely arbitrary. *Common sense requires that the acts of society shall be governed by the same rules which govern the ordinary acts of an individual, or of two, three, six, or a score, of individuals acting together, since society is no more than a larger aggregate of exactly the same nature.* If this is kept clearly in mind, I apprehend little disagreement of a vital nature with what is to follow.

BOOK III
THE TECHNOLOGY OF HAPPINESS
PART TWO—APPLIED

CHAPTER X

THE SOCIAL MECHANISM

In seeking the solution of the problem of happiness the unchangeable laws of creation are our only limitations. In the preceding book we have been engaged in examining the most vital of those laws in order to deduce from them criteria from which to evolve, and by which to test, means adapted to the solution of that problem. This examination has led to the substitution of eight criteria for one as a guide to the conduct of society, with an accompanying loss in generality, but a more than compensating gain in concreteness. The first stage of our task is thus completed — we have formulated the theory of the technology of happiness — we must now apply it — we have gained in concreteness, but we have not gained enough. Mechanical technology is not confined to the consideration of statics, kinematics, and kinetics — these merely embody the theory of the subject. Applied mechanics concerns itself with the practice of that theory — with the application of mechanical laws to concrete material mechanisms. Similarly, the technology of happiness is not confined to the mere theory of the subject. To attain the usefulness of which it is capable it must direct itself to the practice of that theory — to the application of the appropriate laws of nature and human nature to concrete non-material mechanisms — to social systems — whose modes of operation must be adjudged good or bad according as they are adapted or unadapted to achieve the object of utility. In the present book I intend thus to apply the theory formulated in Book II directly to the conduct of society — to exhibit it as an actual working test of proposed or practised policies.

The future conduct of society must and will consist of some definite assemblage of voluntary acts occurring in a definite order of succession, and while the law of causation remains intact the output of happiness of society will be a function of its future conduct. Experience yields ample reason to believe that of the indefinite number of congeries of acts which might constitute the conduct of society, all are not equally adapted to the end of utility, but that some are better adapted than others. This being the case, it is clear that to guide the conduct of society toward utility and away from inutility would be a useful thing to do. But to guide society in any direction is to do neither more nor less than to control its acts, and to exercise control, a means of exercising it must be available. Two distinct methods of exercising control over the conduct of society are proposable: (1) The *anarchical:* (2) the *non-anarchical*.

The anarchical method consists simply in leaving everything to nature, permitting each individual to do as he pleases and follow his own impulses which, as they impel him toward personal pleasure and away from personal pain, will tend — according to the anarchist — on the whole, to attain the end of utility. *Anarchy requires the absence of all artificial control of the conduct of society.* The objections to this method are sufficiently treated in other portions of this work.

As the anarchical method of control is control by nature alone, the only alternative to it must be some method in which men voluntarily modify the course of nature in order to deflect the conduct of society in a greater or less degree from that which would result under anarchy. The device, or instrument, by means of which this is accomplished is known as *government*. The non-anarchical methods of control may be divided into two classes: (1) The *oligarchical:* (2) The *democratic*.

The first method consists in controlling the conduct of society in conformity with the approval or disapproval of some person, or class of persons, constituting a small fraction of the total, the selection of said person or persons being determined by some means other than the will of society itself. *Oligarchy requires that the conduct of society shall be subject to artificial control, but that said control shall not be exercised by society.* The extreme case of oligarchical control is autocratic control, the approval or disapproval of a single person controlling public conduct. Oligarchical control of government is practically universal at the present time. It is typical of all forms of monarchy, and is an essential feature thereof. It is also typical of all actual examples of democracy, though it is not an essential feature thereof.

Were it possible to so select the ruling body in an oligarchy that its inclinations were identical, or approximately identical, with those of Justice, this form of control would be a just one. But no method of doing this has ever been proposed. Thus some form of control which consults the will and interest of the persons controlled is preferable. As Leibnitz says: " Men will prefer to have their own will, and look themselves after their own welfare, until they have confidence in the supreme wisdom and power of their rulers." In an oligarchy there is no presumption that the approval or disapproval which constitutes the guide to social conduct will be identical with that of Justice, or even approximately so. This is the peculiar defect of oligarchical control, and it is manifest throughout all history, and never more manifest than at the present time.

The second or democratic method consists in making the approval or disapproval of a majority of the adults (usually the male adults) of a community, the test of what the community as a whole shall do. The theory of democratic control is simple. The nearest approach possible to the will of Justice will be the will of that portion of society capable of employing common sense as a guide to conduct. Hence their control will approximate more closely to the control of Justice than that of any portion selected by other means. The Declaration of Independence affirms that governments derive " their just powers from the consent of the governed," and no other just source of governmental power has ever been consistently maintained. *Democracy requires that conduct affecting the interests of society shall be controlled by society.*

Any attempt to put the theory of democracy into practice, however, encounters serious obstacles. The difficulty of distinguishing those who are capable of exercising judgment from those who are not is such that distinctions so loosely approximate as to be almost arbitrary have to be resorted to. Thus the separation of voters from non-voters by an arbitrary age limit is a very unsatisfactory expedient, and the employment of sex as a distinction is still less defensible. Another difficulty arises from the great number of persons whose will is the source of control. In small communities, such as the towns of New England, it is practical for the whole voting community to meet in one spot and express their will, but in large communities this is impossible — hence the resort to representative government, in which communities are represented by individuals, who themselves exercise control. The introduction of this expedient, whereby the people and their government are distinct, makes it possible to defeat the will of society by controlling its government, and in every community there are large classes of persons willing and anxious to do this, in order to further their own interests. Thus far every attempt at the application of the democratic theory of control has been thwarted by the activity of such self-seeking classes; hence all democracies are, in reality, but mitigated oligarchies. Whether we consider the states of Greece in ancient times, or the United States of America in modern times, the same deterioration of democracy into oligarchy is to be observed. There are plenty of nominal democracies in the world, but no real ones. Whatever the form of government, it is probable that any community divided into two or more classes of antagonistic interests will sooner or later become of the oligarchical type; though it is not to be denied that a mechanism sufficiently adapted to the expression of the people's will might prevent this. It is no part of the purpose of this work to enter into a general discussion of the proper structure of such a mechanism, though it may be remarked in passing that means are proposable much better adapted to this end than any now practised.

Among the most important of them are the *initiative* and *referendum*, constituting means whereby an approximation to direct legislation may be secured. These devices are, in reality, extensions of the town meeting principle, whereby the people vote directly for measures, instead of for men, and thus legislate for themselves instead of trusting to the readily deranged and corrupted representative system. The details of the initiative and referendum I shall not discuss here — they are capable of much variation and have stood the test of long trial — notably in Switzerland. Every democracy should adopt them as the most efficient means yet proposed of preventing lapse into oligarchy. The referendum has been occasionally employed in this country by states and municipalities, and it is one of the means prescribed in the Federal Constitution for securing amendments to that instrument. No evils have thus far developed in its employment. The fact that in many instances of the use of the referendum a majority of the voters have not troubled themselves to record their preferences has often been cited as a reason why the opportunity to record them should be denied the people altogether. Such a criticism is shallow. Because a majority does not care to express its preferences on some matter in which it is not interested affords no reason for believing that it does not care to express them on matters in which it *is* interested. Whenever the measures on which the people are called upon to directly decide have an essential relation to their happiness they will take sufficient interest to vote upon them, and the state in which the opportunity to do so is denied them has but an inferior claim to the name of a democracy. As a supplement to direct legislation, an indirect system is essential in all large communities, but as the sole means of transcribing the will of the people into law it is imperfect and unsafe. The present party system in the United States, for example, is but a bungling affair, and self-seekers have not usually encountered much difficulty in using it to defeat the people's will. Despite its defects, the democratic theory is the only reasonable one thus far proposed, since no other creates even a moderate presumption that the control of the conduct of society will be in the interests of Justice.

There is, nevertheless, one serious objection to the democratic theory of control, viz., that the interests of a vast majority of those affected by the conduct of the present generation are not represented in, nor often consulted by, the controlling government. I refer to the interests of posterity, whose right to be considered is immeasureably greater than that of any single generation. This objection, however, is one which applies to all systems and is probably irremediable. Were a system devisable which recognized and preserved the paramount rights of posterity, it would be more just than any yet proposed. Apparently the best that can be done is to make manifest to the public in how many particulars the interests of one generation are actually identical with those of their posterity, and in those particulars in which they are not, to trust to the sense of justice which a cultivated understanding of the nature of morality tends to develop. To trust to the sense of justice of a community will, under any system, afford a less presumption of success than to trust to its self-interest, but the presumption will be greater when morality is subject to the test of common sense than when, as at present, it is subject to that of intuition, since to make conscience the criterion of right instead of right the criterion of conscience is not likely to result in a reign of righteousness.

The anarchical, the oligarchical, and the democratic, forms of control are the only distinct forms which have ever been proposed, but there are many indistinct forms, founded on no definite principle and having their origin in the accidents of history. These comprise all forms in actual practice, and they consist of the first two, or of all three, forms in combination. It would be futile to attempt to distinguish in what degree the three forms or methods of control share in determining the conduct of society. The anarchical form, of course, predominates, determining the bulk of all human activities throughout the world.

As science first encroaches upon intuitionism from the material side, its effect upon nations emerging from mediævalism is to promote an industrial development out of proportion to their moral development. The means of producing desiderata are stimulated beyond the capacity of the community to put them to useful purposes, and the efficiency of production is increased far more than that of consumption. Thus have arisen the great commercial nations of modern times — all hands and no head — with great capacity for doing things, but without capacity to distinguish what things are useful to do. Like ships with huge engines, but rudderless, they rush feverishly and aimlessly about, not knowing their goal and hence powerless to lay their course. They use common sense as a guide to proximate ends, but intuition as a guide to ultimate ends. Thus, materially they are modern, but morally they remain mediæval.

In the discussion which follows I shall confine attention to social mechanisms which embody the democratic principle of control, since no other has any interest to utilitarianism. In the particular stage of development in which modern democracies find themselves, there are open four forms of social mechanism to one or the other of which they must resort. Though there may be variation in detail, it is difficult to see how an industrial state not belonging to one or the other of these forms can remain in any degree democratic. They may be called in the order of their development in time (1) *Natural competition,* (2) *Artificial competition,* (3) *Pseudo-socialism,* (4) *Socialism.* I shall in the chapters following test these alternative forms by means of the criteria formulated in the preceding book, and from the data thus obtained shall attempt the construction of a concrete social mechanism which shall fulfil the requirements of common sense, and be adapted to attain the end of utility.

CHAPTER XI

COMPETITION

Among the proposed methods of attaining the object of society is that embodied in competition. It may be contended that competition is not a method deliberately employed by society to gain its ends, because by simply letting things alone competition operates automatically, and hence is not a means voluntarily selected, but is something which " just happens." Such a contention can be allowed only on the supposition that society has no alternative — that no other means of accomplishing her ends can be suggested — for it is undeniable that where no alternatives exist there can be no voluntary act. Such other alternatives exist, however, and therefore we must regard competition as a means deliberately selected by men on account of its supposed adaptability to the attainment of their ends. The fact that it involves inactivity does not make it any the less a voluntarily selected alternative. To let things alone is to exercise volition so long as they are let alone voluntarily. To maintain otherwise is but the claim of the fatalist, and fatalism in a community cannot escape the charge of absurdity on the ground that it avoids volition, any more than in an individual.

The theory of competitive beneficence is a direct corollary of the theory of natural beneficence and none is more widely accepted and more dogmatically maintained. Competition, we are told, is a law of nature and therefore beneficial. Such benefit as competition in nature involves may be revealed by a brief examination of the subject, for it may be admitted that competition is a law of nature in the sense in which writers on social topics use that term; that is, it is a process to be observed in nature. Perhaps the character of the perfectly natural process cannot be better described than in the words of that famous observer of nature — Charles Darwin. In his work on the Origin of Species he remarks that " The elder De Candolle and Lyell have largely and philosophically shown that all organic beings are exposed to severe competition," and adds: " Nothing is easier than to admit in words the truth of the universal struggle for life." He then proceeds to describe the process as follows:

"A struggle for existence inevitably follows from the high rate at which all organic beings tend to increase. Every being, which during its natural lifetime produces several eggs or seeds, must suffer destruction during some period of its life, and during some season or occasional year, otherwise, on the principle of geometrical increase, its numbers would quickly become so inordinately great that no country could support the product. Hence, as more individuals are produced than can possibly survive, there must in every case be a struggle for existence, either one individual with another of the same species, or with the individuals of distinct species, or with the physical conditions of life. It is the doctrine of Malthus applied with manifold force to the whole animal and vegetable kingdoms; for in this case there can be no artificial increase of food, and no prudential restraint from marriage. Although some species may be now increasing, more or less rapidly, in numbers, all can not do so, for the world would not hold them.

"There is no exception to the rule that every organic being naturally increases at so high a rate, that, if not destroyed, the earth would soon be covered by the progeny of a single pair. Even slow-breeding man has doubled in twenty-five years, and at this rate, in less than a thousand years, there would literally not be standing-room for his progeny."[1]

Competition in nature, then, is a struggle for existence — a process whereby continually increasing numbers of individuals contend with one another for the available means of subsistence. As observed in human society, however, competition is restricted in many different modes and degrees. It is only in communities which have not a trace of government that it is unrestricted. When each individual is able to act upon the impulse of the moment, unrestrained by any legal regulation, competition is unrestricted. Such a condition obtains among animals, and perhaps among such communities as those of the pygmies of Africa. It is the only pure individualism, and involves the maximum legal liberty. As soon as legal restraint upon the acts of individuals in the interest of society is imposed, pure individualism is at an end and anti-individualism begins. The term *socialism* is evidently adapted to stand for that which is opposed to individualism, but as it happens, this term has already been confined to certain relatively high degrees of anti-individualism, and hence is not available for this purpose. It is

---

[1] Origin of Species; Chap. 3.

no part of my object to discuss the various forms of restricted competition which human society in its various stages presents, nor to trace how, by the slow change of custom and the substitution of one dogma for another, the present system of competition has been evolved. Karl Marx has already treated this subject historically with great thoroughness. The particular stage at present attained by European countries and America has been appropriately called the *capitalistic system*. It is to the effect upon happiness of competition as observed under the capitalistic system that I wish to direct discussion. Its political philosophy is embodied principally in the *laissez faire* school of economics already referred to.

Capital is defined as wealth devoted to purposes of production. It is generally divided into two classes — *circulating* and *fixed* capital. Mill thus discusses them:

" Of the capital engaged in the production of any commodity, there is a part, which, after being once used, exists no longer as capital; is no longer capable of rendering service to production, or at least not the same service, nor to the same sort of production. Such, for example, is the portion of capital which consists of materials. The tallow and alkali of which soap is made, once used in the manufacture, are destroyed as alkali and tallow; and cannot be employed any further in the soap manufacture, though in their altered condition, as soap, they are capable of being used as a material or an instrument in other branches of manufacture. In the same division must be placed the portion of capital which is paid as the wages, or consumed as the subsistence of labourers. That part of the capital of a cotton-spinner which he pays away to his workpeople, once so paid, exists no longer as his capital, or as a cottonspinner's capital: such portion of it as the workmen consume, no longer exists as capital at all: even if they save any part, it may now be more properly regarded as a fresh capital, the result of a second act of accumulation. Capital which in this manner fulfils the whole of its office in the production in which it is engaged, by a single use, is called Circulating Capital. The term, which is not very appropriate, is derived from the circumstance, that this portion of capital requires to be constantly renewed by the sale of the finished product, and when renewed is perpetually parted with in buying materials and paying wages; so that it does its work, not by being kept, but by changing hands.

" Another large portion of capital, however, consists in instruments of production, of a more or less permanent character; which produce their effect not by being parted with, but by being kept; and the efficacy of which is not exhausted by a single use. To this class belong buildings, machinery, and all or most things known by the name of implements or tools. The durability of some of these is considerable, and their function as productive instruments is prolonged through many repetitions of the productive operation. In this class must likewise be included capital sunk (as the expression is) in permanent improvements of land. So also the capital expended once for all, in the commencement of an undertaking, to prepare the way for subsequent operations: the expense of opening a mine, for example: of cutting canals, of making roads or docks. Other examples might be added, but these are sufficient. Capital which exists in any of these durable shapes, and the return to which is spread over a period of corresponding duration, is called Fixed Capital." [1]

The owner of capital is called a *capitalist*. The manipulator or localizer of capital, or he who employs it for productive purposes, is called a *laborer*. Now the distinguishing characteristic of the capitalistic system is that the capital of a community is not owned by those who employ it. Hence arises the familiar wage system whereby one man or set of men induce other men to manipulate or localize their capital for them; the wealth received in exchange for the result of said manipulation or localization being divided between capitalist and laborer. The part received by the capitalist is called *profit*; that received by the laborer is called *wages* or *salary*. In other words, the capitalist employs the laborer and the laborer employs the capital; the result is profit for the capitalist, and wages for the laborer — both resulting from the employment of capital by labor. Of course, in any stage of capitalism but the most primitive there are many kinds of labor which do not involve the actual handling of the material of production. The machinery of modern production is so complex that in addition to the laborers who actually manipulate the materials, or localize the products, there are many other laborers, such as managers, clerks, salesmen, office boys, watchmen, etc., all having their part in the mechanism of production. Sometimes capitalists take part themselves in the business of production, acting usually in the capacity of managers, directing the activities of their employees. In this case, of course, they are both capitalists and laborers, and their recompense, therefore, is partly wages and partly profit. Frequently, however, no distinction is made between them, and hence the general implication that all capitalists perform productive functions because some of them do. We shall confine the term *profit* to dividends, rent, and in-

[1] Political Economy; Book I, Chap. 6.

terest, or receipts properly creditable to one or the other class; that is, profit is what the capitalist receives for the use of his capital. The land-holder is a capitalist by virtue of his title to the most universally essential kind of fixed capital, viz., land. The recompense received by small merchants, farmers, blacksmiths, etc. is, according to this definition, rather wages than profits. Their profits so-called are in reality due only in small part to their possession of capital, most of it being recompense for the labor performed by them. This is shown by the fact that they would receive but a very small part of their actual recompense, did they simply sell the use of their capital.

The opposition of interest which competition under the capitalistic system brings about is of four classes: (1) The opposition between capitalists and their competitors, whereby profits tend to a minimum: (2) The opposition between laborers and their competitors, whereby wages tend to a minimum, and duration of labor to a maximum: (3) The opposition between buyer and seller, the one striving to decrease, the other to increase the price of commodities: (4) The opposition between capitalists and laborers, the one striving to increase profit at the expense of wages, the other striving to increase wages at the expense of profit. The fourth class of opposition is but a special case of the third; the capitalist being the buyer and the laborer the seller of labor.

This opposition of interest between the individuals and classes of a community is, according to the prevailing school of economy, a source of benefit; and in theory most men appear to agree with this view. In practice, however, all classes seek to avoid it. Everyone is willing that others should meet competition but no one likes to meet it himself, and with the process of time and increase of intelligence, men have found a way to avoid certain classes of competition. Thus by combination between capitalists, private monopolies are formed and the first class of opposing interests is abolished. By similar combinations between laborers into labor unions, or private labor monopolies, the second class of opposing interests is abolished. To abolish the third and fourth classes of competitive opposition, great efforts have been expended, but so far without much success. A brief discussion of the fourth class will show why.

The opposed interest of the buyer and seller of labor constitutes the so-called labor problem of the present day. To solve it one or both of two objects must be attained. Either (1) A way must be found whereby the relation of profits and wages may be made such that neither can be increased by a decrease of the other: or (2) A way must be found of making men as much interested in the happiness of their fellow men as they are in their own. The first requires an alteration in the wage system — the second an alteration in human nature. Attempts to solve the problem by both methods have been made.

The attainment of the first object has been sought by the expedient of profit-sharing in various forms, including the issue of dividend-bearing stock to employees. This expedient has met with some success, but wherever labor is organized its success is likely to be inversely proportional to the intelligence of the laborers, for the increase in recompense from profit-sharing is necessarily so slight as compared with that to be derived from even a small percentage increase of wages, that the latter method of bettering their condition will be preferred by laborers who understand their own interest; since the resulting loss in their dividends cannot be nearly equivalent to the gain in their wages. It is obvious that it would be perfectly possible to distribute all profit as wages. Profit, therefore, may be regarded as a fund withdrawn from wages. To restore a fraction of what has already been withdrawn, clearly cannot compensate for the original withdrawal. So long as a business is making any profit at all there is a prospect of increasing wages at its expense, and the laborers, if the means are available, will attempt to do so. Whether this attempt is just or not will depend, of course, upon its effect upon happiness, a subject to which we shall presently revert. Where labor is not organized, profit-sharing will doubtless tend to harmonize the interests of capitalist and laborer; but unfortunately it is usually fear of the power of labor organization which has prompted capitalists to share their profits with their employees — hence, where labor is unorganized, profit-sharing is not generally a popular policy among capitalists.

The attainment of the second object has been sought by the establishment of boards of conciliation and arbitration, or other means of inducing the parties to a labor controversy to consider the just claims of their opponents. The difficulty is that in the absence of any definition of *justice,* no one can agree upon what constitutes a just claim. Hence it must be decided by some purely arbitrary standard, generally founded upon prevailing customs. If men were unselfish, and each party to the controversy were as much concerned in the happiness of the other as in his own, the strife between capitalist and laborer could be ended with little difficulty. Hence those who maintain that the

Golden Rule, if applied, would solve the labor problem are correct. But it is equally true and equally pertinent that if human beings could live on a diet of stones it would solve the problem of feeding the poor. If men would apply the Golden Rule, most problems which plague humanity would be solved. The question is: how are you to induce them to apply it? Certainly not by simply telling them to do so. Had that method been effectual the end would have been accomplished long ago.

But if those who maintain the beneficence of competition are correct, the contention and competition of capitalist and laborer for an increased share in the product to be divided between them is not a harm, but a benefit; the labor problem is no problem at all. Its solution would be a misfortune — since this constant strife is but one manifestation of wholesome competition, and of that beneficent institution communities cannot have too much. To abolish the labor problem would be a blow at competition, of course, and hence would be harmful, just as trusts and labor unions are harmful according to the same school of economy.

Now, there are reasons to believe that while human nature remains as it is, a real solution of the labor problem is incompatible with the capitalistic system. Competition is its cause, and it can be cured only by abolishing its cause. Should some palliative come to be mistaken for a cure, I believe it would be a public misfortune. The reasons for this belief will appear in the discussion which follows, in which the relation of capitalistic competition to happiness will be examined. The way to discover the effect of competition upon happiness is to discover its effect upon the elements of happiness separately. To attempt to ascertain its total effect in any other way would but lead to the confusion and inconclusiveness so familiar in the current discussions of this all-important question, wherein the effort is made to evaluate the complex effect of competition without any analysis of each effect separately. In other words, if competition is beneficial to society, it is beneficial by virtue of its effect upon one or more of the elements of happiness. Let us then examine its effect upon each of the elements of happiness, in order that we may, if possible, locate the point at which its beneficence enters.

First: What is the effect of competition on the first element of happiness? Does it tend to improve the quality of human beings? Does it tend to the development of a high level of intellect and character? If it does, it must be through some effect upon inheritance, or education, or both, since the qualities of human individuals are functions of these factors and of no others. First, then, let us consider inheritance.

As acquired characters are not inherited the only mode in which competition can affect the inheritance of the race is through selection. Does competition tend to cause those who possess intelligence, altruism, and will, in marked degree, to breed faster than those who possess them in less marked degree? Does competition tend to improve the human race by its effect upon breeding? It is a familiar claim that competition does tend thus to improve the human breed through the effect of natural selection or the survival of the fittest. Let us then examine this claim. On page 362 we have quoted Darwin's description of competition in nature, or the struggle of individuals with one another for the means of subsistence. Now, members of all species of organisms are subject to variation — no two individuals are exactly alike. Moreover, variations are transmissible by inheritance. On these simple facts Darwin founded his famous induction of natural selection thus:

"How will the struggle for existence, briefly discussed in the last chapter, act in regard to variation? Can the principle of selection which we have seen is so potent in the hands of man, apply under nature? I think we shall see that it can act most efficiently. Let the endless number of slight variations and individual differences occurring in our domestic productions, and in a lesser degree, in those under nature be borne in mind; as well as the strength of the hereditary tendency. Under domestication, it may truly be said that the whole organization becomes in some degree plastic. But the variability which we almost universally meet with in our domestic productions is not directly produced, as Hooker and Asa Gray have well remarked, by man; he can neither originate varieties nor prevent their occurrence; he can only preserve and accumulate such as do occur. Unintentionally he exposes organic beings to new and changing conditions of life, and variability ensues; but similar changes of conditions might and do occur under nature. Let it also be borne in mind how infinitely complex and close-fitting are the mutual relations of all organic beings to each other and to their physical conditions of life; and consequently what infinitely varied diversities of structure might be of use to each being under changing conditions of life. Can it then be thought improbable, seeing that variations useful to man have undoubtedly occurred, that other variations useful in some way to each being in the great and complex battle of life should occur in the course of many successive generations? If such do occur, can we doubt (remembering that many more individuals are born than can possibly survive) that individuals having any advantage, however slight, over others, would have the best chance of surviving and procreating their kind? On the other hand, we may feel sure that any variation in the least degree injurious would be rigidly destroyed. This preservation of favorable individual differences and variations, and the destruction of those which are injurious, I have called Natural Selection, or the Survival of the Fittest." [1]

Thus nature, by always producing many more of a species than can survive to propagate, and marking those for death who are least fitted for life, leaves those to propagate who are best fitted, and hence only a few of the best adapted individuals survive to perpetuate the species out of the vast number supplied by each generation. That is to say, nature selects a few from a great many as breeders of the species, and as these few are selected because of certain characteristics which distinguish them as best fitted to survive, these characteristics tend to become fixed, by inheritance, in the species. Competition, it is to be observed, is a necessary factor in this process, and Darwin calls attention to the fact that it is keenest between organisms which are closely related. He says:

"As the species of the same genus usually have, though by no means invariably, much similarity in habits and constitution, and always in structure, the struggle will generally be more severe between them, if they come into competition with each other, than between the species of distinct genera." [2]

From this it appears that the struggle for existence between individuals of the same species must be very keen indeed. Now, among primitive men the process of competition is essentially similar to that among organisms in general; but in civilized society it assumes a new form. The contention between individuals is one, not for the means of subsistence alone, but for the means of happiness. The essential feature of the process is, however, preserved — it is a contention — the gain of one individual is the loss of another, the success of one implies the failure of others, and the greater the success of one, the greater the failure of others.

It will be observed that Darwin employs the word "useful" in describing the characters which tend to be preserved by the

[1] Origin of Species; Chap. 4.
[2] Ibid.

process of natural selection. Does he express by that word the same meaning which we have agreed to express by it? If so, then we can see at least one beneficent result of competition, for if through the struggle for existence useful characters tend to be more and more preserved and perpetuated in organisms, then competition must — at least in effecting this result — be a useful process. If the "fittest" characters mean the "most useful" characters, then certainly a process which involves the survival of the fittest will be a beneficent one. We should then be justified in accepting the reasoning of so many modern writers who are fond of dwelling on the innate beneficence of evolution as a natural process. These writers tell us that the characters which are fittest must be valuable, and a valuable character is, of course, beneficial. This is very much like the reasoning employed by physicians of the time of Paracelsus, when the science of medicine was about in the stage in which the science of politics is now. They reasoned like this: "That which is valuable is valuable as a cure." "Diamonds, gold, and frankincense are valuable." "Therefore, diamonds, gold, and frankincense will be curative." Acting upon this ratiocinative process they prescribed for their patients various elaborate mixtures of pulverized jewels, precious metals, and rare oils and spices. Specimens of such prescriptions are still preserved in ancient works on medicine. When it occurred to these practitioners that gold and jewels were valuable, they neglected to ask themselves the question: Valuable for *what?* Similarly authors who write of the value of individuals, or characteristics thereof, which are *fit,* neglect to ask themselves: Fit for *what?* Natural selection produces individuals who are fit to live under conditions of competition. It is a process of *the survival of the fittest to survive.* But individuals, or individual characteristics are useful in the degree in which they tend to increase the total happiness. Those, however, who are fittest to survive are not necessarily those fittest to increase the total happiness, any more than things of a high financial value are necessarily of a high curative value. *Apriori,* they are as likely to be the reverse. Thus we see that the human mind preserves the same kind of deviation from common sense whether in the stage of medical or political quackery. In fact, Darwin does not employ the word "useful" in the meaning in which we employ it. Useful as a means of survival does not mean useful as a means of happiness, because survival does not necessarily imply happiness. "But," it may be replied, "the characters which have enabled individuals to live are certainly useful, since without life there can be no happiness, and it is these characters which must be possessed by those who survive." Without dwelling upon the fact that competition does not create these characters, but only determines their perpetuation when created, we may point out that although life is a *necessary,* it is by no means a *sufficient* condition of happiness. Any particular life interval to be useful as an end must reveal a surplus of happiness; otherwise, oblivion or no life at all is preferable (p. 127). We may point out also that life supplies likewise a necessary condition of unhappiness, and we shall presently point out that we have but to add competition, to obtain the sufficient conditions as well.

It is clear that the reasoning on this subject, so far as reason has been applied to it at all, fails for the same reason that most sociological and political reasoning fails. Men are not clear in their own minds as to the nature of usefulness — they do not know just what it is that individuals, or those aggregates of individuals called nations, are, or should be, trying to attain; hence failure in the attempt to specify the means of attaining it. In the case under discussion the end of nature is continually confounded with the end of man. These ends are totally different. Hence we should expect to find that the means of attaining them are different, and this is what we do find. Nature, so far as the process of natural selection reveals her design, (and we here speak of design figuratively, since there is no evidence of deliberate intent) aims to adapt organisms more and more completely to their environment — to make it increasingly difficult for related varieties to arise which are better adapted — the test of their degree of adaptation being their ability to survive in competition. So far as I am aware, non-sentient nature employs pleasure and pain as means, but never seeks them as ends. Pain, or the expectation of pain, warns animals of danger to their lives and prompts them to seek food when hungry, and hence is a "useful" means of insuring the survival of the individual. Pleasure, or the anticipation of pleasure, prompts them to consume their food when found, and to seek mates for the purpose of breeding — hence pleasure is a "useful" means of insuring the survival of the individual and of the race. But neither pleasure nor pain are of the slightest value to nature as ends — mere survival and perpetuation is all she seeks. The aim of man, on the other hand, is, or should be, the maximum output of happiness. With ends so distinct it is inevitable that the means to be adopted to attain them must be distinct. If all we seek is survival, nature's methods will serve our purpose, but if we seek happiness, we must devise very different ones.

I now propose to show that were modern competitive ideals realized, the process of the survival of the fittest to survive would tend to deteriorate, rather than to improve, the human breed — to destroy, rather than to develop, intelligence and character. In Chapter 6 notice has been taken of several influences thus tending to race deterioration. A more potent influence still, threatens, due directly to competition. This influence has little if any effect upon adjustability since that quality is developable solely, or at least principally, through education; neither is it materially concerned with health; but upon the other determinants of efficiency of conversion its effects must of necessity be marked.

It is universally observed and universally conceded that competition results in widespread poverty. Now, the effort of the enlightened communities of to-day is to make competition *fair*, i. e., to make each individual's success in the world depend upon his own intrinsic qualities, and not upon accidents of birth or station. Success in this effort to give every individual a fair chance means that those whose intrinsic qualities are not such as to make them succeed in competition will tend more and more, through failure, to sink into the poorer, less educated and less fortunate class, while those whose qualities are such as to lead to success will tend to become prosperous and wealthy. Now, what are the intrinsic qualities which, on the average, tend to increase a man's chance of success in the modern struggle for wealth and opportunity? They are (1) Intelligence, (2) Will, and (3) Egotism. The third quality is seldom seriously lacking in any individual — hence it is not likely to be a critical factor. But if these are the qualities which tend to success, those which tend to failure must be (1) Unintelligence, (2) Lack of will, and (3) Altruism; and it is these, particularly the first two, which — so far as competition determines their distribution — will tend to become the characteristics of the poorer classes. But the poorer and less educated classes — as all students of sociology admit — are the very ones which breed the fastest — they are the classes which contribute the greater number of individuals to each succeeding generation. As men and women become prosperous they breed more slowly. Hence if we divide society into a prosperous slow-breeding, and a less prosperous fast-breeding class, and by giving all men a fair chance, tend to locate the intelligent and potent in the first class, and the unintelligent and impotent in the second, race deterioration is inevitable, since each generation will be recruited in much greater degree from the second class than from the first. As results prove, under competitive conditions, the members of the second class are those best fitted to survive, and this despite their higher death rate — but they are not those best fitted to produce a happy communiy. Hence the competitive process of the survival of the fittest to survive results in the survival of the unfittest to produce happiness. We may call this the *law of the survival of the incompetent*. If the process of race deterioration implied by this law were permitted to proceed indefinitely, the human breed would rapidly retrograde toward the simian level, for the effects of such a process are cumulative or accelerative, and in accelerative processes the most pronounced effects are only a matter of time. This process has little effect upon tastes or needs, or upon altruism, and, indeed, such effect as it has upon the latter quality is good rather than bad. In times past the race has been protected from the evil effects described, by the universal prevalence of poverty and poor education. The intelligent and the unintelligent, the strong and the weak-willed have, on the average, been kept in the poorer, fast-breeding class; only a favored few, as often incompetents as not, finding their way into the opulent, aristocratic, slow-breeding class. Thus the very universality of poverty in the past, and the presence in the poorer classes of an even quota of the intelligent and potent has prevented this source of race deterioration. It is only in recent times, with the advent of universal education and the opening of an approach to equal opportunity, that the effect we have pointed out tends to come into operation. To neutralize it without abolishing equality of opportunity we must abolish poverty, or else base the division into slow and fast breeding classes upon some other distinction than that between the competent and the incompetent. So far as I am aware, no practical method of doing this has as yet been suggested. Exhortation will not serve the end. Reference to race-suicide will not make any class in the community increase or decrease its rate of breeding. Until some other method is suggested, we must regard the abolition of poverty itself as the only just remedy for this source of race-degeneracy. This may be unattainable, but its attainment is at least worth attempting, and if not attainable, then the deterioration of the race by the selection of the incompetent is probably destined to proceed, unless by natural or artificial means a thoroughgoing inequality of opportunity is established. Developed capitalism indeed destroys equality of opportunity, as is obvious at the present day. Hence this source of race-degeneracy is scarcely a danger any longer; but by thus banishing the menace of degeneracy, capitalism will have destroyed the best ideal of the modern competitive system — the ideal of equal opportunity. No lover of justice can be satisfied with such a solution of the dilemma, yet if poverty cannot be abolished there is no other.

Little need be said of the effect on public education of competition since even by the *laissez faire* theorists it is acknowledged that nothing is to be hoped for from leaving the education of the people to the unguided beneficence of nature. They are, to be sure, convinced that as regards most factors in the welfare of society, nature is beneficent and should be "let alone" to work out its own ends, but for some unexplained reason beneficence appears to desert the operations of nature in the domain of education, and hence society, by deliberate effort, must provide for it. Competition, of course, trains men in many things — in particular it teaches them how to get the best of their fellows; developing quickness of intellect to be sure, but at the same time fostering dishonesty, suspicion, and other egotistic traits. There is no community in which such characteristics are not sufficiently developed. As no one proposes to return to the system of education provided by nature, however, we need not discuss the subject. It is in operation wherever barbarism prevails.

The system of public schools, which, in opposition to the theory of *laissez faire,* all enlightened states have adopted, is one of the most satisfactory efforts of modern society toward its own betterment. We have already pointed out some of the defects of that system — due to the self-perpetuating power of dogma. These defects and many others, however, may be in time eliminated by the deliberate application of the common sense of the community — whereas if left to themselves — or to nature — there would be little prospect of improvement.

Second: As the life of man should be divided between production and consumption, his desires should be adapted to both these classes of acts and, other things being equal, the system which breeds the most satisfaction in work and in recreation will be the best one.

In promoting adjustability as it affects production, the capitalistic system has no advantages. It does not tend to reconcile men to excessive labor or to create in them a taste for it. It makes neither retrospection nor anticipation pleasing. In the degree in which it discourages hope and tames aspiration it is successful in producing resignation — a resignation too frequently cynical. So far as this adapts the laborer's desires to inevitable conditions it augments the efficiency of conversion. Where unpleasant conditions are inevitable it is better to be resigned than not resigned, but where they are not inevitable, resignation is bad, since it inhibits the search for, and application of, remedies. One of the commonest and bitterest criticisms of those who, through agitation, seek a happier condition for mankind is that they make men dissatisfied with their lot in life. Such criticism is quite unreasonable. With the knowledge at present available the unpleasant conditions of production which prevail are *not* inevitable; hence it is not well that the laborer should be satisfied with his non-self-supporting life. If he is satisfied, he should be made unsatisfied. To sleep well at night is a poor goal for ambition. Those who die sleep better. A nation whose object is the maximum output of happiness has no place in its economy for individuals who are "satisfied" to be unhappy, any more than an engineer whose object is the maximum generation of steam has a place for boilers which are "satisfied" to consume coal without producing steam. What useful end is to be subserved if the forests are cleared from the wilderness only to be replaced by a plantation of human vegetables?

The effect of competition on adjustability as it affects consumption cannot be deemed beneficial. The dire consequences of failure in the struggle for existence fill men's minds with misgiving, even when they are prosperous, haunting the hours of relaxation of those engaged in the fierce struggle to avoid them. The desire for competence and independence is the hope of the many — it is the realization of the few; and such a hope, forever deferred, and lapsing into hopelessness rather than resignation as time goes on, maketh sick the heart of the multitude. The consumption of a few in the zone of overconsumption involves the consumption of the many in the zone of underconsumption, and the same system which makes permanent the first makes the second permanent also. That which secures to the wealthy their wealth, secures their poverty to the poor. It is idle to say there is plenty of room at the top and to point to isolated examples of men who have made their way there —

often by devious methods. There is just as much room at the bottom, and what is more to the point, competition insures that it shall be occupied. It is not the desires of the few at the top, but that of the many who are far from the top which must be fulfilled if the happiness output of the community is to be positive. The necessity which competition imposes of becoming independent by the acquisition of wealth or suffer ceaseless struggle, implants in men's minds a fierce desire for money, and they ceaselessly strive to attain it. They usually fail, but whether they fail or succeed in their search for money, they lose in their search for happiness, for win or lose they are never satisfied. This money-lust, which is but a form of avarice, is becoming the besetting sin of modern life. It is a taste neither simple nor adaptable and it seems to preclude variety. It is hard to satiate, and satiable only at the expense of others, for under competition there are few ways of acquiring wealth except by attaining a position in which we are enabled to share in what labor produces without sharing in the labor, or sharing in it in an insignificant degree. To accomplish this is what the world calls success, and the great success of one means the great failure of many. Wealth does not fall from the moon. Hence if there are those in the community who can avail themselves of more labor than they perform, it can only be because in the same community there are those who can avail themselves of less than they perform. The working classes feel this, though by the vagueness of the prevailing morality it is concealed from their understanding. They feel convinced that there is something wrong in such inequality, though they cannot answer the current sophistries which prove that as it originates in inalienable rights it must be right — it is legal and hence it is just. This tends to breed in the minds of the poor envy, or at least suspicion, and the response of the rich is distrust. Such qualities do not promote a high efficiency of conversion, and the alienation of classes, however produced, is evidence of an uneconomic attitude of mind.

Perhaps nothing illustrates better how uneconomic a taste money-lust is than its failure to give happiness, even to those who have attained wealth beyond the dreams of avarice, nor is there any better illustration of the popular confusion regarding the goal of society than the frequent citation of this failure to justify, instead of to condemn, the system which produces it. When it is pointed out that the present system breeds misery among the poor, there are those who appear to think that the criticism loses its force because it may be shown that it breeds misery among the rich also. They tell us that wealth only leads to anxiety and care — that the capitalist carries a heavier burden than the laborer — that despite his riches he cannot be happy, for the cares of wealth are more irksome than the privations of poverty; such is the law of compensation. Who has not heard this strange plea advanced as evidence of the inherent justice of the prevailing condition of things? Yet if it be true, then is the present system doubly damned. If those whose rate of consumption is too high are as unhappy as those whose rate is too low it but accentuates the injustice of the prevailing unequal distribution. It is unfair to both parties and only emphasizes the need of equal distribution. The only possible benefit of a high rate of consumption is the happiness it may yield, and yet we are told that it fails even in this. This is strange justification. Misery cannot compensate for misery. Only happiness can compensate for misery, as every man can learn from a simple inspection of his own mind. Could it be shown that, under the present system, the happiness of the rich was so great as to more than compensate for the unhappiness of the poor, it might afford justification of the system, but if, in spite of their high rate of consumption, the rich are not happy, it but emphasizes how ill adapted is the competitive system to the requirements of human nature.

It is unnecessary here to emphasize the poor economy of conversion involved in luxurious tastes. The evils of excessive luxury are a familiar subject of discussion. While such evils may not be confined to the competitive system, they are inseparable from any condition involving great inequality in the distribution of wealth, for, as was long since remarked, it is human nature that increase of appetite should grow by what it feeds on. Hence they are inseparable from the competitive system. Competition, indeed, cannot be credited with any tendency to promote adjustability. Its inevitable separation of society into classes has the contrary effect, for it breeds desires in all classes which it cannot satisfy.

The effect of competition upon the health of a community is acknowledged to be bad. The strain, anxiety, and uncertainty of life wears out the nervous system, and poisons many, even of the few, leisure hours vouchsafed to the average man. The capitalist is, if anything, worse off than the laborer in this particular, and frequently trades health for wealth — a poor bargain for a business man, since it sacrifices the greater value to obtain the less.

Third: It is obvious that the natural resources of the earth cannot be increased by the acts of man, although their accessibility can. Resources created by man are not natural, but artificial. But, though natural resources cannot be increased by man they may easily be diminished. The effect of competition upon utility in diminishing them we may estimate more readily after a consideration of its effect upon the efficiency of consumption and upon population has been examined, since it is upon these factors that it depends. We shall therefore defer discussion of this element to page 405.

Fourth: Passing to the effect of competition on the employment of the non-sentient factor — of machinery — in production, we at once encounter that which most economists agree is the strongest claim of capitalism to beneficence. The development of the wage system under competition has led to production on a large scale. Huge factories have displaced the small workshop of other days, and in every variety of manipulation and localization the division of labor has adapted modes of production to the introduction of machinery. Now under competition, other things being equal, that individual, firm, or corporation will succeed in highest degree — will make the greatest profits — which can produce most cheaply; hence those who receive the profits will be stimulated to introduce labor-saving machinery into their operations, because they may thereby dispense with the wages of laborers, since a machine which will do the work of ten men when operated by one, will obviously dispense with nine men. Thus production is cheapened, not directly by dispensing with labor, but by dispensing with laborers employed in a given operation, and liberating their labor so that it may be employed in other operations. The stimulus to this mode of increasing the efficiency of production is justly represented by economists as a very effectual one, since the desire for wealth in all men is strong, and is not less strong among capitalists than among other classes of the community. Hence if the reward of capitalists, whether laboring or non-laboring, is made a direct function of their success in introducing machinery into production, their zeal and ingenuity will be assiduously directed to that end. The opinions of economists on this point are well represented in the words of Mill, who says:

"We have observed that, as a general rule, the business of life is better performed when those who have an immediate interest in it are left to take their own course, uncontrolled either by the mandate of the law or by the meddling of any public functionary. The person, or some of the persons, who do the work, are likely to be better judges than the government of the means of attaining the particular end at which they aim. Were we to suppose, what is not very probable, that the government has possessed itself of the best knowledge which had been acquired up to a given time by the persons most skilled in the occupation; even then, the individual agents have so much stronger and more direct an interest in the result, that the means are far more likely to be improved and perfected if left to their uncontrolled choice." [1]

Let us acknowledge that competition by this mode of increasing the efficiency of production has strong claims to approval and, so far as its immediate, proximate ends are concerned, affords an excellent means of attaining them. Nevertheless we must not forget that all means must be judged by their *total* — not their *partial* effect — in the attainment of happiness. Hence if it should appear that the remote effects of competition in this particular, neutralize, or more than neutralize, its immediate effects, we cannot approve the system on these grounds. We shall presently consider some of these more remote effects. But before leaving the present subject, it should be remarked that the same stimulus which is so strong in inducing capitalists to introduce labor-saving machinery into production is equally strong in inducing them to introduce devices designed, not to save labor, but to produce inferior products. This subject is so familiar to everyone and has been so often treated by economists that it would be superfluous to dilate upon it. The innumerable adulterations, impostures, and cheats that are everywhere manufactured and sold, from wooden nutmegs to watered stocks, are products of this stimulus to gain. The development of means of imposition and corruption, like that of other kinds of mechanism, accelerates as time goes on. It is but a special case of the progress of an art, and the man who lays the foundation of his success by adulterating sugar with sand, or salting a mine, crowns it by purchasing a legislature, or perverting public opinion through the power of the press. It is characteristic of the *laissez faire* economists that for this condition of things they have no remedy but preaching. Thus Herbert Spencer, after pointing out many of these products of competition, observes:

[1] Political Economy; Book V, Chap. 11.

"As for remedy, it manifestly follows that there is none save a purified public opinion. When that abhorrence which society now shows to direct theft, is shown to theft of all degrees of indirectness; then will these mercantile vices disappear. When not only the trader who adulterates or gives short measure, but also the merchant who overtrades, the bank-director who countenances an exaggerated report, and the railway-director who repudiates his guarantee, come to be regarded as of the same genus as the pickpocket, and are treated with like disdain; then will the morals of trade become what they should be.

"We have little hope, however, that any such higher tone of public opinion will shortly be reached." [1]

We agree with Spencer that if we must wait for public opinion to remedy this condition, the prospect is far from encouraging. The evil is a growing, not a diminishing, one and has vastly increased since Spencer wrote. New forms of corruption and imposture develop every day. Unorganized public opinion such as Spencer appeals to cannot check it, and were he consistent he would have made no appeal to it. Why should he attempt artificially to influence public opinion to condemn such evils — why not let things take their naturally beneficent course? Why will not these evils remedy themselves, like all the other ills which the operation of natural law incidentally develops? Why should the *laissez faire* economist appeal to unorganized, any more than to organized, public opinion? This is not a consistent "let alone" policy; it is not evidence of faith in the doctrine of beneficent drift.

Fifth: The effect of the competitive system upon the skill and interest of labor is not uniform. Those who direct are usually interested in the profits to be made and hence have an incentive to apply themselves in the business of production and to obtain the maximum production from others at the minimum wage. For the directive class of labor then, there is incentive to application, and in a less degree to the acquisition of skill. Interest and application, indeed, will lead to skill even if no deliberate means are adopted to attain it.

To the executive class of laborers, however, there is in the competitive system but little incentive to either interest or skill; since normally they can derive but little advantage therefrom. It is, naturally, the practice of the capitalist to convert into profit any increase in the returns from labor which may result from an increase in the application and skill of his employees. Where labor

[1] The Morals of Trade.

is unorganized this practice is almost universal, and, indeed, when competition between capitalists is keen it is essential to the maintenance of any profit at all, for keen competition makes failure the price of benevolence on the part of employers. Wherever labor is organized, however, and competition in some degree eliminated, the incentive to application is somewhat increased, because organization confers the power upon employees of forcing their employers to share with them the increased return resulting from increased application. Among some labor organizations, however, a policy is adopted which more than offsets this incentive — that of limitation of output — a practice of limiting the output per capita by mutual agreement among laborers. This policy is adopted in order to distribute opportunity for work more uniformly among members of the organization. It increases the *money* cost, but not necessarily the *labor* cost of commodities. It is particularly frequent where the system of piece-work prevails and is adopted to offset the policy of employers of diminishing the price paid per piece as the skill and application of employees and the introduction of machinery enable the production per capita to increase. It is simply a method of forcing the employer to forego part of his profit for the benefit of his employees. The effect of the policy of limitation of output upon the efficiency of production will depend upon the degree to which it is carried. If carried beyond a certain point it will increase the labor cost as well as the money cost of production. Nevertheless, as we shall presently see, the effect of such a policy on the efficiency of consumption is, in general, so excellent that it more than offsets any loss resulting from diminished efficiency of production. Such a situation appears, and is, an anomaly, but it is a direct result of a vaster anomaly — the capitalistic system — and is one evidence of how opposed that system is to the interests of society.

Another result of the absence of interest on the part of the wage earner in the efficiency of production is found in the innumerable strikes and labor disturbances so common during the last generation. The immediate effect of these disturbances is to diminish the efficiency both of production and consumption, but in the aggregate, their remote effect upon the efficiency of consumption is good, and good in the degree in which it tends to suspend the effects of competition. We have already discussed the essentials of the labor question, and have made evident the antagonism of interest which it implies.

Sixth: If there is one effect of the capitalistic system **more** generally acknowledged than another it is its effect upon the distribution of wealth. The "prodigious inequality" of which Mill speaks in a previous quotation (p. 292) is an inequality of wealth and such unequal distribution appears inseparable from all varieties of the competitive system, ancient and modern. In a new country like the United States inequality in the distribution of wealth is not nearly so marked as in Europe and Asia. Still, it has already become a pronounced feature of our civilization and is, of necessity, increasing. In colonial days there was little inequality, but from the conditions of those days we are departing more and more. The distribution of wealth among the 12,500,000 families in the United States in 1890 may be gathered from the following table, which probably embodies the best figures available:

THE UNITED STATES 1890 [1]

Estates	Number of Families.	Aggregate Wealth.	Average Wealth.
The Wealthy Classes $50,000 and over.......	125,000	$33,000,000,000	$264,000
The Well-to-do Classes $50,000 to $5,000......	1,375,000	23,000,000,000	16,000
The Middle Classes $5,000 to $500..........	5,500,000	8,200,000,000	1,500
The Poorer Classes under $500	5,500,000	800,000,000	150
Total	12,500,000	$65,000,000,000	$ 5,200

So universal is this symptom that men very generally have come to regard it as a sort of law of nature — an unavoidable and ineradicable ill — and yet it is no more universal than the competitive system. Because it is inseparable from that system is no reason for claiming that it is inseparable from any and all systems. Those who maintain the unavoidableness of inequality are fond of pointing out that, if by some extraordinary agency wealth were equally distributed to-morrow it would be but a few years before the old condition of inequality would again be attained. The significant thing about this assertion is that it is true. Instead, however, of seeing in its truth the condemna-

[1] Charles B. Spahr, "The Present Distribution of Wealth," p. 69.

tion of the system which produces such an anomaly, the man of average training can see nothing but an excuse for doing nothing — for letting things drift — since if a condition of equal distribution, if attained, is destined so soon to lapse again into one of inequality, it is scarcely worth while to attempt its attainment.

If wealth is observed to inevitably gravitate to a condition of unequal distribution, it must be because something causes it to do so, must it not? And if this be true, it surely is worth while to discover the cause or causes of so unfortunate a tendency, since there is no more essential factor in an economic system than that of a distribution of wealth at least approximately equal. I shall not here discuss these causes in detail, but shall deem it sufficient to remark that if the competitive system were of such character that under it the acquisition of wealth by an individual set in operation causes which made further acquisition increasingly difficult, any great inequality in distribution would be unknown, since accumulation in a few hands would be automatically checked. Instead of being of this character, however, the competitive system is so constituted as to produce a contrary result. Inequality, instead of equality, of distribution is the condition of equilibrium. The more wealth an individual acquires, the more likely is he to acquire more — wealth breeds wealth — and hence the desiderata of a community tend to accumulate in the hands of but a small fraction of the community. The process is a maleficently accelerative one, and even more marked in civilized than in savage communities. Nature then, despite its beneficence, supplies no automatic check to this increasing inequality of distribution. Hence if a check is to be supplied, it must be supplied by man. Whether a method of accomplishing this desirable result consistent with the characteristics of human nature can be suggested, I shall not at this point in the discussion attempt to say. It is sufficient to emphasize the fact that equality of distribution is vital to an economic system of society, and that competition supplies no means of attaining it; but, on the contrary, is acknowledged to be inconsistent with its attainment.

Seventh: Quite as essential to sound economy as the possession by the average member of a community of an approximately equal share of its wealth is adequate leisure wherein to consume it. Under the capitalistic system, not only are wages too low through the abstraction of profit for the realization of equal distribution, but the hours of labor are too long to sustain a self-supporting indicative ratio; not only do wages tend to a minimum but the hours of labor tend to a maximum. The effort to cheapen production in order to increase profits is the rock on which the system founders. For the comprehension of this matter a rather more critical examination of the present wage system will be necessary.

There are two kinds of wages — *nominal* and *real*. Nominal wages are measured by the actual number of money units — of dollars or cents — paid out as recompense to labor. Real wages are measured, so far as measurable, by the amount of production represented in the desiderata purchasable by said number of money units. It is obvious that real wages are those which have a direct relation to utility. Nominal wages are of no consequence, since an average wage of $10.00 per hour would be no better than one of $ .10, if prices were a hundred times as high under the first system as under the second. Under a competitive system, both nominal and real wages tend to a minimum, though this is often denied. It is a familiar argument among economists that the tendency of competition under the wage system to depress wages neutralizes itself through its effect upon the purchasing power of wages. Laborer competing with laborer and capitalist with capitalist, they say, causes both nominal wages and profits to tend to a minimum; thus prices tend to a minimum; but in just the degree that prices diminish, the purchasing power of nominal wages increases — hence a general fall of nominal wages does not interfere with the economy of consumption, since such a fall causes a corresponding fall in prices, and thus real wages remain as before. This argument is frequently urged in favor of the *laissez faire* doctrine of free trade, i. e., free competition between nations.

Of course, economists never refer to the economy of consumption in so many words; but it is that economy which they tacitly recognize as of importance when they propound this theory of the compensating effect of competition in depressing wages. The theory is easily proven fallacious in two ways. (1) Prices do not fall simultaneously with wages, but there is a considerable lag, owing to the fact that capitalists generally try to keep their prices high until forced by competition to lower them, and when so forced, responding by a shortening of wages. Indeed, it is this fall of prices which permits, or would permit, an indefinite fall of nominal wages. Laborers must, naturally, receive *some* wages; they must consume *some* wealth in order to live and to labor; hence there is a point below which their wages cannot be forced; this point will depend upon the purchasing power of wages — it will depend upon prices; hence as prices fall, nominal wages can and will fall, and this fall of nominal wages will be a fall of real wages — since prices will not fall simultaneously. So long as real wages are more than sufficient to just permit the laborer to live and labor it is possible to lower them, and if competition is keen they will be lowered — what can prevent it? Certainly not competition — and if something else prevents it — as at present, in fact, often happens — it cannot be credited to competition. A general decline of nominal wages and a simultaneous and proportional decline of prices would not indeed affect real wages; but this is not what normally occurs. Hence a fall of nominal, means a fall of real wages. (2) Even if the fall of prices prevented a fall of real wages, it could not compensate for the decrease in the indicative ratio which competition inevitably effects. The pleasure derived from consumption increases with the rate of consumption and with its duration, but as already pointed out, it is not proportional to either. For example, eight hours of consumption at a moderate self-supporting rate cannot be compensated for by one hour of consumption at a rate eight times as great. No degree of cheapness of products can compensate for an almost total loss of leisure such as unrestricted competition entails. It is of slight service to men to have commodities cheap if they must spend practically all of their waking life in producing them. As Lubbock says: " If wealth is to be valued because it gives leisure, it would be a mistake to sacrifice leisure in the struggle for wealth."

To these considerations, it is probable that two objections will be made: (1) That under the capitalistic system unrestricted competition does not determine profits and wages, but that these are determined by competition and *custom*. (2) That even under unrestricted competition profits and wages are functions of the demand for, and supply of, capital and labor respectively, and do not always tend to a minimum.

We may admit both of these propositions without invalidating our contention that competition is destructive of the efficiency of consumption. Many of the customs which limit the influence of competition have arisen from the imperative need for protection against the intolerable evils of competition. This is certainly the origin of trusts, labor organizations, and protective tariffs, all of which are restrictive of competition. If through its modification by certain customs competition is rendered less intolerable, this may be deemed a tribute to those customs, but

25

certainly not to competition. In fact, were competition not tempered by custom, and custom tempered by common sense, those who so stoutly maintain its beneficence would, by the most superficial observation, see their error. It is because competition is, in our day, and particularly in our country, so much modified by agencies restrictive thereof that delusions regarding its beneficence prevail. We shall shortly (p. 401) bring to the reader's attention data from which he may judge what competition can, and actually does, accomplish when its restrictions are few and feeble, and the reader may then confirm for himself our contention respecting the effect of competition on the economy of consumption. He will then discover that, left to itself, capitalism makes the indicative ratio depend upon the endurance of the workers and nothing else. Were no modifying agencies set in operation by common sense, that race of men who possessed the greatest capacity for endurance would soon kill by starvation all others who tried to engage in labor. The Chinese, for instance, would, in fair and free competition, probably supplant all other men as laborers in a few generations, and could another sufficiently prolific race be found with greater endurance as physical engines than the Chinese, they in turn would supplant the Chinese, and the population of the earth would, after a while, consist of little more than a race of toiling vermin whose "fitness" to survive would be founded upon their capacity for enduring privation and misery. What use has Justice for such happiness-producing mechanisms as these?

As to the assertion that real wages are a function of supply and demand and will therefore, under competition, not tend to a minimum, but will rise when the demand for labor increases or the supply decreases and will fall under contrary conditions, this may be admitted without any substantial change in our contention. In new countries where the supply of labor is inadequate, or in occupations where the demand is very variable depending, as in agriculture, for example, on the season of the year, the demand for laborers may exceed the supply. Such a condition, however, is but spasmodic and the rise of wages is transient. In old countries, where competition has long prevailed, the supply of labor practically always exceeds the demand — one of the normal products of the capitalistic system is a great army of unemployed who by their competition tend to keep wages at a minimum. This has been shown very clearly by Marx, and it needs but the slightest inspection to confirm it. New countries cannot remain forever new, and if the competitive system shall continue to prevail it is only a question of time when the whole earth will have reached a condition that the longer settled parts have already reached. Let us hope that the people of those countries whose labor market is not yet hopelessly overstocked may be delivered from their delusions before it is too late. To this subject we shall return. At present we desire to emphasize the effect of competition on the seventh element of happiness — the primary adjustment.

The indicative ratio, which probably requires a value greater than one — that is, a consuming day of more than eight hours, even to make the average life self-supporting, is, by competition, forced to approach a minimum; thus precluding all chance of a self-supporting community. It is to the interest of the capitalist to make the systematic working day as long as possible, since by that means his profit is augmented. It is idle to ignore or to attempt concealment of this obvious fact. Hence so long as his interests are consulted and his influence prevails the indicative ratio will tend to a minimum instead of to the point of maximum efficiency. In other words, this uneconomic tendency is a direct result of capitalism.

Failure to adjust the indicative ratio to productive and consumptive power in the manner specified in Chapter 7 results in another source of wretched economy. I refer to the recurrent industrial crises or eras of "hard times" which are directly traceable to this failure. The introduction of labor-saving machinery by the capitalist is for the purpose of enhancing his profits by saving him the wages of laborers. The laborers thrown out of employment by machinery increase the supply of labor, and by making competition keener, tend to lower the wages and increase the working hours of laborers in general. Hence, while the introduction of machinery increases the productive power, it does not increase the consumptive power, and what is of vital importance it tends rather to diminish than to increase the indicative ratio. What is the consequence? While the production of commodities is greatly stimulated their consumption is not stimulated in the same degree, if at all. Hence commodities are not consumed as fast as they are produced and they begin to accumulate in the warehouses. After a while the supply exceeds the demand and prices begin to fall. Even this does not stimulate consumption much because the rich are already largely supplied; the employed poor have such low wages and so little time to consume that their consumption is of necessity largely negative, and their consuming power small; and the unemployed poor are reduced to a minimum of consumption. Even with falling prices and no profits, however, the capitalist cannot afford to stop production since, where costly machinery is employed, the capital invested is so great and the deterioration so rapid that to suspend operations is ruinous and capitalists prefer to run even at a loss. When the market is already overstocked such a policy but makes matters worse, and the overproduction becomes more marked. Finally suspension has to come; but while this tends to rectify matters by diminishing production, it makes them worse by diminishing consumption, for all the laborers thrown out of employment are reduced to the minimum of consumption. This still further demoralizes the market, and other plants suspend, and consumption is still further reduced. Pauperism and crime increase, more and more firms fail, each failing firm weakening its creditors, who fail in their turn — all but the strongest go down like a row of dominoes and their employees cease to be factors in consumption. The whole machinery of industry is thrown out of gear and we have the disconcerting spectacle of a great surplus of commodities whose owners are only too desirous to sell, an army of laborers desperately in need thereof and anxious to buy, but unable to get work and hence unable to buy. So defective is the capitalistic mechanism that in this condition of affairs there is nothing to do but wait until those still able to consume have depleted the accumulated stocks and increased the demand for commodities. To supply this demand plants begin again to operate, the laborers therein again to consume above the minimum, the market gradually strengthens and finally industry is at its height again. But the growing demand at the beginning of a period of prosperity over-stimulates the means of supply — machinery is still further improved — production overtakes consumption again, and again comes a crisis due to overproduction, or what is a more appropriate term, to *underconsumption;* since it is because production is stimulated while consumption is not, or not stimulated in proportion, that these periodic depressions of business occur. In fact, while the capitalistic system promotes efficiency of production in some degree, it destroys efficiency of consumption by emphasizing the unequal distribution of wealth, which is a symptom of all competition, and by failing to increase the indicative ratio, thus inducing periodic panics. That these panics are due to the capitalistic system is shown by the fact that they were unknown before the growth of that system began.

During the last century they have recurred, on the average, once every ten or eleven years.

To avert crises of this character it is necessary to stimulate consumption in the same degree as production, but capitalism has no tendency to do this. Every far-sighted capitalist would be glad to have his fellow capitalists increase the wages and diminish the hours of labor of their employees, for thereby his market would be improved, but he does not want to initiate such a policy among his own employees, since he would lose more than he would gain. Hence, instead of thus stimulating the market at home, capitalists seek to extend their markets into other lands, for only by so doing can they find an outlet for the commodities which they produce in excess of the home demand. Thus arises the race for foreign markets in the effort to capture which industrial nations compete with one another, and that nation which oppresses its producing classes the most will — other things being equal — win the prize.

Eighth: The tendency of organic beings to increase in geometric ratio, upon which Darwin founded his theory of natural selection through the struggle for existence, finds no exception in man. Under ordinary conditions of competition the propagation of human beings is determined by the same impulses and proceeds according to the same law as that of cats, or rabbits, or grasshoppers. The population of any given area tends to increase until it has reached equilibrium with the capacity of that area to support further increase of population. This law is as true for men as for animals and vegetables. Throughout the organic world, where no artificial restraint is met, the check to propagation is starvation. Owing to the laws of diminishing and dwindling returns of labor the pressure of population upon its means of subsistence begins to produce painful results long before equilibrium is actually reached. Poverty steadily increases until it is checked by death — that is, by the death rate becoming equal to the birth rate. All uncivilized countries which have been long enough settled are at or near such a point of equilibrium. This tendency of populations to increase faster than their means of subsistence is called the *Law of Malthus* and was expressed by its alleged originator as follows:

"Throughout the animal and vegetable kingdoms Nature has scattered the seeds of life abroad with the most profuse and liberal hand; but has been comparatively sparing in the room and the nourishment necessary to rear them. The germs of existence contained in this earth, if they could freely develop themselves, would fill millions of worlds in the course of a few thousand years. Necessity, that imperious, all-pervading law of nature, restrains them within the prescribed bounds. The race of plants and the race of animals shrink under this great restrictive law; and man cannot by any efforts of reason escape from it.

" In plants and irrational animals, the view of the subject is simple. They are all impelled by a powerful instinct to the increase of their species, and this instinct is interrupted by no doubts about providing for their offspring. Wherever, therefore, there is liberty, the power of increase is exerted, and the superabundant effects are repressed afterwards by want of room and nourishment.

" The effects of this check on man are more complicated. Impelled to the increase of his species by an equally powerful instinct, reason interrupts his career, and asks him whether he may not bring beings into the world for whom he cannot provide the means of support. If he attend to this natural suggestion, the restriction too frequently produces vice. If he hear it not, the human race will be constantly endeavoring to increase beyond the means of subsistence. But as, by that law of our nature which makes food necessary to the life of man, population can never actually increase beyond the lowest nourishment capable of supporting it, a strong check on population, from the difficulty of acquiring food, must be constantly in operation. This difficulty must fall somewhere, and must necessarily be severely felt in some or other of the various forms of misery, or the fear of misery, by a large portion of mankind.

" That population has this constant tendency to increase beyond the means of subsistence, and that it is kept to its necessary level by these causes will sufficiently appear from a review of the different states of society in which man has existed." [1]

The resemblance of this quotation to that from Darwin, already cited, is at once noticeable, and illustrates the close relation between competition and Malthusianism.

The Law of Malthus, if left uninterpreted, is easily misunderstood and its validity has often been attacked, notably by Henry George in his work on " Progress and Poverty." In fact, if we understand this law to assert that at every moment throughout the history of every country the population is, and has been, increasing faster than the means of subsistence, then the law is certainly false, but it should not be understood as so asserting. It merely means that, in the future as in the past, the population will finally overtake the means of subsistence, provided the causes which have operated in the past continue to operate in

[1] Malthus: The Principle of Population.

the future — provided the conduct of society is left to nature. Such a statement is incontrovertible, since there is obviously some density of population too large for the earth to support, and if the population of the earth is continuously increasing, it must be continually approaching that density. There have been many periods in the history of many countries when the means of subsistence increased faster than the population which was dependent upon them, and the present period in all civilized countries is the most notable of them. This is due to the operation of the law of increasing returns which may, and at present does, more than offset the law of diminishing returns. Owing to the application of science or common sense to the business of production, the law of increasing returns never operated with such power as to-day, and were wealth fairly equally distributed, poverty would now be diminishing throughout the civilized world. Indeed, it *is* diminishing in some lands, notably in Australia, and New Zealand, and even in the United States its increase, except locally, is a matter of debate.

As the pressure of a population upon its means of subsistence becomes greater, effort is made to find a means of relief, and this is found in migration. Migration always takes place from points where the pressure of population is greater to points where it is less, just as water in two vessels communicating with one another always flows from the higher level to the lower. Such was the cause of the great influxes which successively flooded Europe from the East in the early part of the Christian Era, and such is the cause of the migration from Europe and Asia to America in our day. Precisely the same phenomenon is to be observed among animals — they continually extend their range in search of the means of subsistence until checked by some natural agency. Migration, while it tends to relieve temporarily the pressure of population in the country from which it takes place, increases that pressure in the country to which it proceeds, just as water moving from a higher vessel to a lower one, while it lowers the level in the first, raises it in the second vessel. Left to itself, the process of migration will continue, until in all accessible countries the pressure of population upon resources has been brought to the same point, and then by the increase of population, all will increase their pressure together. That is, migration at best can result only in temporary relief, and in the end it merely hastens the day of final equilibrium. Population will finally come to the same pressure in all lands having intercommunication, just as water will finally come to the same level in all vessels having inter-communication. The rate of migration will depend upon facility of communication and transportation, just as the rate at which water flows from one vessel to another will depend upon the friction in the passage by which they communicate. Where the facilities of inter-communication between countries are primitive and poor, migration will be slow; where they are perfected, it will be rapid. Two or three centuries ago migration across the Atlantic was a slow operation, because the means of communication were poor. With the means furnished to-day a whole nation can migrate in a single year.

The tendency under competition then is for population to increase in quantity and extend in range. Whether this tendency is a good or a bad one will depend upon whether the output of happiness of the average individual is positive or negative, and if positive, whether the consumption of said individual is above or below the point of maximum efficiency. In the chapter on the third factor of happiness, we have shown under what conditions increase of population is good, and under what conditions it is bad. Nothing can be more fatal and fatuous than the prevailing idea that a large population is a good thing for a nation. Until the conditions of life are at least such that the average man can produce a positive surplus of happiness an increase of population is not so good as a decrease. It appears to be the prevailing opinion that one hundred miserable persons are better than ten happy ones, and that the ideal of a modern state should be to become overpopulated like India and China. Hence that state whose rapidity of approach to such an overpopulated condition is the highest — other things being equal — is considered the most successful. Wherever any considerable degree of poverty prevails increase of population is a national disease, for poverty is an unfailing sign that the conditions insuring an average positive output of happiness have not been met; much less the conditions insuring maximum efficiency of consumption.

It is clear that if everything is left to nature the time must eventually come, if it has not come already, when the world will be overpopulated, and when each human being born will but add to the surplus of misery. Now if we are to judge a system by its effects upon happiness it is a matter of indifference when its effects are produced. Happiness or misery are no better and no worse in the year 10,000 B. C. than in the year 10,000 A. D. If they are, then there is no reason why they are not better or worse on Wednesdays than on Thursdays. Whatever checks may be locally or temporarily applied, there is but one way of preventing final overpopulation, and that is by stopping the growth of population before it reaches, or even remotely approaches, the point where nature will stop it by starvation. It is universally admitted that competition will not do this, and has not the slightest tendency to do it — hence on this ground alone, beneficence must be denied it. The output of misery of a world brought to equilibrium by nature's expedient — starvation — would be beyond computation. Perhaps, however, it may be objected that the discussion of this question is too remote for any human interest, since the earth is yet very far from overpopulated, and our concern is with the present. Such an objection, I apprehend, will occur to many readers. But it should not be forgotten that our primary purpose in this examination is to discover whether or not competition is a beneficent process. If it is, it will meet the test we have applied — otherwise not.

Perhaps, however, to the objection mentioned, a more cogent reply may be made, viz., that if overpopulation means a population whose output of happiness under the conditions actually existing is negative, then the world is now, and always has been, overpopulated — the popular opinion to the contrary notwithstanding. In a world where there is more unhappiness than happiness a population of *one* is too great. Can it be then that the average man in the world to-day produces a negative output — a surplus of unhappiness? If so, the output of the world must be negative. Perhaps the reader may admit this is no more than an axiom. Perhaps, on the contrary, he may regard it as utterly absurd. It depends very much upon his knowledge of the world. All men are prone to judge of the world by the portion of it which surrounds them. If they and their friends are happy, they deem the world happy — if they and their friends are unhappy, they deem the world unhappy, for verily one-half the world knows not how the other half lives. No statistics exist which can substantiate our assertion, and if the declamations of exuberant politicians can refute anything we are refuted. But a moderately accurate test is available — let us apply it — it will be better than none.

The United States of America is generally conceded to be the most successful country in the world — at least, that is the prevailing opinion here, and even Europe is inclined to share it. In our day success is judged by trade, and in trade we are preeminent. In the United States of America the most successful locality would generally be conceded to be the city of New York.

Great cities are peculiarly the product of modern civilization, and if we would judge that civilization we must judge it by its products. New York is the richest, the most prosperous, and possesses the greatest trade of any city in America. If the capitalistic system has produced a success anywhere, it should be here. Hence, if we select New York as a test of what that system can do as a mechanism for producing happiness we cannot be accused of choosing an unfavorable example of its handiwork; for it is the most successful city of the most successful country in the world.

Now according to the utilitarian standard no individual or aggregate of individuals can be considered a success whose contribution to the total happiness of society is negative. A city to be a success must produce, in any given time, hedon-hours in excess of pathon-hours. Its output per day or per year must be positive. Is this true of New York City? To this question the reader will answer either *yes* or *no*. If his answer is *no*, he thereby concedes that the capitalistic system is a failure — that the best it can produce is worse than nothing. If he answers *yes*, I invite him to apply two tests, which, if he is familiar with the metropolis, or with any great city, he can do with no more trouble to himself than five minutes candid reflection. First, I invite him in imagination to walk the streets and visit the habitations of the great metropolis by day and by night, and carefully to note the evidences of pleasure and pain with an impartial eye. Let him visit the houses of the rich, the well-to-do, and the middle classes, and observe their habits and their means of happiness. Are they ever unhappy — if so, how many hours a day and what is the intensity of their unhappiness — he may be sure that during their hours of production they are, on the average, not happy, though the intensity of pain during those hours may be but slight — and certainly half of their waking life is spent in production. Are they ever happy — if so, it is generally during hours of consumption, while eating, attending entertainments, driving, reading, playing some game, or sitting quietly at home with family or friends. How many hours a day are they doing these things, and what is the average intensity during these hours? Is it one, three, six, ten hedons — it must be of *some* average intensity — we cannot determine what, but let the reader estimate from his own experience. Let him repeat these observations among the much greater multitude who live by the labor of their hands, ranging from the moderately poor to the destitute — what is their average duration of consumption, and what the intensity thereof? Let him go through the magnificent palace of the millionaire, but let him also visit the squalid tenement of the victim of poverty, outnumbering the first, five hundred to one. Let him not ignore the happiness to be found in the homes of the well-to-do, the healthy, the morally wholesome — but neither let him ignore the unhappiness to be found in the tenement houses, the hospitals, the alms-houses, the gutters, the jails, and the dives. Taking a bird's eye view of these things, let him candidly ask himself this question: Would you, or would you not, be willing to experience all the pain felt in New York in a year, for all the pleasure felt there in the same time? This is but inquiring whether the totality of life in New York is self-supporting. An affirmative answer means that the total product of the city is, at least, better than nothing. A negative answer means that it is worse than nothing. How many men who knew that they would be taken literally at their word, would dare to answer in the affirmative?

A second test is suggestible which may perhaps be more readily put into practice than this one. If, as we have contended, the test of equivalence of pleasure and pain is preference, as determined by memory rather than anticipation, then the test of whether a given period has resulted in a surplus of pain or pleasure to an individual is best ascertained by determining whether that individual would prefer living over again that period, or one containing exactly the same quantities of pleasure and pain, to not living it over again. Let this test be applied to the average citizen of New York for an average day or an average year — not to an exceptional citizen for an exceptional day or an exceptional year. The average man in New York is a laborer; he can avail himself of no more, and generally of less, labor than that which he himself supplies. The average woman in New York is a laborer also, though not necessarily a wage laborer. Let inquiry be made of the average adult dweller in New York at the close of an average day whether he or she is glad or sorry that the day is done — whether he or she would prefer living it over again to not living it over again, just as it was. Can there be any doubt of the result of such an inquiry? If so, I have yet met nobody who cherished one. If it be objected that the fatigue felt at the close of a day of labor precludes a fair judgment at that time (a fair objection) the inquiry may be varied, applying to a week, a month, a year or a life-time. The period matters little. Few, even among the **well-to-do**, have a balance of happiness in their favor, and the life of the average man or woman undoubtedly produces a surplus of unhappiness. The average child in New York is not a laborer and not exposed directly to the attrition of competition, and it is among the children, if anywhere, that a surplus of pleasure will be found; yet, when the conditions of the average child's life in New York are considered, it will be acknowledged that modern industrial conditions tend to diminish the output even of these, the most immediately useful members of the human race; and it is very doubtful, considering the prevalence of illness, whether the average child's life in New York is self-supporting. If it be objected that the average individual must deem life worth living or he would not consent to live, we may reply that incurable invalids, life convicts, and many who cannot possibly produce a positive surplus, consent to live and are reluctant to die. It is not because they have any reasonable expectation that the future will be an improvement upon the past that men consent to live — it is from the fear of death — an ineradicable instinct, common alike to men and animals. Men do not live from reason but from impulse. They live in perpetual hope that the next day will be better than the last, and they are perpetually disappointed. It is not only in great cities that the average individual produces a negative surplus. It is a universal condition and it has always been so. The relation between man and his environment has never been such as to produce a positive surplus over any considerable period of time, and keen observers of human life have not failed to record the fact. Men live on hope. They "eat the air promise crammed." Says Montgomery:

"Who that hath ever been
Could bear to be no more?
Yet who would tread again the scene
He trod through life before?"

Dryden has expressed the same idea more perfectly in his Aurengzebe:

"When I consider life, 'tis all a cheat.
Yet fool'd with hope, men favour the deceit;
Trust on, and think to-morrow will repay.
To-morrow's falser than the former day;
Lies worse, and while it says we shall be blest
With some new joys, cuts off what we possest.
Strange cozenage! none would live past years again,
Yet all hope pleasure in what yet remain;

And from the dregs of life think to receive
What the first sprightly running could not give."

Pope condenses the same sentiment into his famous couplet:

" Hope springs eternal in the human breast;
Man never is, but always *to be* blest."

Shakespeare in Hamlet's well known soliloquy says that only " the dread of something after death " induces men " to grunt and sweat under a weary life " and Byron in defending his own estimate of the " nothingness of life " shows that he is but expressing an opinion common to the thinking portion of mankind:

" I say no more than has been said in Dante's
Verse, and by Solomon and Cervantes;"

" By Swift, by Machiavel, by Rochefoucault,
By Fenelon, by Luther, and by Plato;
By Tillotson, and Wesley, and Rousseau,
Who knew this life was not worth a potato."

But if all this be true, if the human race inevitably achieves more unhappiness than happiness as a result of its existence, what shall we say of the system which produces this result? Perhaps we cannot condemn it for no better may be attainable; but this much, at least, may be said, that under such a system the less the number of human beings who exist the better; for the less the number the less will be the surplus of unhappiness, and none at all will be the ideal number. In other words, the annihilation of the human race is a better policy — a more just policy, than any form of competition thus far known. Annihilation would, to be sure, extinguish human happiness, but it would at the same time extinguish human unhappiness, and it is as true of an aggregate of individuals as it is of a single one, that nonexistence is better than a surplus of pain, however slight. This conclusion follows from the very meaning of the word *better,* and if the reader thinks that he has in mind a meaning of that word which does not involve such a conclusion, I recommend that he attempt to express it to himself.

From these considerations then, we may infer that the city of New York, the crowning achievement of the modern competitive system in the western world, yields a less output of happiness per acre per day or year than when Hendrick Hudson discovered its site — that it was more useful as an undiscovered wilderness than it is to-day, and contributed more to that output which it is the only useful object of society to produce — happiness. What then shall we think of all the lucubration about prosperity and national greatness so frequently heard? What relation, if any, have these things to utility? It would seem to be the height of presumption for any nation, or any representative of a nation, to boast of its success when universal annihilation would result in still greater success — at least a greater success in the production of anything which it is worth while to produce.

If we go outside the great cities of America into the rural districts and apply either of the tests we have suggested, there can be little doubt that the same condition will be discovered — a surplus of unhappiness is produced — few will be found who would wish to live their lives over again year by year; but it is significant that the output of unhappiness is less. Not only less per square mile, but less per average individual than in the city. The least unhappy portions of a great industrial country are the quiet farming districts, and these are precisely the parts of the country in which the capitalistic system of competition has reached the least development. Few will be inclined to deny this proposition, and yet what a commentary it furnishes upon the achievements of modern civilization. It is true that the city more and more attracts the dweller in the country, but this is because he counts the chances of success and discounts the chances of failure. He notices the luxury — he ignores the squalor. He enters city life as he would a gigantic lottery, seeing only the prizes; but, as in any lottery, the prizes are for the few — the blanks for the many — and this is particularly true of the great lottery of competition. The few who succeed are conspicuous; the many who fail are not; and thus the real condition of things is concealed. In the country, competition is less severe, wealth more evenly distributed, health more general, and were the indicative ratio and with it the education of the people increased, the country districts of America would doubtless begin to produce a positive output even with no other change.

The normal operation of competition to continually increase population then is simply a means of increasing unhappiness, and the migrations which result from this increase are a means of equalizing unhappiness — of insuring that wherever free communication between one nation and another exists that the level of happiness shall everywhere seek the lowest point — for under such conditions if one nation maintains a low level of happiness it is only a question of time when all others will sink to the same level. The pressure of population upon subsistence will tend always to increase and to equalize, just as among animals.

If, as we have sought to show by the best tests available, the United States is not a self-supporting community, how much greater must be the negative margin of self-support in those countries from which the pressure of population continually forces a stream of migration to our shores. In Europe, with the possible exception of France and Switzerland, despite the simpler tastes of the people, the output of misery per capita is doubtless higher than in the United States. All the baleful effects of competition contribute to this result, but the most potent is that caused by overpopulation which is greater in Europe than in America simply because the unrestricted natural laws of increase have operated for a longer period there than here. In yet more ancient communities where competition has been unrestricted for longer periods the conditions are worse than in Europe. In India and China the output of misery is appalling. So closely have these, the most ancient nations in the world, approached the limit of their means of subsistence, that even a partial crop failure means a famine in which hundreds of thousands, and often millions, die of starvation. The population of all these old countries is almost at the point of equilibrium, but it is not a beneficent equilibrium — it is the equilibrium of nature where starvation places a limit which propagation forever strives to exceed. It is the ideal furnished by these densely populated countries that the publicists of our time would have us approach, and approach as quickly as possible. The population cannot grow fast enough to suit them, and they seek to stimulate it in every way. Without seeking to inquire whether the average individual produces a positive or negative surplus, they would hurry the nation toward the point of natural equilibrium and maximum output of misery as rapidly as possible, on the principle that a great number of miserable beings are better than a less number of happy ones. It is perhaps useless to seek to eradicate this notion of the economists of the age, but we may at least refute the argument by which they seek to justify their opinions. This is, in effect, that, owing to the advance in the arts and the improvements in the efficiency of production, the civilized countries of the western world can support a much denser population in comfort than the backward countries of the East can support in discomfort, and hence there is no fear of overpopulation at this stage of our progress. Now it may be acknowledged that with the means of production at hand America, for example, *can* support a large population in comfort, but this does not involve the acknowledgment that it *does* so. It may be acknowledged that owing to the causes mentioned, the condition of the average man in western countries is better than it ever was before; nevertheless this is far from acknowledging that any community yet produces a positive surplus of happiness. This cannot be until the average man is willing and anxious to live his average day, or month, or year, over again — and even could it be shown that a given community was self-supporting, this would not mean that an increase in its numbers would be desirable. Only communities whose consumption per capita is greater than that required for maximum efficiency of consumption can economically increase in numbers, and will anyone contend that any community has yet attained such a stage?

But perhaps in the last paragraph we have made an admission which is significant. If it must be acknowledged that in this, the era of the capitalistic system of competition, the condition of the average individual is better than ever before, surely the capitalistic system cannot be wholly bad. It must have its advantages if it is responsible for such a state of things. The fact is, the capitalistic system is not wholly bad. It has one great advantage, and it is due to this, and to a variety of restrictions upon competition, that the present improvement in man's estate has been brought about — an improvement slight indeed compared with what is accomplishable by a different adaptation of the same means. Intelligent men believe competition beneficent because they are ignorant of its effects when really unrestricted. If they are interested to learn what these effects *would be,* they need but to ascertain what they *have been.* Let them read the story of English industrial life during the first two-thirds of the 19th century, as told by Marx in his work on " Capital," or that by Dr. Kay on the " Moral and Physical Condition of the Laboring Classes in England," or let him read any of the reports so liberally used by these authors. The story is too long to quote in detail here; it must be read in detail to be appreciated, but as a brief and inadequate condensation of its tragic details the following account by E. J. James is worth inspection:

"The doctrine so long current in political economy and expressed in the motto *laissez faire passer,* has been thoroughly exploded by the logic of circumstances. No better proof of this could be desired than the factory laws of modern industrial nations, laws which have been of late warmly defended by economists of every school. The reaction begun by Adam Smith against the paternal theory and practice of contemporary governments resulted in an illogical and untenable theory of the state and its functions. 'Free Competition' was the panacea for all economical ills of society. Everyone was to be free to sell his own labor and that of his family where he could obtain the most for it, and free to make such contracts as he would or could. As England was the first great industrial state of modern times, so in England the results of such a policy first showed themselves in all their nakedness. The most merciless exploitation of the weaker elements of society by the stronger became the rule. The manufacturers, in their thirst for wealth, paid as little attention to the health of their operatives as they chose. The laborers in their necessity were compelled to accept what terms were offered. The labor of the father soon became insufficient to support the family. The mother had to go into the coal mine or factory. It was not enough; the children were sent into the mines and factories. They were compelled to work ten or fifteen hours a day for seven days in the week, in narrow, illy ventilated and dirty factory rooms or in still more unhealthy mines. The result of such work was, of course, the moral and physical deterioration of the children and a steady degeneration of the laborers from decade to decade. The conditions prevailing in Great Britain during the latter part of the last century (the 18th) and the early part of the present century would be entirely incredible were they not well attested by the testimony of unimpeachable witnesses. So crying did the evil become that in 1802, an act was passed 'for the preservation of the health and morals of apprentices and others employed in cotton and other mills and cotton and other factories.' This bill owed its passage to the ravages of epidemic diseases in the factory districts of Manchester. The illy fed and overworked children in the factories formed the very best field for the development and spread of epidemic and contagious diseases. Pauper children were sent in crowds from the agricultural districts of the Southern counties to the manufacturing regions of the northern counties. They were apprenticed to the mill owners and mercilessly overworked and underfed."[1]

The narration of which this extract is the commencement shows what unrestricted competition does for the producers of

[1] Cyclopædia of Political Science, edited by John J. Lalor, Vol. II, p. 151.

a nation. It illustrates what competition would do were the restrictions imposed by labor organizations and the government removed. If let alone the conditions described would extend to practically all industries, and finally affect the whole laboring population. They represent what the dogmatic economist calls the most "economic" conditions of production, conditions which, if attained, will assure the most complete success in the race for commercial supremacy. Indeed, the business men of that day contended that to interfere with these conditions meant ruin to England's industries. When things became so bad that the English government prepared to "meddle" by passing the Factory Acts there was great alarm and indignation among the conservative and respectable factory operators whose "rights" were threatened. They protested with all the vehemence of disinterested patriotism against any interference with the beneficent natural laws which were doing so much for England's commercial prosperity. The Factory Acts, nevertheless, were passed, interfering with "prosperity" in the interests of happiness. As they merely dabble with the matter, however, they have not done much toward abolishing the vast annual deficit of happiness produced by the British people; though they certainly have diminished it.

Advancement in the arts then does not insure happiness, though doubtless it can be made the means of supporting in comfort a greater population than in its absence can be supported in discomfort, but not while competition is in control. In fact, it may be shown that even the single and much proclaimed advantage of the capitalistic system — its stimulus to the use of machinery in the arts — is in reality a disadvantage. Suppose, for example, that modern methods of production were introduced into India and the competitive system were permitted to remain in control. What would happen? A temporary slight rise in the rate of consumption per capita would be the first effect, but the increase in the means of subsistence would promptly result in a decrease of the death rate, and an increase in the population — the faster the means of subsistence increased the faster would the population increase to meet it, until the limit of the agricultural resources of the country, on which depends the limit of the population, would, even with improved methods, be again practically attained. Perhaps in India where the population is already dense, it might by this means be stimulated to increase several fold, and what would be the result — the same final rate of consumption per capita, the same final output of misery per capita would be attained, and the total output of misery would be increased several-fold. Such would be the result of improving methods of production by the application of science and leaving consumption to the beneficence of nature. Indeed, science thus *half* applied is a curse instead of a blessing. That which advancement in the arts would do for India it will do for the United States under competitive conditions; for the population of the country will either increase as fast as in the past, or it will not. If it does its failure to increase as fast as in the past can only mean that the sole competitive check which exists — the Law of Malthus — has begun to operate and will continue to do so until natural equilibrium, like that in India, is attained. If, on the contrary, it does not, it will show that the Law of Malthus is not operative. In the past, the population has several times doubled in less than thirty years, say three times in a century. Assuming the present population to be 80,000,000 and this rate of increase to be maintained, the population in one century will be 640,000,000, in two centuries will be over 5,000,000,000, and in three centuries will be over 40,000,000,000. Does any one suppose the country can support the last two numbers in comfort, or even in a condition of self-support? Do they suppose it can support even 640,000,000 at, or anywhere near, the point of maximum efficiency? Certainly not with competition, and it is doubtful if, with the most perfect system devisable, it could be done, even with half such a population. As Sir William Crookes has shown, the wheat acreage is already approaching its limits, and though these can be extended and the yield per acre increased by the application of science, the yield cannot be indefinitely augmented. The same thing is true of other agricultural resources. The law of diminishing returns cannot forever be more than neutralized by the law of increasing returns; and what is true of agriculture is true of mineral resources, particularly of the coal supply.

Of course, no such rate of increase of population as that we have assumed will or can be maintained; for the very reason that it will be checked by the Law of Malthus. A glance at Fig. 15, showing the rate of increase of population in various countries during the 19th century, according to the report of the 12th Census of the United States, exhibits the effect of this law. Thus the sparsely settled countries (the United States and Russia) have increased most rapidly; the acceleration in the case of the former country being due in part to

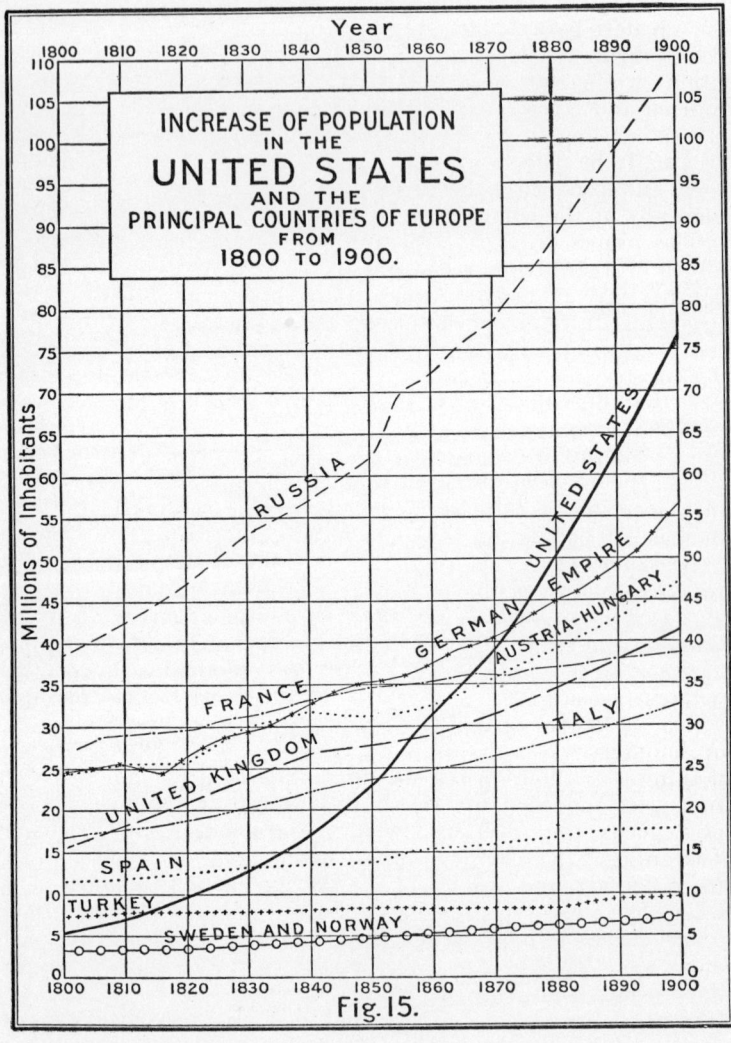

Fig. 15.

immigration. Among densely populated countries it is those in which the operation of the law of increasing returns has been most stimulated by improvement in the arts that have made the greatest gains (The United Kingdom, Germany, and Austria-Hungary). Italy and France occupy an intermediate position, while the most backward industrial countries (Spain, Sweden and Norway, and Turkey) have increased least in population. Owing to our proficiency in the arts, however, we shall eventually be able to support a much greater density of population, and produce a far greater output of wealth and misery than any of the countries of Europe and Asia do now.

The proper way of adjusting population to a diminishing return of wealth is by a decrease in the birth rate, but this is not nature's way in man any more than in animals. Only a relatively high rate of consumption per capita can set in operation the prudential motives which keep human beings from breeding too fast, and this cannot be attained by any system, which, like that of competition, destroys the efficiency of consumption, however much it may increase the efficiency of production. Thus it becomes clear that the improvement in the arts which the modern form of competition promotes is a temporary good, but a permanent evil, or certain to become so if the increase of population is left to nature.

And now to return to the effect of all this on the natural resources of the earth (p. 378). The greatly increased facility of developing nature's resources through improvement in the arts and the great increase in the number of human beings engaged in their development, simply accelerates their depletion without accomplishing anything useful by it. The resources which, if properly applied, would result in a vast production of happiness are, by the competitive system, dissipated with nothing — with less than nothing — to show for their dissipation. In the modern world the prevailing production-madness goads the capitalist, who has everything to gain from "skinning" the country, into opening up and "developing" its resources, and what is the final result — abandoned farms where once were virgin soils — treeless wastes where once stood great forests — huge water-filled caverns in the earth where once was valuable ore. The resources are certainly "developed," but what has the nation to show for it — a vast and increasing surplus of misery, and this we are told is *success*. Such a policy as this may please a few capitalists in one generation, but what of posterity? If, under the present system, men cannot produce a surplus of happiness while living on the cream of the earth's resources, what will they do under the same system when, with numbers indefinitely increased, they must live on the skimmed milk? So abysmal is the ignorance on this matter that the very men who are hailed as public benefactors because of their haste to develop the resources of the nation, are in reality the worst enemies of the state.

If the rapid development of the nation's resources is indeed a desideratum, then let us by all means hasten it. Let us in America, for example, bring in hordes of laborers from China, supply them with the most improved machinery, make them work sixteen hours a day at the minimum wage, and work day and night shifts to "develop" our resources. Let them exhaust the soils, deplete the mines, level the forests, and exterminate the beasts of the field and the birds of the air, and let them keep at it until they have accomplished their work. By this means the land may be made a desert several centuries sooner than it could by the methods now in use — and thus our success will be the wonder and the admiration of the age. If we adopt this policy no nation can hope to compete with us for the commercial supremacy of the earth. England and Germany, unless they imitate our methods, will not be factors in the race for a moment. If an enormous rate of production of wealth is the object of national existence, this is the way to obtain it, and the sooner we get at it the better. If the practomaniacs of the age dare to be consistent with themselves, let them advocate this policy. If, on the other hand, our object is an enormous rate of production of happiness, we should pursue the opposite policy. The resources of the country should be conserved and husbanded with the greatest care; their development should be delayed as long as possible; the activities of men should be turned to developing individuals who are fitted to convert the potentiality of happiness involved in national resources into actual happiness; the efficiency of consumption should be stimulated and then, when the husbanded resources are at last developed, the nation will have something to show for their dissipation. On page 318 we have already discussed this matter and further repetition is not required here. All we need point out is that the capitalistic system, in developing a country, wastes its resources instead of using them.

In Chapter 8 we have set forth the effects on the several elements of happiness required of a just social system. We are now in a position to compare these effects with those which modern competition tends to produce. Thus:

(1) A just system aims to improve the quality of human beings.

Competition tends to deteriorate it.

(2) A just system seeks a high degree of adjustability and health.

Competition secures a low degree.

(3) A just system conserves natural resources until a high efficiency of consumption is developed.

Competition dissipates natural resources, at the same time maintaining a low efficiency of consumption.

(4) A just system substitutes machinery for men in production, simultaneously increasing the indicative ratio.

Competition displaces men with machinery, without simultaneously increasing the indicative ratio.

(5) A just system stimulates a high degree of skill and interest in labor.

Competition stimulates a low degree of skill and interest in all save directive labor.

(6) A just system seeks equality in distribution of wealth and leisure.

Competition secures inequality in both.

(7) A just system seeks to so adjust the indicative ratio as to secure maximum efficiency per capita, by making it a direct function of productive power, productive intensity, and consumptive power.

Competition tends only to make it an inverse function of endurance and diminish it indefinitely.

(8) A just system seeks to adjust a population to its means of happiness so as to maintain it at the point of beneficent equilibrium.

Competition adjusts population only to its means of subsistence, leading to natural equilibrium.

Competition then has not a single good point. On every vital issue it is opposed to a just system. It deteriorates the quality of the population, it destroys the efficiency of consumption, and even such good effect as it has on the efficiency of production is thereby turned into an evil which is only made more terrible by its effect in indefinitely increasing the population. In other words, the system of competition is to-day but a more efficient form of what it always has been — a mechanism for maintaining and continually increasing an output of unhappiness.

Perfected by science, this mechanism if its use be persisted in, will cause the earth eventually to become a very hell in which the sensitive organization of human beings is utilized in the highly successful manufacture of misery. There is no more dismal delusion than that of the beneficence of competition. It is a political myth as gross as, and vastly more harmful than, the myths of ancient and modern mythology, and by coming generations it will be placed in the same category. It remains to be seen whether common sense can, with sufficient promptness and completeness, triumph over custom to destroy this delusion and the system founded upon it, and substitute therefor an applied science whose object is the manufacture of happiness. The signs of the times give reason to believe that such a triumph is coming soon, and in the following chapter we shall attempt to point out the course of events by which this "consummation devoutly to be wished" is to be attained.

CHAPTER XII

PRIVATE AND PUBLIC MONOPOLY

Human society, like much else in nature, is a product of evolution, and evolution consists either in progress or in retrogression. In the history of the forms of animal and vegetable life both processes have occurred, and both have occurred in the history of human society. In the eleventh chapter has been discussed the effect upon human happiness of the modes of activity of that phase in the evolution of society denominated the capitalistic system. This form of social mechanism was developed out of the feudal system of mediæval Europe through several intermediate stages and at the present time is in process of undergoing transformation into another form. What that form is to be was foreshadowed by Marx in his discussion of the "Historical Tendency of Capitalist Accumulation," as follows:

"What does the primitive accumulation of capital, i. e., its historical genesis, resolve itself into? In so far as it is not immediate transformation of slaves and serfs into wage-laborers, and therefore a mere change of form, it only means the expropriation of the immediate producers, i. e., the dissolution of private property based on the labour of its owner. Private property, as the antithesis to social, collective property, exists only where the means of labour and the external conditions of labour belong to private individuals. But according as these private individuals are labourers or not labourers, private property has a different character. The numberless shades that it at first sight presents, correspond to the intermediate stages lying between these two extremes. The private property of the labourer in his means of production is the foundation of petty industry, whether agricultural, manufacturing, or both; petty industry, again, is an essential condition for the development of social production, and of the free individuality of the labourer himself. Of course, this petty mode of production exists also under slavery, serfdom, and other states of dependence. But it flourishes, it lets loose its whole energy, it attains its adequate classical form, only where the labourer is the private owner of his own means of labour set in action by himself; the peasant of the land which he cultivates, the artizan of the tool which he handles as a virtuoso. This mode of production pre-supposes parcelling of the soil, and scattering of the other means of production. As it excludes the concentration of these means of production, so also it excludes co-operation, division of labour within each separate process of production, the control over, and the productive application of the forces of Nature by society, and the free development of the social productive powers. It is compatible only with a system of production, and a society, moving within narrow and more or less primitive bounds. To perpetuate it would be, as Pecqueur rightly says, 'to decree universal mediocrity.' At a certain stage of development it brings forth the material agencies for its own dissolution. From that moment new forces and new passions spring up in the bosom of society; but the old social organization fetters them and keeps them down. It must be annihilated; it is annihilated. Its annihilation, the transformation of the individualized and scattered means of production into socially concentrated ones, of the pigmy property of the many into the huge property of the few, the expropriation of the great mass of the people from the soil, from the means of subsistence, and from the means of labour, this fearful and painful expropriation of the mass of the people forms the prelude to the history of capital. It comprises a series of forcible methods, of which we have passed in review only those that have been epoch-making as methods of the primitive accumulation of capital. The expropriation of the immediate producers was accomplished with merciless vandalism, and under the stimulus of passions the most infamous, the most sordid, the pettiest, the most meanly odious. Self-earned private property, that is based, so to say, on the fusing together of the isolated, independent labouring-individual with the conditions of his labour, is supplanted by capitalistic private property, which rests on exploitation of the nominally free labour of others, i. e., on wages-labour.

"As soon as this process of transformation has sufficiently decomposed the old society from top to bottom, as soon as the labourers are turned into proletarians, their means of labour into capital, as soon as the capitalist mode of production stands on its own feet, then the further socialisation of labour, and further transformation of the land, and other means of production into socially exploited, and, therefore, common means of production, as well as the further expropriation of private proprietors, takes a new form. That which is now to be expropriated is no longer the labourer working for himself, but the capitalist exploiting many labourers. This expropriation is accomplished by the action of the immanent laws of capitalistic production itself, by the centralization of capital. One capitalist always kills many. Hand in hand with this centralization, or this expropriation of many capitalists by few, develops, on an ever extending scale, the co-operative form of the labour-process, the conscious technical application of science, the methodical cultivation of the soil, the transformation of the instruments of labour into instruments of labour only useable in common, the economizing of all means of production by their use as the means of production of combined, socialized labour, the entanglement of all peoples in the net of the world-market, and with this, the international character of the capitalistic regime. Along with the constantly diminishing number of the magnates of capital, who usurp and monopolise all advantages of this process of transformation, grows the mass of misery, oppression, slavery, degradation, exploitation; but with this too grows the revolt of the working class, a class always increasing in numbers, and disciplined, united, organized by the very mechanism of the process of capitalist production itself. The monopoly of capital becomes a fetter upon the mode of production, which has sprung up and flourished along with, and under it. Centralization of the means of production and socialization of labour at last reach a point where they become incompatible with their capitalist integument. This integument is burst assunder. The knell of capitalist private property sounds. The expropriators are expropriated.

"The capitalist mode of appropriation, the result of the capitalist mode of production, produces capitalist private property. This is the first negation of individual private property, as founded on the labour of the proprietor. But capitalist production begets, with the inexorability of a law of Nature, its own negation. It is the negation of negation. This does not re-establish private property for the producer, but gives him individual property based on the acquisitions of the capitalist era: i. e., on co-operation and the possession in common of the land and of the means of production.

"The transformation of scattered private property, arising from individual labour, into capitalist private property is, naturally, a process, incomparably more protracted, violent, and difficult, than the transformation of capitalistic private property, already practically resting on socialized production, into socialized property. In the former case, we have the expropriation of the mass of the people by a few usurpers; in the latter, we have the expropriation of a few usurpers by the mass of the people." [1]

Thus, more than fifty years ago, Marx predicted the evolution of the capitalistic system of competition into a system of private monopoly. He predicted also the leadership of the United States in this movement, and he points out its inevitable development into a system of public monopoly. It is interesting

[1] Capital; pp. 786–789.

to observe this evolution now in actual process of operation. As Marx says, the fall of capitalism is to be much more rapid than its rise. The system of private monopoly had its inception only about twenty-five years ago and yet its practical replacement in the United States by public monopoly will, in all probability, be witnessed by the rising generation.

Private monopoly follows capitalistic competition as effect follows cause. Were the industrial conditions existing two generations ago to be re-established, they would again pass through the same stages and develop the same condition of private monopoly which they did before. The inconvenience, worry, and loss occasioned the capitalist by competition prompts him to seek a way to escape it. This can only be done by combination between competitors, and when by the coalescence of many small concerns into a few large ones the number of competitors has diminished, this becomes a relatively easy task. The earliest form of combination, known as *pooling*, consists simply of verbal agreements among competitors not to compete. The output of the commodity sold by them is restricted and the price fixed. Thereby the fearful wastes of competition are avoided and a profit to the combine insured. But, of course, the seller's gain is the buyer's loss; and as the public is directly or indirectly the buyer, the profit of the pool is at the cost of the public. To protect themselves against pooling most of the states of the Union, during the '80's, passed laws making it illegal; and in 1890 Congress passed the Sherman anti-trust act to the same effect. In other words, by "meddling" legislative enactment the law-makers attempted to induce *artificial competition*. The *laissez faire* theory had already been converted into a dubious doctrine by the Factory Acts and other legislation. The Sherman law converted it into a farce. Competition, that beneficent natural law, develops by a natural process into private monopoly. Thereupon the learned law-givers, imbued with the innate beneficence of natural law, proceed to enact one, since nature fails them; the result being that curious anomaly — an artificial natural law — a law which is both natural and unnatural. Is it therefore both beneficent and not beneficent? We leave this question to political metaphysicians; but one thing is sure — it has not stopped pooling. As pooling agreements are merely verbal, it is very difficult to get evidence of them except by the confession of one of the parties. They may be dissolved to-day and renewed to-morrow. The Sherman act, therefore, has remained little more than a dead letter.

To keep pooling agreements in moments of temptation, however, requires a sense of honor, and this is something that business does not breed. The parties to the various pools formed, when they saw an opportunity of gain would frequently break their agreements and the combine would immediately crumble. Thus pools were continually dissolving, and though they continually reformed under the blistering blows of competition, they were a very unsatisfactory form of combination. The pool, therefore, soon developed into the *trust,* so-called because it consisted of a company whose function was to hold the stock of competing companies in trust. Through the trustees or officers of the trust, the various companies were each assigned their part in the total production, the output was restricted and the price fixed as under the old pool, but the trust agreements were matters of record and could be legally enforced, and thus it was believed the ills developed under pooling could be remedied. But this source of strength was also a source of weakness. The trust agreements not being secret could be adduced as evidence in the courts and hence were subject to the attack of the anti-trust laws. These were, in many cases enforced, and a number of trusts lost their charters and were forced back into the pooling stage.

The legal position of the trust becoming thus untenable through enforcement of state laws, a new device was tried. *Holding companies* were formed whose sole purpose of existence was the ownership of the stock of other companies. At first only one state, New Jersey, permitted the incorporation of such companies, but one was enough. The competitors formerly combined into trusts now combined into holding companies, secured a charter in New Jersey, and were then free to operate in any state they pleased without interference, since the attempt by any state to discriminate against a company not incorporated therein was, by the courts, interpreted as a regulation of interstate commerce and hence illegal. The trust was thus displaced by the holding company and this is the device which prevails very largely to-day, though charters for such companies are now obtainable in several states. Holding companies, or in their absence, pools, have now multiplied in number to such a degree that the sale of all the principal articles of commerce in the United States is either wholly, or in large measure, removed from the realm of competition. Capitalists, coerced by competition, have very generally ceased to compete. Laborers, in the formation and consolidation of labor organizations, have followed the same trend and competition between laborers is diminishing from year to year. Thus private monopoly, predicted by Marx as the inevitable outcome of competition, is in process of realization. The attempt of the anti-trust legislation to stop and reverse the evolution of society by inducing artificial competition is a practical failure. The much vaunted victories of the Sherman law are technical victories only. That law was not made to be impartially enforced. To do so in the case of all railroads doing interstate business would result in chaos, and except in one or two cases it has not been attempted, though the abolition of competition by combination among railroads is all but universal to-day. The enforcement of the Sherman law is, in fact, left to the discretion of the executive and is thus a practical reversion to monarchical theories of government. It is a legislative license for executive fiat.

The attempt to induce artificial competition having failed, the next step is acquiescence in, and national regulation of, private monopoly. President Roosevelt, in his message to Congress of December 5th, 1905, suggests such acquiescence, and commends such regulation in the following words:

" The fortunes amassed through corporate organization are now so large, and vest such power in those who wield them, as to make it a matter of necessity to give to the sovereign — that is, to the Government, which represents the people as a whole — some effective power of supervision over their corporate use. In order to insure a healthy social and industrial life, every big corporation should be held responsible by, and be accountable to, some sovereign strong enough to control its conduct. I am in no sense hostile to corporations. This is an age of combination, and any effort to prevent all combination will be not only useless, but in the end vicious, because of the contempt for law which the failure to enforce law inevitably produces."

The policy thus suggested may be denominated *pseudo-socialism*; and to it the nation is now proceeding — with what result it is too soon to say; but we may with very slight knowledge of human nature rest assured that difficulties will be encountered — not transient, but permanent difficulties — for this solution of the problem leaves untouched the cause of the trouble — the eternal antagonism between the self-interest of the buyer and seller — between *public* interests and *vested* interests. This is the splinter that produces the fester. A poultice may reduce the inflammation some, but to effect a cure the splinter must be removed. The only way to relieve the public from the exaction of private monopoly is to diminish the profits of the monopolists. They will not submit to this without a struggle and however sincere the attempt may be to accomplish it, organized wealth wields too many weapons to make the permanent success of such an undertaking much more probable than that of achieving artificial competition. Not only can organized wealth, through its representatives in Congress, delay the passage of any act adverse to its interests, but it can have incorporated in such acts various ingenious provisions which make their evasion easy, or other acts may be passed making them unenforcible. Even if it is successful in passing the legislative stage unmutilated, means may be found for causing the prosecuting officers to suspend their activities, and if this fails, the thousand technicalities of judicial procedure for delay and evasion are still available. By the time these difficulties have been surmounted the monopolies may have changed their form, reverted to the secret pooling stage, making the act inapplicable, or devised some new method of evasion. But even if they fail in all attempts at evasion what eternal vigilance will it require to keep them under control. Publicity of all their transactions will be an essential feature of government control. To insure accuracy in the reports of these transactions in the case of several hundred monopolies is in itself no small undertaking. The myriad modes known to bookkeeping of concealing profits under other names must all be understood and met, and this by men whose temptation to opacity of understanding may be made very great by the interested parties. But let us assume that all these and many other difficulties are surmounted, in what a dangerous position will the government find itself, surrounded by these colossi of capitalism whose interests are in eternal antagonism to that of the people. Will they forever submit tamely to regulation? Will the government control the monopolies or will the monopolies control the government? Judging by their present hold upon various departments of government the latter alternative appears at least plausible. In a land where a double standard of honor exists — a personal and a political standard — the people cannot hope for much from their representatives when subjected to temptation to conduct, not judged publicly or privately by the personal standard. They will not accord more than the people expect, and so long as the people expect politics to be "practical," they will not be disappointed. So long as they condone corruption they will find those willing to have it condoned. It is not more the people's representatives than their own blindness which betrays them.

But again, let us assume that all difficulties in government regulation of monopolies, without corruption, are surmounted, and that the monopolists are completely submissive to the people's will, seeking no advantage not freely accorded them — what has been accomplished? If regulation is to relieve the people of exaction, at least one of the results must be the restriction of profits to some specific maximum — to a fair rate, whatever that mystic figure may be — say 7% on the actual capital invested — a rate frequently set in the franchises of street railway companies. A result such as this would undeniably be of benefit to the people and relieve them of much exaction; but what effect would it have upon improvement in the arts — that much vaunted advantage of the capitalistic system — that benefit to mankind for the sake of which, we are told, the community may well ignore all the evils of the system? Competition being abolished, the hope of increased profit being abolished, what incentive is there to the capitalist to promote improvement in the arts? He has nothing to gain from it — any increase of profit which might accrue will be confiscated by the community. His interest is confined to keeping his profits from falling below the maximum allowed him. If they threaten to fall he can check the tendency more easily by oppressing his employees or by producing an inferior product than by the expensive operation of junking old machinery and installing a new and improved type. Thus, even if the people succeed in regulating monopoly they will at the same time have deprived the capitalistic system of its only excuse for existence — of its one beneficent effect upon the elements of happiness. What has the capitalist apologist to say to this dilemma? Can it be a delusion? Is beneficence indeed so inseparable from capitalism that it survives every mutation? Is it the inevitable product of competition, and the no less inevitable product of the absence of competition? Doubtless our economists will be able in some manner to show that it is. To the dogmatist, eternal ingenuity is the price of consistency.

When the stage of pseudo-socialism has been reached in an industrial community the capitalistic system is *in extremis*. The attempt to support the collapsing structure is doomed to failure. No sooner is one portion strengthened by a statutory prop or brace than another portion gives way. Law is piled on law, regulation on regulation, in a vain attempt to rehabilitate a piece of industrial and political junk by the mere force of overlegislation. In fact, government control with retention of capitalism is — like the attempt at artificial competition — a kind of political quackery. It is a thing of *laissez faire* shreds and legislative patches and cannot endure. It will either develop into a condition of consistent public monopoly, or of consistent private monopoly in which government control is a mere form. *If the nation does not own the monopolies, the monopolies will own the nation.*

But if government control of monopoly *with* retention of capitalism involves the permanent evils we have mentioned, would they or their equivalents be involved in government control *without* retention of capitalism? Is public monopoly better than public control of private monopoly? Those who claim that it is are called *socialists,* and their doctrine *socialism. Socialism requires that all socialized means of production shall be owned by society, and not by individuals.* Ownership is but one form of control. Is it better that the people should control their own industries, or simply share in their control? And if they should share in control, by what principle of economics are we to discover the degree in which they should be permitted to share? Government regulation, of course, outlaws the *laissez faire* theory. If now we reject socialism by what principle shall we be guided? Economists can, of course, supply none, but they can reject socialism. Consistency requires that they shall, because for years they have been frightening the public with the threat of socialism, just as nurses sometimes frighten children with tales of the bogey-man. If we examine current newspaper criticism of socialism it will appear that it seldom gets beyond the name. To say that a proposal is "socialistic" is to condemn it. It seems to be a word, not a doctrine, to which objection is made. In his polemics against socialism the average editor opposes not a political theory, but a mode of spelling. Indeed, the only consistent opponent of socialism is the anarchist or the oligarchist. *Socialism is but consistent democracy.* It is democracy applied to all forms of conduct which affect the interests of society instead of to a few traditional forms only.

The government of a nation is a means of attaining certain proximate ends. By definition, therefore, it is a *means of production.* The oligarchist claims that this means of production should be in private hands. The democrat claims that it should be in public hands. During feudal times, those archaic capitalists the seigniorial lords competed for its possession. The monarchies founded by the conquerors among these competitors displaced competition with private monopoly. The replacement of a monarchy by a republic is the substitution of public for private monopoly. In the United States this was accomplished at one stroke by the Revolution. In Europe it has come about — or rather is coming about — through a series of compromises between public and private monopoly. That is, the people do not control the government, but merely share in its control — in some cases more — in others less. The democrat claims that as the government of a nation should be managed in the public interest it should be controlled by the public. Otherwise it will be managed — not in the public interest, but in the interest of those who control it — and experience confirms the claim. The oligarchist denies the claim, and appeals to custom to sustain his position. The socialist claims that as the industries of a nation should be managed in the public interest, they should be controlled by the public. Otherwise they will be managed — not in the public interest, but in the interest of those who control them — and experience confirms the claim. The dogmatic economist denies the claim and appeals to custom to sustain his position. The socialist claims that *all* such means of production should be in the hands of the public — his opponent claims that only those which it is customary to have in public hands should be placed there.

The position of the utilitarian on this question, as on all questions, is, of course, determined strictly by utility. When competition is more useful than other proposed policies, adopt it; when private monopoly is more useful adopt *that;* when public monopoly is more useful, then adopt *that*. Does this simple course appear reasonable? I believe it will so appear. Very well then. Socialism is entitled to be judged on its merits and not on its spelling. We have examined seriatim the alleged advantages of competition. Briefly we have pointed out the modifications introduced by the system now commonly proposed, viz., pseudo-socialism, or private monopoly under public control. Let us now see what is claimed for public monopoly.

Socialism proposes to abolish the individual capitalist working in his own interest, and substitute for him the nation working in its own interest. When by the suppression of the first two classes of competition (p. 365) private monopoly has been attained, the socialist proposes to suppress the second two classes also. Instead of perpetuating the antagonism between vested interests and public interests, and then attempting to restrain and check it by a complex regulating mechanism he proposes to abolish the antagonism, and thus dispense with the necessity of restraint. Instead of a system whereby the people sell their labor to a capitalist and then buy back the product of that labor from the capitalist, leaving at each transaction a margin of profit in his hands, the socialist proposes that the nation shall labor for itself, and buy from itself, all profit accruing to the nation. Thus the antagonism between buyer and seller, between laborer and employer of labor, is abolished, for the nation is both buyer and seller, both laborer and employer of labor. Through ownership of the means of production the nation becomes its own capitalist. In effect, the advantage claimed for this system is its improvement in the economy of consumption. By its abolition of the competitive system it abolishes the unequal distribution of wealth which characterizes that system. Inequality in the distribution of wealth is merely inequality in the opportunity possessed by individuals of availing themselves of their own labor. The rich man has an advantage over the poor man simply because the first can avail himself of more labor than he performs, the second of less labor than he performs, provided we measure labor by its cost. In purchasing commodities we avail ourselves of the labor involved in their production. He who can purchase commodities of the highest labor cost therefore, can avail himself of the most labor. Capitalists do not employ laborers merely to satisfy a whim — they employ them that they may avail themselves of a portion of their labor — as large a portion as possible. To this portion Marx has given the name " surplus labor; " it appears in the profit of the capitalist. Now, as equality in the distribution of wealth promotes utility, equality should be sought, and the socialist claims that the shortest way to achieve it is to abolish profit and to make, on the average, each individual able to avail himself of his own labor and no more; or, rather, as children and other helpless persons, for obvious reasons, either cannot or should not be laborers, to make each normal family able to avail themselves of their own labor and no more, i. e., to make them self-sufficient. This is the object of socialism.

Inequality of distribution in wealth is, of course, one of the chief defects of the capitalistic system; hence any device which promises to remedy it is worth considering. The question is — Does socialism, in diminishing one defect, increase others? Its opponents claim that it does, and in this country their real criticisms are practically confined to three.

The first is that socialism would lead to widespread corruption. Government in America is certainly corrupt, and if corruption is confined to the operations of the government this is a serious criticism. General corruption would not only cause general demoralization of character, but it would impair the efficiency of production everywhere. It is, however, generally acknowledged that the demoralized condition of the government is due to the influence of capitalism. The transfer of the debased business standards of morality fostered by the competitive system into politics brings politics down to the level of business. In fact, in our country, politics is a kind of business and is pursued for profit. The control of legislative bodies and other departments of government by great business interests is notorious. This is the source of all the grand corruption to be found in the government, and this socialism would abolish by the destruction of capitalism. As to petty corruption, that is fully as prevalent in great corporations as it is in the government service. Rebates, commissions, rake-offs, and jobs of every description, are so common in business transactions as not to cause comment; and when we consider the gigantic operations of "frenzied finance," speculation, stock watering, cornering, corporation-wrecking, fraudulent bankruptcy, embezzlement, and every form of stock-jobbery, the petty stealings of subordinate government officials which occasionally occur, sink into insignificance. In the abolition of capitalism, socialism would abolish thousands of times the corruption it would cause. Professor Parsons of Boston University states the case with brevity thus:

"The causes and conditions of corruption are mainly (1), private monopoly; (2), political influence in appointment, and (3); secrecy.

"Private ownership of public utilities leaves all three causes in full bloom and feeds their roots.

"Public ownership eliminates two of the causes — private monopoly and secrecy — and if established under reasonable civil service regulations it eliminates the other cause also."

In fact, it is difficult for an impartial observer to take seriously such a criticism as this one of socialism. It is, indeed, a strong, and not a weak feature of the socialistic doctrine that is here criticized. Public monopoly offers a remedy for the

CHAP. XII]   PRIVATE AND PUBLIC MONOPOLY   421

present capitalistic control of the government which regulated private monopoly does not offer. To license private monopolies while leaving them the incentive and the power to corrupt those who are employed by the people to supervise their operations is to invite disaster. The simplest common sense is all that is required to dispose of this first objection to socialism.

The second objection is that control of the means of production by the nation would put in the hands of the party in power a political machine so strong as to be detrimental to the interests of the community. Those who offer this objection have in mind the capitalistic method of influencing elections. They can only mean that it would put in the hands of a machine the power of defeating the will of the majority. The opposition of parties, when it is real, is generally an opposition between classes whose interests are antagonistic. The abolition of capitalism would abolish any marked distinction of the people into antagonistic classes, and it is the claim of socialists that, with the disappearance of class antagonism, party antagonism will disappear, the interests of the whole people being the same. It is the aim of socialism, as of less consistent democracy, to do away with all class distinctions save those established by nature herself. In the absence of the corruption caused by capitalism it is difficult to see how public monopoly could result in the defeat of the will of the majority, particularly when by the abolition of classes the majority would be practically the whole people.

The third objection is one which critics of socialism are unanimous in urging. The claim is made that whatever gain socialism might effect in the efficiency of consumption would be more than offset by the loss in efficiency of production due to the abolition of the class whose zeal to improve the arts is directly due to their self-interest. In a state which is its own capitalist the incentive to the introduction of labor-saving machinery, including skilful organization and management, discussed on page 378, will be lacking. It is justly urged that if mankind is to produce a surplus of happiness, means must be discovered of producing desiderata at a less cost of labor than at present, for it is doubtless true that not only is the distribution of wealth at the present day bad, but the amount of wealth per capita is, and always has been, inadequate. Hence, if socialism does, as a matter of fact, check improvement in the art and organization of industry, and while improving the distribution of wealth diminishes the amount per capita — a valid objection has been lodged against it.

Many facts appear to bear out this criticism of socialism. In America it appears to be a general rule that enterprises carried on by governments are expensive. It appears to cost the government more to accomplish any given amount of production than it does private parties. Such facts lose much of their force, however, when we recall that efficiency of production is inversely proportional, not to *money* cost, but to *labor* cost. The confusion of these two things, so common in our day, is a heritage from the obsolete mercantile system. We cannot infer from money cost to labor cost, as they are by no means proportional to one another. The incentive of the capitalist is to reduce *money* cost — *labor* cost is a matter of indifference to him. Hence it will be found that the private individual derives most of his advantage over the government from the cheaper and more oppressed labor that he employs. The government has no incentive to oppress its employees, since it seeks no profit from their surplus labor. Hence the money cost of governmental production, as a rule, ranges higher than that carried on by private capitalists, but the labor cost is not, therefore, necessarily higher.

The vast strides in mechanical improvements made by industries in private hands is often adduced as evidence of the effectiveness of the incentive to capitalists to improve the arts, and yet what art has advanced so rapidly in the last generation as the art of warfare — an art which has no part in the business of private individuals and which has been developed without the incentive of the capitalist to profit. A modern war vessel is one of the most complex and ingenious machines of modern times, and it has been developed by the government for its own purposes.

But if governmental administration is so unsatisfactory, why is it that it is continually encroaching on the field of private enterprise, and this in spite of the powerful opposition of capitalism. It is significant that, with a few trifling exceptions in the case of municipal governments, the assumption by the government of any activity is always permanent. It holds all the ground it gains, and no one proposes the re-substitution of private enterprise. Does any one suggest placing or replacing the schools, the public buildings, the post-office service, the lighthouse service, the life-saving service, the service of the agricultural department, or the geodetic survey, in private hands?

They are no more public services than the administration of the railroads, the telegraphs, the iron mines, or the flour mills of the country. It would be perfectly possible for the government to turn them over to private parties. Why, if the government is so lax, is this not done or at least proposed? Does any one suppose that if the government once assumed control of the railroads, the coal mines, the steel works, or any other public utility, that there would be any national demand for their return to the control of capitalists? If so, it would be a complete reversal of all former experiences. No: the first two forms of competition when once abolished are abolished permanently, and the same will be true of the last two. In this country there has been little opportunity to compare governmental with capitalistic efficiency, but when we examine the experience of other countries we are confirmed in the view that any great activity once undertaken by the government is found so much more satisfactory than the same activity in private hands, that no one proposes to return. To this statement there are relatively few exceptions. In New Zealand the success of public monopoly has been so pronounced that a general knowledge of its benefits is probably all that would be required to cause the United States to adopt a similar policy.[1] What is true of New Zealand is true elsewhere. In Europe practical socialism is advancing rapidly, and even in our own backward country the advantage of public over private enterprises is generally recognized by candid observers. Governor Douglas, of Massachusetts, in his inaugural address, remarks:

" Whatever doubts may exist as to the expediency of State or Federal ownership of public utilities, the operation of such undertakings has now passed the experimental stage. It has been demonstrated by the experience of towns and cities in this Commonwealth, both with regard to water supply and public lighting, that under favorable conditions and proper management the business of gas, electric lighting, and water supply can be conducted by municipal corporations with profit to the inhabitants, both in price and service."

" It is not disputed that as a rule, private corporations conduct their business more economically than do public corporations. It is, however, disputed that the public usually obtains the benefit of this economical management. In most cases, therefore, the

[1] An excellent discussion and comparison of the industrial system of New Zealand and the United States is that of H. H. Lusk in " Our Foes at Home." 1899.

publicly owned and operated waterworks, sewers, gas and electric lighting plants have given the public cheaper and better service than have the privately owned concerns."

What is true of water works and gas plants and means of transportation, is equally true of any and every public utility. The principle that activities carried on in the public interest should be controlled by the public is as generally sound as any other political principle, and it is the only justification of democracy. When the effects of national policies are estimated in units of happiness, instead of units of money, confusion on this subject will largely disappear.

Nor are public utilities limited to those enterprises to which the public, through its government, grants a charter or franchise. In a primitive condition of society, when each family produced what it consumed and consumed what it produced, public utilities did not exist. But as soon as the division of labor, and with it the system of exchange arose, public utilities came into being, since the mode of operation of producers no longer concerned themselves alone. In early times each family was a self-sufficing unit, and was independent of other units. To-day each family should be a self-sufficing unit, but it should not be, and cannot be, independent of others. It cannot produce exactly what it consumes, but it can, and should, produce the equivalent of what it consumes, and by the modern system of industry it can make a given amount of labor indefinitely more effective than under the old system of self-sufficiency. This gain in efficiency, however, converts all industries into public utilities, since each family is no longer dependent for its desiderata upon its own activities, but is dependent upon others. If the public is entitled to life, liberty and the pursuit of happiness only by sufferance of those private persons or corporations who produce the desiderata which the public consumes, then, indeed, an oligarchy of industry exists, more unjust than the military oligarchies of ancient times. To claim, as some writers do, that the public are entitled to control only those industries which operate under a franchise is to found public conduct upon a purely arbitrary distinction. *Public utilities are those whose operation affects the interests of the public* and it is on this account, and on this account alone, that the public are entitled to control them. If democracy requires that conduct affecting the interests of society shall be controlled by society (p. 357), then the public control of public utilities is the only course of conduct consistent with democracy. Capitalism, indeed, is but the form of oligarchy which the application of the scientific method to production alone, happens to generate. Though in form it may be democratic, in substance it is as far removed from democracy as the true monarchies of Europe or Asia.

Assuming that the third objection to public monopoly is valid — it is no less valid as an objection to publicly controlled private monopoly. If socialism withdraws the existing incentive to improve the arts without supplying any other, the same may be said of pseudo-socialism, which has all the disadvantages of socialism, and most of those of competition, without the advantage of socialism in promoting efficiency of consumption, nor that of competition in promoting efficiency of production. He who would condemn genuine socialism on these grounds must doubly condemn the pseudo-socialism which the leaders of public opinion in America are now proposing as a substitute therefor.

Besides those we have considered, there are five popular criticisms of socialism which arise from a misunderstanding of its tenets.

First. There is a very common confusion of socialism with anarchism. This implies gross ignorance since the two schools are antithetical, the first advocating more government, the second less. Anarchism is simply consistent *laissez faire* doctrine, and is the purest individualism, whereas socialism is anti-individualistic. A point of resemblance between these opposite schools may, nevertheless, be detected. Anarchism would abolish law, because it interferes with "individual liberty" so-called. Socialism proposes to abolish it by dispensing with the necessity for it. It is the claim of socialists that by abolishing the division of society into antagonistic classes, and raising the whole population to a standard of living and morals such that all will have a stake in the order and well-being of society, that crime will dwindle and tend to disappear, that courts, prisons, and police, will become superfluous, and that the conscience of the community will take the place of law. This expectation is not without foundation, since it is from the desire for profit, the antagonism of classes, and the ignorance and poverty which are the universal concomitants of capitalism, that most of the crimes of the community arise.

Second. There is frequent confusion of socialism with communism. The latter embodies the doctrine of community of goods — the principle of dividing the wealth of a community so that each member has the same share. Although socialism, by its tendency to equalize the distribution of wealth, tends to accomplish a result resembling that of communism, it imposes upon no one any obligation not already imposed, to divide his wealth with other members of the community. Within such limits as are prescribed by the principle of self-sufficiency — that each self-sufficing unit may consume the equivalent of what it produces — socialism permits of the accumulation of wealth to any extent whatever. It involves no principle of "dividing up" irrespective of the industry or indolence, the capacity or incapacity, of individuals.

Were it indeed true that socialism put a premium upon indolence, and forced the industrious to support the idle, it would show that socialism had a distinct resemblance to capitalism, but it is not true, though perhaps the mistake is a natural one, since some socialists have advocated a policy which would result in such a condition. I refer to those who claim that justice requires a distribution of wealth according to the need for it. Were this a practical policy it would be a just one; but with human beings as they are it is inoperative, since to disburse desiderata according as persons need or do not need them would put a premium upon the cultivation of needs, or of requirements which would be accepted as needs. Hence those who most dissipated their resources would receive the most from society. Such a policy would develop more requirements than could be supplied, and soon prove suicidal. In other words, a policy of distribution according to needs is, like competition, a maleficently accelerative policy, and is not adapted to its end. During the last century it was embodied in the poor laws of England and stimulated pauperism so fast that it had to be abandoned. The policy is only practical when restricted to persons who are incapacitated. It has no relation to socialism.

Third. There is a very widespread misapprehension that socialism would diminish the liberty of individuals, and force everyone to adopt a cut-and-dried mode of life, having no relation to their tastes and aspirations. This notion arises from the assumption that socialism in *production* implies socialism in *consumption*. No such implication is justified. Indeed, one of the objects of socialism is to increase the real liberty of the individual by abolishing as far as possible that individualism in production which is so notoriously inefficient; thereby freeing his life sufficiently from the necessity of labor to enable him to increase the duration of consumption. Socialism in consumption would be as inefficient as individualism in production, and neither policy is consistent with economy in the generation of happiness.

Fourth. There is a popular notion that socialism is destructive of the family and is opposed to the institution of marriage. It is obvious that public ownership of the means of production, which is all that socialism involves, can have no relation to such a matter as this. Socialism includes no peculiar views on marriage, though doubtless some socialists may hold such views; but if so, it is a mere coincidence, just as some socialists may be bow-legged or cross-eyed. Capitalism, indeed, is much more destructive of the family than socialism. Child-labor would not be tolerated under the latter system, and the employment of women would be much restricted, whereas under capitalism, unrestrained by the state, women and children are drafted into the ranks of labor and made to grind out their lives in toil that commerce may flourish and profits increase. It was this evil that brought about the enactment of the Factory Acts — those earliest offspring of socialism.

Fifth. Another popular idea associates socialism with atheism and the destruction of religion. There is, of course, no such connection. To place public utilities in the control of the public would no more tend to promote irreligion than to place the Post Office in the control of private parties would tend to promote religion.

I have not deemed it necessary to examine seriatum the effects upon the elements of happiness of the social mechanisms embodied either in artificial competition, pseudo-socialism or socialism. All these are attempts to improve upon competition, and are directed primarily to remedying its most conspicuous defect — inequality in the distribution of wealth. The first two, even if adapted to their end — which they are not — would ignore seven of the eight elements of happiness. All we can say of them is that, as improvements upon the present system, they are the first which would suggest themselves to minds trained in the dogmas of the prevailing school and yet forced to acknowledge the inadequacy of those dogmas to deal with modern problems. They are feeble compromises between anarchism and socialism and not consistent with themselves. As intermediate stages in progress toward a scientific system it is to the interest of the public to make them as short as possible. These intermediate stages always occur in the transition from dogma to common sense; hence the present trend of politics is quite normal, as the history of the inductive sciences amply illustrates.

As to socialism, though it is founded upon a sound principle — the same principle, indeed, upon which democracy itself is founded — it has not, at present, sufficient definiteness to permit of a systematic test by means of the elements of happiness. It is a groping effort after a better state, and necessarily groping, since it does not start out with a definite recognition of what it is supposed to accomplish. Hence it ignores almost as many of the elements of happiness as artificial competition and pseudo-socialism. Nevertheless it is a step in the right direction, and upon its foundation principle that those things which affect the happiness of the whole people should be controlled by the whole people, I shall attempt to build a mechanism adapted to the end of utility. In this attempt I shall construct not an indefinite, but a definite, system, capable as far as any system built on paper can be, of test by the criteria laid down in Chapter 8. I do not claim that the system to be expounded in the chapter following is the *only* common sense system: I claim that it is *a* common sense system; to be promptly ignored and discarded if a better one may be proposed.

CHAPTER XIII

PANTOCRACY

In discussing the third objection to socialism in the preceding chapter we have discovered a valid criticism of all systems which have thus far been proposed for the guidance of society. To cure poverty and to make the average individual self-supporting, a better distribution of wealth is a necessary, but not a sufficient, condition. A greater rate of consumption per capita is essential and the only means of attaining it is to make greater the rate of production per capita. We shall point out later that the population of a community is entirely beyond human control when the consumptive rate is of low value, and hence cannot be brought to beneficent equilibrium. The first essential then of an economic system is to simultaneously raise the efficiency of production and of consumption. Capitalism, whether competitive or monopolistic, admits of no means of accomplishing such a result. Socialism does. I propose, then, to undertake the exposition of a modification of socialism which will presumably combine all the advantages of public monopoly with the single advantage of competition, at the same time augmenting that single advantage in a degree impossible under competition. To understand the relation of this proposed system to that at present in operation a slight analysis of profit will be necessary.

Profit under the present system accomplishes two and only two useful objects. (1) It induces men to undertake the production of desiderata: (2) It induces them to undertake to improve the means of production. Economists claim no other element of utility in profit. Aside from these two objects the incentive furnished by profit, or the hope of profit, is not an incentive to useful acts, but to harmful ones. Under the wage system the recompense of the laborer for his labor is his wages — of the capitalist for his capital is his profit. The capitalist will not permit his capital to be utilized in the production of commodities without the promise of profit — hence, under the present system of private capital, profit is essential, since without it capitalists would not engage, or permit their capital to engage, in production at all, since they would have no motive to do so. This first object of profit, socialism accomplishes without the necessity of profit by making production a regular and customary function of government. Under socialism all kinds of industries would be undertaken as regular departments of government, and would be carried on just as the military or naval establishments, the geological survey, or the post-office department are carried on, without the necessity of, or incentive to, profit. Hence socialism, as it is, would accomplish the first object of profit.

As to the second object of profit, all systems proposed or practised are but lame substitutes for a systematic application of common sense. We have cited reasons for believing that the popular opinion which holds socialism inferior to competition in the attainment of this end is, in considerable measure, a delusion, but whether this be so or not, nothing can be done with competition to improve it in this respect, since its supreme virtue becomes manifest only when " let alone." Socialism, on the other hand, has no such limitation, and admits of any improvements which common sense may suggest. Its doctrines, therefore, afford a foundation for an applied technology of happiness.

The first question before us is, how may the efficiency of production be increased simultaneously with an increase in the efficiency of consumption? The profit of the capitalist is supposed by the *laissez faire* theorists to be a means of inducing him to accomplish the first half of this service for society, but we have seen how ill he accomplishes it. Nevertheless, is it not possible to obtain from the capitalistic system one valuable suggestion — to extract from it one feature — which, when applied to socialism, remedies its worst defect, and at the same time leaves capitalism without a single point of superiority, real or imaginary? Could society contrive a method of simultaneously stimulating in a high degree the efficiency of both production and consumption it would certainly be worth paying for — it would be worth much sacrifice — indeed, if poverty is to be permanently cured, and the total activities of society placed upon a self-supporting basis, some method of achieving this result must be devised. It is not only desirable — it is essential. If the stimulus of profit under the capitalistic system fails, as it certainly does, why can we not adapt the same stimulus to the socialistic system so as to succeed? Why can we not harness the power of individual self-interest to the mechanism of public monopoly so as to drive it with all the speed of which that power is capable toward the goal of all human endeavor — happiness? Now, there is reason to believe that precisely this thing can be done — that society, through organization, can be converted into a great happiness-producing mechanism, and that self-interest can be utilized to drive it. Thus we shall not have to essay the hopeless task of destroying egotism in men, but simply by diverting its channel from competition to co-operation convert it into a mighty power for the good — instead of the harm — of mankind. To destroy human egotism is impossible. Therefore let us direct it so as to make it serve the ends of society instead of subverting them. To the construction of such a happiness engine I propose to devote the remainder of this work. With the material at present available it will, of necessity, be very imperfect — a rude and clumsy affair with many of the details lacking — to be compared with the early efforts of Newcomen or Watt to construct a steam engine. But perhaps in the future from this crude beginning a structure may be developed which will bear the same relation to the original that a modern marine engine bears to Newcomen's atmospheric engine of 1705. Possibly such a hope is delusive and such a comparison presumptuous. But this much is certain — to produce the maximum output of happiness society must be organized into a happiness-producing mechanism — and to drive it no less powerful an agent will be required than the one permanent force inherent in human nature — self-interest.

That such a mechanism is constructible may be inferred from two propositons whose soundness has been established in the discussion of the second factor of happiness: (1) *The rate of production per capita can be increased — therefore the rate of consumption per capita can be increased.* (2) *The time required for a given amount of production can be decreased — therefore the time occupied in consumption can be increased.* With these two inferences assuring the soundness of our theory, and with the analysis of the factors of happiness into their elements as our guide to its application, we may proceed to our task with confidence that we are on solid ground. At least we know definitely what we desire to accomplish, and that it is theoretically accomplishable. The only question which remains is: Have we the ingenuity to devise a mechanism, however crude, for its accomplishment? A similar situation confronted those who first undertook the construction of the steam engine, and we shall endeavor to profit by their example. At this point I shall make no attempt to show how the mechanism proposed may be substituted for the one at present in operation, deeming it best to postpone the discussion of that matter to the following chapter.

The mechanism I propose has eight different features, and may conveniently be expounded in eight sections, concerned with the following topics:

(1) Public ownership of the means of production. Retention of the wage system and abolition of profit.

(2) Organization of a system of distribution, whereby supply of, and demand for, products may be adjusted.

(3) Organization of a national labor exchange, whereby supply of, and demand for, labor may be adjusted.

(4) Organization of an inspection system, whereby the quality of products may be maintained at a definite standard.

(5) Application of labor to production.

(6) Organization of invention.

(7) Old age insurance.

(8) Reform of education.

The system to be elucidated under these eight headings I shall call *pantocracy* (Gr. παν = all : κρατέω = to rule), because it involves the control of human activities in the interest of all.

Section (1) The foundation of pantocracy is simply the socialism of Marx and his co-workers. All industries capable of being converted into monopolies are so converted, and title to the means of production appertaining thereto vested in the government — that is, in the people — the government being merely their instrument; local industries, of course, to be owned by local governments, national industries by the national government. Capitalists in control of those industries capable of being converted into monopolies (and they include practically all important industries) are dispensed with, the nation acting as its own capitalist. With this change, profit is abolished, and can be converted entirely into wages, the wage system being retained. The system of socialism is so well known as to require no discussion here. It has been tried and not found wanting. The Post Office department is an example of its application to a national industry formerly in the hands of private parties. Indeed every department of government is an example of applied socialism. Even the army and navy might be placed in private hands, and trusted to private benevolence, and were the *laissez faire* economists consistent, they would advocate such a policy. Socialism began with democratic government.

Section (2) It has been shown in a former chapter that real liberty increases as liberty to consume increases. But real liberty is proportional to opportunity for happiness, and as happiness will, in general, be proportional to the opportunity for it, an economic system should stimulate the liberty to consume as much as possible. Now the *demand,* or what economists call the *effective demand* is proportional to *real,* not to *legal,* liberty. The man who gets $5.00 a week wage may have as much legal liberty as he who gets $50.00, but he has not, in general, as much real liberty, and his effective demand is less. Demand, however, can lead to consumption only if it is supplied. Production is necessary to consumption, and in a common sense system it is essential that the demand for, and supply of, desiderata be adjusted to one another. We have seen how competition accomplishes this — or rather fails to accomplish it — resulting in all sorts of unnecessary labor, reduplication of plants, failures, enforced idleness, and crises, with their attendant ills. Private monopoly does better. A monopoly like the Standard Oil Company has main distributing agencies scattered throughout the territory it supplies; each of these has branch agencies and there is an organized system of distribution. Reports of the demand from these various agencies are received regularly by persons whose function it is to regulate the supply by the demand. If the demand slackens, the supply is made to slacken; if the demand accelerates, the supply is accelerated. Thus production is adapted to consumption, there is no overproduction, and one result of competitive chaos is eliminated. Private monopoly has no tendency to equality of distribution in demand, whereby the demand would become a real index of happiness output, but so far as it goes it accomplishes an excellent result — it adjusts supply to demand, and this feature of private monopoly should be adopted by public monopoly.

The output of every industry should be controlled by an organized department called the *Department of Output Regulation.* This department should be in communication with a national system of warehouses or distributing agencies. Its sole function should be to keep records of the stock on hand of all commodities in all distributing agencies, and the rate at which they are being distributed in supplying the demand. Through the knowledge thus recorded it should regulate the rate of production in each industry, keeping it in constant adjustment to consumption. Each month, or quarter, it should call for a definite output from the plants of the nation, and just that output, and no more, should be supplied. Obviously, a stock sufficient to supply the demand for several months in advance should always be kept on hand — a policy pursued by every prudent storekeeper, and essential to the prompt filling of orders. In the case of necessities this reserve stock should be greater than in the case of other commodities, except, of course, in the case of perishable commodities, for which an adapted system of distribution should be provided.

A single *Distributing Department* should be organized whose function should be to distribute the output of the plants of the country to the various distributing stations. Such an organized department would save a vast amount of unnecessary labor and duplication of effort. It should be operated on the same principle as a commodity producing industry (See section 5) and possess a completely independent organization. Both the department of output regulation and that of distribution should, of course, be divided into subordinate divisions, corresponding to the various departments into which the industries of the country are divided; and the organization should be such that delays and interruptions are reduced to a minimum. An organized system of regulation, such as described, could regulate the supply of practically all commodities to the demand for them, just as the Post Office department regulates the supply of stamps, postal cards, stamped envelopes, newspaper wrappers, etc., to the demand for them, in all the sixty-odd thousand postal distributing stations throughout the United States.

Section (3) So long as men are not at liberty to perpetually consume — so long as they must produce — it is desirable that they should be at liberty, as far as possible, to engage in that kind of production which suits best their tastes. Not only is the labor cost of desiderata less when the laborer's tastes are consulted in assigning him his task, but he will turn out better products, and at a greater speed, for a man will generally succeed best in the kind of work he likes the best. Hence the greatest liberty in choosing or changing their employment should be accorded all laborers. To facilitate this a *National Labor Exchange* should be organized. Each department of government should make periodic — say monthly — reports to the labor exchange of existing vacancies, if any, specifying wages, prevailing hours of labor, character of work, location etc. These reports, converted into properly classified lists, should be published monthly by the labor exchange and distributed, so that every one in the country could have easy access to them without leaving his own town. Every post office, library, etc., should receive copies. Every person qualified, whether employed or not, should be entitled to apply for the positions thus vacant. Besides this there should be published and distributed less frequent reports setting forth all positions in all departments, whether vacant or not, so that persons could apply for positions not vacant with the object of anticipating future vacancies. Applications for any or all these positions should be made in writing to the labor exchange, and the same man should be permitted to apply for as many positions as he chose, so that he would have a wide latitude of choice and a better chance of changing his occupation if that in which he was engaged failed to suit him. All applications should be filed in one department, organized for the sole purpose of facilitating the adaptation of producers to their work. In those industrial departments in which the supply of, exceeded the demand for, labor these applications would constitute a waiting list from which should be selected those to fill the vacancies caused by death, retirement, or exchange in, or expansion of, the operating force. It should be required of every candidate for a particular position that he show himself by examination, previous training, or otherwise, well fitted to fill it. To each of his various applications for employment each candidate should be required to affix one and only one number, (1), (2), (3), (4), etc., called a *preference number,* indicating whether the position was his first, second, third, fourth, etc., choice among those for which he applied, and he should be at liberty to amend these numbers at any time he pleased. Of course, no candidate could apply for a position which he did not prefer to the one held by him at the time of his application, or amendment thereof. Of several candidates shown to be fitted for any position that one should be selected whose preference number was the lowest. If several were equally low, the selection between them should be by lot, precedence of filing, or by some other method shown by experience to be better than these. In those industrial departments in which the demand for, exceeded the supply of, labor there would be no waiting list, or only for certain positions. The mode of filling these vacancies will be considered under section (5).

Under competition there is no more provision for adjusting

the supply of, to the demand for, labor than in the case of commodities. Everything is left to chance. A man must do the best he can. If he loses his position he must either obtain another one through the influence of friends — often something he does not want — or go wandering about "looking for a job," glad if he can get anything. He does not know what positions throughout the country are vacant, nor do those who desire particular services always know where they can obtain men to perform them. In an inadequate manner, advertising fulfils this function locally, but it is a poor substitute for a national labor exchange. With the organization of society into a mechanism for the production of happiness, and the establishment of a bureau for the purpose of deliberately adapting a man's occupation to his powers and preferences, far more real liberty would be gained by the average laborer — that is the people — than was gained by the abolition of slavery and serfdom and the establishment of so-called free labor. Real liberty was doubtless, in the end, increased by this step, and yet the curse of competition immediately ensuing on the liberation of labor, set in operation a compensating influence which largely neutralized the increase. We have only to read Marx's account of the "free" agricultural laborers of England just after the downfall of feudalism to become convinced that their real liberty was less than before they had been liberated from serfdom and divorced from the soil, although their legal liberty was certainly greater. The gain from exchanging slavery for free labor is frequently a gain of legal, more than of real, liberty. The establishment of the so-called "free laborer" is, however, merely a step in the evolution of society which will eventually produce laborers who are really free, emancipated not only from the labor imposed by man, but from that imposed by nature. The real freedom of the laborer consists in freedom from labor — and common sense will eventually accomplish it. Some human labor will always be necessary, but it will involve little labor cost and its burden will be negligible.

A policy very different from that which we have propounded in this section is often imputed to socialism. It has been seriously proposed by some persons who agree with the doctrines of Marx that the assignment of men to their vocations shall be determined — not by their own preference — but by a governmental commission which shall pronounce upon their qualifications and assign each his place in the mechanism of social production, according to its notions of his fitness. This policy has no relation to socialism and it is obviously utterly repugnant to utility. Some socialists may perhaps advocate it, but this does not make it socialism. It is interesting to observe that the dogmatic school takes violent exception to this doctrine and very justly points out that it would lead to a most uncomfortable condition of society. Blind beings — do they not recognize their own offspring? Of course it would make life uncomfortable, but if wealth is the object of national existence, why should we scruple about comfort? Do we not defile our cities with soot and vile effluvia, pollute our streams, disfigure and destroy the beauties of nature, dissipate her resources, waste the lives of men and women, and even of children, in the pursuit of wealth? If it is worth while to sacrifice so much to Mammon, why should we feel delicacy in sacrificing a little more? The motto of the commercial moralist of the day is "business before pleasure," and in this so-called socialistic policy such a motto is consistently applied. We sacrifice most things now to business, why not sacrifice men's inclination to a vocation as well? If it is sensible to sacrifice the end to the means once, then it is sensible to do so twice, thrice, or any number of times. The motto of the utilitarian is "pleasure before business," although not necessarily antecedent thereto. He therefore always considers the end before the means, and instead of sacrificing men's inclinations to business, sacrifices business to their inclinations. He lets men determine their own vocations instead of letting business determine them. The policy here criticised is not only not socialistic, but it is a typical product of the dogmatic school and in harmony with its theory and practice.

Section (4) A third department of government should comprise a *Bureau of Inspection* whose function should be to keep the quality of all products at a required standard. Its agents should be in every government plant and should be held jointly responsible with the directors of that plant for the quality of the product there turned out; so that if the consumer found it otherwise than as represented the responsibility would be at once fixed. Of course, with the abolition of capitalism most of the temptation to the production of inferior products would be done away with, and little more would be required than to guard against the effects of hasty work. For the purpose of improving the quality of products, premiums could be placed upon such improvements, corresponding to those which governments often place upon the speed of war-vessels. In this manner the quality of all commodities could be maintained and improved, and the purchaser could have confidence in what he bought. Adulteration would cease, salesmen could be believed, the necessity for each plant maintaining an inspection bureau of its own, as at present required, would be dispensed with, and the demoralization inseparable from systematic adulteration, substitution, and misrepresentation, would be abolished. Judging from the incomplete statistics of adulteration published, the saving to the nation from this source alone would be several hundred million dollars a year, not to speak of the saving in the health, physical and moral, of the community. The bureau of inspection would thus control the quality of products, while the department of output regulation would control their quantity. Upon the conditions under capitalistic production it is unnecessary to dwell. We have already briefly referred to them. Under capitalism cheating occurs because there is profit to be made by cheating — there is a virtual premium upon it — with human nature as it is then can we expect anything different? Government inspection of the products of private monopoly would be an expensive and doubtful expedient, which would but tempt capitalists to corruption in their effort to evade the objects of inspection.

The departments of output regulation, of distribution, the labor exchange, and the inspection bureau, have been but briefly and broadly described, because their organization is quite normal and familiar. It would be as easy to organize these parts of the pantocratic mechanism as it would be to organize the War department or that of the Interior. Any skilled administrator could accomplish it. Under section (5) we shall describe a system which is not so familiar and possessing features requiring more specific exposition. It is the critical feature of the pantocratic mechanism, the " very pulse of the machine," and it is important that its operating principle should be understood. I shall not discuss every detail, nor anticipate every objection, but the exposition of the section will, nevertheless, be more complete than any other.

Section (5) Each commodity producing industry, or group of closely related industries, should constitute a separate department of government. To illustrate the organization of these departments I shall describe one, which may be considered typical of all. It may be discussed in two parts: (1) The disposition of receipts and expenditures. (2) The disposition of personnel. In describing the system I shall employ a month as a unit of readjustment, but a unit consisting of a quarter, or some other period, might serve as well, or perhaps better.

(1) Corresponding to each industrial department a separate division of the Treasury department should be created, controlled by a separate governing body or *board*. The receipts from the sale of all commodities should be transmitted to the Treasury, or one of the sub-treasuries, and duly credited to the proper industrial department. The gross monthly receipts of each department should be divided into four funds.

(a) *The expense fund*— the money properly creditable to the operating expenses of the month, exclusive of compensation to personnel, including expenditures for material, machinery, repairs, insurance, deterioration, etc.

(b) *The improvement fund*— a sinking fund for improvements and enlargements of plant, the monthly amount of which should depend upon the fund already accumulated, and determinable for each month by the local board of improvement. This fund itself should be divided into two. (1) A smaller part, consisting of a predetermined percentage of the whole, expendable at the discretion of the chief directors, called the *active* fund; and (2) A larger part, expendable only at the discretion of the board of improvement, and called the *reserve* fund.

(c) *The tax fund*— a tax levied on each revenue-producing department by the government, for the support of those departments which have no independent means of support, such as the Army and Navy, the Pension Office, etc. It should be proportional to the number of the personnel, and to the average compensation per capita, in each department. In an advanced stage of public monopoly such a method of taxation would be a substitute for the present tariff and internal revenue, and would be much more equable. The disposition of the fund collected from taxes should of course be, as at present, determined by the legislature.

(d) *The wages fund*— consisting of the gross receipts, less funds (a), (b), and (c), to be distributed as compensation to the personnel in the manner to be hereafter specified.

(2) The personnel should be divided into two corps: (A) *Wage earners.* (B) *Directors.*

(A) The function of the wage earners should be to carry out the orders of the directors. They constitute the bulk of the personnel and should be divided into many classes. For example, in such an industry as that of steel making, they would consist of ordinary laborers, foundrymen, machinists, engineers, carpenters, draughtsmen, clerks, etc. A regular scale of wages, corresponding to that established in such a department as the Post Office, should be prepared, the wage of each wage earner being proportioned to the skill and experience required of him — with this exception, that length of service should be deemed a factor and an advance made for each year that the wage earner served the state. Should wages fall, for reasons hereafter to be specified, they would, of course, fall by the same percentage for all wages. No wage earner should be dischargeable except upon written charges, as at present under the civil service. Proved wilful inefficiency should be a ground for discharge. Proved involuntary inefficiency a ground for decrease of wages.

(B) The directors should be divided into one or more chief directors, corresponding to the president or general manager of a great corporation, and various subordinate directors in charge of important divisions of the industry. The function of the directors should be to manage the work of production and direct the wage earners. They should be required to attain two objects: (1) To deliver to the department of distribution the quantity of product called for by the regulator of output. (2) To improve the efficiency of production by the introduction of labor-saving machinery, and economies in division of labor, manipulation, or other details of management. Corresponding to these two objects their compensation should be of two kinds.

(1) A *wage,* as in the case of a wage-earner, proportioned to the skill and experience required. This would be as constant as any other wage. (2) *Conditional compensation* determined as follows:

Every industry produces one or more products. The average time expended in producing each product is determinable. Call this the *producing time.* It should be reported to the governing board of the department, monthly. If the producing times of the several products contained in the output be added together, and the same divided by the number of products, the quotient will be the *average producing time* for the output of the industry. This will be a function of the average productive capacity. On the date upon which any director assumes office the average producing time should be considered that recorded at the last monthly report. Now in addition to his wage, each director should receive compensation whose amount is conditioned upon the decrease in the average producing time since he entered office. If this time increases, of course, he receives only his wage; if the arts and economies of production continually improve — as they should do — the producing time will decrease, and his conditional compensation will be greater the longer he holds office, and the more successful he is in promoting improvement in the arts and in industrial organization. The conditional compensation of the chief directors should be greater than for their subordinates, and should, in fact, be graded according to the importance of each man as a factor in production. It should be great enough in every case to afford a keen incentive to every director to expend his zeal and ingenuity in diminishing the average producing time — in increasing the efficiency of production. The precise manner in which the shortening of the producing time is made to accrue to the benefit of the producer will be explained presently. Each director on first assuming office should receive only his wage, because conditional compensation should be a recompense for service in increasing the efficiency of production, and no man who had not rendered such service would be entitled to it. The award of conditional compensation in the manner specified is no more than an extension of the ordinary principle of awarding compensation for services rendered. Improvement in the arts is something useful to society, just as bricks, or bolts, or horseshoes are useful to society; and just as those who produce bricks, or bolts, or horseshoes for society are compensated in proportion to the amount of those commodities which they respectively produce, so those who produce improvements in the arts for society should be compensated in proportion to the amount of improvement they produce.

In the fulfilment of their functions the directors have power to direct the labors of all wage earners during working hours, to readjust the character of their employment as much as they deem necessary within the industry, and they have complete control over the active portion of the improvement fund. They have no power of discharge, or alteration of wage except upon written charges to a civil service board; they must keep the hours of labor of all wage earners equal, or introduce inequality only with the consent of the parties concerned, and they have only an advisory power in determining how the hours of labor of the operating force, as a whole, shall be distributed through the month.

It is clear that by this expedient we have accomplished two

objects: (1) We have supplied the directors of industry with an incentive to improve the arts — the same incentive furnished by profit, viz., increased compensation conditioned upon success in improving said arts, and (2) We have altered their incentive to *increase* the hours of labor of wage earners into one to *diminish* them — thus making the interest of directors and wage earners identical instead of antagonistic; and with wages, neither director nor wage earner should have anything to do, this being fixed by law. Having thus made the interest of laborer and director of labor identical, is it possible to make that of both identical with the interest of the consumer, thus abolishing the one remaining industrial antagonism — that between buyer and seller? There is but one method of accomplishing this — that of diminishing the price of commodities as their producing time diminishes. This, of course, would benefit consumers, but would it not be a harm to producers by diminishing the wage fund? We propose to show that under any but abnormal conditions it would not; and under conditions where it would, only temporary inconvenience would result.

On first assuming the management of any industry, the governing board, after an analysis of production, should determine the producing time of all products. Call the time so determined the *initial producing time*. The initial prices should be fixed in conformity therewith. To make plain the subsequent mode of operation in a commodity producing industry, I shall describe the precise procedure for a sample industry, but to simplify the explanation shall assume that its output consists of but one commodity, and that only two classes of wage earners are engaged in its production.

Assume that the directors of all industries receive from the regulator of output on the first of each month a requisition which shall specify what commodities, and what quantity thereof, shall be produced and delivered to the distributor for the month next but one following. Thus on the 1st of May the requisition which shall determine the output for June would be received. Suppose the directors of the sample industry to receive such a report on May 1st, 19—, requiring that they deliver to the distributors by July 1st, 1,020,000 of the commodity which they produce.

Under these conditions there are six different possibilities all of which should be considered. (a) Any desired increase in the personnel can be secured through the labor exchange. (b)

It cannot. An industry in condition (a) may be called in a *supplied* condition; one in condition (b) in an *unsupplied* condition. Under each of these conditions three cases should be discussed. The output required for the month of June will be either (1) Greater than the amount which can be delivered by the operating force without increase in the hours of labor beyond the standard time (See p. 445) for June, (2) Equal to the amount, or (3) Less than the amount. Let us call an industry subject to the first condition *overstimulated,* that subject to the second *unstimulated,* and that subject to the third *understimulated*. This exhausts all possibilities, and if the industrial mechanism we propose is so constructed as to automatically adjust itself to each and all of these conditions, then it cannot be thrown out of gear, except by a social convulsion such as would wreck any system proposable. As the advance in the arts will diminish the price of commodities without diminishing nominal wages, consumption, and therefore demand, will be stimulated more and more, and the normal condition of an industry will be one of overstimulation. That is, on the introduction of the pantocratic system into any community (a)1 would be the normal condition of industry, and in the later stages (b)1. Under any conditions, unstimulated and understimulated industries would be exceptional.

Let us consider each case in order, and first let us assume the sample industry to be in the condition represented by (a) 1.

(a)1. The problems which the directors have to solve are (1) How to fill the requisition, i. e. how to supply the demand, with the least labor cost, and (2) How to adjust the price to the hours of labor and the number of workmen, so that price and hours of labor shall both diminish. Under the conditions represented by (a)1 both of these ends many be attained by a mode of procedure adaptable to all commodity producing industries, and with slight alterations to all industries. This mode of procedure is as follows:

The information needed by the directors and the governing board in guiding their policy is provided by the monthly report required of every industry. The report of the sample industry for the month of April, issued May 1st, would, among other information, include the following: (Specific data are furnished in order to make the explanation clear.)

No. of wage-earners of Class 1 receiving a nominal wage of $94.64 per month 1,000
No. of wage-earners of Class 2 receiving a nominal wage of $78.78 per month 4,000
Total commodities produced in April 1,000,000
Average duration of a day's labor .... 6 hours, 4 minutes
Total time spent in producing 1,000,000 commodities, 47,320,000 minutes
Producing time for April .... 47.32 minutes

The report for March 1st would contain the following:

Producing time for February .... 47.872 minutes

From this information can be calculated, in the first place, the decrease in producing time for two months: 47.872 − 47.32 = .552 minutes. One assumption, and a sufficiently safe one, is now necessary to adjust the industry to the task required in June, and we shall see later that if the assumption proves erroneous, the system is not disturbed (p. 455). It is assumed that the average decrease in the producing time between May 1st and July 1st will be equal to that between March 1st and May 1st. That is, it is assumed that the producing time will diminish as much in one month as in another closely contiguous thereto. If this assumption be sound, the 5,000 wage earners who produced 1,000,000 commodities in April in 47,320,000 minutes, will in June, if they work the same length of time, produce 1,011,800 commodities. Now, if they should work the same length of time in June as in April, the whole gain resulting from the decreased producing time would go to the consumer. If, on the other hand, they worked only just long enough to produce the 1,000,000 commodities which they produced in April, the whole gain would go to the producer. How then shall we divide the advantage derived from improvement in the arts between producer and consumer? This is accomplished by a device which I shall call the *industrial coefficient*. Normally it would be fractional. The best value for the industrial coefficient cannot be predicted *apriori*. Experience alone can determine it, and it probably should be changed from time to time. Let us assume that in May, 19—, it is $\frac{1}{4}$. If now we multiply the assumed gain in producing time by this fraction we shall obtain the product .138 and this number, instead of .552, will be used to determine the number of commodities to be produced by the 5,000 workmen in June. That is, they will be required to labor such time as will suffice to produce 1,002,920 commodities. Call this the *standard number* of commodities for June. It is obtained by multiplying the assumed gain in producing time by the industrial coefficient, subtracting the product so obtained from the producing time for April, and dividing the remainder into the time required to produce the April output.

Thus in June the number of minutes labor required of each wage earner will be about 9,381, which is equivalent to six hours, one minute per day, a decrease since April of three minutes per day in hours of labor. This is called the *standard time* for June in the sample industry; that is, the standard time is the number of minutes per day or per month required to produce the standard number of commodities. But 1,020,-000 commodities were called for, and this only accounts for 1,002,920. Hence, 17,080 commodities must be produced by other laborers. The number of laborers required for this purpose, assuming for simplicity that none were added May 1st, can be discovered by the proportion:

$$1,002,920 : 5,000 :: 17,080 : X$$

X in this case is 85. The kind of workmen to be secured must be determined in each case by the directors, since they know what kind are required, but they will probably be of the same kind and in the same relative proportion as those already employed, viz., one of class (1) to every four of class (2). That is, of the 85 new men, 17 will be of class (1) and 68 of class (2). One month will then be available to obtain the new men through the labor exchange. It may happen that some of the wage earners in the sample industry will, in the meantime, withdraw to other industries, but by having a month's leeway all these inter-industrial adjustments should take place with the minimum disturbance of industry, all men reporting for work at their new places on the first of the month, and not leaving their old until the last of the month, unless they require time to traverse the distance from their old to their new place of employment. Of course, inter-industrial exchanges of wage earners could take place at other times, but industry would suffer least disturbance by having the principal change come at definite periods. Thus a means is provided for absorbing new wage earners into an industry who will enter it under the same favorable conditions of wages and hours as those already there; at the same time insuring that the demand shall be supplied.

The mode of making the *producer* gain by a decrease in the producing time is now obvious. Next let us see how the *con-*

sumer is to gain by it. How shall the price be adjusted to give him his share in the industrial advance?

It should be the function of the governing board to fix prices. These, of course, will depend upon the total expense, and this will be the sum of the expenses attributable to the four funds (a), (b), (c), (d); that attributable to funds (b) and (c) evidently being very slight compared to that for funds (a) and (d). The price for June need not be fixed until July 1st, by which time the following information will be available:

Expense per commodity for June attributable to fund (a).. 19.75 cents
Expense per commodity for June attributable to fund (b).. 00.70 cents
Expense per commodity for June attributable to fund (c).. 00.30 cents

Sum.. 20.75 cents

To this must be added the main expense — that attributable to the wages fund:

No. of wage-earners of Class (1) — 1,017 at a wage of $94.64 per month.................................... $ 96,248.88
No. of wage-earners of Class (2) — 4,068 at a wage of $78.78 per month.................................... 320,477.04
Compensation of Directors (assumed 4 per cent of compensation of wage-earners)............................ 16,669.04

Sum $433,394.96

Dividing this total wages fund by 1,020,000, the number of commodities produced in June, the quotient is 42.50 cents per commodity. The total expense is then $42.50 + 20.75 = 63.25$ cents. This is the price at which the whole 1,020,000 commodities are delivered to the distributor at the works. The price to the consumer is this sum, plus the cost of distribution calculated in the same manner.

The expense in April would appear in the report of May 1st. The expense per commodity attributable to fund (a) would normally be greater than for June, because this fund goes for services and supplies, and these are constantly cheapening through the same process as that by which the commodity of the sample industry cheapens. Thus, the fall in the price of commodities produced by any industry will be a function, not alone of the decrease in the producing time in that industry, but in all industries from which it draws its supplies of raw material, machinery, etc., or whose services it requires in **any**

Chap. XIII] PANTOCRACY 447

capacity. The expense per commodity attributable to funds
(b) and (c) would normally also be slightly larger for April
than for June, but for simplicity we shall assume that they are
the same. The April expense per commodity then would be
something like this:

Expense per commodity attributable to fund (a).......... 20.00 cents
Expense per commodity attributable to fund (b).......... 00.70 cents
Expense per commodity attributable to fund (c).......... 00.30 cents

Sum... 21.00 cents

To this the wages fund should be added.

1,000 wage-earners at $94.64 per month.................. $ 94,640.00
4,000 wage-earners at $78.78 per month.................. 315,120.00
Compensation of Directors (4 per cent of compensation of
wage-earners) 16,390.40

Sum $426,150.40

Dividing by 1,000,000, the number of commodities, we get
42.615 cents as the expense per commodity attributable to fund
(d). Adding this to the other expenses, we have $21 + 42.615 = 63.615$ cents as the price at which the commodity is delivered
to the distributor in April. Comparing this with the price in
June, we see that it has fallen 00.365 cents in two months, a
gain to the consumer of about 00.6%. To make these same
calculations for any industry is merely a matter of bookkeeping.

All fiscal transactions between the various industrial departments, whereby the accounts of each with the others are adjusted, would be carried on between the respective governing
boards. In other words, all such transactions would be confined to the Treasury department, and with them neither the
directors nor the wage earners of any industry would be concerned. Their whole attention would be focussed on the problems of production, the resulting fiscal transfers being removed
from their consideration.

Although normally the expense per commodity, as calculated by the method explained above, will fall — in exceptional cases it will rise. In any given industry, the rise may
be due to: (1) Bad management in the industry itself, whereby the producing time increases instead of decreasing: (2)
Bad management in industries from which supplies are drawn:
or (3) The exhaustion of natural resources upon which the
given industry depends for its raw materials: that is, the usual

order of things may be reversed, and the law of diminishing returns of labor operate to increase the labor cost of commodities more effectively than the law of increasing returns can operate to diminish it. Whenever, from any of these causes, the labor cost of a commodity increases, the price, calculated as we have indicated, will rise instead of fall, and this is just what it should do to maintain the industry in a position of self-support. Besides fluctuations from the causes mentioned, slight fluctuations would perhaps occur from another cause. The expense fund (fund a) will, if the system of bookkeeping is defective, fluctuate considerably, because repairs, additions, and other sources of expense, are not uniformly distributed throughout the year; and were this not allowed for, inconvenient fluctuations in prices would result. With a scientific system of bookkeeping, however, such lack of uniformity can be equalized, and the share of the total expense properly attributable to each commodity for each month adjusted in such a manner as to avoid inconvenient fluctuations. The devices for accomplishing this are not suited to explanation here, but are sufficiently familiar to those who are concerned with the technicalities of bookkeeping.

We thus see how, under the conditions postulated, the sample industry would conduct itself on the receipt of the report of the regulator of output embodying the demand of the nation. If it continued in condition (a) 1, this same procedure would be repeated each month, the industry growing with the demand which it was called upon to supply. If it did not continue in condition (a)1, it would revert to one of the other conditions mentioned on page 443, which will be discussed in their order.

The reason why any industry the demand for whose products is sufficient, can continuously increase the benefit accruing both to consumer and producer is obvious. It is because the price can be lowered, thus benefiting the consumer, and at the same time the number of commodities to be produced so increased as to keep wages as high as before, because, though the price per commodity is less, the number of commodities sold is more. Now if the arts are advancing, every overstimulated industry while steadily lowering prices will, at the same time, shorten the hours of labor and absorb the unemployed. This reacts on all industries; increasing the consumption per capita of those already employed, and at the same time converting non-producers into producers and thus increasing their consumption per capita.

Perhaps the reader may consider that the fall in price and reduction of hours we have cited in our specific example is insignificant, but if he will make a slight calculation he can assure himself that the same rate of advance in all industries would in ten years (1) Absorb a greater army of unemployed than any nation ever had. (2) Increase the purchasing power of every dollar nearly thirty per cent. (3) Decrease the hours of labor about thirty per cent. Thus it would increase by nearly one-third the real wages of every wage earner, and if the hours of labor had originally been nine a day, they would, in the ten years, fall to about six and a quarter. Moreover there would be no army of unwilling unemployed. Such a rate of improvement, if maintained for a single generation, would make every member of the community well-to-do, and reduce the working day to about three hours. Of course, the example given is but an example, but it is doubtless an *under* rather than an *over* estimate of what the conversion of politics into a branch of technology would do for humanity.

From the example given it will be clear why no provision is made for any general advance in wages in any industry. It would be useless, since a general rise in nominal wages would not in itself raise the real wages of any one. The system proposed, however, by constantly diminishing prices while holding nominal wages constant, increases the purchasing power of the dollar and thus *continuously raises the real wages of every wage earner in the community, and this simultaneously with a decrease in his hours of labor.*

(a)2. An industry is unstimulated if the demand for its products is just that which is required to occupy the personnel already employed by it for the standard time, i. e. for the number of hours and no more which they would have been called upon to work had the industry been overstimulated. Thus in the example cited, had the sample industry been called upon to supply 1,002,920 commodities in June instead of 1,020,000, it would have been unstimulated. In this case the price and the hours of labor will fall just as in (a)1 but there will be no increase in the personnel. Otherwise all is as in (a)1.

(a)3. In overstimulated and unstimulated industries the normal fall in price of commodities is due to two main causes: (1) The decrease of expense per commodity due to fund (a) attributable to advance in related industries. (2) The decrease per commodity due to fund (d) attributable to advance in the industry itself, both resulting from increase in the productive power per capita. In understimulated industries only the first of these causes of a diminished price is operative, because the demand is insufficient to cause each operative to increase his production. Hence for understimulated industries the price should be determined as in the case of overstimulated and unstimulated ones so far as it is attributable to funds (a), (b), and (c) — but that part of the price per commodity attributable to fund (d) should remain stationary, that is, it should be precisely as in the month preceding. Thus in understimulated industries prices will not fall as rapidly as in others.

As the demand in such industries can be supplied by less than the standard labor time, the hours of labor of those engaged in the industry will diminish; their wage will also diminish, because after paying the expenses attributable to funds (a), (b), and (c), there will not be enough to pay the nominal wage. In this case all wages are diminished *pro rata.* Otherwise all is as in (a)1. It may be deemed by some critics a fault in the system that there is not some provision to prevent the decline of wages in an understimulated industry, but any such provision would be a bad — not a good feature. An increase in the price might be such a provision or it might not, but in any case it would be an incorrect policy. The proper response to make to understimulation is not increase in price, but decrease in personnel, and this would take place automatically. For every understimulated industry there would, in any normal condition of society, be many that were overstimulated, and if wages continued to fall, wage earners would — without any break in production or intermediate period of unemployment — withdraw from understimulated industries to overstimulated ones. This would be accomplished without difficulty or hitch through the labor exchange. In other words, the laborers would discharge *themselves,* not into an unemployed condition, as in the competitive system, but directly into an overstimulated industry. In fact, under all conditions, labor will tend to flow from understimulated to overstimulated industries by a never-failing law of human nature — that of self-interest. Thus any industry would adjust itself automatically to local understimulation, for the decrease in personnel would leave the available wages fund to be divided among fewer wage earners — the wages would return to their nominal value, the hours of labor to the standard, and the industry would pass into the unstimulated class.

This is the point to discuss the question of fluctuating industries, or those the demand for whose products varies with the time of the year. Under present conditions there are many such, and the periodic stimulation and slackness which results is a cause of much chaos in industry, and distress among wage earners. The system of pantocracy has peculiar advantages in dealing with industries of this class. Fluctuating industries may be divided into two classes. (1) Those whose fluctuations are foreseeable. (2) Those whose fluctuations are not. The first include almost all fluctuating industries, and it is obvious that they can be converted into non-fluctuating industries by means of the department of output regulation, which, anticipating the fluctuations, can provide against them, and requisition for every month approximately the same output as for every other in the year. This steadying is not possible for such industries as fluctuate irregularly and in a manner which cannot be anticipated, and such must adjust themselves by corresponding irregular fluctuations in personnel.

(b)1. When we turn our attention to the condition of industry represented by (b)1, an interesting situation is encountered. In the first place, no such condition could exist while any but voluntary vagrants were unemployed. In other words, if we admit that an unsupplied industry can exist, we admit that poverty can be cured; for, with the equal distribution of wealth and the vast increase of leisure and productive power per capita under pantocracy, an employed person and a person emancipated from poverty, would be synonymous. To this it may be objected that there might be many persons unemployed so lacking in skill or experience as to be unadapted to the work required in such unsupplied industries as existed, and to this objection there are two replies. (1) Only to industries requiring skilled labor would the criticism apply in any case, and more and more as the arts advance skilled labor is dispensed with in production. Machinery makes it superfluous, as the skill required to run a machine can be acquired in a few days or weeks, or at most, months, by a totally inexperienced person. Thus any but an exceptional industry could absorb even the most inexperienced laborers, so long as they were able-bodied and possessed their faculties. The average producing time, of course, would not decrease so fast with green laborers, but this difficulty would be merely temporary. It would delay, but not check, progress. (2) The system of technical education under pantocracy to be described under section (8) would insure that all men would be skilled in one or more productive arts — hence totally inexperienced and unskilled men would not be common.

Now an unsupplied industry may either (1) Lose in number of wage earners through more leaving than can be supplied, (2) Remain stationary in number of wage earners, as many being supplied as are lost, or (3) Gain in number of wage earners, but gain less than the number called for. In any case, it simply means that the wage earners called for through the labor exchange cannot be supplied, through lack of applications for the positions open. Failure to obtain the supply required, however, will not throw the industrial mechanism out of gear. The price is calculated precisely as in the case of (a)1 and the hours of labor of the short-handed operating force are extended beyond the standard point sufficiently to supply the demand. The result will be longer hours of labor, but the excess wages fund will be divided equally among the wage earners. Thus, for example, suppose the sample industry discussed under (a)1 was unable to get new laborers, but able to hold all it had. The hours of labor under the conditions named would then have been extended from six hours and four minutes per day in April to six hours and seven minutes per day in June; the wages of class (1) advancing from $94.64 per month to $96.04 per month, and of class (2) from $78.78 per month to $80.17 per month.

After absorption of the unemployed, the first industries to feel the lack of labor would be (1) Those the demand for whose products was rapidly increasing, (2) Those in which the labor was unpleasant. It is possible that one or both of these classes of industry would become so unsupplied that in spite of every advance in the arts which science could achieve, and in spite of the advance in wages incident thereto, the hours of labor might so increase as to become excessive. It is perhaps hardly worth while to speculate as to the best course to pursue in such an emergency, since by the time it could arise, experience would have taught men the best means of meeting it; but it would not be difficult to meet in any event. A set of rules adapted to each industry, specifying a progressive rise in nominal wages as the hours of labor increased, would doubtless suffice. This would act in two ways: (1) By increasing the price it would check demand, and (2) By increasing the wages it would draw more wage earners from other industries. The unwillingness of men to work long hours at unpleasant occupations would produce such a condition of undersupply therein that particular inducements would be required to tempt wage earners to enter them from pleasanter industries. A sufficiently high wage would, however, secure enough operatives to make possible abnormal subdivision of the tasks to be done. Thus in unpleasant industries the hours of labor would tend to become unusually short and the wages unusually high. This would, of course, tend to increase the prices of the desiderata produced, but such a result would not be an evil, since by no other means can unpleasant occupations be brought into a condition of self-support.

Of course, the arts will improve faster in some industries than in others. Backward industries, like unpleasant ones, in order to avoid a condition of undersupply, would be compelled to raise wages. By thus attracting a sufficient operating force they could, by dividing the tasks to be done among a greater number, maintain the working day as low as in progressive industries. Thus improvements in the arts in one industrial field would react upon all others, tending to free men from labor as well in unprogressive as in progressive industries. In this way all productive operations would automatically adjust themselves to a condition whose margin of self-support approximated a maximum.

(b)2. and (b)3. The industrial conditions represented by these two symbols will obviously be similar in every respect to those of (a) 2 and (a) 3, since as they do not need to absorb labor, difficulty in its absorption will not affect them.

Thus we have considered all six of the cases specified on page 443, and it is plain that the system proposed will automatically adjust itself to any and all of them. It provides a complete means of adjusting the supply to the demand, both of commodities and of labor, coincident with a simultaneous increase in the efficiency of production and of consumption. Incidentally, moreover, it opens the way to an important expansion in the liberty of the community — in real liberty — not in mere nominal liberty. This is rendered possible by the fact that as production is not carried on blindly — as each operating force knows precisely what it must accomplish during each month — it can adapt its hours of labor to its tastes more economically than in the present treadmill mode of procedure. Thus at the first of each month, or a few days previous, the requisition from the regulator of output specifying exactly what commodities, and what quantity thereof, are to be produced by the industry in the month next ensuing, should be posted in every plant in said industry. With it should be connected a tabulation showing the time which will be required, with the means at hand, to produce the output thus specified. Suppose, for example, it was estimated that the work could be accomplished by the force available by working six hours a day for each working day in the month, that is for 26 days. Each man then knows exactly what the task required of his plant is — viz., to deliver to the distributors, commodities of the kind and quality specified in the requisition of the department of output regulation, of the quality required by the bureau of inspection. He knows also, very closely, the time which will be required to perform the task. It will require of each man $6 \times 26 = 156$ hours of work during the month. Now it makes no difference to the consumer of commodities under what conditions they are produced, so long as they are of the quality required, and this is insured by the bureau of inspection. Hence the ends of utility will best be subserved by permitting the producers, as a body, to fix for themselves, by a majority vote, the conditions which will best suit them, instead of having these conditions irrevocably fixed for them, as at present. The 156 hours work per man required during the month can obviously be distributed in a great many ways. For example the required work can be accomplished:

(1) By working 6 hours per day for 26 days
(2) "   "   6   "   30 minutes per day for 24 days
(3) "   "   7   "   5   "   "   "   "   22 "
(4) "   "   7   "   48   "   "   "   "   20 "
(5) "   "   8   "   40   "   "   "   "   18 "
(6) "   "   9   "   45   "   "   "   "   16 "

At the beginning of each month then the entire personnel could decide by vote which of the various modes of distribution of labor was to be adopted for the month next ensuing, the mode receiving the greatest number of votes being adopted. In this manner producers could determine to suit themselves the way in which they would distribute their labor with the same liberty — in fact with much greater liberty — than in the case of small farmers, blacksmiths, or merchants, who are not employees at all. They could, if they pleased, by working long hours each day, give themselves a vacation of a week, or even two weeks, at the end of each month in which to employ themselves in adding to the output of the nation's happiness which, as it is the primary purpose of a nation, is their first duty to society. On the other hand, they might prefer shorter hours each day and no vacation, or they might prefer some intermediate mode of distributing their time and labor. Whatever the majority preferred they could determine to suit themselves without prejudice to the consumer. It might even be so arranged that they could, if they pleased to so predetermine, work overtime during some months, anticipating the requisition of the months ensuing, so as to have a long vacation at times of the year in which they could most enjoy themselves, but in what degree such anticipation would be allowable experience alone could determine. Some limits would certainly have to be placed upon it, since otherwise difficulties might be met in adjusting production to consumption — a vital object of the pantocratic system.

Of course it would not be possible for each man to choose for himself the time in which he would perform his labor, since the successful operation of a great plant requires a systematic and simultaneous co-operation between laborers, which could not be achieved if each man selected his own time for working; but a definite plan of work, predetermined by a majority vote, would involve no such difficulty as this.

Before going further two objections should be discussed, since they may enter the reader's mind and cause unnecessary misgivings. These are:

(1) The time assumed as that required to produce the monthly output called for by the regulator of output may be a miscalculation, resulting in inadjustment of supply to demand.

(2) Leaving the control of their hours of labor so largely in the hands of the wage earners might result in considerable periods in which the machinery of production was idle, which is undesirable.

The first objection is easily answered. Every industry should keep in stock a surplus of every commodity they produce, sufficiently large to eliminate the danger of a short supply. Now if the time calculated as that required to produce the output is incorrect, it will be either too long or too short. If it is too long, then the residuum is simply added to the hours of leisure of the wage earners — the producer gains and the consumer does not lose. If it is too short the supply is made up from the surplus, and the following month extra work will have to be done to bring the surplus back to its normal level; the labor required for this, of course, not being considered in fixing the price of the commodity.

In answering the second objection, answer will incidentally be made to one which perhaps occurred to the reader on page 445, viz., how can an industry expand in men without simultaneously expanding in the machinery which they require in production. This is simple. Every industry should keep its plant considerably larger than is required for immediate needs, even at the risk of some idle machinery. In no other way is it possible to progressively absorb the surplus labor of a state whose population is increasing, nor to provide against rapid expansion in demand. The equipment of modern industry is complex, and each addition to a plant requires time to construct. The proper time for these enlargements should be decided upon by the board of improvement, as will appear later. Economy in the employment of machinery normally requires that it be operated night and day, for by this policy less machinery is required for a given rate of output than if it is allowed to remain idle all night. To work a plant night and day requires a succession of shifts, and without making elaborate explanations, it is obvious that simply by varying the length of the shifts according to the will of the majority the distribution of time spent in labor could be adapted to the taste of the majority without involving that idleness of machinery which would require an unnecessarily large plant. If, for example, the operating force should vote to so lengthen the hours of labor per day in a given month as to leave two weeks of complete freedom to each operative, this would not mean that the plant would operate for two weeks and then shut down for two weeks. It would mean that half the operating force worked the first two weeks and the other half the last two, the shift of each man being twice as long as if he worked every working day in the month. The details of assignment of duty, etc., would, of course, be left to the directors.

The founders of the American Republic in order to "establish justice, insure domestic tranquility, provide for the common defense, promote the general welfare, and secure the blessings of liberty" to themselves and their posterity, invented and put in operation a social mechanism which, since 1789, has served to guide the nation in its attempt to achieve the ends specified. This mechanism is called the Constitution. It is a purely artificial device, providing, or seeking to provide, a means whereby the people in their collective capacity may adopt such policies as appear to them most desirable. To this end it provides for a system of officials, legislative, executive, and judicial, designed to carry into effect the will of the people, and directly or indirectly selected by the people. This is the principle which sanctions all representative government and it is a sound one. It is no part of my purpose at this point to show the manner in which this purpose of the Constitution has been defeated, nor to trace in detail how by control of the machinery through which the people must express their choice of officials a small minority now determines for its own purposes the conduct and destiny of the nation. It is sufficient to remark that in accomplishing this end the dominant class of the community have simply availed themselves of that universal quality of human nature which ordains that men shall think in symbols, shall be guided by names, instead of by that for which the names are symbols. Having obtained control of the party names, the capitalistic class thereby control the party policy which, without any change of name, may be anything they choose to make it. Secure in this possession, they have at their leisure determined the policy of the nation with a view to promoting their own welfare, and having capitalized all the material sources of profit available, have proceeded to capitalize the habits of a people who, unwitting if unwilling servants of the merest symbols, are held in bondage by those shrewd enough to profit by their infirmity. However successfully this particular intent of the Constitution builders has, through defective construction, been thwarted, the fact remains that the principle they had in mind was thoroughly sound in general. No better way of selecting those who are to fulfil a particular function has been discovered than by leaving their selection to those who are interested in having that function efficiently fulfilled.

Now pantocracy provides for a class of officials (the directing class) who may be considered homologous with capitalists under the present system. We know how capitalists are selected — through inheritance — through accident — through unusual intelligence, unusual unscrupulousness, or both. Were the capitalistic system so constituted that those whose will and ability to increase the efficiency of production and consumption was the greatest tended to come into control of industry, much might be said in its favor; but this is obviously not the case. The system of conditional compensation insures that the directing class under pantocracy shall have the *will* to serve the community. How shall we insure that they shall have the *ability?* This may best be done by providing that they be selected by those whose interest it is that they have it. But it is to the interest of all classes of the community that they have it, since under pantocracy the interest of all classes is identical. Hence perhaps as convenient a manner as any of selecting the chief directors of industry would be to have them appointed by the President, as a representative of the consuming class in general, the appointment to be confirmed by a vote of the personnel of the industry to which they are to be assigned. The subordinate directors should, in general, be selected by the chief directors. The directors of any industry would probably be selected from those who had worked their way up in that industry, since they would be most likely to have the experience required to make them efficient, and the immediate self-interest of all concerned in their choice would be opposed to the selection of any but those who were efficient.

One other feature of the pantocratic system should be left to the will of the people as a whole. This is the industrial coefficient. A low value of the industrial coefficient would represent a rapid decrease in hours of labor, a slow rise of wages, and relatively great inter-industrial adjustment. A high value of the coefficient would represent a slower decrease of hours of labor, a rapid rise of wages, and less inter-industrial adjustment. Experience alone could determine what value of the coefficient best suited the tastes of the people. Hence they should determine it for themselves by the ballot. This, of course, is an element of great flexibility in the pantocratic system, and could be fixed, once a year, once every two years, or at any interval found to be desirable. In this way the advantage of improvement in the arts could be divided between producer and consumer in any ratio which the desires of the people might suggest.

The principles explained in this section are applicable to other than commodity producing industries. Indeed they may be applied to all industries. Suppose, for example, the government should take over the fire insurance business of the country, abolish profit and put in its place a system of conditional compensation, whose amount should depend upon the simultaneous shortening of hours of labor of employees and fall in premiums.

Improvements in fire prevention, economies in business methods and organization, and expansion of business would in a few years practically emancipate the employees from labor and reduce the premiums of all policy holders to a small fraction of what they are at present called upon to pay, and the same policy in life insurance would, in a less degree, benefit that branch of insurance. Similarly the system could be adapted to transportation and to agriculture, though the precise mode of application would have to be patiently worked out experimentally in each industry.

Section (6). It should never be for a moment forgotten that the deliberate object of the mechanism we are engaged in describing is the emancipation of mankind from misery by the application of science — the substitution for the present pain producing system of a pleasure producing system. One of the conditions essential to the fulfilment of this object is the development of a high efficiency of production, and upon the efforts to attain one all the forces of science should be focussed. So far the principal means we have proposed to secure that end consists in the diversion of the power of self-interest from a destructive into a constructive channel. By making the self-interest of director and wage earner identical with one another and with that of the consumer, the first step has been taken, for this means that the interest of each member of the community is identical with that of the whole community, and it is to the interest of the community that the efficiency of production be increased to the utmost. But this is only a first step. Having so ordered the system that every individual has the desire to increase the efficiency of production, we should next supply him with the means of gratifying that desire. He has the will — all that is now required is the knowledge.

Now upon what kind of knowledge is applied science founded? It is founded upon a knowledge of pure or unapplied science. And what provision does capitalism make for this foundation of all improvement in the arts? None. As usual, it leaves it to chance. It is left to such isolated, disinterested students as may, by occupying in research the scant leisure left them by the struggle for existence, formulate the uniformities of nature upon which are founded the vast network of inventions which make modern industry possible. Practically the whole of modern science, and hence of modern civilization, has been developed by a few men who had only the love of truth as an incentive. Almost always poorly equipped, and having to waste the bulk of their immeasurably valuable lives in getting a living, unaided and unrecognized by the powerful of their time, they pursued the thankless task of raising mankind from savagery.

Society, like some stupid dog, lacerating the hand which would bind its wounds, has too often sought to oppress and discourage its greatest benefactors. Galileo persecuted, Columbus betrayed and imprisoned, Copernicus ridiculed, Bentham ignored, Paine hounded and impoverished, Marx exiled, and Darwin denounced, are typical illustrations of the treatment received by those who have sought to deliver men from the bondage of their ignorance. And more illustrious cases may be cited. Socrates and Christ sought to deviate mankind into common sense so abruptly that the dogmatists of their time rewarded them with death. The conservatives of every age have been the bitterest foes of progress, and wherever dogma dominates it must always be so. The real builders of civilization — those whose pursuit is truth — cannot hope for recognition from their own generation, and must work with what chance tools opportunity may grant them. Those to whom society awards her greatest prizes are those who most injure and exploit her. To the monopolist she assigns wealth and power — to the material or moral pioneer, poverty and ridicule.

A people aware of their own interests would never tolerate such a condition as this. The knowledge upon which the emancipation of mankind depends should not be left to chance development. To promote such knowledge a *Department of Industrial Improvement* should be organized. Under it a system of extensive national research laboratories should be established in every department of science, physical, chemical and biological. They should be equipped with every appliance required for research, including skilled workers in glass, wood, metal, etc., besides instrument makers, and men skilled in every variety of laboratory manipulation. The institutions thus equipped should be put at the service of the ablest investigators in the country, drawn from the universities, technical schools, and institutions of learning. Systematic campaigns of research should be planned and carried out by an army of investigators working in concert. They should be offered such inducements that the vocation of investigator would be the most sought of any in the country, and the best minds drawn to the service. Their whole attention, undisturbed by the necessity of making a living or teaching, should be centered upon research. Each year a certain number should be taken from those nominated by the universities and technical schools — private and public — and the system should expand as the country increased in population. Division of labor should be introduced — not alone a separation of investigators into specialists, but a separation of investigators and manipulators; and the latter should outnumber the former at least four or five to one. As it is at present, the most gifted investigators are required to spend most of the little time they have in assembling and setting up apparatus. This is as wasteful in research as it would be in business if the managers of great enterprises were compelled to write their own letters, file their own papers, clean their own inkstands, and attend to the thousand details which should be attended to by those whose time is less valuable. In practically all experimentation, preparation for experiment consumes 90 per cent. of the time. By introducing the principle of the division of labor, which has done so much for the mechanical arts, the art of investigation could be proportionally improved. The time of the best investigators could be confined to thought and study, as it should be; most of the actual manipulation could be left to men of the artisan class, trained to that art, and the great institutions of research could be run night and day like factories. By this policy results could be accomplished in a fraction of the time now required, and the few men out of each generation whom nature endows with great talents could make the most of their rare ability to serve the human race. In this way results which would take a thousand years to accomplish under the present system could be accomplished in fifty. The substitution of socialized for individualized research would increase the per capita output of discoveries in the same degree as the substitution of socialized for individualized industry has increased the per capita output of commodities.

Not the least important among these institutions of research should be those devoted to the study of medicine. Disease is the most appalling enemy of organic beings. Could it be conquered the greatest single step toward solving the awful problem of pain would have been taken. No effort should be spared in this difficult field of investigation. It should not be left to such chance efforts as may be made by specialists in the intervals of practice or teaching; but disease should be made the object of organized attack. Every important variety of it should be studied by a body of specialists, equipped with the best apparatus available, and with every facility which ingenuity can devise. Those who carried on these investigations should have not a part, but the whole, of their time to devote to the subject, and all portions of the work not requiring highly trained men should be performed by assistants. These investigations should be carried on night and day, until disease, mental, moral, and physical is abolished or reduced to a minimum. Compared with a work like this, the building of railroads, the development of water-powers, and the dredging of canals, is of such slight consequence as to be negligible. He who can think otherwise has had his sense of proportion hopelessly distorted by the strange commercial ideals of the time, ideals so devoid of common sense as to constitute a distinct variety of mania.

Nor should scientific investigation be confined to those realms in which it is now customary to regard it as legitimate. It should enter the psychical and moral fields now occupied by visionaries, cranks, and madmen; fields which develop the intellectual fungi of occultism, with its spooks, its oriental orgies, its lurid mysticism, its improvised religions, and all the other paraphernalia of pseudo-science or imaginative philosophy. There is much to learn concerning these little investigated phenomena of mind, but the way to learn it is to apply the method of common sense, the method by which we have learned all we know, and in the absence of which the word *knowledge* is meaningless. Ignorance has always regarded the unfamiliar as the supernatural, but whatever basis in reality the delvers in psychical research may have for their observations, they will be best revealed by open-minded and systematic investigation. Much that is of vital interest to the happiness of mankind might be revealed by such an investigation, and should preliminary examination justify it, this would be as reasonable a field of research as any other.

Associated with the institutions of pure research should be a system of laboratories devoted to applied science. Each great industry, or division of industry, should have its own laboratories whose sole business it would be to devise and bring to perfection improvements in the arts. To these laboratories the best inventors should be given every encouragement to come. By the same system of divison of labor as that suggested for the research laboratories they should be relieved of every task which would divert them from the immediate end sought. The most successful laboratories now pursue this policy, and with the organization and equipment which the government could afford to install, the efficiency of co-operative invention could be vastly improved.

The force employed in these technical laboratories would be in communication with the masters of science in the research laboratories, on the one hand, and with the workmen and foremen engaged in the actual operation of the processes of production, on the other. Thus the pure theorist, the trained engineer, and the practical mechanic, would co-operate in every industry to develop those improvements in the arts upon which the emancipation of mankind depends; and every facility for, and incentive to, improvement should be afforded them. There would be no trade secrets, no concealed methods, because competition would be abolished and every one's interest would be the same. The operation of every great industry would be open to the inspection of all who could suggest modes of improvement therein. Specific rewards should be offered by the government for specific improvements in methods, and those arts which were backward should be thus stimulated in the highest degree. Every inventor should be given incentives of this kind. As in the case of the director class of laborers, his reward should be made proportional to his success in achieving his ends. Similarly no limits should be placed upon the time that he should devote to invention and experiment, for it is to the interest of all concerned that those men upon whom the advance of human society depends should put as much of their time as possible into efforts to that end. Their capacity for benefiting society is greater than that of other men, and that capacity should not, by society, be permitted to go to waste. Moreover no work is pleasanter and more inspiring than theirs, particularly when relieved of the drudgery of detail, the minor manipulation of experiment, and in inciting them to work with zeal and persistence, society would but increase the stimulus afforded by their natural inclinations. Governmental activity in developing the arts is but an extension of governmental activity in applying them to production. Just as the nation should support and control vast industries whose sole object is the production of commodities; so it should support and control a vast industry whose sole object is the production of improvements in the means of producing those commodities.

It is obvious, however, that a governmental system of organized and co-operating laboratories should not be a substitute for, but an addition to, such as are carried on by private individuals and institutions. Neither private nor public monopoly of knowledge is desirable, because knowledge is something which is increased by division. In the transfer of knowledge, the gain of one is not the loss of another, as in the case of wealth. No man or nation can lose knowledge by giving it to others, and no man or nation can have too much of it.

Closely affiliated with the department of industrial improvement should be a body composed of trained technologists and statisticians, which may be called the *National Board of Improvement*. Its function should be the control of the reserve portion of the improvement fund (fund b) of all industries. Before the directors of an industry could undertake any great enlargement or improvement involving a heavy drain on the improvement fund it would be necessary to obtain the approval of the board of improvement, or of a local board selected by it. This would tend to insure all industries against excessive or unwise expenditure as a result of the zeal of the director class to reduce the producing time of commodities.

The national board of improvement should be in general charge of advancing the industry of the nation. Besides controlling the expansion of manufacturing industries, it should superintend the exploration of the country by experts with a view to developing its mineral and agricultural resources in conformity with a systematic and comprehensive policy of development, with a view to the interests of posterity. The extension of railroads, the erection of irrigation works, and the improvement of navigation on scientific and maturely considered principles, should be left in its hands. In this way the haphazard, chaotic, wasteful, unrelated, unorganized and unsystematic development of private and conflicting interests would be done away with, and the resources of the country preserved for the benefit of its inhabitants, instead of being dissipated for the benefit of a few land-grabbers and capitalists. Organization should take the place of disorganization in the preparatory development of the country, as in every other branch of industry.

The organization of invention, embodying the principles of the co-operation and division of labor would produce results in the modes of improving the arts as great as it has in the mode of producing commodities. By organizing the manufacture of shoes, for example, one man to-day can turn out fifty or a hundred times the product that he could two generations ago. By similarly organizing the manufacture of improvements in the arts, those improvements will be turned out at an equally accelerated rate. When it is so plain that the emancipation of men from poverty and toil depends upon this improvement, can common sense do less than undertake the means of accomplishing it?

Section (7). As a considerable portion of the ills of life are those resulting from the anticipation of evil, means of insuring the security of the future have always been sought by prudent men and communities. One of the chief objects of the institution of property is to attain such security, and the various forms of insurance are provisions against future contingencies which operate to promote tranquillity of mind. As all human beings have a greater or less prospect of reaching old age, and outliving their capacity for systematic production, means which will secure to this period of life peaceful existence without labor are highly desirable. In a number of modern states — notably in Germany — the government has assumed the function of providing this security to laborers, and it is a function which all governments should undertake. There are various forms of old age insurance, but they are all alike in principle, and when most of the laborers in a state are employed by the state itself, the application of the system is particularly simple. It should consist in withholding from each wage-earner a certain small percentage of his monthly wage, and placing it to his credit; the fund thus accumulated to be paid back to him when incapacitated from age, or to his heirs, should he not survive so long. Such a system would insure the country against all pauperism not resulting from defective mind or body, and each man could enjoy life as it passed without fear of the future, knowing that from his own industry a fund was accumulating which would secure his old age, and of which he could avail himself without the humiliating knowledge that he was dependent upon the community. This is a subject already well understood, and requires no extended treatment here. Its relation to utility is obvious. Not less obvious is the expediency of providing in a similar manner against sickness, accident, or other calamity, and such insurance the government should provide. Whether it should be made compulsory or not may be open to debate — but the probabilities are that it should be.

Section (8). The educational system of the United States and of most, if not all, nations is local in character and varies from place to place within the nation. In all countries, not archaic in political practice, education is provided by the community, the theory being that as education is vital to the interests of the community it should be provided by the community and not left in private hands. If experience proves the education thus provided by local communities to be adequate it may perhaps be left to them, but in a thoroughly organized condition of society it is probable that a national system of education will be found preferable. It would be independent of local enterprise or local competence, and the nation would be justified in undertaking such a task, because in the absence of adequate education no nation can hope to attain the primary end of utility — a self-supporting community. To the attainment of this end, of course, any means is justifiable, and all obstacles to its attainment may justly be removed by deliberate acts of the state itself.

Very briefly I shall attempt to outline the scope of a national system of education which will embody the principles enunciated in Chapter 6, not attempting to enter into details or methods of organization, but confining attention to fundamentals.

Assuming then that every community is provided with facilities for education, school-houses, equipment, teachers, etc., adequate to its population — what essential changes in present modes of education should be introduced? They may be divided into changes of quantity and of kind.

As to quantity there are three alternatives open in the future. (1) The nation can provide less education than at present. (2) The same amount of education as at present. (3) More education than at present. I believe it safe to assert that experience has shown that nothing is to be gained by less education, and that if there is to be gain, it must be by more. If education thus far has not accomplished all that might have been hoped, it is not because there is too much of it, but too little. The fact is that the things which it is important for the members of society to know cannot be quickly acquired. Knowledge of reading, writing, and arithmetic, is not sufficient for the average man. The primary schools are essentially means of imparting the notation of knowledge — the symbols or instruments of thought. Secondary schools should be provided wherein all members of society should be taught the use of those symbols in thinking. The youth of the nation should be taught how to apply them in all cases by systematic instruction in how to apply them in the most typical and important cases. Besides this, economic tastes should be deliberately cultivated, and the amount of education of both kinds should be as great as society can afford. And society cannot afford to pursue any parsimonious policy in regard to education. Reckoned even in money cost ignorance is costly, while if its cost be reckoned in happiness it is ruinous. In the present condition of per capita wealth, every child in the country should have not less than an amount of schooling equivalent to a high-school course. This would be an expensive operation, and might require the withdrawal of some labor now expended in the development and dissipation of natural resources; but though an expensive policy it would be an economical one. Economy does not consist in spending little money — it consists in obtaining the equivalent of what money is spent — be it much or little. When by advance in the arts the per capita wealth increases there is no reason why every youth — male and female — in every civilized country, should not obtain an education superior to that provided by colleges of the present day.

In asserting that every child in modern communities should receive an amount of schooling at least equivalent to that now received in a high school course I do not mean to imply that as much time need be consumed as at present. The same amount of information and training could be obtained with far less consumption of time. There is no reasonable excuse for keeping children in school a specified number of hours each day, independent of what they accomplish. This tends to make dullards of them by encouraging a drowsy, indifferent, diffused, condition of mind, inconsistent with that concentration which is essential to vigorous thought. Hence even if successful in mere acquisition of information the finished product of this system too often becomes

"The bookful blockhead ignorantly read,
With loads of learned lumber in his head."

The same principle applicable to industry is applicable to education. Self-interest should be made to aid, instead of to oppose, the inculcation of knowledge. Definite tasks should be assigned each scholar each day, and when performed to the satisfaction of the teacher, he should be permitted his freedom. Perhaps a system of this kind would involve some inconveniences to the teacher, but it would cultivate quickness and concentration of mind in the scholar and provide an immediate incentive to application. As things are at present a student in any school below the college grade is compelled to dilly-dally in the school-room a certain number of hours each day whether he be the brightest or the dullest scholar there. It makes no difference what he does or does not do, he must be in school the same length of time. Hence his task becomes a bore — he drones through with it, and his capacity for mental concentration diminishes, because habits of mental diffusion are encouraged by the educational system. A premium should be put upon concentration, and none would be more available or tend more to convert study into a pleasure than to make the hours of study an inverse function of accomplishment, just as in industry, the pantocratic system makes the hours of labor an inverse function of production.

This might not be possible with the very lowest grade schools, where the perpetual presence of a teacher is necessary, but in those where written tests are possible such a system would not be difficult to devise. Suppose, for example, the first hour of each school day was devoted to written tests of the lessons assigned the day before; the understanding being that the school hours of the following day would be an inverse function of the success achieved in these examinations. The result would be that the brightest scholars would remain in school perhaps not more than two hours a day, while the duller would remain longer and receive the more exclusive attention of the teachers. This is just as it should be. The present system of holding all scholars down to, or near, the rate of advance possible to the dullest in the same number of hours of work, is nonsensical. The incentive to concentrated and alert effort by such a system would be vastly greater than that afforded by a weekly chromo, and it would lengthen the hours of play — a great desideratum with children of all ages. To read and mark so many written tests every day would perhaps be more work than could be expected of a teacher, but it would not require a teacher to do it. A corps of assistants consisting of more advanced students could divide the work between them at a trifling cost to each. The total result of such a system, modified perhaps to meet particular exigencies, would be a vast saving of time and labor, and would involve just as much or more acquisition of information and much better mental training. It is not my intention, however, to discuss pedagogical methods, and the suggestion here given is mentioned incidentally, merely as an example of the application of the pantocratic principle of utilizing self-interest as a motive power.

To specify anything about amount of education without specification as to kind can afford little useful information. No amount of education of some kinds would be of any use to men. The Chinese system of education is adequate as to quantity, but is of a useless kind, consisting principally of memorizing the works of ancient writers. It is a mere training in tradition and tends to little more than mental ossification. A system of education essential to a self-supporting modern community should consist of two kinds — *academic* and *technical*. The first everyone should have, and it is desirable that all men should have more or less of the second also.

The first function of academic education is to cultivate economic tastes, the love of the beautiful in nature and art, a taste for history, literature, and other fine arts, and the capacity to express thought and emotion in language. The second function is to supply such information as is of universal interest — the knowledge of conventional symbols involved in reading and writing, geography, history, mathematics, the elements of physics and biology and the laws of health. These two functions are recognized to-day. Their relation to utility requires no explanation. An increase in the quantity of such studies, together with the abolition of Greek and Latin in public schools, except as electives, could easily be made to bring these offices of education up to a standard sufficient for the purposes of an adequate system. The third, and not the least important, function of academic education is the study of common sense, and this might well take the place of the study of the dead languages in the high school. The study of languages, other than the vernacular, is a waste of time unless it is thorough, and it is never thorough in any school below the college grade — excepting of course in schools devoted to languages exclusively. Common sense is a subject of universal application and universal interest, and its principles should be universally known, instead of universally unknown as at present. As heretofore shown, a knowledge of common sense includes a knowledge of (1) The nature of intelligibility, including the principles of the universal symbolic mechanism of thought, in the absence of which, reasoning can not advance beyond the stage achieved by an intelligent animal. (2) The nature of truth, including the principles of logic; the modes by which valid are distinguished from invalid expectations or beliefs. (3) The nature of usefulness, including the principles of morals; the mode of distinguishing degrees in the utility of acts. This knowledge does not arise spontaneously in every mind, as some persons appear to believe. If it did, disagreement between the judgments of men would be a rare occurrence. It requires to be deliberately taught — nor is it easy to acquire. As already shown, common sense is a universal guide in common affairs, but in other affairs it is usually abandoned. To prevent this its principles should be known. Common sense may be considered a branch of technology; in truth it is its foundation, and because of this it should be included in an academic instead of confined to a technical education. The principles of logic are the foundation of pure science; the principles of morals of applied science; and without observing the principles of meaning, neither kind of science would exist at all.

Dogmas should not be taught in schools. The dogmatic infection arising from family traditions is bad enough. Hence no criterion of truth or of utility, not dependent upon the universal structure of the mind should be recognized in public instruction. Logic and utilitarianism as herein expounded are, however, founded upon the structure of mind and are independent of the previous history of *any* mind. The fitness of teaching the principles of logic in public schools would perhaps be conceded; but about the principles of morals there would be disagreement. No system of morals is taught in any public school, and yet it is clear that nothing is more important than a knowledge of the principles of morals. A system of morals should be taught in the public schools, but it should not be a dogmatic system; it should not be the system of the Baptists, or the Catholics, or the Jews, or the *laissez faire* economists, or the Mohammedans, or any other system whose criteria are dependent in any degree upon the accidents of history. The utilitarian system of morals is not a dogmatic system, but is a branch of common sense. And yet it cannot be denied that there would be widespread opposition to the teaching of this system in the public schools — not because it is dogmatic, but because it is *not* dogmatic. A little examination, however, would show the opposition to be rather verbal than real.

That the utilitarian system of morals is founded upon real and vital distinctions in experience would not be denied by any person with mental capacity enough to comprehend it. Nor would there be opposition to expressing these distinctions so long as such expression was confined to verbal symbols like "surplus of happiness," "utility," etc. But should the words "right" and "wrong" be employed, opposition would develop at once. These modes of spelling are consecrated to dogmatic purposes, and should they be given any definite meaning of universal interest, and that meaning taught in the public schools, it would give much offense. It is probable therefore that, so far as public instruction goes, these terms, for a while at least, would have to be left in their present state of equivocality and uselessness, expressing nothing of importance to mankind, and yet appearing to do so. Nevertheless the distinction which we have expressed by these opposed terms could perhaps be brought out in public instruction by changing the spelling of the words. The meanings we have expressed by the words *conscientious* and *unconscientious* might, for example, be expressed by the words *aequum* and *inaequum,* and those for *right* and *wrong* by *bonum* and *malum* respectively. Certainly it is useful for all men to clearly apprehend the vital distinctions in experience which these words are designed to express, and so long as they are clearly apprehended, the sound or spelling of the words employed to express them is of slight consequence. We might, if we pleased, employ the expressions x and *not x,* and y and *not y* for this purpose, and I should have pursued such a policy in this work, were it not that thought and the symbols of thought are so intimately related in the minds of men, that to employ a symbol of unfamiliar sound would have been equivalent to failure in achieving familiarity of sense. Perhaps by some such device as suggested a complete code of common sense could be taught in public schools. The methods employed should be identical with those used in teaching mathematics. The principles and rules should first be explained. Examples, using abstract symbols should then be worked out by the student to familiarize him with the abstract application of the principles, and lastly examples of concrete application, particularly political application, should be worked out, to familiarize him with the concrete application. This is precisely the method employed in teaching algebra, which is a special branch of logic, and were a demand created, graded text books of common sense would be written through which the theory and practice of common sense could be made familiar to every person of competent understanding.

A people so trained would be capable of self-government in a degree unknown at the present time. They would be dogma and demagogue proof. They could not be led like sheep to the sacrifice, betrayed by their own ignorance into the hands of selfish tyrants or unselfish fools. They could no longer be deceived by the mere sound of words, whether used by the dishonest demagogue, deliberately meaningless, or the political mystic — *well* meaning but *un*meaning. With common sense once thoroughly mastered by a whole people the road to happiness would be very easy. It is ignorance of common sense which has held, and still holds, the world in bondage. While this ignorance persists it cannot be free, for it cannot adapt its means to its ends.

Moreover an educated populace would not easily lose its equilibrium. Appeals to its passions and prejudices would have slight chance of success, and in such a society the occupation of the agitator would be gone. Mob-rule is, if anything, more intolerable than autocratic rule, and it is a danger from which capitalism is never free. The only way to abolish the possibility of mob-rule is to abolish the materials out of which mobs are made, and the universality of education and of opportunity under pantocracy would accomplish precisely such a result. Men are what their inheritance and education make them; and if there are classes in the community who are, or may become, a menace to the stability of organized government, it is because the prevailing social system sets in operation causes which produce them. Repression cannot forever free us from the danger of anarchy, but the abolition of ignorance and poverty can.

Of technical education little need be said, except that the nation should provide trade schools and schools of technology wherein the practice of the industrial arts should be taught. All men could not become thoroughly trained engineers, but all could become proficient in one or more trades and fit to play their part efficiently in the industrial mechanism. Certificates from the technical schools should be accepted as guarantees of competence by the various industrial departments of government, and the kind of position a man inexperienced in actual production would be fitted to apply for, would depend upon the kind and amount of technical education he was able and willing to secure. The more universal and thorough technical education, the greater the number of skilled mechanics and inventors per thousand of the population would be developed, and the greater the number of such, the more rapidly would the arts improve under their direction. The technical schools would thus be feeders, not alone of the commodity producing industries, but of the invention producing industry, and would augment the efficiency of both. Incidentally the widespread study of science required in technical education would develop the most economical of tastes — the love of truth — of which modern science is the product. Next to the love of usefulness this is the loftiest and most satisfying of passions, and its gratification reacts beneficently upon the whole community. The encouragement of such an intellectual passion by the organization of research and invention, together with the diffusion of scientific education by an organized system of technical schools, would develop a nation of investigators and technologists whose knowledge and control of the forces of nature would rapidly emancipate the world. We have the same reason for expecting such a result to follow the adoption of pantocracy as we have, in general, for expecting effect to follow cause.

Some of the suggestions made in this section are doubtless too radical to be taken seriously at the present time, but as I am concerned neither with radicalism nor conservatism, but with common sense, I give them for what they are worth. At the present day the suggestion that all human beings should be taught the difference between right and wrong, for example, may sound radical, but in the future it will probably appear conservative.

Having thus described in outline the system of pantocracy, let us now, following the same course as in Chapter 11, examine the presumable effect of such a system upon each of the elements of happiness; at the same time comparing them with the effects of the competitive system. In thus testing the mechanism of pantocracy it should be remarked that to compare it with a perfect mechanism — one which admitted of no criticism, theoretical or practical, would be idle. I do not claim that the mechanism of pantocracy is defectless, but I do claim that it is less defective than any of its alternatives. To compare it with its antithesis, the competitive system, will sufficiently indicate its status as compared with the related systems which we have discussed.

First: How does pantocracy compare with competition in its effects upon the first element of happiness — the quality of the sentient agent? In Chapter 11 we have shown that competition, if its ideals are realized, tends, through inheritance, to deteriorate the human breed by means of the survival of the incompetent, and that its principal educative tendency is toward the development of craft, dishonesty, and general egotism.

In contrast to these, what effects would pantocracy presumably produce? Pantocracy claims to be a means of curing poverty — at any rate it will either cure it or it will not. Should it fail as completely as competition to cure it — an absurd supposition — race deterioration would go on as under competition, but it would not be accelerated. On the other hand, should it succeed in curing poverty it would thereby suspend the operation of the law of the survival of the incompetent by bringing competent and incompetent into the prosperous, educated, slow breeding, class; i. e., it would cause the prudential restraint upon propagation to operate upon all natural classes of the population instead of upon the naturally competent alone. This would open the way to a practical means of improving the human breed by some such method as that proposed by Galton on page 206. It would be premature to discuss at this point the possible modes of stimulating artificial selection among human beings as a means of improving the breed. To cure poverty is to suspend the Law of Malthus, and it cannot be suspended without curing poverty. Moreover until that law is suspended, no efficient mode of improving the human breed can be suggested; but once the indefinite increase of population can be controlled, the most potent of all instruments for increasing the happiness of the world is placed within reach of humanity — the possibility of improving the sentient agent itself — an agent at present wretchedly adapted to its end — for man is not only weak, stupid, and egotistic, but he is thousands of times more sensitive to pain than to pleasure — all of which is precisely the reverse of what an efficient happiness producing mechanism should be. Pantocracy offers the opportunity of changing such conditions, and of conferring upon posterity the unequalled blessing of an increasing superiority of parentage — a heritage greater than wealth or power — or even knowledge. Such would be the effect of pantocracy upon the factor of inheritance.

As to education it would but extend and emphasize the socialistic practice of public education already so well begun. Much money is now expended by the state in education, but not nearly enough. Realizing that the development of the human mind and character is indefinitely more important than the development of the natural resources of a country, particularly at this stage of human progress, pantocracy would, by the necessary taxation, deliberately divert money, that is labor, which under capitalism is employed in development of the latter kind, to development of the former kind.

Second: Under pantocracy the factor of adjustability during production ought to be higher than under competition. It is true the work would be more intensive — while the men worked they would work faster — but it would not be the hopeless treadmill work of the present system. There would be an incentive to it — it would be like an interesting game, for the duration of labor would be an inverse function of the speed of work. There would probably be no dawdling, but this would be a small loss, even assuming dawdling to be a source of pleasure, since the less dawdling the more play — the more hours of unhampered consumption. Moreover there would be hope in work under pantocracy; not the kind of hope which partakes little of expectation, but expectant hope, since each year, each month even, would see the conditions of industry improve — there would be no fear of discharge, no insecurity of employment to dread — each year would see an increase in the wages of the workmen, depending directly upon the rate of improvement in the arts and upon their own capacity to rise. Every wage-earner would have opportunity to reach the director class, independent of his social connections, since the more capable he showed himself, the more would it be to the interest of appointing and confirming power alike, to elevate him to a position of responsibility. Thus hope would replace despondency, and all men, whether of exceptional talents or not, could anticipate secure, peaceful and continually improving, conditions of employment. Moreover congenialty of employment would in most cases be assured through the use of preference numbers in assigning positions through the labor exchange; and in those industries in which the work was inevitably uncongenial, there would be compensation in increased wages. Thus under pantocracy, wage-earners would have something better to look forward to during their work than sleeping well at night. They would have something to live for, and they would work willingly, knowing that the more willingly and efficiently they worked the more would life be worth living, for themselves and for others; whereas under the chaos of competition, rapid and efficient labor leads to no shortening of hours, and merely hastens the inevitable day of overproduction and crisis, when, as a penalty of work only too well done, the laborer finds himself out of employment and reduced to want. No wonder the labor organizations under the unadjusted conditions of supply and demand prevalent under competition sometimes seek to limit production. It is simply a question of self-defense — a means of postponing the ever impending industrial crisis inseparable from the production-madness of capitalism.

Adjustability during consumption is likewise promoted by pantocracy. Under competition the desire for wealth can be gratified by only a small proportion of the population; with the great majority it must remain ungratified; and the conditions of its attainment under that system are such that many, if not most, of those who attain it are no better satisfied than those who remain poor. Thus the only useful purpose of wealth is defeated in both cases. Pantocracy, however, solves the problem by making happiness independent of wealth, or rather of any quantity of wealth greater than is accessible to everyone in the community, not defective in faculty. It provides that any great accumulation of wealth is impossible, but it insures happiness without such accumulation. Under no possible system can everyone in a community be wealthy, but under a commonsense system all can be happy — and if happy they have no need of wealth. By bringing all able adult males into the working class, and then, by the substitution of machinery for men, converting the working class into a leisure class, society is completely emancipated; and as independence and happiness is to be had without wealth, money-lust and its attendant ills will· disappear. The desires of the people will be such as may be fulfilled under the conditions by which they find themselves surrounded. Success under competition means the accumulation of wealth, which is, as we have pointed out, no more than the acquisition of means by which one set of men are enabled to avail themselves of the labor of another set. Under competition, in other words, the success of one man is at the cost of the failure of other men, and the greater the success of one, the greater the failure of others — this is the *essence of competition*. Under pantocracy, on the other hand, things are so devised that the only means by which an individual can attain success is by benefiting society — hence the success of one means the success of all, and the greater the success of one, the greater the success of all — this is the *essence of pantocracy*. There is just as much room at the top under pantocracy as under competition, but as most men cannot reach the top, means must be provided for being happy even at the bottom if the ends of utility are to be met, and these means pantocracy seeks by practical and definite devices to provide.

The nervous strain and anxiety inseparable from life under the uncertainty of the competitive system would, under pantocracy, be replaced by a justified tranquility of mind due to ample insurance against sickness, old age, or other source of incapacity in an institution of practically perfect security —, the government itself. Moreover the danger to health involved in long hours, in unsanitary places of occupation, in the congestion and vice inseparable from great manufacturing centres under competition, in the ignorance and carelessness of the submerged and spawning millions which are the normal products of capitalism would, under pantocracy, disappear with the causes which produce them. The labors of the national medical laboratories, established for the sole purpose of diminishing and finally abolishing disease, would augment the efficacy of all these improved conditions, and in the end, the co-operative efforts of science would do away with ill health, as with all the other ills to which mortality is subject.

Third: As to the effect of pantocracy on natural resources, we shall, as with competition, postpone specific consideration of the subject until we have examined the effect of our system upon the efficiency of consumption, and quantity of population.

Fourth: Comparison of the effect of competition with that of pantocracy in promoting the use of machinery in the arts is of particular importance in our inquiry. This is deemed by its advocates the strongest point in the system of capitalistic competition, its strength arising from the stimulus afforded capitalists by the promise of profit to improve the arts and save the labor of men, thus providing the means of saving the expenditure required for their wages. This undoubted advantage, however, we discovered to be offset by certain disadvantages. (1) The same stimulus which induces improvement in the arts of production, induces improvement in the arts of adulteration, substitution and misrepresentation. (2) The practice of throwing men out of employment through the introduction of machinery, leaving them without employment for varying periods, and re-employing them under conditions no more advantageous as to hours of labor than before, prevents the improvement in the economy of consumption which ought to accompany improvement in the economy of production, besides leading to overproduction, crises, and chaos. Pantocracy, on the other hand, retains all the advantages of competition, replacing the effective stimulus of profit by the no less effective stimulus of conditional compensation, at the same time eliminating its disadvantages by taking away temptation to adulteration, substitution, and misrepresentation, and utilizing machinery, not to deprive men of employment, but to save them labor, not to discharge them into a condition of non-production, but to permit them to discharge themselves from understimulated into overstimulated industries whenever the activities of industry require it, at the same time providing a channel whereby the change may be made quickly, easily, and conformably to the taste of the producer. Under capitalism a decrease in the operating force of an industry where a decrease is called for, is accomplished by the wretchedly uneconomic policy of forcing one set of workmen into a non-producing and underconsuming condition and throwing all the labor upon the remainder. Instead of this foolish policy, pantocracy divides the labor among all the workmen and permits the resulting decrease of wages to cause the surplus labor power to flow spontaneously to industries where an increase of operating force is called for. Moreover by fixed and uniform rules the hours of labor are reduced as the reduction in the producing time of commodities permits, and by the device embodied in the industrial coefficient the price of commodities is lowered without the discharge of a single wage-earner; producer and consumer thus sharing immediately in the benefit arising from improvement in the arts — and as the industrial coefficient, which determines in what ratio they shall share in said benefit, is fixed by the people themselves, no cause of complaint can arise from this source. Hence economy of consumption increases simultaneously with economy of production, and as demand and supply are adjusted by the department of output regulation, overproduction, or underconsumption, and consequently crises, cannot occur.

If it be objected that conditional compensation can never be so effective a stimulus as profit, since profit is so much greater in amount, we may reply that the degree of stimulus does not depend upon *absolute,* but upon *relative* increase of compensation. To a director whose salary is $5,000 per year, an increase of $1,000 a year for every per cent by which the average producing time of commodities is reduced, is as effective as an increase in dividends of $1,000,000 a year would be to a capitalist whose dividends were already $5,000,000. These enormous profits are rare; they practically always go to men who have little or nothing to do with the actual work of production, or even of organization; and they are generally the reward of ingenious or dishonest speculation rather than of any improvement in the arts. To permit these vast sums to be withdrawn from the compensation of the wage earners would defeat the ends of justice. No such withdrawals are required, and the profits which Mill and other economists have had in mind as effective stimulants are of no such dimensions. It is probable that conditional compensation, amounting in all to not more than one per cent on the capital invested in an industry, would provide more stimulus to improvement in the arts than the present profits — varying from nothing or less than nothing to three hundred per cent on the investment. There is much discussion as to what a "fair rate" of profit is — a fair rate according to the dogmatic standard is, of course, a customary rate. The doctrine of utility enables us to comprehend this matter more clearly. The lowest rate of conditional compensation which will keenly stimulate directors to reduce the producing time of commodities by substituting machinery for men is a fair rate — any lower rate is unfair because it will sensibly diminish the rate of improvement in the arts which society has a right to expect — any higher rate is unfair because it will produce inequality of distribution in wealth without any compensating advantage.

Besides the stimulus to improvement in the arts and organization of industry provided by conditional compensation, pantocracy increases many times the efficiency of the means of accomplishing such improvements by the organization of invention, and technical education. Thus the one advantage of competition over socialism (and that a temporary one) is by pantocracy, adopted, augmented, purified from its accompanying disadvantages, and made permanent, by the application of the ordinary methods of science in technology.

One of the greatest gains in the mechanism of production which would be accomplished by the conversion of all socialized industries into public monopolies would be the co-ordination of effort effected. The lack of such co-ordination is the cause of the vast waste of labor under competition. The partial organization of industry under private monopoly has done something toward abolishing this source of productive inefficiency. The complete organization of industry under public monopoly would do very much more. The present work of the world could thus be accomplished in less than half the time now required, and under a pantocratic system this saving of labor could be reflected directly in a corresponding shortening of the working day. To appreciate the possibilities from this source of improvement in the machinery of production, the twenty-second chapter of Edward Bellamy's "Looking Backward" should be read.

Fifth: By its effect upon the interests of all classes of laborers, pantocracy would not only make more effective the handling of the methods of production, but it would solve the labor problem; for the interests of the laborer and of the director of labor would be identical. The only way in which the directors could acquire additional compensation would be to shorten the hours of labor, while leaving nominal wages stationary; and to shorten the hours of labor means, by the principle we have enunciated, to lower the price of commodities; this taking place in all industries means raising the real wages of every one in the community. Hence the interests of director, wage-earner, and consumer being identical, the cause which has given rise to the labor problem would no longer exist. Lock-outs could not occur, for it would be in no one's power to discharge wage-earners without charges of wilful incompetence. Strikes would not occur, for against whom would an operating force strike? They would have to strike against a nation the industrial relations of which were in every part identical — they could not strike for lower hours, for they already work the minimum necessary to supply the demand — nor for higher wages, since these are fixed by law according to definite principles, and not by the caprice of an employer. The general rate of wages of an industry would be raised only as that industry became undersupplied — hence dissatisfaction with the wages in a given industry would automatically raise the wages therein, since the wage earners would prefer other industries, and thus induce a condition of undersupply. The transactions of all industries would be a matter of public record, there would be no secrecy as at present, there would be no profits eating up the wages of labor, and the principles governing the relation of wage earners to their employer — the nation — would be the same in all industries. Under such circumstances the unanimous verdict of public opinion would alone prevent strikes, assuming any set of men ingenious enough to imagine a cause for them, and even should a strike occur, it would be immediately broken unless the whole nation struck against itself, since striking would be voluntary discharge, and would be treated like any other case thereof — the wage earners required would be obtained through the labor exchange.

The limitation of production would be against the interest of both director and wage earner, lowering the conditional compensation of the first, and lengthening the hours of labor of the second — this would be enough to prevent it. It would be to the interest of every man to work with zeal and enthusiasm, since the more efficiently he worked when he did work, the shorter would his hours be. For the same reason it would be to the interest of all to get the best men into places of responsibility. Similarly wage earner and director alike would be interested in handling the materials of production economically, and of minimizing the deterioration of plant, since every expense would, by raising the price of the commodity produced, tend to the understimulation of the industry and the consequent fall of wages. Thus as a means of increasing the efficiency of production through stimulus of skill and interest in the use of machinery, pantocracy is immeasurably superior to competition.

Applying now the auxiliary criterion of the adaptive principle another marked advantage is disclosed. Under capitalism, public utilities are placed in the control of persons whose interests are exactly opposed to those of the public. The great multitude are, and must always be, both producers and consumers. As producers it is to their interest to have their working day shortened, and their real wages increased. As consumers it is to their interest to have prices fall, and to obtain the best products possible for .the price paid. The interests of capitalists are exactly the reverse. It is to *their* interest to lengthen the working day of their employees and to reduce their wages — it is to *their* interest to obtain the highest prices they can from all consumers, and to give them the poorest products possible for the price paid — for by all these means their profit will be increased. Under such conditions it is to be expected that capitalists will be forever oppressing both producer and consumer, and the expectation is not disappointed, for this is precisely what they do and always will do while human nature remains what it is. A community so stupid as to make the interests of those who control the desiderata upon which it depends for its happiness diametrically opposed to its own must expect to be oppressed — it puts a premium upon oppression, and it cannot escape the consequences of the law of human nature which it has invoked. It utilizes the adaptive principle to oppose, instead of to achieve, the end of utility. After production has become thoroughly socialized, society at last perceives its mistake — it sees that vested interests and public interests are antagonistic and clumsily attempts to remedy matters — not by abolishing the antagonism directly — but by attempting to nullify the effect of the positive adaptive principle already in operation, by superimposing upon it the effect of the negative adaptive principle. It first makes it to the interest of capitalists to oppress both producer and consumer; and then threatens to punish them if they do so. This is regulated capitalism — it is the pseudo-socialism which the dominant school of politicians propose as a remedy for existing evils. On the other hand, pantocracy abolishes the primary antagonism of interest, and substitutes for it an identity, using the positive adaptive principle to attain the end of utility, thereby adapting the social mechanism to human nature instead of leaving it hopelessly unadapted, as at present.

Sixth: As to the distribution of wealth — pantocracy provides for substantial equality by doing away with the chief means provided by the capitalistic, and every other variety of competition, whereby inequality is attained. It will be noticed, however, that pantocracy does not seek absolute equality in the distribution of wealth. Successful directors, that is, directors who have been instrumental in permanently decreasing the hours of labor and increasing the real wages of a community, for example, could accumulate considerable fortunes through the conditional compensation received for their service to the community. They could not become multi-millionaires, but their fortunes might become from 10 to 100 times as great as that of the average member of the community. Besides this, pantocracy provides for higher wages for skilled and experienced workers than for unskilled and inexperienced. This perhaps may be deemed a fault in the system, and were it devoid of compensating advantages, such a departure from equality would be a fault in any system. But the equal distribution of wealth is a means — not an end, and if, as a means, it does not attain the end of utility as successfully as some other specifiable means, then it should be abandoned in favor of that other means. The proposition that wealth should be equally distributed is true as a general, but not as a universal, proposition. This is why in constructing the pantocratic mechanism, I have departed, in some degree, from means of completely equalizing wealth. It is important to efficiency of production that skilled workmen should be developed to fulfil certain productive functions. The acquisition of skill, however, requires time and trouble. Hence unless there is some incentive to do so, men will not take the trouble and time required to develop it. The higher price of skilled labor under pantocracy therefore, is simply compensation for the hours of labor — that is of life — spent in developing the skill required to make men of more service to the community; and the inequality of wage involved is required by the general, though not universal, rule that the compensation for any given quantum of labor should be proportional to its labor cost. Reasons of a similar kind justify the inequality of wealth involved in the institution of conditional compensation. By the stimulus it affords to improvement in the arts the community will gain in happiness far more than it will lose through the departure from equality involved; and this is sufficient for the utilitarian. Knowing what end he seeks, he can adapt his means to attain it, unconfounded by confusion of a proximate with an ultimate end.

Seventh: The means adopted by pantocracy of progressively increasing the indicative ratio as the arts improve have already been explained and their effect on this element of happiness is obvious. The theory of utility demands an increasing indicative ratio, and pantocracy provides definite means for supplying it. The effect of increasing the hours of leisure and at the same time increasing the real wages of all producers by the fall in the price of desiderata is to bring the whole population into the condition of an emancipated middle class, and this condition is that at which consumption at the point of maximum efficiency will occur. There would, under such circumstances, be no consumers in the zone of either under or overconsumption; each average family would be self-sufficient, and the whole population self-supporting. Once this emancipated condition is obtained, however, it is probable that the actual indicative ratio would spontaneously diminish, because for the first time men would be brought into the condition where they would have not only the taste for pleasant forms of labor, but the education and freedom from unpleasant forms necessary to gratify it. Hence art, literature, music, and science, would be pursued, not by the few, but by the many. Not by one per cent, but by ninety-nine per cent of the population. As the necessity for consuming life in systematic and unpleasant labor in the "useful arts" diminished by the substitution of machinery for men, opportunity for consuming it in pleasant labor in the fine arts and the pursuit of the humanities would increase. Thus the avocation, instead of the vocation, would occupy the principal place in the life of each individual, spontaneous would replace compulsory labor, and the inversion of the indicative ratio would indicate a gain, instead of a loss, in the economy of happiness. Such at any rate would be the presumable result of the combined industrial and educative systems involved in pantocracy.

In vivid contrast to this common sense procedure consider that of capitalism. Instead of using labor-saving devices to increase the leisure of the producer and thus emancipate mankind from labor, it seeks to make the indicative ratio a function of endurance only, and to make men work as long as they did when their labor was not nearly so productive. Even for the shortening of the working day already obtained labor has had to struggle mightily, and were it not for the activity of labor unions, men would now be working twelve and fourteen hours a day — as they still do where competition is unrestricted. Mill, in his Principles of Political Economy says: " It is questionable if all the mechanical inventions yet made have lightened the day's toil of any human being." Such a statement is not true to-day — thanks to the activity of competition suppressing agencies — but what a commentary it is on the practomania of the capitalistic age. With the vast strides in industry of the last century or two the productive power of the American laborer is to-day, on the average, probably a hundred times greater than in colonial times — and yet his working day is only a little shorter. Of course it would be unwise to reduce the working day in the same proportion as the producing time is diminished — this would prevent increase in the per capita rate of consumption — but surely when the producing time has been diminished a hundred fold the working day might be cut down at least three-quarters, and yet provide for a vast increase in the rate of consumption per capita. Had this been done in the past, the laborer of to-day would not require to work more than four hours per day at the utmost, and yet live twenty times as well as his forefathers of pre-revolutionary days. Thus does capitalism throw away the great opportunity offered by socialized production.

Eighth: In considering the effect that the adoption of a system of pantocracy would have upon the eighth element of happiness — the quantity of the population, its contrast to competition is marked. Competition insures perpetual poverty, restricts the prudential restraint upon propagation to the successful classes, and thus limits population only by starvation, deteriorating the race and wasting the resources of nature by making them support an unhappy population. The extinction of the human race would thus achieve a better object than competition.

We have made the claim that the adoption of a pantocratic system would lead to the abolition of poverty and have given reasons in support of that claim, but whether this claim is just or not, it is certainly not too much to say that if pantocracy will not cure poverty then nothing will. Poverty is simply a name for a low rate of consumption per capita. If it is to be cured at all it must be by adopting such means that (1) The production per capita per unit of time will be made to approach as near as possible to a maximum, and that (2) The wealth thus produced shall be well distributed.

If focussing all the power represented in the stimulus of enlightened self-interest, and all the knowledge and ingenuity furnished by organized scientific research and co-operative invention upon this single object cannot accomplish the result, then by what means *can* it be accomplished? Certainly not by letting everything alone. Drifting can not cure poverty. If it could, it would have done so long ago, for mankind since its first advent on the earth, has done little else than drift. If through the operation of the law of increasing returns the tendency to increase the production per capita per unit of time can be made to offset the tendency of the law of diminishing returns to decrease it, then poverty can be cured. Otherwise it cannot be cured. Now, pantocracy stimulates the operation of the law of increasing returns in a degree impossible under any other system. Its whole construction is deliberately designed to stimulate it. Hence we say if pantocracy, or some variation of it embodying the same principles, cannot cure poverty then no system can. Pantocracy is primarily a means of applying science to the cure of poverty as the most pressing and universal ill of mankind, and as Lubbock says in this connection, "we must choose between science and suffering." There is no other alternative.

But once poverty is cured — and enlightenment substituted for ignorance by the diversion of human effort from the dissipation of natural resources to the development of man, consequences of transcendent import inevitably follow. The causes which now operate to restrict propagation in the well-to-do classes will operate to restrict it in all classes, since all classes will be well-to-do — the Law of Malthus will be suspended and deterioration of the breed checked in the manner noticed under section one. The eighth element of happiness can only be controlled by increasing the efficiency of consumption, and if uncontrolled, the population will increase until it reaches a position of natural equilibrium. At this point its rate of production of misery approaches a maximum.

A pantocratic system will, of course, have the effect of diminishing the resources of nature — any policy other than the extinction of humanity must have that effect; but in the dissipation thereof, and as a result of it, happiness will be produced instead of unhappiness, as under competition. There will be something instead of less than nothing to show for the resources dissipated. Instead of utilizing the increased means of subsistence derived from improvement in the arts to increase the mere numbers of an underconsuming population, pantocracy would utilize them to increase the consumption per capita until the average member of the community was consuming at the point of maximum efficiency, or as near that point as possible. Thenceforth, increase in the population instead of being checked by starvation would be controlled by the prudence of the emancipated community itself, and maintained at such a rate as to keep the average member of the community consuming at the point of maximum efficiency. Thus the production-madness, inseparable from capitalism, which wastes alike the lives of the present generation and the substance of their posterity, would be replaced by the sanity of common sense. Labor would be recognized for what it is — a means to an end, and not an end in itself — and the end to which labor is, or ought to be, the means would be recognized no less specifically. That end is not to develop and diminish nature's resources with maximum speed, but to convert the potentiality of happiness resident in said resources into actual happiness with maximum efficiency. These two contrasted views of the object of labor represent the difference between the ideals of the commercial and of the utilitarian schools of political economy — they represent the difference between practomania and common sense.

Thus if we test pantocracy by the same criteria whereby we tested competition, viz., its effect upon each of the elements of happiness separately, we discover that the former stands every test while the latter stands none. Between them is all the difference between justice and injustice. Pantocracy is an adapted, competition an unadapted, means of attaining the end of utility, and a moment's consideration will serve to banish all surprise at this result. Both competition and pantocracy are neither more nor less than social mechanisms, to be deliberately employed by society to attain its end — viz. happiness. Competition is a mechanism which, speaking figuratively, nature employs to attain her end — adaptability to survive — an object which has no particular relation to the object of society, except that survival is a necessary element in both. Now no one possessing common sense would expect a mechanism designed to produce one specified result to be adapted incidentally to produce another one totally different from the first. No one would expect a nail making mechanism to be adapted to the manufacture of washing soda. No more would any one with common sense expect a mechanism designed to attain the end of nature to be adapted to attain the end of man — and it is not so adapted, as the tests we have applied demonstrate. Pantocracy, on the other hand, is a mechanism deliberately designed to produce that end, designed by the same methods of common sense that would be employed in designing a mechanism for the manufacture of nails or of washing soda. Hence it is only to be expected that it will be successful in meeting the very tests which have served as a guide to its construction. But while we should have reason to expect pantocracy to be a system adapted to attain the end of society — it would be a great mistake to suppose it to be the only one, though doubtless it embodies the essential elements of any successful system. There is more than one system for making sulphuric acid, though all systems require the presence of the elements essential to that acid, viz., hydrogen, oxygen, and sulphur. Other political systems differing in many details from pantocracy might be proposed, and were pantocracy once adopted the details of its operation might turn out to be quite distinct from those I have suggested or might suggest. Hence I have not attempted to specify details, except so far as was necessary to demonstrate that the system is practical and will operate in a definite manner while the properties of nature and of human nature remain what they are. There are several forms of mechanism whereby the energy latent in steam may be converted into mechanical motion, but all of them must take advantage of the properties of steam; and though several forms of mechanism may be proposed for converting the world's latent potentialities of happiness into actual happiness, all of them must take advantage of the properties of nature and of human nature in order to achieve success, and every social mechanism should be judged — just as a steam engine should be judged — strictly according to its adaptability to attain its end.

Once more let me emphasize the dilemma in which society finds itself to-day. It finds that its activities are not self-supporting; that more unhappiness than happiness is produced by humanity; that the present system is a failure while human nature retains its properties. In this situation three alternatives and only three are open. (1) Human nature may be changed. (2) The system may be changed. (3) Both may be changed. There is a prevalent school of moralists, of whom

Tolstoy is the type, who seek the first way out of the dilemma. They claim that the trouble with the present situation is that men themselves are at fault — that human nature must be altered before society can produce a surplus of happiness, and they propose to change human nature by *telling* it to change. If they are correct, the situation is indeed hopeless. The method of changing human nature they propose is not adapted to its end. Preaching will do no more in the future than it has done in the past. Human nature has not changed much during historic times, though its customs have, and if it is to be radically changed, changes will be necessary in that part of the social system which affects inheritance and education, for it is by these influences and these alone that human nature can be changed. But to adopt such changes would be to select the third way out of the dilemma, since it would be changing human nature by first changing the social system. It is obvious that it is by this route that pantocracy seeks a way out of the present unhappy situation. The reaction of the present system upon human nature results in misery. To change human nature is hopeless — at least immediately — hence our only alternative, if we would escape misery, is to change the system — and it is by a change in the social system that every advance in the past has been made. The changes from religious intolerance to religious tolerance, from slavery to free labor, from aristocracy to democracy, have all been changes in the social system which have left human nature intact, merely changing its customs. Selfishness remains the dominant characteristic of organic beings, and it cannot be ignored in man. Pantocracy recognizes this, and instead of employing the great power of self interest to defeat the end of utility, as competition does, it employs it to accomplish that end. It seeks not to destroy selfishness by telling men to be good — that would be futile, but to divert it from competitive into anti-competitive channels. What good does it do to tell men to be good and they will be happy? Does any one seriously believe that propounding this platitude will make men good? No, the proper way is to make them happy, and then they will be good. Although to abolish self-interest is impossible, to change its mode of application to the social mechanism is not. Should we attach a dozen horses to a mired vehicle, and then let each pull in the direction in which he felt inclined, we should not accomplish much, but with precisely the same power we could pull the load out of the mire by making the horses all pull in one direction. In such a situation co-operation will accomplish what competition will not, and in hauling society out of the slough in which it is gradually sinking the same methods must be employed. To produce happiness, co-operation is required — not the mere co-operation of good-will, but organized co-operation, amounting to a change in the social system. A convenient form of that organization I have already explained, and to the provisions therein for accomplishing the change desirable in human nature I need not again revert.

It is a common claim that socialism cannot succeed because it is unadapted to human nature. Such a criticism applies with greater force to competition than to socialism. It is because competition as a means to happiness is so utterly unadapted to human nature that it is, and always has been, a failure. The only reason why the failure of competition is not more generally recognized is that men, having no test by which to distinguish success from failure, cannot tell the difference between the two even when they see it. Not knowing what society is, or ought to be, endeavoring to accomplish, they, of course, are unable to tell whether it is accomplished or not. Hence they mistake mere human activity, the movement of persons and things from one place to another on the earth's surface, for success. They gauge success by the activity of industry — by the mere motion of material bodies. They are in precisely the position of one who, entering a factory of the purpose of which he is ignorant, mistakes the motion of the countershafting for the production of output. He cannot tell whether or not the factory is accomplishing its purpose, because he does not know what its purpose is. It is futile for men to attempt the guidance of public policy who are ignorant of the direction in which public policy should lead. The output of a nation in bushels of grain, tons of pig iron, or coal, or steel rails, can tell us little or nothing about a nation's success, since, though these products may be *necessary,* they are not *sufficient,* conditions of happiness. And yet it is of such products that politicians perpetually prate. In this connection the commentary of Mill upon the folly of the mercantilists, who confused money with wealth, is peculiarly appropriate. He says:

"It often happens that the universal belief of one age of mankind — a belief from which no one *was,* nor without an extraordinary effort of genius and courage, *could* at that time be free — becomes to a subsequent age so palpable an absurdity, that the only difficulty then is to imagine how such a thing can ever have appeared credible. It has so happened with the doctrine that money is synonymous with wealth. The conceit seems too preposterous to be thought of as a serious opinion. It looks like one of the crude fancies of childhood, instantly corrected by a word from any grown person. But let no one feel confident that he would have escaped the delusion if he had lived at the time when it prevailed. All the associations engendered by common life, and by the ordinary course of business, concurred in promoting it. So long as those associations were the only medium through which the subject was looked at, what we now think so gross an absurdity seemed a truism. Once questioned, indeed, it was doomed; but no one was likely to think of questioning it whose mind had not become familiar with certain modes of stating and of contemplating economical phenomena, which have only found their way into the general understanding through the influence of Adam Smith and of his expositors." [1]

Oh, ingenuous Mill — do you remember what the pot called the kettle? In this quotation, if the word "wealth" is substituted for the word "money" and the word "happiness" for the word "wealth," we shall have a commentary whose striking application to the present system is incapable of happier expression. Is it any more absurd to mistake money for wealth than to mistake wealth for happiness? Incredible as to a subsequent age it will appear, those who guide the policy of modern states make this very mistake, apparently unconscious that they are but mercantilists who have changed the form of their folly. It was not surprising that after the adoption of a system of exchange by means of money that the medium of exchange should, by the worthy predecessors of modern economists, be mistaken for something having ultimate intrinsic value, and it was perhaps inevitable that between this vulgar error and the explicit recognition of happiness as alone possessing such a quality, an intermediate delusion should be cherished — the delusion that wealth has ultimate intrinsic value. Since the laws of the evolution of human thought required this step Adam Smith did the world a service in taking it, but it is calamitous that men thus deluded should be selected to guide the policy of nations, particularly as "all the associations engendered by common life, and by the ordinary course of business" concur in rendering them as blissfully oblivious of their preposterous situation as were the mercantile theorists of theirs. To be sure, happiness is recognized to-day as an incidental desideratum, as wealth was similarly recognized previous to the publication of

[1] Political Economy, Chap. 1.

the "Wealth of Nations," but incidental recognition will not do in the one case any more than in the other. Happiness must be recognized explicitly, as a definite product of the activity of society, expressible in definite units — a product having at any given time a definite magnitude, expressible by a definite intensity into a definite time interval, and increasable only by increase of that intensity or that time interval, or both — a product requiring cultivation by organized and directed effort — effort as organized and directed as that of a shoemaker in turning out his shoes. We cannot too often insist that the only units in which the success or failure of society may be estimated are such as express quantity of happiness or unhappiness, and until we have determined the relation that wealth bears to happiness, the output of wealth can give us no more clue to the output of happiness than the weight of precious metal possessed by a state can give to its wealth. Could the people of our day and country learn this one lesson it would be worth all their other political knowledge combined, and they *will* learn it when common sense displaces common nonsense.

It is the duty, and it should be the delight, of the economists of our time to purge their science of the archaic dogmas of Adam Smith, and to found it directly upon the foundation of ethics itself — namely, utility — the only sound foundation for any applied science. In so doing they will have accomplished for economics what Copernicus accomplished for astronomy — they will have replaced the geocentric system of commercialism with the heliocentric system of utilitarianism — they will have fixed the centre around which revolves the stupendous system of human effort and human interest — not in the dead world of wealth, but in the living sun of happiness.

CHAPTER XIV

THE NEXT STEP

To any proposal for substituting an uncustomary for a customary policy in the affairs of society the first objection, of course, will proceed from the ever prevailing conservatism of mankind — that ubiquitous form of fatalism which confounds inaction with prudence through misapprehension of the nature of a use-judgment. Assuming the law of causation, it is obvious that if with any given act of a man or a nation the same natural causes are combined, the effect of the given act will always be. the same; and we may assume that if the man or the nation is careful not to alter his or its acts, then he or it may be assured that the effects thereof will, at any rate, not be worse in the future than they have been in the past. If the same natural causes are always combined with the same modes of human activity then conservatism may be caution. The difficulty is that they are not. By suspending change in their modes of activity men do not suspend change in the modes of activity of nature. The inaction of men does not involve the inaction of nature, and it must not be forgotten that human nature is a part of nature, and as subject to the law of causation as any other part. The alleged attempt of the ostrich to escape danger by hiding its head in the sand is a mental operation similar to the one we are criticizing. The ostrich apparently thinks that by suspending its own visual powers the visual powers of all creation will thereby be suspended, and similarly the conservative thinks that by suspending his own activity he will thereby suspend the activities of the rest of creation. His caution is that of the ostrich. Nature's policies are usually accelerative and, as we have seen, they are usually maleficently accelerative. Hence man can counteract such acceleration only by changing his policies to meet it. He must be radical in order to be cautious. Such caution is by the incautious conservative deemed incaution, and he consistently protests against it. If these protests prevail and radical action is postponed too long, calamity frequently follows, and this the conservative attributes to radicalism instead of to its real cause — conservatism. Thus Archbishop Whately justly remarks:

"The mass of mankind are, in the serious concerns of life, wedded to what is established and customary; and when they make rash changes, this may often be explained by the too long *postponement* of the requisite changes; which allows (as in the case of the Reformation) evils to reach an intolerable height, before any remedy is thought of. And even then, the remedy is often so violently resisted by many, as to drive others into dangerous extremes. And when this occurs, we are triumphantly told that experience shows what mischievous excesses are *caused* by once beginning to innovate. 'I told you that if once you began to repair your house, you would have to pull it all down.' 'Yes; but you told me wrong; for if I had begun sooner, the replacing of a few tiles might have sufficed. The mischief was, not in taking down the first stone, but in letting it stand too long.'"[1]

Revolutions are the result of conservatism. The English Revolution was caused by the conservatism of the House of Stuart, the American Revolution by the conservatism of the House of Hanover, and the French Revolution by the conservatism of the Bourbons. The way to avoid revolution is through radicalism; but although cautious policies are almost always radical, radical policies are not necessarily cautious. Obviously it is easy to suggest thousands of harmful radical policies. Now in the preceding chapter I have outlined a national policy, adoptable by any state which has attained a condition of civilization equivalent to that of Western Europe. So far as I am aware, only four general policies are proposed as alternatives. (1) Natural competition: (2) Artificial competition: (3) Pseudo-socialism: (4) Socialism: and the first is hardly a possible alternative in the United States at the present stage of its development. Pantocracy is more radical than any of these; that is, it departs more from prevailing policies. To the man whose judgment has no taint of fatalism, however, this will make no difference. All he will ask is: Is it or is it not, more useful than any of its alternatives? Is its end that of utility, and is it or is it not, better adapted than other suggested policies to that end? I have attempted, by noting its effect upon each of the elements of happiness, to show that it is. Were politics judged by the standards employed in science it would be difficult to doubt that the attempt had been successful; but with the

[1] Elements of Logic.

political standards at present prevailing there is a wide chasm between the establishment of a reasonable presumption and the production of conviction, since wherever dogma prevails, conviction is not a function of reasonableness but of priority, and the suspension of this law of human cerebration is not to be expected in one department of knowledge more than in another. It has beset the early stages of every science from mathematics to medicine, and politics will be no exception to these.

It must, of course, be admitted that the only presumption thus far established in favor of the policy proposed is an *apriori* one, and presumptions established *apriori* should not be depended upon when *aposteriori* evidence is obtainable. The question is then, can *aposteriori* evidence of the operation of a pantocratic system of the character desired be obtained, and if so, how? To answer this question we have but to mark the procedure followed in those arts where the method of common sense already prevails — where science has already been applied. Suppose, for example, a cautious cotton manufacturer should have submitted to his attention the design of a mechanism which promised *apriori* to be an improvement upon the prevailing method of cotton manufacturing. What would he do? Would he reject the scheme at once on the ground that it was not a customary mechanism and therefore useless? No; he might pursue such a policy if he were merely a conservative manufacturer, but not if he were a cautious one. Would he, on the other hand, immediately dismantle his whole plant and re-erect it equipped throughout with machinery identical with that called for in the design submitted to him? No; a cautious man would not pursue this policy unless the *apriori* evidence of success was overwhelming. He would do what every experienced manufacturer, whether of cotton or anything else, would do — he would try it on a small scale, approximating as closely as possible the conditions to be met on a large scale. That is, he would experiment, and from the *aposteriori* evidence thus furnished would judge of the wisdom of installing the proposed mechanism on a large scale. This simple and safe procedure is the one adopted in all branches of applied technology, and it should be adopted in politics.

In proceeding toward any given goal we must proceed by steps, but it is important that the steps should be in the direction of the goal. At any given stage of progress there is always a next step which will lead more directly in the desired direction than any other, and if common sense is taken as our guide, we may usually distinguish it. The next step in any progression is always the most important step at the moment it is to be taken, for if we make no mistake in each successive step as we are called upon to take it, we need not worry about the sum of the steps. Now we have ascertained what the goal of society ought to be — the maximum output of happiness — we have examined the several proposed routes whereby modern states, proceeding from the stage they have already attained, may seek that goal. They are: through competition, natural or artificial: through pseudo-socialism: through socialism: through pantocracy. We have submitted strong evidence to show that of these routes, competition leads away from the goal, that pseudo-socialism either leads to private monopoly, a route which everyone acknowledges leads away from the goal, or into socialism; that socialism leads toward the goal, but that pantocracy leads more directly to the goal than any of its alternatives. This much being ascertained the next step becomes clear — the *apriori* evidence here submitted should be supplemented by *aposteriori* evidence. Pantocracy should be tried on a small scale, the conditions of operation on a large scale being approximated as closely as possible. In each of the several states which have reached the stage where this step is the next one to be taken the precise mode of taking it would have to be adapted to the conditions there prevailing. I shall not attempt the discussion of these conditions in any other state than that of the United States of America, but the principles involved are of course adaptable to any other nation.

Should the United States as a nation elect to experiment with the industrial application of pantocracy on a small scale it is obvious that it could be done without any alteration of her present relations with other nations; but should she attempt to extend the system it is equally obvious that the policy of international exchange of men and of commodities could easily be such as to interfere with, if not to upset, the whole system. The industrial reorganization of the country would involve a reorganization of its relations with other countries. Now it is important for our purpose to be able to see clearly, not only how pantocracy might be tried on a small scale in the United States, but to see no less clearly how it might be indefinitely extended, should experiment justify its extension. This can only be done by first showing how the relations of this country with others can be adjusted so as to prevent interference with the objects of pantocracy; and in order to show this it will be necessary to apply the principles of utility directly to the questions of immigration and of free trade and protection — to the international exchange of men and of commodities as it applies to America.

For the sake of clearness I shall first discuss these questions as if they were questions of patriotism alone. I shall make a provisional assumption that it is right to ignore the interests of all nations except our own. Afterwards I shall show that the policies proposed are those demanded by humanitarianism as well as patriotism. And first it should be remarked that the present policy of America is inconsistent with itself as a result of the dominance of capitalism. On the theory that the interests of Americans should be protected the United States adopts a policy of protection, protecting from foreign competition all products produced here with one exception — labor. It is to the interest of the capitalist to protect all products except labor — hence it is the policy of the United States to do so. Thus results the inconsistent policy of restricted trade in commodities but free trade in labor. The product of labor must pay an importation tariff, but immigration is free or practically so. It is not to the purpose to object that protection of commodities incidentally protects the labor that produces them. This is true, but were it the purpose of those who control the trade policy of the United States to protect labor they would do so by protecting it from immigration. It is not their purpose to do it and hence it is not done. The restriction of Chinese immigration is a sop thrown to the labor element which only serves to make the inconsistency of the present policy the more glaring. Our country is to-day as completely capitalist-ridden as India is caste-ridden, or as mediæval Europe was priest-ridden.

In Chapter 6 we have asserted that the most important problems of any country are those of race, and we have given there the reasons for so asserting. Hence the most important problems before the American people to-day are the negro problem, and the immigration problem, both of them involving the future of the race. The negro problem has been forced upon the present generation in America by the ignorance and selfishness of their ancestors. The country drifted into it, and consistently with the time honored theory of *laissez faire,* it is invited by enlightened publicists and politicians to drift out of it again. It is easier for a ship to drift on than off a lee shore, though *laissez faire* navigators may claim that it will not always be so. Perhaps they are right — at any rate they should receive the support of their doctrinal brethren, the economists. When it becomes as easy to drift to windward as it is to drift to leeward, then we shall drift out of the negro problem, but probably not before. It is an evil that will not "cure itself." I shall not attempt the discussion of the negro problem in this work. It requires separate treatment and should the occasion arise I may return to it. It may be remarked, however, that the policy of drift which permitted the immigration of the negro is practically the same to-day as it always has been. Whether it will give us other race problems is a question I shall not discuss, but if it does not it will not be to the credit of the nation's foresight. Men are taught through dear bought experience, but apparently dear bought experience cannot teach nations. It is bad enough to have to pass through the experience, but it is worse to learn nothing from it. Let us examine the immigration problem as a problem in simple common sense and see if a definite policy is not suggested by it.

The question of immigration, as it applies to the United States, may most conveniently be discussed in two parts. (1) The effect of immigration upon the quality of the population of America. (2) The effect of immigration upon its quantity.

And first as to quality. There are two current delusions which must be removed before this question can be intelligently understood. The first is that a race can be improved by education. The second is that a blend of several races produces a race superior to any of the elements of the blend. It has already been shown in Chapter 6 that as acquired characters are not inheritable the racial characteristics of immigrants cannot be changed either for better or worse by education. Hence I need not further consider the first delusion at this point. As to the second delusion — for it is a delusion — it apparently arises from the well-known fact that the repeated breeding together of consanguineous individuals frequently — though not always — results in deterioration, usually physical and sometimes mental. Opposed to this close-breeding or in-breeding, as it is called, is cross-breeding, which results from the mating of individuals far removed from consanguinity. Cross-breeding of distinct varieties or races gives rise to mongrels or hybrids, and among breeders periodic cross-breeding is often employed to prevent local deterioration from in-breeding. Now if the American race were in any danger of deterioration from in-breeding the immigration of distinct races would be a good thing, but it is in no such danger. Deterioration from in-breeding, whether among animals or men is a local phenomenon — it only occurs in small communities in which for many generations little or no intermarriage with outside communities has taken place. There are quite a number of such communities in New England where everyone is a cousin to everyone else, and in some of them there are signs of sporadic deterioration. Where there is no circulation of the population, in-breeding is a threatening evil, but with the improved facilities of communication of our day stagnant communities, already rare, will become rarer, and were we as secure from other sources of race deterioration as we are from this one we should have no cause for complaint. If the United States with a population of 80,000,000 requires immigration from other continents to save it from the ills of in-breeding, then the world requires immigration from other planets to save it from the same ills.

But besides being a means of preventing deterioration from in-breeding, cross-breeding is utilized by breeders to improve races, and those who do not know just how it is utilized to that end may have acquired and spread the prevailing delusion that to blend races necessarily improves them. Those familiar with the facts, of course, know better. What cross-breeding does accomplish is an increase of variability. Now the more variable a species the more effectively can artificial selection be employed in improving it; hence crossing is employed by breeders to obtain the variations from which to select. If they obtain the variations and then fail to make any selection they have accomplished nothing whatever. In other words, cross-breeding can only aid in the improvement of a race when it is combined with selection — otherwise it is useless. Hence the blending of races caused by immigration may produce a more variable race, but it affords no more presumption of improvement than of deterioration, because the only real instrument of race improvement — selection — is not employed. If, as many quick judging authors of our day assume, cross-bred or mongrel races are the best — then half breeds should always be superior to either of the races from which they spring. If this be so excellent results should be obtained from crossing Chinese, Negroes and Malays with the Caucasian race, though observation cannot be said to confirm such a claim.

The real facts about the cross-breeding of different races, so far as they relate to the immigration problem, may be summarized thus: If two races of men or other organisms — a superior race A and an inferior race B of practically equal numbers are blended without selection the resulting race will probably, though not certainly, be intermediate between them in characteristics. That a race superior to A or inferior to B *might* be obtained by this means cannot be denied, since we are ignorant of the causes of variation; but so far as I am aware no specific case of either kind has been recorded. The chances against it in any given case are very great. Whether the race resulting from the cross of A and B would, as a race, be just half way between them, would depend upon whether the two parent races were equally pre-potent. Unless we have information about the relative pre-potence of the races, that is, their relative power to transmit their characteristics, the assumption that the mongrel race will be half way between the parent races will be more probable than any other equally specific assumption, but that it will be superior to the inferior race and inferior to the superior race we may safely assume. Of course, if the races are unequal in number the mongrel race will tend to approximate more closely in characteristics to the race which is most numerous. The effect of crossing two races is well illustrated in the breeding of mulattoes. As a race, mulattoes are intermediate in color between the parent races, the white and the black. The more white blood they have in them the whiter they are, the more black blood the blacker they are, as a rule. It would have been very surprising had the crossing of a white and a black race produced a mongrel race blacker than the black race or whiter than the white one. Now what is true of color is, in general, true of all other characteristics of organisms, physical and mental — they will tend, on the average, to be intermediate between those of the parents. This is not true of man alone, but of all organisms, and is thoroughly recognized by biologists. As regards any given characteristic or aggregate of characteristics in respect to which two races differ, one race must be the superior of the other, since otherwise they would not differ. Now the chance of getting a race superior to the superior race from crossing two such races is the same as getting a race whiter than the white race from crossing the white and black races, i. e., it is very small indeed. The principle thus expounded as holding true of a cross between two races is equally applicable to crosses between more than two.

Having disposed of the current delusions on this subject, we may apply this organic law to the solution of the immigration problem, and if we care to make the comparison we shall find that we have applied neither more nor less than the simple rule of common sense which every farmer applies to the breeding of his horses or corn or wheat.

There are certain qualities desirable in the American race affectable by inheritance. The most essential are health, intelligence, altruism and will. They are qualities which every person would wish to inherit from his parents and transmit to his offspring. Considering these qualities in the aggregate the American race, as at present constituted, possesses them, on the average, in a certain definite degree. Now, on the average, the immigrants at present coming to our shores in such numbers are, as regards this aggregate of qualities, either (1) Superior to the American race, (2) Just equal to it, or (3) Inferior to it. There is no fourth alternative.

(1) If evidence that they are a superior race is adducible then, on the score of quality, there can be no criticism of immigration; indeed, the more of it the better, and the sooner the old race is replaced by the new, as is at present occurring, the more fortunate it will be for the future of America and the world. Such evidence, however, has never been adduced and probably is not adducible. It is generally acknowledged that the American race is one of unusual capacity; that so far as intelligence and will is concerned at least, it takes high rank, and if this be true the chance that the average of a random immigration is its superior would not be great. Statistics on this vital matter are entirely wanting, nor would those relating to the pauperism or literacy of the immigrant class compared with the natives be of any service in forming a judgment. Acquired characters being uninheritable the chance of generating a superior race from a community of paupers and illiterates is as great as from a community of the rich and educated. The characteristics observable in any man or aggregate of men are due to inheritance and education combined, and those due to education must first be eliminated before we may judge of those due to inheritance. Hence to compare the congenital or permanent qualities of two races we should compare representative aggregates thereof which have been subjected to the same amount and kind of education. Statistics of crime, literacy, and capacity will then be of value, but not otherwise; just as in comparing two kinds of seed-corn we must compare them when sown in the same kind of soil and subjected to the same influences of cultivation — otherwise we shall not be comparing the permanently transmissible qualities of the seed, but merely these qualities as temporarily modified

by cultivation. It is only when one race is very much superior to another that a marked discrepancy of education cannot disguise the fact. Individuals and communities of unusual superiority are recognizable under any circumstances if subjected to careful inspection, but such inspection of our present class of immigrants has not revealed any unmistakable signs of superiority. We may then regard it as quite certain that the immigrant class have not, by this means, been shown to be the superiors of those at present inhabiting America.

(2) The probability that the two races are exact equals is very remote indeed. It would be practically impossible that any two races whatever should be identical with regard to any qualities whatever. Hence this alternative need not be discussed.

(3) The probability that our immigrants are, on the average, the inferiors of the people at present inhabiting America is considerable, and were it necessary, evidence tending to establish such a presumption might be presented. It is not necessary, however — hence we need not stop to discuss it. Failure to adduce reasons for believing the incoming races superior to our own is sufficient to answer the question whose answer we seek. Simple common sense is all that is required. When a prudent farmer has a good and well proved variety of cattle, he will not permit them to breed promiscuously with any that may come along. The possibility that his breed *might* not be deteriorated by such a blend would not be sufficient for him — he would want a probability, and a very strong one, against deterioration before he risked the permanent qualities of a breed already well above the average. Now the qualities of men are surely as important as those of cattle, and the prudence which every farmer exercises with respect to his herds should at least be equalled when the qualities of a human breed are in question. Is this asking too much of the intelligence and patriotism of our law-givers? As Robert Hunter says of the question of immigration:

"It is a question of babies and birth-rates, and whatever decision is made regarding immigration, it is perforce a decision concerning the kind of children that shall be born. The decision for Congress to make consciously and deliberately is simply whether or not it is better for the world that the children of native parents should be born instead of the children of foreign parents. The making of the decision cannot be avoided. It is made now, although unconsciously, and it is a decision against the children of native parents. . . . This is the race-suicide, the annihilation of our native stock, which unlimited immigration forces upon us, none the less powerfully because it is gradually and stealthily done. The native stock of America, possessed of rare advantages, freed by its own efforts from oppression and the miseries of oppression, might have peopled the United States with the seventy millions which now inhabit it. It has not done so for the reason that 'we cannot welcome an indefinite number of immigrants to our shores without forbidding the existence of an indefinite number of children of native parents who might have been born.'" [1]

The problem of the statesman, so far as it relates to the establishment of an efficient race, is, indeed, practically that of the farmer so far as it relates to the breeding of cattle or the selection of seed; but it is only in new countries like America and Australia that the conditions are such as to leave him much choice. It is in the power of the United States and Canada, for instance, to determine, in large measure, the character of the population which shall people the area of North America, and by becoming the ancestors of its future inhabitants, irrevocably determine the future character of the American race. Although a factor totally ignored by political economists as deserving no attention from those who control the policy of nations, the factor of race is the most vital with which a nation has to deal — it is the factor which must finally determine its destiny, for with an inferior population, an inefficient breed, no nation can do otherwise than decay; and if its decay involves the extinction of the race the sooner it decays the better. Acquired characters not being inheritable the characteristics of the race which first occupies America will — unless their fecundity becomes impaired — remain the characteristics of the American race forever. It is this which makes the matter so vital. Educational policies, financial policies, trade or tariff policies, if found wanting, may be altered; the ills which mistakes in judgment on such issues involve may be remedied by a change in policy; the evil is a temporary one only; but it is totally different with the policy of immigration, for it is by the control of immigration and by its intelligent restriction that the character of the American race is to be determined, so far as it is determinable at this stage in our history; and any mistake in that policy now, can never be remedied by a change of policy in the future. Whatever ills are involved are irremedi-

[1] "Poverty," pp. 313, 314.

able ills — they are as permanent as the race itself. The present generation holds in its hands the fate of posterity, and by the policy it adopts the happiness of posterity will be, in great measure, determined. Never before in the history of the world has the opportunity been offered any state to deliberately construct a race, and as all the present unoccupied land areas are rapidly being populated it is probable that the opportunity will never be offered again. The knowledge of what means to adopt to attain the end, and the power to adopt those means are both available at the present time, and they never before have been available. Though in the past the power may have been available, the knowledge was not. That has only been acquired by relatively recent advances in the study of heredity. Nor are the means to be employed such as would be repugnant to the sentiment and customs of the community. The self-interest of a relatively few persons is opposed to their adoption. The responsibility is not a light one, nor can it be discharged by ignoring the evidence we have adduced or the presumptions established thereby.

Having thus considered the probable effect of immigration upon the quality of the American population, let us turn to the effect upon its quantity. We have shown that if there is one thing which nations need not fear it is a paucity of population. Without any outside aid, nature will rapidly remedy any scarcity of population, if it needs remedying. The Law of Malthus requires no aid to stimulate its operation, for practically every community is increasing in numbers in a geometrical progression toward natural equilibrium. The difficulty is, not how to increase the population, but how to keep it from increasing, and it is an ominous one. Adam Smith and his followers looked forward with dread to the condition of society at the period when it should have attained the so-called "stationary state"— the state of natural equilibrium; but they could offer no remedy and no hope; since the cause which perpetually impels society toward that state with ever increasing acceleration, was deemed by them an unalterable law of nature. As already pointed out, that cause is *competition,* resulting in industrial chaos, unequal distribution of wealth, and the consequent over-propagation of the poorer classes; and it is no more unalterable than the law of nature which decrees that animals shall not wear clothes. Clothes are now worn by men in defiance of that "law" and the law of competition can be as successfully defied. Now immigration simply stimulates the operation of the Law of Malthus. The immigrants coming to us are poor and ignorant and hence are very fast breeding, as are all peoples in that condition. They crowd the cities, swamp the labor market, lower the standard of living, and render hopeless the task of increasing the rate of consumption per capita. To attempt taking the pressure of poverty off the population of America while leaving the channels of immigration open would simply cause an increased flow of population from foreign lands where such pressure is higher; for the law of equilibrium of populations in communication is similar to the law of equilibrium of liquids in communication; populations like liquids seek a common level — the lowest they can find. Poverty is certainly incurable with unrestricted immigration, and the continuance of the present policy in America simply means that within a century or two we shall be in the condition of India and China — the simplest calculation proves it. (See p. 403.)

This brings us to the question of the international exchange of commodities — the question of protection and free trade — a matter slight in consequence compared with that of immigration, but essential to a clear comprehension of just how pantocracy would operate if adopted as a national policy by the United States.

It is certain that with free trade in commodities it could not be made to operate any more successfully than with free trade in men. With commodities freely admitted into the United States from countries where pantocracy was not practised it is doubtful if any great success in the extension of that beneficent system would be possible. Perhaps this assertion may be deemed a confession of weakness in the pantocratic system. The dogmatic economist will be tempted to say: "If pantocracy cannot hold its own with the present system in full and free competition then it is the inferior of the present system, and is unworthy of adoption." This is the typical attitude of those afflicted with production-madness. It is a fact that, under the conditions named, pantocracy probably could not hold its own with capitalism in keeping down the money cost of commodities — though it would more than hold its own in keeping down their labor cost. To make perfectly clear, even to a professional economist, the mode by which free trade would interfere with a pantocratic system, or any other system designed to increase the economy of consumption, I shall discuss a specific case.

Suppose the pantocratic system had been applied to the production of a given commodity in the United States for a number of years, and by the automatic operation of that system the hours of labor of the operatives engaged in producing it had been reduced to four a day, the price having fallen in proportion. Let us assume the average wage of the operatives to be $24.00 a week. Assuming free trade in that community the question is — could an enterprising capitalist located let us say in Europe, or in China, produce said commodity at a lower money cost than the American factories, and thus successfully compete with them. It is, of course, true that the national system of promoting invention under pantocracy would result in a much more perfect system of labor-saving machinery than any capitalist, by his unaided efforts, could develop. But to an enterprising capitalist this would prove no obstacle. He would simply keep himself informed concerning the machinery and methods of production employed here. In his plants in Europe he would duplicate said machinery and methods, and then employ men at an average wage let us say of $12.00 a week, who would work twelve hours a day instead of four; that is, he would pay 16⅔ cents per hour for his labor instead of $1.00 as here, just one-sixth as much. Free competition, of course, would permit him to get this cheap labor without difficulty. To make three men working four hours per day do work which one man working twelve hours a day might do, is, to be sure, utterly repugnant to the dogmatic economist; he deems it an uneconomic proceeding. He thinks in this way because he has production-madness. To the utilitarian it appears quite economic, provided machinery has been so developed that an average of four hours of labor a day maintains a thoroughly self-supporting rate of consumption per capita. Any other policy would but lead to overproduction, and would be uneconomic however considered, because the object of utility is not the economic production of wealth, but the economic production of happiness. Production is for purposes of consumption, not consumption for purposes of production. It is uneconomic to waste the time of a happiness-producing mechanism in the production of anything but happiness so long as it is possible to devote its time to the manufacture of that commodity — for happiness may be considered as a sort of commodity of commodities. One minute unnecessarily employed in the production of anything else is just one minute wasted.

Now it is altogether probable that the well paid, ambitious, and happy laborers of America could do more work in an hour than the ill paid and exhausted laborers of Europe could do in the same time, but they could not do *six times as much,* and hence they could not compete with said ill paid laborers. We often hear it said that well paid labor need not fear the competition of labor that is ill paid, because well paid labor is, in the end, the cheapest. It *is* cheapest in *misery* — but not in *money,* and success in competition depends on low *money* cost — not low *labor* cost. Hence under a competitive system, poorly paid labor is generally the cheapest. Were it not so, capitalists would refuse to pay low wages, and he who charged most for his services would in every case be employed. It is unnecessary to remark that this condition of things is not to be discovered by much searching. Even in those exceptional industries where the skill of the workman is such a critical factor that highly paid labor can more than hold its own with cheap labor, little is gained by the community at large, since under conditions of free competition attempts to compete by parties employing cheap labor are continually made, and though in the end they may be unsuccessful they involve the perpetuation of those unhappy conditions of industry which it should be the object of society to avoid.

In short the notion with which free traders in this country attempt to deceive themselves and others viz.: that the use of improved machinery in America would prevent deterioration in the standard of living here, is a delusion. It would do so only so long as capitalists, American or foreign, were so stupid as not to perceive that the use of the same machinery in Europe, where cheap labor is available, would yield a greater margin of profit than here where it is not. Well paid labor and improved machinery may compete with ill paid labor and antiquated machinery, but where cheap labor is superimposed upon improved machinery, the competition of well paid labor becomes impossible.

Now by the superimposition of labor at one-sixth the cost of that required in America upon the same machinery there employed the foreign competitor with pantocracy, although he might not be successful in lowering his wage-fund to one-sixth that required in America, could probably lower it to one-quarter of that amount. This would enable him to undersell the American factories, and how could those factories meet such competition except by discharging nearly two-thirds of their employees, cutting the wages of the remainder in half, and extending their hours of labor from four to twelve; in other words, they would have to come down to the level of their competitors and lose all

they had gained in economy of consumption. It might be that
the cost of freightage would save them from coming quite to
the level of their foreign competitors, or it might not, for the
cost of freightage on the raw material might be such as to favor
said competitors as much as that on the finished product opposed
them. The absence of profit would also be in favor of the
American producer, but the margin would be small at best and
continually dwindling. To meet foreign competition the general
lowering of wages, if such were required, would be of no consequence,
since a general fall or rise of nominal wages does not
affect real wages; but the discharge of men into the non-producing
and non-consuming class, and the lengthening of the
hours of labor would destroy the very economy of consumption
which it is the object of pantocracy to promote, and the whole
system would be thrown into the chaos inseparable from competition;
for free trade is but free competition between nations
— it is as destructive of the end of utility as that between individuals
— and the policy of protection is an interference with
it distinctly socialistic. It is a definite recognition of the
beneficence of suppressed competition, and is a step in the right
direction, a means of maintaining the economy of consumption
in countries where it is not a minimum. Countries like China,
where labor is the cheapest on earth, require no protection, but
free trade as a policy of the United States would be calamitous
even under our present system, and under pantocracy it would
be impossible. The whole misunderstanding about free trade
arises from mistaking wealth for happiness, and thinking in
terms of *money cost* instead of in terms of *labor cost*. Thus
arises the ridiculous notion that the cheapening of products is
equally useful to a community whether it arises from exploitation
of the *sentient* factor of production with an *increase* of
labor cost, or of the *non-sentient* factor of production with a
decrease thereof. To seek the elevation of the standard of living
by the first method — to cheapen products by cheapening labor,
is to emulate the dextrous feat of Baron Munchausen who pulled
himself out of a bog by his boot-straps — and the ingenious
economists who, by ignoring the distinction between the sentient
and non-sentient factors of production, sanction this mode of
rescuing society from the industrial slough in which it is mired,
are entitled to the same meed of admiration which is due the not
less ingenious Munchausen. Both must be commended for their
dexterity — of wit.

From the foregoing consideration of the questions of immigration and protection the immediate policy of the United States is plain. Immigration should not only be restricted — it should be prohibited. All immigrants of the laboring class who tend to swamp the labor market should be kept out as completely as the Chinese are now. An exclusion law operating for say ten years, and renewable at the end of that period, should be passed, and rigidly enforced. If any great harm were coming to the country from this policy it would be evident within ten years, but let it be distinctly understood that delay in the development and dissipation of nature's resources is not a harm, but a benefit, in a country whose economy of consumption is as wretched as that of the United States. What is the hurry about developing the resources of the country? They have existed here for a long time and they are not going to vanish spontaneously. The forests will not fly away — the ore deposits are not going to sink into the inaccessible bowels of the earth — the elements of the soil's fertility will not evaporate. Why not let them alone until they become assets of utility? They constitute potentialities of great happiness — why not wait until those potentialities can be realized? Why should we hasten to develop them now when only their potentialities of unhappiness can be realized? By postponing their development a few years until the economy of consumption in this country is improved we can reap from these resources a vast harvest of happiness. Why not husband them till then? Prohibition of immigration may lead to the husbandry of these resources, but this is just what is wanted. The object of utility is not merely to build towns — it is to build *happy* towns. It is not sufficient to make the country support a population — it must be a *happy* population, and any rate of happiness production less than that involving maximum efficiency is uneconomic.

Thus rendered consistent by the protection of labor, the general policy of protection should be continued, and as soon as the nation began the manufacture of any commodity under a public monopoly the importation of that commodity should be thenceforth prohibited altogether. Thus interference with the progress of the nation through the importation of commodities or of men would be prevented.

With such policies adopted, or definitely in view, the United States could enter upon experimentation with a pantocratic system upon a small though conclusive scale; but a small scale of experiment would mean a large scale of production — for a small scale of production would not lead to conclusive results,

Modern industry requires production on a large scale — and it derives its high economy therefrom, for only on a large scale can the division of labor and the extended use of machinery be introduced to advantage. The pantocratic system could be applied most easily and simply to commodity producing industries — hence to these it should be first applied. A few typical, extensively consumed, commodities should be selected, and experiment at first confined to these. Steel-making, meat-packing, coal-mining, cotton-growing, and perhaps lumbering, would be convenient and typical classes of industry to start with. Public monopoly would not be necessary at first, though perhaps in the case of coal mining it might be desirable even at first. The promptest mode of procedure would be to take one or more large plants of the first two named industries by right of eminent domain, paying for them as for any condemned property. Through the exercise of the same right, suitable tracts of coal-mining and cotton-raising land should be acquired. The tracts for lumbering have already been acquired — they are the forest reserves, and by the extension of the same principle, tracts for other public purposes could, and should, be reserved. Having acquired the appropriate properties the government should assign them to the management of a definite department of government, called, let us say, the *Department of Industry*, either created for the purpose, or organized as a bureau of some department already in existence. Having conducted such statistical inquiries as are required to establish the various items of expense, the initial producing times of the various commodities, etc., the department of industry should draw up definite plans of procedure, fix the scale of wages and of conditional compensation, and enter upon the several industrial operations specified — or others equally appropriate — on a large scale; the definite object being the reducing of hours of labor and the fall of prices by the introduction of improved machinery, social and material, and the practice of all economies of production other than the oppression of the sentient factor.

As these experimental applications of pantocracy would not simulate the consistent and fully grown system exactly certain allowances would have to be made, and certain expedients adopted, which would be unnecessary at a later stage. Thus the industrial coefficient should be arbitrarily fixed at a low value, the bulk of the benefit of curtailment of the producing time accruing directly to the producer. The reasons for this are obvious. (1) Such a policy would more rapidly abolish the army of unemployed. (2) Were all industries conducted under a pantocratic system, then the fall in price of commodities incident thereto would be a fall in the price of most, or all, commodities. Hence if the industrial coefficient were the same in all industries, a large value thereof would be tolerable, since each producer would gain by the increase in the purchasing power of his wages what he failed to gain in the decrease of his hours of labor. But where only a few industries are practising pantocracy no such compensation to the producer is to be obtained. Hence the industrial coefficient should be low, and the bulk of the benefit of the system go to the producer. This would not materially interfere with the acquisition of the information which the experiment is designed to yield, since it is obvious that by such change in the industrial coefficient as the community might subsequently deem best the benefit of all economies of production could be distributed between producer and consumer in any desirable ratio.

Another difference between such a local and a general system of pantocracy would be the absence of any adequate substitute for the department of output regulation. This would be serious, and involve the loss of some of the main benefits of the system. Hence to test this part of the system it would be desirable to establish at least one public monopoly — say the coal mines — or perhaps the anthracite mines alone. With such an experiment almost every feature of the system could be thoroughly tested, and the conditions of general pantocracy simulated quite closely.

In those experiments involving competition with private competitors, however, many features besides that of conditional compensation could be tested sufficiently for guidance in their ultimate conversion into public monopolies. Thus the ordinary channels of distribution could be used, and each industry could have its own labor exchange — organized preferably under the national civil service bureau. Inspection of products would also be easy. Experimental laboratories, stimulated by conditional compensation, should, without fail, be organized in every experimental industry. Should it care to protect itself by patents it is probable that thus equipped, the government would soon outstrip all its competitors in lowering the price of commodities, even with the advantages in this respect which said competitors would have in their liberty to oppress at will the sentient factor of production; since pantocracy would have in its favor compensating advantages more than equivalent thereto, such as freedom from labor troubles, enthusiasm, and zeal on the part of laborers and directors alike, and harmonious co-operation between them, a more rapid improvement in the machinery of industry, and the absence of any necessity to make a profit. Conditional compensation would not be comparable to profit, and would be no drain upon industry, first because it would only be slight compared with the amounts paid in normal dividends, and second because it would be proportional to, and conditional upon, improvements in the arts. If these advantages of pantocracy over private enterprise were not sufficient the industrial ratio could be increased until they became so. Thus even without any definite fiat government activity under pantocracy would, with little doubt, soon extend itself into public monopoly, because of the impossibility of successful competition by any private enterprise, and it would only need to fear foreign competition because of its cheap and indefinitely oppressible labor, and its power to adopt the machinery developed here without our consent. Of course the government might overcome this last difficulty, in some degree, by taking out foreign patents, but foreign patent laws could be changed at the will of foreign governments, and it would be cheaper and easier to forbid importation altogether, since it would accomplish precisely the same result in the end.

The system of pantocracy would require to be adapted to each industry by careful trial, because every industry has conditions peculiar to itself, and the mode of applying the principles of pantocracy could only be learned experimentally. In the case of most commodity-producing industries the mode of application would be practically the same for all; hence in such industries relatively little experimentation would be required, but to agricultural industries whose activities fluctuate with the seasons, and to transportation, the adaptation of the system would be less easy, and would probably involve some preliminary failure. The initial stage in all industries, however, should be careful and conclusive experimentation. This would thoroughly insure the community against calamity.

Assuming the preliminary experimentation to be over, what should be the next step? How should the transfer from capitalism to pantocracy, in the case of each industry, be accomplished? How should the means of production, now in the hands of private parties, be transferred to the people? Four modes of accomplishing this may be suggested. (1) By confiscation. (2) By destructive competition. (3) By purchase. (4) By gradual sequestration. Let us examine the advantages of each of these modes.

(1) Confiscation is merely the expropriation of property by the state without compensation to the owner or owners thereof. It is a method familiar enough in time of war, but practically unknown at any other time. The American nation was founded upon such an act of confiscation, and by a similar act President Lincoln emancipated the slaves in 1863. It is, of course, unconstitutional under our system of government except as a war measure; few persons would sanction it, and any attempt by such a method to obtain control of the means of production would require a profound change of sentiment in the American people. It is hardly worth while therefore to discuss the matter or its morality, and we shall pass to more practical suggestions.

(2) Destructive competition is a method familiar in private industry and, as suggested on page 511, the government under a system of pantocracy would possess such advantages over private competitors that it could probably ruin them and acquire their property through bankruptcy proceedings. In order to do this, however, it might be necessary to increase the producing ratio more than is desirable. In opposition to the advantages of pantocracy private enterprise would have but one weapon — the oppression of its wage earners — and it would be a difficult weapon to wield with labor organized as it is to-day. Indeed this mode of acquiring private property is as undesirable between the government and private enterprise as it is between one private enterprise and another. It would be practically confiscation by competition, since the capitalist would be forced to part with his property without compensation, or at any rate, with slight compensation. It would involve, as it always involves, great hardships and unnecessary suffering, and any act or policy involving unnecessary suffering must be unjust. Yet most men would consider competitive confiscation a just mode of acquiring the property of private individuals — and why — simply because it is a customary mode, and wherever dogma prevails, custom determines justice. To ruin competitors by "fair" and free competition is a commonplace affair in business, and hence is sanctioned by current morality, which in this case, as in others, reverses common sense, justifying the end by the means instead of the means by the end. A better method than the slow and painful one of competitive confiscation is available.

(3) The method of acquisition by purchase is familiar and requires little comment. Applied to the acquisition of the means

of production of the country it would almost of necessity take the form of bond issues. Title to the property to be taken would be transferred to the government by right of eminent domain — interest-bearing bonds of the value of said property would be issued in exchange, redeemable during a term of years — thirty, forty, fifty, or even more. At the end of the period, the bonds having been all redeemed, the property would belong to the government without further payment of interest. Such a method of purchase should be as constitutional in the case of great properties as it certainly is in the case of small properties. Nevertheless, it contains elements of injustice which will become apparent by discussion of the fourth alternative.

(4) Gradual sequestration might be of several kinds. I shall suggest two — either of which would presumably be preferable to the foregoing methods. These are (a) Acquisition by the issue of non-inheritable bonds, and (b) Acquisition by payment of diminishing interest.

(a) Acquisition by the issue of non-inheritable bonds may be explained as follows: Title to the property should be secured, as in the case of simple purchase, by right of eminent domain, interest-bearing bonds of the value of the property should be issued in exchange, but these should be non-redeemable, non-transferable, and on the death of the holder should become void, the property represented by them reverting to the government. Thus by the simple expedient of making bonds issued in payment for the means of production non-inheritable said means of production would become the property of the people without further expense than that involved in the payment of a low rate of interest on the value of the property during the lifetime of the original bondholders. This expense should be carried by fund (a) (p. 439) and would be continually dwindling as more and more of the bonds were rendered void by the death of their holders, the advantage of the diminishing expense fund accruing to the community by the resulting fall in the price of commodities.

I am well aware that the method of acquisition here proposed will be criticized. The charge will doubtless be made that it is merely confiscation in the guise of purchase, and that it is an invasion of the sacred and inalienable rights of property. It certainly is an invasion of the sacred and inalienable right of bequest of property, but as that right is as non-existent as any other inalienable right of individuals no moral right whatever is invaded. The so-called right of bequest is a privilege which time has altered into a right, or alleged right, and when such privileges are invaded history shows that there is always much protest against the invasion of rights. It is the old story — the sanction of tradition is substituted for the sanction of justice. It must be admitted that the expedient proposed is uncustomary — it may even be unconstitutional — but it is not unjust. Let us look at the facts candidly. In substance they are as follows. Every particle of man-created capital in this country has been created by the labor of the people. Through the operation of the machinery of the capitalistic system, title to the capital so created has become vested in a small class of the people. This has been accomplished through the accumulation of surplus values. Now by the system of purchase through redeemable bonds what is asked of the people? Nothing more nor less than this: that they buy back the capital which they have themselves created from persons who, for the most part, had nothing whatever to do with its creation, and many of whom were not even born when it was created. This, we are told, is justice. But would Justice approve it? Clearly not. Very well then, it is not justice but injustice. Hence, it should not be tolerated by a just nation, nor advocated by a just man.

I believe a little candid consideration will convince any reasonable man that some such restriction upon the accumulation of wealth as the one proposed will become necessary if the liberty of the people is to endure. With the present facilities of accumulation the unrestricted privilege of bequest and inheritance simply means that, in two or three generations at the most, practically all the wealth of the country will be in the hands of a few hundred families, or perhaps a few score families. The people will be practically slaves; they will be in the condition of the people of Attica at the accession of Solon — held in bondage by the money lenders. Solon freed his country by abrogating the "inalienable right" of the Athenian capitalists to hold their creditors in servitude, and there can be no doubt that the "inalienable right" of unrestricted bequest will have to be abrogated if the people of this country are to be anything better than bondsmen. A society like our own, divided into classes on the basis of wealth, is unstable. It is but a special case of a nation "half slave and half free," or rather nine-tenths slave and one-tenth free. Wealth is the foundation of power, and history proves that no class has ever possessed power without using it to further its own ends. This can only mean that the inequality of wealth in a society where there is no restriction upon accumulation will become greater and greater until the masses either become permanent bondsmen, or revolt and reestablish equality by confiscation, and the process will repeat itself until some restriction is placed upon accumulation, for otherwise the establishment of equality is not permanent.

Thus the acquisition of the means of production by non-inheritable bonds would accomplish two useful objects at the same time. It would place the ownership of public utilities in the hands of the public, where alone they belong, and it would allay the congestion of wealth which menaces the life of the republic. Abrogation of the right to bequeath property in means of production, such as is here proposed, leaves intact, of course, the right to bequeath other kinds of property. It is private property in public utilities alone which the expedient proposed is designed to abolish.

(b) Acquisition by payment of diminishing interest is an alternative means of acquiring public utilities which would have some advantages over the preceding, and would perhaps be less disturbing to the business interests of the country during the period of transition. The nature of this means may be indicated by the following example: Suppose the purchasing price of a given plant to be A dollars. For the first three years the government would pay interest on A dollars; for the next three on ninety per cent of A dollars; for the following three on eighty per cent of A dollars, and so on. Carrying out this principle, title to the property would become completely vested in the government at the expiration of thirty years; the transition from private to public ownership being immediate so far as concerned operation, but gradual so far as concerned the division of profit. In the beginning profit, represented by interest on the full value of the property, would be given the original owners: at the end this would all accrue to the public in the form of diminished prices: in the intermediate stages it would be divided between the original owners and the public. By a device of this general character, or of that involved in the issue of non-inheritable bonds, the means of production could be gradually restored to the community which created them without any violent disturbance of private interests.

It should not be forgotten, however, that by whatever mode the acquisition of the public utilities of the United States might or may be accomplished it is not of necessity permanent. In acquiring control of the industries in which their welfare is bound up the people will have done nothing irrevocable. They can always reverse their action if they conclude they have made a mistake. Many earnest persons believe that the cessation of individual ownership in the means of production would leave the people in a hopeless, ambitionless, and dejected condition — would deprive them of initiative and thrift. He who has carefully considered what has preceded in this work will, I believe, be unable to accept such a view. It is, indeed, diametrically opposed to the truth, and arises from the confusion of socialism in production with socialism in consumption. The present system it is which is destructive of ambition and initiative — not indeed completely so, but tending to confine these traits to a favored few. The great mass of the industrial army must always consist of laborers engaged in the execution — not in the direction of the tasks of the world, just as the great mass of an ordinary army must consist of privates — very few can be colonels and generals. Hence a system which would make mankind hopeful must hold out hope to the executive laborers — not alone the hope of rising into the directive class; this must in the very nature of things be delusive to the average man, and is indeed conspicuously so under the present system — but it must hold out the hope of happiness to the wage-earner *while he remains a wage-earner* — it must render him a joyous being whether or no he rises into the directing class. This, pantocracy is designed to accomplish, which capitalism is not. But if, under the former system, any particular acquisition of a public utility by the public should turn out to be a mistake, or seem to do so — if it should tend to diminish hope and stifle ambition — the people could readily reverse their action if they desired to; and this would be particularly easy provided they had established the essentially democratic principle of direct legislation. A referendum vote would suffice to put any public utility back into the hands of private capitalists. For example, suppose our people at the present time had power of direct legislation, and concluded that the public ownership of the Post Office was making them ambitionless and dejected. They could easily, by means of the referendum, direct the authorities to transfer the whole system to capitalists. This might be done in any one of a variety of ways. The government might agree to accept the bonds of a syndicate formed to conduct the post office business of the country, and experience proves that it would probably not be difficult to find a syndicate willing to serve the public in such a capacity. On receipt of properly guaranteed bonds the post office property would be turned over to the syndicate, and they would proceed to conduct it in such a manner as would be most profitable to themselves, that is, by instituting the normal process of giving as little to, and getting as much from, the public as possible. In this way perhaps the ambition of the people might be revived, and their dejection turned into hope, and the same course could be pursued with any public utility which the nation might acquire under pantocracy. Thus the people would be fully guaranteed against the dismal and dejected conditions which certain unobservant theorists are convinced must inhere in freedom from capitalistic control of industry, and could proceed with the successive aquisition of the various utilities now in private hands with full consciousness that the old conditions could be re-established in any particular case, should a careful trial show such a course to be desirable.

The centralization so dreaded by political dogmatists is dangerous only under oligarchical conditions. Direct legislation would render it innocuous. The remedy for present evils is not less centralization combined with industrial oligarchy; it is more centralization combined with industrial democracy. We should substitute direct for indirect control of the people, by this means avoiding the dangers not only of capitalistic, but of bureaucratic, despotism.

We have thus outlined a policy suggested solely by the principles of utility which, if adopted, would tend to bring the United States as a nation into a condition of self-support, and make it the first nation in the history of the world to attain that condition. The beneficent effects of the policy would not be fully felt by the present generation, for the progress of science, though rapid, cannot undo the evil of a thousand generations of dogma in one of common sense; but if we will put ourselves in the place of our posterity we shall discover that in adopting the policy of common sense we have adopted the Golden Rule — we shall have done to our posterity as we would that our ancestors had done unto theirs. For, had we the power to choose, under what conditions would we desire to be brought into the world, and what conditions would we desire to find there? Would we desire ancestry of a superior or of an inferior race? Surely we would not desire an inferior ancestry. Very well then — if holding the fate of posterity in our hands we fail to make such provision as is supplied us by the current knowledge of heredity to insure to our posterity an undegenerate ancestry, we have violated the Golden Rule, and have failed in our duty to the coming generations. Would we desire to be born into an overpopulated world the cream of whose resources had been dissipated by our ancestors, and take up the struggle for existence with nature and with man after the first had been rendered niggardly by "development" and the second desperate by want; or would we desire to find the population adapted to its means of support by a low birth rate instead of a high death rate; to find the resources of nature husbanded and rendered accessible by science, and the interests of men identical with, instead of opposed to, our own? There can be no doubt that the second of these alternatives would be selected by any sane man. Very well then — the Golden Rule requires that we adopt the means necessary to attain such ends, and common sense alone can distinguish them.

Let no man repeat the stale objection that, as this world is a school of adversity, it is good that men should be born to pain — that suffering and hardship are better than happiness and ease — if he is sincere, let him wear a hair shirt — that act will speak louder than many words. His consistent predecessor, the ascetic of the Middle Ages, thus proved his adherence to the moral code of unhappiness, and as much should be required of the modern ascetic before we accept his preaching as sincere. If this world is indeed a school of adversity — if those who preach the duty of unhappiness are sufficiently in the confidence of Omnipotence to know that it is His design that we be unhappy here, then why do they attempt to thwart that design by preaching and practising charity? Why do they labor to relieve the poor and unfortunate, and thus render less effective the moral discipline which it is the object of life to supply? If they practised what they preached they would seek to intensify, and not to relieve, the suffering of mankind. They do not practise what they preach because their heart is a better guide than their head, and the morality of their instincts repudiates the immorality of their theology. It is a triumph of common sense over sophistry. If once we accord men the right to charity we cannot withhold from them the right to justice; and were justice done, charity would be superfluous. The confusion of this whole matter would be abolished if he who preaches the glory of suffering and its power to develop character would but distinguish between self-sacrifice *with* an object, and self-sacrifice *without* an object; if he would but recognize that character is not an end, but a *means* to an end. The modern ascetic is not a follower of Christ, for Christ was a utilitarian, and practised what He preached. His object was — not to cause men suffering, but to save them from it. He recognized that conscience must first be guided by right before the conduct of men can safely be guided by conscience. Had He been an intuitionist, adopting conscience as a guide, He might just as well have accepted the moral code He found, instead of erecting a new one; for if conscientiousness is all that is required of men it can be secured as well by adherence to one code of morals as to another. A man can be as conscientious about burning his fellow-man alive as about curing his sickness or relieving his poverty. Let all such confusion about the morality of suffering be repudiated once for all — pain is an unmitigated evil, and its causes are evils — sickness is an evil, selfishness is an evil, ignorance is an evil, poverty is an evil, only because they are causes of suffering, and pain is only to be deliberately sought, or deliberately tolerated, when it is a presumable means to an ultimate gain in happiness.

The policy herein suggested for the American nation has thus far been supported only on grounds of patriotism, and were custom our guide, such grounds would be sufficient. Few, if any, nations determine their policies by the presumable effects thereof upon other nations, but utility requires a broader morality than this. It requires the application of the Golden Rule as between one nation and another on the same ground that it requires the application of the same rule as between one generation and another. Therefore, we must justify our policy on humanitarian grounds as well as on patriotic grounds.

There is a school of patriotism more or less popular which teaches that a man owes to his country a duty which he owes to no other aggregate of the human race, and that he should render service to the constituted authorities thereof, whatever policies they may choose to pursue. The motto of this school is "My country, right or wrong." Had it been the motto of Washington and his compatriots the United States would still be a part of the British Empire. The particular aggregate of men which constitutes a nation is a matter of the merest accident. Since the first confederation of the thirteen colonies at the time of the American Revolution it has been a matter of debate whether the United States is one nation, or an aggregate of nations, as its name implies. At the time of the Civil War, the North held to the former view, the South to the latter, and those who contended that each state was sovereign and independent and entitled to their first allegiance were as patriotic as those who contended for the opposite view. Indeed, the patriotism whose dictum is "My country, right or wrong" is but one degree of egotism, for if my country right or wrong, why not my state right or wrong, if my state right or wrong, why not my town right or wrong, if my town right or wrong, why not my neighborhood right or wrong, if my neighborhood right or wrong, why not my family right or wrong, if my family right or wrong, why not my great-uncle right or wrong, if my great-uncle right or wrong, why not *myself* right or wrong? If patriotism, why not phyliotism, if phyliotism, why not oeciotism, if oeciotism, why not *egotism*? It would seem as if he whose only reason for judging a nation worthy of service and support was because he happened to be a citizen thereof was guilty of the apotheosis of egotism. The utilitarian cannot sanction such a view; he has but one test, and judges of the value of a nation by the same standard as he judges of the value of everything else — from a toothpick to a code of morals — that nation is the best which contributes most to the happiness of humanity, and the ambition of the true patriot is to make his country occupy that proud position. Now I claim that the adoption of a pantocratic policy would make the United States in the future, what she has been in the past, the greatest contributor to the happiness of humanity of any nation on earth; and that, unless she abandons her present capitalistic system, and adopts a policy of consistent democracy, she will cease to be the greatest nation of the world, and other states, imitating her past instead of her present example, will supersede her in that position.

To justify the claim thus made it will be sufficient to expound the utilitarian theory of free trade as applied to nations like the United States. It is quite distinct from the *laissez faire* theory of free trade, and has an exactly opposite effect upon the happiness of humanity.

We have asserted that the United States, on assuming the production of any commodity, should prohibit the importation of that commodity into the country. This is certainly not much like free trade and the free trader would criticize it. He would argue thus: Nature has endowed different portions of the earth's surface with different resources of use to man. Some portions she has made favorable to one class of industries, other portions to another class: In certain portions, for example, she has placed rich deposits of iron ore, and in juxtaposition thereto the coal and limestone required in its reduction. In those portions, therefore, the manufacture of pig iron, and steel ingots, and of articles manufactured therefrom, can be carried on with less labor than is required in parts of the earth's surface where the conditions of mining and smelting are less favorable. Similarly she has rendered certain other portions particularly well suited to the manufacture of porcelain, leather, wood-pulp, or other articles of commerce, and other portions she has adapted to the growth of cotton, or wheat, or potatoes, etc. Now it is obvious that articles of commerce can be produced with least labor in those portions of the earth which nature has adapted best to their production, and the free trader claims that free trade, through the free play of competition, will make industries gravitate to those parts of the earth which are thus best suited to their operation. Protection, on the other hand, by artificial interference with trade, really enriches nobody since, if a country is best adapted to the production of a given commodity, free trade will insure that it shall be produced there, whereas if it is not adapted, the attempt to produce the commodity is attended with more labor than would have been required had the country confined its efforts to producing products which by nature it was adapted to produce, and exchanging them for the given commodity with some country which was better adapted to produce it. I believe this to be a fair epitome of the argument for free trade. To those who have read what is remarked on this subject on pages 504 to 507 its fallacy will be obvious. The facilities afforded by nature constitute but one of the factors which enter into the labor cost or the money cost of commodities. By sufficient oppression of the sentient factor of production it is easy to compensate for very great differences in natural adaptability; hence success in competition, which is a function of money cost, affords no criterion by which we may judge of the relative natural advantages of two countries — it tells us nothing about relative labor cost. It is only when natural advantages are very decided that free importation into a country whose standard of living is high, is admissible. For example, it would be absurd for Canada to attempt to grow its own oranges. Even assuming its standard of living to be higher than that of the United States it would be cheaper in labor cost to import them from Florida or California than to attempt to grow them in hot houses, as the climate of Canada would require. It is worth observing that when free traders choose an example by which to emphasize the point of their doctrine they generally seem to select some agricultural product in whose production, climate is a critical factor.

Success in competition then affords no criterion by which

to judge of the labor cost of producing a given commodity, but a method of thus judging may nevertheless be suggested. It should be the policy of the United States, on assuming the production of a given commodity (A) under pantocracy, not only to prohibit the importation of that commodity, but to freely proclaim its intention of abandoning said prohibition and said production in favor of any country which would meet the following conditions: (1) Adopt and maintain a pantocratic system of production, not necessarily identical in every detail with our own, but deliberately designed to increase the efficiency both of production and consumption. (2) Prove its ability to produce said commodity (A) at a less labor cost, by producing and delivering it in the United States at a less money cost than that required here, after bringing the wage earners engaged in its production there to the same level of consumption as those engaged in its production here — that is, to the same real wages and same hours of labor. This process I shall call the *equalization of the sentient factor of production*. (3) Provide a market for some other commodity or commodities whose labor cost here would, under the same system, be less than there; said market to be substantially as great as that provided by the United States for commodity (A). This policy embodies the *utilitarian theory of free trade*. It provides for the determination of the relative natural advantages of two or more nations in the production of any commodity by comparison of the relative money cost of that commodity in said nations, not under conditions of unequal economy of consumption, as is the case with ordinary free trade, but under conditions of *equal* economy. It provides that the low money cost of a commodity shall really represent the great natural advantages utilized in the production thereof, and not the low standard of living imposed upon the producers thereof. In addition to this it requires a market in exchange for that abandoned here, since otherwise the United States could export no commodities in exchange for those imported. This would result in an unfavorable balance of trade, and the final loss by the United States of all its gold, which, in the absence of a market for anything else, it would be forced to export in exchange for imports. Such a condition would involve inconvenience, but worse than this, it would involve the enforced migration of laborers who, deprived of their means of support here, would be forced to seek it elsewhere. It is not common sense thus to force men to follow an industry out of a country. Industries should be the servants, not the masters, of men, and it is better

CHAP. XIV] THE NEXT STEP 523

to submit to a slightly increased labor cost than to force unwilling migration. The happiness involved is the only criterion in judging of this as of any policy. It is well to locate an industry where it is most favored by nature; but it is better to locate it where it will produce the most happiness, and in selecting the locality of any industry the second consideration should always prevail over the first — provided, of course, there is any conflict between them.

The mutual interchange of markets under utilitarian free trade would obviously be an advantage to both nations taking part therein, since the very conditions of exchange require that it shall be accomplished only when it involves a decrease in the labor cost of all the commodities concerned. The mode of effecting the exchange of markets should and could be made to exclude all disturbance in the labor market of both countries. Suppose, for example, upon careful examination by experts it is discovered that, under a pantocratic system, the labor cost of producing commodities A, B, and C, in the United States is less than that involved in their production in Germany under a similar system, and that the labor cost of commodities D, E, and F, is less in Germany than in the United States; the markets for said commodities being essentially the same. Unless the labor cost of transportation nullified these differences, Germany, by agreement with the United States would cease to produce commodities A, B, and C — the United States would cease to produce commodities D, E, and F — all restrictions upon the importation of these commodities being, of course, removed. In order not to disturb the labor market, however, the exchange of commodity markets should not be effected suddenly, but as the plants in Germany engaged in the production of commodities A, B, and C, were dismantled, those engaged in D, E, and F would be erected and the same labor, though not necessarily the same wage earners, formerly engaged in the production of A, B, and C, would, without interruption, proceed to engage in the production of D, E, and F. Similar operations would occur simultaneously in the United States. Besides this, such parts of the machinery for producing the respective commodities as were worth while transporting could be exchanged between the two countries, and thus the labor cost of re-erecting the plants in more favorable situations minimized. As the whole transaction would be carried out deliberately and after thorough investigation by experts of its total effect upon both production and consumption, and as neither nation would have anything to gain by concealment or misrepresentation, nothing but good could result to both nations, and the exchange would be a mutual benefit. The contrast of such a sane and common sense mode of taking advantage of natural facilities with the destructive and chaotic method involved in the *laissez faire* policy of free trade, is too obvious to require comment. The latter attains its object only after the sentient factor of production has been oppressed to the point of exhaustion — the former requires as a condition of its consummation that means deliberately designed for the emancipation of the sentient factor shall be adopted before the exchange of markets shall occur. The United States, on account of its vast market and its extraordinary natural advantages, occupies a unique position. It is by nature adapted to play the part of the greatest nation on earth, because by the proper use of its natural advantages it can contribute more to the happiness of humanity than any other nation. Should it adopt the *laissez faire* policy of free trade it would simply employ its unique position to contribute to the unhappiness of humanity. Suppose it should adopt that policy, what would happen? Every industrial nation in the world under the capitalistic system would bend every effort to capture its vast markets; each would vie with the other, not only in introducing improvements in the arts, but in oppressing labor to the breaking point. The laboring population of industrial Europe and of the United States in competition therewith, would engage in a death struggle for commercial supremacy — the products of industry would be coined in agony — and year by year conditions would become worse as each nation tried to bankrupt its competitors; and what would be the end? Other things being equal, that nation would win whose population could be forced to the lowest level of living and the maximum misery per capita — it would probably win even from the nation possessing the greatest natural advantages, provided that nation were peopled by men who would not or could not live so cheaply and labor so long. Such a policy would but put a premium upon the oppression of labor, and while forcing down the standard of living in Europe, it would force it down in the United States as well. It would be an invitation to every industrial nation on earth to outdo its neighbor in oppressing the sentient factor of production.

On the other hand, what would be the effect should the United States adopt a system of pantocracy, and at the same time its logical concomitant, the utilitarian policy of free trade. It would be an invitation issued to all the world to emancipate its people. That nation and that nation only whose policy was guided by the economy of happiness could hope to capture the markets of the United States, or to benefit by its great natural advantages. It would put a premium, not upon the oppression, but upon the uplifting, of wage earners, and would divert the ingenuity and effort of the directing class abroad, as well as at home, from expedients to defeat the demands and aspirations of the laboring class to expedients for so improving the arts of production as to accomplish the very object for which the laboring population are everywhere striving. While recognizing the fundamental truth at the foundation of the ordinary theory of free trade, pantocracy would employ that recognition to accomplish the end of utility. It would make the capture of our markets by foreign countries, as well as the capture of foreign markets by our own, depend upon success in the exploitation of the *non-sentient* instead of the *sentient* factor of production, by making the equalization of the sentient factor a condition thereof. It would freely recognize the importance of everywhere taking advantage of the bounty of nature, and for that very reason would insist that success in the capture of the world's markets, so far as the United States could affect the matter, should really be determined by the bounty of nature, and not by the misery of man. This is the true theory of reciprocity, for the exchange of markets under such conditions would bring benefit to all nations without bringing harm to any, and moreover it is but consistently carrying out the general policy of pantocracy of saving the sentient at the expense of the non-sentient factor of production; for to so readjust industry as to make more accessible to mankind the most available resources of nature is equivalent to increasing the availability of her resources by the improvement of machinery, and has a similar effect upon the economy of production.

Incidentally our exposition of the utilitarian theory of free trade shows why, in the pantocratic scheme expounded in Chapter 13, no provision was made for exploiting foreign markets. What is the use, under pantocracy, of producing a lot of articles we do not want, and then having to dispose of them abroad, in order to postpone (for it does not prevent) a crisis from overproduction? The United States can exercise no control over the tariff or other policies of foreign countries under the present system, and an industry depending for its market upon foreign trade may be thrown out of gear at any time by a change in the policy of some foreign country. A foreign trade (unless under the conditions just expounded) would preclude the adaptation of the supply to the demand and would thus throw the pantocratic mechanism into disorder. Except as a means of obtaining articles, such as coffee and spices, which she does not attempt to produce at all, the United States has no more need of a trade with foreign countries than the earth has need of a trade with Mars. Products such as those mentioned, not producible in the United States, should be, as now, obtained by exchange for those produced here; and the trade in such commodities should be the only trade with countries too unenlightened to adopt a pantocratic system.

Success in imposing upon other countries the recognition and practice of the economy of happiness would have remote effects even more valuable to humanity than the immediate effect involved in the mutually advantageous exchange of markets. By raising the standard of living and of education abroad the same effect would be produced there as here, viz., suspension of the Law of Malthus. By the powerful effect of a pantocratic system upon the law of increasing returns the pressure of the population upon its means of subsistence and of happiness would be relieved — it would no longer be necessary for the inhabitants of foreign lands to seek relief from misery by exile. Emigration would cease because the necessity for it would disappear. Thus by its immigration and trade policy our country would not only insure its own posterity against over-population, but it would make relief from over-population in other countries the very means of that insurance. The unequal pressure of population is the cause of migration, and to permanently dispense with the necessity of migration the pressure must be equalized. The present immigration policy of the United States proposes to equalize it by *increasing the pressure here* — the proposed pantocratic policy would equalize it by *decreasing it abroad*. Of what use is it to give a few immigrants temporary relief from the burden of over-population only to produce finally the very conditions here from which they sought, and are seeking, to escape abroad. Their temporary relief only insures to their posterity and ours permanent impossibility of relief. If through improved facilities of communication the unoccupied areas of the earth are, in the next few generations, to be populated as densely as Europe or China, what is to become of the numberless generations which are to follow? The time is rapidly approaching when relief from over-population cannot be obtained from migration unless we establish communication with the moon.

The United States should not permit the transient effect of immigration upon the actual immigrants themselves to blind it to the permanent effect thereof upon posterity. The impulse to relieve the misery we see is a commendable one; but the misery we do not see is as real as that we see. We shall not live to witness the full measure of misery which posterity must pay for our present policy, but our failure to witness it will not reduce its poignancy one iota. The misery we relieve now by that policy is not as a drop in the bucket to that which will be caused by it hereafter. It may gratify our impulses to relieve the poor immigrant fleeing from the over-population of Europe, but what right have we to secure such gratification at the cost of the embittered lives of future generations? It is profoundly unjust thus to allow sentiment to dominate reason. It is the merest pathomania and no less dangerous than dogma.

Paralleling the argument for unrestricted immigration arising from short-sighted sentiment, there is another having its origin in religious dogma which, if consistently applied, would lead back to fatalism. Thus, it is often remarked that men should not meddle with the interests of posterity, because though those interests may be affected by their acts, the effects are not immediately observable, and such matters should be left to the care of God, the assumption being that God will attend to that which man neglects. This is perhaps the last concretely baneful religious dogma which survives in the western world. It is applied under various circumstances where no other pretext can be conveniently cited as justification for a prevailing custom. Of course it is never consistently applied, since if it is indeed safe to leave things to the care of God, one thing can be as safely left to His care as another, and neither men nor nations would need to take thought for the morrow, but could trust to Heaven for food, raiment, and protection from the elements. Labor could be dispensed with, and it could be said of men as of the lilies " They toil not neither do they spin," and yet are provided for by the Creator. How fallible man is enabled to distinguish those things which it is safe to leave to God from those which it is not, is a question which must be left to such persons as possess supernatural means of communication with the Author of the Universe But this much is certain — if their counsel prevails and leads to the neglect of the immigration problem, posterity must pay a mighty price for the ignorance of their ancestry. Experience teaches that there is no more reason to believe in the intervention of God to prevent the misery of posterity than to prevent the poverty, and crime, and dishonor, which we observe about us. To attempt to place the responsibility for human inaction upon God is a dismal piece of superstition. If the world is to be successful in the production of happiness, it must be through the voluntary acts of man, and God will not nullify his negligence in one department of conduct more than in another. The law of increasing population and its direct consequence, the law of increasing migration, cannot be counteracted by neglect. To attempt to follow the policy of drift in the future, as it has been followed in the past; to attempt to equalize the pressure of population upon subsistence by increasing its *final* pressure, instead of decreasing its *initial* pressure is hopeless, because it leaves the operation of the Law of Malthus intact. It will but hasten the day when the population of the earth attains *natural,* instead of *beneficent,* equilibrium. It will but reduce the whole world to a common level of misery, and

"Shut the gates of mercy on mankind."

Besides its effect upon terrestrial over-population, the reciprocal exchange of markets under pantocracy would have an effect upon international amity and union only less beneficent, because as each great nation fell into its natural place as an international producer of those commodities which it was by nature best fitted to produce, the interdependence of nations would increase, and the incentive to international strife would disappear with the disappearance of the occasion therefor. With the extension of the organization of industry under pantocracy the departments of output regulation, distribution, etc., would become international instead of national, since not otherwise could the supply be adjusted to the demand. Instead of striving to outdo its fellow nations in the world's markets, each nation would strive to outdo its fellows in raising the level of its own happiness, for this would be the condition of capturing those markets. That is, the self-interest of each nation would become identical with the self-interest of all nations. This is obviously no more than the principle of pantocracy applied to the relations of nations. With such an international policy war would become extremely improbable since no nation seeks to wage war upon its own interests, and having once entered into the relations of mutual interdependence implied in the utilitarian policy of free trade, the interests of the great nations of the earth would become identical, and any nation entering into war with its neighbors would, by that act, deprive itself of things essential to its life, or happiness, or both. Thus pantocracy would seek to attain universal peace by so adjusting the relations of nations as to make them have everything to lose and nothing to gain by war, and an essential part of its policy would consist in so directing education that not only would this be the case, but that everyone would know that it *was* the case, and would govern his conduct accordingly. As with individuals, so with nations, it would seek to divert the power of self-interest from destructive into constructive channels, since to abolish self-interest entirely is out of the question. Thus patriotism would become identical with humanitarianism, and the sentiment of Thomas Paine would become that of every patriot: " The world is my country and to do good is my religion."

This is but a recognition of the assertion made in Chapter 3 that the distribution of pleasure and pain in space or time is of no consequence. It matters not when or by whom these sensations are felt, whether now or a thousand years hence, whether by white man, black man, dog, toad, or worm; the form, size, or constitution of tissues of the sentient being concerned have nothing to do with the question. Intensity and duration are the only factors which may justly be considered. There is in the universe but one good and that is happiness, and there is but one evil and that is unhappiness: all things else are to be deemed good or evil only because of their relation to these through the law of causation. To contradict this assertion either leaves the words *good* and *evil* without any useful meaning, or it deprives them of all meaning whatever.

Here ceases our exposition of the economy of happiness. As a treatise on the technology of that subject it is primitive and incomplete, but as it is the first of its kind, perhaps no more can be expected of it. When contrasted with treatises of a future generation, I hope and I expect, that it will appear a poor and feeble thing. I believe, however, that, as a structure, it will stand. Its details doubtless will be profoundly modified and amplified, but its principles appear to be as eternal as the structure of the mind from which they are deduced. This conviction may be a delusion. If so, the sooner it is overthrown the better, and none will be readier to assist in its overthrow than he who now sustains it. Science cannot live on delusions, whereas dogmatism cannot live on anything else, and if the present work is infected with dogma, let no method of disinfection known to the candid critic be spared.

But before the system herein submitted is judged, one point should be brought to a distinct focus in the critic's mind. Any criterion of criticism, whether applied to art or agriculture, to potatoes or politics, to mud-pies or morals, must be either intuitionistic or it must not. If it is, then the ultimate dictum of criticism can be no more than "I like it" or "I don't like it." With such a criterion there are no issues except between individual tastes, and to dispute about a right or a wrong — a better or a worse — whether in morals or anything else, is idle, since *de gustibus non est disputandum*. He who fails to clearly comprehend this truth is ignorant of the A B C of criticism. If, on the other hand, the criterion employed is not intuitionistic, it must be utilitarian, or founded on some other distinction in experience as independent of approval and disapproval as is the criterion of utility. As already shown, (p. 257) such a distinction no one has ever deemed it worth while to seek, nor is any one likely to. Hence the criterion of utility is the only one by which any system may usefully be judged, and directed by that criterion the controversy of keen and discriminating criticism becomes the champagne of philosophy.

But of the many varieties of criticism by intuition there is one requiring neither discrimination nor keenness which may as well be anticipated, since no proposed innovation has ever escaped it and none ever will. I refer to that form of censure which labels all new proposals "impractical." Critics subject to this infirmity confound the impractical with the uncustomary. They assume that what they cannot conceive, the universe cannot realize. They limit the capacity of all human effort by their own. Every age has had critics of this calibre and none is commoner to-day than the political pessimist who complains that there is really no use in trying to do anything to the present situation except apply a few palliatives, warranted to disturb no respectable gentleman in the enjoyment of his immemorial privileges. They admit that the world progresses, but only at a rate, and in a direction, which they are peculiarly fitted to prescribe. These critics, I am sure, will be able to tell "by intuition" that the proposals herein put forth are impractical. They are of the same class as those who, by the sound of the name, can tell that socialism is impractical. But can any presumption be established that the judgment of these men is such as to afford a safe guide to the conduct of society? Are their attainments and training of the character required, and do they approach the subject with an open mind? Have the distinctions and principles herein set forth been long familiar to their meditations, and are the doctrines founded upon them rejected by critics whose mature judgment has weighed them in the balance and found them wanting? By no means. The men who make "practicalness" the test of every proposed system are fitted neither by training nor judgment to apply that test. They consist of pedagogues whose highest ambition is to teach what they have been taught, editors dominated by the dogmas of a past generation, law-givers whose political philosophy is a mitigated anarchy, business men who mistake a knowledge of finance for omniscience. If their private cogitations have been centered long upon the technics of human happiness no one has ever suspected it. They are political mystics who use the terms *liberty, prosperity, patriotism, public welfare, justice,* as their metaphysical prototypes use the terms *substance, noumenon, thing-in-itself, ego* — not as signs of, but as substitutes for, ideas. As critics, they are of that common class

"Who now to sense, now nonsense leaning,
Mean not, but blunder round about a meaning."

It is scarcely possible that they can be practical — since if the word *practical* is to be employed in any useful meaning the practical man is one who adapts his means to his ends; hence in order that he who would adapt the means of society to its end may be practical, the first requisite is that he shall know *what that end is;* and this is just what no critic of the prevailing school of economy *does* know. Therefore, he cannot be practical. It may be that the dogmatic critic can show common sense to be "impractical," but in order to do so he must first emasculate his term.

Perhaps it may be deemed impractical — as it certainly is uncustomary — to begin a work on political philosophy with an analysis of common sense. Is it impractical because everyone understands the nature of common sense "by intuition," or because political philosophy requires no such foundation? If everyone does understand common sense how is it that most of us discover that other people have an aggravating habit of departing from it; and if political philosophy is not to be founded on common sense, on what is it to be founded? Does the critic deem that a shallower foundation would be a surer one? Is superficiality a guarantee of security? There appears to be a popular idea that in such a "practical" thing as politics the superficial man is the safest, but that in engineering, or navigation, or medicine, he is not. Such a delusion is not derived from experience, though it is well adapted to furnish nations with experience sufficient to correct it. Those who are subject to this delusion are usually subject to another, viz., that the practical man is not a theorist. The doctrines of the economy of happiness therefore being theories, must be impractical, but they ignore the palpable fact that as opponents of those theories they are themselves theorists, since a political theory can be opposed only by advocating one of its alternatives. And advocates of any of the alternatives of pantocracy, except socialism, are not only theorists — not only advocates of a theory — but of a theory absurd *apriori* and *aposteriori* — not only wrong in principle, but a failure in practice. No political theory thus far put in operation has been anything but a failure — none has ever produced a permanent surplus of happiness — and none ever will until morality, political and personal, is recognized as within the domain of common sense. When that time comes, politics will take its place with applied mechanics, electricity, and chemistry, as a branch of technology, and will become as thoroughly revolutionized as were alchemy, astrology, and the other varieties of mysticism from which the sciences of to-day have been evolved.

It is a view very commonly held that, somehow or other, science will better the existing order of things — and so it will — but in so doing, it will apply the methods it has always applied; it will proceed by definite steps in a definite direction. Science has already done more for humanity than the sum of all the other forces set in motion by human effort. In her achievements, to quote Archdeacon Farrar,

". . . there is not only beauty and wonder, but also beneficence and power. It is not only that she has revealed to us infinite space crowded with unnumbered worlds; infinite time peopled by unnumbered existences; infinite organisms hitherto invisible but full of delicate and iridescent loveliness but also that she has been, as a great Archangel of Mercy, devoting herself to the service of man. She has labored, her votaries have labored, not to increase the power of despots, or to add to the magnificence of courts, but to extend human happiness, to economize human effort, to extinguish human pain. Where of old, men toiled, half blinded and half naked, in the mouth of the glowing furnace to mix the white-hot iron, she now substitutes the mechanical action of the viewless air. She has enlisted the sunbeam in her service to limn for us, with absolute fidelity, the faces of the friends we love. She has shown the poor miner how he may work in safety, even amid the explosive fire-damp of the mine. She has, by her anæsthetics, enabled the sufferer to be hushed and unconscious while the delicate hand of some skilled operator cuts a fragment from the nervous circle of the unquivering eye. She points not to pyramids built during weary centuries by the sweat of miserable nations, but to the lighthouse and the steamship, to the railroad and the telegraph. She has restored eyes to the blind and hearing to the deaf. She has lengthened life, she has minimized danger, she has controlled madness, she has trampled on disease."

And this is but the beginning — these are merely the incidental achievements of a power destined to convert the present material civilization into a moral one. If civilization is one-sided and materialistic it is only because science has not yet taken possession of her legitimate province — morality. When she does, the moral civilization of the future will have dawned, and the long night of dogma will be over. Mankind have always hoped for happiness, and they have hoped in vain. If they will but follow common sense their hope, by fulfilment, will be converted into expectation. Science will solve the problem which metaphysics and theology have tried but failed to solve, and unlike her predecessors she will not be satisfied to offer a pain-ridden world those empty substitutes for a solution —

"That keep the word of promise to our ear,
And break it to our hope."

Morality is the last citadel of the dynasty of dogma. That citadel once captured by common sense, truth will replace untruth, and right will replace wrong Men will at last be free to seek the one eternal aspiration of the human heart, unappalled by the hideous idols of ignorance and asceticism, and unenthralled by the stolid custodians of imperial or sacerdotal authority, whose combined power has wrought the tragedy of history. Suffering will no longer be the portion of sentience, and the morality of happiness will rule the conscience and the conduct of mankind, world without end.